PAGE 50

ON THE ROAD

YOUR COMPLETE DESTINATION GUIDE
In-depth reviews, detailed listings and insider tips

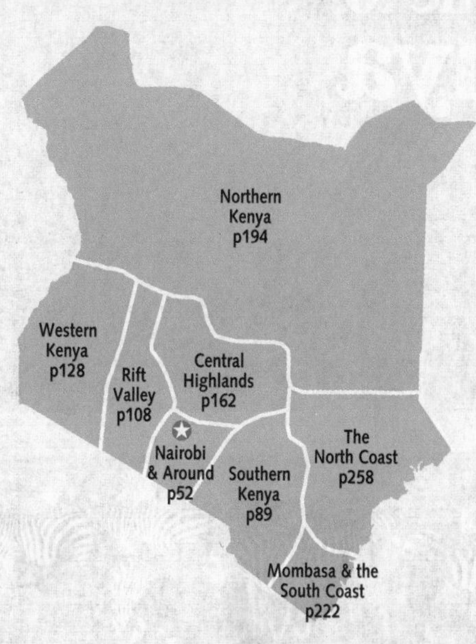

PAGE 359

SURVIVAL GUIDE

VITAL PRACTICAL INFORMATION TO HELP YOU HAVE A SMOOTH TRIP

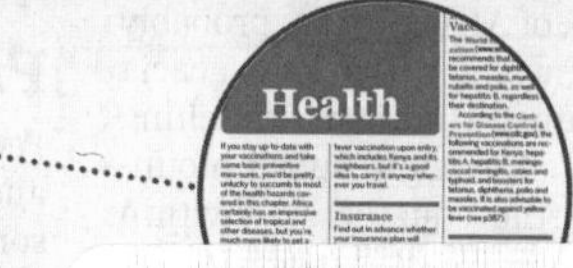

THIS EDITION WRITTE

Anthony Ham, Stuart Butler, Dean Starnes

Stirring Landscapes

When you think of Africa, you're probably thinking of Kenya. It's the lone acacia silhouetted against a horizon stretching into eternity. It's the snowcapped mountain almost on the equator and within sight of harsh deserts. It's the lush, palm-fringed coastline of the Indian Ocean, it's the Great Rift Valley that once threatened to tear the continent asunder, and it's the dense forests reminiscent of the continent's heart. With so much variety, Kenya's landscapes are far more than a mere backdrop to the country's wildlife and peoples. Instead, Kenya has soul, a gravitas bequeathed to it by epic landforms and a natural environment that stirs our deepest longings for this very special continent.

Proud Peoples

Peopling that landscape, adding depth and resonance to Kenya's age-old story, are some of Africa's best-known peoples. The Maasai, the Samburu, the Turkana, Swahili, the Kikuyu: these are the peoples whose histories and daily struggles tell the story of a country and of a continent – the struggle to maintain traditions as the modern world crowds in, the daily fight for survival in some of the harshest environments on earth, the ancient tension between those who farm and those who roam. Drawing near to these cultures, even coming to

Kenya is the Africa you always dreamed of. This is a land of vast savannahs, immense herds of wildlife and peoples with proud traditions on the soil where human beings were born.

(left) Zebras and Mt Kilimanjaro, Amboseli National Park (p92)
(below) Maasai men, Masai Mara National Reserve (p129)

understand them a little better through your presence among them, could just be a highlight of your visit. And it's not only about tradition: this may be a country of many tribes, but it's also a fiercely proud and modern country, one where being called Kenyan is increasingly seen as a badge of honour.

Abundant Wildlife

Then, of course, there's the wildlife. This is the land of the Masai Mara, of wildebeest and zebras migrating in their millions, with the great predators of Africa – lions, leopards, cheetahs and hyenas – following in their wake. This is the land of the red elephants and black rhinos of Tsavo, a wilderness almost brought to its knees by poaching and yet which somehow survived to thrive again. And this is a place where you'll have so many experiences that will come back to you in vivid detail long after you've returned home: elephant families wallowing in swamps in the shadow of Mt Kilimanjaro, the massed millions of pink flamingos bathing elegantly in lake shallows, the landscape suddenly fallen silent and brought to attention by the arrival of an as-yet-unseen predator. Africa is the last great wilderness where these creatures survive. And there's nowhere better than Kenya to answer Africa's call of the wild.

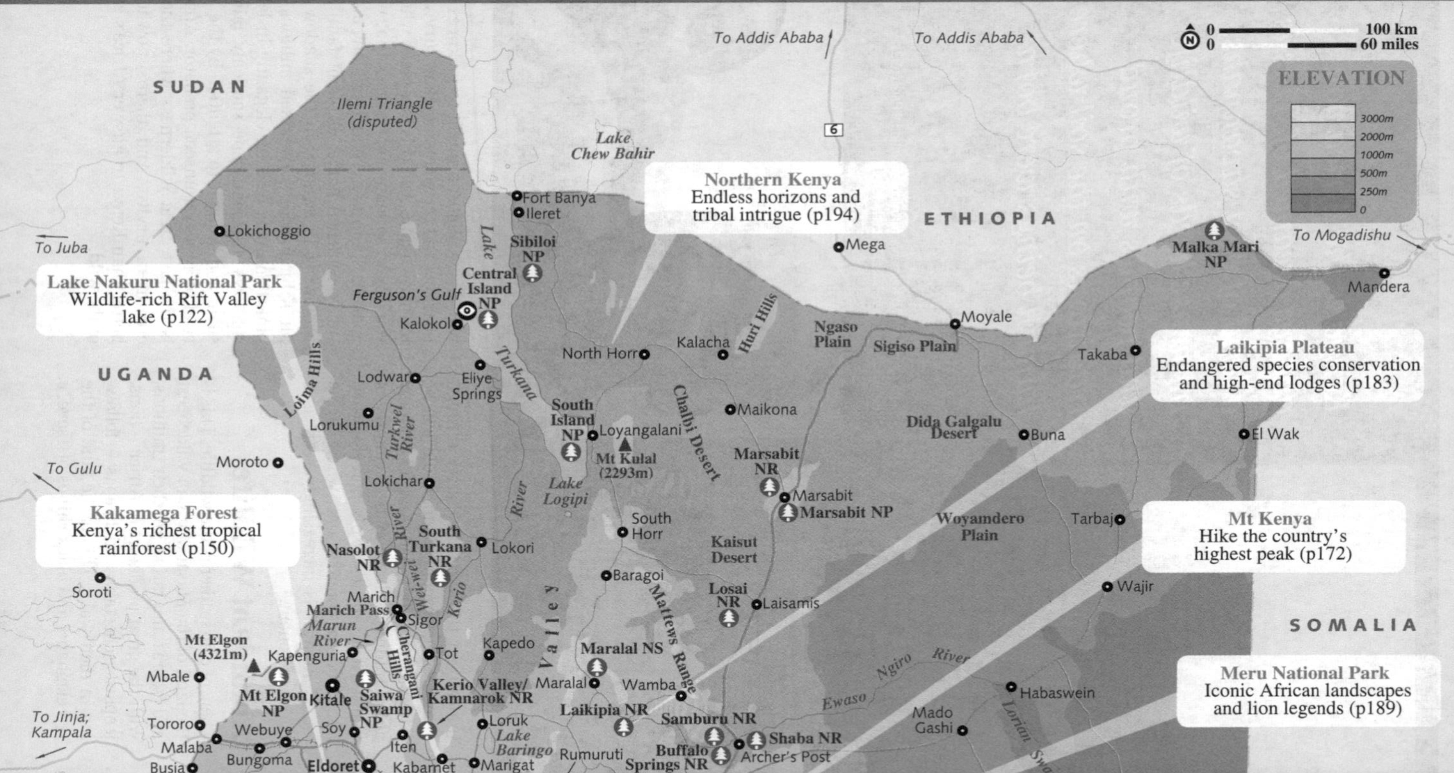

Lake Nakuru National Park
Wildlife-rich Rift Valley lake (p122)
Kakamega Forest
Kenya's richest tropical rainforest (p150)
Northern Kenya
Endless horizons and tribal intrigue (p194)
Laikipia Plateau
Endangered species conservation and high-end lodges (p183)
Mt Kenya
Hike the country's highest peak (p172)
Meru National Park
Iconic African landscapes and lion legends (p189)
ELEVATION
3000m
2000m
1000m
500m
250m
0
0
100 km
0
60 miles
SUDAN
UGANDA
ETHIOPIA
SOMALIA
Ilemi Triangle (disputed)
To Juba
To Gulu
To Jinja; Kampala
To Addis Ababa
To Addis Ababa
To Mogadishu
6
Lake Chew Bahir
Lokichoggio
Fort Banya
Ileret
Sibiloi NP
Central Island NP
Ferguson's Gulf
Kalokol
Lake Turkana
Lodwar
Eliye Springs
Loima Hills
Lorukumu
Turkwel River
Moroto
Lokichar
South Island NP
Loyangalani
Mt Kulal (2293m)
Lake Logipi
North Horr
Kalacha
Huri Hills
Chalbi Desert
Maikona
Mega
Ngaso Plain
Sigiso Plain
Moyale
Takaba
Malka Mari NP
Mandera
Dida Galgalu Desert
Buna
El Wak
Marsabit NR
Marsabit
Marsabit NP
Woyamdero Plain
Tarbaj
South Horr
Kaisut Desert
Soroti
Nasolot NR
South Turkana NR
Lokori
River
Baragoi
Losai NR
Laisamis
Wajir
Marich
Marich Pass
Sigor
Wei-wei
Kerio
Marun River
Cherangani Hills
Mt Elgon (4321m)
Kapenguria
Tot
Kapedo
Valley
Mattews Range
Maralal NS
Mbale
Mt Elgon NP
Kitale
Saiwa Swamp NP
Kerio Valley/ Kamnarok NR
Maralal
Wamba
Ngiro River
Ewaso
Habaswein
Mado Gashi
Lorian Swa
Laikipia NR
Samburu NR
Shaba NR
Tororo
Webuye
Soy
Loruk
Lake Baringo
Malaba
Bungoma
Iten
Busia
Eldoret
Kabarnet
Marigat
Rumuruti
Buffalo Springs NR
Archer's Post

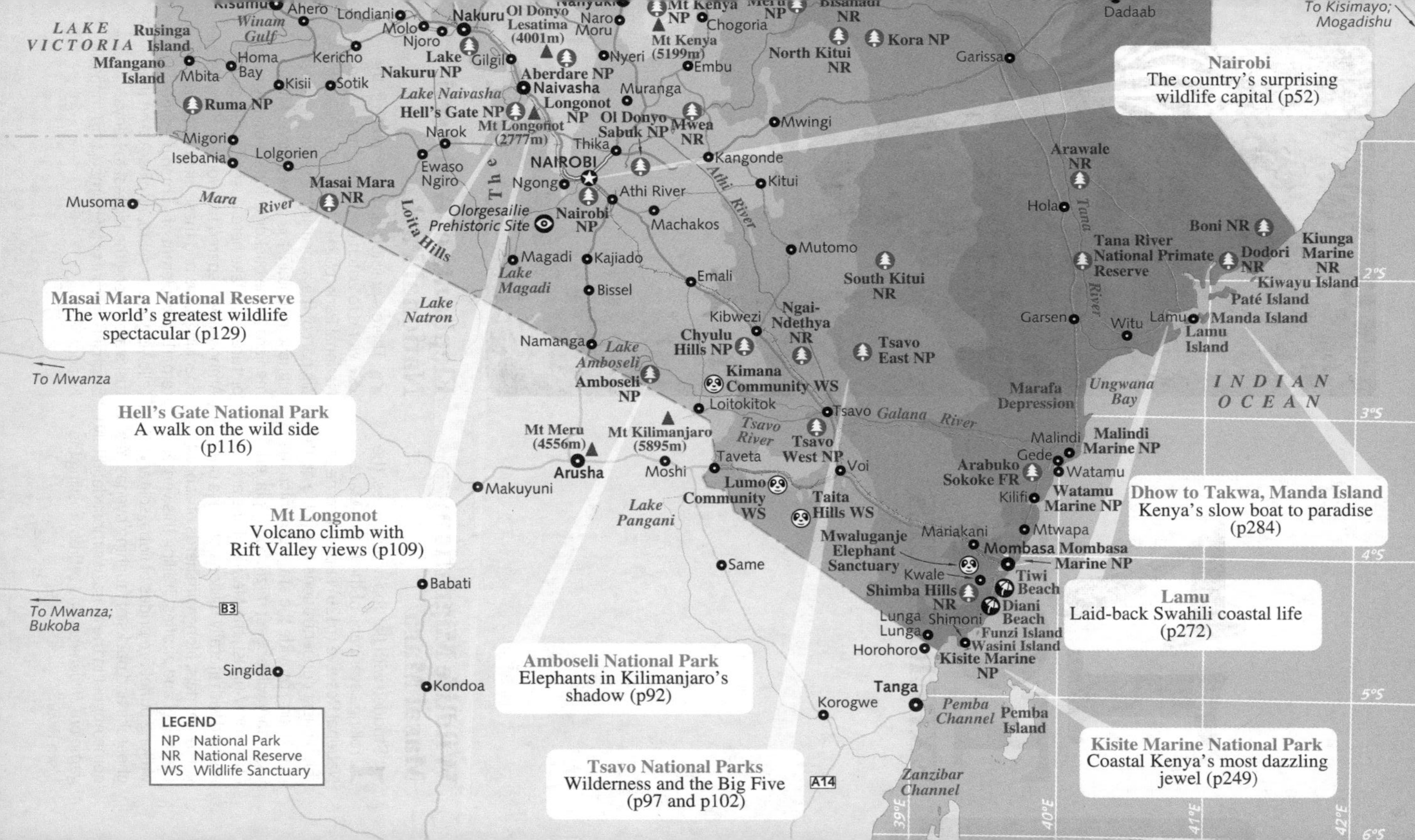

Nairobi
The country's surprising wildlife capital (p52)
Masai Mara National Reserve
The world's greatest wildlife spectacular (p129)
Hell's Gate National Park
A walk on the wild side (p116)
Mt Longonot
Volcano climb with Rift Valley views (p109)
Amboseli National Park
Elephants in Kilimanjaro's shadow (p92)
Tsavo National Parks
Wilderness and the Big Five (p97 and p102)
Dhow to Takwa, Manda Island
Kenya's slow boat to paradise (p284)
Lamu
Laid-back Swahili coastal life (p272)
Kisite Marine National Park
Coastal Kenya's most dazzling jewel (p249)
LEGEND
NP National Park
NR National Reserve
WS Wildlife Sanctuary
LAKE VICTORIA
INDIAN OCEAN
To Kisimayo; Mogadishu
To Mwanza
To Mwanza; Bukoba
Rusinga Island
Mfangano Island
Winam Gulf
Ahero
Londiani
Molo
Njoro
Nakuru
Lake Nakuru NP
Gilgil
Ol Donyo Lesatima (4001m)
Naro Moru
Nyeri
Mt Kenya NP
Mt Kenya (5199m)
Chogoria
Embu
Muranga
North Kitui NR
Kora NP
Garissa
Dadaab
Homa Bay
Mbita
Kericho
Kisii
Sotik
Ruma NP
Aberdare NP
Naivasha
Lake Naivasha
Hell's Gate NP
Mt Longonot (2777m)
Longonot NP
Ol Donyo Sabuk NP
Mwea NR
Mwingi
Migori
Isebania
Lolgorien
Narok
Ewaso Ngiro
Thika
NAIROBI
Kangonde
Kitui
Ngong
Athi River
Masai Mara NR
Mara River
Musoma
Olorgesailie Prehistoric Site
Nairobi NP
Machakos
Loita Hills
Magadi
Lake Magadi
Kajiado
Bissel
Emali
Mutomo
South Kitui NR
Arawale NR
Hola
Tana River
Boni NR
Tana River National Primate Reserve
Dodori NR
Kiunga Marine NR
Kiwayu Island
Paté Island
Lamu
Manda Island
Lamu Island
Witu
Garsen
Lake Natron
Namanga
Lake Amboseli
Amboseli NP
Kibwezi
Chyulu Hills NP
Ngai-Ndethya NR
Tsavo East NP
Kimana Community WS
Loitokitok
Tsavo
Galana River
Marafa Depression
Ungwana Bay
Mt Meru (4556m)
Mt Kilimanjaro (5895m)
Arusha
Moshi
Tsavo River
Tsavo West NP
Taveta
Voi
Malindi
Malindi Marine NP
Gede
Watamu
Arabuko Sokoke FR
Makuyuni
Lumo Community WS
Taita Hills WS
Lake Pangani
Kilifi
Watamu Marine NP
Mtwapa
Mariakani
Mombasa
Mombasa Marine NP
Mwaluganje Elephant Sanctuary
Same
Babati
Kwale
Tiwi Beach
Shimba Hills NR
Diani Beach
Lunga Lunga
Shimoni
Funzi Island
Wasini Island
Horohoro
Kisite Marine NP
Singida
Kondoa
Tanga
Korogwe
Pemba Channel
Pemba Island
Zanzibar Channel
B3
A14
2°S
3°S
4°S
5°S
6°S
39°E
40°E
41°E
42°E

17 TOP EXPERIENCES

Wildlife Migration, Masai Mara

1 Studded with flat-top acacia trees, the rolling savannahs of the Masai Mara National Reserve (p129) support some of the highest concentrations of wildlife on the planet, and provide the stage on which the legendary wildebeest migration is played out. From August, the Mara's plains are flooded with literally millions of these ungainly animals, along with herds of zebras, elephants and giraffes. Trailing this veritable walking buffet are prides of lions, solitary cheetahs and packs of laughing hyenas. Yes, come August in the Mara, it's most definitely *game on*. Wildebeest and zebras crossing the Mara River

Elephants of Amboseli National Park

2 There's possibly no better place in the world to watch elephants than Amboseli National Park (p92) in the country's south. A big part of the appeal is the setting – Africa's highest mountain, the snowcapped Mt Kilimanjaro, is the backdrop for seemingly every picture you'll take here. Just as significant, Amboseli was spared the worst of Kenya's poaching crisis and these elephants are remarkably tolerant of human presence (allowing you to get *really* close). And their tusks are among the biggest in Kenya. Elephants in front of Mt Kilimanjaro, Amboseli National Park

1

MARTIN HARVEY/GETTY ©

2

SEAN CAFFREY/LONELY PLANET IMAGES ©

Wandering Lamu Backstreets

3 Lamu (p272) is surely the most evocative destination on the Kenyan coast. With no cars around, the best way to get to know this graceful town is by wandering its backstreets, admiring the grand old Swahili doors, peeking into hidden courtyards bursting with unexpected colours, slipping into an easy chair and sipping on fruit juices, and accepting all invitations to stop and shoot the breeze (chat). Do all this and the backstreets of Lamu will become a place you'll dream of forever.

Hiking Mt Kenya

4 Mt Kenya (p172) is the country's highest peak and the second highest on the continent. Located in the heart of the country and in the hearts of the Kikuyu people, this is not a mountain to be admired from afar. With four days, some determination and several layers of warm clothing, you could find yourself standing on the frozen summit of Point Lenana, mere minutes from the equator, but a whole world away from the other African experiences. Chogoria route, Mt Kenya

Kakamega Forest

5 Paths lace the Kakamega Forest (p150) and offer a rare opportunity to ditch the safari 4WD and stretch your legs. This ancient forest is home to an astounding 330 bird species, 400 butterfly species and seven different primate species. Like all rainforests, though, the trees themselves are the chief attraction here, and in the forest gloom you'll stumble upon the botanical equivalent of beauty and the beast: delicate orchids and parasitic figs that strangle their hosts as they climb towards the light. African map butterfly, Kakamega Forest

4

GRANT DIXON/LONELY PLANET IMAGES ©

5

NIGEL PAVITT/JAI/CORBIS ©

6

7

Dhow to Takwa

6 Set sail with the salty monsoon winds on a creaky dhow: the sleepy Swahili ruins of Takwa (p284) are your goal. To get there you must plot a course between the Seven Isles of Eryaya and navigate the narrow maze of the mangrove forests. On the way you can swim and snorkel with fish as bright as the morning sun, and eat coconut rice as ghost crabs play at your feet. Never does the Kenyan coast feel more romantic than when seen through the eyes of a dhow trip around the Lamu archipelago.

Nairobi

7 Nairobi's (p52) reputation precedes it, and not always in the most enticing way. And yet Nairobi is an essential (and very often immensely enjoyable) element of the Kenyan experience. No other city in the world can boast a national park (which is home to four of the Big Five) within sight of city skyscrapers, the chance to feed orphaned baby elephants, immerse yourself in the place that inspired *Out of Africa* and visit an outstanding national museum all in a single day. Uhuru Park, Nairobi

ARIADNE VAN ZANDBERGEN/LONELY PLANET IMAGES ©

DAVE LEWIS/LONELY PLANET IMAGES ©

The Remote North

8 No matter how you look at it, northern Kenya (p194) spells adventure. This vast emidesert wilderness is one of the last great ınknowns of East Africa. Its scrublands are lled with elephants and antelopes, its forests ontain creatures still unknown to science and ts deserts contain the secrets to the earliest ıumans. You can ride across it in a 4WD, ounce through it in the back of a goods truck r, best of all, saddle up your ship of the desert nd ride across by camel. Ewaso Ngiro River, Samburu National Reserve

Kisite Marine National Park

9 Hiding away like a secret jewel is the laid-back isle of Wasini (p248), close to the border of Tanzania. You can sail to it from Diani Beach (p242) like an Omani sultan in a magnificent dhow, and dive overboard to snorkel with fish big and small in the stunning Kisite Marine National Park (p249), which fringes the island. Or you can come under your own steam and walk the footpaths to the near-forgotten village of Mkwiro (p249) – the perfect spot to be engulfed by Swahili culture.

10

ARIADNE VAN ZANDBERGEN/LONELY PLANET IMAGES ©

11

Lions at Tsavo National Park

10 The two Tsavo (East and West) National Parks (p102 and p97) are wilderness experiences par excellence: vast and dramatic landscapes where wildlife lurks in the undergrowth. All of Africa's charismatic megafauna are present here, but it's the cats – leopards, lions and cheetahs – who bring this ecosystem to life. Against a backdrop of red soils, volcanic outcrops and sweeping savannah plains, these lions of legend (it was here that the man-eaters of Tsavo once struck fear into the hearts of locals) laze about in the shade, waiting for the right moment to pounce.

Hell's Gate National Park

11 It's one thing to watch Africa's megafauna from the safety of your safari vehicle, quite another entirely to do so on foot or from astride a bicycle. Hell's Gate National Park (p116) – a dramatic volcanic landscape of red cliffs, otherworldly rocky outcrops and deep canyons in the heart of Kenya's Rift Valley – may lack predators, but this chance to experience the African wild at close quarters certainly gives most people frisson. By placing you in the landscape, Hell's Gate heightens the senses, bringing alive the African wild like nowhere else in Kenya.

Lake Nakuru National Park

12 Another of Kenya's world-class parks, this park is dominated by one of the Rift Valley's most beautiful lakes. The waters are lined on one side by an abrupt escarpment and the shoreline is at times given colour and texture by masse[d] flamingos and pelicans. But Lake Nakuru (p122) is also a wildlife haven for land-borne mammals, home as it is to lions, leopards, the highly endangered Rothschild's giraffes, zebras, buffaloes, various primate species and Kenya's most easily spotted rhinos. No wonder it's regularly ranked among Kenya's top five parks. Flamingos, Lake Nakuru National Park

12

TOM COCKREM/LONELY PLANET IMAGES ©

Mt Longonot

13 Mt Longonot (p109) not only has the near-erfect shape we imagine ll volcanoes to have, it's lso the most accessible of enya's Rift Valley climbs. nlike the more famous Mt enya ascent, the climb to ne crater rim is more of a trenuous 90-minute hike nan a serious expedition; ven the climb, circumnavi-ation and descent can be ccomplished in four hours. he rewards are glorious ift Valley views (including verlooking Hell's Gate) and bird's-eye view down to the st forests of the crater floor. homson's gazelles in front of It Longonot

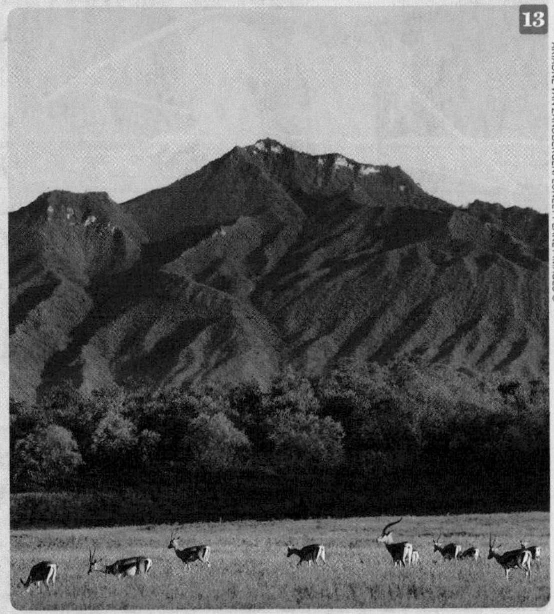

13

ARIADNE VAN ZANDBERGEN/LONELY PLANET IMAGES ©

Laikipia Plateau

14 In the shadow of Mt Kenya, this network of conservancies and private wildlife reserves (p183) is both beautiful and one of the most exciting stories in African conservation. At the forefront of efforts to save endangered species such as lions, African wild dogs, Grevy's zebras and black rhinos, the plateau's ranches offer an enticing combination of high-end lodge accommodation, big horizons and charismatic megafauna. Best of all, this is a more intimate experience than your average national park, with scarcely another vehicle in sight. A Maasai guide and young tourist, Laikipia plateau

Meru National Park

15 One of Kenya's most underrated park Meru (p189) is a beguiling mix of icon African landscapes (fertile hills, river forests, baobabs and doum palms) and a fine range of fauna (including black and white rhinos, elephants, lions and zebras). Meru is also where the lion legends of George Adamson's *Born Free* came into being. But above all else Meru is the safari as it used to be, with unusual quiet trails and the thrill of stumbling upon wildlife when you least expect it. Zebra, Meru National Park

15

TOM COCKREM/LONELY PLANET IMAGES ©

16

MARK DAFFEY/LONELY PLANET IMAGES ©

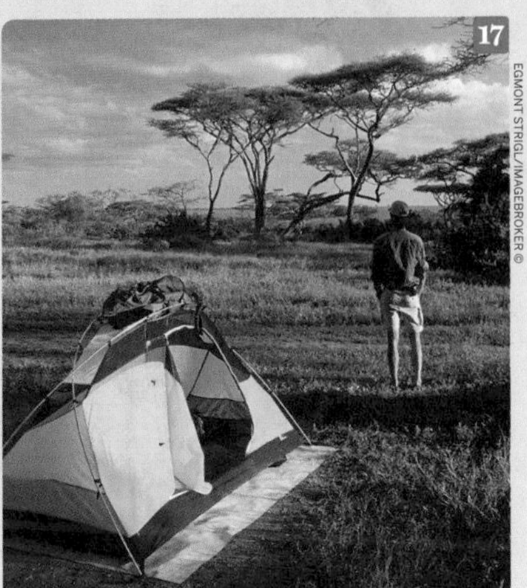

17

EGMONT STRIGL/IMAGEBROKER ©

Kenyan Beaches

16 Kenya's Indian Ocean coast (p222) is one of Africa's prettiest shores. Long tretches of white sand, translucent waters nd coves sheltered by palm trees would be ufficient reason for most travellers to visit. ut trade winds through the centuries have rought an intriguing mix of African and Arab ultures, resulting in a coastline with attitude: t once laid-back in the finest spirit of *hakuna natata*, yet bristling with ruins and the evocative ignposts of Swahili culture. Tiwi Beach, south f Mombasa

Camping Out on Safari

17 There's nothing quite like it for sharpening your senses and heightening your awareness of Africa. Sleeping under the stars is a soulful experience and the antithesis of the modern world's clamour – an infinity of stars, the crackle of the campfire, the immensity of the African night. But it's not for the faint-hearted, with wind whistling through the guy ropes, the not-so-distant roar of a lion and the knowledge that only flimsy canvas separates you from a rampaging rhino.

need to know

Currency

» Kenyan shilling (KSh)

Language

» English and Swahili; other tribal languages also spoken

When to Go

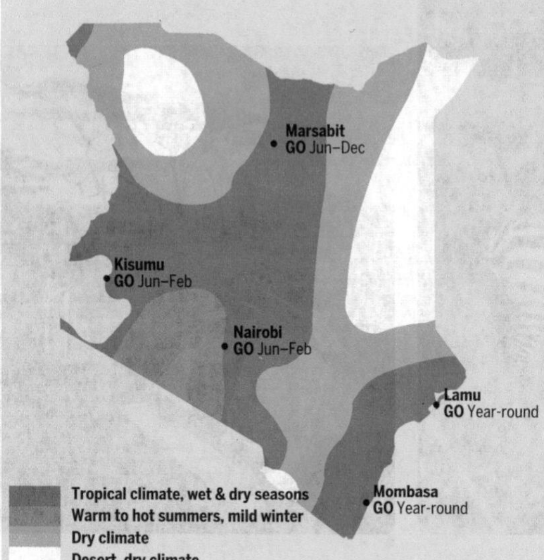

High Season
(Jun–Oct, Jan & Feb)

» Wildebeest in the Mara migrate from June to October.

» January and February offer hot, dry weather good for wildlife watching.

» Sky-high lodge prices. Book coastal accommodation months in advance.

Shoulder
(Nov & Dec)

» Short rains fall in October and November.

» Prices at most lodges and parks drop on 1 November, but advance reservations are still required.

Low Season
(Mar–May)

» Long rains mean accommodation is much quieter and prices are low, but wildlife is harder to spot and mosquitoes are rife.

Your Daily Budget

Budget less than US$50

» Cheap hotels (US$5–10) and camping (from US$15)

» Eat in local restaurants (meals US$1–4)

» Stock up in supermarkets; carry own camping equipment

» Travel by matatu

» Occasional splurge on wildlife drives with other travellers

Midrange US$50–200

» Double room in midrange hotel: US$50-200

» Independent safaris with car rental: US$75-100 per day

» Full board in lodges

Top End more than US$200

» Double room in top hotel: US$200 and up

» No-expenses-spared safaris in luxury tented camps

Money

» ATMs in major towns only. All banks change US dollars, euros and pounds. Credit cards accepted in most midrange and top-end hotels, restaurants and shops.

Visas

» Issued on arrival at Nairobi's Jomo Kenyatta international airport and valid for three months. Otherwise obtain in advance from Kenyan embassy overseas.

Mobile Phones

» Local SIM cards widely available and can be used in most international mobile phones. Mobile coverage extensive but patchy in wilderness areas and parks.

Driving/ Transport

» Drive on the left; steering wheel is on the right side of the car. Buses and matatus provide intercity public transport; also some internal flights.

Websites

» **Kenya Wildlife Service** (www.kws.org) Conservation news and information on national parks and reserves.

» **Kenya Association of Tour Operators** (www.katokenya.org) Full list of KATO-approved member companies.

» **Lonely Planet** (www.lonelyplanet.com/kenya) Destination information, hotel bookings, traveller forums and more.

» **Magical Kenya** (www.magicalkenya.com) Kenya Tourism Board official website.

» **Nation Newspaper** (www.nation.co.ke) Kenya's foremost newspaper.

Exchange Rates

Australia	A$1	KSh100
Canada	C$1	KSh95
Europe	€1	KSh132
Japan	¥100	KSh122
New Zealand	NZ$1	KSh76
UK	UK£1	KSh153
USA	US$1	KSh95

For current exchange rates see www.xe.com.

Important Numbers

Kenyan regions have area codes which must be dialled in full, followed by the number, if calling from within Kenya; the code's '0' is dropped if calling from overseas.

International access code	☎000
Kenya country code	☎254
Directory enquiries	☎991
Police, ambulance & fire	☎999
Tourist helpline (24hr)	☎020-604767

Arriving in Kenya

» **Jomo Kenyatta international airport, Nairobi**

City bus – bus 34 (one-way KSh30); danger of theft so best avoided

Taxis – KSh1200–1500; 30 minutes to one hour to the city centre, depending on traffic; book at 'information' desk in arrivals hall; only option at night

» **Moi Internationa Airport, Mombasa**

Public transport – none

Taxis – KSh1200; 20 to 30 minutes

Choosing Your Safari

For most visitors to Kenya, the single most important decision you'll make when preparing your trip is choosing a safari. It may sound simple, but the most useful part of your preparations comes before you begin making contact with the various safari companies out there. Decide on exactly what kind of safari you dream of. Which parks do you want to visit? Do you want a specialist safari (such as birdwatching) or a general overview of the major parks? Which wildlife do you most want to see? What's your budget? Do you want to travel independently or as part of a group? Thus armed with at least general answers to these questions, and having read our definitive guide to Kenyan safaris (p28), you're well placed to start making enquiries.

if you like...

Big Cats

The sight of prowling predators is guaranteed to produce a frisson of excitement, and it's the big cats – lions, leopards and cheetahs – that most visitors come to see. Lions sleeping under a tree, a lone leopard draped along a branch, a cheetah accelerating across the savannah – these are some of Kenya's most unforgettable experiences.

Masai Mara National Reserve The best place to spot all three cats, often on a kill from June to October (p129)

Tsavo East National Park Another good spot for relatively easy sightings of all three (p102)

Tsavo West National Park Big cats elusive but tracking them down is half the fun (p97)

Amboseli National Park Good for lions in dry season (p92)

Meru National Park Lions and cheetahs both present (p189)

Lake Nakuru National Park Resident leopards and lions (p122)

Nairobi National Park All three present within sight of the capital (p58)

Elephants & Rhinos

The African elephant and the rhinoceros are the enduring icons of a continent. Whether you're watching elephant families strung-out across the savannah or encountering elephants and rhinos bathed in the ochre-tinted mud of Tsavo, you'll be spellbound.

Amboseli National Park As close as you'll ever get to a big-tusked elephant with Mt Kilimanjaro in the background (p92)

Tsavo East National Park Kenya's largest elephant population, with over 11,000 (p102)

Lake Nakuru National Park One of the best places in Kenya to see the highly endangered black rhino (p122)

Aberdare National Park Elephants and black rhinos in the Central Highlands' forested slopes (p168)

Tsavo West National Park An important sanctuary for black rhinos; also 'red' elephants (p97)

Marsabit National Park Kenya's northernmost elephants (p208)

Birdwatching

Kenya is one of Africa's premier destinations for twitchers, with around 1200 bird species recorded – even amateur birdwatchers will find the thrill of safari enhanced by spotting and ticking off the country's weird and wonderful bird species. Northern migrant species escaping Europe's winter begin arriving in November.

Lake Nakuru National Park Flamingos in their tens of thousands (sometimes), and 400 other species (p122)

Amboseli National Park Over 370 bird species, including raptors and the grey-crowned crane (p92)

Lake Bogoria National Reserve Another flamingo spectacular, with internationally recognised wetlands (p124)

Kakamega Forest Reserve Rainforest habitat and over 330 recorded species (p150)

Saiwa Swamp National Park Over 370 bird species in just over 15 sq km (p160)

Lake Baringo Over one-third of Kenya's species have been recorded here (p125)

If you like...climbing extinct volcanoes, Mt Longonot offers some of the finest Rift Valley views in Africa (p109)

Beaches

Kenya's coastline is utterly gorgeous: no amount of overdevelopment in some areas can detract from that. The large resorts are easy to avoid, but people come here for a reason – some pretty idyllic beaches. Elsewhere, there remain some stunning, remote stretches of sand yet to be discovered – the places you'll always remember as your own slice of paradise.

Takaungu Fishing village, empty sand, this is Indian Ocean perfection (p257)

Shela Beach With 12km of white sand and one of Lamu's most beautiful beaches (p281)

Watamu Enjoy 7km of unspoiled beach with a lovely fishing village nearby (p260)

Manda Island The land time forgot, with sand dunes, mangroves and quiet beaches (p283)

Tiwi Beach The alter ego to Diani Beach and its equal in beauty (p240)

Diani Beach A crowded but still stunning beach (p242)

Dhow Trips

Travelling the East African coast in a dhow (ancient Arab sailing vessel) is as old as the spice coast itself and there are few more agreeable ways to experience this beguiling coastline. So much more than a means of transport, this is a way of life that carries echoes of ancient civilisations and trade winds past. Apart from anything, travelling by dhow forces you to slow down to a languid pace of life that peoples of the Kenyan coast long ago perfected.

Mkwiro There's no other way to reach this quieter-than-quiet village (p249)

Matandoni Watch dhows being built, then sail around the Lamu archipelago for a day (p283)

Funzi Island Charter a dhow for a day and go crocodile spotting on this mangrove island (p248)

Lamu Find yourself a good captain and sail between Lamu and Manda Island for the day (see the boxed text, p280)

Takwa The pick of the Lamu archipelago trips (p284)

Diving & Snorkelling

Reefs proliferate all along Kenya's coastline and the diving and snorkelling here rank among the best in East Africa. It's not quite the Red Sea, but casual divers and snorkellers will find more than enough to marvel at, from abundant marine life to an exceptional array of coral. Some top-notch dive schools operate in the big resorts, but most snorkelling is done by diving off the back of a dhow – very cool.

Malindi Marine National Park Excellent diving from July to February (p265)

Manda Toto Island The snorkelling here is highly favoured among devotees of the Lamu archipelago (p284)

Kisite Marine National Park Snorkel with the dolphins, with diving also possible (p249)

Watamu Marine National Park Fabulous reefs, fish and sea turtles (p260)

Diani Beach Professional dive schools and even a purpose-sunk shipwreck (p243)

» Rothschild's giraffes outside Giraffe Manor, Nairobi (p73)

Luxury Lodges

Kenya does luxury extremely well, and nothing quite beats the experience of returning from a day's safari to be pampered with luxury accommodation, spa and massage packages and impeccable standards of personal service.

Giraffe Manor, Nairobi Top-end luxury wedded to a sense of world-class service, and a Rothschild's giraffe looking in your window (p73)

Finch Hatton's Safari Camp, Tsavo West National Park Dress for dinner and eat from bone china deep in the African wilds (p102)

Tortilis Camp, Amboseli National Park Fine Kilimanjaro views from this ecolodge; the family rooms are simply extraordinary (p94)

Basecamp Masai Mara, Masai Mara National Reserve Ecolodge par excellence, with luxury tents close to the world's greatest wildlife spectacular (p135)

Lewa Wildlife Conservancy Gets everything right, from its conservation and social programs to luxury of the highest standard (p199)

Escaping the Crowds

The wildebeest migration is not the only mass migration in Kenya from June to October – this is also when visitors arrive in the millions. While there's good reason to join them, there are alternatives for those who blanch at the sight of 20 tour vans clustered around a pride of sleeping lions or beach resorts casting beautiful beaches into the shade.

Meru National Park A match for the more famous parks of Kenya's south, but without the crowds (p189)

Ruma National Park Wild Africa all to yourself, with fascinating antelope species (p143)

Loyangalani The essence of remote northern Kenya, with fascinating cultures and Lake Turkana (p216)

Paté Island Leave the modern world behind on this enchanted island in the Lamu archipelago (p284)

Mt Susua Fabulous Rift Valley views and a volcano all to yourself and the Maasai (p113)

Mfangano Island Lake Victoria islands with rock paintings and blissful quiet (p145)

Culture & Wildlife Immersion

Community-run projects are increasingly found all over Kenya. Their aims range from environmental sustainability and conservation to finding ways for tourism revenues to flow back into local communities. The best do both, and can provide experiences of a lifetime. If you've ever felt uncomfortable as you drive past a Maasai village with tourists lined up for a photo opportunity, these may be for you.

Lewa Wildlife Conservancy Local health-care, education and other community projects depend on this fantastic place (p199)

Lion Guardians An innovative approach to conservation that saves lions and fortifies Maasai traditions (p95)

Kimana Community Wildlife Sanctuary Maasai-run park with strong roots in the local community (p96)

Maasai Manyatta Visit Catch a glimpse of Maasai life on relatively equal terms (p133)

David Sheldrick Wildlife Trust Orphaned elephants en route to freedom (p62)

month by month

Top Events

1. **Annual wildebeest migration**, June–October
2. **Migrating bird species**, October–March
3. **Maulid Festival**, February or March
4. **Kenya Music Festival**, August
5. **International Camel Derby**, August

January

One of the most popular months for visiting Kenya. Animals congregate around waterholes and bird migration is well and truly under way. Days are usually warm and dry.

Dry-Season Gatherings

All but perennial water sources have dried up, drawing predators and prey alike to the last remaining waterholes. Wildlife watching at this time can be tense, exhilarating and intensely rewarding.

Birds in Abundance

Migratory bird species have by now arrived in their millions, giving Kenya close to its full complement of more than 1100 bird species. Rift Valley lakes and other wetlands are a birdwatcher's paradise.

February

High season in Kenya. Days are hot and dry, accommodation is often full, there's excellent wildlife watching around waterholes, and countless bird species on show.

Maulid Festival

This annual celebration of the Prophet Mohammed's birthday rouses Lamu (p272) from its slumber. Muslims from up and down the coast converge on the town. Everyone is welcome.

March

Kenya's big annual rains begin, flooding much of the country and making wildlife viewing difficult. But if the rains are late, it may be worth visiting now: prices are rock-bottom.

Late-Rains Safari

The cheapest time to visit Kenya – roads can be impassable, mosquitoes are everywhere and wildlife heads for shelter. But if the rains are late, conditions couldn't be better, with wildlife desperate for a drink and most birds still around.

April

The inundation continues to batter the country. Getting around is difficult. Unless the rains have failed entirely, avoid visiting now.

May

The rains usually continue well into May; when they stop and you can see the horizon, the country is wonderfully green. By late May, the rains may have subsided.

June

Kenya emerges from the rains somewhat sodden but ready to make up for lost time. The annual migration of wildebeest and zebra in their millions begins midmonth.

Wildlife Spectacular

Following the rains, wildebeest begin to arrive in the Masai Mara National Reserve (the Mara) in mid-June, with predators following in their wake. It's the greatest wildlife show on earth.

Rhino Charge

This charity cross-country rally in aid of

Rhino Ark (www.rhinoark.org) and other worthy conservation causes challenges mad motorists to reach the finish line in the straightest line possible, whatever the crazy obstacles. The location changes annually.

Kenya Fashion Week

Fashion shows may not rank highly on the list of Kenyan attractions, but this expo-style event is a fascinating insight into regional styles and designers from all across the country. It's held in the Sarit Centre, in Westlands, Nairobi.

July

The wildebeest and zebra migration is in full swing. So too is the annual migration of two-legged visitors who converge on the Mara. Weather is fine and warm, with steaming conditions on the coast.

Return to Amboseli

When the rains begin in March the herbivores of Amboseli (p92) (elephants, antelope, zebras...), followed by the predators, leave for grasslands outside the park. By July, they're on their way back within park confines.

August

The mid-year high season continues; the Mara is still the focus, but other parks are also rewarding. Europeans on holiday flock to Kenya; prices go up, room availability goes down.

Kenya Music Festival

The country's longest-running music festival (see p67) is held over 10 days in Nairobi, drawing worthy international acts along with its predominantly African cast of stars.

Camel Racing

Maralal's International Camel Derby (see p214) is at once about serious camel racing and a chance to join the fun. A huge event.

September

Crowds drop off ever so slightly, but the weather remains fine and the Mara is still filled to bursting with wildlife, so prices and visitor numbers remain high.

October

A great time to visit; the wildebeest are around until mid-October, and migratory birds begin arriving. The best season for diving and snorkelling begins and visitor numbers start to fall.

Here Come the Rains

Unlike the main rainy season from March to May, the short rains that usually begin in October and continue into November cause only minor disruptions to safaris. Rains are generally localised and heavy, but only last for an hour or two each day.

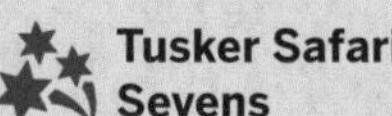

Tusker Safari Sevens

Nairobi hosts this highly regarded international rugby tournament (www.safarisevens.com). Drawing world-class rugby-union players, the tournament spills over into November (p67).

November

In normal years, the short rains appear almost daily throughout this month, but disruptions are minimal. Some animals range beyond the parks, birds arrive in great numbers and prices fall.

Migratory Birds

Birdwatchers couldn't hope for a better time to visit, as millions of birds and hundreds of species arrive for their wintering grounds while Europe shivers.

East African Safari Rally

This classic-car rally (www.eastafricansafarirally.com) in late November is over 50 years old and there's more than a whiff of colonial atmosphere about it. The rally traverses Kenya, Tanzania and Uganda and is open to pre-1971 vehicles only.

December

A reasonable time to visit, with lower prices and fine weather, plenty of migratory birds in residence and much of the country swathed in green.

Whether you've got six days or 60, these itineraries provide a starting point for the trip of a lifetime. Want more inspiration? Head online to lonelyplanet.com/thorntree to chat with other travellers.

SOUTH SUDAN
ETHIOPIA
UGANDA
SOMALIA
NAIROBI
Masai Mara NR
Amboseli NP
TANZANIA
INDIAN OCEAN

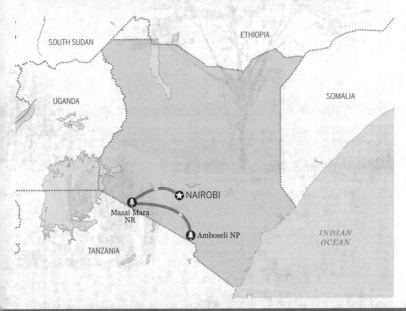

One Week
Safari Njema

Ideal for those with limited time, this classic safari route brings you face to face with the continent's most charismatic creatures. *Safari njema* – have a good trip!

Begin in **Nairobi**. Kenya's (in)famous rough-and-ready capital is not without charm; if nothing else, it's the only capital city with a national park on its doorstep – watch lions, leopards and cheetahs against the backdrop of distant skyscrapers. This is just a taster for the world-renowned **Masai Mara National Reserve**. Between July and October, the Mara hosts the annual wildebeest migration, which offers an iconic slice of safari Africa, and one of the greatest wildlife concentrations on earth. If you can't time your visit to coincide with this epic event, the Mara is worth visiting any time.

Staying in Maasailand and tracing its trajectory across Kenya's south, head to **Amboseli National Park**, where you can get closer to elephants than almost anywhere else in Africa. From here, the views of Mt Kilimanjaro, Africa's highest peak, are without rival in Africa.

» (above) White rhinos, Lake Naku (p122)
» (left) Leopard, Masai Mara Natio Reserve (p129)

CHRISTER FREDRIKSSON/LONELY PLANET IMAGES ©

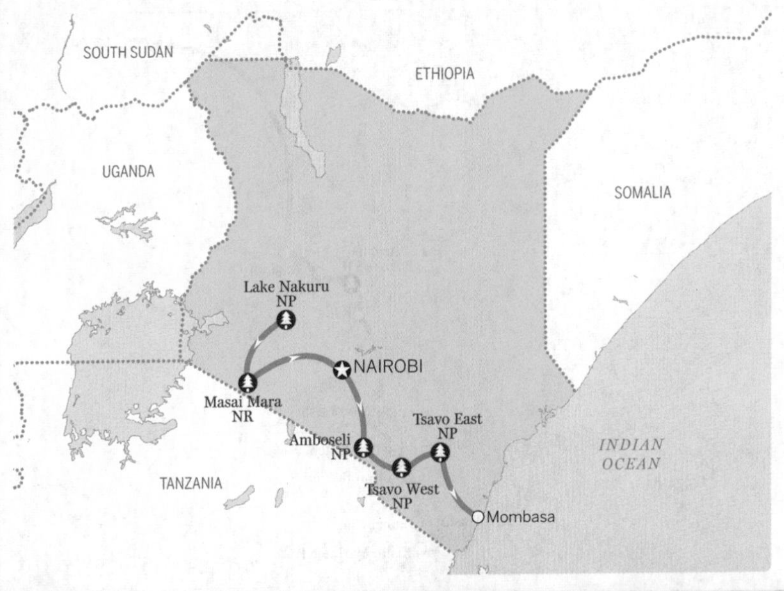

Three Weeks
In Search of the Big Five

Seeing the 'Big Five' has become a mantra for African wildlife watchers, but few know it was coined by white hunters for those five species deemed most dangerous to hunt: elephant, lion, leopard, rhino and buffalo. Seeing all five is relatively easy in Kenya; it's even possible to spot them all in a single day, although you'd have to be pretty lucky.

Start your search at **Lake Nakuru National Park**, a stunning alkaline lake in the Rift Valley. The lake's population of many thousands of pink flamingos and pelicans is one of Kenya's signature images – the sort to make you gasp at the sheer beauty of it all. This vitally important national park also protects the country's largest population of endangered black rhinos, as well as large herds of buffalo; the black rhino is present elsewhere, but sightings are almost guaranteed here.

From Lake Nakuru, your next stop is the obligatory safari in **Masai Mara National Reserve**, which is lion country – your chances of seeing lions on a kill are nowhere higher than in the Mara during the annual wildebeest migration from July to October. With a little luck, you can also spot leopards lounging in trees, and cheetahs prowling around the savannah. From the Mara, head southeast, passing through Nairobi, to **Amboseli National Park** for a wildlife drive in the shadow of Mt Kilimanjaro. Here you'll see elephants at nearly every turn (there are around 1200 in just 392 sq km), while lion sightings are also common; buffaloes lurk in the swamps, although generally in small numbers.

From Amboseli it's a straightforward drive to **Tsavo West National Park** and **Tsavo East National Park**, Kenya's largest wildlife parks and a real taste of the African wilderness. The chances of spotting wildlife are higher in Tsavo East, where the vegetation is less dense, but Tsavo West has the advantage of being home to all of the Big Five – see them all in one day and you've hit the safari jackpot.

From here you can head down the highway to the ancient Swahili port of **Mombasa**, where you can either fly straight home, or start a whole new journey exploring the Kenyan coast.

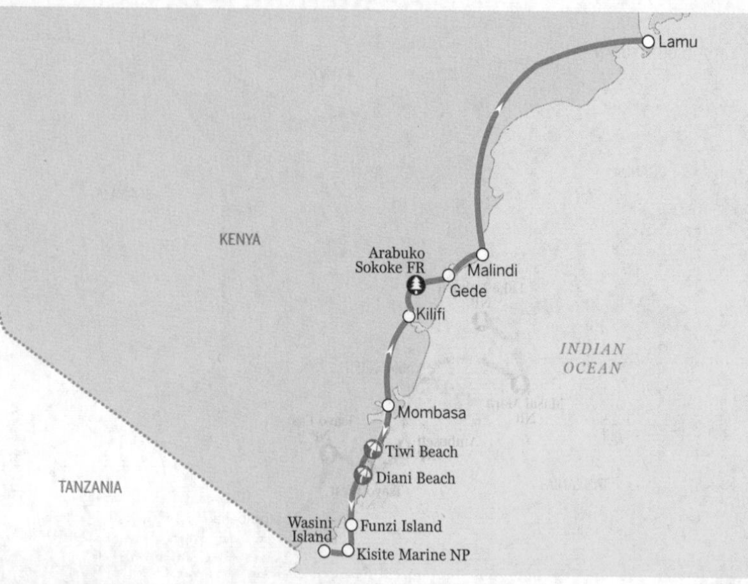

Two to Three Weeks

Sun, Surf & Swahili

Whether you're interested in exploring the remaining vestiges of Swahili culture or simply kicking back on the beach for days on end, don't miss the chance to explore Kenya's sun-drenched coast.

Before setting out, explore the coastal gateway of **Mombasa**, one of the truly great port cities on earth and the essence of East Africa. It gets steaming hot here, so your first stop heading south should be **Tiwi Beach**, a tranquil white-sand paradise popular with independent travellers. Just down the road, you can head on to the package-holiday destination of **Diani Beach** for a taste of the full-on resort experience.

Near the Tanzanian border, **Funzi** and **Wasini Islands** provide a dose of unspoilt coastal life; on the latter **Mkwiro** is somewhere close to paradise. These islands also afford easy access to the excellent **Kisite Marine National Park**. Whether you spot crocodiles along the banks of mangrove-lined rivers or dolphins crashing through the surf, a visit to the marine park is a wonderful complement to Kenya's terrestrial wildlife destinations. Offshore, humpback whales are a possibility from August to October. A trip in a traditional dhow is also a must.

Heading north back on the coastal trail, make a quick stop in the charming town of **Kilifi** before pressing on to **Arabuko Sokoke Forest Reserve**. One of the largest remaining tracts of indigenous coastal forest in East Africa, the reserve plays host to prolific birdlife and forest elephants, and is a last refuge of the golden-rumped elephant shrew.

Further north are the **Gede ruins**, an ancient Swahili city dating back to the 13th century. Another historic destination along the Swahili coast is **Malindi**, a 14th-century trading post that's now one of the country's leading beach destinations for Italian holidaymakers. While it can be something of a scene, it has bucketloads of charm once you get beyond the beach.

This itinerary ends (and peaks) at the wonderful **Lamu archipelago**, a veritable tropical paradise and Swahili heritage gem. However, you should check the security situation before travelling here (see boxed text on p279).

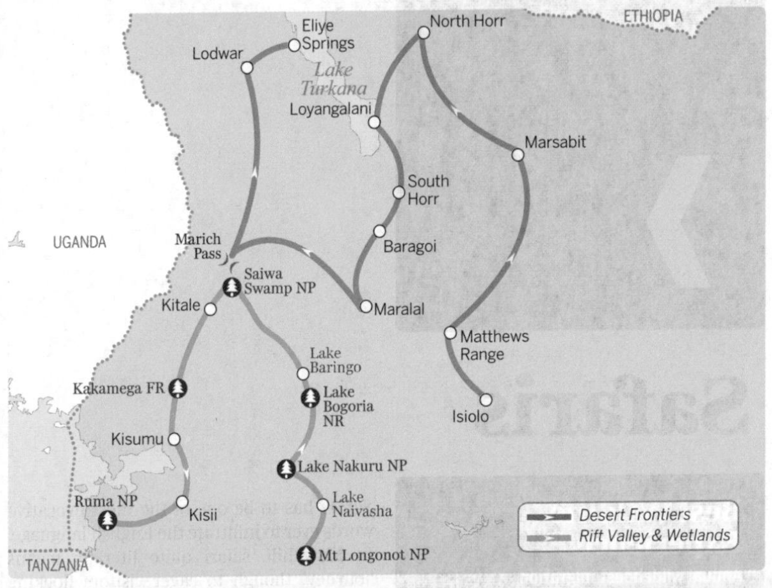

Two to Three Weeks

Rift Valley & Wetlands

The Rift Valley is one of Africa's defining geological marvels. West and northwest of Nairobi lie some of the country's most fertile and scenic spots, characterised by still, tranquil bodies of water.

An excellent place to start is **Lake Naivasha**, a popular freshwater lake close to the starting point of the climb to the summit of **Mount Longonot**, one of the Rift's prettiest vantage points. Then it's an easy hop to **Lakes Nakuru**, **Bogoria** and **Baringo**, all of which support a wealth of birdlife.

Take the loop through the Cherangani Hills to the agricultural town of **Kitale** and the lovely **Saiwa Swamp National Park**, a real wetland treat.

Heading south, you'll come across the **Kakamega Forest Reserve**, an essential stop for walkers and bird lovers alike. Continue down the road to the region's main city, **Kisumu**, on the shore of Lake Victoria. Skirting the Winam Gulf, you reach busy **Kisii**, a handy hub for Lake Victoria's small islands, and tiny **Ruma National Park**, a rarely visited gem.

Two to Three Weeks

Desert Frontiers

This adventurous trail winds through the barren but beguiling landscape around Lake Turkana. The eastern gateway to this region is the small town of **Isiolo**, just north of Mt Kenya; a side trip to **Matthews Range** is great for walkers.

Alternatively, plough straight into the desert route, heading up the rough road to **Marsabit**, the dusty tribal centre of this remote area, which boasts a fine national park.

Assuming you're not tempted to hop across to Ethiopia at Moyale, take the western loop to Turkana via **North Horr**, heading for the tiny lakeside settlement of **Loyangalani**, a base for trips into even more remote parts.

From here the trail leads south again, passing all kinds of scenic zones and the stopover towns of **South Horr** and **Baragoi**. It's worth stopping for a couple of days in **Maralal**, to replenish supplies and sample the joys of camel trekking.

You could end the trip here, but for the full effect head up to the other side of Turkana, passing through the lush western area around **Marich Pass** to reach sweltering **Lodwar** and the lovely lakeshore at **Eliye Springs**.

Safaris

Best Wildlife Experience

Annual wildebeest migration
Location Masai Mara National Reserve
Season Jul–Oct

Best Birdwatching Experience

Flamingos
Location Lake Nakuru & Lake Bogoria, Rift Valley
Season Year-round

Best Times to Avoid

Rainy Season late Mar–May

Best Safari Planning Resources

Ecotourism Society of Kenya (p34)
Kenyan Association of Tour Operators (KATO; p34)
ResponsibleTravel.com (p34)

Best Safari Circuits

The Mara Circuit (p32)
The Southern Circuit (p32)

Best Specialist Safaris

Birdwatching Origins Safaris (p35)
Camel Desert Rose (p35)
Cultural IntoAfrica (p35)
Cycling Bike Treks (p32)
DIY Adventure Upgrade Safaris (p36)

Safari has to be one of the most evocative words ever to infiltrate the English language. In Kiswahili, safari quite literally means 'journey', though to eager visitors flocking to the Kenyan national parks, it means so much more. From inspiring visions of wildebeests fording raging rivers and lions stalking their heedless prey through the savannah grass, to iridescent flamingos lining a salty shore at sunset, a safari into the wild is untamed Africa at its finest.

Planning a Safari

Booking

Many travellers prefer to get all the hard work done before they arrive in Kenya by booking from home, either through travel agents or directly with safari companies. This ensures that you'll be able to secure a spot at the more famous lodges, especially during peak seasons when places start filling up months in advance. However, while most safari operators will take internet bookings, making arrangements with anyone other than a well-established midrange or top-end operator can be a risky business. If you're going for a budget option, you should certainly wait and do your research on the ground when you arrive.

If you want to book a safari once in Kenya, allow at least a day to shop around, don't rush into any deals and steer clear of any attempts of intimidation by touts or dodgy operators. The best way to ensure you get what you pay for is to decide exactly what you want, then visit the various companies in person and talk through the kind of package you're looking for. Budget travellers should also check out the various backpackers' accommodation choices around Nairobi, as most also organise safaris.

Costs

Compared to other countries on the continent, Kenya is not always the cheapest destination for safaris. That said, most safari operator quotes include just about everything, such as park entrance fees, the costs of accommodation or tent rental, transport costs from the starting base to the park, and the costs of fuel plus a driver/guide for wildlife drives. However, this varies enough that it's essential to clarify before paying. Drinks (whether alcoholic or not) are generally excluded, and budget camping safari prices usually exclude sleeping-bag hire. Prices quoted by agencies or operators usually assume shared (double) room/tent occupancy, with supplements for single occupancy ranging from an additional 20% to 50% of the shared-occupancy rate.

If you're dealing directly with lodges and tented camps rather than going through a safari operator, you may be quoted 'all-inclusive' prices. In addition to accommodation, full board and sometimes park fees, these usually include two 'activities' (usually wildlife drives, or sometimes one wildlife drive and one walk) per day, each lasting about two to three hours. They generally exclude transport costs to the park. Whenever accommodation-only prices apply, and unless you have your own vehicle, you'll need to pay extra to actually go out looking for wildlife, and costs can be considerable.

Budget Safaris

Most safaris at the lower end of the price range are camping safaris. In order to keep costs to a minimum, groups often camp outside national park areas (thereby saving camping fees) or – alternatively – stay in budget guesthouses outside the park. Budget operators also save costs by working with larger groups to minimise per-person transport costs, and by keeping to a no-frills set-up with basic meals and a minimum number of staff. For most safaris at the budget level, as well as for many midrange safaris, daily kilometre limits are placed on the vehicles.

For any budget safari, the bare minimum cost for a registered company is about US$75 to US$100 per person per day, which should include transport, food (three meals per day), park entry and camping fees, tents and cooking equipment. Sleeping-bag hire will cost you an additional US$10 to US$15 for the duration of the trip.

BEATING SAFARI SCAMS

Every year we get numerous letters from readers complaining about bad experiences on safari, such as dodging park fees and ignoring client requests, to pure rip-offs and outright criminal behaviour. For the most part, these incidents are perpetrated by Nairobi's budget companies, which shave every possible corner to keep their costs down.

One persistent feature of Kenya's safari scene is the street tout, who will approach you almost as soon as you step out of your hotel in the streets of Nairobi and Mombasa. They're not all bad guys, and the safari you end up with may be fine, but you'll pay a mark-up to cover their commission.

We can't stress enough how important it is to not rush your booking. Talk to travellers, do as much research as possible, insist on setting out every detail of your trip in advance, don't be pressured into anything and don't pay any substantial amounts of cash up front. If in doubt, think seriously about stretching your budget to use a reputable midrange firm. And even though we recommend some operators in this chapter, satisfaction is by no means guaranteed whoever you go with.

Of course, we receive plenty of positive feedback as well, so don't let potential problems put you off. Indeed, wildlife safaris can be utterly unforgettable experiences for all the right reasons, so it's certainly worth making the effort to book one – just keep your wits about you...

» (above) Safari vehicles in Tsavo National Park (p97 and p102)
» (left) Young cheetah, Masai Mara National Reserve (p129)

Midrange Safaris

Most midrange safaris use lodges, where you'll have a comfortable room and eat in a restaurant. Overall, safaris in this category are reliable and reasonably good value. A disadvantage is that they may have somewhat of a packaged-tour or production-line feel. This can be minimised by selecting a safari company and accommodation carefully, by giving attention to who and how many other people you travel with, and by avoiding the large, popular lodges during peak season.

In high season you're looking at US$150 to US$200 per person per night (usually full board) for staying in lodges or tented camps, though these prices do drop a bit in the low season.

Top-End Safaris

Private lodges, luxury tented camps and even private fly-in camps are used in top-end safaris, all with the aim of providing guests with as 'authentic' and personal a bush experience as possible without forgoing the creature comforts. For the price you pay (from US$220 up to US$600 or more per person per day), expect a full range of amenities, as well as top-quality guiding. Even in remote settings without running water you will be able to enjoy hot, bush-style showers, comfortable beds and fine dining. Also expect a high level of personalised attention and an intimate atmosphere – many places at this level have fewer than 20 beds.

Tipping

Assuming service has been satisfactory, tipping is an important part of the safari experience, especially to the driver/guides, cooks and others whose livelihoods depend on tips. Many operators have tipping guidelines, although in general you can expect to tip about US$3 to US$5 per staff member per day from each traveller. This value should increase substantially if you're on a top-end safari, part of a large group or if an especially good job has been done.

Also, it's never a mistake to err on the side of generosity while tipping. Remember that other travellers are going to follow you and the last thing anyone wants to find is a disgruntled driver/guide who couldn't care less whether you see wildlife or not.

When to Go

Wildlife can be seen at all times of year, but the migration patterns of the big herbivores (which in turn attract the big predators) are likely to be a major factor in deciding when to go. From July to October, huge herds of wildebeest and zebras cross from the Serengeti in Tanzania to the Masai Mara. This is probably prime viewing time as the land is parched, the vegetation has died back and the animals are obliged to come to drink at the ever-shrinking waterholes. However, most safari companies increase their rates at this time. Birdwatching is especially good from October to March.

The long rains (from March to May) transform the national parks into a lush carpet of greenery. It's very scenic, but it does provide much more cover for the wildlife to hide behind, and the rain can turn the tracks into impassable mush. Safaris may be impossible in the lowland parks during this time. Such problems are also possible during the short rains (from October to November), although getting around is rarely a problem.

Itineraries

Most itineraries offered by safari companies fall into one of three loosely defined 'circuits', which can all be combined for longer trips. Treks up Mt Kenya (p172) are a fourth option, sold separately or as an add-on.

For an idea of what's feasible in the time you have available, turn to p23.

DON'T HURRY

When planning your safari, don't be tempted to try to fit too much in to your itinerary. Distances in Kenya are long, and hopping too quickly from park to park is likely to leave you at the end tired, unsatisfied and feeling that you haven't even scratched the surface. Try instead to plan longer periods at just one or two parks – exploring in depth what each has to offer, and taking advantage of cultural and walking opportunities in park border areas.

The Mara Circuit

The standard safari itinerary centres on the **Masai Mara** (p129). The shorter versions generally involve two nights in the park and two half-days travelling. Possible add-ons include **Lake Nakuru National Park** (p122), **Samburu National Reserve** (p201), **Lake Baringo** (p125) and **Lake Bogoria** (p124).

The Southern Circuit

Offered as the main alternative to the Mara, southern itineraries make a beeline for **Amboseli National Park** (p92) and its famous Kilimanjaro backdrop. Anything longer than a three-day trip here should allow you to also visit **Tsavo West** (p97) for a couple of nights, with a couple more days required to add on **Tsavo East** (p102) as well. Most companies will give you the option of being dropped in Mombasa at the end of this route rather than heading back to Nairobi.

The Northern Circuit

The focal point of any northern safari is **Lake Turkana** (p211), which requires at least a week to visit effectively due to the long distances involved. Depending on how long you take, and which side of the lake you visit, possible stops include the **Rift Valley lakes** (p108), **Marsabit National Park** (p208) and **Samburu National Reserve** (p201) – a two-week safari could even cover all of these.

Types of Safaris

For a list of recommended safari companies who may cover one or more of the following types of safari, turn to p35.

Birdwatching Safaris

Most of the safari companies listed in this chapter offer some kind of birdwatching safaris, though the quality is not always up to par for serious birders – if you're a serious birdwatcher, quiz any prospective companies at length before making a booking. **Origins Safaris** (p35) is one reliable specialist.

Camel Safaris

This is a superb way of getting right off the beaten track and into areas where vehicle safaris don't or can't go. Most camel safaris go to the Samburu and Turkana tribal areas between Isiolo and Lake Turkana, where you'll experience nomadic life and mingle with tribal people. Wildlife is also plentiful, although it's the journey itself that is the main attraction.

You have the choice of riding the camels or walking alongside them. Most caravans are led by experienced Samburu *moran* (warriors), and accompanied by English-speaking tribal guides who are well versed in bush lore, botany, ornithology and local customs. Most travelling is done as early as possible in the cool of the day, and a campsite established around noon. Afternoons are time for relaxing, guided walks and showers before drinks and dinner around the campfire.

All companies provide a full range of camping equipment (generally including two-person tents) and ablution facilities. The typical distance covered each day is 15km to 18km so you don't have to be superfit to survive this style of safari.

The following companies offer camel safaris of varying lengths:

Bobong Camp (p211)

Desert Rose (p35)

Yare Camel Club & Camp (p212)

Camping Safaris

Few things can match the thrill of waking up in the middle of the African bush with nothing between you and the animals except a sheet of canvas and the dying embers of last night's fire.

Camping safaris cater for budget travellers, the young (or young at heart) and those who are prepared to put up with a little discomfort to get the authentic bush experience. At the bottom of the price range, you'll have to forgo luxuries such as flush toilets, running water and cold drinks, and you'll have to chip in with chores such as putting up the tents and helping prepare dinner. Showers are provided at some but not all campsites, although there's usually a tap where you can scrub down with cold water. The price of your safari will include three meals a day cooked by the camp cook(s), although food will be of the plain-but-plenty variety.

There are more comfortable camping options, where there are extra staff to do all the work, but they cost more. A number of companies have also set up permanent campsites where you can just drop into bed at the end of a dusty day's drive.

» (above) Samburu man (p201) on camel safari
» (left) A luxury tent in the Masai Mara (p129)

Cultural Safaris

With ecofriendly lodges now springing up all over Kenya, remote population groups are becoming increasingly involved with tourism. There is also a growing number of companies offering cultural safaris, allowing you to interact with locals in a far more personal way than the rushed souvenir stops that the mainstream tours make at Maasai villages. The best of these combine volunteer work with more conventional tour activities, and provide accommodation in tents, ecolodges and village houses.

One company that receives consistently good reviews for its cultural safaris is **IntoAfrica** (p35).

Flying Safaris

These safaris essentially cater for the well-off who want to fly between remote airstrips in the various national parks and stay in luxury tented camps. If money is no object, you can get around by a mixture of charter and scheduled flights and stay in some of the finest camps in Kenya – arrangements can be made with any of the lodge and tented-camp safari operators. Flying safaris to Lake Turkana and Sibiloi National Park are an interesting alternative and most safari companies will be able to sort out a countrywide itinerary.

Lodge & Tented-Camp Safaris

Safari lodges make up the bulk of most safari experiences, ranging from five-star luxury to more simple affairs. In the lodges you can expect rooms with bathrooms or cottages with air-conditioning, international cuisine, a terrace bar beneath a huge *makuti* (palm-thatched) canopy with wonderful views, a swimming pool, wildlife videos and other entertainments, and plenty of staff on hand to cater for all your requirements. Almost all lodges have a waterhole and some have a hidden viewing tunnel that leads right to the waterside.

If you can't do without luxuries, there's a whole world of luxurious lodges with swimming pools and bars overlooking waterholes, and remote tented camps that re-create the way wealthy hunters travelled around Kenya a century ago. Some of the lodges are beautifully conceived and the locations are to die for, perched high above huge sweeps of savannah or waterholes teeming with African wildlife. Most are set deep within the national parks, so the safari drives offer maximum wildlife-viewing time.

The luxury-tented camps tend to offer semipermanent tents with fitted bathrooms (hot showers are standard), beds with mosquito nets, proper furniture, fans and gourmet meals served alfresco in the bush. The really exclusive ones are even more luxurious than the lodges and tend to be *very* expensive: many of the guests fly in on charter planes, which should give you some impression of the kind of budget we're talking about.

Motorcycle Safaris

Operating out of Diani Beach, **Fredlink Tours** (p247) runs motorcycle safaris to the Taita Hills, Rift Valley, Tsavo West and the Kilimanjaro foothills.

Walking & Cycling Safaris

For the keen walker or cyclist, and those who don't want to spend all their time in a safari minibus, there are a number of options. For information on treks in Mt Kenya National Park, see p172.

Booking a Safari

The service provided by even the best safari companies can vary, depending on the driver, the itinerary, the behaviour of the wildlife, flat tyres and breakdowns and, of course, the attitude of the passengers themselves. We've tried to recommend some of the better companies later in this section, but this shouldn't take the place of your own hands-on research.

Useful Resources

Ecotourism Society of Kenya (ESOK; ☎020-2724755; www.ecotourismkenya.org) Maintains a list of member companies and lodges who subscribe to its code of conduct for responsible, sustainable safaris.

Kenyan Association of Tour Operators (KATO; ☎020-2713348; www.katokenya.org) It may not be the most powerful regulatory body in the world, but most reputable safari companies subscribe, and going with a KATO member will give you *some* recourse in case of conflict.

Kenya Professional Safari Guides Association (KPSGA; ☎020-2342426; www.safariguides.org) Your guide's accreditation by this body is a good indicator of quality and experience.

ResponsibleTravel.com (www.responsibletravel.com) A good place to start planning a culturally and environmentally responsible safari.

Uniglobe Let's Go Travel (p83) A searchable database of lodges and other forms of accommodation as well as a useful safari finder.

Safari Companies

The following list of safari companies is by no means exhaustive. We've chosen these places either because of first-hand experience, consistently positive reports from travellers, and/or the fact that they've been around for a while. Most are members of the Kenyan Association of Tour Operators.

Abercrombie & Kent (Map p64; ☎020-6950000; www.abercrombiekent.com; Abercrombie & Kent House, Mombasa Rd, Nairobi) Luxury travel company with excellent safaris to match.

Basecamp Explorer (off Map p56; ☎0733333709; www.basecampexplorer.com; off Ngong Rd, Nairobi) Scandinavian-owned ecotourism operator offering comprehensive and often luxurious camping itineraries with an environmentally sustainable focus.

Bike Treks (off Map p77; ☎020-2141757; www.biketreks.co.ke; Kabete Gardens, Westlands, Nairobi) Just about every possible combination of walking and cycling safaris, from quick three-day jaunts to full-on expeditions.

Bushbuck Adventures (off Map p56; ☎020-7123090; www.bushbuckadventures.com; Peponi Rd, Westlands, Nairobi) Small company specialising in personalised (including walking) safaris. It has a private, semipermanent camp in the Masai Mara.

Desert Rose (www.desertrosekenya.com) Walking camel-train safaris (everything from bare bones to luxury) leave from the remote Desert Rose lodge just north of Baragoi in northern Kenya.

Eastern & Southern Safaris (Map p60; ☎020-2242828; www.essafari.co.ke; 6th fl, Finance House, Loita St, Nairobi) Classy and reliable outfit aiming at the midrange and upper end of the market, with standards to match. They do all the classic Kenyan trips.

Eco-Resorts (☎0733618183; www.eco-resorts.com) US-based company with a variety of activity-based volunteer and cultural packages and customised safaris around Kenya. A proportion of profits go to community and conservation projects.

Gametrackers (Map p60; ☎020-2222703; www.gametrackersafaris.com; 5th fl, Nginyo Towers, cnr Koinange & Moktar Daddah Sts, Nairobi) Long-established and reliable company with a full range of camping and lodge safaris around Kenya; one of the best operators for Lake Turkana and the north.

IntoAfrica (☎UK 0114-2555610; www.intoafrica.co.uk; 40 Huntingdon Cres, Sheffield, UK) One of the most highly praised safari companies in East Africa, IntoAfrica specialises in 'fair-trade' trips providing insights into African life and directly supporting local communities. Combining culture *and* wildlife viewing is a speciality.

Natural Tours & Safaris (www.naturaltoursandsafaris.com) Mombasa (☎041-2226715; Jeneby House, Moi Ave); Nairobi (Map p60; ☎020-2216830; 1st fl, Gilfillan House, Nairobi) Well-organised safaris visiting all the major parks.

Origins Safaris (Map p60; ☎020-3312137; www.originsafaris.info; EcoBank Towers, Standard St, Nairobi) A natural history and cultural focus, with everything from expert birdwatching to Samburu circumcision ceremonies, as well as other more mainstream safaris.

Pollman's Tours & Safaris (Map p64; ☎020-3337234; www.pollmans.com; Pollman's House, Mombasa Rd, Nairobi) Kenyan-based operator that covers all the main national parks, with coastal and Tanzanian trips as well.

GUIDE ACCREDITATION

A good indicator of any guide's level of expertise and experience is the accreditation system run by the Kenya Professional Safari Guides Association. It isn't perfect, but all applicants must sit for an exam to progress to the next level and it remains a fairly effective system. A full (although not always updated) list of accredited guides can be found on the website (www.safariguides.org).

» **Bronze**: basic knowledge of guiding and wildlife

» **Silver**: advanced knowledge of guiding and wildlife, and at least three years' experience

» **Gold**: the elite, with (at last count) just 13 in the whole country

Private Safaris (www.privatesafaris.co.ke) Mombasa (☎041-476000; Safari House, Kaunda St); Nairobi (☎020-3607000; 2nd fl, Mobil Plaza, Muthaiga) Another safari agent offering trips that can be highly customised, Private can book trips all throughout sub-Saharan Africa.

Safe Ride Tours & Safaris (Map p60; ☎020-2229484; www.saferidesafaris.com; 2nd fl, Ave House, Kenyatta Ave, Nairobi) A relatively new budget operator recommended by readers for camping excursions around the country.

Samburu Trails Trekking Safaris (UK ☎0131-6256635; www.samburutrails.com) Small British specialist outfit offering a range of foot excursions in some less-visited parts of the Rift Valley.

Savage Wilderness Safaris (Map p77; ☎020-7121590; www.whitewaterkenya.com; Sarit Centre, Westlands, Nairobi) Kenya's premier white-water rafting company also offers organised and customised walking, climbing and mountaineering trips.

Somak Travel (www.somak-nairobi.com) Mombasa (☎041-5486326; Somak House, Nyerere Ave); Nairobi (Map p64; ☎020-535508; Somak House, Mombasa Rd) Kenyan-based operator with more than 30 years of experience on the safari circuit, Somak is a home-grown favourite.

Southern Cross Safaris (www.southerncrosssafaris.com) Mombasa (☎041-2434600; Kanstan Centre, Nyali Bridge, Malindi Rd); Nairobi (Map p64; ☎020-3884712; Symbion House, Karen Rd) Professional Kenyan company Southern Cross is a good choice for individually designed safaris.

Tropical Winds (Map p60; ☎020-3341939; www.tropical-winds.com; Lower ground fl, Barclays Plaza, Loita St) Nairobi's STA Travel representative with the full safari range.

Do-It-Yourself Safaris

A DIY safari is a viable and enticing proposition in Kenya. Doing it yourself has several advantages over organised safaris, primarily total flexibility, independence and being able to choose your travelling companions. However, as far as costs go, it's generally true to say that organising your own safari will cost at least as much, and usually more, than going on an organised safari to the same areas. And you will, of course, need to book your own accommodation well in advance (if you're staying in lodges or tented camps) or carry your own camping equipment. For advice on renting a car or 4WD in Kenya, see p379.

Four local car-hire companies that we recommend:

Adventure Upgrade Safaris (Map p60; ☎0722529228; www.adventureupgradesafaris.co.ke)

Central Rent-a-Car (Map p60; ☎020-2222888; www.carhirekenya.com)

Tough Trucks Kenya (Map p60; ☎020-2228725; www.toughtruckskenya.com)

Uniglobe Let's Go Travel (Map p64; ☎020-4447151; www.uniglobeletsgotravel.com)

Camping Equipment

For a list of companies offering camping equipment for rent, see p81.

One of the better places is **Atul's** (Map p60; ☎020-2228064; Biashara St) in Nairobi. Expect to pay KSh180 to KSh250 per day for a sleeping bag with liner, KSh450 for a two-person dome tent and KSh100 per day for a gas stove (gas canisters are extra). On most items there is a deposit of KSh1500 to KSh3000.

It's also possible to hire a vehicle and camping equipment as one package. **Adventure Upgrade Safaris** (☎0722529228; www.adventureupgradesafaris.co.ke) is one such operator.

BUDGET SAFARIS

In addition to the larger safari companies, numerous budget accommodation options in Nairobi organise camping safaris for budget travellers. These include the following:

Milimani Backpackers & Safari Centre (p71)

Upper Hill Campsite & Backpackers (p71)

Whistling Thorns (p87)

Wildebeest Camp (p71)

Outdoor Activities

Best Ballooning
Masai Mara National Reserve
Location Western Kenya
Season Jul-Oct

Best Mountaineering
Mt Kenya National Park
Location Central Highlands
Season Jun-Oct

Best Diving & Snorkelling
Manda Toto Island
Location Lamu Archipelago
Season Oct-Mar

Best Mountain Trekking
Mt Elgon or Mt Longonot
Location Western Kenya or Rift Valley
Season Jun-Feb

Best Forest Trekking
Kakamega Forest
Location Western Kenya
Season Jun-Feb

Best Windsurfing
Lamu & Manda Islands
Location Lamu Archipelago
Season Dec-Mar

Best for Watersports
Diani Beach
Location South of Mombasa
Season Year round

Planning Your Trip

When to Go

Kenya is a fantastic year-round activities destination, with one exception: we generally recommend that you avoid the long rains which run from sometime in March (or later) through to May. At this time trails (and access roads) can be impassable, and underwater visibility is generally poorer. The shorter rains in October and November tend to be more localised and heavy downpours rarely last longer than an hour or two. These 'short rains' (as they're known locally) will rarely disrupt your plans to get active.

What to Take

There are few requirements for most activities. Operators who organise whitewater rafting and other similar sports will provide the necessary equipment; bicycles and mountain bikes can be rented in Kenya, but serious cyclists and bikers may want to bring their own. Most hikers head out onto the trail under their own steam, but even those who plan on joining an organised hike with a guide will usually need to bring their own equipment.

Land Activities

If bumping around national parks in a safari bus in search of wildlife isn't your thing, or if you'd like to add an extra dimension to your time in Kenya, there's an amazing range of distractions and diversions to keep you on your toes from dusk till dawn. Trekking is among the most popular pursuits, as it doesn't require expensive equipment and can be arranged very easily locally; for a different thrill try an aerial adventure from balloons to gliders. For more ideas on organised trips and activities, see p28.

Ballooning

Balloon trips in the wildlife parks are an absolutely superb way of seeing the savannah and, of course, the animals. The almost ghostly experience of floating silently above the plains with a 360° view of everything beneath you is incomparable, and it's definitely worth saving up your shillings to take one of these trips.

The flights typically set off at dawn and go for about 1½ hours, after which you put down for a champagne breakfast. You will then be taken on a wildlife drive in a support vehicle and returned to your lodge. Prices start at around US$500. Check out the following companies:

» **Governors' Balloon Safaris** (www.governorscamp.com) This company operates out of Little Governors' Camp in the Mara.

» **Transworld Balloon Safaris** (www.transworldsafaris.com/ballooning.php) Based at the Sarova Mara Lodge in the Mara.

» **Kilimanjaro Ballooning** (www.kilimanjaroballooning.co.ke) Amboseli National Park.

» **Go Ballooning Kenya** (www.goballooningkenya.com) Lake Elmenteita.

Where to Balloon

» **Masai Mara National Reserve** (p129)

» **Lake Elmenteita** (p118)

» **Amboseli National Park** (p92)

Climbing & Mountaineering

Kenya isn't particularly well-known for its rock-climbing, but that's more to do with a lack of infrastructure rather than a lack of suitable places. One professional outfit, **Savage Wilderness Safaris** (☎020-521590; www.whitewaterkenya.com; Sarit Centre, Westlands, Nairobi), offers mountaineering trips to Mt Kenya, as well as other activities elsewhere around the country.

Another useful resource is the **Mountain Club of Kenya** (MCK; www.mck.or.ke; Wilson Airport) in Nairobi. Members have a huge pool of technical knowledge about climbing in Kenya.

Where to Climb

» **Mt Kenya** (p172)

» **Tsavo West National Park** (p97)

» **Ndoto Mountains** (p205)

» **Hell's Gate National Park** (p117)

Cycling & Mountain-Biking

An increasing number of companies offer cycling trips in Kenya. The best operator is **Bike Treks** (☎020-2141757; www.biketreks.co.ke), which has specialised trips for around US$120 per day; it might even have you cycling through the Masai Mara...

If you're just after a trundle rather than some serious cycling, many local companies and accommodation places around the country (particularly campgrounds) can arrange bicycle hire. Prices generally start at KSh500 to KSh700 per day, but always check the quality of the bike as standards vary wildly.

For more information, visit the website of the **Mountain Club of Kenya** (MCK; www.mck.or.ke).

See also p376 for more information on cycling in Kenya.

Where to Cycle

» **Masai Mara National Reserve** (p129)

» **Hell's Gate National Park** (p117)

» **Central Highlands** (p162)

» **Arabuko Sokoke Forest Reserve** (p263)

Gliding & Flying

The **Gliding Club of Kenya** (off Map p164; ☎0733760331; gliding@africaonline.co.ke; Nyeri), near Nyeri in the Central Highlands, offers silent glides over the Aberdares.

Flying lessons are easily arranged in Nairobi and are much more affordable than in Europe, the USA and Australasia. Contact the **Aero Club of East Africa** (☎020-6000479; www.aeroclubea.com) and **Ninety-Nines Flying Club** (☎020-6006935; www.99flying.com), both at Wilson Airport.

RESPONSIBLE TREKKING & CLIMBING

Help preserve the ecology and beauty of Kenya by observing the following tips:

Rubbish

» Carry out all your rubbish.

» Never bury rubbish: digging disturbs soil and ground cover and encourages erosion. Buried rubbish will likely be dug up by animals, which may be injured or poisoned by it.

» Minimise waste by taking minimal packaging and no more food than you will need. Take reusable containers or stuff sacks.

» Sanitary napkins, tampons, condoms and toilet paper should be carried out despite the inconvenience. They burn and decompose poorly.

Human Waste Disposal

» Where there is a toilet, please use it. Where there is none, bury your waste. Dig a small hole 15cm deep and at least 100m from any watercourse. Cover the waste with soil and a rock.

Washing

» Don't use detergents or toothpaste in or near watercourses, even if they are biodegradable.

» For personal washing, use biodegradable soap and a water container at least 50m away from the watercourse. Disperse the waste water widely to allow the soil to filter it fully.

» Wash cooking utensils 50m from watercourses using a scourer, sand or snow instead of detergent.

Erosion

» Stick to existing tracks and avoid short cuts.

» If a well-used track passes through a mud patch, walk through the mud so as not to increase the size of the patch.

Fires & Low-Impact Cooking

» Don't depend on open fires for cooking. Cook on a lightweight kerosene, alcohol or shellite (white gas) stove and avoid those powered by disposable butane gas canisters.

» Ensure that you fully extinguish a fire after use.

Wildlife Conservation

» Discourage the presence of wildlife by not leaving food scraps behind you. Place gear out of reach and tie packs to rafters or trees.

» Do not feed the wildlife as this can lead to animals becoming dependent on handouts, to unbalanced populations and to disease.

Trekking

Kenya has some of the best trekking trails in East Africa, ranging from strenuous mountain ascents to rolling hill country and forests. It is, of course, always worth checking out the prevailing security situation in the area you wish to trek, not to mention the prevalence of any wild animals you might encounter along the trail. In some instances, it may be advisable to take a local guide, either from the Kenyan Wildlife Service (KWS) if they operate in the area, or a local village guide.

Where to Trek

The following places are all good for proper mountain trekking in varying degrees of difficulty:

- **Mt Kenya** (5199m; p172)
- **Mt Elgon National Park** (4187m; p158)
- **Mt Longonot** (2776m; p109)
- **Cherangani Hills** (p160)
- **Lesiolo Loop** (p214)
- **Mt Kulal** (p216)
- **Aberdares** (p168)
- **Ndoto Mountains** (p205)

For forest hiking, we especially like the following:

- **Kakamega Forest** (p150)
- **Matthews Range** (p204)
- **Arabuko Sokoke Forest Reserve** (p263)

Useful Trekking Resources

For more trekking information, refer to the relevant chapters in this book or get hold of a copy of Lonely Planet's *Trekking in East Africa*; it may be out of print but remains the definitive guide to trekking the region.

Also be sure to contact the **Mountain Club of Kenya** (MCK; www.mck.or.ke) in Nairobi. The club meets at 8pm every Tuesday at the clubhouse at Wilson Airport. Members organise frequent climbing and trekking weekends around the country.

Savage Wilderness Safaris (☎020-521590; www.whitewaterkenya.com; Sarit Centre, Westlands, Nairobi) offers trekking around the country.

PERSONAL TREKKING EQUIPMENT CHECKLIST

- ☐ Sturdy hiking boots
- ☐ A good-quality sleeping bag – at high altitude (such as Mt Kenya), nights can be bitterly cold and the weather can turn nasty at short notice
- ☐ Warm clothing, including a jacket, jersey (sweater) or anorak (windbreaker) that can be added or removed
- ☐ A sleeping sheet, a warm, but lightweight sleeping bag
- ☐ A sturdy but lightweight tent
- ☐ Mosquito repellent
- ☐ A lightweight stove
- ☐ Trousers for walking, preferably made from breathing waterproof (and windproof) material such as Gore-Tex
- ☐ Air-filled sleeping pad
- ☐ Swiss Army knife
- ☐ Torch (flashlight) or headlamp with extra batteries

Water Activities

A whole world of water activities awaits in Kenya. Snorkelling is popular and can easily be arranged locally and inexpensively. Some of the larger resorts have water-sports centres giving visitors the opportunity to try out everything from jet skis and banana boats to bodyboarding and surfing.

Diani Beach (p243), south of Mombasa, is the best place to go if you want to try any (or all) of these activities. **Malindi** (p265) can also be good.

Diving & Snorkelling

The Kenyan coast promises some of the best diving and snorkelling in Africa beyond the Red Sea. There are a number of professional dive centres, but many visitors' first experience of the world beneath the Indian Ocean's surface comes by diving off the back of a boat in the course of a languid dhow (Arab sailing boat) journey. In addition to myriad fish species and colourful coral, charismatic marine mammals – including dolphins, sea turtles, whale sharks and humpback whales (August to October) – also frequent these waters.

If you aren't certified to dive, almost every hotel and resort on the coast can arrange an open-water diving course. They're not much cheaper (if at all) than anywhere else in the world – a five-day PADI certification course will cost between US$400 and US$500. Trips for certified divers including two dives go for around US$100.

When to Dive & Snorkel

There are distinct seasons for diving in Kenya. October to March is the best time; from June to August it's often impossible to dive due to the poor visibility caused by the heavy silt flow from some rivers. That said, some divers have taken the plunge in July and found visibility to be a very respectable 7m to 10m, although 4m is more common. So don't decide not to dive just because you find yourself here in the underwater-visibility low season – particularly if you're a first timer, you're unlikely to leave disappointed.

» (above) Sailing the Indian Ocean, off Diani Beach (p242)
» (left) Spotting zebras on a hot-air-balloon safari, Masai Mara National Reserve (p129)

Where to Dive & Snorkel

There is a string of marine national parks spread out along the coast between Shimoni and Malindi. As a general rule, these are the best places to dive and snorkel, and the better marine parks are those further away from Mombasa.

» **Kiwayu Island** (p286)

» **Malindi Marine National Park** (p265)

» **Manda Toto Island** (p284)

» **Kisite Marine National Park** (p249)

» **Diani Beach** (p243)

» **Wasini Island** (p249)

» **Malindi Marine Natinal Park** (p265)

» **Watamu Marine National Park** (p260)

Fishing

The **Kenya Fisheries Department** (☎020-3742320; www.fisheries.go.ke; Museum Hill Rd, Nairobi), operates a number of fishing camps in various parts of the country, and also issues mandatory fishing licences.

There is, however, a downside to fishing in the country – for a sobering look at the ecological state of Kenya's fisheries, see p249.

Where to Fish

For freshwater fishing, there are huge Nile perch as big as a person in **Lake Victoria** (p137) and **Lake Turkana** (p194). Some of the trout fishing around **Mt Kenya** (p172) and the **Aberdares** (p163) is exceptional.

The deep-sea fishing on the coast is some of the best in the world, and various private companies and resorts in the following places can arrange fishing trips. Boats cost from US$250 to US$500 and can usually fit four or five anglers. The season runs from August to April.

» **Diani Beach** (p243)

» **Watamu** (p263)

» **Malindi** (p265)

» **Shimoni** (p248)

» **Mtwapa** (p255)

Sailing

Kilifi (p256), **Mtwapa** (p255) and **Mombasa** (p223) all have sailing clubs, and smaller freshwater clubs can also be found at **Lake Naivasha** (p111) and **Lake Victoria** (p137), which both have excellent windsurfing and sailing. If you're experienced, you may pick up some crewing at the yacht clubs; you'll need to become a temporary member. While not hands-on, a traditional dhow trip out of **Lamu** (p280) is an unforgettable sailing experience.

Water Sports

Windsurfing

Conditions on Kenya's coast are ideal for windsurfing – the country's offshore reefs protect the waters, and the winds are usually reasonably strong and constant. Most resort hotels south and north of Mombasa have sailboards for hire.

Where to Windsurf

» **Lamu and Manda Islands** (p282) The sheltered channel between Lamu and Manda Islands is one of the best places for windsurfing on the coast.

» **Watamu** (p260)

» **Malindi** (p270) Also good for kitesurfing.

White-Water Rafting

The people to talk to are **Savage Wilderness Safaris** (☎020-521590; www.whitewaterkenya.com; Sarit Centre, Westlands, Nairobi), run by the charismatic Mark Savage. Depending on water levels, rafting trips start from four to five hours, but longer trips (450km, three weeks' duration) are also possible; most trips last one to four days and cover up to 80km.

The most exciting times for a white-water rafting trip are from late October to mid-January and from early April to late July, when water levels are highest.

Where to Go Rafting

The **Athi/Galana River** has substantial rapids, chutes and waterfalls and there are also possibilities on the **Tana River** and **Ewaso Ngiro River** near Isiolo.

Travel with Children

Best Regions for Kids

Western Kenya

A safari in the Masai Mara, particularly during the extraordinary spectacle of the massed wildebeest migration, is surely one of the most memorable experiences your child will ever have in nature. If you take your kids to one wildlife reserve, make it the Masai Mara.

Southern Kenya

In Amboseli National Park, you're still in the heart of Maasai country and you'll never get as close to an elephant as you will here. The other parks in the region require more patience, but provide more of a wilderness experience which may be better appreciated by older kids.

The North Coast

You could go anywhere along Kenya's coast and find your family's own little slice of paradise. But there's something about the languid pace of life in and around Lamu that seems perfectly suited to a family holiday.

Kenya is a wonderful destination in which to travel as a family. Yes, there are vaccinations to worry about and Africa can seem like a daunting place to take the kids, but just about any kind of trip is possible. You're more likely to have a hassle-free time if you're prepared to spend a little extra and take comfort over adventure for the core of the trip. And it's worth remembering: loads of families simply cast their worries aside and have the holiday of a lifetime.

Kenya for Kids

Families travelling with kids have long been an established part of Kenyan travel and most Kenyans will go out of their way to make your children feel welcome.

Beach Holidays

Beach holidays are a sure-fire way to keep the kids happy, and factoring in some beach time go with the safari can be a good idea. Kenya's beaches alone should be sufficient, but some of the watersports on offer, such as snorkelling, may be suitable for children, depending on their age. And packing a picnic lunch and sailing out to sea on a dhow (a traditional old sailing boat) is a fine way to spend some fun family time.

Culture

Children find it so much easier to break down the barriers of language and culture than do adults, and watching your child play in the dust with a Maasai boy or girl of their own age is an unforgettable experience for children and parents alike. Learning a little of the language and getting to know how children from different cultures spend their days will grab the attention of most children. Better still, their interactions may even help the adults among you to find your entry point into conversations that you'd never dream of starting on your own.

Safaris

The safari could have been custom-built for children. Driving up almost to within touching distance of elephants, watching lion cubs gambolling across the plains or holding their breath as a cheetah accelerates across the plains – these are experiences that will stay with your kids for a lifetime. There are so many lessons to be learned here, from conservation to natural history and geography, and never has learning been so much fun. You'll never be able to visit a zoo again…

Children's Highlights

National Parks & Reserves

» **Masai Mara National Reserve** Africa's charismatic mega-fauna in abundance

» **Amboseli National Park** Get up close and personal with elephants

» **Lake Nakuru National Park** Lions, leopards and playful monkeys

» **Nairobi National Park** A kids'-sized park with no time for interest levels to flag

» **Tsavo East & West National Parks** Tick off the Big Five and marvel at red elephants

» **Mwaluganje Elephant Sanctuary** Accessible but wild enough to be exciting

WHAT TO PACK

While supplies of the following are available in most large supermarkets, they can be expensive. Bring as much as possible from home:

- ☐ canned baby foods
- ☐ child-friendly insect repellent (not available in Kenya)
- ☐ child seat if you're hiring a car or going on safari
- ☐ disposable nappies
- ☐ powdered milk

Beaches

» **Diani Beach** Plenty of child-friendly facilities

» **Malindi** Ditto

» **Shela** White sand and plenty of space close to Lamu

» **Watamu** Another quiet but fabulous beach close to a fishing village

» **Manda Island** Show the kids what East Africa's beaches used to be like

» **Kipungani** A Lamu favourite largely devoid of hassle

Activities

» **Ballooning** Ride high over the Masai Mara in a balloon

» **Dolphin watching** Swim with the dolphins at Kisite Marine National Park

» **Snorkelling** Snorkel at Manda Toto Island to discover a whole new underwater world

» **Sailing** Take a dhow trip from Lamu for a picnic lunch on the beach

» **Elephant feeding** Feed the elephants at Nairobi's David Sheldrick Wildlife Trust

Planning

Local attitudes towards children vary in Kenya just as they do in the West, but kids will generally be welcomed anywhere that's not an exclusively male preserve, especially by women with families of their own.

Accommodation

Safari lodges can handle most practicalities with aplomb, whether it's an extra bed or cot, or buffet meals that will have something even the fussiest of eaters will try. Some lodges have children's playgrounds, and almost all have swimming pools. In non-lodge accommodation, your chances of finding what you need (such as cots) increase the more you're willing to pay.

Budget hotels are probably best avoided for hygiene reasons. Most midrange accommodation should be acceptable, though it's usually only top-end places that cater specifically for families. Camping can be exciting for the little ones, but you'll need to be extra careful that your kids aren't able to wander off unsupervised into the bush.

Most hotels will not charge for children under two years of age. Children between two and 12 years who share their parents' room are usually charged 50% of the adult

» (above) Schoolgirls in uniform near Kisii (p146)

» (left) African elephants at Mwaluganje Elephant Sanctuary (p241)

TOP KENYA BOOKS FOR KIDS

Aimed at children learning about the diverse peoples of the region, the Heritage Library of African Peoples: East Africa is an excellent series. Otherwise, here are some of our favourites:

» *Mama Panya's Pancakes: A Village Tale from Kenya* by Joyce Cooper Arkhurst (suitable 4 to 8 years)

» *Maasai & I* by Virginia Kroll

» *Kenya (Discover Countries)* by Chris Ward

» *Kenya: Letters from Around the World* by Ali Brownlie Bojang

» *For You Are a Kenyan Child* by Kelly Cunnane

» *Jambo Means Hello* by Muriel L Feelings

rate; you'll also get a cot thrown in for this price. Large family rooms are sometimes available, and some places also have adjoining rooms with connecting doors. Be warned that some exclusive lodges impose a minimum age limit for children.

Eating

Kenyans are family-friendly, and dining out with children is no problem. Hotel restaurants occasionally have high chairs, and while special children's meals aren't common, it's easy enough to find items that are suitable for young diners. Avoid curries and other spicy dishes; uncooked, unpeeled fruit and vegetables; meat from street vendors (as it's sometimes undercooked); and unpurified water. Supermarkets stock boxes of fresh juice, and fresh fruit (tangerines, bananas and more) are widely available.

Health

Consult your doctor well in advance of travel as some vaccinations or medications (including some for preventing malaria) are not suitable for children under 12. For detailed health advice for both adults and children, see p383.

Things to Consider

Temperatures can be fiercely hot in southern Kenya (especially around the two Tsavo parks) and extremely humid along the coast. At the other extreme, temperatures in the Rift Valley and Central Highlands can be surprisingly cool, and downright cold at night – come prepared. You might also want to consider flying some parts of the journey in order to avoid long road journeys.

Transport

Safari vehicles are usually child-friendly, but travelling between towns in Kenya on public transport is not always easy with children. Car sickness is one problem, and young children tend to be seen as wriggling luggage, so you'll often have them on your lap. Functional seatbelts are rare even in taxis, and accidents are common – a child seat brought from home is a good idea if you're hiring a car or going on safari.

When to Go

Kenya is a decent year-round destination for kids, with one exception: avoid the wet season from March to May when roads can become impassable, wildlife disperses and the risks from mosquito-born diseases is much higher. Your chances of easily accessible wildlife encounters in the Masai Mara National Reserve are definitely higher during the annual migration from mid-June to mid-October.

regions at a glance

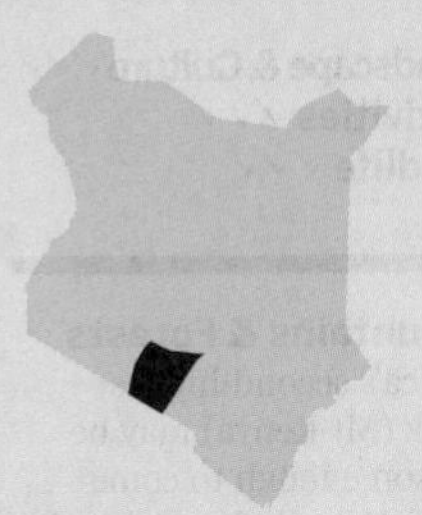

Nairobi

Wildlife ✓✓
Museums & Galleries ✓✓
Food ✓✓

City-fringe Wildlife

Forget elephant herds framed by Mt Kilimanjaro and instead consider the thoroughly modern vision of Africa's free-ranging iconic wildlife set against an unlikely backdrop of not-so-distant skyscrapers. Nairobi National Park's proximity to the capital is matched by its proliferation of wildlife: the big cats, giraffes, rhinos and rich birdlife. Throw in a giraffe-breeding centre and orphaned elephants and Nairobi ranks among Kenya's most surprising wildlife-watching experiences.

Kenya's Storied Past

Kenya's National Museum is an intriguing journey through Kenya's natural and human past, with everything from life-sized elephant models to geological specimens with detours en route into the lives of Kenya's tribal groups. *Out of Africa* fans will find the Karen Blixen Museum takes you back into the fabled Ngong Hills of early-20th-century Kenya, while a host of other museums and galleries showcase Kenya's rich artistic and architectural heritage.

Kenya's Table

Nairobi's culinary variety far surpasses anything you'll find elsewhere in the country, especially out on the safari trail. Here there's everything from fast and furious places where the locals get their fill, through pan-African and Asian choices to upmarket options that evoke Nairobi's colonial past. And then there's Carnivore, one of Africa's most celebrated restaurants.

p52

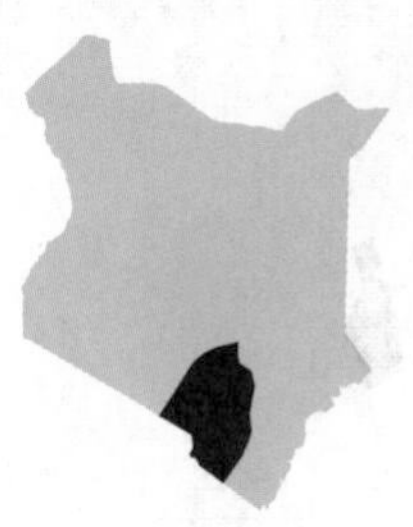

Southern Kenya

Wildlife ✓✓✓
Landscape & Culture ✓✓✓
Activities ✓✓

Pick of the Parks

There's a hint of legend about southern Kenya's parks, from the elephant-and-Kili views from Amboseli to the vast, rugged beauty of the Tsavo parks with their history of man-eating lions, and rescued rhino. Put simply, some of Kenya's most soulful wildlife experiences are found here.

The Maasai Heartland

Southern Kenya occupies the heart of Kenya's Maasai country, the homeland of a people whose presence lends personality to a thinly populated landscape that encompasses sweeping savannah plains, volcanic cinder cones, natural springs and jagged peaks.

Caves & Climbing

Aside from the obvious appeal of safari expeditions in the region's parks, spelunkers will relish the prospect of the world's longest lava tube in the Chyulu Hills National Park, while climbing is also possible in Tsavo West.

p89

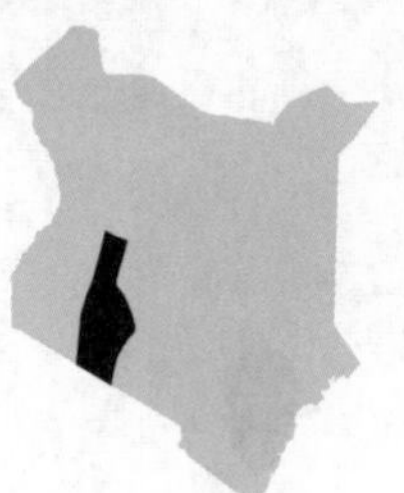

Rift Valley

Landscape ✓✓✓
Wildlife ✓✓
Activities ✓✓✓

The Rift Fracture
The drama of Kenya's Rift Valley is one of natural Africa's grand epics, with astonishing rock formations and expansive lakes that are the aesthetic antidote to the horizonless world of the Masai Mara savannah.

Flamingo & Rhino
The Rift Valley lakes are such rare natural phenomena that strange bedfellows are drawn here to cohabit. Delicate flamingos and prehistoric rhinos are the headline acts among many, with fantastic birdlife (over one-third of Kenya's species) guaranteed.

Hike the Rift
While Mts Kenya and Kilimanjaro get all the attention, discerning hikers look to the relatively untrampled summits of Mt Longonot and Mt Susua. And there's nothing like a foot safari through Hell's Gate National Park for heightening the senses.

p108

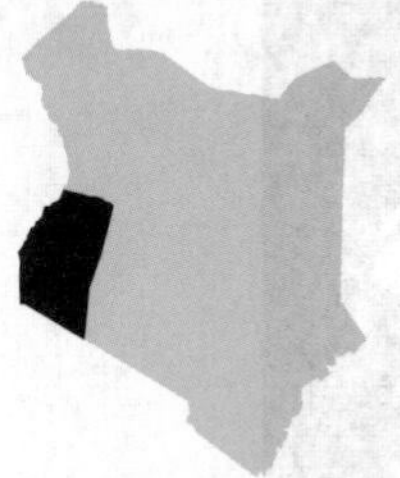

Western Kenya

Wildlife ✓✓✓
Landscape ✓✓✓
Food & Drink ✓

Great Migrations
Western Kenya's Masai Mara, together with the Tanzania's Serengeti, is home to the greatest wildlife show on earth. The great predators – lions, leopards, cheetahs – share the plains with the vast congregations of zebras and wildebeest, while elephants and giraffes look on.

Africa in Microcosm
The vast savannah plains of the Masai Mara may grab the headlines, but Western Kenya also boasts Lake Victoria, one of Kenya's most underrated natural wonders, as well as soaring mountains and forests that evoke the endless stands of green in Central Africa.

Food & Drink
Kenya's tea-growing capital of Kericho is a place to step beyond the clamour of modern Africa, while cheese-lovers should on no account miss Eldoret.

p128

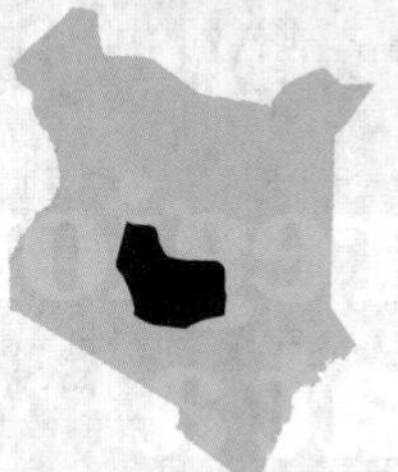

Central Highlands

Landscape & Culture ✓✓✓
Activities ✓✓✓
Wildlife ✓✓✓

Mountains & Forests
Africa's second-highest peak (Mt Kenya) may be reason enough to come here, but rainforest, jungle and savannah somehow also cram into this homeland of Africa's largest tribe, the Kikuyu.

Stairway to Heaven
Trek to Point Lenana, Mt Kenya's third summit, or join the professionals on the climb to its highest point (5199m). Either way, the incongruity of snows this close to the equator and the sweeping views have few peers on the continent.

The Aberdares
Africa's highest-dwelling elephant herd inhabits this forested realm that's a world away from the Africa of popular imagination. And then there's black rhinos and hyenas, the everywhere-you-look baboons and the rarer-than-rare bongo antelopes and black leopards.

p162

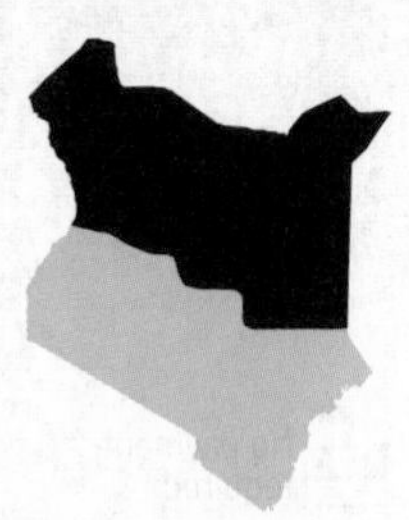

Northern Kenya

Adventure ✓✓✓
Wildlife ✓✓
Tribes ✓✓✓

The Road Less Travelled

These remote frontier lands where Kenya, Ethiopia, South Sudan and Somalia collide are only just starting to register with foreign tourists, thus giving wannabe explorers a genuine opportunity to go where few have trodden before.

Wild Africa

There are few other places in Kenya where it's possible to stumble upon large mammals outside of the protected areas, but in northern Kenya that is not just a possibility, it's almost a given.

A Tribal Heartland

From butterfly-bright Samburu warriors, to the dramatically pierced Turkana women and the elegant Gabbra peoples who wander the burning deserts with their camels, northern Kenya is arguably the tribal heartland of Kenya – and rest assured almost nothing is put on for the benefit of tourists!

p194

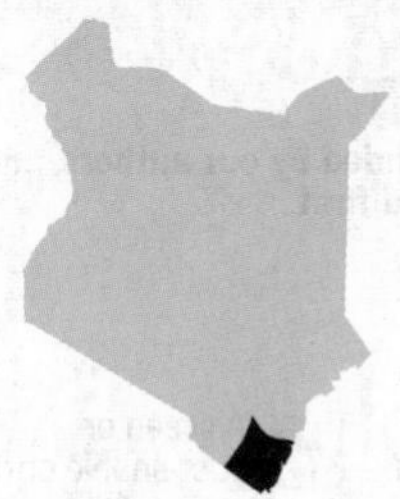

Mombasa & the South Coast

Beaches ✓✓✓
Wildlife ✓✓
Culture ✓✓

Sun, Sand & Sea

Despite the occasional rash of package-tourism development, some of the finest beaches in the country are to be found on Kenya's south coast. Away from sands that sparkle like crystals, there are islands galore and world-class diving.

Beach & Safari

From elephants, buffaloes and giraffes in the inland reserves to whale-sharks and dolphins by the dozen in the oceans, there's a lot of wildlife to be tracked down around here, but it's the profusion of tweeting birds that really stands out.

Cultural, Coastal Vibes

Choose from the big-city attractions of Mombasa, with its ancient fort, twisting streets and bubbling contemporary character, or the quiet life found in fishing villages up and down the coast – getting wrapped up in the coast's Swahili culture couldn't be easier.

p222

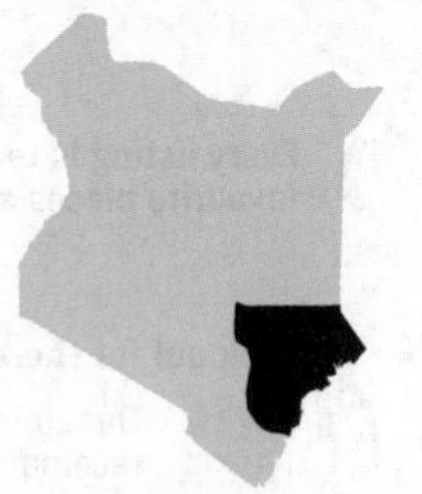

The North Coast

Beaches ✓✓
Wildlife ✓✓
Culture ✓✓✓

Beach Safari

Pack a bucket and spade and struggle to choose between the lively beach at Malindi, the mellow vibes of Watamu or, maybe best of all, an island-hopping trip by dhow around the sublime sands of the Lamu archipelago.

Butterflies & Elephant Shrews

For most wildlife-watchers the north coast is all about the birds. Everywhere you go around here you'll be accompanied by the sing-song notes of hundreds of different birds, but look a bit harder and you'll find elephant shrews, thousands of butterflies and fish in a plethora of colours.

Live Like a Swahili

Put simply, Lamu is the ultimate immersion in all things Swahili. This gorgeous town of narrow streets and *bui-bui*-clad women is the oldest in Kenya and the most complete Swahili settlement in existence.

p258

Every listing is recommended by our authors, and their favourite places are listed first.

Look out for these icons:

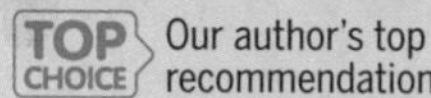
Our author's top recommendation

A green or sustainable option

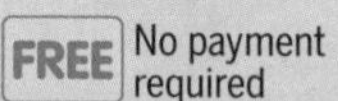
No payment required

See the Index for a full list of destinations covered in this book.

On the Road

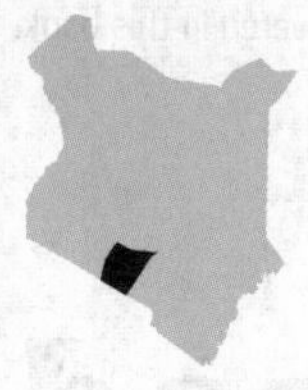

Nairobi

POP 3.5 MILLION

Includes »

Best of Nature

- Nairobi National Park (p58)
- David Sheldrick Wildlife Trust (p62)
- Giraffe Centre (p59)
- Ngong Hills (p86)

Best of Culture

- Bomas of Kenya (p66)
- National Museum (p55)
- African Heritage House (p66)
- Karen Blixen Museum (p64)
- Carnivore (p75)

Why Go?

Nairobi's reputation for crime is well-known, but the horror stories obscure a vibrant and cosmopolitan city full of attractions. Primary among these is the world's only national park on the cusp of a capital city – a park packed with the free-roaming megafauna more associated with remote African plains. There's also an elephant orphanage and a brilliant park that has played a crucial role in saving the Rothschild's giraffe from extinction – a visit to both promise experiences that will rank alongside your favourite wildlife memories of your time in Kenya. Not far away, the former home of Karen Blixen (of *Out of Africa* fame), an outstanding museum and fantastic restaurants and hotels all add to the city's appeal. And those horror stories? Yes, many of them are true. But the majority of visitors to Kenya's capital never experience a problem. If you keep your wits about you, you're far more likely to leave with a lasting impression of Kenya's dynamism than tales of personal disaster.

When to Go

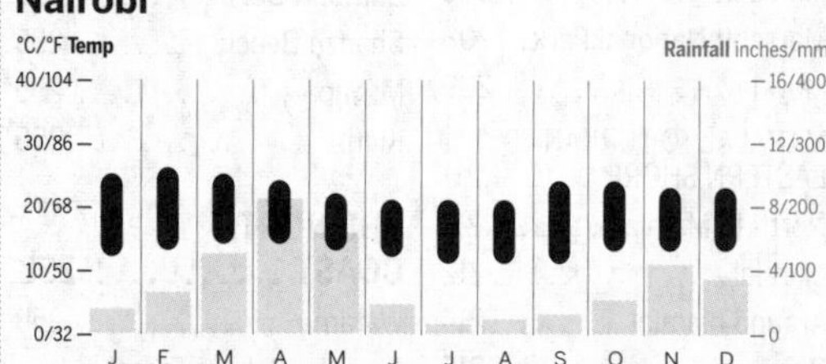

Jan & Feb, Jun–Sep The driest months; Nairobi National Park is at its best

Oct & Nov The rain cools things off without causing more than the usual traffic jams

Mar–May You don't want to be here when it rains, and rains, and rains...

History

Nairobi is a completely modern creation, and almost everything here has been built in the last 100 years. In fact, until the 1890s the whole area was just an isolated swamp. But, as the tracks of the East African Railway were laid down between Mombasa and Kampala, a depot was established on the edge of a small stream known to the Maasai as *uaso nairobi* (cold water). The Maasai were quickly and forcibly removed from the land, as the British East Africa protectorate had ambitious plans to open up the interior to white colonial settlement.

In addition to its central position between the coast and British holdings in Uganda, Nairobi benefited from its extremely hospitable environment. Its proximity to a network of rivers meant that water was abundant, and its high elevation and cool temperatures were conducive to comfortable residential living without fear of malaria. Although Nairobi did struggle in its early years, with frequent fires and an outbreak of the plague, by 1907 the booming commercial centre had replaced Mombasa as the capital of British East Africa.

Even after the first permanent buildings were constructed, Nairobi remained a frontier town, with rhinos and lions freely roaming the outskirts. As a result, the colonial government built some grand hotels to accommodate the first tourists to Kenya – big-game hunters, lured by the attraction of shooting the country's almost naively tame wildlife. In 1946, Nairobi National Park was established as the first national park in East Africa. It remains the only wildlife reserve in the world bordering a capital city.

After achieving independence in 1963, Nairobi grew too rapidly, by most accounts, putting a great deal of pressure on the city's infrastructure. Power cuts and water shortages became a common occurrence, and enormous shanty towns of tin-roofed settlements sprung up on the outskirts of the capital. In the name of modernisation, almost all of the colonial-era buildings were replaced by concrete office buildings, which today characterise much of the modern city.

However, Nairobi has been successful in establishing itself as East Africa's largest city and main transport hub. The capital is also situated firmly at the centre of national life and politics, though this position did the city no favours in 1998 when the US embassy on Moi Ave was bombed by militants with links to al-Qaeda. More than 200 Kenyans were killed in the attack, and although four suspects were convicted and sentenced to life without parole, many locals were angered by what they considered lenient sentences (they had wanted the death penalty) and meagre compensation.

In December 2007, the shanty towns of Nairobi were set ablaze as riots broke out following a disputed presidential election.

NAIROBI IN...

Two Days

Start by getting up close and personal with wildlife at the **Giraffe Centre** and the **David Sheldrick Wildlife Trust**. A visit to the **Karen Blixen Museum** is recommended for *Out of Africa* fans, then go shopping at the **Kazuri Beads & Pottery Centre** and **Utamaduni**. In the evening, dine at **Carnivore** and dance at the **Simba Saloon**.

On day two, head downtown to visit the **National Museum**, view the city from the **Kenyatta Conference Centre**, and step back in colonial time at the **Railway Museum**. Have a drink at the legendary **Thorn Tree** or **Lord Delamere Terrace & Bar**. In the evening, eat posh at **Tamarind Restaurant** and have a whole lot of fun at **Simmers**.

Four Days

Spend the best part of your third day in **Nairobi National Park**, but leave enough time for a tour of **Kibera** shanty town. For dinner, eat at either **Rusty Nail** or the **Karen Blixen Coffee Garden**.

For your final 24 hours, branch out into the **Ngong Hills** and the **grave of Denys Finch Hatton**, do a bit of shopping in the **curio markets**, eat at **Haandi**, Kenya's best Indian restaurant, then drink the night away at **Gypsy's Bar**.

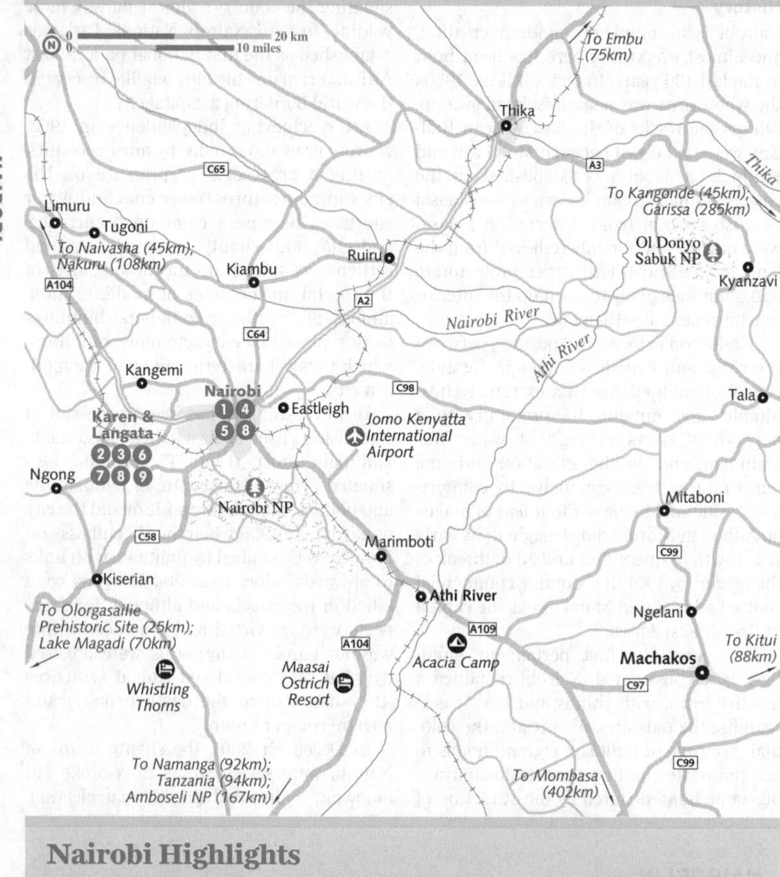

Nairobi Highlights

1. Searching for wildlife in the most incongruous of places at **Nairobi National Park** (p58).
2. Watching a gleeful group of baby elephants being bottle-fed at the **David Sheldrick Wildlife Trust** (p62).
3. Tangling tongues with an endangered Rothschild's giraffe at Langata's **Giraffe Centre** (p59).
4. Broadening your appreciation of all things Kenyan at the **National Museum** (p55).
5. Surveying the city from above the clamour at the **Kenyatta Conference Centre** (p55).
6. Making the essential foodie pilgrimage to **Carnivore** (p75).
7. Striking out for the scenic **Ngong Hills** (p86).
8. Sampling two different vestiges of colonial past at the **Karen Blixen Museum** (p64) and **Lord Delamere Terrace & Bar** (p74).
9. Learning how much of Nairobi lives by taking a tour of **Kibera** (p69).

Hundreds of homes were burnt to the ground by protestors, and many suffered violent attacks. Deep scars remain, especially among those who were internally displaced.

In recent years, the growth of the city has led to tremendous pressure being put on the government to develop protected lands such as Nairobi National Park. But the government has so far resisted, as these lands continue to support traditional migration routes for herd animals.

Sights

CITY CENTRE

TOP CHOICE National Museum MUSEUM

(Map p56; www.museums.or.ke; Museum Hill Rd; adult/child KSh800/400, combined ticket with Snake Park KSh1200/600; 8.30am-5.30pm) Kenya's wonderful National Museum, housed in an imposing building amid lush, leafy grounds just outside the centre, has a good range of cultural and natural history exhibits. Aside from the exhibits, check out the life-sized fibreglass model of pachyderm celebrity Ahmed, the massive elephant who became a symbol of Kenya at the height of the 1980s poaching crisis, and who was placed under 24-hour guard by Jomo Kenyatta; he's in the inner courtyard next to the shop.

The museum's permanent collection is entered via the **Hall of Kenya**, with some ethnological exhibits, but this is a mere prelude. In a room off this hall is the **Birds of East Africa** exhibit, a huge gallery of at least 900 stuffed specimens. In an adjacent room is the **Great Hall of Mammals**, with dozens of stuffed mammals, as well as a skeleton reproduction of Ahmed the elephant. Accessible off the mammals room is the **Cradle of Humankind** exhibition, the highlight of which is the **Hominid Skull Room** – an extraordinary collection of skulls that describes itself (with some justification, it must be said) as 'the single most important collection of early human fossils in the world'; the information panels in this room are worth poring over.

Upstairs, the **Historia Ya Kenya** display is an engaging journey through Kenyan and East African history. It's well-presented, well-documented and offers a refreshingly Kenyan counterpoint to colonial historiographies. Also on the 1st floor, the **Cycles of Life** room is rich in ethnological artefacts from Kenya's various tribes and ethnic groups. There are also plans to reinstall the **Joy Adamsons Exhibition** on the 1st floor, including the 'Peoples of Kenya' series of tribal portraits by the author of *Born Free*.

Snake Park ZOO

(Map p56; www.museums.or.ke; Museum Hill Rd; adult/child KSh800/400, combined ticket with National Museum KSh1200/600; 8.30am-5.30pm) In the grounds of the National Museum, the zoo-like Snake Park has some impressive snake species, including the puff adder, black mamba, African rock python and the Gaboon viper (which rarely bares its 4cm-long fangs, the longest in the world). There are also local fish species, lizards, turtles and some sad-looking crocodiles.

> **NATIONAL MUSEUM & SNAKE PARK GUIDES**
>
> If you're keen to really get under the skin of the collection, consider the volunteer guides who linger close to the entrance of both the National Museum and Snake Park. Tours are available in English, French and possibly other languages. There's no charge for their services, but a donation to the museum or a tip for the guides is appropriate.

Kenyatta Conference Centre LOOKOUT

(Map p60) Towering over City Square on City Hall Way, Nairobi's signature building was designed as a fusion of modern and traditional African styles, though the distinctive saucer tower looks a little dated next to some of the city's flashier glass edifices.

Staff will accompany you up to the **viewing platform** (adult/child KSh500/250; 9.30am-6pm) and helipad on the roof for wonderful views over Nairobi. The sightline goes all the way to the suburbs and on clear days you can see aircraft coming in to land over Nairobi National Park. You're allowed to take photographs from the viewing level but not elsewhere in the building. Access may be restricted during events and conferences.

Railway Museum MUSEUM

(Map p56; Station Rd; adult/child KSh400/100; 8am-5pm) The main collection at this interesting little museum is housed in an old railway building and consists of relics from the East African Railway. There are train and ship models, photographs, tableware, and oddities from the history of the railway, such as the engine seat that allowed visiting dignitaries like Theodore Roosevelt to take potshots at unsuspecting wildlife from the front of the train.

In the grounds are dozens of fading locomotives in various states of disrepair, dating from the steam days to independence (which puts the museum's more recent trains on a par with those still being used on the Nairobi–Mombasa line). You can walk around the carriages at your leisure.

Nairobi

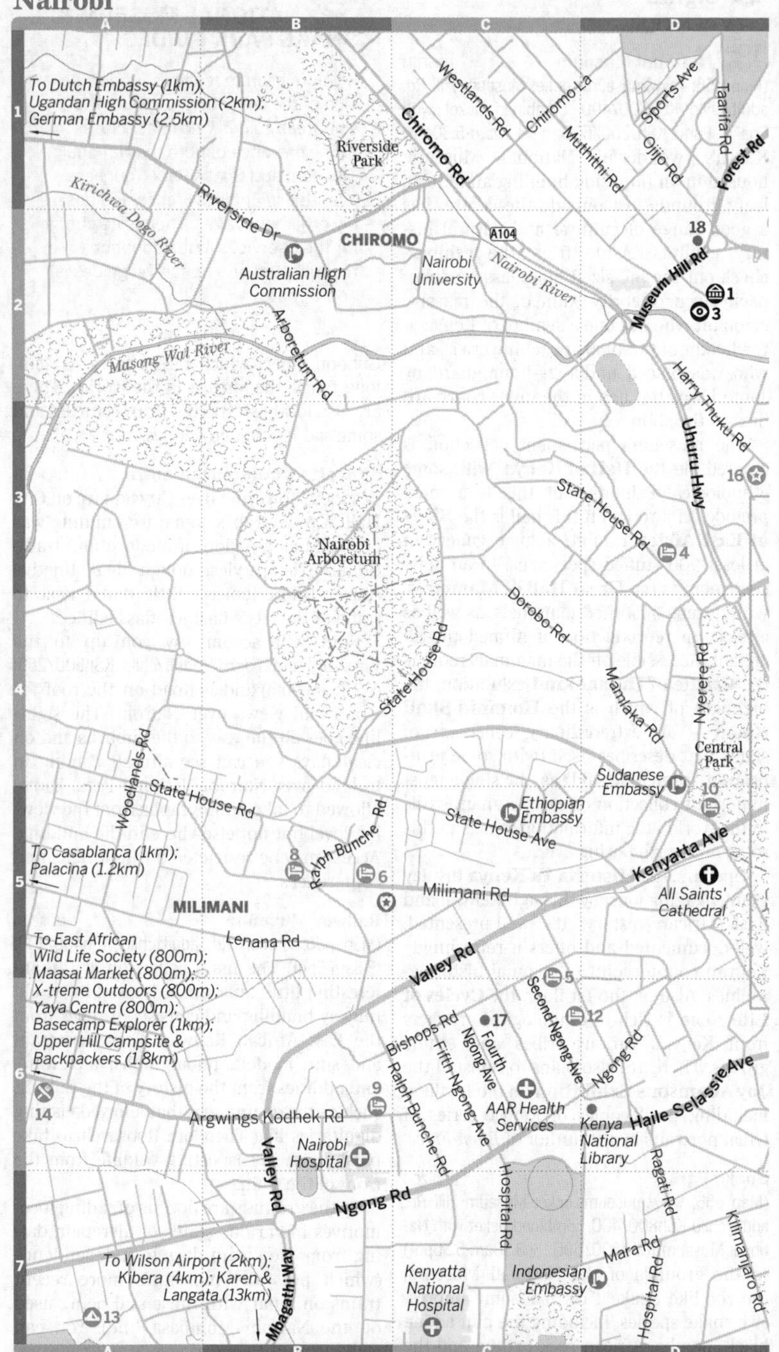

To Dutch Embassy (1km); Ugandan High Commission (2km); German Embassy (2.5km)
Riverside Park
Kirichwa Dogo River
Riverside Dr
CHIROMO
Australian High Commission
Nairobi University
Westlands Rd
Chiromo Rd
Chiromo La
Muthithi Rd
Sports Ave
Ojijo Rd
Taarifa Rd
Forest Rd
A104
Nairobi River
Museum Hill Rd
18
1
3
Masong Wai River
Arboretum Rd
Harry Thuku Rd
Uhuru Hwy
16
State House Rd
4
Nairobi Arboretum
Dorobo Rd
State House Rd
Mamlaka Rd
Nyerere Rd
Central Park
Woodlands Rd
State House Rd
Sudanese Embassy
10
Ethiopian Embassy
State House Ave
Ralph Bunche Rd
To Casablanca (1km); Palacina (1.2km)
8
6
Milimani Rd
Kenyatta Ave
All Saints' Cathedral
MILIMANI
Lenana Rd
To East African Wild Life Society (800m); Maasai Market (800m); X-treme Outdoors (800m); Yaya Centre (800m); Basecamp Explorer (1km); Upper Hill Campsite & Backpackers (1.8km)
Valley Rd
5
Second Ngong Ave
12
17
Bishops Rd
Fourth Ngong Ave
Fifth Ngong Ave
Ngong Rd
Haile Selassie Ave
14
9
Ralph Bunche Rd
AAR Health Services
Kenya National Library
Argwings Kodhek Rd
Nairobi Hospital
Valley Rd
Ragati Rd
Hospital Rd
Ngong Rd
Kilimanjaro Rd
To Wilson Airport (2km); Kibera (4km); Karen & Langata (13km)
Mbagathi Way
Kenyatta National Hospital
Indonesian Embassy
Mara Rd
Hospital Rd
13

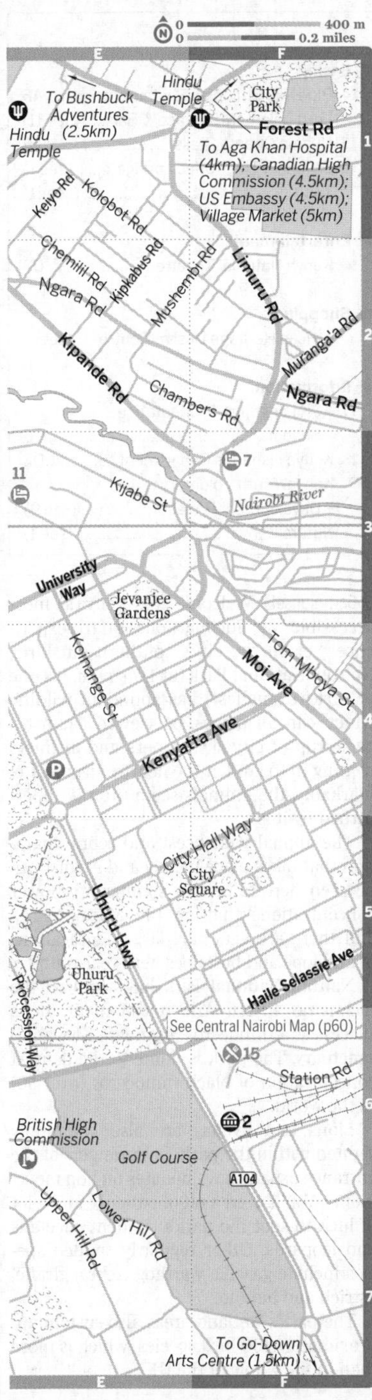

At the back of the compound is the steam train used in the movie *Out of Africa*. It's a fascinating introduction to this important piece of colonial history.

The museum is reached by a long lane beside the train station.

National Archives LIBRARY

(Map p60; Moi Ave; admission free; ⏲8.30am-5pm Mon-Fri, 9am-1pm Sat) Right in the bustling heart of Nairobi is the distinctive National Archives, the 'Memory of the Nation', a vast collection of documents and reference materials housed in the former Bank of India building. It's mainly used by students and researchers, but the ground-floor atrium and gallery display an eclectic selection of contemporary art, historical photos of Nairobi, cultural artefacts, furniture and tribal objects, giving casual visitors a somewhat scattergun glimpse of East African heritage.

Uhuru Park PARK

(Map p60; admission free; ⏲dawn-dusk) An expanse of manicured green on the fringe of the CBD, this attractive city park is a popular respite from the mean city streets. It owes its existence to Wangari Maathai, a Kenyan Nobel Peace Prize winner; in the late 1980s, she fought to save the park from the bulldozers of the former Moi government. Moi had famously suggested that Maathai should be more of a proper woman in the 'African tradition'. Upon her death in late 2011, her funeral was held in the park and attended by thousands of mourners. During the day, the park attracts picnicking families, businessmen stepping out of the office and just about anyone in need of a little green. It's not safe after dark.

Parliament House NOTABLE BUILDING

(Map p60; ☎2221291; Parliament Rd) If you fancy a look at how democracy works (or doesn't) in Kenya, it's possible to obtain a free permit for a seat in the public gallery at parliament house; ring ahead to secure your permit and remember that applause is strictly forbidden. If parliament is out of session, you can tour the buildings by arrangement with the sergeant-at-arms.

Jamia Mosque MOSQUE

(Map p60; Banda St) Amid the clutter of downtown, Nairobi's main mosque is a lovely building in typical Arab-Muslim style, with all the domes, marble and Quranic

Nairobi

Sights

1	National Museum	D2
2	Railway Museum	F6
3	Snake Park	D2

Sleeping

4	Central YMCA	D3
5	Fairview Hotel	C5
6	Heron Hotel	B5
7	Kahama Hotel	F3
8	Milimani Backpackers & Safari Centre	B5
9	Nairobi International Youth Hostel	B6
10	Nairobi Serena Hotel	D5
11	Norfolk Hotel	E3
12	Upper Hill Country Lodge	C6
13	Wildebeest Camp	A7

Eating

14	Blue Nile Ethiopian Restaurant	A6
	Lord Delamere Terrace & Bar	(see 11)
15	Nyama Choma Stalls	F6
	Savanna: The Coffee Lounge	(see 1)
	Tapu	(see 11)

Entertainment

16	Kenya National Theatre	D3

Shopping

	African Heritage Design Centre	(see 1)

Information

17	ACK Language & Orientation School	C6
18	Kenya Fisheries Department	D2
	Kenya Youth Voluntary Development Projects	(see 9)
	Nature Kenya	(see 1)

inscriptions you'd expect from an important Islamic site, plus the traditional row of shops down one side to provide rental income for its upkeep. Non-Muslims are very rarely allowed to enter, but the appealing exterior is visible from the street.

American Embassy Memorial Garden GARDEN

(Map p60; Moi Ave; admission KSh20; ⌚8am-6pm) This well-tended walled garden occupies the former site of the American embassy, which was destroyed by terrorist bombings in 1998. It's a lovely spot, despite being right between busy Moi and Haile Selassie Aves. The entrance fee pays for maintenance, and keeps numbers down.

KAREN & LANGATA

These posh suburbs south of Nairobi bear little resemblance to the urban sprawl of the capital. Inhabited mainly by the descendants of white settlers and foreign expats, these leafy environs conceal extensive ranks of houses and villas, all discreetly set in their own colonial-era grounds. The genteel atmosphere and wealth of attractions make Karen and Langata appealing destinations for an easy escape from city life.

TOP CHOICE **Nairobi National Park** PARK

(Map p64; www.kws.org/parks/parks_reserves/NANP.html; adult/child/student US$40/20/15; ⌚6am-sunset) Welcome to Kenya's most accessible yet incongruous safari experience. Set on the city's southern outskirts, Nairobi National Park (at 117 sq km, it's one of Africa's smallest) has abundant wildlife which can, in places, be viewed against a backdrop of city skyscrapers and airliners coming in to land at the nearby airport. Remarkably, the animals seem utterly unperturbed by it all.

The annual wildebeest and zebra migration that takes place in July and August can be seen here (albeit in significantly lower concentrations than in the Masai Mara), and there are generally large aggregations of antelope and buffaloes here year-round.

Nairobi National Park has acquired the nickname 'Kifaru Ark', a testament to its success as a rhinoceros (*kifaru* in Kiswahili) sanctuary. The park is home to the densest concentration of black rhinoceros (over 50) in the world.

Lions and hyenas are also commonly sighted within the park; park rangers at the entrance usually have updates on lion movements. You'll need a bit of patience and a lot of luck to spot the park's resident cheetahs and leopards. Other regularly spotted species include gazelle, warthog, zebra, giraffe, ostrich and buffalo.

The park's wetland areas also sustain approximately 400 bird species, which is more than in the whole of the UK.

A little further into the park, the Ivory Burning Monument marks the spot where, in 1989, Kenyan President Daniel arap Moi burnt 12 tons of ivory at a site near the main gate. This dramatic event improved Kenya's conservation image at a time when East African wildlife was being decimated by relentless poaching.

The park's main entrance is on Langata Rd. Other entrances are on Magadi Rd and the Athi River Gate; the latter is handy if you're continuing on to Mombasa, Amboseli or the Tanzanian border. The roads in the park are passable with 2WDs, but travelling in a 4WD is never a bad idea, especially if the rains have been heavy.

Unless you already have your own vehicle, the cheapest way to see the park is on the **park shuttle** (adult/child US$20/5), a big KWS bus that leaves the main gate at 2pm on Sunday for a 2½-hour tour. You need to book in person at the main gate by 1.30pm.

Nairobi Safari Walk ZOO

(Map p64; www.kws.org/parks/education/nairobi_safariwalk; adult/child US$20/5; 6am-sunset) Just outside the main entrance into Nairobi National Park, this safari walk is a sort of zoo-meets-nature boardwalk with lots of birds as well as other wildlife, including a pygmy hippo and a white rhino. Children in particular love the chance to get up close and personal with the animals.

Animal Orphanage ZOO

(Map p64; adult/child US$15/5; ⏲8.30am-5.30pm) Just inside the main gate to Nairobi National Park, this animal orphanage houses formerly wild animals that have been recovered by park rangers. Although it's something of a glorified zoo and the conditions in which the animals are kept are less than inspiring, the orphanage does protect animals that would have died without human intervention. It also serves as a valuable education centre for Nairobi-ites and school children who might not otherwise have the chance to interact with wildlife.

TOP CHOICE **Giraffe Centre** WILDLIFE RESERVE

(Map p64; www.giraffecenter.org; Koitobos Rd; adult/child KSh700/250; ⏲9am-5.30pm) This is one of Kenya's good-news conservation stories. In 1979 Jock Leslie-Melville (the Kenyan grandson of a Scottish earl) and his wife Betty began raising a baby giraffe in their Langata home. At the time, when their African Fund for Endangered Wildlife (AFEW) was just getting off the ground, there were no more than 120 Rothschild's giraffes (which differ from other giraffe subspecies in that there is no patterning

NAIROBI NATIONAL PARK: A NECESSARY PARK

There's one very good reason why Nairobi has its own national park: cities and wildlife don't mix. As Nairobi boomed in the early 20th century, conflicts between humans and animals were rampant. Early residents of the capital were forced to carry guns at night to protect themselves from lions, while herd animals routinely raided country farms. As a result, the colonial government of British East Africa set about confining the game animals to the Athi plains to the west and south of Nairobi. In 1946, Nairobi National Park became the first national park in British East Africa, although the event was not without controversy, as the Maasai pastoralists were forcibly removed from the parklands.

The conflict between human and wildlife continues in the park today. The park is fenced in parts to keep the wildlife out of the city, although it's not a closed system and is instead kept open to allow animals to migrate along a narrow wildlife corridor to southern Kenya or the Masai Mara. With human settlements almost completely encircling the park, however, such corridors are almost completely closed and the migrations will soon be a thing of the past. What that means for animals that survive by following the rains or for the ecosystems within the park is a topic of great concern for conservationists.

Friends of Nairobi National Park (FoNNaP; Map p64; ☎500622; http://fonnap.wordpress.com; Kenya Wildlife Service Headquarters, Langata Rd) The society aims to protect migration corridors connecting the park with other Kenyan regions as well as raising awareness about the park.

Central Nairobi

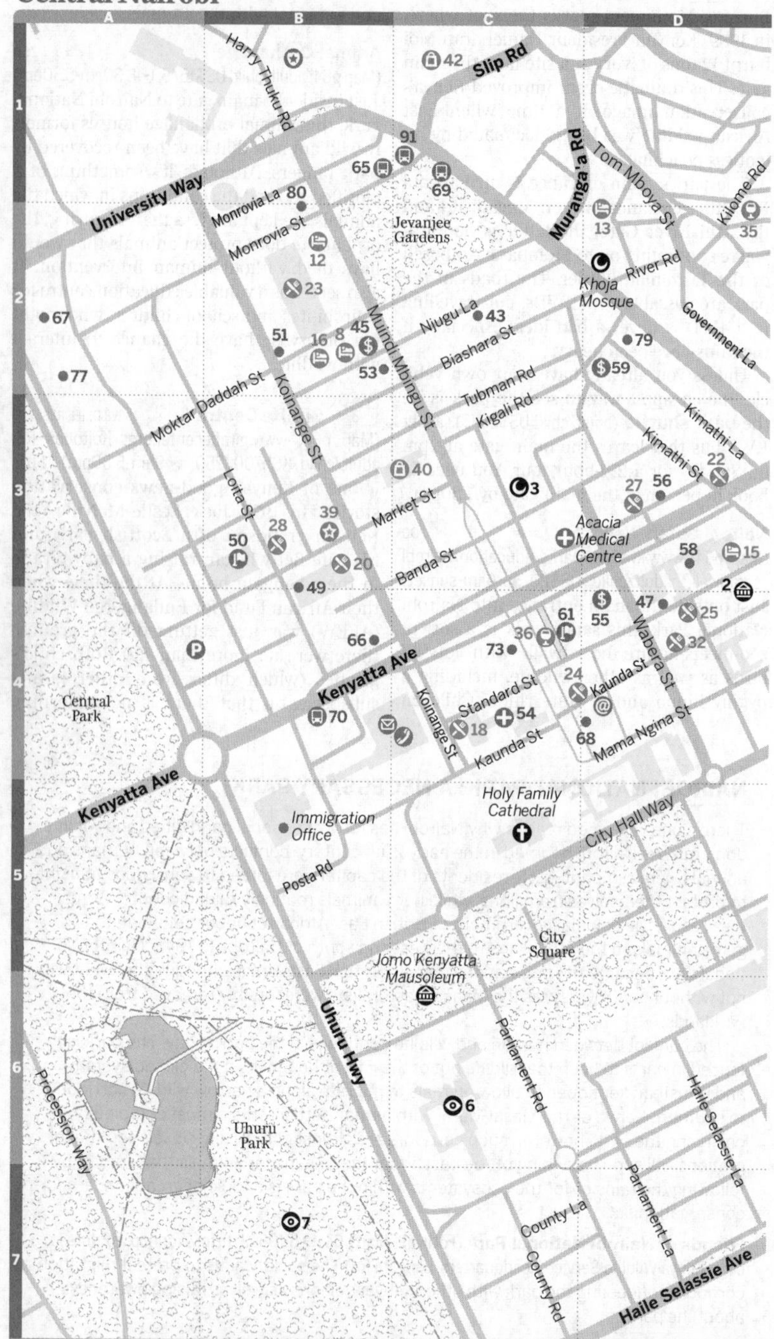

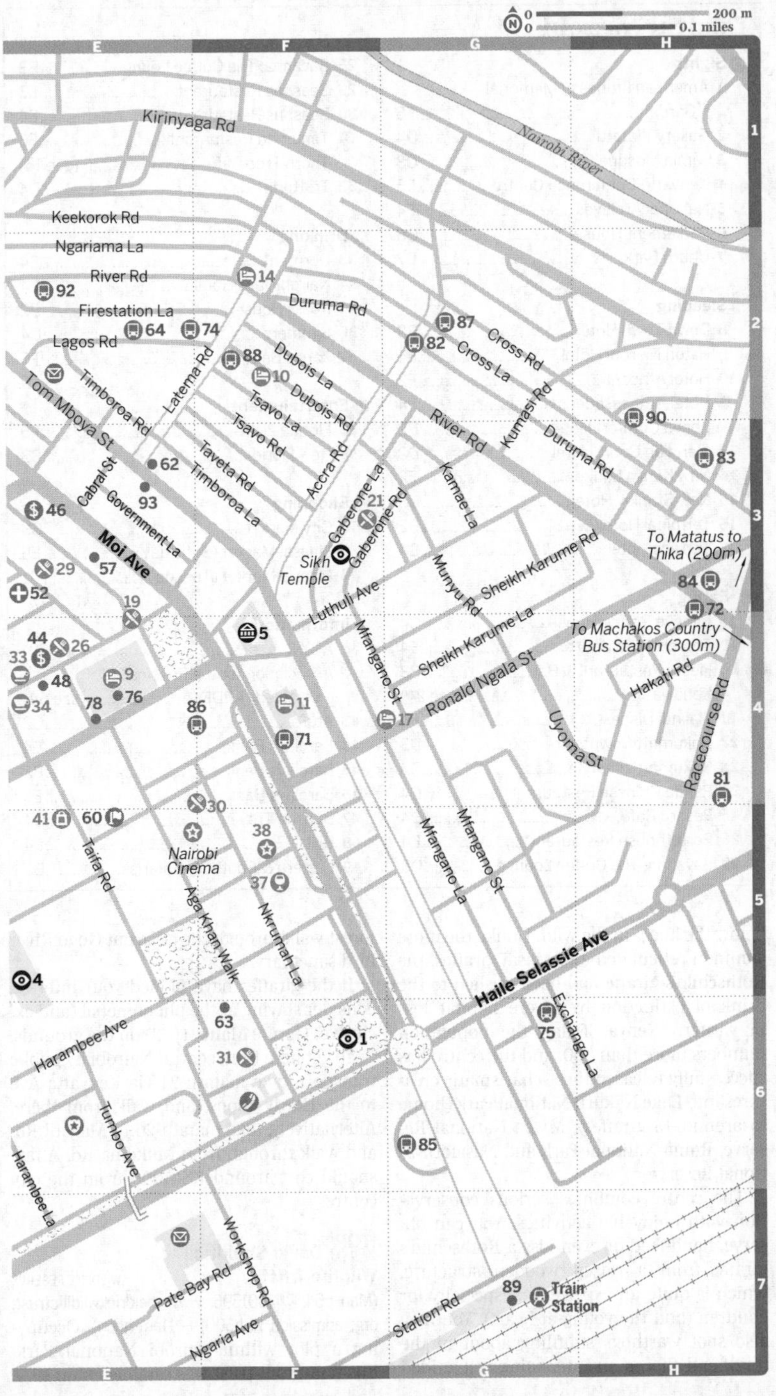
0 200 m
0 0.1 miles
E
F
G
H
1
2
3
4
5
6
7
Kirinyaga Rd
Nairobi River
Keekorok Rd
Ngariama La
River Rd
Firestation La
Lagos Rd
Duruma Rd
Cross Rd
Cross La
Kumasi Rd
Laterna Rd
Dubois La
Dubois Rd
Tsavo La
Tsavo Rd
River Rd
Duruma Rd
Timboroa Rd
Tom Mboya St
Taveta Rd
Timboroa La
Accra Rd
Gaberone La
Gaberone Rd
Kamae La
Cabral St
Government La
Moi Ave
Sikh Temple
Luthuli Ave
Munyu Rd
Sheikh Karume Rd
Sheikh Karume La
To Matatus to Thika (200m)
To Machakos Country Bus Station (300m)
Mfangano St
Ronald Ngala St
Hakati Rd
Uyoma St
Racecourse Rd
Nairobi Cinema
Taifa Rd
Aga Khan Walk
Nkrumah La
Mfangano La
Mfangano St
Haile Selassie Ave
Exchange La
Harambee Ave
Turnbo Ave
Harambee La
Workshop Rd
Pate Bay Rd
Ngaria Ave
Station Rd
Train Station
92
64
74
14
88
10
87
82
90
83
62
93
46
21
29
57
52
84
72
19
5
44
26
33
48
9
76
34
78
86
11
17
71
81
41
60
30
38
37
4
63
1
75
31
85
89

Central Nairobi

Sights

1 American Embassy Memorial Garden ... F6
2 Gallery Watatu ... D4
3 Jamia Mosque ... C3
4 Kenyatta Conference Centre ... E5
5 National Archives ... F4
6 Parliament House ... C6
7 Uhuru Park ... B7

Sleeping

8 Down Town Hotel ... B2
9 Hilton Nairobi Hotel ... E4
10 Hotel Africana ... F2
11 Hotel Ambassadeur Nairobi ... F4
12 Kenya Comfort Hotel ... B2
13 Meridian Court Hotel ... D2
14 New Kenya Lodge ... F2
15 New Stanley Hotel ... D3
16 Terminal Hotel ... B2
17 Terrace Hotel ... G4

Eating

18 Beneve Coffee House ... C4
19 Etouch Food Court ... E4
20 Fiesta Restaurant & Bar ... B3
Kahawa ... (see 24)
21 Malindi Dishes ... F3
22 Nakumatt Downtown ... D3
23 Nakumatt Lifestyle ... B2
24 Panda Chinese Restaurant ... C4
25 Pasara Café ... D4
26 Porterhouse Restaurant ... E4
27 Savanna: The Coffee Lounge ... D3
28 Savanna: The Coffee Lounge ... B3
29 Seasons Restaurant ... E3
30 Seasons Restaurant ... E4
31 Tamarind Restaurant ... F6
Thorn Tree Café ... (see 15)
32 Trattoria ... D4

Drinking

33 Dormans Café ... E4
34 Nairobi Java House ... E4
35 Roast House ... D2
36 Simmers ... C4
37 Zanze Bar ... F5

Entertainment

38 Florida 2000 ... F5
39 New Florida ... B3

Shopping

40 City Market ... C3
41 Maasai Market (Saturday) ... E5
42 Maasai Market (Tuesday) ... C1

Information

AGX ... (see 50)
Association for the Physically Disabled (APDK) ... (see 64)
43 Atul's ... C2
44 Barclays Bank ... E4
45 Barclays Bank ... B2
46 Barclays Bank ... E3
47 Bunson Travel ... D4
48 DHL ... E4
49 Eastern & Southern Safaris ... B3

below the knee) in the wild. Unlike the more common reticulated and Masai giraffes, the Rothschild's giraffe had been pushed to the brink of extinction by severe habitat loss in western Kenya. Today, the population numbers more than 300, and the centre has successfully released these charismatic creatures into Lake Nakuru National Park (home to around 45 giraffes), Mwea National Reserve, Ruma National Park and Nasalot National Reserve.

The centre combines serious conservation with enjoyable activities. You can observe, hand-feed or even kiss a Rothschild's giraffe from a raised wooden structure, which is quite an experience, especially for children (and the young-at-heart). You may also spot warthogs snuffling about in the mud, and there's an interesting self-guided forest walk through the adjacent Gogo River bird sanctuary.

If the giraffes have piqued your interest, consider staying at the phenomenal (and exclusive) Giraffe Manor (p73) on the grounds.

To get here from central Nairobi by public transport, take matatu 24 via Kenyatta Ave to the Hardy shops, and walk from there. Alternatively, take matatu 26 to Magadi Rd, and walk through from Mukoma Rd. A taxi should cost around KSh1000 from the city centre.

TOP CHOICE David Sheldrick Wildlife Trust WILDLIFE RESERVE

(Map p64; ☎2301396; www.sheldrickwildlifetrust.org; admission KSh500; ⏰11am-noon) Occupying a plot within Nairobi National Park, this non-profit trust was established in 1977,

50 French Embassy B3
51 Gametrackers B2
Goldfield Forex .... (see 24)
52 KAM Pharmacy E3
53 Kenya Canvas Ltd B2
Link Forex .... (see 61)
54 Medical Services Surgery C4
Origins Safaris .... (see 24)
55 Postbank D4
56 Safe Ride Tours & Safaris D3
57 Sana Highlands Trekking Expeditions E3
58 Savuka Tours & Safaris D3
Spanish Embassy .... (see 48)
59 Standard Chartered Bank D2
60 Tanzanian High Commission E5
Tropical Winds .... (see 50)
61 Ugandan High Commission (Consular Section) C4

Transport

62 Adventure Upgrade Safaris E3
63 Air India F6
Airport Bus Departure Point .... (see 86)
64 Akamba E2
65 Akamba Booking Office & International Departures B1
66 Avenue Car Hire B4
67 Avis A2
68 Budget D4
69 Bus & Matatu Stop C1
70 Bus & Matatu Stop (to Hurlingham & Milimani) B4
71 Bus Stop (to Langata, Karen & Airport) F4
Bus Stop (to Westlands) .... (see 69)
72 Buses to Kisii & Migori H3
73 Central Rent-a-Car C4
74 Coastline Safaris E2
75 Easy Coach Office G6
76 Egypt Air E4
77 Emirates A2
Ethiopian Airlines .... (see 54)
Gametrackers .... (see 51)
78 Glory Car Hire E4
79 Glory Car Hire D2
80 KBS Booking Office B2
81 KBS Bus Station H4
Kenya Airways .... (see 50)
82 Main Bus & Matatu Area G2
Matatus to Eldoret .... (see 75)
83 Matatus to Kericho & Kisumu H3
Matatus to Kibera .... (see 71)
84 Matatus to Naivasha, Nakuru, Nyahururu & Namanga H3
85 Matatus to Wilson Airport, Nairobi National Park, Langata & Karen G6
86 Metro Shuttle Bus Stand E4
87 Modern Coast (Oxygen) G2
88 Mololine Prestige Shuttle F2
89 Nairobi Train Station Booking Office G7
90 Narok Line H2
91 Riverside Shuttle C1
92 Scandinavia Express E2
93 Tough Trucks Kenya E3

shortly after the death of David Sheldrick, who served as the anti-poaching warden of Tsavo National Park. Together with his wife Daphne, David pioneered techniques for raising orphaned black rhinos and elephants and reintroducing them back into the wild, and the trust retains close links with Tsavo for these and other projects.

After entering at 11am, visitors are escorted to a small viewing area centred on a muddy watering hole. A few moments later, much like a sports team marching out onto the field, the animal handlers come in alongside a dozen or so baby elephants. For the first part of the viewing, the handlers bottle-feed the baby elephants – a strangely heartwarming sight.

Once the little guys have drunk their fill, they proceed to romp around like big babies, though it's serious business keeping them in line as they each weigh a few hundred kilos. The elephants seem to take joy in misbehaving in front of their masters, so don't be surprised if a few break rank and start rubbing up against your leg! While the elephants gambol around, the keepers explain the background of each of the animals.

The baby elephants also use this designated timeslot for their daily mud bath, which makes for some great photos; keep your guard up as they've been known to spray a tourist or two with a trunkful of mud.

Once the show ends, you're permitted to check out the orphaned rhinos, which are a bit feistier and a whole lot more dangerous than the elephants. Although it can be a little depressing to see these majestic animals

Nairobi National Park

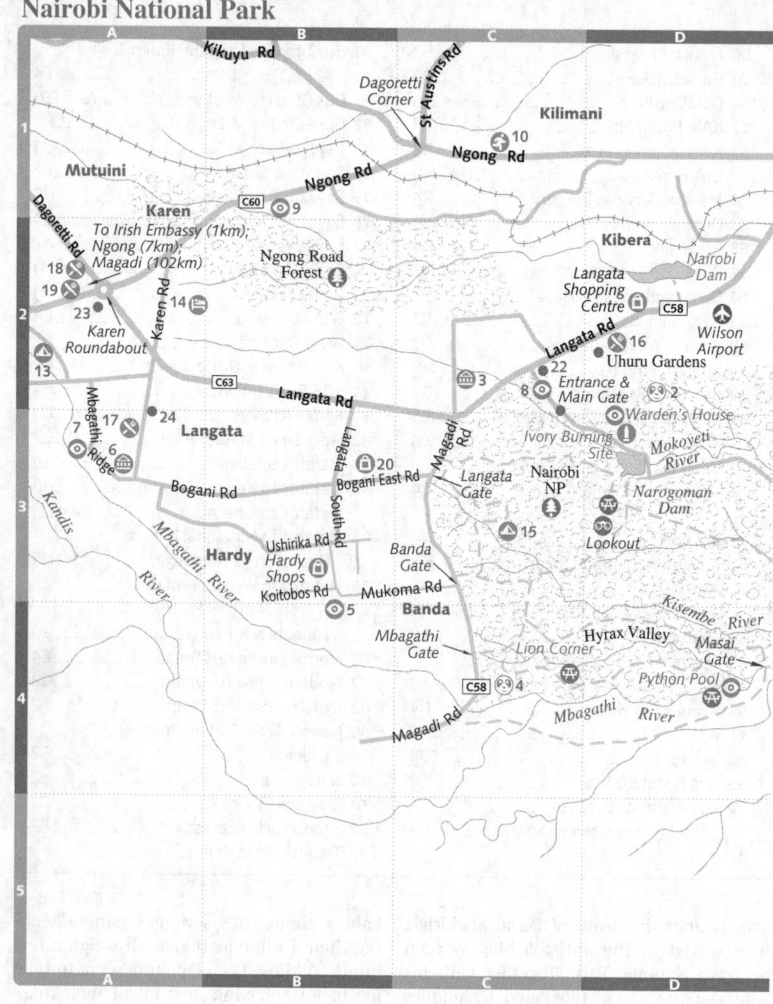

in cages, remember that they are being rehabilitated, and will eventually be released into the wild.

To get here by bus or matatu, take 125 or 126 from Moi Ave and ask to be dropped off at the KWS central workshop on Magadi Rd (KSh50, 50 minutes). It's about 1km from the workshop gate to the Sheldrick centre – it's signposted and KWS staff can give you directions. Be advised that at this point you'll be walking in the national park, which does contain lions, so stick to the paths. A taxi should cost between KSh1000 and KSh1500 from the city centre.

TOP CHOICE Karen Blixen Museum HISTORIC BUILDING

(Map p64; ☎8002139; www.museums.or.ke; Karen Rd; adult/child KSh800/400; ⊙9.30am-6pm) This museum is the farmhouse where Karen Blixen, author of *Out of Africa*, lived between 1914 and 1931. She left after a series of personal tragedies, but the lovely colonial house has been preserved as a museum. It, along with the adjacent agricultural college, was presented by the Danish government to the Kenyan government at independence. The museum is set in expansive gardens, and is an interesting place to wander

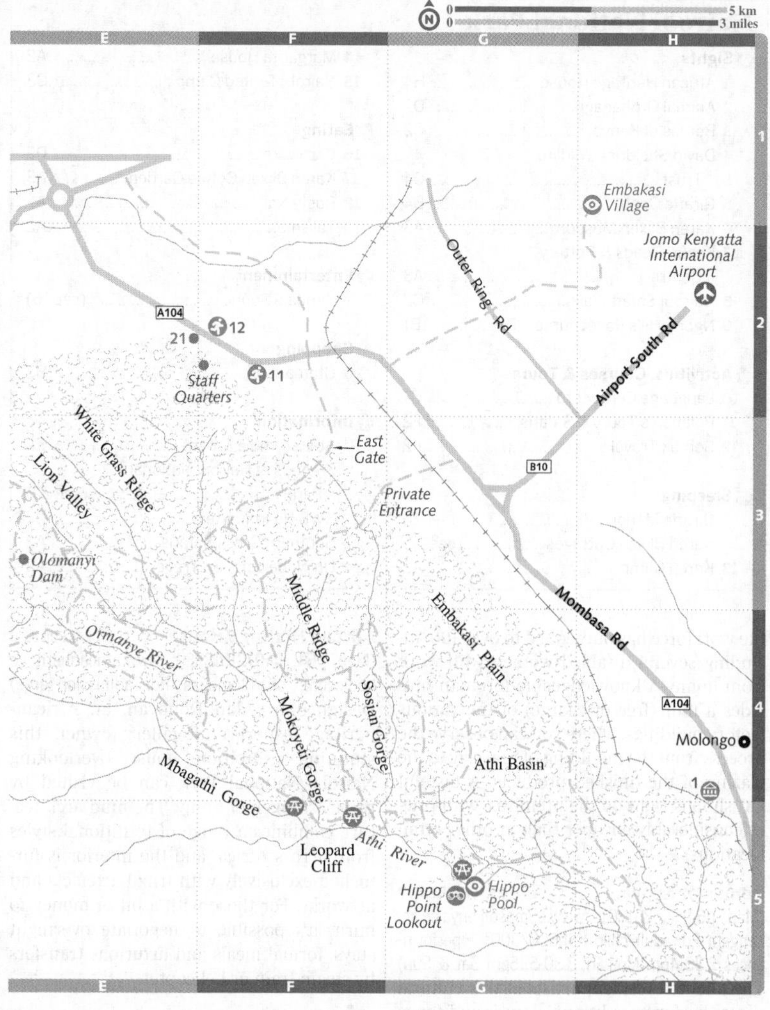

around, especially if you're a fan of the Hollywood classic. That said, the movie was actually shot at a nearby location, so don't be surprised if things don't look entirely right! Guides (non-mandatory, but useful) are included in the admission fee, but they do expect a tip.

Just down the road you'll find the Karen Blixen Coffee Garden (p77) and the Karen Blixen Cottages (p72), just in case you want to make the most of your *Out of Africa* experience.

The museum is about 2km from Langata Rd. The easiest way to get here by public transport is by matatu 24 via Kenyatta Ave, which passes right by the entrance. A taxi should cost between KSh1000 and KSh1500 from the city centre.

Kazuri Beads & Pottery Centre CRAFT CENTRE

(Map p64; ☎3883500; www.kazuri.com; Mbagathi Ridge; ⏲shop 8.30am-6pm Mon-Sat, 9am-5pm Sun, factory 8am-4.30pm Mon-Fri, 8am-1pm Sat) An interesting diversion in Karen, this craft centre was started up by an English expat in 1975 as a place where single mothers could learn a marketable skill and achieve self-sufficiency. Beginning with just two employees,

Nairobi National Park

Sights
1 African Heritage House....H4
2 Animal Orphanage....D2
3 Bomas of Kenya....C2
4 David Sheldrick Wildlife Trust....C4
5 Giraffe Centre....B4
6 Karen Blixen Museum....A3
7 Kazuri Beads & Pottery Centre....A3
8 Nairobi Safari Walk....C2
9 Ngong Hills Racecourse....B1

Activities, Courses & Tours
10 Language Center Ltd....C1
11 Pollman's Tours & Safaris....F2
12 Somak Travel....F2

Sleeping
Giraffe Manor....(see 5)
Karen Blixen Cottages....(see 17)
13 Karen Camp....A2
14 Margarita House....A2
15 Nairobi Tented Camp....C3

Eating
16 Carnivore....D2
17 Karen Blixen Coffee Garden....A3
18 Rusty Nail....A2
19 Talisman....A2

Entertainment
Simba Saloon....(see 16)

Shopping
20 Utamaduni....B3

Information
21 Abercrombie & Kent....E2
Freonds of Nairobi National Park....(see 22)
22 KWS Headquarters....C2
23 Southern Cross Safaris....A3
24 Uniglobe Let's Go Travel....A2

the workforce has burgeoned to over 100, including several disabled women who work from home. A knowledgeable foreman provides a tour (free of charge) of the various factory buildings, where you can observe the process from the moulding of raw clay to the glazing of the finished products. A tasteful gift shop is right on the premises, with prices considerably cheaper than at other retail locations.

Bomas of Kenya CULTURAL CENTRE
(Map p64; ☎891801; www.bomasofkenya.co.ke; Langata Rd; adult/child KSh600/300; ⊙performances 2.30-4pm Mon-Fri, 3.30-5.15pm Sat & Sun) The talented resident artists at this cultural centre perform traditional dances and songs taken from the country's various tribal groups, including Arabic-influenced Swahili *taarab* music, Kalenjin warrior dances, Embu drumming and Kikuyu circumcision ceremonies. It's touristy, of course, but still a spectacular afternoon out.

The centre is at Langata, near Nairobi National Park's main gate. Bus or matatu 125 or 126 runs here from Nairobi train station (KSh40, 30 minutes). Get off at Magadi Rd, from where it's about a 1km walk, clearly signposted on the right-hand side of the road. A taxi should set you back between KSh1000 and KSh1200.

African Heritage House CULTURAL BUILDING
(Map p64; ☎0721518389; www.africanheritagebook.com; off Mombasa Rd; admission free) Designed by Alan Donovan, an African-heritage expert and gallery owner, this stunning exhibition house overlooking Nairobi National Park can be visited by prior arrangement only. The mud architecture combines a range of traditional styles from across Africa, and the interior is furnished exclusively with tribal artefacts and artworks. For those with a bit of money to burn, it's possible to negotiate overnight stays, formal meals and luxurious transfers by steam train or helicopter.

Activities

Most international tourist hotels have swimming pools that can be used by nonguests for a daily fee of between KSh200 and KSh500.

Nature Kenya BIRDWATCHING
(☎3749957; www.naturekenya.org; per person KSh200) Organises a variety of outings, including half-day bird walks that depart from the National Museum. Contact them for more information.

Mountain Club of Kenya CLIMBING
(MCK; www.mck.or.ke; Wilson Airport) The club meets at 8pm every Tuesday at the clubhouse at Wilson Airport. Members organise frequent climbing and trekking weekends around the country and have a huge pool of technical knowledge about climbing in Kenya.

Tours

Some travel agencies (p83) and safari companies (p35) offer full- or half-day tours that take in some of the city's major attractions. Prices vary from one company to the next, and also depend on how much ground you cover, how many people take the tour and how long the tour lasts.

An increasingly popular tour is a walk through the Kibera shanty town. See p69 for details.

People to People Tourism TOURS
(☎0722750073; www.peopletopeopletourism.com) This company does city tours and can take you further afield, with an emphasis on cultural encounters. Ask whether it's still running its introduction to the world of *jua kali,* Kenya's open-air manufacturing industry; it sometimes combine tours of the usual tourist sights with visits to *jua kali* workshops producing crafts and other goods.

Festivals & Events

Kenya Fashion Week FASHION
(Sarit Centre, Westlands) An expo-style event held in June, bringing together designers and manufacturers from all over the country.

Kenya Music Festival MUSIC
(Kenyatta Conference Centre) Kenya's longest-running music festival was established almost 80 years ago by the colonial regime. African music now predominates, but Western and expat musicians still take part. It's held over 10 days in August.

Tusker Safari Sevens SPORT
(http://safarisevens.com; Nyayo National Stadium) A high-profile, international seven-a-side rugby tournament. It's always hotly contested and the Kenyan team has a strong record in the tournament, reaching the semi-finals in 2011. It's held in October and November.

Sleeping

Nairobi has something for everyone when it comes to accommodation, from rough-and-ready cheapies on the wrong side of the tracks to palatial colonial-era hotels rich in history to fabulously priced options out in the verdant suburbs.

> **NAIROBI NATIONAL PARK**
>
> **Why Go** The park has high novelty value as a city-fringe park, with savannah and swampland, 400 bird species, highly endangered black rhinoceros, lions, cheetahs, zebras and giraffes.
>
> **When to Go** Year-round. July and August are best for wildebeest and zebra migration; January, February and June to October are good for the highest wildlife concentrations.
>
> **Practicalities** The park is just 7km from the CBD. Matatus 125 and 126 (KSh50, 30 to 45 minutes) pass by the park entrance from the train station. You can also go by private vehicle. Nairobi tour companies offer half-day safaris (from US$75 per person).

You can expect to pay a bit more in Nairobi than you would for the same facilities elsewhere in Kenya. However, in a city where personal safety is something of an issue, it's worth shelling out more for secure surroundings, especially if you're travelling with expensive gear. The majority of mid-range and top-end places also tend to throw in a hearty buffet breakfast, which can certainly keep you going throughout the day.

In this section, accommodation is broken down by neighbourhood and then by author preference. Keep in mind that inflation and political instability in Kenya can have drastic consequences, and prices are likely to change: use the prices here as general comparisons as opposed to fixed and non-negotiable rates. Also, rates vary considerably at the top-end properties, so it's best to contact them in advance as you can usually secure small discounts.

CITY CENTRE

TOP CHOICE **Kahama Hotel** HOTEL $
(Map p56; ☎3742210; www.kahamahotels.co.ke; Murang'a Rd; s/d from KSh3100/3700) Almost equidistant between the city centre and the National Museum, this place is a terrific choice. Its catchcry is 'Economy with Style' and it pretty much lives up to it, with pleasant rooms, comfy beds and free wireless

NAIROBI ART GALLERIES

The **Go-Down Arts Centre** (off Map p56; ☎0726992200; www.thegodownartscentre.com; Dunga Rd; admission free; ⏲9am-5pm Mon-Fri) contains 10 separate art studios, and is rapidly becoming a hub for Nairobi's burgeoning arts scene. It brings together visual and performing arts with regular exhibitions, shows, workshops and open cultural nights. It's in a converted warehouse in the Industrial Area just south of the CBD.

One of Nairobi's longest-established galleries is the central **Gallery Watatu** (Map p60; ☎2024857; Lonhro House, Standard St). It has regular exhibitions of paintings, photography and some sculpture, and many of the items are for sale; be prepared to part with upwards of KSh20,000. It also has a good permanent display.

access (no Yahoo! for some reason). The only downside? The new highway passes by the front door – ask for a room at the back.

TOP CHOICE **Norfolk Hotel** HOTEL $$$
(Map p56; ☎2265000; www.fairmont.com/norfolkhotel; Harry Thuku Rd; s/d from US$275/300; P❄☎≋) Built in 1904, Nairobi's oldest hotel was *the* place to stay during colonial days. The hotel remains the traditional starting point for elite safaris, and the Lord Delamere Terrace is still Nairobi's most famous meeting place. Thanks to the leafy grounds, it has an almost rustic feel, providing an appealing contrast to the modern bent of more central options, and it is by far the best spot in town for those looking for a bit of historical authenticity. To learn more about the colourful antics of Lord Delamere, one of the Norfolk's legendary patrons, see p295.

Nairobi Serena Hotel HOTEL $$$
(Map p56; ☎2842000; www.serenahotels.com; Central Park, Procession Way; s/d from US$290/320; P❄☎≋) Consolidating its reputation as one of the best top-flight chains in East Africa, this entry in the Serena canon has a fine sense of individuality, with its international-class facilities displaying a touch of safari style. Of particular note is the onsite Maisha health spa, which offers a wide range of holistic cures aimed at soothing your travel-worn bones and balancing your wanderlust-ridden mind. Opt for one of the amazing garden suites, where you can take advantage of your own private patio, complete with mini-pergola for dining outside. As the hotel is right opposite Uhuru Park, avoid walking anywhere from here at night.

New Stanley Hotel HOTEL $$$
(Map p60; ☎2757000; www.sarovahotels.com/stanley; cnr Kimathi St & Kenyatta Ave; s/d from US$421/468; P❄☎≋) A Nairobi classic. The original Stanley Hotel was established in 1902, though the latest version is a very smart and modern construction run by the sophisticated Sarova Hotels. Rooms are large and luxurious, and colonial decor prevails inside, with lashings of green leather, opulent chandeliers and old-fashioned fans, though the real highlight (at least from our perspective!) is the Thorn Tree Café (see p74), which inspired Lonely Planet's online community. Online rates are often considerably lower than the rack rates listed here.

Meridian Court Hotel HOTEL $$
(Map p60; ☎2220006; www.meridianhotelkenya.com; Muranga'a Rd; s/d from KSh7850/8950; P☎≋) The elaborate lobby here is rather more prepossessing than the grey concrete blocks above it, but it's hardly worth complaining when you're essentially getting a suite for the price of a standard room. There's no great luxury involved and some of the furnishings have seen better days, but the pool, bar and restaurants make it terrific value in this price range. The superior rooms are rarely worth the extra.

New Kenya Lodge HOTEL $
(Map p60; ☎2222202; www.nksafari.com; River Rd; dm/s/d with shared bathroom KSh600/700/1200) This classic, long-standing shoestringer's haunt has seen better decades (some of the beds sag prodigiously), though it's got an aged charm if you're not too fussy about things like, well, cleanliness. Staff here are friendly, and there's hot water in the evening (or so they claim).

Terminal Hotel HOTEL $
(Map p60; ☎2228817; Moktar Daddah St; s/d/tr KSh1700/2000/2300) Although it's lacking in quality compared to other midrange offerings, the Terminal Hotel is preferable to the rock-bottom budget crash pads in the

KIBERA

Kibera (which is derived from a Nubian word *kibra,* meaning forest) is a sprawling urban jungle of shanty-town housing. Home to an estimated one million residents, Kibera is the world's second-largest shanty town (after Soweto in Johannesburg, South Africa). Although it covers 2.5 sq km in area, it's home to somewhere between a quarter and a third of Nairobi's population, and has a density of an estimated 300,000 people per sq km. The neighbourhood was thrust into the Western imagination when it featured prominently in the Fernando Meirelles film *The Constant Gardener,* which is based on the book of the same name by John le Carré. With the area heavily polluted by open sewers, and lacking even the most basic infrastructure, residents of Kibera suffer from poor nutrition, violent crime and disease.

Although it's virtually impossible to collect accurate statistics on shanty towns, with the demographics changing almost daily, the rough estimates for Kibera are shocking enough. According to local aid workers, Kibera is home to one pit toilet for every 100 people; its inhabitants suffer from an HIV/AIDS infection rate of more than 20%; and four out of every five people living here are unemployed. These stark realities are compounded by the fact that the social services needed to address the situation are largely absent from governmental policies.

History

The British established Kibera in 1918 for Nubian soldiers as a reward for service in WWI. However, following Kenyan independence in 1963, housing in Kibera was rendered illegal by the government. But this new legislation inadvertently allowed the Nubians to rent out their property to a greater number of tenants than legally permitted and, for poorer tenants, Kibera was perceived as affordable despite the legalities (or lack thereof). Since the mid-1970s, though, control of Kibera has been firmly in Kikuyu hands, who now comprise the bulk of the population.

Orientation

Kibera (Map p64) is located southwest of the CBD.

The railway line heading to Kisumu intersects Kibera, though the shanty town doesn't actually have a station. However, this railway line does serve as the main thoroughfare through Kibera, and you'll find several shops selling basic provisions along the tracks.

Visiting the Shanty Town

A visit to Kibera is one way to look behind the headlines and touch on, albeit briefly, the daily struggles and triumphs of life in the town; there's nothing quite like the enjoyment of playing a bit of footy with street children aspiring to be the next Pelé. Although you could visit on your own, security is an issue, and such visits aren't always appreciated by residents. The best way to visit is on a tour, allowing you to explore a little of Kibera in the company of a trustworthy local resident. But be aware that a number of establishments in Nairobi are starting to offer 'cultural tours' to Kibera, many of which visitors may feel are not much more than organised voyeurism promoting little human interaction. If you are considering a visit, ask questions about the nature of your trip, and consider the potential positive and negative impact that it may have on the community. One company we recommend is **Kibera Tours** (☎0723669218; www.kiberatours.com; per person KSh2500).

Getting There & Away

You can get to Kibera by taking bus 32 or matatu 32c from the Kencom building along Moi Ave. Be advised that this route is notorious for petty theft, so be extremely vigilant and pay attention to your surroundings.

WHERE TO STAY IN NAIROBI?

Your experience of bedding down in the capital will be largely dependent on where you choose to lie, since Nairobi's neighbourhoods vary considerably in character.

The heart and soul of Nairobi is the city centre, so if you want to go to bed and wake up in the centre of it all, look no further. The main budget area is between Tom Mboya St and River Rd, where you'll find dozens of small hotels and guesthouses, though most of the rock-bottom cheapies are usually brothels or dosshouses for drunks. Staying in this area is something of a budget-travellers' tradition, but remember that these are some of Nairobi's meanest streets. The area west of Moi Ave is generally fine, and has a range of options.

Of the outlying areas, the eastern districts of Nairobi Hill and Milimani have the most promising selection, catering for all budgets. This is where you'll find a clutch of reliable business hotels and upmarket lodges, and the city's top three backpacker spots, all pleasantly removed from the congestion of the city centre. If you want to be a bit further out, there's expat-friendly Westlands and Parklands.

For a decidedly different take on Nairobi, consider heading right out into the 'burbs, namely Karen and Langata. For the most part, accommodation out here is at the top end, though the bucolic charm exuded by many of these properties is worth every shilling. If that's out of your price range, however, there are a couple of campsites that are worth checking out.

If Karen and Langata aren't far enough away from the city centre for you, then consider bedding down among the famed Ngong Hills, home to a popular ranch and a world away from the urban bump and grind. Near the Athi River, also on the south side of the city, is another recommended spot, **Acacia Camp** (see boxed text p88), especially good if you want to get up close and personal to some fine, feathered friends.

city centre. The emphasis here is on doing the basics well, with no overblown attempts at tourist frills, and the clean and adequate rooms speak for themselves.

Hotel Ambassadeur Nairobi HOTEL $$
(Map p60; ☎2246615; Tom Mboya St; s/d from US$80/100; P wi-fi) Believe it or not, this big hotel opposite the National Archives once belonged to the posh Sarova chain, and while structurally not much has changed, we do suspect room standards were rather more exacting in those days. Rooms are large and relatively plain with worn carpet a recurring theme. That said, it's central, and offers decent value in this price range.

Hilton Nairobi Hotel HOTEL $$$
(Map p60; ☎2250000; www.hilton.com; Mama Ngina St; s/d from US$200/250; P air-con wi-fi pool) A distinct Nairobi landmark, the Hilton dominates the centre of town with its somewhat dated round tower, occupying virtually an entire block with rooms, restaurants, shops and a whole slew of business facilities. Although its overwhelming modernity isn't as atmospheric as some of Nairobi's more seasoned top-end hotels, the Hilton remains one of the best deals in town for upmarket travellers.

Kenya Comfort Hotel HOTEL $$
(Map p60; ☎2317605; www.kenyacomfort.com; cnr Muindi Mbingu & Monrovia Sts; s/d from US$45/60; wi-fi) This cheerily painted place is kept in reasonable nick, offering a selection of tired but well-valued tiled rooms and a lift for easy access. Meals are also available in the popular 24-hour Sokoni bar-restaurant, and the rooftop guest lounge is a nice place to survey the city.

Hotel Africana HOTEL $
(Map p60; ☎0726243840; Dubois Rd; s/d KSh1050/1400) The Africana has clean, bright rooms, and is better maintained than many places in its class. It has a TV room and a roof garden offering a bird's-eye view of the busy streets. The surrounding area is pretty seedy, but it's a 15-minute walk to the centre.

Central YMCA HOSTEL $
(Map p56; ☎2724116; State House Rd; dm/s/d from KSh1000/1400/2100; P) While it might not inspire the Village People to dedicate a song to it, this central spot has a decent range of passable rooms. Note that you don't need to be a man or a Christian to stay at the YMCA, though you'll certainly be in the majority here if you're either. Breakfast is available for KSh400, and other meals for KSh600.

Terrace Hotel HOTEL $
(Map p60; ☎221636; Ronald Ngala St; s/d with shared bathroom KSh700/1000) One of the better deals you'll get at the budget end, the hotel wears its worn atmosphere like a badge of honour. It compares favourably to some of the cell-like establishments around, but it's still spartan by any standard.

Down Town Hotel HOTEL $
(Map p60; ☎2240501; downtownhotel2000@yahoo.com; Moktar Daddah St; s/d KSh1900/2200) A few doors up from the Terminal Hotel, Down Town doesn't have quite the personality of its neighbour, but provides similar standards for a similar price. If the Terminal's full, chances are this is where they'll send you for alternative accommodation, and you're unlikely to hold it against them. That is, unless they're still demolishing the building next door and noise levels haven't abated.

MILIMANI & UPPER HILL

TOP CHOICE **Upper Hill Country Lodge** HOTEL $$
(Map p56; ☎2881600; www.countrylodge.co.ke; Second Ngong Ave, Milimani; s/d from KSh11,400/15,600; P) This fantastic property was constructed by the owners of the adjacent Fairview Hotel, though rather than striving for over-the-top opulence, the focus here is on affordable luxury for business travellers. Despite a recent price hike, it remains one of the best-value midrange options in Nairobi – its minimalist yet stylish living quarters can compete with the best of them. Travellers can also unwind in the small gym, relax in the rock garden or take advantage of the bars and restaurants at the Fairview next door.

TOP CHOICE **Palacina** BOUTIQUE HOTEL $$$
(off Map p56; ☎2715517; www.palacina.com; Kitale Lane, Milimani; 1-/2-person ste US$270/409, penthouse US$690; P) The fabulous collection of stylish suites – at what is possibly the first genuine boutique hotel in Kenya – is perfect for well-heeled sophisticates who still like the personal touch. Intimate rooms are awash with calming tones, boldly accented by rich teak woods, lavish furniture and private jacuzzis.

Wildebeest Camp BACKPACKERS $
(Map p56; ☎2720740; www.wildebeestcamp.com; Milimani Rd, Milimani; camping KSh1000, dm/s/d KSh1250/2500/3500, s/d garden tent from KSh3500/4500; P@) This fabulous place, next to the Royal Nairobi Golf Course west of Upper Hill, is another of Nairobi's outstanding budget options. The atmosphere is relaxed yet switched on, and the accommodation is spotless and great value however much you're paying. A great Nairobi base.

Heron Hotel HOTEL $$
(Map p56; ☎2720740; www.heronhotel.com; Milimani Rd, Milimani; s/d from KSh9995/11,995; P) It's hard to see why anyone would pay top-end prices when places like the Heron are around. Rooms are modern, extremely comfortable and well-appointed, while the staff are attentive and professional. The location is quiet and there's not even the merest trace of Buffalo Bill's, a notorious brothel that once occupied the site. Highly recommended.

Upper Hill Campsite & Backpackers BACKPACKERS $
(off Map p56; ☎2500218; www.upperhillcampsite.com; Othaya Rd, Kileleshwa; camping KSh450, dm/d KSh700/KSh3000, d without bathroom KSh2000; P@) An attractive, secure compound and an oasis from the mean city streets, Upper Hill offers a range of accommodation, attracting a loyal following of overland trucks groups and an international mix of backpackers and budget travellers. It's centred on an elegant, restored colonial house on a sprawling estate in the embassy district of Kileleshwa. Competing for the title of Nairobi's top backpacker spot, Upper Hill organises just about every kind of safari and outdoor excursion you can imagine, and it will even take the time to tune up your ride if you're on a self-drive expedition. To get here, take matatu or bus 46 along Othaya Rd until you pass the Egyptian embassy on the left-hand side; the entrance to the property is just past here on the right-hand side.

Milimani Backpackers & Safari Centre BACKPACKERS $
(Map p56; ☎2724827; www.milimanibackpackers.com; Milimani Rd, Milimani; camping KSh600, dm KSh750, s/d cabins KSh2200/2500, with shared bathroom KSh1500/2000; P@) This terrific place is one of the friendliest accommodation options in town, and whether you camp out back, cosy up in the dorms or splurge on your own cabin, you'll end up huddled around the fire at night, swapping travel stories and dining on home-cooked meals (KSh450) with fellow travellers. The friendly

staff can also help you book a safari, organise onward travel or simply get your bearings. Take matatu 46 (KSh30) from the city centre.

Nairobi International Youth Hostel HOSTEL $

(Map p56; ☎2738046; www.yhak.org; Ralph Bunche Rd, Milimani; dm KSh700-900, d KSh3000; P@) This well-looked-after budget option isn't as atmospheric as the Upper Hill Campsite and Milimani Backpackers, but Kenya's HI instalment is still a comfortable and relaxed spot to meet other travellers. It offers the usual range of hosteller-catered amenities including an activity centre, booking desk, cybercafe, bar-restaurant and a communal lounge. It's preferable that you have an HI card, but you'll still be let in if you don't. Any matatu or bus going down either Valley or Ngong Rds will get you here; always take a taxi when returning at night.

Fairview Hotel HOTEL $$

(Map p56; ☎2711321; www.fairviewkenya.com; Bishops Rd, Milimani; s/d/ste from KSh14,800/17,300/24,000; ❄📶🏊) An excellent top-end choice that puts many of the more prestigious and pricier places in town to shame. The Fairview is nicely removed from the central hubbub and defined by its winding paths and green-filled grounds. It all creates a refined atmosphere, especially around the charming courtyard restaurant.

PARKLANDS

Southern Sun Mayfair HOTEL $$$

(Map p77; ☎3740920; http://southernsun.co.ke; Parklands Rd, Parklands; s/d from US$299/324; P❄📶🏊) If you're looking for discreet luxury away from the city centre, the Mayfair is a 1930s Edwardian place with classy rooms arrayed around a mature internal garden. The furnishings have colonial charm that's rarely overdone.

KAREN & LANGATA

Staying in Karen and Langata puts you pretty far from the city centre, though that's precisely the point. These leafy suburbs are a welcome respite from the grit of the CBD, and you'll be within striking distance of some of Nairobi's top tourist attractions.

TOP CHOICE **Karen Blixen Cottages** BOUTIQUE HOTEL $$$

(Map p64; ☎882130; www.karenblixencoffeegarden.com; 336 Karen Rd, Karen; s/d US$300/465; P📶🏊) Located near the Karen Blixen Museum, this gorgeous clutch of spacious cottages is centred on a formal garden, and adjacent to a small coffee plantation and a country restaurant. It's sophisticated, supremely comfortable and if you're keen on having an *Out of Africa* experience, then look no further.

Nairobi Tented Camp TENTED CAMP $$$

(Map p64; ☎2603337; www.nairobitentedcamp.com; Nairobi National Park; s/d full board US$405/770; P🏊) The only accommodation inside Nairobi National Park, this luxury tented camp offers the full-on safari experience, even though you've scarcely left the city. The tents are like those you'll find in Kenya's better-known parks, and with just eight of them there's a real (and somewhat incongruous) sense of solitude. Prices

KAREN BLIXEN

The suburb of Karen takes its name from Karen Blixen, aka Isak Dinesen, a Danish coffee planter and aristocrat who went on to become one of Europe's most famous writers on Africa. Although she lived a life of genteel luxury on the edge of the Ngong Hills, her personal life was full of heartbreak. After her first marriage broke down, she began a love affair with the British playboy Denys Finch Hatton, who subsequently died in a plane crash during one of his frequent flying visits to Tsavo National Park.

After the farm came close to bankruptcy, Blixen returned to Denmark, where she began her famous memoir *Out of Africa*. The book is one of the definitive tales of European endeavour in Africa, but Blixen was passed over for the 1954 Nobel Prize for Literature in favour of Ernest Hemingway. She died from malnutrition at her family estate in Denmark in 1962.

Out of Africa was made into a movie in 1985, starring Meryl Streep, Robert Redford and one of the retired trains from Nairobi's Railway Museum. The final production was terrific from a Hollywood perspective, but leaves out enough of the colonial history to irk historians and Kenyan nationalists alike.

include airport transfers, a game drive and park entrance fees.

Margarita House GUESTHOUSE $$
(Map p64; ☎2018421; www.themargaritahouse.com; Lower Plains Rd, Karen; s/d from US$85/125; P) Tucked away on a quiet street on Karen's north side, this tranquil guesthouse is one of the few midrange options in the area, and thankfully it's a good one. Rooms are large and comfortable, contemporary artworks adorn the walls, and Elizabeth and Joel are welcoming hosts. The roads can be a little confusing around here – print out the detailed directions from its website.

Giraffe Manor HISTORIC HOTEL $$$
(Map p64; ☎8891078; www.giraffemanor.com; Mukoma Rd, Karen; s/d full board US$660/960; P) Built in 1932 in typical English style, this elegant manor is situated on 56 hectares, much of which is given over to the adjacent Giraffe Centre. As a result, you may have a Rothschild's giraffe peering through your bedroom window first thing in the morning, which is just about one of the most surreal experiences you could imagine. And yet, the real appeal of the Giraffe Manor is that you're treated as a personal guest of the owners – which means you can use their chauffeur, sample their wines and dine in lavish excess. Literary buffs should ask for the Karen Blixen room, decked out with furniture the famous author gave the owners when she left Africa for the last time.

Karen Camp CAMPGROUND $
(Map p64; ☎8833475; www.karencamp.com; Marula Lane, Karen; camping US$6, s/d walk-in tent US$20/30, r from US$40; P) You wouldn't expect to find a backpacker-friendly option out here in affluent Karen, which is why we like this friendly little spot so much. The quiet location and smart facilities are reason enough to make the trek out to the shady campsites, spick-and-span dorms and permanent safari-style tents.

Eating

Nairobi is well stocked with places to eat, particularly in the city centre, where you can choose anything from the cheap workers' canteens around River Rd to Chinese feasts and full-on splurges off Kenyatta Ave. For dinner it's worth heading out to the suburbs, where there are dozens of choices of cuisine from all over the world. Karen and Langata have the best range, though there are some good choices in Westlands and Parklands, and in Milimani and Upper Hill.

As in the rest of the country, lunch is the main meal of the day, and city workers flock to the numerous canteens dishing up simple, classic Kenyan and Swahili dishes along with Western staples like chicken and chips.

Nairobi has plenty of upmarket restaurants serving internationally inspired cuisine. The capital is also famous for its Indian cuisine, which makes an appearance in some form or another on just about every menu.

Note that in this section, eating options are broken down by neighbourhood and then by author preference. Also be advised that restaurants come and go quickly in the fickle capital, though the places we cover in this section have thus far stood the test of time.

HAVE YOUR SAY

Found a fantastic restaurant that you're longing to share with the world? Disagree with our recommendations? Or just want to talk about your most recent trip?

Whatever your reason, head to lonelyplanet.com, where you can post a review, ask or answer a question on the Thorntree forum, comment on a blog, or share your photos and tips on Groups. Or you can simply spend time chatting with like-minded travellers. So go on, have your say.

CITY CENTRE

Nairobi's lifeblood flows through the CBD, which is why you'll find the lion's share of restaurants here. Cheap canteens and fast-food eateries fuel a good number of Nairobi's office workers, though there are several upmarket places that can set the scene for that crucial business lunch. If you're planning on having dinner anywhere in the city centre, be sure to take a taxi back to your accommodation as the streets empty out once the sun goes down.

TOP CHOICE **Savanna: The Coffee Lounge** CAFE $
(snacks from KSh180, mains KSh440-590; ⏲7am-8pm Mon-Sat, 9am-6pm Sun) National Museum (Map p56; Museum Hill Rd); Central Nairobi (Map

p60; Loita Street); Central Nairobi (Map p60; Kenyatta Ave) This classy little chain has outposts across Nairobi, including two in the town centre, but we particularly like the tranquillity of the branch inside the grounds of the National Museum. Decor is safari chic without being overdone, service is friendly and unobtrusive, and dishes include pies, wraps, samosas, sandwiches, burgers, pasta, soup and salads.

TOP CHOICE Lord Delamere Terrace & Bar INTERNATIONAL $$$
(Map p56; ☎2265000; www.fairmont.com/norfolkhotel; Norfolk Hotel, Harry Thuku Rd; mains KSh1450-2575; ⊙lunch & dinner) This popular rendezvous spot at the Norfolk Hotel has existed as the unofficial starting and ending point for East African safaris since 1904. While it has been patronised by almost all of the first European pioneer settlers, it is named after the colourful character that is Lord Delamere (see p295). While the atmosphere may be a bit too colonial for some people's tastes, there's no denying the palatable sense of history that ebbs from the walls. The restaurant inside the Norfolk Hotel, **Tapu** (mains KSh1450-2750; ⊙lunch & dinner), shares a similar menu, with wonderful steak and seafood and dishes that range from Lamu crab cakes and Indian Ocean lobster to crocodile kebabs and ostrich fillets.

Tamarind Restaurant SEAFOOD $$$
(Map p60; ☎2251811; www.tamarind.co.ke; off Harambee Ave; mains KSh1000-2500; ⊙lunch & dinner Mon-Sat) Kenya's most prestigious restaurant chain runs Nairobi's best seafood restaurant, located in the monumental National Bank Building. The splendid menu offers all manner of exotic flavours, and the lavish dining room is laid out in a sumptuous modern Arabic-Moorish style. Starters range from Kilifi oysters to red snapper in spicy harissa, though save room for the crustacean onslaught of flambéed lobster with cognac, sunset Pwani crab and tikka masala prawns. Smart dress is expected, and you'll need to budget at least KSh2500 for the full works – much more if you want wine or cocktails and lobster – though seafood gourmands agree that it's money well spent.

Thorn Tree Café INTERNATIONAL $$
(Map p60; ☎2757000; New Stanley Hotel, Kimathi St; mains KSh950-1950; ⊙lunch & dinner) The Stanley's legendary cafe still serves as a popular meeting place for travellers of all persuasions, and caters to most tastes with a good mix of food. The original thorn-tree noticeboard in the courtyard gave rise to the general expression, and inspired Lonely Planet's own online Thorn Tree Travel Forum. While the cafe is now on its third acacia, and the noticeboard's not quite the paperfest it once was, a little nostalgia is de rigueur, even if only to pause and recognise an original landmark on the Cape to Cairo overland trail. The menu ranges from grilled giant prawns to Kenyan-style chicken stew. It also does a four-course business lunch (KSh2100) Monday to Friday.

Beneve Coffee House KENYAN $
(Map p60; cnr Standard & Koinange Sts; mains KSh180-250; ⊙lunch & dinner Mon-Fri) This small self-service cafe has locals queuing outside in the mornings waiting for it to open. Food ranges from African- and Indian-influenced stews to curries, fish and chips, samosas, pasties and a host of other choices, all at low, low prices.

Pasara Café INTERNATIONAL $
(Map p60; ground fl, Lonrho Bldg, Standard St; dishes KSh275-395; ⊙7am-midnight Mon-Sat) At the forefront of Nairobi's burgeoning cafe culture, this stylish, modern bar-brasserie has a nifty selection of snacks, sandwiches, grills and breakfasts, always offering something that bit more ambitious than the usual cafeteria fare; try the chicken tikka burger and a milkshake for example. The atmosphere equals that of a European coffeehouse, making it a fine place to relax with a newspaper away from all the stresses of the capital's streets.

Nyama Choma Stalls KENYAN $
(Map p56; Haile Selassie Ave; lunch around KSh400) A definite step down the scale, but worth it for the atmosphere, are the backstreet stalls near the Railway Museum, behind the Shell petrol station. Foreigners are a rare sight, but you'll be warmly welcomed and encouraged to sample Kenyan dishes such as *matoke* (cooked mashed plantains).

Malindi Dishes KENYAN $
(Map p60; Gaberone Rd; mains KSh80-250; ⊙lunch & dinner) This small Swahili canteen serves great food from the coast, including pilau (curried rice with meat), birianis (spicy rice casseroles) and coconut fish,

FOR THE LOVE OF MEAT

Love it or hate it, **Carnivore** (Map p64; www.carnivore.co.ke; off Langata Rd; meat buffet lunch/dinner KSh2530/2835, veg buffet KSh2150/2410, child 5-12 half price; ⏲lunch & dinner; Ⓟ) is hands down the most famous *nyama choma* (barbecued meat) in Kenya, an icon among tourists, expats and wealthier locals for the past 25 years.

Owned by the Tamarind chain, Carnivore was voted by UK magazine *Restaurant* to be among the 50 best restaurants in the world in 2002 and 2003. This honour was largely in recognition of the fact that you could dine here on exotic game meats. In recent years, however, strict new laws mean that zebra, hartebeest, kudu and the like are now off the menu, and you have to be content with camel, ostrich and crocodile in addition to the more standard offerings. You also get soup, salads and sauces to go with the meats.

At the entrance is a huge barbecue pit laden with real swords of beef, pork, lamb, chicken and farmed game meats. As long as the paper flag on your table is flying, waiters will keep bringing the meat, which is carved right at the table; if you're in need of a breather, you can tip the flag over temporarily. Note that dessert and coffee (but not other drinks) are included in the set price.

This meat-fest does have its critics – prices *are* high and the waiters, hats and all, can seem like the ringmasters of a circus with their enthusiastic bonhomie. But if you take it for what it is, you'll leave satisfied.

At lunchtime, you can get to Carnivore by matatu 126 from the city centre – the turn-off is signposted just past Wilson Airport, from where it's a 1km walk. At night, it's best to hire a taxi, which should run to about KSh800 each way depending on your bargaining skills.

At night you may wish to stay on for an all-night dance-athon at the adjacent Simba Saloon (p79).

with side dishes such as *ugali* (maize- or cassava-based staple), naan and rice. You'll get a grand halal feed here, but true to its Muslim roots, it's closed for prayer at lunchtime on Friday.

Trattoria ITALIAN $$

(Map p60; ☎340855; cnr Wabera & Kaunda Sts; mains KSh850-1300; ⏲7am-midnight) This popular and classy downtown Italian restaurant, swathed in trellises and plants, offers excellent pizzas, homemade pasta, risottos, varied mains and a whole page of desserts. The atmosphere and food are excellent. It's packed every night, especially the upstairs balcony section.

Kahawa INTERNATIONAL $

(Map p60; EcoBank Towers, Kaunda St; mains KSh320-620; ⏲lunch & dinner daily) Kahawa has an unusual coastal theme – the counter even resembles a traditional dhow (Arabic sailing vessel), complete with mast. The menu, however, is anything but old-fashioned, proffering an ever-changing cavalcade of unexpected specials to complement the grills and steaks. Servings are generous.

Seasons Restaurant KENYAN $

(mains KSh390-500, buffets KSh500; ⏲24hrs) Nairobi Cinema (Map p60; Uchumi House, Aga Khan Walk); Kimathi St (Map p60; Mutual Bldg) The cafeteria vats here always brim with cheap Kenyan and Western favourites, which is probably why this local chain has a strong following. The buffet is small but (unusually for those who've been staying in safari lodges) entirely African in orientation. It claims to open 24 hours, but we didn't pass by at 4am to check. The Nairobi Cinema outlet has a popular bar and beer garden, where you can bring your own alcoholic beverage and pay a small corkage fee.

Fiesta Restaurant & Bar INTERNATIONAL $$

(Map p60; Koinange St; mains KSh620-980; ⏲7am-midnight) Despite the Latin resonances of the name and the bright adobe-style decor, the Fiesta doesn't have anything remotely Tex-Mex on offer. It concentrates instead on mixed grills and other international dishes, with an upmarket version of Kenya's *nyama choma* (barbecued meat) obsession thrown in. Come here on a slow afternoon and it all falls a bit flat, but the atmosphere livens up most evenings.

CREDIT CARDS?

At budget and some midrange eateries, it's recommended that you pay in cash, especially if you haven't racked up too large a bill. All of the upmarket places listed in this section do accept credit cards, though most add 17% VAT to the bill. Be sure to check your bill carefully before signing your name.

Panda Chinese Restaurant CHINESE $$
(Map p60; EcoBank Towers, Kaunda St; mains KSh420-1300; ⌚lunch & dinner) This spacious, classy restaurant hidden away on Kaunda St is where you should head if you have a sudden, incurable craving for beef and broccoli. The staff are attentive (sometimes overly so, especially when it's quiet), but the food is some of the best Chinese chow you'll find in these parts.

Porterhouse Restaurant STEAKHOUSE $$
(Map p60; ☎221829; Mama Ngina St; mains KSh480-690; ⌚9.30am-10.30pm Mon-Sat) Steak-lovers should make this 1st-floor restaurant their first port of call: apart from a few token dishes such as chicken Kiev, the menu here is entirely dedicated to the art of carving chunks of cow. Locals worry that it's not what it use to be, but it still has few steak rivals in the downtown area.

Etouch Food Court FAST FOOD $
(Map p60; Union Towers, cnr Moi Ave & Mama Ngina St; meals KSh350-550; ⌚lunch & dinner) We all need a bit of greasy comfort food from time to time, and Nairobi-ites are certainly no exception. If you find yourself craving a quick fix, head to the Etouch Food Court, a central collection of cheap 'n' easy fast-food joints such as Nando's, Chicken Inn, Creamy Inn, Pizza Inn...you get the idea.

MILIMANI

TOP CHOICE **Blue Nile Ethiopian Restaurant** ETHIOPIAN $$
(Map p56; ☎2271851; bluenile@yahoo.com; Argwings Kodhek Rd, Hurlingham; mains KSh400-700; ⌚lunch & dinner) One of those rare places with a character all its own, Blue Nile's quirky lounge, painted with stories from Ethiopian mythology, couldn't be mistaken for anywhere else. For the full, communal, African eating experience, you could order the five- to seven-person *doro wat* (spicy traditional chicken stew, KSh4500), but the *yebeg key wot* (spiced goat meat sauce marinated in butter and spicy berebere) is much more manageable.

WESTLANDS

TOP CHOICE **Haandi Restaurant** INDIAN $$
(Map p77; ☎4448294; The Mall Shopping Centre, Ring Rd, Westlands; mains KSh750-1500; ⌚lunch & dinner; ❄) This international-award-winner is widely regarded as the best Indian restaurant in Kenya. While you might not expect to find a restaurant of this calibre in a shopping mall, your doubts will disappear the moment the waiter brings the tome of a menu to your table. Indeed, it reads something like a recipe book crossed with a guide to Indian cuisine, and includes wonderful Mughlai (North Indian) spreads, tandoori dishes and plenty of vegetarian curries. Be sure to come here with an empty stomach as it isn't exactly the lightest fare, especially when served with Haandi's signature stacks of naan and piles of basmati rice. It has sister restaurants in Kampala and London, and even sells its own souvenir T-shirts.

Siam Thai THAI $$
(Map p77; ☎3751728; Unga House, Muthithi Rd, Westlands; mains KSh760-2500; ⌚lunch & dinner) While Asian food in Kenya tends to gravitate towards greasy Chinese, this attractive restaurant has an extensive menu of authentic Thai food. Curries here are rich, thick and spicy, which is exactly the way they're supposed to be. Unga House can be reached from either Woodvale Grove or Muthithi Rd.

Sarit Centre Food Court FAST FOOD $
(Map p77; Sarit Centre, Parklands Rd, Westlands; prices vary; ⌚lunch & dinner) This large food court on the 2nd floor of this popular shopping mall has a good variety of small restaurants and fast-food places catering to discerning palates. Standard Kenyan and Indian offerings are available here, as are other international eats including Italian and Chinese cuisines.

KAREN & LANGATA

TOP CHOICE **Talisman** INTERNATIONAL $$
(Map p64; ☎3883213; 320 Ngong Rd, Karen; mains KSh950-1800; ⌚breakfast, lunch & dinner Tue-Sun) This classy cafe-bar-restaurant is incredibly fashionable with the Karen in-crowd, and rivals any of Kenya's top eateries for imaginative international food. The comfortable

Westlands

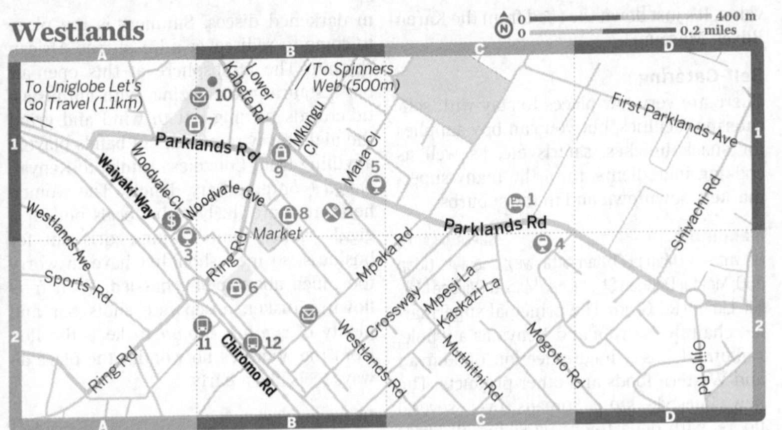

Westlands

Sleeping

1 Southern Sun Mayfair C1

Eating

Haandi Restaurant .... (see 6)
Sarit Centre Food Court .... (see 7)
2 Siam Thai B1
Uchumi .... (see 7)

Drinking

3 Gypsy's Bar A1
4 Klub House C2
5 Soho's B1

Shopping

Banana Box .... (see 7)
6 Mall Shopping Centre B2
7 Sarit Centre A1
8 Undugu Craft Shop B1
9 Westlands Curio Market B1

Information

AAR Health Services Clinic .... (see 7)
Automobile Association of Kenya .... (see 7)
Barclays Bank .... (see 7)
DHL .... (see 7)
EasySurf .... (see 7)
10 Savage Wilderness Safaris B1
Text Book Centre .... (see 7)
Travellers Forex Bureau .... (see 6)

Transport

11 Bus & Matatu Stands B2
12 Bus & Matatu Stands B2

lounge-like rooms mix modern African and European styles, the courtyard provides some welcome air, and specials such as chili coconut mangrove-crab curry perk up the palate no end.

Rusty Nail INTERNATIONAL $$

(Map p64; ☎3882461; Dagoretti Rd, Karen; mains KSh950-1300; ⌚lunch & dinner) The relaxed atmosphere of this pavilion restaurant sits nicely with the wide range of food on offer. Lunch and dinner menus change weekly, although steaks and fish dishes are mainstays. It also serves lighter meals such as burgers and salads, and traditional Sunday roasts cater for nostalgic English foodies.

Karen Blixen Coffee Garden INTERNATIONAL $$$

(Map p64; ☎0719346349; www.tamarind.co.ke; Karen Rd, Karen; mains KSh790-1690; ⌚7am-10pm) This upmarket option, run by the ubiquitous Tamarind group, offers diners and snackers five different areas in which to enjoy a varied menu, including the plush L'Amour dining room, the historic 1901 Swedo House and the main section, which is a smart restaurant set in a veritable English country garden. The food is excellent, especially the mixed grill 'chapa kazi choma sampler', an upmarket version of Kenya's favourite dish. Its Sunday lunch buffet (KSh1490) is popular, and excellent value. It's just down the road from the Karen Blixen Museum.

Self-Catering

There are very few places to stay with self-catering facilities, but you can buy supplies for snack lunches, safaris etc, as well as cooking ingredients, from the many supermarkets downtown and in the suburbs.

Nakumatt SUPERMARKET $

Downtown (Map p60; Kenyatta Ave); Lifestyle (Map p60; Moktar Daddah St); Village Market (Village Market, Limuru Rd, Gigiri) The principal supermarket chain in Nairobi and Kenya as a whole, Nakumatt has a huge selection of Kenyan and Western foods and other products. The new Lifestyle store spreads over several floors, with departments stocking all kinds of useful household and outdoor goods.

Uchumi SUPERMARKET $

(Map p77; Sarit Centre, Parklands Rd, Westlands) Once the main supermarket chain in town, Uchumi has faded fast in Nakumatt's wake and several central branches have closed. It has a good range of items.

Drinking

Western cafe culture has hit Nairobi, and been seized upon enthusiastically by local expats and residents pining for a decent cup of Kenyan coffee. This is the best place in the country for *real* coffee. All of the cafes reviewed here offer at least some form of food, whether it's a few cakes or a full menu, but none serve alcohol.

As for bars, there are plenty of cheap but very rough-and-ready bars around Latema Rd and River Rd, although these places aren't recommended for female travellers, and even male drinkers should watch themselves. There are some safer and friendlier watering holes around Tom Mboya St and Moi Ave, and many of the restaurants and hotels reviewed in our Sleeping and Eating sections are fine places for a drink. You can also head to Westlands and Karen, where the drinking scene brings in a lot more expats. Even in the 'burbs, however, foreign women without a man in tow will draw attention.

CITY CENTRE

TOP CHOICE **Simmers** BAR

(Map p60; cnr Kenyatta Ave & Muindi Mbingu St; ⏲8am-1am) If you're tired of having your butt pinched to the strains of limp R&B in darkened discos, Simmers is the place to come to rediscover a bit of true African rhythm. The atmosphere at this open-air bar-restaurant is amazing, with enthusiastic crowds turning out to wind and grind the night away to parades of bands playing anything from Congolese rumba to Kenyan *benga* (contemporary dance). The women here are more likely to be locals out for a giggle rather than working girls out for business, so men shouldn't have to worry too much about being hassled. With free-flowing Tusker, a separate shots bar and plenty of *nyama choma* to keep the lion from the door, it's no wonder the place always feels like a party.

Dormans Café CAFE

(Map p60; Mama Ngina St; coffee KSh110-340; ⏲6.30am-8.30pm Mon-Sat, 9am-7.30pm Sun) Established in the 1960s, this venerable firm has only recently branched out into the cafe business, but has certainly made an aggressive Starbucks-style start, opening a shiny pine outlet right opposite its main rival, Nairobi Java. The coffee's good (everything from cappuccino to iced coffee and hazelnut mocha), the selection of teas is impressive, and the food (main dishes and light meals) definitely hits the spot.

Nairobi Java House CAFE

(Map p60; www.nairobijava.com; Mama Ngina St; coffee KSh120-280; ⏲6.30am-10pm Mon-Fri, 7am-9pm Sat, 8am-8pm Sun) This fantastic coffeehouse is rapidly turning itself into a major brand, and you may see its logo on T-shirts as far afield as London and beyond. Aficionados say the coffee's some of the best in Kenya, and there are plenty of cakes and other sweet and savoury treats (even New York cheesecake).

Roast House BAR

(Map p60; Kilome Rd; ⏲noon-late) This split-level bar-restaurant is one of the better specimens in the River Rd area, with regular DJ nights. Caution is advised if you're coming here at night – bring a local friend if you want to take part in the action.

Zanze Bar BAR

(Map p60; Kenya Cinema Plaza, Moi Ave; ⏲6pm-late) A lively and friendly top-floor bar with pool tables, a dance floor, cheap beer and reasonable food. During the week things are relatively quiet, but from Friday to Sunday it rocks until the early hours, with a much more relaxed vibe than the big clubs.

WESTLANDS & PARKLANDS

TOP CHOICE Gypsy's Bar BAR

(Map p77; Woodvale Grove; ⊙11am-4am) This is probably the most popular bar in Westlands, pulling in a large, mixed crowd of Kenyans, expats and prostitutes. Snacks are available, and there's decent Western and African music, with parties taking over the pavement in summer.

Klub House BAR

(Map p77; Parklands Rd; ⊙24hr) At the western end of Westlands, the Klub House is another old favourite. The spacious bar has more pool tables than other bars, and is a good place to party until late. Music is predominantly Latin, Caribbean and home-grown Swahili, and every night has a different theme, from chillout (Monday) and live jazz (8pm to 11pm Tuesday) to disco (Friday) and live bands (Saturday)

Soho's BAR

(Map p77; Parklands Rd; ⊙6pm-late) A lively and popular place that pulls in a smart Kenyan and expat crowd. As well as the crisp cold beers, there's a good selection of wines and cocktails.

MILIMANI

TOP CHOICE Casablanca BAR

(off Map p56; ☎2723173; Lenana Rd, Hurlingham; ⊙hours vary) This Moroccan-style lounge bar continues to be a hit with Nairobi's fastidious expat community, and you don't have to spend much time here to become a convert. Shisha pipes, wines and cocktails conspire to ease you into what's bound to end up a late night.

☆ Entertainment

There's a good selection of dance clubs in Nairobi's centre and there are no dress codes, although there's an unspoken assumption that males will at least wear a shirt and long trousers. Beer in all these places is reasonably priced at about KSh150, but imported drinks cost a lot more. Due to the high number of female prostitutes, men will generally get the bulk of the hassle, though even women in male company are by no means exempt from approaches by either sex.

For information on entertainment in Nairobi and for big music venues in the rest of the country, get hold of the *Saturday Nation*, which lists everything from cinema releases to live-music venues. There are also plenty of suggestions in the magazine *Going Out*. Nightclubs usually open from 9pm until 6am, although they may close earlier if things are quiet.

Nightclubs

Florida 2000 NIGHTCLUB

(Map p60; http://floridaclubskenya.com; Moi Ave; men/women KSh250/150) This big dancing den, known by everyone as F2, is near City Hall Way. It works to the same formula of booze, beats and tightly packed bodies. As is typical in Nairobi, every night is a little different: Thursday is techno trance, Friday is rumba and so on.

New Florida NIGHTCLUB

(Map p60; floridaclubskenya.com; Koinange St; men/women KSh250/150) The 'Madhouse' is a big, rowdy club housed in a bizarre, blacked-out saucer building above a petrol station. The music ranges from jazz to the customary weekend mish-mash of Western pop. Whatever night you choose, it's usually mayhem, crammed with bruisers, cruisers, hookers, hustlers and curious tourists, but it's great fun if you're in the right mood (or just very drunk).

Simba Saloon NIGHTCLUB

(Map p64; off Langata Rd; admission KSh200-300) Next door to Carnivore out on the road to Karen, this large bar and nightclub, which is partly open-air, pulls in a huge crowd, particularly on Wednesday, Friday and Saturday. There are video screens, several bars, a bonfire and adventure playground in the garden, and unashamedly Western music on the dance floor, although you might get the occasional African superstar playing live. It's usually crammed with wealthy Kenyans, expat teenagers, travellers and NGO workers, plus a fair sprinkling of prostitutes. You can get a range of well-priced food at all hours, and there's a Dormans coffee stall to keep those eyelids open until closing.

Theatre

Kenya National Theatre THEATRE

(Map p56; ☎2225174; Harry Thuku Rd; tickets from KSh250) This is the major theatre venue in Nairobi. As well as contemporary and classic plays, there are special events such as beauty pageants, which are less highbrow but still culturally interesting. Check out the *Daily Nation* to see what's on. It's opposite the Norfolk Hotel.

Shopping

Nairobi is a good place to pick up souvenirs before heading home. There are loads of souvenir shops downtown and in the area northwest of Kenyatta Ave, so you're spoilt for selection. Be warned though that prices are usually higher than elsewhere in the country.

Although most places sell exactly the same things, there are a few speciality shops with better-than-average crafts. The 'Little India' area around Biashara St is good for fabric, textiles and those all-important souvenir Tusker T-shirts. If you're interested in buying local music, just wander around the River Rd and Latema Rd area and listen out for the blaring CD kiosks.

TOP CHOICE Utamaduni HANDICRAFTS
(Map p64; www.utamaduni.com; Bogani East Rd, Karen; ⌚9am-6pm) Utamaduni is a large crafts emporium, with more than a dozen separate rooms selling all kinds of excellent African artworks and souvenirs. Prices start relatively high, but there's *none* of the hard sell you'd get in town. A portion of all proceeds goes to the Kenya Wildlife Foundation. There's an on-site restaurant and playground. It's close to the Giraffe Centre.

African Heritage Design Company HANDICRAFTS
(Map p56; Museum Hill Rd; ⌚9am-6pm daily) With various outlets around town, including this one opposite the entrance to the National Museum, African Heritage Design Company has a classy range of statues, ceramics and textiles. Not all of the items are from Kenya, but the quality is good.

Banana Box HANDICRAFTS
(Map p77; www.bananaboxcrafts.com; Sarit Centre, Westlands; ⌚9.30am-6pm Mon-Sat, 10am-2pm Sun) Amid the rather less-altruistic commercialism of the Sarit Centre, Banana Box works in conjunction with community projects and refugee groups and offers modern uses for traditional objects. It's one of the better handicrafts stores around town, with an upmarket feel but reasonable prices.

Spinners Web HANDICRAFTS
(off Map p77; www.spinnerswebkenya.com; Getathuru Gardens, off Peponi Rd, Spring Valley; ⌚9.30am-6.30pm Mon-Fri, 9.30am-5.30pm Sat & Sun) This place works with workshops and self-help groups around the country. It's a bit like a handicrafts version of Ikea, with goods displayed the way they might look in a Western living room. There are some appealing items, including carpets, wall-hangings, ceramics, wooden bowls, baskets and clothing.

Undugu Craft Shop HANDICRAFTS
(Map p77; www.undugukenya.org; Woodvale Grove, Westlands; ⌚8.30am-5.30pm Mon-Fri, 9am-2pm Sat) This nonprofit organisation supports community projects in Nairobi and has top-quality crafts including wood and soapstone carvings, basketwork and fair-trade food products.

Maasai Market MARKET
Central Nairobi (Map p60; off Slip Rd; ⌚Tue); Gigiri (Village Market, Limuru Rd; ⌚Fri); City Centre (Map p60; opposite Reinsurance Plaza, Taita Rd; ⌚Sat); Yaya Centre (off Map p56; Argwings Kodhek; ⌚Sun) These busy curio markets are held every Tuesday on the waste ground near Slip Rd in town, Friday in the rooftop car park at the Village Market shopping complex, Saturday in the city centre and Sunday next to the Yaya Centre. The markets, where Maasai handicrafts dominate although you'll find handicrafts from other ethnic groups as well, are open from early morning to late afternoon. Check with your accommodation as locations and schedules do change.

City Market MARKET
(Map p60; Muindi Mbingu St; ⌚9am-5pm Mon-Fri, 9am-noon Sat) The city's souvenir business is concentrated in this covered market, which has dozens of stalls selling wood carvings, drums, spears, shields, soapstone, Maasai jewellery and clothing. It's a hectic place and you'll have to bargain hard (and we mean *hard*), but there's plenty of good stuff on offer. It's an interesting place to wander around in its own right, though you generally need to be shopping to make the constant hassle worth the bother.

Westland Curio Market MARKET
(Map p77; Parklands Rd, Westlands) This complex of stalls, located at a road junction, has the usual tourist kitsch as well some genuine tribal objects, such as Turkana wrist-knives and wooden headrests. Like at the City Market, you're going to need to bargain hard here, though the sales pressure is a bit softer. It's near the Sarit Centre in Westlands.

Village Market SHOPPING CENTRE
(www.villagemarket-kenya.com; Limuru Rd, Gigiri) This beautifully conceived shopping centre has a selection of entertainment activities to help you while away an afternoon, including a cinema, bowling alley, pool hall, water slides, minigolf and a children's playground complete with toy-car rides and a minitrain circuit. You can get here with matatu 106 (KSh40) from near the train station.

Information

Camping Equipment

Atul's (Map p60; ☎2225935; Biashara St; ⊙9am-1pm & 2-5pm Mon-Fri, 9am-4pm Sat) Hires out everything from sleeping bags to folding toilet seats – see p36.

Kenya Canvas Ltd (Map p60; ☎2223045; www.kenyacanvas.com; Muindi Mbingu St)

X-treme Outdoors (off Map p56; ☎2722224; www.xtremeoutdoors.co.ke; Yaya Centre, Hurlingham)

Dangers & Annoyances

First-time visitors to Nairobi are understandably daunted by the city's unenviable reputation. 'Nairobbery', as it has been nicknamed by jaded residents and expats, is often regarded as the most dangerous city in Africa, beating stiff competition from Johannesburg and Lagos. Read the local newspapers and you'll quickly discover that carjacking, robbery and violence are daily occurrences, and the social ills behind them are unlikely to disappear in the near future. However, shell-shocked first-timers should take comfort in the fact that the majority of problems happen in the shanty towns, far from the main tourist zones.

The most likely annoyance for travellers is petty theft, which is most likely to occur at budget hotels and campsites. As a general rule, you should take advantage of your hotel's safe and never leave your valuables out in the open. While you're walking around town, don't bring anything with you that you wouldn't want to lose. As an extra safety precaution, it's best to only carry money in your wallet, and hide your credit cards and bank cards elsewhere.

The downtown area bound by Kenyatta Ave, Moi Ave, Haile Selassie Ave and Uhuru Hwy is unthreatening and comparatively trouble-free as long as you use a bit of common sense. Walking around this area by day is rarely a problem. There are also plenty of *askaris* (security guards) about in case you need assistance. In fact, compared to Johannesburg and Lagos – where armed guards, razor-wired compounds and patrol vehicles are the norm rather than the exception – Nairobi's Central Business District (CBD) is quite relaxed and hassle-free. As long as you stay alert, walk with confidence, keep a hand on your wallet and avoid wearing anything too flashy, you should encounter nothing worse than a few persistent safari touts and the odd con artist.

Once the shops in the CBD have shut, the streets empty rapidly and the whole city centre takes on a deserted and slightly sinister air. After sunset, mugging is a risk anywhere on the streets, and you should always take a taxi, even if you're only going a few blocks. This will also keep you safe from the attentions of Nairobi's street prostitutes, who flood into town in force for a bit of moonlighting.

There are a few other places where you do need to employ a slightly stronger self-preservation instinct. Potential danger zones include the area around Latema and River Rds (east of Moi Ave), which is a hot spot for petty theft. This area is home to the city's bus terminals, so keep an eye on your bags and personal belongings at all times if passing through here. Uhuru Park is a very pleasant place during daylight hours, but it tends to accumulate all kinds of dodgy characters at night.

Nairobi's infamous reputation is largely the result of its horrific shanty towns, which lie on the outskirts of the city. These expansive areas, largely devoid of electricity, plumbing and fresh water, are tense places where opportunism can quickly lead to violent crime. If you want to visit these places to get a better sense of how Nairobi's less-fortunate inhabitants live, do so with a reliable local friend or as part of an organised tour (see p69).

In the event that you are mugged, never, ever resist – simply give up your valuables and, more often than not, your assailant will flee the scene rapidly. Remember that a petty thief and a violent aggressor are very different kinds of people, so don't give your assailant any reason to do something rash.

Finally, the majority of foreign visitors and resident expats in Nairobi never experience any kind of problem, so try not to be paralysed with fear. Again, it's important to understand the potential dangers and annoyances that are present, though you shouldn't let fear exile you to your hotel room. Exude confidence, practise street smarts, and chances are you'll actually end up really enjoying your time in Nairobi.

SCAMS Nairobi's handful of active confidence tricksters seem to have relied on the same old stories for years, and it's generally easy to spot the spiels once you've heard them a couple of times.

It is almost a certainty that at some point during your time in Nairobi you will be approached on the street by safari touts. Most of these persistent guys are hoping to drag you into an operator's office, where they can expect to receive a small commission. A small minority are hoping to

SCAMMERS

One classic Nairobi con trick that you'll likely be subjected to is the refugee story, commonly combined with the equally well-worn university scam. In this gambit, it turns out that your interlocutor has coincidentally just won a scholarship to a university in your country (the amount of research they do is quite astounding), and would just love to sit down and have a chat with you about life there.

Then at some point you'll get the confidential lowering of the voice as the story kicks in with 'You know, I am not from here...', leading into an epic tale of woe that involves them having walked barefoot all the way from Juba or Darfur to flee the war. While once restricted to stories with a Sudanese focus, they could include stories from Zimbabwe, Somalia or just about any troubled African nation.

Of course, once you've shown due sympathy they'll come to the crux of the matter: they have to get to Mombasa or Dar es Salaam or elsewhere to confirm their scholarship and fly out for their studies, and all they need is a few thousand shilling – not that they could ask you, their new friend, for that much money, though anything you could spare to help them out would be greatly appreciated (you get the idea).

There are variations on the theme. One traveller wrote telling us how, after refusing to give anything, he was approached by two 'policemen' who promptly arrested the scammer and warned the traveller that he was in trouble for conspiring with an illegal immigrant. If this happens to you, ask for to see police ID and try to enlist the help of people around you.

distract you with their glossy brochures while they deftly lift your wallet.

This is not to say that safari touts are bad people – a good number of them really do want to help you make a booking. With that said, it's better to err on the side of caution and work directly with a reliable operator. For more information, see the Safaris chapter (p28).

Apart from the regular safari rip-offs, you should be careful of something known as the 'Nairobi bump'. The usual tactic is for a scammer to bump into you in the street, and then try to strike up a small conversation. If this happens, keep walking, as it's probably the most effective way of preventing your wallet or backpack from being stolen.

You should also be wary of anyone who says they work at your hostel/hotel/campsite, even if they actually know the names of the staff there. We have received countless letters from travellers who have been duped into handing over money on the street for seemingly valid reasons, such as buying groceries for the evening's dinner. If someone claiming to be from your accommodation asks for money, be sceptical and just walk away.

Given the continuing severity of the conflicts in countries close to Kenya, another local speciality is the refugee scam.

In short, always exercise caution while talking to anyone on the streets of Nairobi. While there are genuinely good people out there, the reality is that foreign tourists are an easy target for scamming.

Emergency

Aga Khan Hospital (off Map p56; ☎3662020; Third Parklands Ave) A reliable hospital with 24-hour emergency services.

Emergency services (☎999) The national emergency number to call for fire, police and ambulance assistance. A word of warning, though – don't rely on prompt arrival.

Police (Map p56, Map p60; ☎2240000) Phone for less-urgent police business.

St John's Ambulance (☎2210000)

Tourist helpline (☎604767; ⏲24hr)

Internet Access

There are hundreds of internet cafes in downtown Nairobi, most of them tucked away in anonymous office buildings in the town centre. Connection speed is decent assuming you're not streaming YouTube, though machine quality varies wildly. Rates range from KSh1 to KSh4 per minute. It can be difficult to find any cyber cafe open in the downtown area on Sunday.

AGX (Map p60; Barclays Plaza, Loita St; per min KSh1; ⏲8am-6pm Mon-Fri, to 3pm Sat) Best connections in town, with a choice of browsers.

EasySurf (Map p77; Sarit Centre, Westlands; per hr KSh180; ⏲8.30am-8pm Mon-Fri, 10am-7.30pm Sat, 10.30am-3.30pm Sun)

Perm Enterprises (Map p60; cnr Muindi Mbingu & Kaunda Sts; per hr KSh60; ⏲8am-6pm Mon-Fri, to 3pm Sat)

Lucille Cyber Café (Map p60; ground fl, Uganda House, Standard St; per hr KSh30; ⌚7am-8pm Mon-Fri, 9am-6pm Sat, 10am-4pm Sun)

Medical Services

Nairobi has plenty of health-care facilities that are used to dealing with travellers and expats, which is a good thing as you're going to want to avoid the Kenyatta National Hospital – although it's free, stretched resources mean you may come out with something worse than you had when you went in.

AAR Health Services (Map p56; ☎2715319; Williamson House, Fourth Ngong Ave) Probably the best of a number of private ambulance and emergency air-evacuation companies. It also runs a private clinic in Westlands.

Acacia Medical Centre (Map p60; ☎2212200; ICEA Bldg, Kenyatta Ave; ⌚7am-7pm Mon-Fri, 7am-5pm Sat, 8am-5pm Sun)

KAM Pharmacy (Map p60; ☎2251700; IPS Bldg, Kimathi St; ⌚8.30am-6pm Mon-Fri, 8.30am-2pm Sat) A one-stop shop for medical treatment, with a pharmacy, doctor's surgery and laboratory.

Nairobi Hospital (Map p56; ☎2846000; www.nairobihospital.org; off Argwings Kodhek Rd; ⌚24hr)

Money

Jomo Kenyatta International Airport has several exchange counters in the baggage reclaim area and a **Barclays Bank** (⌚24hr) with an ATM outside in the arrivals hall.

There are Barclays branches with guarded ATMs on Mama Ngina St, Muindi Mbingu St and on the corner of Kenyatta and Moi Aves. There are also branches in the Sarit Centre and on Woodvale Grove in Westlands, and the Yaya Centre in Hurlingham.

The other big bank is Standard Chartered Bank, which has numerous downtown branches.

Foreign-exchange bureaus offer slightly better rates for cash than the banks. There are dozens of options in the town centre, so it's worth strolling around to see who is currently offering the best deal.

Goldfield Forex (Map p60; EcoBank Towers, Kaunda St; ⌚9am-5pm Mon-Thu, 9am-12.30pm & 2-5pm Fri, 9am-1pm Sat)

Link Forex (Map p60; ☎226212; ground fl, Uganda House, Standard St; ⌚9am-5pm Mon-Fri, 9am-1pm Sat)

Postbank (Map p60; 13 Kenyatta Ave) For Western Union money transfers.

Travellers Forex Bureau (Map p77; The Mall Shopping Centre, Westlands; ⌚8.30am-5pm Mon-Fri, 9am-1pm Sat)

Post

The vast **main post office** (Map p60; ☎2243434; Kenyatta Ave; ⌚8am-6pm Mon-Fri, 9am-noon Sat) is a well-organised edifice close to Uhuru Park. Around the back of the main building is the **EMS office** (⌚8am-8pm Mon-Fri, 9am-12.30pm Sat), for courier deliveries, and there's a Telkom Kenya office upstairs.

If you just want stamps, head to the post offices on Haile Selassie Ave or Tom Mboya St, or in the Sarit Centre and on Mpaka Rd in Westlands.

DHL (www.dhl.co.ke); Downtown (Map p60; ☎6925135; International House, Mama Ngina St); Westlands (Map p77; ☎ 0711017131; Sarit Centre) is a reliable private courier.

Telephone

Telkom Kenya (Map p60; ☎2232000; Haile Selassie Ave; ⌚8am-6pm Mon-Fri, 9am-noon Sat) has dozens of payphones and you can buy phonecards. Many stands downtown sell Telkom Kenya phonecards and top-up cards for prepaid mobiles. Alternatively, there are numerous private agencies in the centre of town offering international telephone services.

Toilets

It may come as a shock to regular travellers to Africa, but Nairobi now has a handful of staffed public toilets around the downtown area offering flush toilets with a basic level of cleanliness. Signs will indicate if you need to pay (about KSh5). Some central shopping centres, such as Kenya Cinema Plaza, have free public conveniences.

Tourist Information

Despite the many safari companies with signs saying 'Tourist Information', there is still no official tourist office in Nairobi. For events and other listings you'll have to check the local newspapers or glean what you can from a handful of magazines, which take a bit of effort to hunt down.

The vast noticeboards found at the Sarit Centre and Yaya Centre are good places to look for local information. All sorts of things are advertised here, including language courses, vehicles for sale and houses for rent.

Travel Agencies

For companies that concentrate exclusively on selling safaris, see p28.

Bunson Travel (Map p60; ☎2248371; www.bunsontravel.com; Pan Africa Insurance Bldg, Standard St) A good upmarket operator selling air tickets and upmarket safaris.

DEPARTURE TIMES

Most long-distance bus services (to Mombasa or Kisumu, for example), leave in the early morning or late evening. If you have a choice, choose the former as travelling after dark on Kenya's roads increases the chances of being involved in an accident.

Uniglobe Let's Go Travel (www.uniglobeletstravel.com) Westlands (off Map p77; 4447151; ABC Place, Waiyaki Way); Karen (Map p64; ☎3882505; Karen shopping centre, Langata Rd) Let's Go is good for flights, safaris and pretty much anything else you might need. It publishes an excellent price list of hotels, lodges, camps and *bandas* (thatched-roofed huts) in Kenya.

Getting There & Away

Air

Nairobi is the main arrival and departure point for international flights, although some touch down in Mombasa as well. For information about international services to and from Nairobi, and domestic and international airlines that serve the city, see p373.

Nairobi has two airports:

Jomo Kenyatta International Airport (NBO; Map p64; ☎6611000; www.kenyaairports.co.ke) Most international flights to and from Nairobi arrive at this airport, 15km southeast of the city.

Wilson Airport (WIL; Map p64; ☎3603260; www.kenyaairports.co.ke) Six kilometres south of the city centre on Langata Rd; mostly domestic flights.

Bus

In Nairobi, most long-distance bus company offices are in the River Rd area, clustered around Accra Rd and the surrounding streets, although some also have offices on Monrovia St for their international services. Prices vary from company to company, and there are many companies servicing these routes. You should always make your reservation up to 24 hours in advance and check (then double check) the departure point from where the bus leaves.

The **Machakos Country Bus Station** (Map p60; Landhies Rd) is a hectic, disorganised place with buses heading all over the country; it serves companies without their own departure point. However, if you can avoid coming here, do so as theft is rampant.

The table below provides a guide to what's possible with the better companies and with orientative prices. For international bus services from Nairobi, see p374.

Of the various bus companies, these are the ones we recommend:

Akamba (Map p60; ☎2365790; Lagos Rd) The biggest private bus company has an extensive network. It's generally safer and more reliable than most other companies. It also has a **booking office** (Map p60; Monrovia St) across from Jevanjee Gardens in the north of the city centre, from where its international buses go to Uganda and Tanzania.

Easy Coach (Map p60; ☎2210711; Haile Selassie Ave) Another reliable company serving western Kenyan destinations as well as running international buses to Uganda and Tanzania.

Modern Coast (Oxygen; Map p60; cnr Cross Lane & Accra Rd) Safer, more reliable and slightly more expensive buses to Mombasa, Malindi and Kisumu. They don't take phone bookings.

BUSES FROM NAIROBI

TO	FARE	DURATION	COMPANY
Eldoret	KSh1050-1100	6-8 hr	Akamba Easy Coach
Kakamega	KSh1150-1300	7-9 hr	Easy Coach
Kisumu	KSh900-1250	5½-7 hr	Akamba Easy Coach Modern Coast (Oxygen)
Malaba	KSh1250	6-7 hr	Easy Coach
Malindi	KSh1500	10-13 hr	Modern Coast (Oxygen)
Mombasa	KSh100-1200	8-10hr	Akamba Easy Coach Modern Coast (Oxygen)

MAJOR MATATU ROUTES

TO	FARE	DURATION	DEPARTURE POINT
Eldoret	KSh700	6 hr	Easy Coach Terminal
Kericho	KSh650	3 hr	Cross Rd
Kisumu	KSh600-900	4 hr	Cross Rd
Meru	KSh550	3 hr	Main Bus & Matatu Area
Naivasha	KSh200-300	1½ hr	cnr River Rd & Ronald Ngala St
Nakuru	KSh400	3 hr	cnr River Rd & Ronald Ngala St
Namanga	KSh300-400	2 hr	cnr River Rd & Ronald Ngala St
Nanyuki	KSh400	3 hr	Main Bus & Matatu Area
Narok	KSh400	3 hr	Cross Rd
Nyahururu	KSh400	3½ hr	cnr River Rd & Ronald Ngala St
Nyeri	KSh350	2½ hr	Latema Rd

Riverside Shuttle (Map p60; ☎0722220176; Monrovia St) Mostly international services to Arusha and Moshi (Tanzania).

Matatu

Most matatus leave from the chaotic Latema, Accra, River and Cross Rds and fares are similar to the buses. Most companies are pretty much the same, although there are some that aim for higher standards than others. **Mololine Prestige Shuttle** (Map p60), which operates along the Nairobi–Naivasha–Nakuru–Eldoret route, is one such company, with others set to follow their example on other routes. Departure points are shown on the Central Nairobi map.

Peugeot (Shared Taxi)

As with matatus, most of the companies offering Peugeot shared taxis have their offices around the Accra, River and Cross Rds area. Departures vary on demand, but you can usually find cars heading to Eldoret, Isiolo, Kabarnet, Kericho, Kisumu, Kitale, Meru, Malaba and Nakuru. Fares are about 20% higher than the same journeys by matatu. Most services depart in the morning.

Train

The train from Nairobi to Mombasa receives divided reviews – some acclaim it as a sociable and comfortable means of avoiding the highway while spotting some wildlife from the windows; for others it's shabby and unnecessarily time-consuming, not helped by inconsistent scheduling and lax timetable enforcement. For more information on train travel in Kenya, see p382.

Nairobi train station has a small **booking office** (Map p60; Station Rd; ⏲9am-noon & 2-6.30pm). You need to come in person to book tickets a few days in advance of your intended departure. On the day of departure, arrive early.

Getting Around

To/From Jomo Kenyatta International Airport

Kenya's main **international airport** (Map p64; ☎6611000) is 15km out of town, off the road to Mombasa. We recommend that you take a taxi (KSh1200 to KSh1500, but you'll need to bargain hard) to get to/from the airport, especially after dark. If you book at one of the 'information' desks at the airport, you'll still end up in a public taxi, but it isn't any more expensive.

A far cheaper way to get into town is by city bus 34 (KSh30), but a lot of travellers get robbed on the bus or when they get off. Always hold onto valuables and have small change ready for the fare. Buses run from 5.45am to 9.30pm weekdays, 6.20am to 9.30pm Saturdays and 7.15am to 9.30pm Sundays, though the last few evening services may not operate. Heading to the airport, the main departure point is along Moi Ave, right outside the Hotel Ambassadeur Nairobi. Thereafter, buses travel west along Kenyatta Ave.

To/From Wilson Airport

To get to **Wilson Airport** (Map p64; ☎3603260), the cheapest option is to take bus or matatu 15, 31, 34, 125 or 126 from Moi Ave (KSh25, 15 to 45 minutes depending on traffic). A taxi from the centre of town will cost you KSh750 to KSh1000, depending on the driver. In the other direction, you'll have to fight the driver down from KSh1250. The entrance to the airport is easy to miss – it's just before the large BP petrol station.

DOMESTIC BAGGAGE

Note that the check-in time for domestic flights is one to two hours before departure. Also be aware that the baggage allowance is only 15kg, as there isn't much space on the small turboprop aircraft.

Bus

The ordinary city buses are run by **KBS** (☎229707) but you shouldn't need to use them much. Forget about them if you're carrying luggage – you'll never get on, and if you do, you'll never get off! Most buses pass through downtown, but the main KBS terminus is on Uyoma St, east of the centre. There are other private companies plying routes within the city, such as City Hoppa and MM.

Car

See p377 for comprehensive information on car hire, road rules and conditions. If you are driving, beware of wheel-clampers: parking in the centre is by permit only (KSH140), available from the parking attendants who roam the streets in bright yellow jackets. If you park overnight in the street in front of your hotel, the guard will often keep an eye on your vehicle for a small consideration.

Matatu

Nairobi's horde of matatus follows the same routes as buses and displays the same route numbers. For Westlands, you can pick up 23 on Moi Ave or Latema Rd. Matatu 46 to the Yaya Centre stops in front of the main post office, and 125 and 126 to Langata leave from in front of the train station. As usual, you should keep an eye on your valuables while on all matatus.

There are plans to phase out matatus and replace them with larger (and fewer) minibuses to reduce traffic congestion. No new matatu licences were being issued at the time of research, but don't expect to notice any difference in the short-term.

Taxi

As people are compelled to use them due to Nairobi's endemic street crime, taxis here are overpriced and under-maintained, but you've little choice, particularly at night. Taxis don't cruise for passengers, but you can find them parked on every other street corner in the city centre – at night they're outside restaurants, bars and nightclubs.

Fares around town are negotiable but end up pretty standard. Any journey within the downtown area costs KSh400, from downtown to Milimani Rd costs KSh500, and for longer journeys such as Westlands or the Yaya Centre, fares range from KSh600 to KS700. From the city centre to Karen and Langata is around KSh1000 one way.

You can also find a few Indonesian-style tuk-tuks operating from Kenyatta Ave, though they're slowly being phased out.

AROUND NAIROBI

Ngong Hills

The green and fertile Ngong Hills were where many white settlers set up farms in the early colonial days. It's still something of an expat enclave, and here and there in the hills are perfect reproductions of English farmhouses with country gardens full of flowering trees – only the acacias remind you that you aren't rambling around the home counties of England.

The hills provide some excellent walking, but robbery has been a risk in the

TRAIN ROUTES

FROM	TO	1ST-CLASS FARE	2ND-CLASS FARE	DEPARTURE TIME	DURATION
Nairobi	Kisumu	KSh2550	KSh1400	6.30pm Mon, Wed & Fri	14½ hr
Nairobi	Mombasa	KSh3660	KSh2640	7pm Mon & Fri	15 hr
Nairobi	Naivasha	KSh1805	KSh1255	6.30pm Mon, Wed & Fri	3 hr
Nairobi	Nakaru	KSh1560	KSh1560	6.30pm Mon, Wed & Fri	6½ hr

WARNING – THINGS CHANGE

Transport information is extremely vulnerable to change. At the time of writing, fuel prices in Kenya were soaring and it is almost certain that prices for bus routes will increase.

You should get local opinions, quotes and advice before parting with your hard-earned cash – a good place to inquire is at your hotel. In addition, tickets for private buses should always be booked at least one day in advance, given the uncertainty of the transport grid.

past; ask locals for the latest information. If you're worried, take an organised tour or an escort from the Ngong police station or KWS office.

Grave of Denys Finch Hatton HISTORIC SITE

(0723758639) Close to Pt Lamwia, the summit of the range, is the grave of Denys Finch Hatton, the famous playboy and lover of Karen Blixen. The site is now almost completely overgrown and is difficult to find 4km up the hill from Kiserian; ask someone to show you the way from Kiserian, and expect to pay a KSh200 tip. A large obelisk marks his grave, inscribed with a line from 'The Rime of the Ancient Mariner', one of his favourite poems. The inscription reads 'He prayeth well, who loveth well/Both man and bird and beast'. There are legends about a lion and lioness standing guard at Finch Hatton's graveside, but these days they'd have trouble getting past the padlocked gate. Call ahead to make sure the custodian of the key is nearby.

Ngong Hills Racecourse STADIUM

(Map p64; 573923; Ngong Rd) Several Sundays a month, hundreds of Nairobi residents flee the noise and bustle of the city for the much more genteel surroundings of the Ngong Hills Racecourse, just east of Karen. In the past, races had to be cancelled because of rogue rhinos on the track, but the biggest danger these days is stray balls from the golf course in the middle! The public enclosure is free to enter; entry to the grandstand is KSh150, or you can pay KSh300 for a platinum pass, which gives you access to the cushioned members' seating and the restaurant overlooking the course. A race card costs KSh50 and you can bet as little as KSh25 with some bookies (minimum KSh100 with the course Tote). There are usually three races every month during the season, which runs from October to July. You can get here on the Metro Shuttle bus (KSh50, 30 minutes) and matatus 24 or 111 (KSh25), all from Haile Selassie Ave.

Sleeping

Whistling Thorns CAMPGROUND $

(Map p54; 3540720; www.whistlingthorns.com; Isinya/Kiserian Pipeline Rd, near Kiserian; camping KSh500, tent hire KSh650, s/tw KSh3000/3500, luxury tent KSh4200, cottage KSh5000; P@) This scenic ranch, located in the Maasai foothills of the Ngong, is a wonderfully rural spot to either launch or wind down your Kenyan holiday. It offers horse-riding safaris through the area, as well as walking trails and birdwatching on the open plains. You can also feast on the delicious home cooking (breakfast KSh450). To get here by public transport, take bus or matatu 111 or 126 from Moi Ave to Kiserian (KSh60, one hour) and change to an Isinya/Kajiado matatu. Ask to be dropped at Whistling Thorns, which is 200m from the roadside. Count on a two-hour trip from central Nairobi, less if you're coming in your own vehicle.

Maasai Ostrich Resort LODGE $$

(Map p54; 350014; www.mericagrouphotels.com; off A104; s/d from US$70/115; P) Combining an ostrich farm and a hotel is a fairly unusual idea, but, then again, why not? Certainly the simple but comfortable farmhouse accommodation and gardens provide a nice setting, and there's a range of activities (including ostrich riding!) to keep you busy in an otherwise unpromising area. To get out here, take the road towards Namanga (A104) and turn left at the sign. Southbound public transport can get you to the turn-off, but it's another 7km to the farm itself.

Kiambethu Tea Farm

Kenyan coffee may be world-famous, but the country is also the world's largest exporter of black tea. A visit to the **Kiambethu Tea Farm** (2012542; www.kiambethufarm.co.ke;

WORTH A TRIP

ACACIA CAMP

Just 36km from central Nairobi, off the busy Nairobi–Mombasa Rd, **Acacia Camp** (Map p54; ☎2529500; www.swaraplains.com; US$102/192;Ⓟ📶), located within the Swara Plains conservancy, is a wonderful escape from city life. The camp itself is extremely comfortable without being over the top, with well-appointed bungalows, good food and lovely gardens in the shade of acacias. The ranch itself is spread out over 81 sq km and is home to giraffes, zebras, wildebeest, warthogs, a host of gazelles and antelopes and more than 270 bird species (but not cheetahs as advertised on its website); the only predator is a resident hyena. For additional charges, there are game drives and a visit to some captive (and still rather wild) lions on the ranch's outer reaches.

guided tour & lunch KSh1700) is a wonderful chance to get an insight into Kenya's tea plantations, as well as being an immensely enjoyable excursion from the city. The guided tour takes you through the history of Kenyan tea-growing, visits the lovely colonial-era farmhouse and can also encompass a nearby stand of primary forest.

Advance bookings are essential and some Nairobi tour companies can make the necessary arrangements, including transport. If you're coming in your own vehicle, print out the detailed directions from its website. The farm is around 25km northwest of central Nairobi.

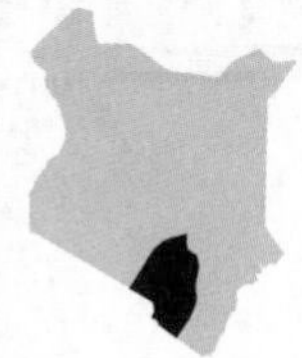

Southern Kenya

Includes »

Best of Nature

- Tsavo West National Park (p97)
- Tsavo East National Park (p102)
- Amboseli National Park (p92)
- Taita Hills Wildlife Sanctuary (p106)
- Chyulu Hills National Park (p96)

Best of Culture

- Lion Guardians (see the boxed text, p95)
- Kimana Community Wildlife Sanctuary (p96)
- Lumo Community Wildlife Sanctuary (p106)

Why Go?

Southern Kenya is one of the great wildlife-watching destinations in Africa. Here you find a triumvirate of epic Kenyan parks – Amboseli, Tsavo West and Tsavo East – that are home to the Big Five and so much more. Big cats roam in relative abundance and large-tusked elephants pass by close enough to touch, set against the backdrop of Africa's highest mountain, Mt Kilimanjaro, and a soulful back-story of wildlife surviving against the odds. Despite the parks' popularity, large tracts of wilderness dominate the two Tsavos in particular and it's possible to spend hours without seeing another safari vehicle. Perhaps best of all, the Maasai roam the areas just beyond park boundaries – the chances to get to know these fascinating people on equal terms, especially through community-run ranches and wildlife sanctuaries, are higher here than perhaps anywhere else in Kenya. In short, this is Kenya at its wildest and yet most accessible.

When to Go

Voi

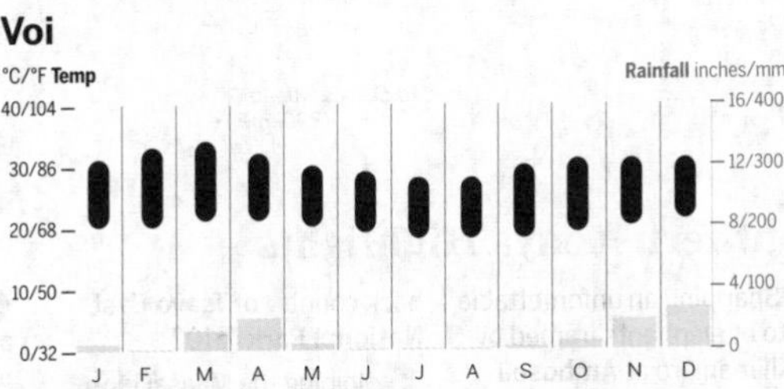

Jul–Oct Far from the Masai Mara, this is prime time for watching wildlife in southern Kenyan parks.

Nov–Feb Good for bird- and wildlife-watching; November rains are a minor inconvenience.

Mar–May Rains here can make roads impassable and wildlife strays beyond Amboseli.

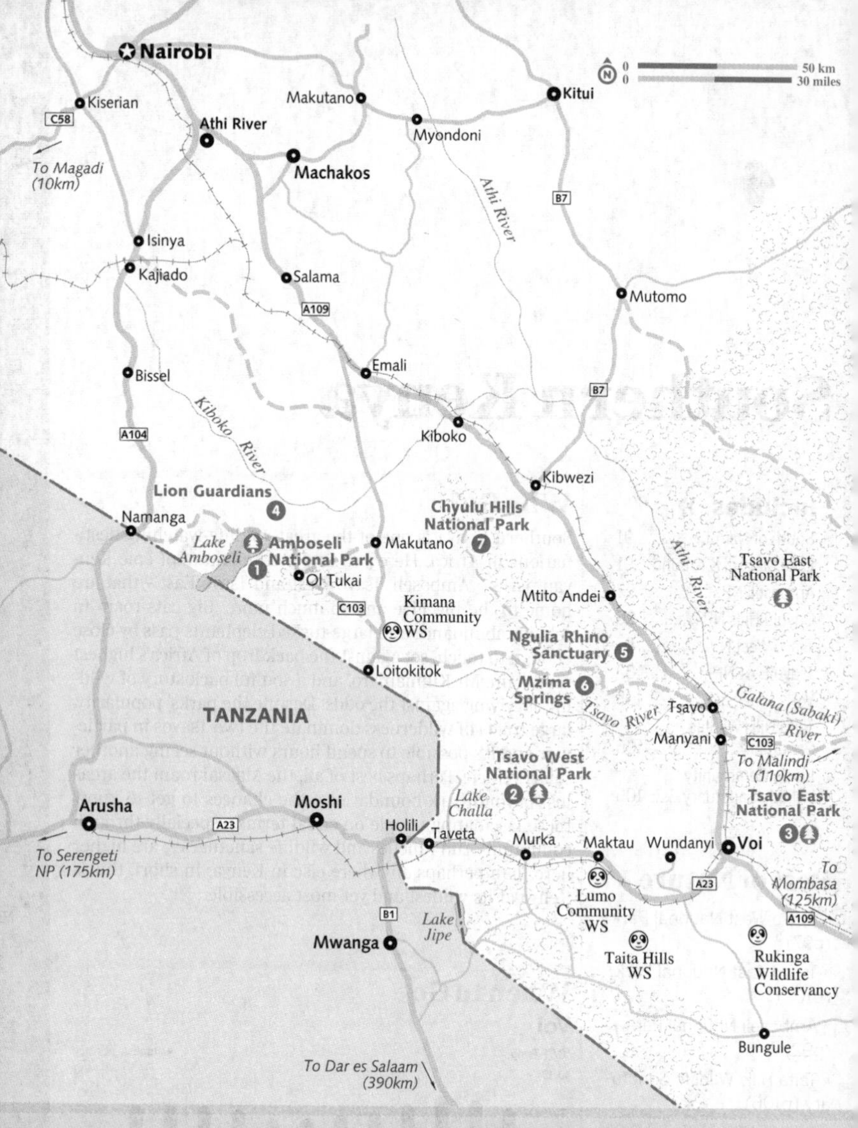

Southern Kenya Highlights

1. Snapping an unforgettable photo of elephants framed by Mt Kilimanjaro at **Amboseli National Park** (p92).
2. Roaming the wilderness of **Tsavo West National Park** (p97), scanning the tree branches for leopards.
3. Braving the country's lions and red elephants in the back country of **Tsavo East National Park** (p102).
4. Joining the Maasai **Lion Guardians** (p95) as they become best friends with lions.
5. Catching a rare glimpse of some of Kenya's last black rhinos at the **Ngulia Rhino Sanctuary** (p97) in Tsavo West National Park.
6. Spotting hippos, crocs and giant kingfishers in the pristine oasis of **Mzima Springs** (p97) at Tsavo West National Park.
7. Spelunking in **Leviathan** (p96), the world's second-longest lava tube in the Chyulu Hills National Park.

SOUTH OF NAIROBI

Lake Magadi & Around

The little-travelled road southwest of Nairobi runs down into the Rift Valley and on to Lake Magadi, the most southerly of Kenya's Rift Valley soda lakes, close to the Tanzanian border. En route, the road passes an intriguing archaeological site and you've a chance of seeing giraffes, zebras and ostriches by the roadside. It all adds up to a rewarding day trip from Nairobi, if you have your own vehicle.

The most mineral-rich of the soda lakes, **Lake Magadi** (off Map p54) is almost entirely covered by a thick encrustation of soda that supports small colonies of flamingos and gives the landscape a bizarre lunar appearance. The thick soda crust is formed when the mineral-rich water, pumped up from hot springs deep underground, evaporates rapidly in the 38°C temperature to leave a mineral layer. A soda-extraction factory 'harvests' this layer and extracts sodium chloride (common salt) and sodium carbonate (soda), which are then put straight onto trains to Mombasa. Not surprisingly, Magadi is purely a company town, run by the unimaginatively named Magadi Soda Co, for factory staff and their families.

To travel beyond the southern end of town, a checkpoint charges KSh300. It's worth it, for the causeway leads across the most visually dramatic part of this strange landscape to a **viewpoint** on the western shore; you'll need a 4WD. Otherwise you can head to the **hot springs** further south. The springs aren't particularly dramatic, but you can take a dip in the deeper pools and there are large numbers of fish that have adapted to the hot water. You may run into local Maasai, who will offer to show you the way and 'demonstrate' everything for you for a small fee.

On your way back to Nairobi, take the turn-off for the famous **Olorgasailie Prehistoric Site** (off Map p54; adult/child KSh500/250; ⏲daylight hours). Several important archaeological finds were made by the Leakeys in the 1940s at this site, 40km north of Magadi, including hundreds of hand axes and stone tools thought to have been made by *Homo erectus* about half a million years ago. Fossils have also been discovered and some are still there, protected from the elements by shade roofs. Supposedly free guided tours are compulsory, although a tip is expected.

Sleeping

Olorgasailie campsite CAMPSITE $
(Hwy C58; camping KSh250, new/old bandas KSh800/500) This campsite, at the gate of the archaeological site, is your only option out here. It's fairly basic (you'll need to bring your own food, bedding and drinking water), but you'll feel like you're properly in the bush and you're likely to have the place to yourself. The newer *bandas* aren't bad at all.

Getting There & Away

Magadi is 105km southwest of Nairobi. The C58 road from Nairobi sees little traffic, but potholes are a constant problem. There's usually one matatu a day to Nairobi (KSh250), leaving in the morning and returning to Magadi in the evening.

The Road to Arusha

Heading south from Nairobi, the A104 runs straight to the Tanzanian border en route to Arusha (Tanzania). The border town of

WILDLIFE OF SOUTHERN KENYA

Few **elephants** in Africa have been as closely studied as those of Amboseli, the scene of decades of elephant research led by Cynthia Moss. As a consequence, there's nowhere else in Africa where you can get closer to these magnificent creatures. The elephants of Tsavo, caked in ochre-red mud, and the **black rhinos** of Tsavo West, have had an entirely different relationship with human beings, having been massacred in their thousands in the 1970s and 1980s by poachers. Their continued survival only adds to the excitement of seeing them in the wild. And then of course there are the world-famous **lions** of Tsavo, descendants perhaps of the world's most notorious man-eaters. **Leopards** are also present in all three parks, while **cheetahs** frequent both Tsavo East and Amboseli, although they're more elusive here than in the Masai Mara. **Hippos**, **crocodiles**, **zebras**, **giraffes**, **antelope** of every imaginable kind and abundant **birdlife** all help to make this a splendid place to go looking for wildlife.

Namanga is a good place to stock up on fuel and supplies.

BISSEL

The first point of interest along this route is Bissel, a vibrant Maasai township with a busy market where there's a petrol station, a handful of *dukas* (small shops or kiosks) and plenty of small bars and *hotelis* (eateries). Not many tourists stop along this route.

Matatus run from Bissel to Nairobi (KSh300, one hour) and Namanga (KSh150, one hour).

NAMANGA

Continuing south, the border town of Namanga has a surprisingly relaxed atmosphere away from the frontier itself. The border crossing is open 24 hours and the two posts are almost next to each other, so you can walk across. Moneychangers do a brisk trade on the Kenyan side of the border, though if you use them don't believe anyone who says you can't take Kenyan shillings into Tanzania or vice versa!

Namanga River Hotel HOTEL $
(☎0722440089; riverhotelnamanga.com; camping KSh500, s/d from KSh3600/4700; P) For one last night in Kenya or to otherwise break up your travels, consider this shady campsite that offers an attractive clutch of cabins of varying levels of comfort, and a decent bar-restaurant that's often frequented by overland truck travellers.

Getting There & Away

Buses between Nairobi and Arusha pass through daily (KSh300 to KSh600, two hours). Matatus and Peugeots (shared taxis) also run here from the junction of River Rd and Ronald Ngala St in Nairobi (KSh300 to KSh400).

Akamba has an office at the Kobil station, where you can book seats on the morning bus to Arusha. Several other companies cover this route, as do matatus and Peugeots from the Tanzanian side of the border. For more details on getting to/from Tanzania see p374.

THE SOUTHEAST

Kenya's southeastern corner, set back from the coast, includes three of the country's most prestigious parks – Amboseli, Tsavo West and Tsavo East. Together, the latter two account for almost 4% of Kenya's surface area. Less well-known but nonetheless rewarding are the private, often community-run wildlife sanctuaries that lie beyond park borders, particularly around the picturesque Taita Hills.

Amboseli National Park

Amboseli (adult/child per day US$75/40) belongs in the elite of Kenya's national parks, and it's easy to see why. Its signature attraction is the sight of hundreds of big-tusked elephants set against the backdrop of Africa's best views of Mt Kilimanjaro (5895m). Africa's highest peak broods over the southern boundary of the park, and while cloud cover can render the mountain's massive bulk invisible for much of the day, you'll be rewarded with stunning vistas when the weather clears, usually at dawn and/or dusk. Apart from guaranteed elephant sightings, you'll also see

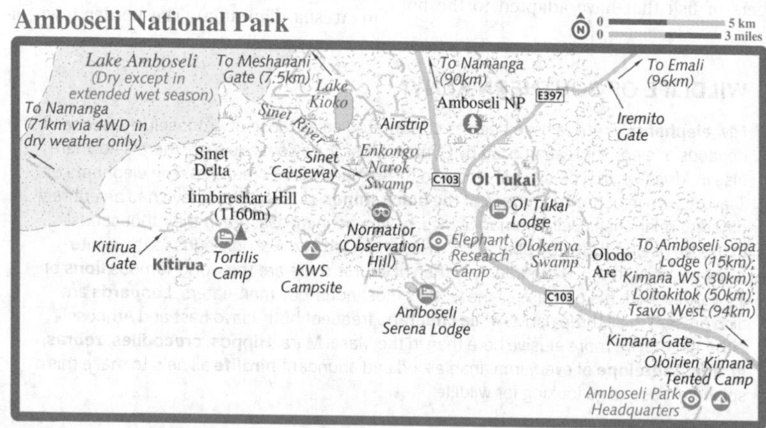

wildebeest and zebras, and you've a reasonable chance of spotting lions and hyenas. The park is also home to over 370 bird species. And with chances to delve a little deeper into the world of wildlife conservation, it all adds up to one of Kenya's premier wildlife experiences.

Sights & Activities

The Swamps LAKE

Amboseli's permanent swamps of **Enkongo Narok** and **Olokenya** create a marshy belt across the middle of the park and this is where you'll encounter the most wildlife. Elephants love to wallow around in the muddy waters and you've also a good chance of seeing hippos around the edge, especially in Enkongo Narok. Birdlife also proliferates here. For *really* close-up elephant encounters, **Sinet Causeway**, which crosses Enkongo Narok near Observation Hill, is often good. The surrounding grasslands are home to grazing antelope, zebras and wildebeest, with spotted hyenas and lions sometimes lurking nearby. Birdlife is especially rich in these swamps when the migrants arrive in November and stay until March.

Normatior (Observation Hill) LOOKOUT

Observation Hill provides an ideal lookout from which to orientate yourself to the plains, swamps and roads below. The views from here are also pretty special, whether south to Kilimanjaro or east across the swamps. Wildlife is generally a fair way off, but the views here put them in their context.

Sinet Delta PARK

From Observation Hill, the northern route runs across the Sinet Delta, which is an excellent place for birdwatching. Commonly sighted species include jacanas, herons, egrets, ibises, geese, plovers, storks, ducks, fish eagles and flamingos. The vegetation is thicker the further south you go, providing fodder for giraffes and also framing some of the park's best Kilimanjaro views.

Lake Amboseli LAKE

Away to the northwest from the delta, this 'lake' occupies a large swathe of the park, but it's usually bone dry except after extended rains. At other times it's worth a journey out here if you've time to spare, not least because few vehicles make it out this way.

Kimana Gate WILDLIFE RESERVE

If you're taking the road that runs east across the park to the Kimana Gate, watch for Masai giraffes in the acacia woodlands; this is the best place inside the park for giraffe-spotting. Here you may also find gerenuks, an unusual breed of gazelle that 'browse' by standing on their hind legs and stretching their necks. There are numerous lodges and campsites just outside the gate, while the road (in poor condition) continues on to Tsavo West National Park.

Elephant Research Camp WILDLIFE RESERVE

(☎0710149131, 0733782851; www.elephanttrust.org; group of 10 or less US$500, group of more than 10 per person US$50; ⊙by prior appointment 3pm Mon-Sat) The elephants of Amboseli are among the most studied in the world, thanks largely to the work of Cynthia Moss, whose books include *The Amboseli Elephants* and *Elephant Memories;* she was also behind the famous documentary DVD *Echo of the Elephants*. The research camp remains in operation in the heart of the park, under the guidance of the **Amboseli Trust for Elephants** (www.elephanttrust.org). Although the camp is not open for casual visits it is possible, with prior arrangement, to arrange a one-hour lecture at the camp, during which the researchers explain their work and other related issues of elephant conservation, with time for questions at the end. The visit

AMBOSELI NATIONAL PARK

Why Go To see big-tusked elephants, the best Mt Kilimanjaro views in Africa, lions, wildebeest and zebras, rich birdlife and elephant and lion conservation programs.

When to Go Year round. The dry season (May to October and January to March) is best for spotting wildlife, while November to March is the best time to see migratory birds. Much of the wildlife moves beyond the park during and immediately after the rains.

Practicalities Drive in from Nairobi or Mombasa; flying is also possible. There are three main gates; approaches to the park from the west (Kitirua and Meshanani gates) are in poor conditions, Iremito (northeast) or Kimana (southeast) gates are in better conditions. The park is accessible in 2WD. Iremito is the only gate where you can top up your safari card.

WHITHER AMBOSELI?

Although it's a prominent part of the country's tourist portfolio, Amboseli has been at the centre of some controversy since President Kibaki's 2005 attempt to downgrade it from a national park to a national reserve, which would have transferred its administration from the Kenya Wildlife Service (KWS) to local authorities. Supporters claim that the move would rightfully return control of the land to the local community, although conservation bodies argue that it could be the beginning of the end for Amboseli. More than that, they fear that degazetting national parks could undermine Kenya's whole wildlife preservation system. Kenya's High Court ruled the move illegal in 2011, but that hasn't put an end to questions over the park's future.

In October 2011, Tourism Minister Najib Balala threatened to close Amboseli for three years to allow the park to recover from drought (much of the park is a dustbowl in the dry season and thousands of animals died during the 2009 drought), over-exploitation by tourism and a massive elephant population; Amboseli's elephant population is now believed to be over 1200, almost double the figures of a decade ago and such numbers are believed to be unsustainable. The vegetation here used to be much denser, but rising salinity, damage by elephants and irresponsible behaviour with safari vehicles has caused terrible erosion.

A moratorium on new tourist developments is a more likely outcome than closing the park, but clouds continue to gather around Amboseli's future, and some are starting to wonder whether its is only a matter of several years before the lack of food makes the animals move on.

doesn't come cheap. But this is one of the mother lodes for elephant research in Africa and a visit here is a rare opportunity to learn more about these soulful creatures. Bookings can be made via the above telephone numbers and email address.

Sleeping & Eating

Accommodation in Amboseli is either top end or budget simplicity, with not much else in between. All prices for the lodges (but not the campsites) given here are for full board.

TOP CHOICE Ol Tukai Lodge LODGE $$$
(020-4445514; www.oltukailodge.com; s/d US $308/385; P @) Lying at the heart of Amboseli on the edge of a dense acacia forest, Ol Tukai is a splendidly refined lodge with soaring *makuti* (thatched roofs of palm leaves) and tranquil gardens defined by towering trees. Accommodation is in wooden chalets, which are brought to life with vibrant zebra prints, while the split-level bar has a sweeping view of Kili and a pervading atmosphere of peace and luxury.

Tortilis Camp TENTED CAMP $$$
(045-622195; www.tortilis.com; s/d US$470/780, family tent US$1950; P) This wonderfully conceived site is one of the most exclusive ecolodges in Kenya, commanding a superb elevated spot with perfect Kilimanjaro vistas. The luxurious canvas tents have recently been given a facelift; the family rooms have the biggest wow factor we found in southern Kenya. The lavish meals, which are based on North Italian traditional recipes from the owner's family cookbook, feature herbs and vegetables from the huge on-site organic garden. Sustainability is a key feature of this site, with solar power used wherever possible.

Amboseli Serena Lodge LODGE $$$
(020-2842000; www.serenahotels.com; US$270/370; P) A classically elegant property in Amboseli, the Serena is comprised of fiery-red adobe cottages, some of which overlook the wildlife-rich Enkongo Narok swamp and are fringed by lush tropical gardens of blooming flowers and manicured shrubs. There are no Kilimanjaro views from the lodge. Service is impeccable.

Oloirien Kimana Tented Camp CAMPGROUND $
(0720951500; per person tent/banda KSh1500/2000; P) Just outside the park boundaries, 2.8km south of the Kimana gate, this camp is bare and dusty but friendly, with basic tents and simple *bandas* with cold showers. There's a kitchen for DIY cooking.

Amboseli Sopa Lodge LODGE $$$
(☎020-3750460; www.sopalodges.com/amboseli/home.html; s/d US$223/314; P≋@) Located 15km outside the park boundaries on the road to Tsavo West National Park, the Sopa Lodge offers clay huts that are decked out in safari spreads and a healthy smattering of Kenyan curios. You're a fair way from the park, and service is not quite up there with other top-end places, but nor are the prices.

KWS campsite CAMPGROUND $
(camping US$25; P) Just inside the southern boundary of the park, the KWS campsite has toilets, an unreliable water supply (bring your own) and a small bar selling warm beer and soft drinks. It's fenced off from the wildlife, so you can walk around safely at night, though *don't* keep food in your tent, as baboons visit during the day looking for an uninvited feed.

Information

Kenya Wildlife Service (☎045-622251; www.kws.org/parks/parks_reserves/AMNP.html; adult/child US$75/40, safari card required)

Getting There & Away

Air

Airkenya (www.airkenya.com; one-way from $101) Daily flights between Nairobi's Wilson Airport and Amboseli. You'll need to arrange with one of the lodges or a safari company for a vehicle to meet you at the airstrip.

Car & 4WD

Whichever route you take, allow around four hours from Nairobi.

VIA NAMANGA 180km sealed road, whereafter the 75km dirt road to the Meshanani Gate is pretty rough but passable.

VIA EMALI 240km sealed road, then 18km graded but not sealed road to Irimeto Gate.

LION GUARDIANS

Because lions are the easiest of the big cats to observe, few people realise that lions face an extremely uncertain future. A century ago, more than 200,000 lions roamed Africa. Now, fewer than 30,000 are thought to remain and lions have disappeared from 80% of their historical range, according to **Panthera** (www.panthera.org), the leading cat conservation NGO based in New York. In Kenya, lion numbers have reached critical levels: less than 2000 adult breeding lions are thought to remain in the country. An estimated 60 of these inhabit the Amboseli ecosystem, which refers to the national park and surrounding Amboseli basin. Around half of these lions (more in the rainy season) live outside the park boundaries, sharing the land with the Maasai and their herds of livestock.

In Maasai culture, young male warriors (the *morran*) have traditionally killed lions and other wild animals as part of proving their bravery and as an initiation rite into manhood. But one organisation has come up with an innovative way of honouring Maasai tradition while protecting lions in the process. The **Lion Guardians** (www.lionguardians.org or www.wildlifeguardians.com) has taken many of these young, traditional warriors and turned them into Lion Guardians, whose task is to protect the Maasai and the lions from each other. Each Lion Guardian, most of whom have killed lions before, patrols a territory, keeping track of the lions through radio transmitters and more traditional means, and warning herders of lion locations and helping them to find lost livestock and even lost children. In areas where the Lion Guardians operate, lion-killings (and livestock lost to lions) has fallen dramatically.

Visiting the Lion Guardians

Although the idea was still on the drawing board at the time of writing, there are plans to allow **guided visits** of the Lion Guardians program, which would include time spent talking with Lion Guardians and possibly even patrolling with them in search of lions. Check the website for a list of participating lodges through which the visits may be booked. The cost of visits is still being worked out, but it is likely to cost around US$250 to US$500 per person, depending on the activity – expensive perhaps, but this is a fabulous opportunity to learn more about the Maasai and lions at the cutting edge of wildlife conservation.

WORTH A TRIP

KIMANA COMMUNITY WILDLIFE SANCTUARY

While it's not as grand in scope as Southern Kenya's signature national parks, this 40-hectare **sanctuary** (admission US$25) protects an impressive concentration of plains wildlife, although you'd be lucky to see any predators. More importantly, any money spent here directly supports the local community. While the foundations of Kimana were established in 1996 by USAID and KWS, the sanctuary has since been owned and managed by local Maasai. Today, Kimana serves as an encouraging template for similar initiatives throughout the continent.

Although a night here is an extremely expensive proposition, **Campi ya Kanzi** (☎045-622516; www.campiyakanzi.com; s/d from US$700/1180; P) is a worthwhile Maasai-run initiative that directly supports education, health care and environmental conservation in local communities. Accommodation is in luxury tents scattered around an enormous ranch that is centred on a nostalgically decorated stone lodge.

Kimana is located about 30km east of Amboseli, just off the road heading to Tsavo West National Park. The only access to this area is the poorly maintained dirt track leading west from Emali (on the Nairobi–Mombasa road) to Loitokitok on the Tanzanian border, or the bumpy road between Amboseli and Tsavo West.

Chyulu Hills National Park

One of Kenya's least-visited national parks, the Chyulu Hills are an oasis of green rising above the arid plains of southern Kenya. The park, just northwest of Tsavo West National Park, is dominated by extinct volcanoes that rank among the world's youngest range of mountains – they were formed perhaps no more than 500 years ago. There are fine views of Mt Kilimanjaro and the Amboseli plains of Maasailand to the east.

At the same time, you're likely to see more herders with their cattle than wildlife, and poaching remains a problem here. Not surprisingly, wildlife populations – elands, klipspringers, giraffes, zebras, baboons, Sykes monkeys and wildebeest, plus a small number of elephants, lions, leopards and buffaloes – are small and generally shy, but you are likely to have them to yourself.

Sights & Activities

Some 15km from the park entrance and well signposted, the aptly named **Leviathan**, the second-longest lava tube in the world at 12km, was formed by hot lava flowing beneath a cooled crust. You'll need full caving equipment to explore it, and perhaps a bit of prior experience spelunking in claustrophobic conditions. Caving and trekking trips in the hills are possible with **Savage Wilderness Safaris Ltd** (Map p77; ☎020-7121590; www.whitewaterkenya.com). Otherwise, you're only allowed to enter the cave in the company of a KWS ranger and with prior permission from the warden.

The track into the hills from the headquarters is tough going, but should be passable in a 2WD if it hasn't rained in recent days. Ask at the park headquarters for the latest situation.

Sleeping

There are no lodges within the park's boundaries.

KWS Campsite CAMPGROUND $
(camping US$15; P) If you're completely self-sufficient, you can spend the night at this basic but functional campsite near the park headquarters.

Ol Donyo Wuas LODGE $$$
(Map p98; ☎020-600457; www.greatplainsconservation.com; s/d from US$550/950; P) If money is no object, Ol Donyo Wuas is a well-established ecolodge constructed entirely of local materials and employs advanced water recycling and solar-power systems. While guests are treated to paramount luxury, the real highlights of this property are the wildlife drives and horse-riding excursions into the national park.

Information

The park headquarters is signposted just outside Kibwezi, about 41km northwest of Mtito Andei. The park headquarters is 1.3km inside the northwest gate, 9km off the Nairobi–Mombasa road.

Kenya Wildlife Service (☎020-2153433; www.kws.org/parks/parks_reserves/CHNP.html; adult/child US$20/10, safari card not valid)

Tsavo West National Park

Welcome to the wilderness. **Tsavo West** (adult/child per day US$60/30) is one of Kenya's larger national parks (9065 sq km), covering a huge variety of landscapes from swamps, natural springs and rocky peaks to extinct volcanic cones, rolling plains and sharp outcrops dusted with greenery.

This is a park with a whiff of legend about it, first for its famous man-eating lions in the late 19th century and then for its devastating levels of poaching in the 1980s. Despite the latter, there's still plenty of wildlife here, although you'll have to work harder and be much more patient than in Amboseli or the Masai Mara to see them all; the foliage is generally denser and higher here. Put all of these things together, along with its dramatic scenery, fine lodges and sense of space and this is one of Kenya's most rewarding parks. If possible, come here with some time to spare to make the most of it.

The northern half of Tsavo West is the most developed, with a number of excellent lodges, as well as several places where you can get out of your vehicle and walk. The landscape is also striking and is largely comprised of volcanic hills and sweeping expanses of savannah. The southern part of the park, on the far side of the dirt road between Voi and Taveta on the Tanzanian border, is rarely visited.

TSAVO WEST NATIONAL PARK

Why Go For the dramatic scenery, wilderness and a good mix of predators (lion, leopard, cheetah and hyena), prey (lesser kudu, gazelle, impala) and other herbivores (elephant, rhino, zebra, oryx and giraffe).

When to Go Year round. The dry season (May to October and January to March) is best for spotting wildlife. November to March is the best time to see migratory birds.

Practicalities Drive in from Kibwezi along the Nairobi–Mombasa Rd. There is a campsite close to the park entrance and lodges throughout the park. The park works on the safaricard system (you can only add credit at Mtito Andei Gate); gates open from sunrise to sunset.

Sights & Activities

TOP CHOICE Ngulia Rhino Sanctuary WILDLIFE RESERVE

(⏲4-6pm) At the base of Ngulia Hills and part of the Rhino Ark program, this recently expanded 90-sq-km area is surrounded by a 1m-high electric fence, and provides a measure of security for the park's last 50-odd highly endangered black rhinos. In the 1960s, Tsavo had Africa's largest population of black rhinos with between 6000 and 9000. There are driving tracks and waterholes within the enclosed area, but the rhinos are mainly nocturnal and the chances of seeing one are slim. If you don't see one, take consolation in the fact that these archaic creatures are breeding successfully and around 15 have been released elsewhere in Tsavo West National Park. The sanctuary is close to Ngulia Safari Lodge but a long drive from anywhere else.

TOP CHOICE Rhino Valley PARK

This is one of our favourite areas for wildlife watching, with plenty of antelope species keeping a careful eye out for the resident lions, leopards and cheetahs. You'll also see elephants, giraffes and, if you're lucky, black rhinos. Birdlife is also particularly diverse here. The signposted 'Rhino Valley Circuit' is a good place to start, while anywhere along the Mukui River's ponds and puddles is a place to watch and wait.

Ngulia Hills MOUNTAIN

Rising more than 600m above the valley floor and to a height over 1800m above sea level, this jagged ridgeline ranks among the prettiest of all Tsavo landforms, providing a backdrop to Rhino Valley. The hills can be climbed with permission from the warden (see p100), while the peaks are also a recognised flyway for migrating birds heading south from late September through to November.

TOP CHOICE Mzima Springs SPRING

Mzima Springs is an oasis of green in the west of the park and produces an incredible 250 million litres of fresh water a day. The springs, whose source rises in the Chyulu

Tsavo East & West National Parks

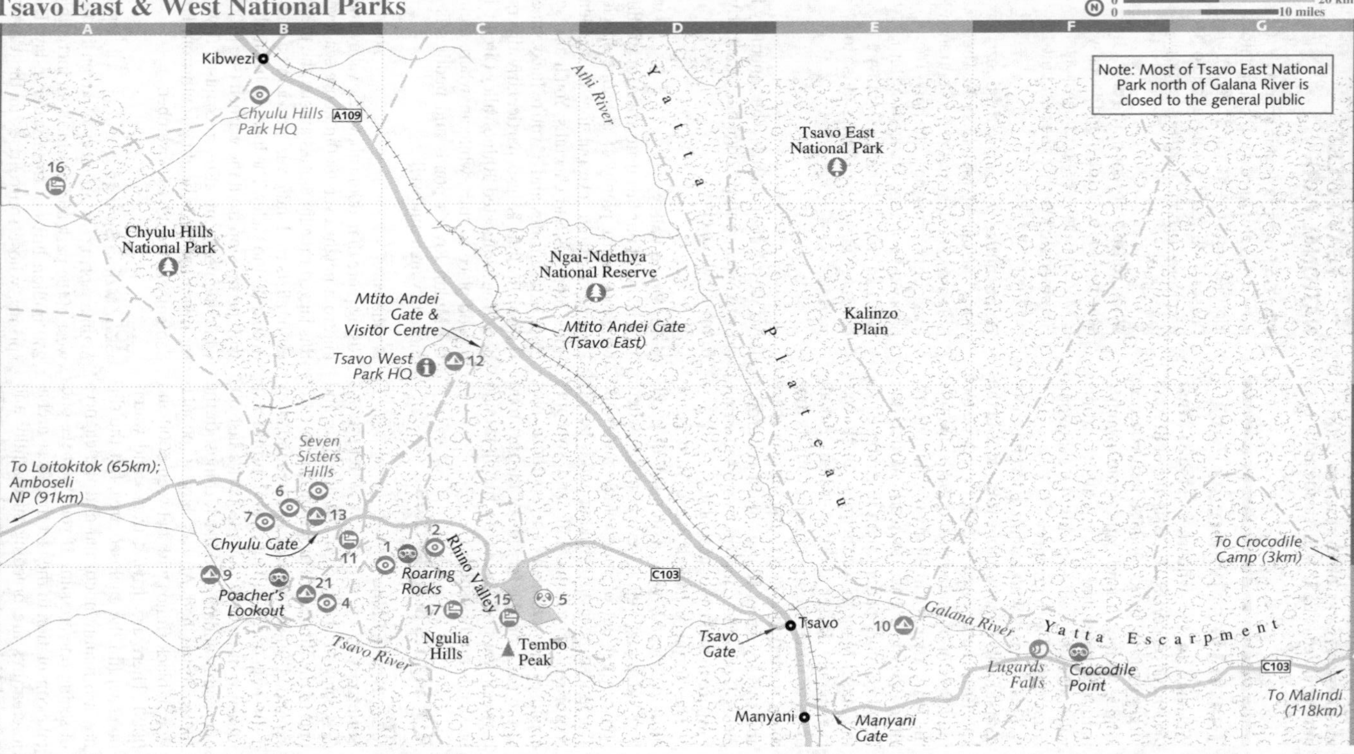

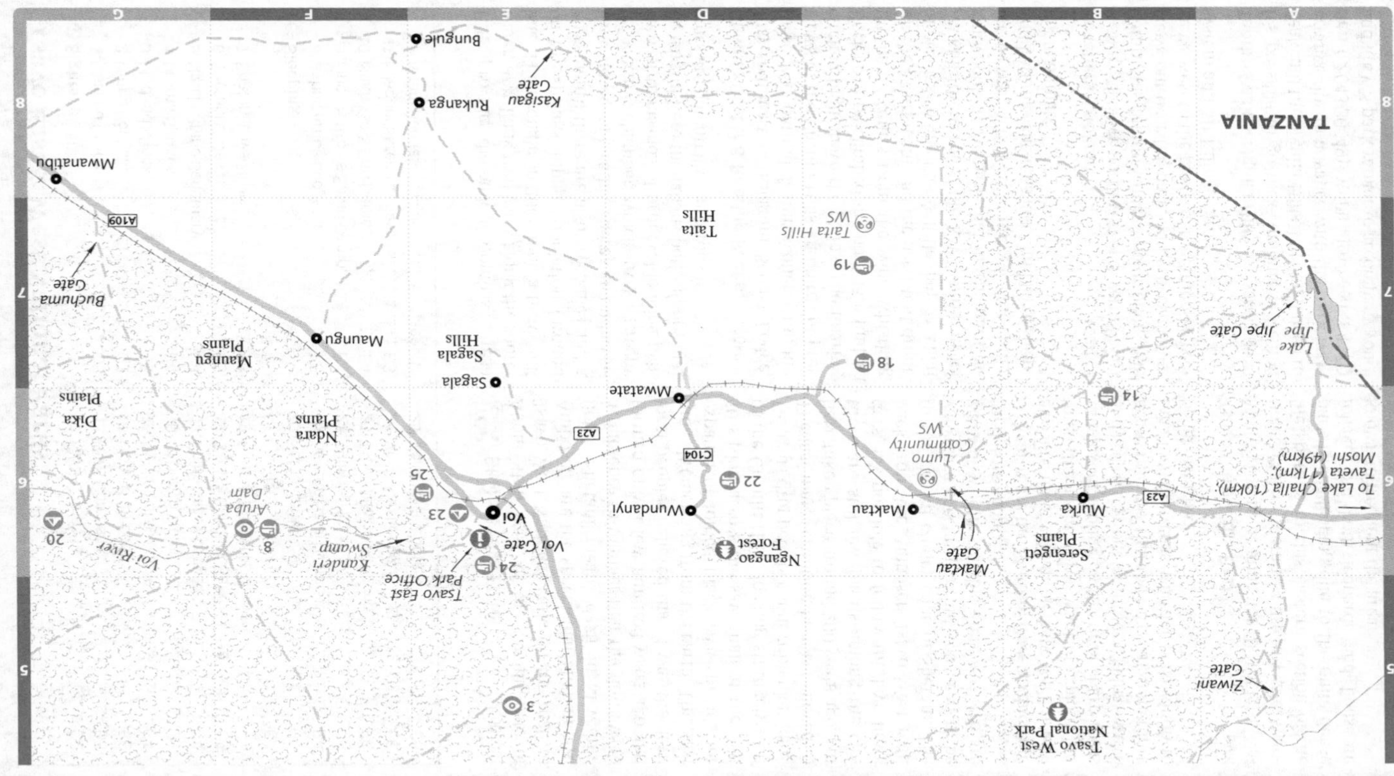
Tsavo West National Park
Ziwani Gate
To Lake Challa (10km); Taveta (11km); Moshi (49km)
A23
Murka
Serengeti Plains
Maktau Gate
Maktau
Lumo Community WS
Lake Jipe
Jipe Gate
14
TANZANIA
18
19
Taita Hills WS
Taita Hills
Ngangao Forest
22
Wundanyi
C104
Mwatate
A23
3
Voi
Voi Gate
24
1
Tsavo East Park Office
23
25
Sagala
Sagala Hills
Kasigau Gate
Rukanga
Bungule
Kanderi Swamp
Ndara Plains
Maungu
8
Aruba Dam
Maungu Plains
Voi River
20
Dika Plains
Buchuma Gate
A109
Mwanatibu
A
B
C
D
E
F
G
5
6
7
8

Tsavo East & West National Parks

Sights

1 Chaimu Crater C3
2 Hippo Pool C3
3 Mudanda Rock E5
4 Mzima Springs B4
5 Ngulia Rhino Sanctuary C4
6 Shetani Caves B3
7 Shetani Lava Flows B3

Sleeping

8 Ashnil Aruba Lodge F6
9 Finch Hatton's Safari Camp B4
10 Galdessa Safari Camp E4
11 Kilaguni Serena Lodge B3
Kitani Bandas .... (see 21)
12 KWS Campsite C2
13 KWS Campsite B3
14 Lions Bluff Lodge B6
15 Ngulia Safari Lodge C4
16 Ol Donyo Wuas A1
17 Rhino Valley Lodge C4
18 Sarova Salt Lick Safari Lodge C7
19 Sarova Taita Hills Game Lodge C7
20 Satao Camp G6
21 Severin Safari Camp B4
22 Taita Rocks D6
23 Tsavo Mashariki Camp E6
24 Voi Safari Lodge E6
25 Voi Wildlife Lodge E6

Hills, provides the bulk of Mombasa's fresh water. A walking trail leads along the shoreline. The drought in 2009 took a heavy toll on the springs' hippo population (around 20 remain); there are also crocodiles and a wide variety of birdlife. There's an underwater viewing chamber, which gives a creepy view of thousands of primeval-looking fish. Be careful here though, as both hippos and crocs are potentially dangerous.

Chaimu Crater & Roaring Rocks LOOKOUT
Just southeast of Kilaguni Serena Lodge, these two natural features offer stunning views of the Chyulu Hills and birds of prey circling high above the plains. The Roaring Rocks can be climbed in about 15 minutes; the name comes from the wind whistling up the escarpment and the persistent drone of cicadas. While there's little danger when walking these trails, the KWS warns in its guidebook to the park that in Chaimu Crater 'be wary when exploring since the crater and lava may shelter snakes and large sleeping mammals'.

Poachers' Lookout LOOKOUT
A short distance northwest of Severin Safari Camp, this hilltop vantage point offers fine views out over the park, and especially fine views west to the plains of the Amboseli ecosystem and Mt Kilimanjaro.

Tembo Peak & Ngulia Hills ROCK CLIMBING
It's possible to go rock-climbing at Tembo Peak and the Ngulia Hills, but you'll need to arrange this in advance with the **park warden** (☎043-30049). You'll also need a 4WD and a KWS park ranger to accompany you.

TOP CHOICE **Shetani Lava Flows** LOOKOUT
About 4km west of the Chyulu gate of Tsavo West National Park, on the road to Amboseli, are the spectacular Shetani lava flows. 'Shetani' means 'devil' in Kiswahili, a reference to the fact that the flows were formed only a few hundred years ago and local peoples believed that it was the devil himself emerging from the earth. This vast expanse of folded black lava spreads for 50 sq km across the savannah at the foot of the Chyulu Hills, looking strangely as if Vesuvius dropped its comfort blanket here. The last major eruption here is believed to have taken place around 200 years ago, but there are still few plants among the cinders. It's possible to follow the lava flows back from the Amboseli–Tsavo West road to the ruined cinder cone of Shetani. The views are spectacular, but you need to be wary of wildlife in this area, as there are predators about.

Nearby are the **Shetani Caves**, which are also a result of volcanic activity. You'll need a torch (flashlight) if you want to explore, but watch your footing on the razor-sharp rocks and keep an eye out for the local fauna – we've heard rumours that the caves are sometimes inhabited by hyenas, who don't take kindly to being disturbed.

Tsavo Gate & the East PARK
Many visitors heading for Tsavo East National Park or Mombasa use this gate. Wildlife spotting in this eastern section of the park is challenging due to the quite dense foliage, but both leopards and lions are known to frequent the area.

TOP CHOICE **Tsavo River & the South** RIVER

Running west–east through the park, this lovely year-round river is green-shaded and surrounded for much of its path by doum palms. Along with Mzima Springs, the river provides aesthetic relief from the semi-arid habitats that dominate the park. The trees all along the river are known to shelter leopards. South of the river, running down to the Ziwani and Maktau gates, the foliage is less dense with cheetah sightings a small possibility.

Lake Jipe LAKE

This lake (pronounced ji-*pay*) lies at the extreme southwestern end of the park and is reached by a desperately dusty track from near Taveta. You can hire boats at the campsite to take you hippo and crocodile spotting on the lake (US$5). Huge herds of elephants come to the lake to drink, and large flocks of migratory birds stop here from February to May.

Sleeping & Eating

TOP CHOICE **Severin Safari Camp** TENTED CAMP $$$

(020-2684247; www.severinsafaricamp.com; s/d full board from US$215/330; P) This fantastic complex of thatched luxury tents just keeps getting better. They've recently overhauled the tents, added a luxury swimming pool and spa and even a tented gym. The staff offer a personal touch, the food is outstanding and the tents are large and luxurious despite costing considerably less than others elsewhere in the park. Environmental sustainability is a high priority here as well. Hippo and lion visits are fairly frequent and there are Kilimanjaro views from some points on the property. Warmly recommended.

TOP CHOICE **Kitani Bandas** BANDAS $$

(020-2684247; www.severinsafaricamp.com; s/d bandas US$55/110, meals US$10-15; P) Run by the same people as the top-end luxury Severin Safari Camp, Kitani is located next to a waterhole, about 2km past its sister site, and offers the cheapest Kili views in the park. These *bandas* (which have their own simple kitchens), have far more style than your average budget camp and you can use Severin's facilities (including the pool and free wi-fi). Great value.

Rhino Valley Lodge BANDAS $$

(Ngulia Bandas; 0721328567; www.tsavocampsandlodges.com; s/d bandas from US$80/130; P) This hillside camp is Tsavo's best luxury bargain and one of the few genuine midrange choices in the parks of southern Kenya. The thatched stone cottages perch on the lower slopes of the Ngulia Hills with sweeping views of Rhino Valley, overlooking a stream where leopards are known to hide out. The decor is designer rustic with plenty of space and private terraces. The setting and standards outdo plenty of the more ambitious lodges, for a fraction of the price. It's still signposted throughout the park under its old name, Ngulia Bandas.

Ngulia Safari Lodge LODGE $$

(043-30000; www.safari-hotels.com; s/d US$140/200; P) Tsavo vantage points don't come any better than this – the surrounding Ngulia Hills attract loads of birds, there's a waterhole right by the restaurant (which attracts buffaloes, elephants and hyenas at night) and a leopard is fed right next to the restaurant every evening. Out the back there are sweeping views down off the escarpment and over the Ngulia Rhino Sanctuary. It's all enough to make you forget that the building itself is a monstrosity and the rooms (especially the bathrooms) are tired and in need of an overhaul; the balcony views from all rooms are wonderful.

POACHING IN TSAVO

As poaching reached epidemic proportions in Kenya in the 1980s, Tsavo was very much on the frontline – not surprising given the park's size and terrain. In a few short years, the elephant population dropped from 45,000 to just 5000, and rhinos were almost wiped out entirely; at the height of the crisis, an estimated 5000 elephants were being killed every year. Populations are slowly recovering, and there are close to 12,500 elephants in the two parks, but less than 100 rhinos, down from about 9000 in 1969. If you're used to the human-habituated elephants of Amboseli, who'll scarcely move when approached in a vehicle, Tsavo's elephants may come as a surprise – they're skittish and prone to sudden retreats. Rhinos, too, can be difficult to see, not just because they're nocturnal.

Kilaguni Serena Lodge LODGE $$$
(045-622376; www.serenahotels.com; s/d US $225/320; P) As you'd expect from the upmarket Serena chain, this lodge is extremely comfortable with semi-luxurious rooms, many of which have been recently renovated. The centrepiece here is a splendid bar and restaurant overlooking a busy illuminated waterhole – the vista stretches all the way from Mt Kilimanjaro to the Chyulu Hills. The best watering-hole views are in rooms 14 to 39. The extravagant suites are practically cottages in their own right, boasting chintzy living rooms and epic balconies.

KWS campsites CAMPGROUND $
(camping US$15; P) The public sites are at Komboyo, near the Mtito Andei gate, and at Chyulu, just outside the Chyulu gate. Facilities are basic, so be prepared to be self-sufficient.

Finch Hatton's Safari Camp TENTED CAMP $$$
(020-3518349; www.finchhattons.com; s/d US $360/560; P) This upmarket tented camp, which is distinguished by its signature bone china and gold shower taps (guests are requested to dress for dinner), was named after Denys Finch Hatton, the playboy hunter and lover of Karen Blixen. He died at Tsavo, despite his obsession with maintaining civility in the middle of the bush. The camp is situated among springs and hippo pools in the west of the park, in grounds so sprawling you have to take an escort at night to keep you safe from the animals.

Information

Kenya Wildlife Service (043-30049; www.kws.org/parks/parks_reserves/TWNP.html; adult/child US$60/30, safari card required)

ONE OF THE WORLD'S RAREST ANTELOPES

Until their partial translocation to Tsavo East, the sole surviving population of hirola antelope was found near the Kenya–Somalia border in the south Tana River and Garissa districts. Intense poaching (for meat) and habitat destruction have reduced their numbers from an estimated 14,000 in 1976 to a pitiful 450 today. At the time of writing, there were approximately 100 left within the park confines, mostly in the little visited southern reaches of the park.

ENTRY Six gates, but safari card can only be topped up at Mtito Andei Gate

FUEL Generally available at Kilaguni Serena Lodge and Severin Safari Camp; fill up before entering park

MAPS *Tsavo West National Park* map and guidebook available from Mtito Andei Gate

Getting There & Away

The main access to Tsavo West is through the Mtito Andei gate on the Mombasa–Nairobi road in the north of the park. Although security is much improved, vehicles for Amboseli travel in armed convoys from Kilaguni Serena Lodge; check at the lodge for departure times.

Tsavo East National Park

043

Kenya's largest national park has an undeniable wild and primordial charm and is a terrific wildlife-watching destination. Although one of Kenya's largest rivers flows through the middle of the park and the contrast between the permanent greenery of the river and the endless grasses and thorn trees that characterise much of the park is visually arresting, the landscape here lacks the drama of Tsavo West. Tsavo East is markedly flatter and drier than its sister park. The flipside is that spotting wildlife is generally easier thanks to the thinly spread foliage.

Despite the size of the park, the area of most wildlife activity is actually quite compact – the northern section of the park is largely closed and can only be visited with advance permission due to the threat of banditry and ongoing campaigns against poachers. The demarcation point is the Galana River.

According to a late-2010 elephant census, over 12,500 elephants call the two Tsavo parks home. This is the largest population of any of the Kenyan parks and a third of the country's total, although herds are quite small. Most people come here to see the famous red elephants of Tsavo – their colour comes from bathing in the red Tsavo mud (to keep the skin cool and prevent insect bites). Lion and cheetah sightings are also common; unusually, the male lions are almost maneless. Other unusual inhabitants of the park include servals (many of which are black or melanistic rather than spotted), the striped hyena and African hunting dog, although all three are extremely difficult to spot.

Sights & Activities

TOP CHOICE Kanderi Swamp & Voi River RIVER

Around 10km from Voi gate, the lovely area of green known as Kanderi Swamp is home to a resident pride of lions, and elephants also congregate near here; this is one of only two water sources in the park during the dry season. The landscape here has a lovely backdrop of distant hills. A number of vehicle tracks also follow the contours of the Voi River; keep an eye on the overhanging branches for leopards.

TOP CHOICE Aruba Dam & the Southeast LAKE

Some 30km east of Voi gate is the Aruba Dam, which spans the Voi River. It also attracts heavy concentrations of diverse wildlife; the park's other regularly spotted lion pride ranges around here. Away to the east and southeast, all the way down to the Buchuma Gate, the open grasslands provide the perfect habitat for cheetahs and sightings are more common here than anywhere else in southeastern Kenya.

Galana River & Around RIVER

Running through the heart of the park and marking the northernmost point in the park that most visitors are allowed to visit, the Galana River, which combines the waters of the Tsavo and Athi Rivers, cuts a green gash across the dusty plains. Surprisingly few visitors make it even this far and sightings of crocs, hippos, lesser kudus, waterbucks, dikdiks and, to a lesser extent, lions and leopards, are relatively common. Watch out also for the distinctive Somali ostrich. There are several places along the flat-topped escarpments lining the river where you can get out of your vehicle (with due caution, of course). Most scenic are **Lugards Falls**, a wonderful landscape of water-sculpted channels, and **Crocodile Point**, where you may see abundant crocs and hippos. The trail that runs from the falls back to Voi follows a river and is good for wildlife-spotting, but the track is impassable after the rains.

The area north of the Galana River is dominated by the **Yatta Escarpment**, a vast prehistoric lava flow which is estimated by some to be the longest lava flow in the world at 300km. However, much of this area is off limits to travellers because of the ongoing campaign against poachers (see also opposite).

TSAVO EAST NATIONAL PARK

Why Go To see wilderness, red elephants and maybe leopards, lions and cheetahs. The park also has close to 500 bird species.

When to Go June to February. Wildlife concentrations are highest in the dry season (September to October and January to early March).

Practicalities Drive in from Voi, Mandanyi or Tsavo gates along the Nairobi–Mombasa Rd. The Sala and Buchuma gates are good for Mombasa. There are a small number of lodges and camps throughout the park or close to Voi Gate. The park works on the safari card system (you can only add credit at Voi Gate); gates open from sunrise to sunset.

Voi Safari Lodge LOOKOUT

If you're staying at this lodge just 4km inside Voi Gate, you're guaranteed great views out over the savannah from high on the hill, with a waterhole down below that's visited by elephants, buffalo, zebra, baboons and other wildlife. Steps lead down to a hide adjacent to the waterhole, where you can watch the wildlife without being seen.

Mudanda Rock MOUNTAIN

Towering over a natural dam near the Manyani gate, this towering natural formation runs for over 1.5km. It attracts elephants in the dry season and is reminiscent of Australia's Uluru (Ayers Rock), albeit on a smaller scale. Leopards and elephants are among the wildlife to watch out for here.

Sleeping & Eating

In addition to the handful of places within the park, a couple sit right outside the gate and are worth considering.

Inside the Park

Voi Safari Lodge LODGE $$$

(☎Mombasa 041-471861; www.safari-hotels.com; s/d US$140/200; P ☒) Just 4km from Voi gate, this is a long, low complex perched on the edge of an escarpment overlooking an incredible sweep of savannah. There's an attractive rock-cut swimming pool, as well as a natural waterhole that draws elephants, buffaloes and the occasional predator; a

MAN-EATERS OF TSAVO

Wild felines the world over are rightfully feared and respected, though the famed 'man-eaters of Tsavo' were probably the most dangerous lions to ever roam the planet. During the building of the Kenya–Uganda Railway in 1898, Engineer Lt Col John Henry Patterson led the construction of a railway bridge over the Tsavo River in Kenya. However, efforts soon came to a halt when railway workers started being dragged from their tents at night and devoured by two maneless male lions.

The surviving workers soon decided that the lions had to be ghosts or devils, which put the future of the railway in jeopardy. This drove Patterson to create a series of ever more ingenious traps, though each time the lions evaded them, striking unerringly at weak points in the camp defences. Patterson was finally able to bag the first man-eater by hiding on a flimsy wooden scaffold baited with the corpse of a donkey. The second man-eater was dispatched a short time later, although it took six bullets to bring the massive beast down.

According to Patterson's calculations, the two lions killed and ate around 135 workers in less than one year. He detailed his experiences in the best-selling book *The Man-Eaters of Tsavo* (1907), which was later rather freely filmed as *Bwana Devil* (1952) and *The Ghost and the Darkness* (1996).

In a vengeful twist, Patterson turned the two man-eaters into floor rugs, which he kept for more than a quarter of a century. In 1924 he finally rid himself of the lions by selling their skins to the Chicago Field Museum for the sum of US$5000. The man-eaters of Tsavo were then stuffed and placed on permanent display, where they remain to this day.

To date, scientists have offered up a number of hypotheses to explain the ferocious behaviour of the man-eaters. Research has shown that Tsavo lions have noticeably elevated levels of the male sex hormone testosterone, which could have been responsible for their hair loss and increased territorial behaviour. The pair themselves had badly damaged teeth, which may have driven them to abandon their normal prey and become man-eaters.

It has also been suggested by historians that an outbreak of rinderpest (an infectious viral disease) might have decimated the lions' usual prey, forcing them to find alternative food sources. Alternatively, the man-eaters may have developed their taste for human flesh after growing accustomed to finding human bodies at the Tsavo River crossing, where slave caravans often crossed en route to Zanzibar.

While the descendants of Tsavo's man-eaters aren't quite the indiscriminate killing machines that their forebears were, they still have a reputation for ferocity and are generally wilder than the lazy kitty cats you come across in Masai Mara. On that note, be aware of your surroundings, sleep in closed campsites and give mother nature's predators a healthy amount of respect and distance.

photographers' hide sits at the level of the waterhole. Rooms are attractive and many have superlative views.

Satao Camp TENTED CAMP **$$$**
(☎Mombasa 041-475074; www.sataocamp.com; s/d US$260/330; P) Located on the banks of the Voi River, this luxury camp is run by the top-class operator Southern Cross Safaris. Intimacy is the theme here, with just 20 canopied tents, all of which are perfectly spaced within sight of a waterhole that's known to draw lions and cheetahs on occasion.

Ashnil Aruba Lodge LODGE **$$$**
(☎020-4971008; www.ashnilhotels.com; s/d US$175/215; P 🏊 @) A stone's throw from the wildlife-rich Aruba Dam, this lodge has attractively decorated rooms decked out in safari prints. In the heart of the park, it's an ideal starting point for most Tsavo East safaris. Wildlife wanders around the property's perimeter at regular intervals.

Galdessa Safari Camp TENTED CAMP **$$$**
(☎040-3202217; www.galdessa.com; s/d from US$500/750; P 📶) Perched on the edge of the Galana River, approximately 15km west of Lugards Falls, this Italian-owned safari camp is by far the swishest property in Tsavo East, especially since it's often booked out entirely by private parties. For a healthy dose of European sophistication in

your bush camping experience (fine wines, gourmet dining, fashionable decor and impeccable service) look no further – assuming of course you've got a whole pile of euros to burn!

Outside the Park

TOP CHOICE Tsavo Mashariki Camp TENTED CAMP $$
(☎2031444; www.masharikicamp.com; per person bed & breakfast from KSh4500, full board from KSh7000; P) The closest camp to Voi Gate just outside the park, this charming Italian-run place has some fine tents made out of all-natural local materials; the family tent is brilliant. Best of all, the prices here put many other tented camps to shame. Highly recommended.

Voi Wildlife Lodge LODGE $$
(☎2031444; www.voiwildlifelodge.com; s/d US $130/180; P 🏊) Close to Voi Gate, this well-run place has large, pleasant rooms, all of which look towards a waterhole that sits inside the park, just on the other side of the fence. The views are better still from the restaurant and viewing platform. There's a spa centre on-site with massage and a range of therapies, and the whole place is infinitely better value if you can get the travel agent's rates.

Information

Kenya Wildlife Service (☎043-30049; www.kws.org/parks/parks_reserves/TENP.html; adult/child US$60/30, safari card required)

ENTRY Six gates, but safari card can only be topped up at Voi or Sala gates

FUEL Available in Voi; fill up before entering park

MAPS *Tsavo East National Park* map and guidebook available from Voi Gate

Getting There & Away

A track through the park follows the Galana River from the Tsavo gate to the Sala gate; others fan out from Voi gate.

TO/FROM NAIROBI OR TSAVO WEST Voi, Tsavo and Manyani gates

TO/FROM MOMBASA Sala or Buchuma gates

Voi

☎043

Voi is a key service town at the intersection of the Nairobi–Mombasa road, the road to Moshi in Tanzania and the access road to the main Voi gate of Tsavo East National Park. While there is little reason to spend any more time here than is needed to get directions, fill up on petrol, change money and buy some snacks for the road, you'll inevitably pass through here at some point.

Sights & Activities

Voi War Cemetery CEMETERY
(Commonwealth War Graves; ⏰vary) On the north side of the road just before the turn-off to Voi Gate on the eastern outskirts of town, this well-tended cemetery contains 137 graves, including those of 70 South African, 44 British, 12 'Rhodesian', nine East African and two Indian graves. The area around Tsavo, particularly the railway, was a major theatre of war between Britain and Germany during WWI. The gate is usually padlocked shut, but ask around the nearest shops and soon enough they'll track down the custodian of the key.

Sleeping & Eating

You'll find simple places serving *nyama choma* (barbecued meat) in numerous places surrounding the main matatu park and market in the centre of town.

Tsavo Lodge LODGE $$
(☎0721328567; www.tsavocampsandlodges.com; s/d full board US$60/90) About halfway between Voi and the park's Voi gate, this simple place has rooms and tents arrayed around a green courtyard. Rooms are large and basic. If you can stay closer to (or inside) the park, do so.

Tsavo Park Hotel HOTEL $
(☎0721328567; www.tsavocampsandlodges.com; s/d US$25/50) If you really must stay in Voi itself, this place is simplicity itself. Rooms are gloomy but fine for a night.

Getting There & Away

Frequent buses and matatus run to/from Mombasa (KSh500, three hours), and buses to Nairobi (KSh800 to KSh 1000, six hours). There are at least daily matatus to Wundanyi (KSh250, one hour) and Taveta (KSh450, two hours), on the Tanzanian border.

See p107 for information about travel to Tanzania.

WORTH A TRIP

WUNDANYI

The provincial capital of Wundanyi is set high in the Taita Hills. Numerous trails criss-cross the cultivated terraced slopes around town, leading to dramatic gorges, waterfalls, cliffs and jagged outcrops. It's easy to find someone to act as a guide, but stout walking boots and a head for heights are essential.

Other attractions in the hills include the butterflies of **Ngangao Forest**, a 6km matatu ride northwest to Werugha (KSh70); the huge granite **Wesu Rock** that overlooks Wundanyi; and the **Cave of Skulls** where the Taita people once put the skulls of their ancestors (and where the original African violets were discovered).

The best of Wundanyi's limited accommodation offerings, **Taita Rocks** (☎0735651349; r KSh700-1500) is perched up a slope off the road on the way into town, with views towards Wesu Rock. The rooms are priced according to size and there's a small restaurant and bar here for getting your feed before hiking.

Semifrequent matatu services run between Wundanyi and Voi (KSh140, one hour). Leave Wundanyi by around 8.30am if you want to connect with the morning buses to Nairobi from Voi. There are also direct matatus to Mombasa (KSh350, four to five hours) and an irregular morning service to Nairobi (KSh700, seven hours).

Taita Hills Wildlife Sanctuary

☎043

The Taita Hills, a fertile area of verdant hills and scrub forest, is a far cry from the semi-arid landscape of Tsavo. Within the hills is the private **wildlife sanctuary** (adult US$25), covering an area of 100 sq km – the landscape is dramatic and all the plains wildlife is here in abundance.

Sleeping & Eating

Sarova Salt Lick Safari Lodge LODGE $$$

(☎30270; www.sarovahotels.com; s/d full board from US$179/239; P❄@≋) The centrepiece of the sanctuary is the upmarket, visually striking complex of mushroomlike houses on stilts surrounding a waterhole. Since the Taita Hills are not an official national park, the sanctuary permits night drives, which provide good opportunities for spotting nocturnal animals as well as watching hunting behaviour. You can organise everything through the Salt Lick.

Sarova Taita Hills Game Lodge LODGE $$$

(☎30540; www.sarovahotels.com; s/d full board from US$143/190; P❄@≋) Another Sarova property within the sanctuary, this place is older and lacks the waterhole-proximity of the Salt Lick but is generally cheaper and rooms are pleasant.

Getting There & Away

You'll need your own vehicle to get to the Taita Hills, which lie south of the dirt road from Voi to Taveta.

Lumo Community Wildlife Sanctuary

☎043

This innovative community-run **reserve** (adult/child US$30/15) of 657 sq km was formed from three community-owned ranches in 1996, but only opened to the public in 2003. It's partly funded by the EU and involves local people at every stage of the project, from the park rangers to senior management.

Birdlife is plentiful and all the Big Five are here, as well as several war relics from WWI. For more information, call the **sanctuary offices** (☎30936) in the village of Maktau, near Maktau gate. If you contact them in advance, the rangers may be able to arrange a wildlife drive or guide for a reasonable price.

Sleeping & Eating

Lions Bluff Lodge LODGE $$$

(☎0735453089; www.lionsblufflodge.com; camping US$20, r per person full board from US$125; P) Accommodation within the sanctuary is provided by this private lodge, a *makuti*-and-canvas compound. It also has the **Cheetah Campsite** close to the lodge.

Getting There & Away

The sanctuary lies on the Voi–Taveta road, so you can, in theory, get here by public bus or matatu, though a private car is helpful for moving around.

The Road to Moshi

Heading west from Voi, the A23 runs straight to the Tanzanian border en route to the city of Moshi. This road will also drop you off at the border town of Taveta, which is a good place to stock up on fuel and supplies before crossing.

Before entering Taveta, there's a worthwhile detour to the rarely visited **Lake Challa**, a deep, spooky crater lake about 10km north of the town. There are grand views across the plains from the crater rim, near the defunct Lake Challa Safari Lodge, with the mysterious waters shimmering hundreds of metres below.

The lake gained notoriety in early 2002, when a gap-year student was killed by crocodiles here. That said, you *can* walk around the crater rim, and down to the water, but be very careful near the water's edge and under no circumstances consider swimming.

The road to Challa turns off the Voi–Taveta road on the outskirts of Taveta, by the second police post. On Taveta market days (Wednesday and Saturday) there are local buses to Challa village (KSh60), passing the turn-off to the crater rim.

Continuing on to **Taveta**, this dusty little town sits on the Tanzanian border; its busy twice-weekly market attracts people from remote villages on both sides of the border.

A pastel-orange building conveniently situated on the main road, **Tripple J Paradise** (☎5352463; r from KSh700; P) is little more than a crash pad for drivers heading back and forth between Kenya and Tanzania, though it'll do in a pinch if you can't make it to Moshi in one go.

The Tanzania border is open 24 hours, but the border posts are 4km apart, so you'll have to take a *boda-boda* (bicycle taxi; KSh40) if you don't have your own wheels. From Holili on the Tanzanian side, there are matatus to Moshi (TSh1200), where you can change on to Arusha (TSh2000).

From Taveta, numerous matatus head to Voi (KSh350, 2½ hours) and Mombasa (KSh750, four hours) throughout the day.

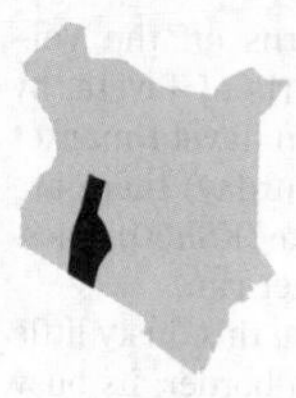

Rift Valley

Includes »

Best of Nature

» Lake Nakuru National Park (p122)

» Lake Baringo (p125)

» Lake Bogoria National Reserve (p124)

» Longonot National Park (p109)

» Hell's Gate National Park (p116)

Best of Culture

» Kikopey Nyama Choma Centre (p120)

» Elsamere Conservation Centre (p113)

Why Go?

Africa's Great Rift Valley is one of the continent's grand epics. Here in Kenya, the battle of geological forces that almost rent Africa in two has left the Rift Valley looking as if it were created by giants: the ribbon of steaming and bubbling soda lakes (inscribed on Unesco's World Heritage list in 2011) scars the valley like the footprints of a massive hippopotamus, and numerous dried-out volcanic cones stand to attention like amplified termite mounds.

The Rift Valley's dramatic landscapes are lent personality by some of central Kenya's most charismatic wildlife. Here, the massed colonies of flamingos turn the earth to pink, endangered rhinos snuffle by the lakeshore and Rothschild's giraffes stride gracefully across lacustrine plains. Lions laze under trees, and leopards lurk in the undergrowth.

It's this combination of stunning natural forms and soulful wildlife that gives the region its charm. And in this sense the Rift Valley is all that's good about Kenya in microcosm.

When to Go

Nakuru

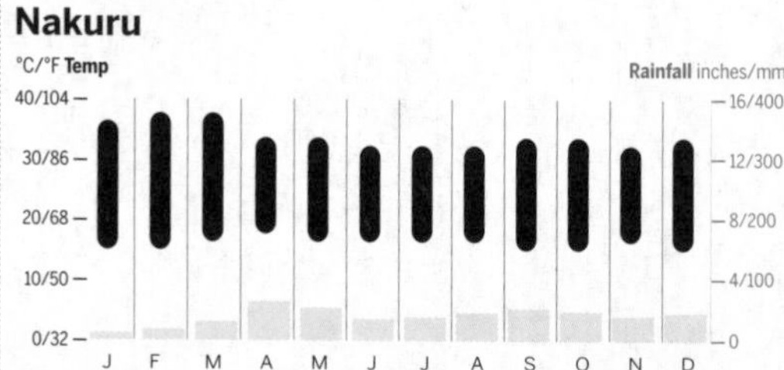

Nov–Mar Migratory bird species abound; weather clear, dry and hot after November rains.

Jun–Oct Generally fine weather, no rains until October; good for climbing Mt Longonot.

April & May Avoid as rains drench the valley, mosquitoes proliferate and some roads are impassable.

Longonot National Park

One of the shapeliest peaks in all the Rift Valley, Mt Longonot (2776m) and its serrated crater rim offer fabulous views. The dormant volcano rises 1000m above the baking hot valley floor and was formed 400,000 years ago; it last erupted in the 1860s. The park itself covers only 52 sq km, and was set up to protect the volcano's ecosystem and little else.

Sights & Activities

Mt Longonot HIKING
(Map p110; adult/child US$20/10; guide to crater rim/summit & back KSh1500/2500) Pull on your hiking boots and enjoy the rare treat of hiking through the Kenyan bush. But this isn't just any hike. The one- to 1½-hour hike from the park gate up to the crater rim (2545m) is strenuous but, without question, worth the considerable effort. There are two steep stretches that will challenge those not used to hiking. On the lower slopes you may spot impala, zebra and occasionally buffalo. Your reward is to emerge at the lip of the crater rim for superb views of the 2km- to 3km-wide crater – a little lost world hosting an entirely different forest ecosystem. The Rift Valley views are also marvellous, but your eyes will be drawn inward to the crater, inhabited only by rarely spotted baboons and klipspringer.

It takes between 1½ and 2½ hours to circumnavigate the crater; watch for occasional steam vents rising from the crater floor. The name 'Longonot' comes from the Maasai name *olo nongot,* which means 'mountain of many summits', and the rim is anything but a flat-level walk; the final push up to Mt Longonot's summit is particularly steep. The prize is fine westerly views towards Hell's Gate National Park.

Including time for pausing to take in the views, this 21km trek from the park gate and back should take about five to six hours.

The trail is clear and easy to follow and taking along a KWS (Kenya Wildlife Service) ranger is not necessary, although a good one will certainly enhance your trek; rangers can be arranged at the main gate as you enter.

Sleeping

Most people stay in Lake Naivasha, a 30-minute drive away.

Oloongonot Campsite CAMPGROUND $
(camping US$15) This campsite sits just beyond the gate on the way up to the crater. There's space to pitch a tent and a toilet and shower block but no firewood; you'll need to bring all your own food and cooking supplies.

Information

Kenya Wildlife Service (☎050-50407; www.kws.org/parks/parks_reserves/MLNP.html; park admission adult/child US$20/10, safari card not valid)

Getting There & Away

If you're driving, Mt Longonot is 75km northwest of Nairobi on the Old Naivasha Rd. If you're without a vehicle, take a matatu from Naivasha to Longonot village, from where there's a path (ask locals) to the park's access road.

Naivasha

☎050

Bypassed by the new A104 Hwy to Nairobi, Naivasha is the gateway town for both Longonot and Hell's Gate National Parks. It's a pleasant enough workaday Kenyan town that now exists primarily to service the area's blossoming flower industry, but it's hard to see why you would choose to stay the night here rather than at the lake shore. If nothing else, it's a good place to change money (banks line Moi Ave), stock up on supplies and check your email.

WILDLIFE OF THE RIFT VALLEY

Kenya's Rift Valley is one of the country's premier birdwatching regions, with an astonishing congregation of species year-round, but especially during the November to March migration period. Flamingos are generally present year-round, but can move from lake to lake.

Lake Nakuru National Park is one of Kenya's finest parks, with both black and white rhinos in residence, as well as lions, leopards, reintroduced Rothschild's giraffes, zebras, buffaloes, olive baboons and black-and-white colobus monkeys.

Rift Valley Highlights

1. Searching for lions, leopards and rhinos, as well as blushing pink flamingos, at **Lake Nakuru National Park** (p122).
2. Being serenaded to sleep by snorting, hungry hippos, then waking to the fish eagles' dawn chorus at **Lake Baringo** (p125).
3. Climbing to the volcanic rim of **Mt Longonot** (p109) and being rewarded with glorious Rift Valley and crater views.
4. Watching a stressed Mother Earth let off steam while flamingos mass nearby at **Lake Bogoria National Reserve** (p124).
5. Trying to out-sprint a buffalo in the red-cliffed gorges of **Hell's Gate National Park** (p116).
6. Stopping for the quintessential Kenyan lunch of *nyama choma* at **Kikopey Nyama Choma Centre** (p120).
7. Visiting the former home of Joy Adamson (of *Born Free* fame) then taking a boat out onto **Lake Naivasha** (p113).

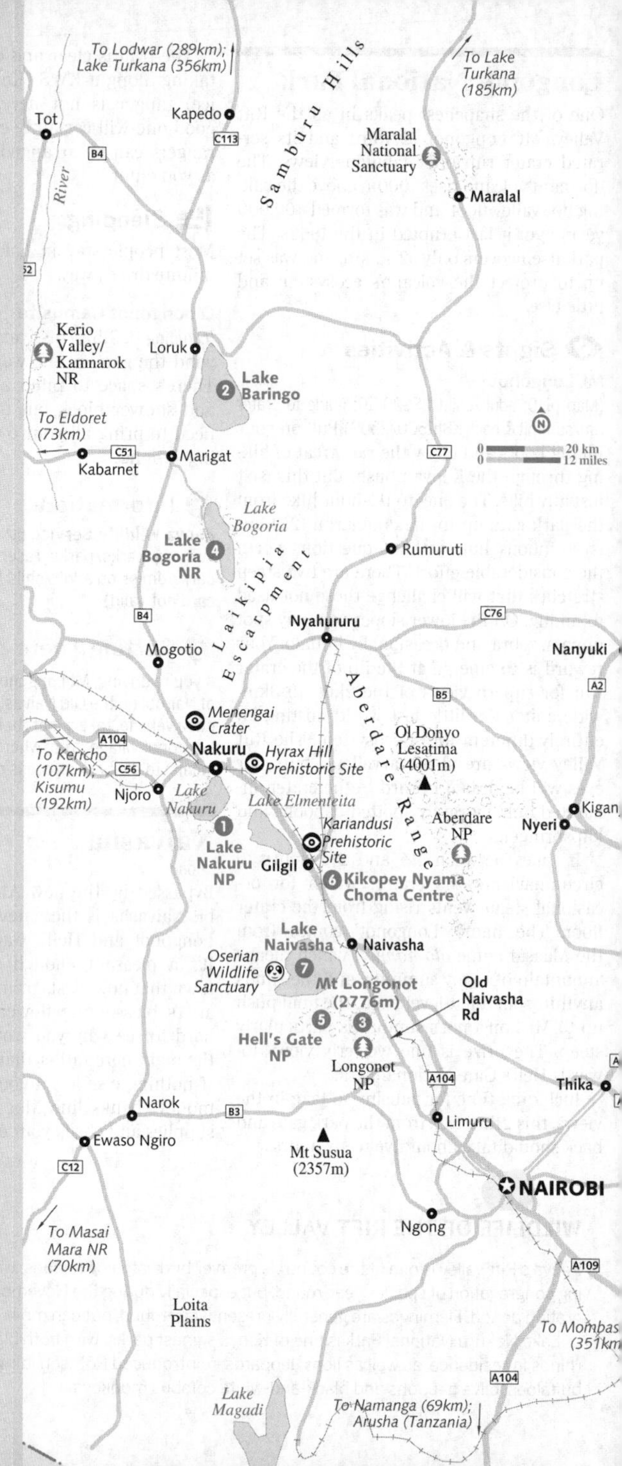

Sleeping

Sam's Holiday Inn HOTEL $

(Mbaria Kaniu Rd; s/tw KSh425/650) The mattresses might be too big for the frames, but the inn still offers the best budget digs in town. All rooms have a private bathroom with hot shower, and there are reasonable views from the roof.

La Belle Inn HOTEL $

(☎2021007; info@labelleinn.com; Moi Ave; s/d KSh3000/3500; wi-fi) Naivasha's oldest hotel was built in 1922 and retains a faded colonial charm. The rooms are fine for a night, if a tad neglected; most are generously sized and all have mosquito nets. Wi-fi is available.

Eating & Drinking

Smiles Café KENYAN $

(Kariuki Chotarai Rd; meals KSh100-150; ⊙breakfast, lunch & dinner) As cheap and cheerful as the name suggests, this little green-and-white treasure offers cholesterol-filled fried breakfasts and hearty stews. It's always busy and conversations come easy.

La Belle Inn INTERNATIONAL $

(Moi Ave; meals KSh400-800; ⊙breakfast, lunch & dinner) The roadside colonial verandah here is the place to choose from a varied menu that includes charcoal-grilled whole tilapia fresh from Lake Naivasha; crayfish cooked in butter, garlic, herbs and green chillies; and, for dessert, apple pie. It also does curries, soup, salads and pasta. Once you're done, head into the Happy Valley bar that gets busy in the evenings.

Getting There & Away

The main bus and matatu station is off Mbaria Kaniu Rd, close to the municipal market. Frequent buses and matatus leave for Nakuru (KSh150 to KSh200, 1¼ hours) and Nairobi (KSh200 to KSh300, 1½ hours).

Frequent matatus run around the south side of the lake to Kongoni (KSh100) and Fisherman's Camp area (KSh70, 45 minutes). They depart from the bus station and from Kenyatta Ave.

Lake Naivasha

☎050

The freshwater Lake Naivasha is the highest of the Rift Valley lakes (1884m above sea level) and is for many travellers the first port of call after Nairobi. With its shores fringed in papyrus and yellow-barked acacias, bulbous snorting hippos playing in the shallows, a cacophony of twittering birds and a gentle climate, there's no denying its appeal over the urban mayhem of Nairobi. Be aware, however, that unless you're staying here, actually getting to the lakeshore can be a challenge – a boat safari is the best way to get a sense of the area's natural beauty and wildlife. There's also a decent (and relatively accessible) flamingo colony at Lake Oloiden, off Lake Naivasha's southwestern corner. If you are staying here, wander down to the water's edge early in the morning when a barely perceptible layer of fine mist hangs above the water's surface – this is when you'll most appreciate being here.

Lake Naivasha has one of the largest settler and expat communities in Kenya, and half of Nairobi seems to decamp here at weekends. It can have a resort-feel to it in high season, when it essentially becomes Kenya's earthier version of St Tropez, with Tusker beer rather than champagne.

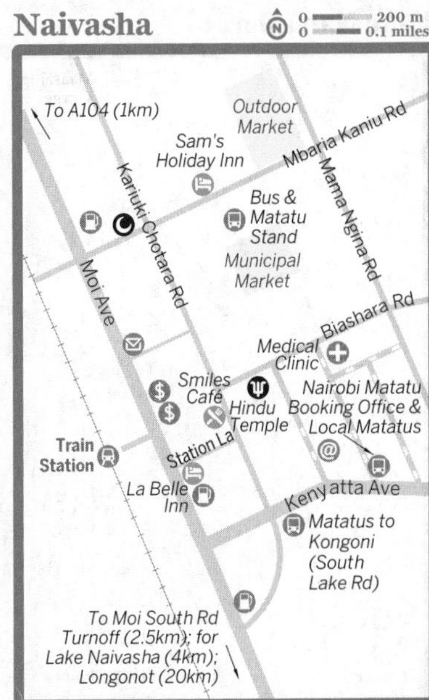

History

A vast range of plains animals and a plethora of birdlife have long called the verdant shoreline home, as have the Maasai, who considered it prime grazing land. Unfortunately for the Maasai, the splendour of the surroundings wasn't lost on early settlers,

Lake Naivasha

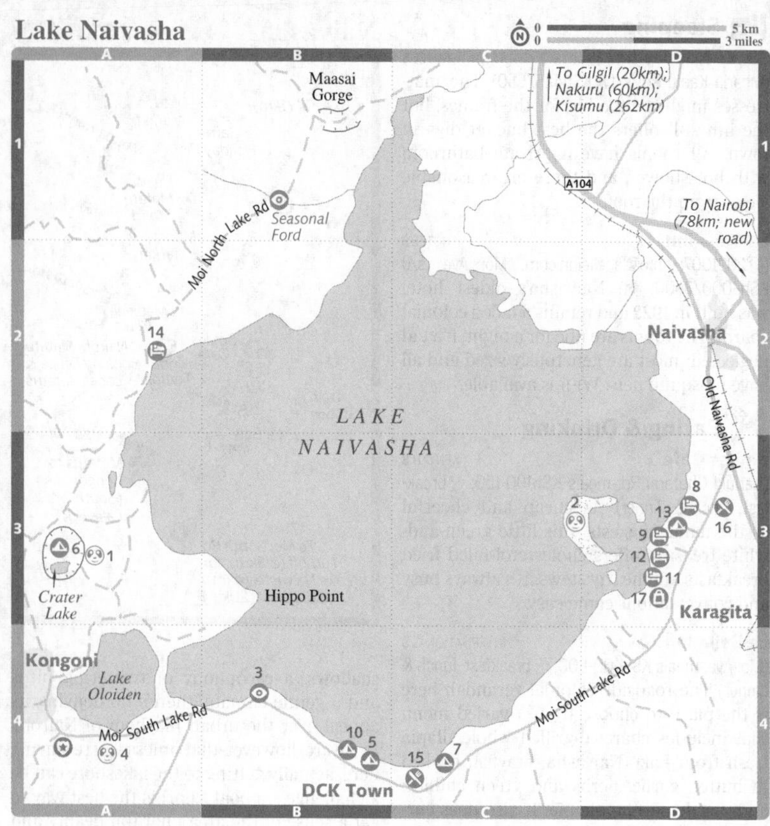

Lake Naivasha

Sights

1 Crater Lake Game Sanctuary ... A3
2 Crescent Island Wildlife Sanctuary ... C3
3 Elsamere Conservation Centre ... B4
4 Oserian Wildlife Sanctuary ... A4

Sleeping

Chui Lodge ... (see 4)
5 Connelley's Camp ... B4
6 Crater Lake Camp ... A3
7 Crayfish Camp ... C4
8 Dea's Gardens Guesthouse ... D3
Elsamere Conservation Centre ... (see 3)
9 Enashipai ... D3
10 Fisherman's Camp ... B4
11 Lake Naivasha Country Club ... D3
12 Lake Naivasha Sopa Resort ... D3
13 Marina's Camp ... D3
14 Olerai House ... A2

Eating

15 Acacia Café ... C4
16 Fischers Tower Hotel ... D3
Fisherman's Camp ... (see 10)

Shopping

17 Elmenteita Weavers Ltd ... D3

and it was one of the first areas settled, eventually becoming the favourite haunt of Lord Delamere and the decadent Happy Valley set of the 1930s (see p295).

Amazingly, between 1937 and 1950, the lake was Kenya's main airport, with British Overseas Airways Corporation's Empire and Solent flying-boats landing here after their four-day journey from Southampton.

WORTH A TRIP

MT SUSUA

Less frequented than Longonot but with a crater that's even more of a lost world, this unique volcano is well worth the considerable effort of visiting. The steep outer crater protects a second inner crater, whose rim peaks at 2357m and begs to be trekked. There's also a network of unexplored caves on the east side of the mountain, some of which are home to baboons.

There's no designated route and all land is owned by local Maasai, so you'll have to find someone from the nearby villages that dot the B3 Nairobi–Narok road to guide you. It's a 90-minute drive from Nairobi to the point where you leave the tarmac road, whereafter it's a further 2½ hours to the crater's outer rim. It takes about eight hours to circumnavigate the outer crater, meaning that you'll need to camp overnight (and be completely self-sufficient in food and water). Is it worth it? Absolutely, not least because you and the Maasai will have it all to yourselves.

Sights & Activities

TOP CHOICE Elsamere Conservation Centre WILDLIFE RESERVE
(☎2021055; www.elsamere.com; admission KSh800; ⏲8am-6.30pm) This conservation centre is the former home of the late Joy Adamson of *Born Free* fame. She bought the house in 1967 with a view to retiring here with her husband, George. Adamson did much of her writing from Elsamere, right up until her murder in 1980. It's now a conservation centre focused on lake ecology and environmental awareness programs, and the site is open to the public. Entry includes afternoon tea, complete with a mountain of biscuits, taken on the hippo-manicured lawns (with a chance to see eastern black-and-white colobus monkeys and over 200 bird species); a visit to the small museum dedicated to the Adamsons; and a showing of the weathered, 40-minute *Joy Adamson Story*. It also rents bicycles (KSh700 per day), can arrange seven-seater boat trips (per hour KSh3000), and you can even sleep here, staying in Joy Adamson's former bedroom (see p115).

Boat Safaris BOAT TOUR
(per boat per hr KSh3000-6000) Most of the camps and lodges along Lake Naivasha's southern shore rent out boats; most boats have seven seats and come with pilot and lifejackets. Places where nonguests can organise a boat rental include Marina's Camp, Fisherman's Camp and the Elsamere Conservation Centre.

TOP CHOICE Crater Lake Game Sanctuary WILDLIFE RESERVE
(admission per person US$15, plus car KSh200) Surrounding a beautiful volcanic crater lake fringed with acacias, this small sanctuary has many trails, including one for hikers along the steep but diminutive crater rim. The jade-green crater lake is held in high regard by the local Maasai, who believe its alkaline waters help soothe ailing cattle. As well as the impressive 150 bird species recorded here, giraffes, zebras and other plains wildlife are also regular residents on the more open plains surrounding the crater, while leopard, serval, caracal and aardvark have also been spotted; when we last visited, a lone hippo had taken up residence. While walking, remember that buffaloes lurk in the woods. There are also night safaris and guided nature walks for those staying at the sanctuary's camp (p115).

TOP CHOICE Lake Oloiden LAKE
(boat safaris per 30/60 min KSh2000/4000) Lake Naivasha may be a freshwater lake, but the alkaline waters of its near neighbour Lake Oloiden draw small but impressive flocks of flamingos. Boat safaris are available here. Apart from anything else, the real appeal here is that it's one of the few stretches of public land in the area where you can walk near to the lakeshore.

Crescent Island Wildlife Sanctuary WILDLIFE RESERVE
(adult/child US$25/12.50, plus car KSh200, horse riding per hr KSh2000; ⏲sunrise to sunset) The curious form left by the protruding rim of a collapsed volcanic crater forms this island on the eastern side of Lake Naivasha. It's a private sanctuary, where you can walk beneath acacias in search of giraffes, zebras, wildebeest, Thomson's and Grant's gazelles, elands, waterbucks and countless bird species.

LAKE NAIVASHA FLOWERS

Not only does Lake Naivasha's fresh water bestow it with a unique ecosystem (in comparison with the vast majority of Rift Valley lakes, which are highly alkaline), but it also means the lake can be used for irrigation purposes. While the surrounding countryside has historically been a major production area for beef cattle and fresh fruit and vegetables, today the flower industry rules the roost. Shade houses have proliferated in the hills, and Lake Naivasha is now the centre of Kenya's US$360 million flower industry. Astoundingly, flowers that are picked here in the early morning can be at Europe's flower auctions the same day.

Oh, and there are some rather gigantic pythons too! If you're renting a boat elsewhere on the lake, this island is a destination worth considering.

Oserian Wildlife Sanctuary WILDLIFE RESERVE
(www.oserianwildlife.com) This wonderful 100-sq-km private reserve serves as a wildlife corridor between Hell's Gate National Park and Lake Naivasha and, as a consequence, wildlife here may include leopard, cheetah, white rhino (which breed here), plains species and over 300 bird species. To visit the sanctuary, you need to be staying at the exclusive Chui Lodge.

Sleeping

Due to its popularity and proximity to Nairobi, Lake Naivasha has the Rift Valley's best range of accommodation. Most places are along the lake's southern shore, but a couple of interesting places can be found on the north side.

Moi South Lake Road

Chui Lodge LODGE $$$
(☎2020792; www.oserianwildlife.com; s/d minimum 2 nights full board US$1360/1250; @) This exclusive collection of luxury stone-and-acacia cottages amid the euphorbia trees of the Oserian Wildlife Sanctuary are impeccably attired with locally produced handicrafts and service is faultless. Other highlights include the heated swimming pool, fabulous meals, four-poster beds and sweeping views.

TOP CHOICE **Dea's Gardens** GUESTHOUSE $$
(☎2021015; www.deasgardens.com; per person half board €60; P) A place with an unusually personal feel along the southern lake shore, this charming guesthouse is run by the elegant Dea. The main house (with two rooms) is a gorgeous chalet of Swiss inspiration, while the two cottages in the lush grounds are large and comfortable. Meals are served in the main house with Dea as your host. Warmly recommended. The guesthouse is reached via a turn-off to the right, 2km after turning onto the Moi South Lake Rd; it's not signposted but it's the first track after the 'Kimwa' sign and signposted as 'Hortitec'.

TOP CHOICE **Marina's Camp** TENTED CAMP $$
(☎0722728054; cottages per person KSh3500, full board KSh4000) The cottages here are nothing to write home about, but the semi-luxurious tents amid the acacia trees that were almost completed when we visited promise to be among the best places to stay around Lake Naivasha. Prices weren't yet available at the time of writing.

Connelley's Camp CAMPGROUND, BANDAS $
(☎50004; camping KSh600, dm/tw KSh800/2500, old bandas from KSh6000, new bandas KSh6000-10,000) Camping here is excellent value, and even at weekends it remains slightly more tranquil than some of its neighbours. The accommodation varies, from old bandas (huts) that inhabit former shipping crates and basic twins to rather lovely new bandas closer to the water.

Lake Naivasha Sopa Resort LODGE $$$
(☎50358; www.sopalodges.com; s/d US$248/347; P) This expansive, verdant property, with roaming gazelle and other wildlife, sweeps down to the lake's edge. The rooms have a slightly dated style but they're large and semiluxurious. All look out onto the lawns where hippos range at night; an escort is required in the evening.

Fisherman's Camp CAMPGROUND, BANDAS $
(☎50462, 0726870590; fishermanscamp@gmail.com; camping KSh400, tents from KSh500, bandas Sun-Thu per person KSh1300, Fri & Sat per banda KSh4000, 6-person cottage KSh8000) Spread along the grassy tree-laden southern shore, Fisherman's is a perennial favourite of campers, overland companies and backpackers. The site is huge, and weekends get busy, with a noisy party atmosphere more akin to Glastonbury than Africa; keep an eye

on your belongings. During the week things are much calmer and, depending on your point of view, more pleasant. Hippos lurk by the lakeshore (they're kept out by an electric fence). Nonguests are charged KSh100 admission.

Crayfish Camp CAMPGROUND $

(☎2020239; camping KSh500, r per person with shared bathroom KSh1700, s/d KSh4000/6000; @) Following Fisherman's lead, the Crayfish Camp can seem more like a beer garden than a campsite, but it's not a bad option. The rooms are simple but adequate (full- and half-board rates are available), but the real novelty is sleeping on a mattress crammed into a converted combivan, car or boat! Meals are available from KSh700.

Lake Naivasha Country Club HISTORIC HOTEL $$$

(☎020-4450636; www.sunafricahotels.com; s/d/tr US$180/245/335; P) Set in manicured lawns and dating back to 1937 – when it was a playground for the Happy Valley set (see p295) of colonial Kenya – this country club has a certain old-world charm. Rooms aren't quite as luxurious as you might expect, but they're a step back in time nonetheless.

Enashipai HOTEL $$$

(☎020-3592627; www.enashipai.com; s/d US$210/295; P@) This swish place opened in April 2011, and is easily the most polished of the places along the southern lake shore. Enashipai is a Maasai name that means 'State of Happiness', and while this lovely place lacks a little character, the rooms are beautifully turned out, and there's an on-site spa resort.

Elsamere Conservation Centre HOTEL $$$

(☎2021055; www.elsamere.com; s/d US$145/240; P) The rooms inside this impressive lakeside conservation centre are a touch overpriced in our book, but one of them has a high-novelty value as the former bedroom of Joy Adamson.

Moi North Lake Road

TOP CHOICE Olerai House GUESTHOUSE $$$

(☎020-8048602; www.olerai.com; s/d full board US$390/600) Hidden under a blanket of tropical flowers, this beautiful house is like something from a fairy tale, where petals dust the beds and floors, zebras and vervet monkeys hang out with pet dogs, and your every whim is attended to. Perhaps best of all, the camp is owned by renowned elephant conservationists Iain and Oria Douglas-Hamilton – if they're at home, there are few more fascinating hosts in Kenya.

Crater Lake Camp TENTED CAMP $$$

(☎2020613; www.mericagrouphotels.com; camping KSh500, s/d full board US$187/280;) This tented camp inside the private Crater Lake Game Sanctuary (p113) places nestles among trees and overlooks the tiny jade-green crater lake. The tents aren't exactly luxurious, but they are extremely comfortable, and the honeymoon tent contains a whirlpool bath and other romantic essentials. Nature walks and night safaris are included in the price.

Eating & Drinking

Since food and drinks can be had at most of the accommodation options mentioned previously, and most offer full-board packages, there's little in the way of independent wining and dining.

Acacia Café KENYAN $

(mains KSh100-150; ⊙lunch & dinner) If the restaurants found at most of the camps just aren't 'African' enough for you (or cost too much) then slide on over to this fine little locals' cafe in DCK Town where you'll get beef stew for KSh125.

Fischers Tower Hotel INTERNATIONAL $

(meals KSh100-500; ⊙7am-midnight) Not long after turning onto the Moi South Lake Rd, this busy place on the left does everything from snacks, salads and burgers to beef kebabs and lamb curry. The garden tables (difficult to snaffle on weekends) are a good place to have a beer.

THE STONE LADY

Fischer's Tower (p116) may look like nothing more than a needle of rock, but if that rock could talk, which it once could, it would tell you how it was actually a pretty young Maasai woman, sent from her home village against her wishes to marry a fearless warrior. As she left she was warned not to turn back, but in her sadness she couldn't resist one last longing glance at her old home. As soon as she did so, she was cast into stone and remains rooted to the spot to this day.

Fisherman's Camp INTERNATIONAL $$
(mains KSh250-500; ⏲lunch & dinner) Everything from fruit smoothies and chicken tikka to burgers and chilli con carne make their way onto plates at this atmospheric restaurant and bar. Be prepared to wait, and wait, and wait for your food. It's easily the most popular spot for well-to-do Kenyans on weekends.

Shopping

Elmenteita Weavers Ltd HANDICRAFTS
(off Moi South Lake Rd; www.elmenteitaweavers.com; ⏲8am-5pm) This small-scale cooperative shares a compound with other like-minded concerns (including a pottery workshop). You can watch them weaving and they turn out a small but lovely range of blankets, rugs and other textiles.

Getting There & Away

Frequent matatus (KSh100, one hour) run along Moi South Lake Rd between Naivasha town and Kongoni on the lake's western side, passing the turn-offs to Hell's Gate National Park and Fisherman's Camp (KSh70).

Getting Around

Most lodges and camps hire mountain bikes if you're heading for Hell's Gate National Park; costs start from KSh700 per day. Check the bikes carefully before paying.

Hell's Gate National Park

Looking at animals from the safety of your car is all well and good, but let's be honest – after a while who *doesn't* get the urge to get out of the vehicle and re-enter the food chain? At Hell's Gate you really can do that, because this unique park actively encourages you to walk or, better still, cycle, through an African savannah teeming with large animals. You'll find that your senses become heightened tenfold when a buffalo starts looking annoyed with you and wow, giraffes really are tall aren't they? It's largely a predator-free zone – a few leopards and hyenas roam the park but they're rarely seen.

The scenery here is dramatic, with rich ochre soils and savannah grasses squeezed between looming cliffs of rusty columnar basalt. It's all aglow in the early morning.

HELL'S GATE NATIONAL PARK

Why Go Dramatic volcanic scenery; a chance to walk or cycle through wildlife areas.

When to Go June to March.

Practicalities Drive, walk or cycle to the main Elsa Gate from Lake Naivasha.

Sights

Hell's Gate Gorge PARK
(adult/child US$25/15) The gorge that runs through the heart of the park is a wide, deep valley hemmed in by sheer, rusty-hued rock walls. Marking its eastern entrance is **Fischer's Tower**, a 25m-high volcanic column named after Gustav Fischer, a German explorer who reached the gorge in 1882. Commissioned by the Hamburg Geographical Society to find a route from Mombasa to Lake Victoria, Fischer was stopped by territorial Maasai, who slaughtered almost his entire party.

All through this valley you'll come across zebras, the occasional giraffe, warthogs and various antelope species, while birds of prey circle overhead. Even if you visit nowhere else in the park, this main valley is worth the entry fee.

Lower Gorge CANYON
(Ol Njorowa; guide per hr KSh500) Rising from the main gorge's southern end is the large **Central Tower**, an unusual volcanic plug. A picnic site and ranger's post are close by, from where an excellent walk descends into the Lower Gorge (Ol Njorowa). This narrow sandstone ravine has been sculpted by water, and the incoming light casts marvellous shadows. In some places the riverbed is broad and dry, in others you'll find yourself wading through a shallow stream and scrambling down a steep and slippery descent. Some steps have been cut into the rock, and although some parts seem perilous, whole school parties manage it on a regular basis. We recommend taking a guide.

Buffalo Circuit PARK
A well-signposted track loops away to the south from close to the main Elsa Gate, climbing up and over the hills before rejoining the main valley after 14km. En route, you'll have some outstanding views of Mt Longonot, and there's generally more wildlife here, including giraffe, various antelope species and the odd buffalo or two. Close to the Elsa Gate end of the trail, a side track

Hell's Gate National Park

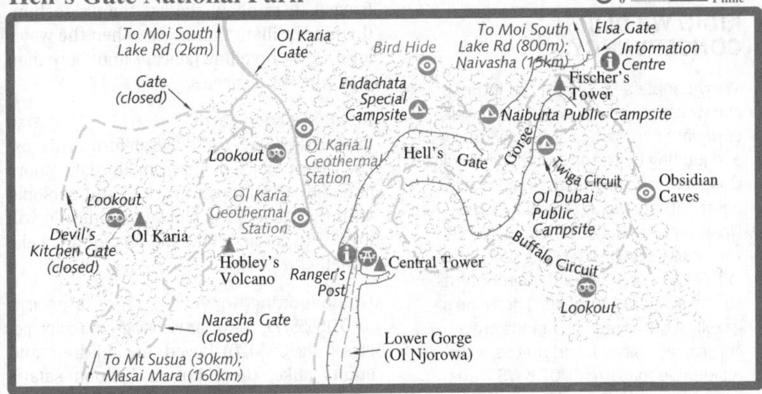

leads for 2km to the Obsidian Cave, where you'll find moderately interesting examples of the glassy black rock so characteristic of Rift Valley lava flows. The Buffalo Circuit would be a fairly strenuous walk or cycle, but it's accessible by 2WD vehicle, except after heavy rain.

Activities

If you intend to **walk** through the park, allow a full day and take plenty of supplies.

Cycling is our favourite way to explore the park, and the main Hell's Gate Gorge is relatively flat; the distance from Elsa Gate to the Lower Gorge is around 7km. Mountain bikes can be rented at Elsa Gate (per day KSh500), but test them out rigorously before handing over the money – dodgy brakes and gears are common problems.

The sheer rock walls of Hell's Gate are just made for **climbing** and, thankfully, the park has two resident climbers, **Simon Kiane** and **James Maina** (☎0720909718, 0727039388), who act as instructors and guides; they also have some basic equipment. They offer relatively easy 10- to 15-minute climbs of Fischer's Tower (US$10) and more challenging routes on the gorge's sheer red walls (US$100). If they're not in their usual place at the base of Fischer's Tower, give them a call or check at the park gate before you enter.

Sleeping

Most visitors stay at one Lake Naivasha's many lodges and camps, but the park has three gorgeous, if rudimentary, campgrounds.

Naiburta Public Campsite CAMPGROUND $
(camping US$15) Naiburta, sitting on a gentle rise on the northern side of the Hell's Gate Gorge and commanding fine views west past Fischer's Tower, is the most scenic site, and has basic toilets, an open banda for cooking and freshwater taps.

Ol Dubai Public Campsite CAMPGROUND $
(camping US$15) Resting on the gorge's southern side and accessible from the Buffalo Circuit track, Ol Dubai has identical facilities to Naiburta. It offers views west to the orange bluffs, and the puffs of steam from the geothermal power station at the far end of the park.

Endachata Special Campsite CAMPGROUND $
(camping US$30) This 'special' campsite has no services, and besides absolute solitude, offers no more ambience than the cheaper public sites.

Information

Kenya Wildlife Service (www.kws.org/parks/parks_reserves/HGNP.html; park admission adult/child US$25/15, safari card not valid).

Information Centre (☎050-2020284; Elsa Gate)

Getting There & Around

The usual access point to the park is through the main Elsa Gate, 1km from Moi South Lake Rd. With the two gates on the northwest corner of the park closed, the only other gate is Ol Karia.

WORTH A TRIP

KIGIO WILDLIFE CONSERVANCY

Many people believe that the future of conservation in Kenya is in the hands of private companies and individuals, and judging by the superb Kigio Wildlife Conservancy, they might just have a point. Situated along the Naivasha–Nakuru road, this 3500-acre reserve was started on a struggling dairy farm in 1997 and has met with phenomenal success. Zebras, impalas, Thomson's gazelles, buffaloes and elands are all commonly sighted, and there's even a resident leopard. In 2002 KWS translocated eight Rothschild's giraffes here and the first white rhinos have recently been translocated.

Unfortunately, casual visitors are not encouraged to drop in: to visit you must be staying in the supremely comfortable colonial-style **Malewa Ranch House** (☎020-3535878; www.kigio.com; s/d full board US$278/340; 📶), which is rented exclusively to one group at a time.

Naivasha to Nakuru

Besides the odd zebra and gangs of hardened road warriors (baboons) dotting the roadside between Naivasha and Nakuru, there are a few reasons to pull over. The frequent matatus plying this route will happily drop you anywhere you like.

KARIANDUSI PREHISTORIC SITE

The **Kariandusi site** (Map p110; adult/child KSh500/250; ⏲9am-6pm) is signposted off the A104 Hwy near Lake Elmenteita. It was here in the 1920s that the Leakeys (a family of renowned archaeologists) discovered numerous obsidian and lava tools made by early humans between 1.4 million and 200,000 years ago. Two excavation sites are preserved and two galleries display a brief history of early human life.

LAKE ELMENTEITA

Sights & Activities

Lake Elmenteita LAKE

(adult/child KSh500/200, car KSh200, guide KSh300) A major tourist attraction with passing water birds, though strangely less popular with passing humans, Lake Elmenteita has a beautiful soda shoreline that is often fringed in rainbow shades, thanks to hundreds of brilliant flamingos (when the water level's low), breeding pelicans and more than 400 other bird species.

Rosalu Ostrich Farm FARM

(adult/child KSh250/150; ⏲8am-5pm) This ostrich park sits not far from the lake shore and allows you to get up close and personal with these oversized chickens. Children will love it. To get here take the turn-off for Lake Elmenteita Lodge.

Go Ballooning Kenya BALLOONING

(☎0715555777; www.goballooningkenya.com; per person 1hr US$420) Loved by children and adults alike, these hot-air balloon safaris promise the best-possible Rift Valley views.

Sleeping

Elementaita Country Lodge LODGE $$$

(☎020-2220572; www.seasonshotelskenya.com; s/d full board from US$131/213, cottages US$191/294; P📶🏊) Opened in 2010, this fine, expansive property on a rise overlooking the lake is probably the pick of a rather expensive bunch. Most rooms are well-sized, all look towards the lake, and the decor, though a little dated, has some character.

Lake Elmenteita Lodge LODGE $$$

(☎050-50648; www.jacarandahotels.com; s/d full board US$210/300; P@🏊) Sitting around a mazelike bougainvillea garden, the slightly dated cottages here are overpriced, but nevertheless are full on a regular basis. The bar's terrace, with good lake views, is crying out for the company of you and a gin and tonic. Numerous activities are on offer, including horse riding (KSh1800 per hour) and nature walks (KSh500 per person).

Nakuru

☎051 / POP 300,000

Despite being Kenya's fourth-largest city and despite its busy markets that crowd the downtown streets, Nakuru still feels like an overgrown country town. Its relaxed atmosphere and proximity to the outstanding Lake Nakuru National Park and the dramatic Menengai Crater make it a good base for a few days.

Sleeping

Don't be surprised if a taxi or safari tries to direct you to the hotel of their choice; we'd advise you not to listen to them.

Nakuru

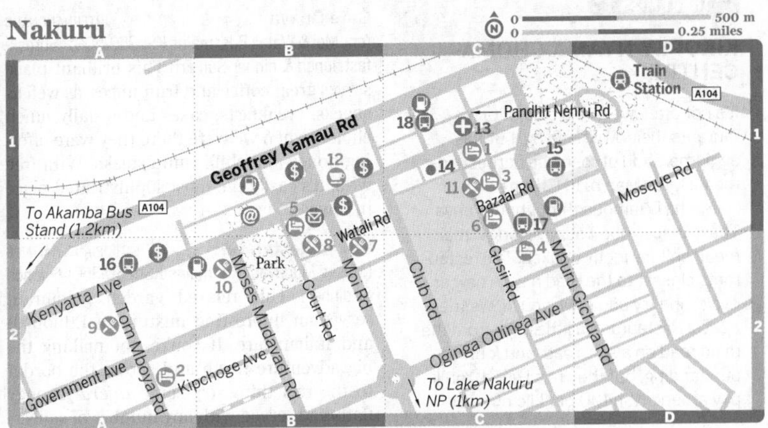

Merica Hotel HOTEL $$
(☎2216013; www.mericagrouphotels.com; Kenyatta Ave; s/d US$80/125; ❄📶🏊) This contemporary tower hosts Nakuru's best rooms. Ride the glass elevators up the sunlit atrium to well-appointed rooms, large enough to host a wildebeest migration. The bathrooms could do with a little freshening up.

New Mount Sinai Hotel HOTEL $
(Bazaar Rd; s/tw with shared bathroom KSh500/600) Foreigners are considered 'special' and therefore get the posh, and clean, rooms right up on the roof (5th floor, no lift), with distant views of Lake Nakuru. The rooms are basic and stripped of anything that's not completely necessary (eg you'll have to be a porcelain jockey – the toilets lack seats), but most rooms have mosquito nets. If there was a fire the numerous padlocked security gates would be a right laugh to get past.

Care Guest House HOTEL $
(Pandhit Nehru Rd; s/tw KSh500/800) This is a surprise: at first glance you fear the worst, but the pokey pink rooms are actually tidy and all have attached bathrooms with hot, OK warm, well all right, possibly tepid, showers.

Carnation Hotel HOTEL $
(☎2215360; Mosque Rd; s/tw KSh1000/1550) Carnation Hotel is the town's prettiest budget rose. Rooms are simple, but with their multicoloured tiled floors and kitsch bed sheets they have plenty of character, as well as hot showers.

Nakuru

Sleeping

1 Avenue Suites Hotel C1
2 Bontana Hotel A2
3 Care Guest House C1
4 Carnation Hotel C2
5 Merica Hotel B1
6 New Mount Sinai Hotel C1

Eating

7 Café Guava B2
8 Courtyard Restaurant B2
9 Hygienic Butchery A2
10 Kokeb Restaurant B2
11 Ribbons Restaurant C1

Drinking

12 Nakuru Coffee House B1

Information

13 Aga Khan University Hospital (Nakuru Medical Centre) C1
14 Crater Travel C1

Transport

15 Bus & Matatu Station C1
16 Easy Coach A2
17 Matatus to Kampi ya Samaki & Marigat C1
18 Mololine Prestige Shuttle C1

Avenue Suites Hotel HOTEL $$
(☎2210607; avenuesuiteshotel@yahoo.co.uk; Kenyatta Ave; s/d/tr KSh1400/2500/3700) The rooms here on busy Kenyatta Ave are probably the best in their price range, but they still have

DON'T MISS

KIKOPEY NYAMA CHOMA CENTRE

It's not often we give a cluster of restaurants their own heading, but this agglomeration of roadside barbecued-meat stalls (Map p110) 31km north of Naivasha is famous throughout Kenya. These places don't survive long if their meat isn't perfectly cooked. The restaurants closest to the road hassle new arrivals, and try and draw you in. We tried Acacia Restaurant, a little back from the main road on a side road, and found it outstanding, but they're all good. You'll pay around KSh400 per kilo of meat.

that uninspiring air that pervades so many Nakuru hotels. Ask for a room at the back; they're quieter.

Bontana Hotel HOTEL $$
(☎2210134; www.bontanahotel-nakuru.com; Tom Mboya Rd; s/d from US$70/110;) Quieter than other downtown options, this place has pleasant rooms with balconies, but the old bathrooms let down the side a little.

Eating

For self-caterers, there are several well-stocked supermarkets on or just off Kenyatta Avenue.

TOP CHOICE **Ribbons Restaurant** KENYAN $
(Gusii Rd; mains KSh80-250; 24hr) One of the best restaurants for cheap Kenyan dishes, this 1st-floor restaurant has a balcony overlooking the street. In addition to whole tilapia with ugali, other local specialties include *githeri* (maize and beans) and *ndengu* (pea stew). Take the staircase signed as Care Guest House to get here.

TOP CHOICE **Hygienic Butchery** KENYAN $
(Tom Mboya Rd; mains KSh180-250; lunch & dinner) Great name, great place. The Kenyan tradition of *nyama choma* (barbecued meats) is alive and well here. Sidle up to the counter, try a piece of tender mutton or beef and order half a kilo (per person) of whichever takes your fancy, along with chapatis or ugali (no sauce!). The meat will then be brought to your table, carved up, and you dig in with your hands. Bliss! It also serves stews, barbecued chicken and other dishes.

Café Guava INTERNATIONAL $
(cnr Moi & Watali Rds; mains KSh350-500; breakfast, lunch & dinner Sun-Fri) This brilliant place serves great coffee and fruit juices, as well as snacks, breakfasts, cakes and a daily lunch choice; when we were there they were offering honey-and-chilli rump steaks. With free wi-fi, it's easily the most sophisticated place in town.

Kokeb Restaurant ETHIOPIAN & ITALIAN $
(Moses Mudavadi Rd; mains KSh260-350; lunch & dinner) This relaxed garden restaurant serves an interesting mixture of Ethiopian and Italian fare. If you're not making the big adventure north and across the border to the real thing, try some *injera* (spongy flatbread served with any number of sauces) and *wat* (stew) here.

Courtyard Restaurant KENYAN & INTERNATIONAL $
(off Court Rd; meals KSh190-350; lunch & dinner) In addition to simple Kenyan fare that includes *matoke* (plantains), a range of stews and fried chicken or fish, this place scratches a variety of itches, from Indian to Italian and from beef stew to seafood, though you'd be lucky to find them all actually available. As the name suggests, there's an outdoor courtyard.

Drinking

TOP CHOICE **Nakuru Coffee House** CAFE
(Kenyatta Ave; coffee cup/mug KSh40/100) For a straightforward caffeine fix, this '50s-style cafe sells excellent freshly roasted coffee, which is surprisingly rare in this coffee-rich country. It also serves breakfast.

Information

Changing cash in Nakuru is easy, with numerous banks and foreign exchange bureaus. Barclays Bank's ATMs are the most reliable.

Aga Khan University Hospital (Nakuru Medical Centre; Kenyatta Ave) Various lab services including malaria tests

Crater Travel (☎2215019; cratertravel@yahoo.com; off Kenyatta Ave) Good for air tickets and excursions into Lake Nakuru National Park.

Petmary Cyber Café (Kenyatta Ave; per hr KSh60; 8am-5.30pm Mon-Fri, to 1pm Sat) Nakuru's fastest connections

Getting There & Away

PARKING Street parking in central Nakuru requires a ticket from the nearest warden; ask at your hotel for help.

SHUTTLE A cut above your average matatus (it only has 10 seats for 10 passengers, and is driven more carefully), **Mololine Prestige Shuttle** (off Geoffrey Kamau Rd) has services to Nairobi (KSh400), Eldoret (KSh400) and Kisumu (KSh600).

MATATUS Most matatus leave from the chaotic stands along Mburu Gichua Rd. Services include Naivasha (KSh150 to KSh200, 1¼ hours), Nyahururu (KSh175, 1¼ hours), Kericho (KSh350, two hours), Nyeri (KSh350, 2½ hours), Eldoret (KSh300, 2¾ hours), Nairobi (KSh400, three hours) and Kisumu (KSh500 to KSh600, 3½ hours).

LAKES BOGORIA & BARINGO Matatus for Lake Baringo (Kampi Ya Samaki; KSh250, 2½hrs) or Marigat (for Lake Bogoria; KSh150, two hours) leave from the southern end of Pandhit Nehru Rd.

BUS **Easy Coach** (Kenyatta Ave) is one of several bus companies offering services to Nairobi (KSh500, three hours), Eldoret (KSh650, 2¾hrs) and Kisumu (KSh750, 3½hrs).

Around Nakuru

MENENGAI CRATER

From town it doesn't look like much, but the striking red cliffs of **Menengai Crater** (adult/child KSh600/50, guides KSh1000; ⏲7am-5pm), which radiate outwards and encircle a 90-sq-km cauldron of convoluted black lava flows, is quite something once you've scrambled up to its summit. While lush vegetation is now proliferating on the harsh crater floor, some 500m below, the violent and dramatic volcanic history is easily seen; the crater was formed over 1 million years ago, although the last eruption was just 350 years back.

A grim local legend states that the plumes of steam rising from the bottom are the souls of defeated Maasai warriors, thrown into the crater after a territorial battle, trying to make their way to heaven.

On the crater's western side is the **Mau Mau Cave**, where guerrillas hid from British colonial forces during the Mau Mau uprising.

James Maina (☎0723031150; jamesmaina11@yahoo.com), a good local guide to the crater, can take you down into the crater and back up again (a four-hour roundtrip) or to the Mau Mau Cave.

There's a small group of *dukas* (shops) at the main viewpoint selling drinks and trinkets.

Security has improved since the Kenya Forest Service took over the site, but it's an isolated 9km walk (or 6km from the main gate). Hikers should never make the climb alone.

There are plans to improve the track leading to the summit. A taxi up and back shouldn't cost more than KSh2000.

HYRAX HILL PREHISTORIC SITE

This **archaeological site** (Map p123; adult/child KSh500/250; ⏲9am-6pm), 4km outside Nakuru, is a great spot for a peaceful amble away from the rhinos and tourists. It contains a museum and the remains of three settlements excavated between 1937 and the late 1980s, the oldest being possibly 3000 years old, the most recent 200 to 300 years old.

You're free to wander the site, but it's rather cryptic and a guide is useful – a tip of KSh150 is plenty. The North-East Village, which is believed to be about 400 years old, sits closest to the museum and once housed 13 enclosures. Only the 1965 excavation of Pit D remains open. It was here that a great number of pottery fragments were found, some of which have been pieced together into complete jars and are displayed in the museum.

From Pit D the trail climbs to the scant remains of the stone-walled hill-fort near the top of Hyrax Hill itself. You can continue to the peak, from where there's a fine view of Lake Nakuru in the distance.

Looking down the other side of the hill, you'll see two 'c'-shaped Iron Age stone hut foundations at the base. Just north of the foundations, a series of Iron Age burial pits containing 19 skeletons was found. The majority were male and lots of them had been decapitated, so a number of colourful explanations have been offered.

Nearby, two Neolithic burial mounds and several other Iron Age burial pits were also discovered. The large collection of items found in these pits included a real puzzle – six Indian coins, one of them 500 years old, and two others dating from 1918 and 1919.

On a more lively note, there's a *bao* (traditional game that's played throughout East Africa) board carved into a rock outcrop between the Iron Age settlements and the museum.

It's possible to camp (per tent KSh250) here, though facilities are basic and you'd need to be entirely self-sufficient.

Local matatus to Naivasha or Nairobi will take you past the turn-off (about 1km from the site), just south of Nakuru.

Lake Nakuru National Park

One of Kenya's finest national parks is just a few kilometres from the hustle of central Nakuru. Although the massive flamingo flocks that made the lake famous aren't always present, there are lions, leopards, endangered Rothschild's giraffes, buffaloes and zebras. Perhaps best of all, this is one of the best places in Kenya to see black and white rhinos. The landscape is fringed with euphorbia trees, acacia forests, an escarpment or two, and at least one lovely waterfall.

Sights

Lake Circuit PARK

The park's relatively small size (188 sq km) makes it easy to get around in a day, including a full lake circuit and time spent exploring the riverine acacia forests and open country in the park's southern reaches. The forests anywhere in the park are good for leopards. If you're very, very lucky, you'll catch a glimpse of a rare tree-climbing lion. The park's rhinos (around 80 white and 60 black) tend to stick fairly close to the lakeshore and sightings are almost a given on the southern shore. The shy black rhinos, browsers by nature and much more aggressive, are more difficult to spot than the white rhinos. Warthogs are common all over the park, as are waterbucks, zebras and buffaloes, while Thomson's gazelles, impala and reedbucks can be seen further into the bush. Around the cliffs you may catch sight of hyraxes and birds of prey amid the countless baboons; black-and-white colobus monkeys are present in small numbers in the forests near the eastern shore of the lake. A small herd of hippos generally frequents the lake's northern shore. Even if the flamingos aren't in residence, the thousands of breeding pelicans still put on a show.

To get the best view that takes in much of the park, head up to **Baboon Cliff**; it's at its best late afternoon as the sun casts a warm glow over the lake. The **Makalia Falls**, at the extreme southern end of the park, are really impressive (by Kenyan waterfall standards) after the rains.

> **LAKE NAKURU NATIONAL PARK**
>
> **Why Go** To see lions, leopards, Rothschild's giraffes, black and white rhinos, and sometimes flamingos, plus the pretty and varied landscape
>
> **When to Go** June to March. For birdwatching, November to March.
>
> **Practicalities** Driving in from Nakuru there are three gates (Main, Lanet and Nderit); Main Gate is the only gate where you can top up your safari card. The park is accessible in a 2WD.

Sleeping & Eating

If you're camping, you'll have to bring your own food. Always make sure your tents are securely zipped or the vervet monkeys and baboons will make a right mess while cleaning you out.

TOP CHOICE **Sarova Lion Hill Lodge** LODGE $$$

(020-2315139; www.sarovahotels.com; s/d full board US$366/486; @) Sitting high up the lake's eastern slopes, this lodge offers first-class service and comfort. The views from the open-air restaurant-bar and from most rooms are great. Rooms are understated but pretty, while the flashy suites are large and absolutely stunning. It's certainly one of the friendlier top-end places, and on quiet days you may even get the residents' rate, which is less than half that quoted here.

TOP CHOICE **Wildlife Club of Kenya Guesthouse** HOSTEL $

(0710579944; r with shared bathroom per person KSh1250) For atmosphere alone, this beats anywhere in Nakuru hands down. It's like staying in a secluded cottage in the countryside, but instead of a garden full of bunny rabbits it's a garden full of rhinos and buffaloes! There are six simple rooms here, as well as an equipped kitchen and a nicely appointed dining room. With advance notice, the guard can cook.

Lake Nakuru Lodge LODGE $$$

(850228; www.lakenakurulodge.com; s/d full board US$250/340; P) Another excellent lodge in the southwestern corner of the park, this place is (like so many national park lodges) overpriced if you look solely at the rooms,

Lake Nakuru National Park

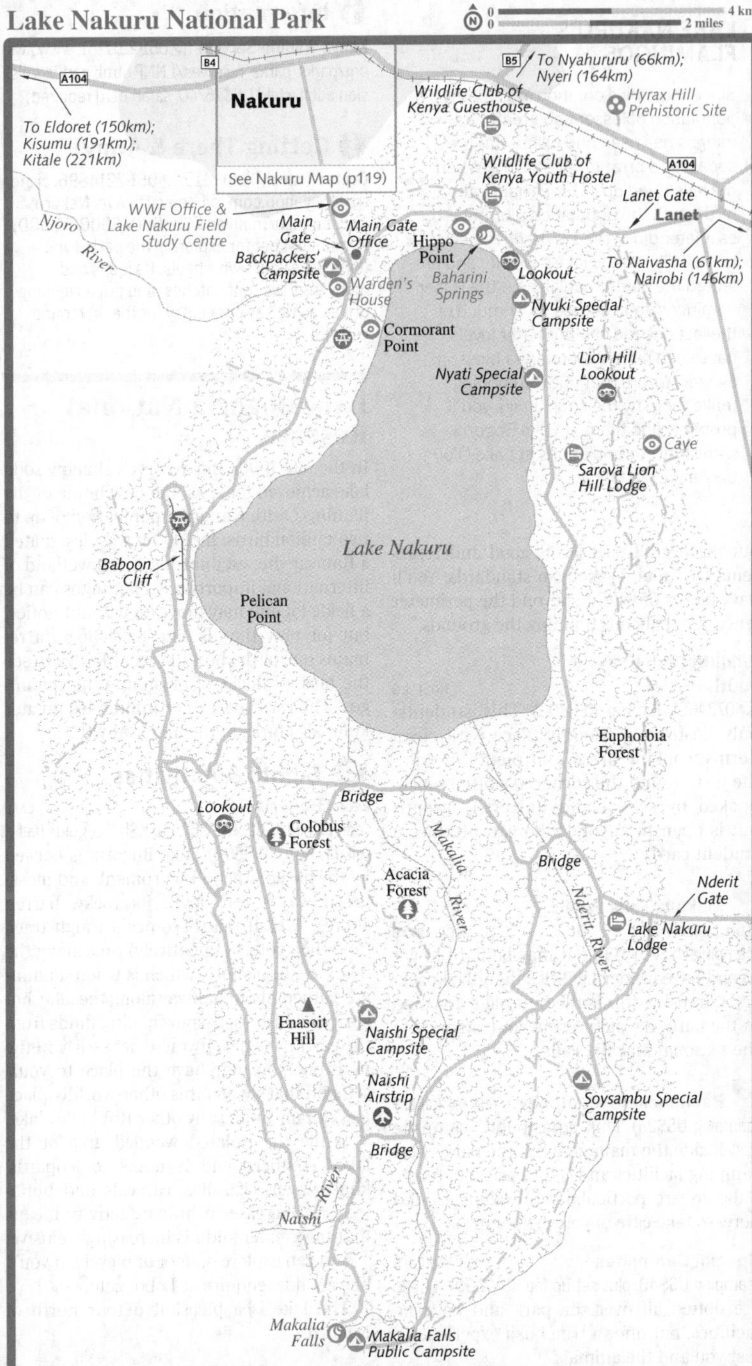

LAKE NAKURU'S FLAMINGOS

Since the park's creation in 1961, the population of lesser and greater flamingos has risen and fallen with the soda lake's erratic water levels. When the lake dried up in 1962 (happy first birthday!), the population plummeted, as it later did in the 1970s when heavy rainfall diluted the lake's salinity and affected the blue-green algae – the lesser flamingos' food source. Over much of the last decade healthy water levels have seen flamingo numbers blossom again. If future droughts or flooding make them fly the coop again, you'll probably find them at Lake Bogoria, with smaller populations at Lake Oloiden and Lake Magadi.

but the overall package is good and represents OK value by Kenyan standards. You'll have plenty of wildlife beyond the perimeter fence, and baboons roaming the grounds.

Wildlife Club of Kenya Youth Hostel HOSTEL $
(☎0734661463; dm KSh800) This students-only hostel is a friendly place with clean dorms, cooking areas and plenty of wildlife just around the corner. It's often block-booked by school and university groups but is open to anyone who can produce a student card.

Makalia Falls Public Campsite CAMPGROUND $
(camping US$25) While it may be hard to get to and have cruder facilities than Backpackers' Campsite, this is the best place to camp in the park. It's picturesque and sits next to the seasonal Makalia Falls.

Backpackers' Campsite CAMPGROUND $
(camping US$25) This large public campsite just inside the main gate has the park's best camping facilities and is the easiest to reach. Baboons are particularly prevalent around here, so take care of your belongings.

Special Campsites CAMPGROUND $
(camping US$40, plus set-up fee KSh7500) These are dotted all over the park and have no facilities, but offer a true bush experience – just you and the animals.

Information

Kenya Wildlife Service (☎051-2217151; www.kws.org/parks/parks_reserves/LNNP.html; park admission adult/child US$75/40, safari card required)

Getting There & Away

Crater Travel (Map p119; ☎051-2214896; cratertravel@yahoo.com; off Kenyatta Ave, Nakuru; 5hr car/jeep/minivan KSh5000/6000/11,000) is your best bet for exploring the park if you don't have your own wheels. Its jeeps and minivans have roof hatches, and prices include driver, as well as park entry for the driver and vehicle.

Lake Bogoria National Reserve

In the late 1990s this reserve's shallow soda lake achieved fame as 'the new home of the flamingo', with a migrant population of up to two million birds. In 2000 it was designated a Ramsar site, establishing it as a wetland of international importance. Flamingos can be a fickle lot and may move on without notice, but for now the alkaline Lake Bogoria remains one of the best places in Kenya to see the massed flocks of blushing pink flamingos. The rare and rather impressive greater kudu also lurks in the undergrowth.

Sights & Activities

Lake Bogoria LAKE
(adult/child KSh2500/250, car KSh750, guide half-/full day KSh750/1500) Lake Bogoria is backed by the bleak Siracho Escarpment, and moss-green waves roll down its rocky, barren shores. A road that becomes a rough track (and then peters out entirely) runs along the lake's western shore, which is where flamingos gather. About halfway along the lake, hot springs and geysers spew boiling fluids from the earth's insides. If you're here early in the morning, you may have the place to yourself and that's when this other-worldly place feels totally unlike any other Rift Valley lake.

While the isolated wooded area at the lake's southern end is home to leopards, klipspringers, gazelles, caracals and buffaloes, an increase in human activity means that the greater kudu is increasingly elusive.

You can explore on foot or bicycle. If you'd like a guide, enquire at Loboi gate.

The lake is a pleasant detour north of Nakuru.

Kesubo Swamp — BIRDWATCHING

Just outside the reserve's northern boundary and on the road in from the main B4 road north, Kesubo Swamp is a birdwatcher's paradise: more than 200 species have been recorded and one lucky person spotted 96 species in one hour – a Kenyan record. You'll need to park your car close to the Lake Bogoria Spa Resort and walk around the perimeter.

Sleeping & Eating

Camping at the pretty **Fig Tree Camp** and **Acacia Camp** are the only sleeping options within the reserve. At the time of research, both of these campsites were inaccessible from the north due to road slippage, and as such were closed. To check whether they're open, ask at the reserve's main gate whether you need to enter via the reserve's southern Emsos Gate.

The nearby town of Marigat is a good place to buy local produce or to have a meal.

Lake Bogoria Spa Resort — HOTEL $$

(051-2216867; www.lbogoriasparesort.com; s/d from US$85/108;) Set in lovely grounds around 2km northwest of the Loboi Gate, the long-standing Lake Bogoria Spa Resort is about to undergo a desperately needed overhaul. If all goes to plan, the prices shouldn't rise too drastically in the process. Until it does renovate, rooms are fine but tired and uninspiring. The pool is fed by a nearby hot spring.

Getting There & Away

GATES Entrances are at Loboi (north), Emsos (south) and Maji Moto (west); only Loboi is accessible by 2WD vehicle.

PETROL The nearest petrol is available in Marigat.

PUBLIC TRANSPORT Matatus run to Loboi Gate from Marigat (KSh100, 30 minutes). Regular matatus serve Marigat from Nakuru (KSh250, two hours) and Kabarnet (KSh165, 1¼ hours).

Lake Baringo

051

This rare freshwater Rift Valley lake, encircled by mountains and with a surface dotted with picturesque islands and hippos batting their eyelids, is probably the most idyllic of the Rift Valley lakes, as well as the most remote. Topping the scenic surrounds is an amazing abundance of birdlife, with over 450 of the 1100 or so bird species native to Kenya present. This is serious birdwatching territory.

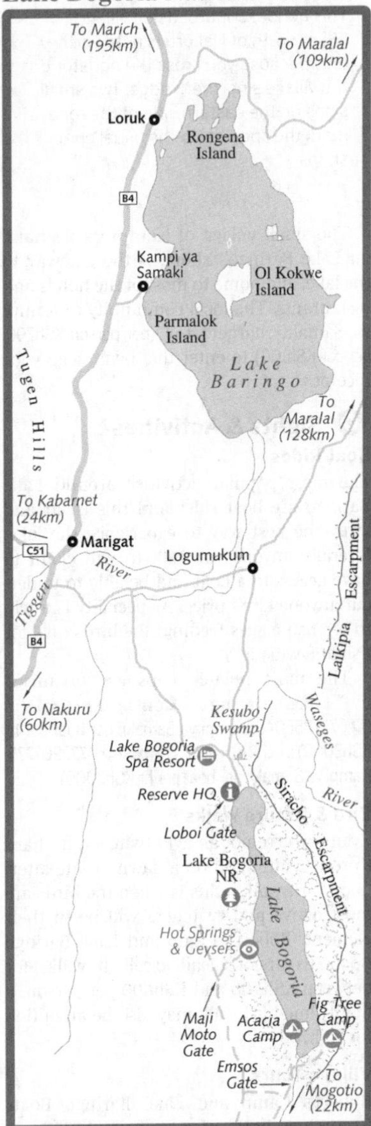

With some of the best-value accommodation in the Kenyan interior and a go-slow vibe, the lake is easily one of the Rift Valley's highlights.

MOGOTIO

This nondescript roadside village 38km north of Nakuru is noteworthy only because you cross the equator on the village's northern edge. Two small signs on the eastern side of the road mark the spot, as do the usual curio shops.

The small village of **Kampi ya Samaki**, on Lake Baringo's shore, is the gateway to the lake, and home to most of the hotels and restaurants. The local community at Kampi ya Samaki charge a toll (per person KSh200, per car KSh100) to enter the town; keep your receipt.

Sights & Activities

Boat Rides

The most popular activities around Lake Baringo are boat rides and this is far and away the best way to experience the lake. Literally anyone you talk to will claim to have access to a boat and be able to undercut anyone else's price. A speciality is a trip to see fish eagles feeding; the birds dive for fish at a whistle.

The most reliable trips are organised by **Lake Baringo Boats Excursions** (0727856048; Kampi ya Samaki; per boat per hr KSh3000) and **Roberts' Camp** (0733207775; Kampi ya Samaki; per boat per hr KSh3000).

Bird & Nature Walks

Even if you're not an avid twitcher, it's hard to resist setting off on a dawn or late afternoon bird walk – this is when the birds are most active and twitchers will be in their element. Robert's Camp and Lake Baringo Boats Excursions lead excellent walks for between KSh400 and KSh600 per person; a night-time bird walk may also be an option for KSh700.

Village Tours

Robert's Camp and Lake Baringo Boats Excursions both offer tours (KSh1200 per person) to Pokot, Tugen and Njemps villages close to the lake; the Njemps are cousins of the Maasai and live on Ol Kokwe and Parmalok Islands and around the lakeshore, mainly practising pastoralism and fishing.

Sleeping

TOP CHOICE **Robert's Camp** BANDA & CAMPGROUND $

(0733207775; www.robertscamp.com; Kampi ya Samaki; camping KSh500, s/d bandas from KSh2000/3400, 4-person cottages KSh7500; P) As one reader said, 'This place keeps getting better and better', and we couldn't agree more. It's right on the lake shore and full of chirping birds, wallowing hippos and toothy crocodiles. It doesn't matter whether you opt for camping in your own tent, or staying in a beautifully furnished banda or extravagant cottage, what you get for your money here is, quite simply, superb value. You could happily stay here for days and days without a care in the world and, for our money, this is as good as Kenya gets. Numerous excursions are organised here too.

Lake Baringo Club LODGE $$

(020-4450636; www.sunafricahotels.com; Kampi ya Samaki; s/d full board US$160/180; P) Set amid lovely grounds that descend gently down to the lakeshore, this old-style hotel has a colonial air and reasonable, if slightly overpriced, rooms. It offers a full (if pricey) array of bird walks and boat tours.

Weavers Lodge HOTEL $

(0721556153; Kampi ya Samaki; r KSh600; P) Down a rocky alley off the town's main drag, you'll find music-filled African fun at this simple lodging, which has clean rooms with attached bathrooms and solid mattresses. This is where the safari drivers stay, which is a good sign.

Bahari Lodge & Hotel HOTEL $

(0726857947; Kampi ya Samaki; per person with shared bathroom KSh300; P) Bahari is as cheap as they come in the village. The rooms are basic and a touch shabby, but the owners are friendly and it's fine for a night.

Eating & Drinking

Self-caterers should note that while some foodstuffs may be available at Roberts' Camp, fresh vegetables and fruit are generally in short supply in Kampi ya Samaki. Bring much of what you need – Marigat usually has a reasonable selection.

TOP CHOICE **Thirsty Goat** INTERNATIONAL $$

(Roberts' Camp, Kampi ya Samaki; mains KSh450-650; breakfast, lunch & dinner) This lovely open-air restaurant and bar serves a welcome

RIFT VALLEY LAKES IN PERIL

Kenya's Rift Valley lakes may seem pristine, but their ecosystems are facing serious threats to their well being.

Despite being listed as Kenya's fourth Ramsar site in January 2002, Lake Baringo faces numerous threats, among them droughts, falling water levels, severe siltation due to soil erosion around the seasonal *luggas* (dry river beds) and overfishing.

In the case of Lake Naivasha, tourism and the wealth generated by the flower farms has spawned massive development. In addition, pesticides and fertilisers are seeping into the lake. Irrigation has further destabilised erratic water levels; the lake is currently receding and now only spreads over 139 sq km, which is, according to the WWF, around half of its original size. The lake's ecology has also been interfered with on a number of other occasions, notably with the introduction of foreign fish (for sports and commercial fisheries), crayfish, the South American coypu (an aquatic rodent that initially escaped from a fur farm) and various aquatic plants, including the dreaded water hyacinth.

For these reasons Naivasha has been the focus of conservation efforts and in 1995, after years of lobbying from the Lake Naivasha Riparian Association (LNRA), the lake was designated a Ramsar site, officially recognising it as a wetland of international importance. Besides educating the locals dependent on the lake about the environmental issues involved, the LNRA, Elsamere Conservation Centre and other organisations work to establish a code of conduct among the local growers that will maintain the lake's biodiversity. Among the positive outcomes is that since 2007, all local businesses have been required to submit environmental-impact statements. But much remains to be done.

variety of foreign fare, with hornbills regular visitors to your table. There's a range of dishes here from Moroccan meatballs or chicken curry to the spicy 'spitting cobra pizza'. Easily the best place to eat in town.

Bahari Lodge & Hotel KENYAN $
(Kampi ya Samaki; mains from KSh300; ⌚lunch & dinner) Of Kampi ya Samaki's few remaining local restaurants, this is the best place for cheap food, with fish, chicken and vegetables all on the menu. You'll need to order at least a couple of hours in advance.

ℹ Getting There & Away

Lake access is easiest from Kampi ya Samaki on the lake's western shore, some 15km north of Marigat.

BUS A 25-seater bus leaves for Nakuru each morning (KSh300) between 6.30am and 9.30am (it departs when full).

PICK-UPS Slightly more regular pick-up trucks head to Marigat (KSh100, 30 minutes) and catch more frequent matatus from there to Nakuru (KSh250, two hours) or Kabarnet (KSh200, 1¼ hours).

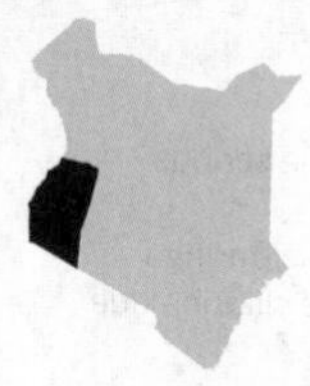

Western Kenya

Includes »

Best of Nature

- » Masai Mara National Reserve (p129)
- » Kakamega Forest Reserve (p150)
- » Saiwa Swamp National Park (p160)
- » Mt Elgon National Park (p158)

Best of Culture

- » Maasai (p136)
- » Kisii soapstone carving (p146)

Why Go?

For most people, the magic of western Kenya is summed up in two poetic words: Masai Mara. Few places on earth support such high concentrations of animals, and the Mara's wildebeest-spotted savannahs are undeniably the region's star attraction. Drama unfolds here on a daily basis, be it a stealthy trap coordinated by a pride of lions, the infectious panic of a thousand wildebeest crossing a river or the playful pounce of a cheetah kitten on its sibling.

But there is much more to western Kenya than these plains of herbivores and carnivores. The dense forests of Kakamega are buzzing with weird and wonderful creatures, the rain-soaked hills of Kericho and their verdant tea gardens bring new meaning to the word 'green', and amid the boat-speckled waters of Lake Victoria lie a smattering of seldom-visited islands crying out for exploration.

When to Go

Kisumu

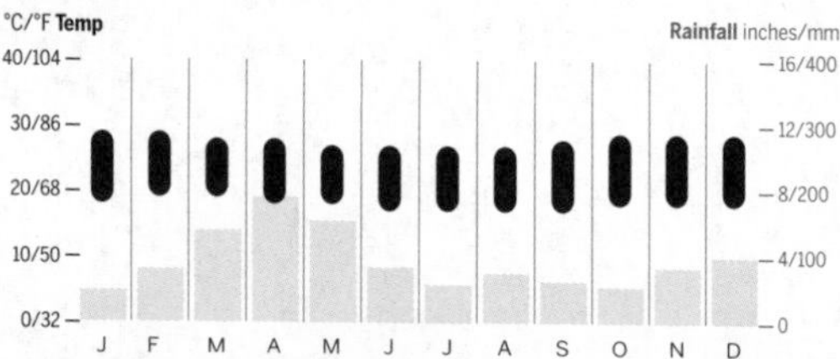

March–May The 'heavy rains' fall at this time, particularly in the cooler Western Highlands.

July–October With the arrival of the wildebeest migration, the Masai Mara groans with herbivores.

November & December The 'lesser rains' appear briefly before things really dry out in January.

MASAI MARA

Dream of Africa and you dream of the Masai Mara. This huge expanse of gently rolling grassland – specked with flat-top acacia trees and trampled by thousands-strong herds of zebra and wildebeest – is the ultimate African cliché. But for once the reality lives up to the image, and for many people this reserve is not just the highlight of their Kenyan adventure but the very reason they came in the first place.

Narok

☎050 / POP 24,000

Three hours west of Nairobi, this ramshackle provincial town is civilisation's last stand before the vast savannahs of the Masai Mara and the region's largest town. It's a friendly and surprisingly hassle-free place, but few travellers have reason to stop. Most people roll on in, browse the curio shops while their driver refuels, then roll on out again.

The town's only attraction is the small **Narok Museum** (adult/child KSh500/250; 9am-6pm Mon-Sun) and its displays on traditional and contemporary Maasai culture, as well as that of other Maa-speaking people.

Sleeping & Eating

Chambai Hotel HOTEL $
(☎22591; s/d from KSh1050/1250; P) The standard rooms out the back are simple, spotless and sport mosquito nets. The newer and pricier 'super' rooms in the main building have inviting beds, balconies, large TVs and huge bathrooms. The waiters here see enough tourists to know you'll want your soda served cold.

Seasons Hotel HOTEL $$
(☎020-2220572; reservationseasonsnarok@gmail.com; B3 Hwy; camping KSh700, s/d from KSh3000/4000; P) While undeniably nicer than anything else around, the Seasons isn't that much better than the Chambai to warrant paying triple. Locally it is regarded as having the best restaurant in town although its buffet (KSh700, lunch and dinner) has seen better days – possibly some time ago.

Information

Barclays Bank (B3 Hwy) With a temperamental ATM.

Info Point Cyberdome (B3 Hwy; per hr KSh60) The last reasonably priced connection before entering the Mara.

Getting There & Away

Narok Line matatus run between Narok and Nairobi (KSh400, three hours) from the Shell petrol station on the B6 Hwy. All other matatus leave from the main matatu stand just around the corner in the centre of town. Destinations include Naivasha (KSh350, 2½ hours), Kisii (KSh400, three hours), Kericho (KSh400, 2½ hours) and Nakuru (KSh400, two hours).

Public trucks also leave from the matatu stand to Sekenani and Talek gates for between KSh300 to KSh400, depending on the condition of the road.

Several petrol stations pump the elixir of vehicular life – fill up, it's much cheaper here than in the reserve.

Masai Mara National Reserve

The world-renowned Masai Mara needs little in the way of introduction; its tawny, wildlife-stuffed savannahs are familiar to everyone who owns a TV set and the scene for umpteen documentaries and movies (most recently Disney's *African Cats*).

The Masai Mara (or Mara as locals affectionately refer to it) is the northern extension of Tanzania's equally famous Serengeti Plains and is jointly managed by the Narok County Council and the Mara Conservancy (on behalf of Trans-Mara County Council). The whole ecosystem is greatly extended by the numerous privately and community owned conservancies and group ranches that surround the reserve.

Reliable rains and plentiful vegetation underpin this extraordinary ecosystem and the millions of herbivores it supports. Wildebeest, zebra, impala, eland, reedbuck, waterbuck, black rhino, elephant, Masai giraffe and several species of gazelle all call the short-grass plains and acacia woodlands of the Mara home. This vast concentration of game accounts for high predator numbers including cheetah, leopard, spotted hyena, black-backed jackal, bat-eared fox, caracal and the highest lion densities in the world.

Sights & Activities

TOP CHOICE **Wildlife Drives** DRIVING TOUR
Whether you're bouncing over the plains in pursuit of elusive elephant silhouettes or parked next to a pride of lions and listening to their bellowed breaths, wildlife drives are *the* highlight of a trip to the Mara.

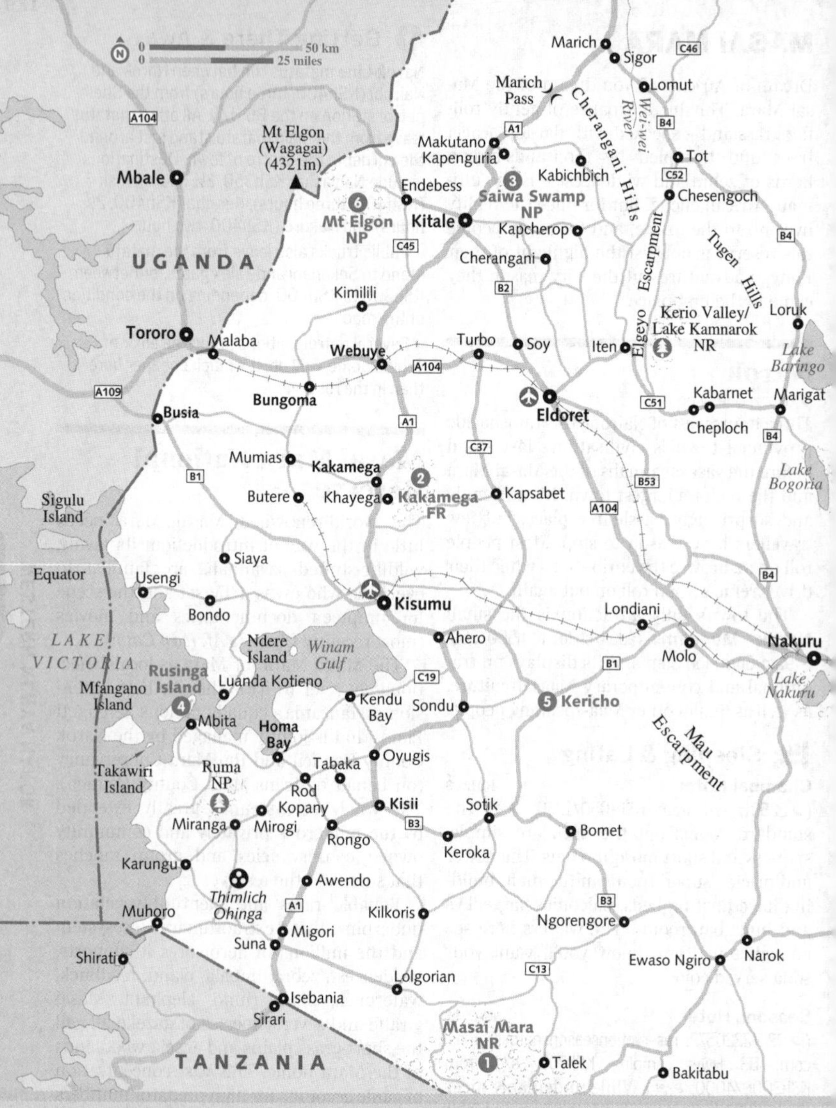

Western Kenya Highlights

1. Getting caught up in the swirling wildebeest traffic jams of the **Masai Mara National Reserve** (p129), the greatest animal show on earth.
2. Scouring the leaf litter for creepy-crawlies and searching for the thumbless colobus in the depths of **Kakamega Forest Reserve** (p150).
3. Wading through the swampy backwaters of **Saiwa Swamp National Park** (p160) in a hunt for paddling antelope.
4. Throwing away your watch and making plans to stay forever on one of **Lake Victoria**'s (p144) idyllic islands, such as **Rusinga Island**.
5. Learning how to brew a proper cuppa in **Kericho** (p147), the tea capital of Africa.
6. Shielding your head from whirling bats while searching for salt-loving elephants in the caves of **Mt Elgon National Park** (p158).

WILDLIFE IN WESTERN KENYA

The Masai Mara National Reserve (p129) is arguably Kenya's most famous park and positively groans with all manner of savannah-dwelling creatures. The annual migration sees the arrival of a million herbivores (principally wildebeest and zebras) from the Serengeti in search of grass, which in turn supports a large number of predators including crocodiles, cheetahs, lions, leopards, hyenas, caracals, black-backed jackals and mongoose.

The dense rainforests of Kakamega Forest Reserve (p150) offer prolific birdlife, seven species of primates including rare de Brazza's monkeys, nocturnal flying squirrels and a staggering array of butterflies and insects.

You might get lucky and spot one of Mt Elgon National Park's (p158) famous mineral-loving elephants that mine bat-infested caves for salt, although waterbucks and colobus monkeys are more readily seen.

More wildlife and unique surrounds can be found at Ruma National Park (p143), home to Kenya's only roan antelope population and a good number of endangered Rothschild's giraffes, and at Saiwa Swamp National Park (p160), which hosts rare swamp-dwelling sitatunga antelope.

During the busy Christmas and migration seasons it can seem that there are as many minivans as animals. Officially the limit is five vehicles around any one animal but when no rangers are present (which is most of the time) this is widely flaunted. A further problem is that despite the risk of being heavily fined for leaving designated tracks, drivers often do so and risk destroying the fragile vegetation that forms a protective cover across the savannah. The resulting erosion causes the formation of dust bowls (and muddy quagmires when it rains) that blight the landscape and cause grave damage to the ecosystem.

Central Plains

The southeast area of the park, bordered by the Mara and Sand Rivers, is characterised by rolling grasslands and low, isolated hills. With the arrival of the migration, enormous herds of wildebeest and zebra, interspersed with smaller herds of Thompson and Grant gazelles, topi and eland, all graze here. The riverine forests that border the Mara and Talek Rivers are great places to spot elephant, buffalo and bushbuck. Leopards are sometimes seen near the Talek and Sand Rivers and around the Keekorok valleys.

Rhino Ridge & Paradise Plains

Rhino Ridge is a good area to see black-backed jackal, as they are known to use the old termitaria here for den sites. Lookout Hill is worth a detour as it offers phenomenal views over the seasonal Olpunyaia Swamp. You may also get lucky and spot one of the few black rhinos that inhabit the reserve anywhere between Lookout Hill and Rhino Ridge and in the vicinity of Roan Hill.

For lions, the Marsh Pride near Musiara Swamp and the Ridge Pride near Rhino Ridge both starred in the BBC's *Big Cat Diary* and are fairly easy to find.

Cheetahs on the other hand are far more elusive but are sometimes found hunting gazelles on the Paradise Plains.

Mara River

Pods of hippos can be found in any of the major rivers, with the largest and most permanent concentrations occurring in the Mara River. The river is also home to huge Nile crocodiles, and is the scene where wildebeest make their fateful crossings during the migration. The New Mara Bridge in the south is the only all-weather crossing point and another great place to see hippos. Rangers here might volunteer to show you these but establish the cost first; you don't want to pay a half-day guiding fee (KSh1500) and just get a two-minute stroll.

The Mara Triangle & Esoit Oloololo (Siria) Escarpment

Unlike the rest of the park, which is under the control of the Narok County Council, the northwest sector of the reserve is managed by the non-profit Mara Conservancy. The only way to reach this part of the park is from either the Oloololo Gate or via the New Mara Bridge. Consequently, this area is less visited than elsewhere, despite having high game concentrations.

The Oloololo Escarpment, which forms the northwest boundary of the park, was

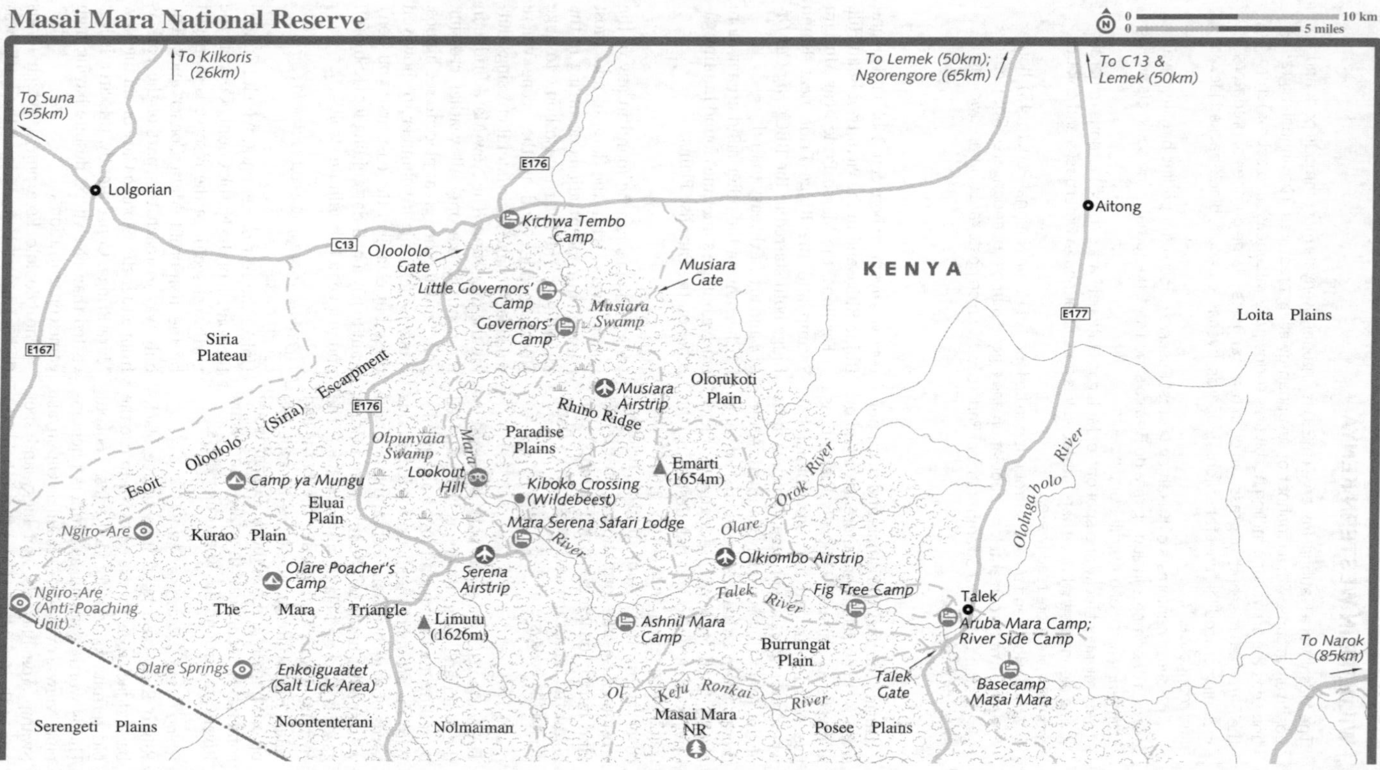
Masai Mara National Reserve
0 10 km
0 5 miles
To Kilkoris (26km)
To Suna (55km)
To Lemek (50km); Ngorengore (65km)
To C13 & Lemek (50km)
Lolgorian
Aitong
KENYA
E176
E167
C13
E177
Kichwa Tembo Camp
Oloololo Gate
Musiara Gate
Little Governors' Camp
Musiara Swamp
Governors' Camp
Siria Plateau
Loita Plains
Escarpment
(Siria)
Oloololo
Esoit
Olorukoti Plain
Musiara Airstrip
Rhino Ridge
Paradise Plains
Olpunyaia Swamp
Mara
Lookout Hill
Emarti (1654m)
Kiboko Crossing (Wildebeest)
Camp ya Mungu
Eluai Plain
Orok River
Oloinga bolo River
Ngiro-Are
Kurao Plain
Mara Serena Safari Lodge
River
Olare
Olkiombo Airstrip
Olare Poacher's Camp
Serena Airstrip
Talek River
Fig Tree Camp
Talek
Ngiro-Are (Anti-Poaching Unit)
The Mara Triangle
Limutu (1626m)
Ashnil Mara Camp
Aruba Mara Camp; River Side Camp
Burrungat Plain
To Narok (85km)
Olare Springs
Enkoiguaatet (Salt Lick Area)
Ol Keju Ronkai River
Talek Gate
Basecamp Masai Mara
Serengeti Plains
Noontenterani
Nolmaiman
Masai Mara NR
Posee Plains

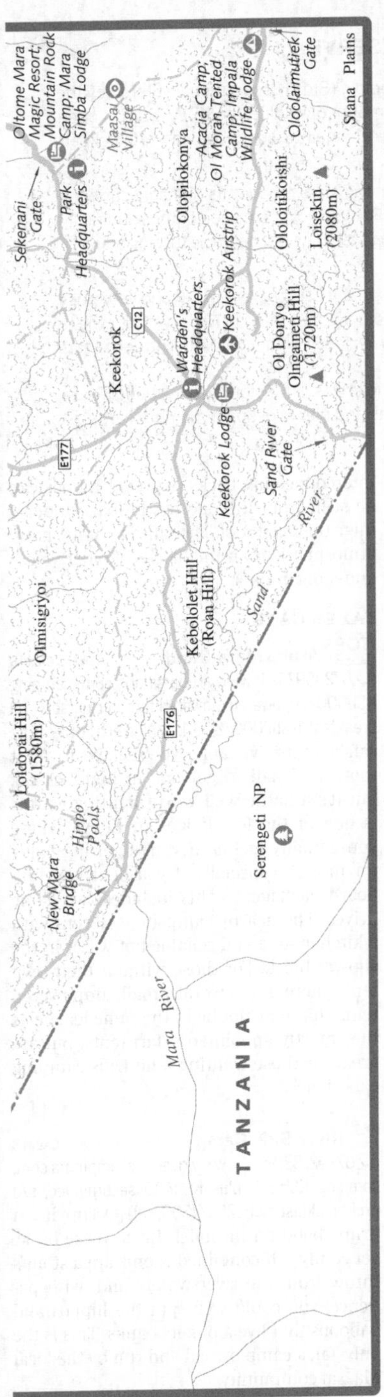

once wooded but fire and elephant damage means that it is now mostly grasslands. Rock hyrax and klipspringer can be readily seen here.

Guided Nature Walk WALKING TOUR

(2hr walk per person KSh1000-2000) Many old Africa hands swear that the best way to experience the African bush is on foot, and doing this is a wonderful experience; you'll learn all about the medicinal properties of various plants, see the tell-tale signs of passing animals and have some heart-in-mouth close encounters with the local wildlife. However, as it is forbidden to walk within the reserve, guided walks generally take place in the company of a Maasai *moran* (warrior) outside the park. Any of the lodges and camps listed in the Sleeping & Eating section can arrange a guided walk, although their rates vary.

Maasai Manyatta Visit VILLAGE

The Maasai are synonymous with the Masai Mara, and their slender frames, blood-red cloaks, ochre hairstyles and beaded jewellery make them instantly recognisable. Despite their reputation as fearsome warriors with somewhat lofty dispositions, many Maasai *manyattas* (villages) now welcome visitors, using the income to fund schools, buy medicine and expand their precious cattle herds.

Unfortunately many tourists find the whole experience so daunting, from the haggling over admission prices at the start to the tireless souvenir sales pitch at the end, that they forget to enjoy the fabulous cultural bits in between. Admission is by negotiation but KSh1000 to KSh1500 per person is reasonable.

Ballooning SCENIC FLIGHTS

(flight per person US$450) Several companies operate dawn balloon safaris and there is no better way to start your day than soaring majestically over the rolling grasslands. Trips can be booked at most of the lodges or campsites. Flights include a champagne breakfast, game drive and transport to and from the launch point. See p38 for more details.

Sleeping & Eating

In general, accommodation in the Masai Mara is insanely overpriced. Don't be at all surprised if you end up paying more for a lacklustre room or tent here than you would

MASAI MARA NATIONAL RESERVE

Why Go Backed by the spectacular Esoit Oloololo (Siria) Escarpment, watered by the Mara River and littered with an astonishing amount of wildlife, the 1510 sq km of open rolling grasslands that make up the Mara offer the quintessential African safari experience, with lion sightings virtually guaranteed.

When to Go Breathtaking at any time of year, the Mara reaches its pinnacle during the annual wildebeest migration in July and August, when over a million of these ungainly beasts move north from the Serengeti seeking lusher grass, before returning south around October.

Practicalities The Masai Mara's fame means that it can get very busy (and very pricey) during the annual migration. To share costs, join a group safari in Nairobi, scour the notice boards at Nairobi backpackers or go to www.lonelyplanet.com/thorntree in search of travel companions.

Bring a windbreaker for early morning game drives, and – for those *National Geographic*–style shots – a 70-300mm zoom lens and plenty of spare memory cards.

for a decent hotel room in a major Western European city.

We have listed accommodation-only rates, where available, although all places also offer full-board options.

SEKENANI GATE

While the places listed here are outside the Sekenani Gate, they are still within the reserve and sleeping here will incur park fees (even if the camps state otherwise).

Mountain Rock Camp TENTED CAMP $
(☎020-2242133; www.mountainrockkenya.com; camping KSh350, tent s/d shared bathroom KSh2000/3000; tent s/d KSh 3000/5000; excl breakfast; P) The simple safari tents here come in two categories; those with private bathrooms, cloth wardrobes and firm beds and those that are smaller and use a shared ablution block. There is also a pleasant camping area, and all guests can use the kitchen if they're not upgrading to the full-board option.

Oltome Mara Magic Resort TENTED CAMP $$
(☎020-2498512, 0727267723; www.oltomemaramagic.com; tent s/tw full board US$145/260; P) This small camp has only seven semi-permanent tents, so there is plenty of privacy and personalised service from the staff. Each tent is tastefully furnished and features stone floors, wooden verandahs and an attached modern bathroom.

Mara Simba Lodge LODGE $$$
(☎020-4343960; www.simbalodges.com; s/tw full board US$495/575; P) Set in the riverine forest on the banks of the Talek River, this large lodge has a series of interconnecting decks (a pod of hippos can be seen from the one by the bar) under a huge thatched roof. The safari tents are more atmospheric than the blocks of older wood-and-stone rooms.

TALEK GATE

TOP CHOICE **Aruba Mara Camp** TENTED CAMP $
(☎0723997524; www.aruba-safaris.com; camping KSh600, unpowered/powered tent per person excl breakfast KSh2000/8000; P) With only five safari tents available, you'll have to fight tooth and nail to get one in high season, but it's a battle well worth fighting as this is one of the few lodges in Kenya where you actually feel as if you're getting value for money, especially if you book the full-board package, as this includes two game drives. The nearby campsite is decent with a kitchen area and reliable hot water in the shower block. For those without their own tent, there are several small, unpowered tents that may not be in the same league as the smartly appointed safari tents, but are great for those wanting a no-frills camping experience.

River Side Camp CABIN $
(☎0720218319; www.riversidecampmara.com; camping KSh400 plus KSh400 security fee, s/d excl breakfast KSh2250/4500; P) Occupying a prime bend on the Talek River, these basic, yet comfy self-contained rooms are a stone's throw from the river waters and, with patience, you could well spot the hippos and baboons that live along its banks. This is the only Talek camp owned and run by the local Maasai community.

Fig Tree Camp LODGE $$$
(☎020-2500273, 0722202564; www.madahotels.com; tent s/d full board US$360/440; P📶🏊) Vegetate on your tent's verandah, watching the Talek's waters gently flow pass this sumptuous camp with a colonial-days feel. The gardens are about the most luxurious you'll ever see, and the bathrooms about the biggest and most inviting you'll find under canvas. To round things off, there is a small but scenic pool and a trendy treetop bar.

Basecamp Masai Mara LODGE $$$
(☎0733333909; www.basecampexplorer.com; tent s/d full board US$290/500; P📶) 'Eco' is a much-abused word in the tourism industry and sadly some so-called 'ecofriendly' establishments are often nothing of the sort. To see what an ecofriendly hotel really looks like come to this upmarket lodge. If all this green scheming makes you worry that the accommodation might be rustic, fear not. The safari tents fall squarely into the luxury bracket with open-air showers and stylish furnishings.

OLOOLAIMUTIEK GATE

Like those at Sekenani Gate, these camps fall within the reserve boundaries (despite being outside the gate) and incur park fees.

Acacia Camp TENTED CAMP $
(☎0726089107; www.acaciacamp.com; camping US$8, tent s/tw excl breakfast US$36/54; P) Thatched roofs shelter closely spaced, spartan, semi-permanent tents in this quaint campground. There are numerous cooking areas, a bar, a campfire pit and a simple restaurant that serves meals for US$7 a pop. The communal bathrooms are clean, and hot water flows in the evening. The only downside for campers is the lack of shade.

Ol Moran Tented Camp TENTED CAMP $$
(☎020-882923, www.olmorantentedcamp.com; tent s/d/tr full board from US$115/150/188; P) The safari tents here come in two flavours; the 'superior' is large with a wooden deck and a smart bathroom while the 14 standard tents are smaller and simpler, but entirely presentable.

Impala Wildlife Lodge TENTED CAMP $$
(☎020-2226189; www.impalawildlifelodge.com; tent s/d full board US$90/160, s/d excl breakfast US$120/180; P🏊) Previously known as Hippo Lodge, the Impala has a combination of safari tents and rooms in circular block *bandas* (huts) that are clean but a little dated.

MUSIARA & OLOOLOLO GATES

Sadly, there are no secure budget or midrange options here.

Kichwa Tembo Camp TENTED CAMP $$$
(☎020-3740920; www.kichwatembo.com, tent full board per person US$375-475; 🏊) Just outside the northern boundary, Kichwa has permanent tents with grass-mat floors, stone bathrooms and tasteful furnishings. Hop in a hammock and take in spectacular savannah views. The camp has an excellent reputation for its food.

Governors' Camp TENTED CAMP $$$
(☎020-2734000; www.governorscamp.com; tent s/d full board US$544/872;🏊📶) This camp, and **Little Governors' Camp** (tent s/d full board US$634/1014; 🏊) are widely regarded as the most magisterial camps in the Mara and offer great service, pleasing riverside locations and activities aplenty. The extraordinary rates include three wildlife drives and someone keen to wash your dirty clothes.

INSIDE THE RESERVE

TOP CHOICE **Keekorok Lodge** LODGE $$$
(☎020-4450636; www.sunafricahotels.com; s/d/tr full board US$320/490/630; P📶🏊) This may be the oldest lodge in the Mara, but thanks to a recent makeover the rooms are modern, bright and tastefully decorated with tribal chic. The bar and restaurant areas also incorporate tribal art to great effect, and flow to manicured gardens and a wooden boardwalk that lead to a gazebo overlooking a hippo pool. Thanks to its central location amid the reserve's savannah, don't be surprised to see zebra prancing past your window. Its website often lists great deals on fly-in packages that include full board and game drives.

Ashnil Mara Camp TENTED CAMP $$$
(☎0717612499; www.ashnilhotels.com, tent full board per person US$299; ❄📶🏊) Despite the 'no new developments within the reserve' rule, this luxury camp was built in 2008 – despite conservationists protests – and now boasts 40 beautifully appointed safari tents that are as close as canvas comes to being an actual hotel room. Tents 1 to 6 and 21 to 40 have views to the Mara River from their private decks.

Mara Serena Safari Lodge LODGE $$$
(☎020-2842000; www.serenahotels.com; s/d full board US$445/595; 📶🏊) Of all the lodges within the park, the Serena has the best

LOCAL KNOWLEDGE

MEETING THE MAASAI

While the Tanzanian and Kenyan governments may have initiated programs to encourage the Maasai to forego their traditional semi-nomadic lifestyle, their culture has proved surprisingly resilient and one of the most enduring in East Africa. We asked Mahna and Everlyn what a curious traveller could do to learn more of their traditional ways.

Mahna Dnkuny: Maasai ilmoran (warrior)

Tourists find it easy to recognise us because most *ilmoran* wear bright red *shukas* (blankets). Some also redden their hair with ochre and cut their ear lobes. We men are very proud because to become a warrior requires a lengthy, solo stay in the bush when we turn 18, after which, our circumcision is celebrated in a huge ceremony.

If you visit a Maasai *manyatta* (village) you could see men leaping high as they dance the *adumu*. If you're brave, ask to try *kule naa-ilanga* – a mixture of blood drained from a cow's neck and milk.

I also recommend going on a guided walk with an *ilmoran*. He will protect you and teach you the names of many medicinal plants.

Everlyn Saiyalei

I recommend visiting one of our villages to meet the women. We work harder than the men and have many responsibilities. You will see us wearing our beautiful, beaded jewellery and the *inkajijik* (homes) that we build from branches, cow dung, grass and mud. If you want to watch us milk the cattle, arrive early. At other times you'll find us tending our children, cooking and washing.

view. Built on a small hill (home to many rock hyraxes), most rooms have commanding views over the Paradise Plains and the Mara River above not one, but two, migration crossing points. The rooms themselves are inspired by Maasai *manyatta* (don't worry, they're not made from dung and sticks) and are perfectly comfortable, although to earn their four-star accolades, are due for a makeover.

Camping CAMPGROUND **$$**
(public campsites per person US$30, special campsites per person US$40) It is only possible to camp within the reserve in the Mara Triangle sector of the park in either the public or special (private campsites that can be reserved) campsites. You will need to be totally self-sufficient to the point of bringing your own firewood (using the deadwood within the park is prohibited) and hire the compulsory two rangers for protection (KSh4000).

Information

Although the main **reserve** (www.maasaimara.com; park entrance adult/child staying within the park US$70/40, adult/child staying outside the park US$80/45; ⏲6am-7pm) is managed by the Narok County Council and the **Mara Triangle** (www.maratriangle.org) is managed by the Mara Conservancy, both charge the same, and an admission ticket brought at one is valid at the other. Keep hold of this ticket, as you will be asked to present it when travelling between the reserve's Narok and Transmara sections and on your eventual exit.

As some gates are located inside the reserve boundary it is easy to enter the Masai Mara unknowingly. Most confusion arises when people camping outside the gates are requested to pay park fees – cue confrontation.

All vehicles seem to get charged KSh1000 at the gates, instead of the KSh400 fee for vehicles with less than six seats – be insistent but polite and all will be well.

Ranger guides are available at the park gates and prices are fixed at KSh1500 for up to six hours, and KSh3000 for anything over this. Note that night game drives and walking safaris are not permitted within the park; they're only possible in the surrounding conservancies.

Getting There & Away

Air

Airkenya (☎020-605745; www.airkenya.com) and **Safarilink** (☎020-600777; www.flysafarilink.com) each have daily flights to any of the eight airstrips in and around the Masai Mara. Flights start at US$250 return.

Matatu, Car & 4WD

Although it's possible to arrange wildlife drives independently, keep in mind that there are few savings in coming here without transport or prearranged game drives. That said, it is possible to access Talek and Sekenani Gates from Narok by matatu (KSh300 to KSh400), and from Kisii a matatu will get you as far as Kilkoris or Suna on the main A1 Hwy, after which you will have problems.

For those who drive, the first 52km west of Narok on the B3 and C12 are smooth enough, but after the bitumen runs out you'll find that there's just as much rattle as there is roll and you'll soon come to dread this road. The C13, which connects Oloololo Gate with Lolgorian out in the west, is very rough and rocky, and it's poorly signposted – a highway it's not.

Petrol is available (although expensive) at Mara Sarova, Mara Serena and Keekorok Lodges, as well as in Talek village.

Getting Around

If you do arrive by matatu, you can organise game drives with most lodges and even some of the cheaper camps. Typically they charge around KSh12,000 for a full day's vehicle and driver hire, which can be split between as many of you as can be comfortably squeezed into the vehicle. There is no public transport within the park.

Maasai Safari Guide (☎0721633864, josef tira@gmail.com), based at Talek Gate, is a reliable local operator, renting 4WDs for KSh12,000 per day or KSh7000 for a game drive.

LAKE VICTORIA

Spread over 68,000 sq km, yet never more than 80m deep, Lake Victoria, the source of the White Nile, might well be East Africa's most important geographical feature, but is seen by surprisingly few visitors. This is a shame, as its humid shores hide some of the most beautiful and rewarding parts of western Kenya – from untouched national parks to lively cities and tranquil islands.

Kisumu

☎057 / POP 322,700

Set on the sloping shore of Lake Victoria's Winam Gulf, the town of Kisumu might be the third largest in Kenya, but its relaxed atmosphere is a world away from that of places like Nairobi and Mombasa.

Until 1977 the port was one of the busiest in Kenya, but decline set in with the demise of the East African Community (the EAC was originally established by Kenya, Tanzania and Uganda to promote a common market within the region, but now also includes Burundi and Rwanda) and the port sat virtually idle for two decades. Recently increased cooperation and the revival of the EAC in 2000 has helped establish Kisumu as an international shipment point for petroleum products. Surprisingly the lake plays no part (raw fuel for processing is piped in from Mombasa and the end products are shipped out by truck) so, while the lake may have been the lifeblood for Kisumu's inception, the city sits with its back to the water. Nonetheless, with Kisumu's fortunes again rising, and the water hyacinth's impact reduced, it is hoped Lake Victoria will once more start contributing to the local economy.

VICTORIA'S UNWELCOME GUESTS

Lake Victoria's 'evolving' ecosystem has proved to be both a boon and a bane for those living along its shores. For starters, its waters are a haven for mosquitoes and snails, making malaria and bilharzia (schistosomiasis) all too common here. Then there are Nile perch – introduced 50 years ago to combat mosquitoes – which eventually thrived, growing to over 200kg in size and becoming every fishing-boat captain's dream. Horrifyingly, the ravenous perch have wiped out over 300 species of smaller tropical fish unique to the lake.

Last but not least is the ornamental water hyacinth. First reported in 1986, this 'exotic' pond plant had no natural predators here and quickly reached plague proportions. Millions of dollars have been ploughed into solving the problem, with controversial programs including mechanical removal and the introduction of weed-eating weevils. The investment seems to be paying off, with the most recent satellite photos showing hyacinth cover dramatically reduced from the 17,230 hectares it once covered.

Kisumu

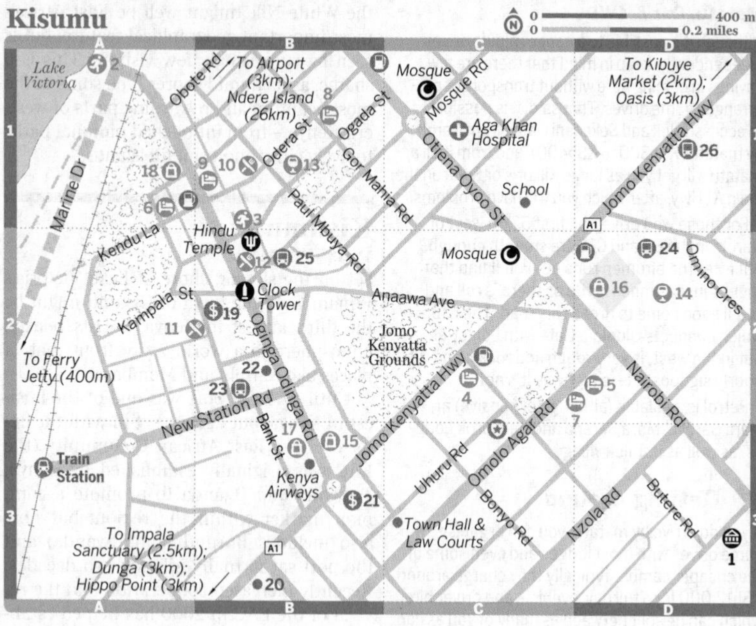

Kisumu

Sights

1 Kisumu Museum....................D3

Activities, Courses & Tours

Integri Tours....................(see 4)
2 Railway Beach Hippo Trips....................A1
3 Zaira Tours & Travel....................B1

Sleeping

4 Duke of Breeze....................C2
5 Hotel Palmers....................D2
6 Lakeside Guest House....................A1
7 New East View Hotel....................D2
8 New Victoria Hotel....................B1
9 Sooper Guest House....................B1

Eating

10 Green Garden Restaurant....................B1
11 Juice Parlour....................B2
Laughing Buddha....................(see 18)
12 Senorita....................B2
The Grill....................(see 18)
Tin-Shack Restaurants....................(see 2)
Ukwala Supermarket....................(see 18)

Drinking

13 Octopus Bottoms-Up Club....................B1
14 Social Centre....................D2

Shopping

15 Al-Imran Plaza....................B3
16 Main Market....................D2
17 Mega Plaza....................B3
18 Swan Centre....................A1

Information

19 Barclays Bank....................B2
Clinipath Laboratory....................(see 17)
20 Immigration Office....................B3
21 Kenya Commercial Bank....................B3
Moscom Cyber....................(see 17)
Post Office....................(see 17)
22 Shiva Travels....................B2

Transport

23 Akamba....................B2
24 Bus & Matatu Station....................D2
25 Easy Coach....................B2
26 Easy Coach....................D1
Jet Link....................(see 15)

Sights & Activities

Kisumu Museum MUSEUM

(Nairobi Rd; admission KSh500; ⌚8am-6pm) Set on sprawling grounds southwest of the town centre, this educational facility has three main sections. The first is a small museum covering Western Kenya's three principal linguistic groups: the Luo, who were predominantly fishermen; the agricultural Bantu; and the Kalenjin, famed for their animal husbandry.

The second attraction is a traditional Luo homestead depicting the fictitious life of Onyango as he undergoes the rite of passage to establish his own family compound.

The last attraction is a crocodile pit, a tortoise pen, a small aquarium displaying the nearby lake's aquatic assets, and a series of vivariums displaying all the local snakes you don't want to meet on a dark night.

Hippo Point Boat Trips BOAT TOUR

Everyone seems to make the pilgrimage out to Hippo Point, sticking into Lake Victoria at Dunga, about 3km south of town, and though it's pleasant enough, there is actually nothing at all to see or do and you're extremely unlikely to see any hippos.

If you want guaranteed hippo sightings, you will have to venture onto the lake. As you might imagine, plenty of people offer just such a boat trip. Prices vary widely but KSh500 to KSh750 per person for a two-hour boat trip in a group of four would be reasonable. Boat trips can also be organised at Railway Beach (at the end of Oginga Odinga Rd).

Impala Sanctuary PARK

(www.kws.go.ke; adult/child US$15/5; ⌚6am-6pm). On the road to Dunga, this 1-sq-km sanctuary is home to a small impala herd and provides important grazing grounds for local hippos.

Ndere Island National Park PARK

(www.kws.go.ke; adult/child US$20/10; ⌚6am-6pm) Gazetted as a national park back in 1986, tourism to this small 4.2-sq-km island has never taken off. It is forested and very beautiful, housing a variety of bird species, plus hippos, impalas (introduced), and spotted crocodiles – a lesser-known cousin of the larger Nile crocodile.

Unfortunately there is nowhere to stay and although twice-daily matatus reach the shore just opposite the island, your only reliable option to get to Ndere is with chartered boats. Expect to pay around KSh2000 per hour, with typical return trips taking five hours (including three hours on shore). Chartered boat trips can be arranged with any of the boat captains offering sightseeing trips from Hippo Point or Railway Beach.

Tours

It is quite feasible to see the sights of Kisumu on your own, but if you don't know your eagle from your snowy egret, or want to visit further afield with limited time, then consider hiring a guide.

Ibrahim Nandi NATURE

(☎0723083045; ibradingo@yahoo.com) A well-known and trusted tour guide to the many sights and sounds of the Kisumu region. He can arrange boat trips, birdwatching tours, nature walks and excursions to Ndere Island National Park. He can be contacted through the New Victoria Hotel.

Integri Tours NATURE

(☎0720647864; www.integritour.com; Duke of Breeze, off Jomo Kenyatta Hwyl) Professional operator with some excellent itineraries for day trips.

Zaira Tours & Travel SAFARIS

(☎0722788879; zairatours@yahoo.com; Ogada St) The best safari operator in town, with pop-top minivans and 4WDs.

Sleeping

At one time or another accusations of poor security have been levelled at all of the cheapies we list here. If you are able, consider using your own padlock to secure your room or deposit valuable items with reception. And, if you are finding the humidity hard to deal with, you'll be pleased to know that all rooms in Kisumu are equipped with fans.

New Victoria Hotel HOTEL $

(☎2021067; newvictoriahotel@yahoo.com; Gor Mahia Rd; s with shared bathroom excl breakfast KSh900, s/tw/tr excl breakfast KSh1450/1950/2700) This Yemeni-run hotel has character in abundance and is something of a focal point for the town's small Arab population. Rooms have fans, mosquito nets and comfy foam mattresses. The next-door mosque will rouse you at 5am, whether you want to be roused or not.

Lakeside Guest House GUESTHOUSE $
(☎2023523, 0725468797; Kendu La; r/tw excl breakfast KSh800/1000) More lake-glimpse than lakeside, the rooms here are larger (and cheaper) than many found at Sooper's, although the staff are far more lackadaisical. Some of the mosquito nets are quite holey and the shower tap snapped off in our hands (sorry) so you may want to avoid room 6. Hot water is available in the mornings and evenings.

Sooper Guest House BACKPACKERS $
(☎0725281733; kayamchatur@yahoo.com; Oginga Odinga Rd; s excl breakfast KSh1000-1200, d excl breakfast KSh 1200-1400, tw/tr excl breakfast KSh1200/1600) Sooper has become the defacto backpackers in town and you have a good chance of meeting other travellers here. The rooms aren't quite the bargain we once found them to be but still offer decent low-cost digs. The rooms in the newer block are larger than those in the old block but cost KSh200 more and suffer from street noise.

New East View Hotel HOTEL $
(☎0722556721; Omolo Agar Rd; s KSh1700-2300, d KSh2300-2800; P) One of the many family homes in the area that have been converted into a hotel. It retains just enough furniture and decoration to give the rooms a homely, pre-loved feel.

Duke of Breeze HOTEL $
(☎0717105444; reservations@thedukeofbreeze.com; off Jomo Kenyatta Hwy; s/d/tr KSh1900/2400/3000; wi-fi) Popular with Peace Corp volunteers, the Duke has large, fan-cooled rooms that have seen better days. The real attractions are the roof-top restaurant, the free wi-fi (but the sodas here are twice the price as elsewhere) and the relaxed, chilled vibe.

Hotel Palmers HOTEL $
(☎2024867; hotel.palmers@yahoo.com; Omolo Agar Rd; s/d/tw/tr KSh1500/2300/2800/3500; P) The doubles here are particularly nice, with large bay windows and enormous double beds. The singles, alas, are far more poky.

Kiboko Bay Resort TENTED CAMP $$$
(☎2025510, 0724387738; www.kibokobay.com; Dunga; s/d/tr US$145/175/195; P ❄ pool) At Kiboko, you will find nine Masai Mara–style safari tents huddled under the trees on the banks of the lake. Each has a hardwood floor, a huge bed, canopy mosquito nets and an attached permanent bathroom. Considering the price (nonresidents pay twice that of residents), we were surprised to find the pool more than a tinge green (nonguests pool use is KSh200).

Eating

The fact that Kisumu sits on Lake Victoria certainly isn't lost on restaurants here, and fish is abundant on menus.

If you want an authentic local fish fry, there are no better places than the dozens of smoky tin-shack restaurants sitting on the lake's shore at Railway Beach at the end of Oginga Odinga Rd. Dive in between 7am and 6pm; a midsized fish served with *ugali* or rice is sufficient for two people and will set you back KSh400.

TOP CHOICE **Green Garden Restaurant** INTERNATIONAL $
(Odera St; mains KSh380-500; ⏲lunch & dinner) Surrounded by colourful murals and potted palms, the Green Garden remains an oasis of culinary delight set in an Italian-themed courtyard. As you would expect, it is an expat hot spot and the word is that the tilapia (fish) in a spinach and coconut sauce is the way to go. Not that we can vouch for this; we were sidelined by the pizzas and banana fritters.

The Laughing Buddha VEGETARIAN $
(Swan Centre, Accra St; mains KSh350-500; ⏲lunch & dinner Tue-Sun; vegetarian) Guaranteed to smack a smile on your face, The Laughing Buddha rounds off its excellent vegetarian menu with treats like sizzling chocolate fudge brownies and Oreo milkshakes (greedy little monkeys take note: the second one is only KSh50). The curb-side dining is a novelty in these parts.

Juice Parlour CAFE $
(off New Station Rd; juice from KSh50; ⏲breakfast, lunch & dinner) You name it and they'll stick it in a blender and pulverise the bejesus out of it. The pumpkin-and-beetroot juice looked foul so we shared a very special moment with a mango and pineapple combo instead.

The Grill INTERNATIONAL $
(Swan Centre, Accra St; mains KSh400; ⏲lunch & dinner) Right next door to The Laughing Buddha, The Grill is *the* place to come if you want to sink your teeth into some excellent steaks and chicken fillets. Steak treatments

OBAMA FEVER

Regardless of your individual politics, it's hard to deny the rock-star status that US President Barack Obama enjoys throughout Kenya. After his convincing win in the 2008 elections, Kenya was swept up in a tide of 'Obama fever' that saw everything from schools, matatus, butcheries, wedding-dress shops and a significant number of newborn babies named in his honour. At this time many Kenyans felt that their 'native son' had ascended the world's highest seat of power to represent not just those who had voted for him, but everyday Kenyans as well.

The strong connection lies in the fact that President Obama is the son of Barack Obama Sr, a Luo from the town of Nyang'oma Kogelo near Kisumu. Barack Sr met the president's mother while attending the University of Hawai'i at Mānoa but separated when young Obama was just two-years old. Tragically, Barack Sr only saw his son once more before dying in an automobile accident in 1982.

Obama Jr travelled to Kenya for the first time in 1988, spending five weeks in the company of his paternal relatives, but his highest-profile visit came in 2006 when tens of thousands of Kenyans lined the streets of Kisumu and greeted him with a hero's welcome. Always the crowd pleaser, the then Senator Obama shouted 'I greet you all!' in the local Luo language. The crowd went wild.

Since then, enthusiasm has waned. President Obama hasn't been the magical 'cure-all' that many Africans had hoped for and, with enough troubles on his plate at home, he's had little time for addressing the problems of his father's nation. Today Kenyans and Obama alike are fiercely proud of his African roots, but this pride is tempered with the realisation that above all, President Obama is an American.

include mushroom, masala, Mexican and garlic sauces. Befitting its name, there is also a charcoal BBQ out front serving *nyama choma* (and smoke, if the wind is blowing unfavourably).

Senorita KENYAN $
(Oginga Odinga Rd; mains KSh150-250; ⌚lunch & dinner) This upmarket locals' restaurant has a great '50s feel, and a menu that covers everything that involves chips and other fried food.

Ukwala Supermarket SUPERMARKET $
(Swan Centre, Oginga Odinga Rd) One of several supermarkets in the city centre.

Drinking & Entertainment

Kisumu's nightlife has a reputation for being even livelier than Nairobi's. Check flyers and ask locals who are plugged into the scene. Be careful when leaving as muggings and worse are not unheard of. Solo women should take a chaperone – Ibrahim Nandi (p139) offers just such a service. The clubs are at their liveliest on Friday and Saturday nights, although folks don't get to bumping and grinding until after 10pm.

Oasis DANCE
(Kondele, Jomo Kenyatta Hwy; club entry KSh150-200) Well-known locally, with live music most nights, this is the place to see Lingala music performed by Congolese bands. Be prepared for a fair bit of shaking and sweating.

Social Centre DANCE
(off Omino Cres; club entry KSh100) Tucked behind the main matatu stage, this club is big on *ohangla* (Luo traditional music) with the odd Kiswahali hip-hop tune thrown in for good measure.

Octopus Bottoms-Up Club DANCE
(Ogada St; bar free, club entry KSh100) This heavyweight bar and club rages all night, but be warned that the scene isn't that pretty.

Shopping

Kisumu's **main market**, off Jomo Kenyatta Hwy, is one of Kenya's most animated markets, and certainly one of its largest, now spilling out onto the surrounding roads. If you're curious, or just looking for essentials like suits or wigs, it's worth a stroll around.

Come past the huge **Kibuye Market** (Jomo Kenyatta Hwy; ⌚Sun) on any quiet weekday and you'll find it as empty as a hyena's heart, but visit on a Sunday and it's transformed into a blossoming spring flower of colour and scents.

Information

Aga Khan Hospital (☎2020005; Otiena Oyoo St) A large hospital with modern facilities and 24-hour emergency room.

Barclays Bank (Kampala St) With ATM.

Clinipath Laboratory (☎2022363; Mega Plaza, Oginga Odinga Rd; ⏰8am-5pm Mon-Fri, 8am-1pm Sat, 10am-noon Sun)

Kenya Commercial Bank (Jomo Kenyatta Hwy) With ATM (Visa only).

Moscom Cyber (Mega Plaza, Oginga Odinga Rd; per hr KSh60; ⏰8am-8.30pm) One of many internet cafes around town; it also has a licence to burn CDs (KSh100).

Police station (Uhuru Rd)

Post office (Oginga Odinga Rd)

Shiva Travels (☎2024331; Oginga Odinga Rd) Airline ticketing and hotel reservations.

Getting There & Away

Air

All three airlines here offer daily morning and afternoon flights to Nairobi (from KSh5500 one way, 50 minutes).

Fly540.com (www.fly540.com) The 5.30pm flight to Nairobi is via Eldoret.

Jet Link (☎0714333377; www.jetlink.co.ke; Al-Imran Plaza, Oginga Odinga Rd)

Kenya Airways (☎2056000; www.kenya-airways.com; Alpha House, Oginga Odinga Rd)

Boat

Despite the reduced hyacinth in the Winam Gulf, ferry services to Tanzania and Uganda haven't restarted. **Earthwise Ferries** (http://earthwiseferries.com) have plans (but then somebody always does) for a ferry to once again link Kisumu with Mwanza (Tanzania) and Kampala (Uganda).

Bus & Matatu

Buses, matatus and Peugeots (shared taxis) to numerous destinations within Kenya battle it out at the large bus and matatu station just north of the main market. Peugeots cost about 25% more than the matatu fares listed.

Akamba (off New Station Rd) has four daily buses to Nairobi (KSh1100, seven hours) via Nakuru (KSh800, 4½ hours). There is also a 1pm departure to Kigali (KSh2500, 20 hours) via Busia (KSh400, three hours) and Kampala (KSh1500, seven hours) and an 11pm departure to Mwanza (KSh1800, 12 hours).

Easy Coach (Jomo Kenyatta Hwy) serves similar domestic destinations, as well as Kakamega (KSh250, one hour), with some added comfort and cost.

Train

Trains have once again sprung (well, spluttered) into life between Kisumu and Nairobi (1st/2nd/3rd class KSh2550/1400/500, 13½ hours) via Nakuru (KSh1560/1125/280, seven hours) and Naivasha (KSh1805/1255/360, 11 hours). All going well (and it often doesn't), the train departs Kisumu at 6.30pm every Tuesday, Thursday and Sunday. It departs Nairobi at the same time on Monday, Wednesday and Friday. Despite passing through some beautiful scenery and skirting the Aberdare National Park, you will see little of it as the train travels at night. From Nairobi sit on the left for views into the sprawling Kibera shanty town.

Getting Around

Boda-Boda & Tuk-Tuk

Both *boda-boda* (bicycle or motorbike taxis) and tuk-tuks (motorised minitaxis) have proliferated, and they are a great way to get around Kisumu. A trip to Hippo Point should be no more than KSh50/150 for a *boda-boda*/tuk-tuk.

Matatu

Matatus 7 and 9, which travel along Oginga Odinga Rd and Jomo Kenyatta Hwy, are handy to reach the main matatu station, main market and Kibuye Market – just wave and hop on anywhere you see one.

Taxi

A taxi around town costs between KSh100 and KSh200, while trips to Dunga range from KSh250 to KSh400, with heavy bargaining.

MATATUS FROM KISUMU

DESTINATION	FARE	DURATION
Busia	KSh300	2 hours
Eldoret	KSh400	2½ hours
Homa Bay	KSh350	3 hours
Isebania	KSh500	4 hours
Kakamega	KSh250	1¾ hours
Kericho	KSh300	2 hours
Kisii	KSh300	2 hours
Kitale	KSh450	4 hours
Nairobi	KSh900	5½ hours
Nakuru	KSh500	3½ hours

Lake Victoria's South Shore

HOMA BAY

059 / POP 42,600

Homa Bay has a slow, tropical, almost Central African vibe, and the near total absence of other tourists means it's extraordinarily and genuinely friendly. There is little to do other than trudge up and down the dusty, music-filled streets or wander down to the lake edge to watch the **marabou storks** pick through the trash as they wait for the fishermen and their morning catch.

Alternatively, the energetic may like to climb some of the cartoon-like hills that surround the town. The easiest summit to bag is the unmistakable conical mound of **Asego Hill**, which is just beyond the town and takes about an hour to clamber up. The town also makes a great base from which to visit Ruma National Park and Thimlich Ohinga.

Sleeping & Eating

TOP CHOICE **Twin Towers Hotel** HOTEL $
(0715032988; s/d/tw KSh1200/1500/2000) Just opened and seriously under-priced, the Twin Towers (slightly unfortunate name that) is easily the town's best-value digs. If all you require is a comfy bed and a bathroom that doesn't require a biohazard suit to enter, then look no further. The restaurant here offers decent, if unimaginative, mains for around KSh300.

Ruma Tourist Lodge HOTEL $
(0717192221; s/d/tw excl breakfast KSh700/900) Don't be put off by the messy entrance – the town's best bar lurks here with cold beers, decent tunes, a rickety pool table and a decent *nyama choma* restaurant (meals KSh150 to KSh250). Rooms are also available but noise can be problematic.

Homa Bay Tourist Hotel HOTEL $$
(072711265; s/d/tw excl breakfast from KSh3000/6200/7500; P@) This lakeside 'resort' is the town's only operation aimed squarely at the tourist sector. The expansive lawns running down to the water's edge surround this ageing but still presentable complex, make it an ideal place to chill with a book.

Information

Barclays Bank (Moi Hwy) With ATM.

Fezza Online (per hr KSh60, closed Sat) Up the hill from Twin Towers Hotel.

WORTH A TRIP

SIMBI LAKE

This pint-sized lakeside village of Kendu Bay, two hours from Kisumu, has little to offer apart from the strange volcanic Simbi Lake a couple of kilometres from town. The circular lake, sunk into the earth like a bomb crater, has a footpath around it and is an excellent twitching spot. The town itself – which is a charming place that feels exactly as you imagine remote Africa would feel – sees very few tourists, and the reception is staggeringly warm.

KWS warden's office (22544) In the district commissioner's compound.

Getting There & Away

Akamba's office is just down the hill from the bus station and its buses serve Nairobi (KSh1200, nine hours, 7.30pm) via Kericho (KSh650, four hours) and Nakuru (KSh900, six hours). Several other companies and matatus (operating from the bus station) also ply these routes, as well as Mbita (KSh250, 1½ hours), Kisii (KSh250, 1½hours) and Kisumu (KSh350, three hours).

Ruma National Park

Bordered by the dramatic **Kanyamaa Escarpment**, and home to Kenya's only population of roans (one of Africa's rarest and largest antelope), is the seldom-visited, 120-sq-km **Ruma National Park** (0717176709, www.kws.go.ke; adult/child US$20/10, plus vehicle from KSh300; 6am-6pm). Due to leopard and hyena predation, the roan population has fallen to a mere 31 individuals but there are plans to make a predator-free sanctuary within the park and possibly bolster the gene pool with roans brought in from Tanzania.

Besides roan, other rarities like Bohor's reedbuck, Jackson's hartebeest, the tiny oribi antelope and Kenya's largest concentration of the endangered Rothschild's giraffe can also be seen here. Birdlife is prolific, with 145 different bird species present, including the migratory blue swallow that arrives between June and August.

The best game viewing is near the new airstrip, as both the giraffes and roans favour that area.

WORTH A TRIP

THIMLICH OHINGA

East of Ruma National Park, this **archaeological site** (admission KSh250) is one of East Africa's most important. The site holds the remains of a dry-stone enclosure, 150m in diameter and containing another five smaller enclosures, thought to date back as far as the 15th century.

Getting to Thimlich is a problem without your own transport, although not completely impossible (with patience). Head down the Homa Bay–Rongo road for 12km, then turn right at Rod Kopany village, heading southwest through Mirogi to the village of Miranga. The site is signposted from there.

Tours

The park is set up for those with vehicles, but if you don't have your own wheels, contact the **KWS rangers** (☎0717176709) at the park gates who may be able to send a local with a pop-top minivan to collect you from Homa Bay. At the time of research, a full-day game drive cost KSh5000 for the vehicle (plus entrance park fees), but as this is drastically out of kilter with the higher charges elsewhere, it is almost certain to rise. The rangers can also accompany you on a **guided trek** (half/full day KSh1500/3000).

Sleeping & Eating

Camping CAMPGROUND $

(camping US$15; P) There are two simple campsites near the main gate. The Nyati special campsite is the more scenic.

Oribi Guesthouse CABIN $$

(☎0717176709, www.kws.go.ke; per cabin excl breakfast US$100; P) Your only other option is the KWS run Oribi Guesthouse, which is extortionate if there are only two of you but quite good value for groups. It has dramatic views over the Lambwe Valley and is well equipped with solar power, hot showers and a fully functioning kitchen.

Getting There & Away

With your own vehicle, head a couple of kilometres south from Homa Bay and turn right onto the Mbita road. About 12km west is the main access road, and from there it's another 11km. The park's roads are in decent shape, but require a mega 4WD in the rainy season.

Mbita & Rusinga Island

POP 26,000

Mbita and Rusinga Island (connected by a causeway) are delightful. Tiny, languid and very rarely visited, they offer a glimpse of an older Africa; an Africa that moves to the gentle sway of the seasons rather than the ticking of a clock. This is the sort of place where school children abandon their classes to see you pass by and old women burst into song at your arrival.

Sights & Activities

Tom Mboya's Mausoleum HISTORIC SITE

A child of Rusinga and a former sanitary inspector in Nairobi, Mboya was one of the few Luo people ever to achieve any kind of political success. He held a huge amount of influence as Jomo Kenyatta's right-hand man and was widely tipped to become Kenya's second president before he was assassinated in 1969. His tomb is on the island's north side.

Mbasa Island WILDLIFE RESERVE

Also known as Bird Island, Mbasa is home to a wide variety of wetland birds including long tailed cormorants (which have a breeding colony here), fish eagles, marsh harriers and little white egrets to name but a few. Bird concentrations are thickest at sunset when peripatetic birds return to roost. To get here you'll need to arrange a boat with a local fisherman; expect to pay between KSh6000 and KSh10,000 per boat, depending on who you talk to.

Sleeping & Eating

TOP CHOICE **Rusinga Guesthouse** GUESTHOUSE $

(☎0735172597; rusingaguesthouse@yahoo.com; Rusinga; s/d/tw KSh1200/1500/1700; P) Far enough away from the bars to offer a quiet night's sleep, this new guesthouse is setting the bar in terms of value for money. The rooms are all freshly painted so they even smell clean, and the mosquito nets are yet to acquire holes. The staff are endearingly shy, the security is good and the restaurant can sort you out with the standard chicken, beef or fish options (mains KSh210 to KSh260).

Lake Victoria Safari Village RESORT $$
(☎0721912120; www.safarikenya.net; Mbita; s/d/tr KSh3900/6000/7800; Ⓟ) A Lake Victoria beachfront haven if ever there was one. Lovely traditionally thatched roofs tower over comfy beds and impressive bathrooms in each of the pretty cottages. The grassy gardens lead down to a private beach with safe swimming, and there's a 'honeymoon suite' inside a mock lighthouse. It's a couple of kilometres south of town.

Bimoss Hotel HOTEL $
(☎0711568875; Mbita; s/d/tw excl breakfast KSh800/1200/1200; Ⓟ) This is a good budget option in town, although the single rooms are slightly crammed and dark and its central location means it's within earshot of local clubs which are quite noisy, unless – and there is a good chance of this – there's a power outage.

Getting There & Away

The best way of getting from Mbita to Kisumu is to take the ferry (foot passenger KSh100, vehicle from KSh700; one hour) to Luanda Kotieno on the northern shore of the narrow Winam Gulf and catch a connecting matatu (KSh250, two hours). Boats leave Mbita at 7am, 9am, 11am, 2pm and 4.30pm. Coming from the other direction, boats depart Luanda Kotieno at 8am, 10am, noon, 3pm and 5.30pm.

If you get off on being placed inside an airless, hot, sticky room and beaten and bruised senseless, you'll love the matatu ride between Mbita and Homa Bay (KSh200, 1½ hours) and on to Kisumu. There is also the odd matatu that heads around Rusinga Island to the mausoleum (KSh50).

Mfangano Island

POP 17,000

If you want to fall totally off the radar then Mfangano Island, sitting out in the placid lake waters, is an idyllic place to get lost. Home to many a monitor lizard, inquisitive locals, intriguing rock paintings and the imposing but assailable Mt Kwitutu (1694m), Mfangano Island is well worth a day or two.

The rock paintings, often featuring sun motifs, are both revered and feared by locals (which has hindered vandalism) and are thought to be the handiwork of the island's earliest inhabitants, Bantu Pygmies from Uganda. The KSh500 entry fee is used to help fund some very needy children at the local orphanage. They (both the orphanage and the rock paintings) are found near the settlement of Kakiimba, a 3km or KSh150 *boda-boda* ride from Sena, the island's 'capital'.

Local **George Ooko Oyuko** (☎0716537317; per day KSh500) can act as a guide to these and other sites. He can also arrange homestays (KSh400) although be prepared for some *extremely* basic conditions, a humbling experience and a warm reception.

Sleeping & Eating

Joyland Hotel HOTEL $
(☎0715165433; Sena, s/tw shared bathroom excl breakfast KSh300/600) Although the basic rooms are essentially clean, those with delicate sensibilities might find the shared toilets a bit grim. Food is available in the attached and only restaurant in Sena.

Mfangano Island Camp RESORT $$$
(☎bookings 020-2734000, camp 0733616224; www.governorscamp.com; 6km north of Sena, per person full board US$450) Nestled into the banks of beautifully maintained gardens alive with monitor lizards and bird life, these stone-and-thatch cottages are the smartest digs on Lake Victoria. The 'honeymoon cottage', with superb 180-degree views, and '*banda* six' are the pick of the bunch and cost no more than the other accommodation options. The camp was formerly a fishing resort, and now offers a number of other watersports, all of which are included in the tariff. If you are planning on dropping in for dinner (meal US$30), give the manager a day's notice.

Getting There & Away

Boats ply the lake waves between Mbita and Mfangano Island daily (KSh150, 1½ hours). In theory they leave at 8am, 10am, 11am, 1pm, 3pm and 5pm returning at 8am, 10am, noon and 3pm. In practice they go only when full and dangerously overloaded. Usually they call in at Takawiri Island en route, stop at Mfangano's 'capital' Sena and then carry on around the island, stopping at most villages on the way.

Private boats can be chartered from the Mbita's Lake Victoria Safari Village for between KSh10,000 and KSh16,000 for a full-day trip.

WESTERN HIGHLANDS

Despite media impressions depicting a land of undulating savannah stretching to the horizon, the real heart and soul of Kenya, and the area where most of the people live, is the luminous green highlands. Benefiting from reliable rainfall and fertile soil, the Western Highlands are the agricultural powerhouse of Kenya; the south is cash-crop country, with vast patchworks of tea plantations covering the region around Kisii and Kericho, while further north, near Kitale and Eldoret, dense cultivation takes over.

The settlements here are predominantly agricultural service towns, with little of interest unless you need a chainsaw or water barrel. For visitors, the real attractions lie outside these places – the rolling tea fields around Kericho, the tropical beauty of Kakamega Forest, trekking on Mt Elgon, the prolific birdlife in Saiwa Swamp National Park and exploring the dramatic Cherangani Hills.

Kisii

☎058 / POP 59,300

Let's cut straight to the chase. Kisii is a noisy, polluted and congested mess, and most people (quite sensibly) roll right on through without even stopping.

While the feted Kisii soapstone obviously comes from this area, it's not on sale here. Quarrying and carving go on in the Gusii village of **Tabaka**, 23km northwest of Kisii. Soapstone is relatively soft and pliable (as far as rocks go) and with simple hand tools and scraps of sandpaper the sculptors carve chess sets, bowls, animals and the unmistakable abstract figures of embracing couples. Each artisan specialises in one design before passing it on to someone else to be smoothed with wet sandpaper and polished with wax. Most pieces are destined for the curio shops of Nairobi and Mombasa, and trade-aid shops around the world. As you would expect, prices are cheaper here than elsewhere. If you are undaunted by adding a few heavy rocks to your backpack, you can save a packet.

Sleeping & Eating

Nile Restaurant, Fast Food & Guesthouse HOTEL $
(☎0710847277; Hospital Rd; s/d excl breakfast KSh650/1000) Clean, cheap rooms and a central location make the Nile the best deal in town. The icing on the cake is that the 2nd-floor restaurant (mains KSh200 to KSh300) has a commanding view of the chaos below, and the menu throws up a few interesting options. Our hopes were high for the chicken tikka (which appears in the Italian section of the menu) but it turned out to be just chicken and chips.

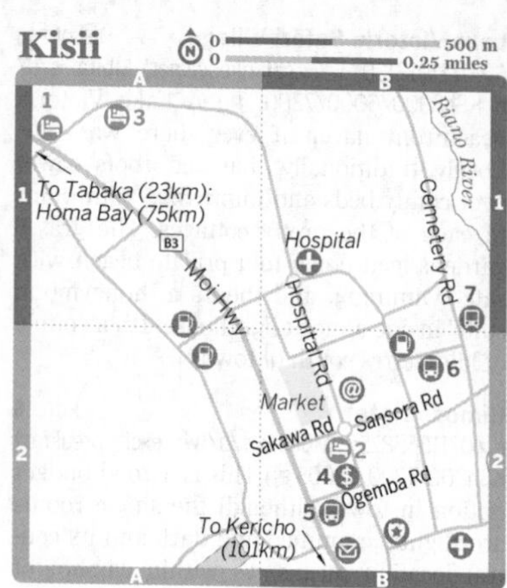

Kisii

Sleeping
1 Kisii Hotel A1
2 Nile Restaurant, Fast Food & Guesthouse B2
3 St Vincent Guesthouse A1

Information
4 Kenya Commercial Bank B2

Transport
5 Akamba B2
6 Matatus B2
7 Matatus to Tabaka B1

Kisii Hotel HOTEL $
(☎30134; s KSh1100/d & tw 1500; P) This is a relaxed place in what feels like an old school building off Moi Hwy. It boasts large gardens and sizeable rooms with decent bathrooms. Like St Vincent's Guesthouse, this is great for those who need quiet surroundings in order to sleep soundly.

St Vincent Guesthouse GUESTHOUSE $
(☎0733650702; camping KSh1000, s/d/tw KSh1500/1850/2450; P) This Catholic-run guesthouse off the Moi Hwy isn't the place for a party, but the rooms are very clean and cosy. Couples travelling together pay a lot less than 'just friends' so, if you are just friends, we'd recommend pushing the beds together and saving 500 bob.

Information

Barclays Bank (Moi Hwy) With ATM.

Fast Web Computer Centre (Hospital Rd; per hr KSh30) Internet and CD/DVD burning facilities.

Post office (Moi Hwy) With cardphones.

Getting There & Away

All hell breaks lose daily at the congested Matatu terminal in the centre of town. Regular departures serve Homa Bay (KSh250, 1½ hours), Kisumu (KSh350, 2½ hours), Kericho (KSh300, two hours) and Isebania (KSh250, 1¾ hours) on the Tanzanian border.

Tabaka matatus (KSh100, 45 minutes) leave from Cemetery Rd. Returning, it is sometimes easier to catch a *boda-boda* (KSh70) to the 'Tabaka junction' and pick up a Kisii-bound matatu there.

Akamba (Moi Hwy) has a daily bus to Nairobi (KSh1000, eight hours) via Nakuru (KSh700, 5½ hours) departing at 9pm – it's wise to book a day in advance. Its Mwanza (Tanzania) bound bus (KSh1600, four hours) from Nairobi calls in at the unseemly hour of 3.30am.

Kericho

052 / POP 82,100

The polar opposite of Kisii, Kericho is a haven of tranquillity. Its surrounds are blanketed by a thick patchwork of manicured tea plantations, each seemingly hemmed in by distant stands of evergreens. With a pleasant climate and a number of things to see and do, Kericho makes for a very calming couple of days.

Sights & Activities

Tea Plantations FARMS

This is the centre of the most important tea gardens in all of Africa, so you might expect tea-plantation tours to be touted left, right and centre. Surprisingly though, they are fairly few and far between. If you just want to take a stroll in the fields, then the easiest plantations to get to are those behind the Tea Hotel.

Otherwise take a guided tour with **Harman Kirui** (0721843980; kmtharman@yahoo.com; per person KSh200). Most tours involve walking around the fields and watching the picking in process (note that the pickers don't work on Sunday). If you want to actually see the process through to the end and visit a factory, you should book at least four days in advance through the Tea Hotel or by emailing Harman directly. The factory most often visited is the **Momul Tea Factory** (per person/group KSh300/1000, Mon-Sat), 28km from Kericho (for those without transport, Harman can arrange a car for KSh2000). The factory has 64 collection sites servicing the area's small-scale farmers and processes a staggering 15 million kilos of green leaf a year.

ANYONE FOR TEA?

Kenya is the world's third-largest tea exporter after India and Sri Lanka, with tea accounting for between 20% and 30% of the country's export income. It is unique in that its small landholders produce the bulk (60%) of the country's tea.

Tea picking is a great source of employment around Kericho, with mature bushes picked every 17 days and the same worker continually picking the same patch. Good pickers collect their own body weight in tea each day!

Despite Kericho producing some of the planet's best black tea, you will have trouble finding a cup of the finest blends here – most of it's exported.

Arboretum GARDENS

(B4 Hwy; closed when raining) Eight kilometres east of town, this tropical park is popular with weekend picnickers and colobus, vervet and red-tailed monkeys (best seen in the early morning). The main attraction here is the shade afforded by the tropical trees planted by estate owner Tom Grumbley in the 1940s. The nearby Chagaik Dam is responsible for the lovely lily-covered pond.

Notable Buildings ARCHITECTURE

Theologically speaking, Kericho is well-represented with the impressive, ivy-clad **Holy Trinity Church**, built in 1952, Africa's largest **Gurdwara** (Sikh place of worship) and a modest Hindu temple on Hospital Rd.

Sleeping & Eating

Being a stronghold of the Kipsigis people, this is good place to try *kimyet* (maize-meal served with vegetables and beef) or *mursik* (soured milk). Naturally, tea is extremely popular and drunk from dawn to supper and every opportunity in between.

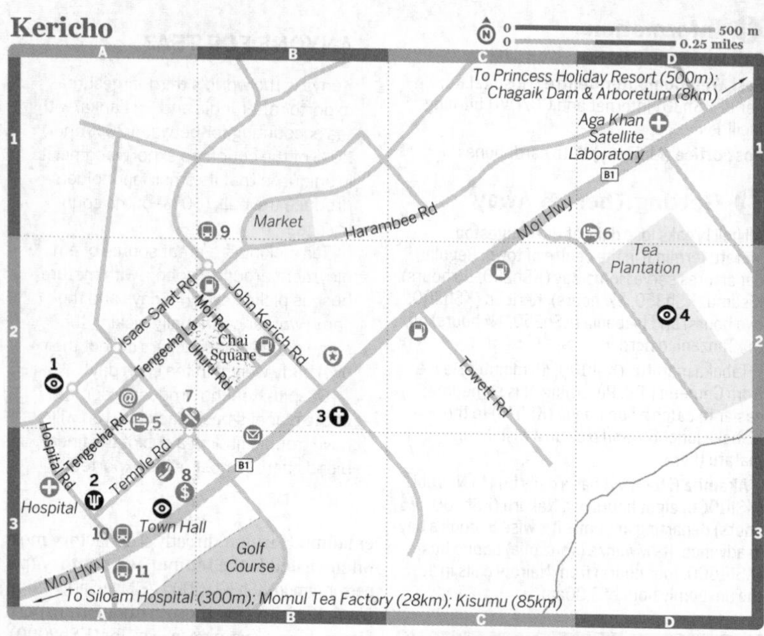

Kericho

Sights

1 Gurdwara A2
2 Hindu Temple A3
3 Holy Trinity Church B2
4 Tea Plantation D2

Sleeping

5 New Sunshine Hotel A2
6 Tea Hotel D1

Eating

7 Litny's Restaurant A2

Information

8 Barclays Bank A3

Transport

9 Bus & Matatu Stand B1
10 Buses (South & West) A3
11 Buses to Kisumu, Kisii & Homa Bay A3
Total Petrol Station .... (see 10)

TOP CHOICE **New Sunshine Hotel** HOTEL $
(0725146601, 30037; Tengecha Rd; s KSh 1500/d & tw 1700) Without a doubt this is the best budget hotel in town (not that the competition is especially stiff). The rooms, while not large, are spotless and the showers are actually hot rather than lukewarm. The attached restaurant (meals KSh320 to KSh550) does a roaring trade, although we found the braised goat must have had the physique of a marathon runner. Two things to note: housekeeping seldom locks doors after cleaning and tariffs are considerably more expensive if you have breakfast included.

Princess Holiday Resort GUESTHOUSE $
(0721254736; off Moi Hwy; s/d KSh2500/3000; P) This is one of many guesthouses-cum-hotels that have sprung up on the side roads around the Tea Hotel. We choose this one over its competitors because the rooms are modern, clean and come with a traditional cooked English breakfast. The management will bend over backwards to be helpful and if you give them a call, they will collect you from town.

Tea Hotel HOTEL $
(020-2050790; teahotel@africaonline.co.ke; Moi Hwy; camping KSh700, s/d excl breakfast US$65/90; P) This grand property was built in the 1950s by the Brooke Bond company and still has a lot of period charm about it. We

liked it in the same way you do a favourite teddy bear despite its missing eye and loose stuffing. The hotel's most notable features are the vast hallways and dining rooms full of mounted animal heads, and its beautiful gardens with their tea-bush backdrops. The latter makes an atmospheric place for afternoon tea, which explains why so many overland trucks choose to camp here. Unfortunately any sentimentality that we found endearing about the communal spaces had worn thin by the time we saw the rooms, which are tired and terribly overpriced.

Litny's Restaurant KENYAN $
(Temple Rd; mains KSh300-500; ⌚lunch & dinner Mon-Sat) Along with New Sunshine Hotel, this is regarded as one of the better restaurants in town, although in truth, the goat here was no different to the goat we ate elsewhere.

Information

Barclays Bank (Moi Hwy) With ATM that accepts Visa and occasionally Mastercard.

Siloam Hospital (☎21200; Moi Hwy) Excellent private hospital.

Post office (Moi Hwy)

Telecare Centre (Temple Rd) Calling cards and cardphones.

World Speed Cyber Cafe (off Tengecha Rd; per min KSh0.80) One of three shacks offering internet browsing in an alley off Tengecha Rd. Groove Cyber next door can also burn CDs and DVDs.

Getting There & Away

Most buses and matatus operate from the main stand in the town's northwest corner, while those heading south and west leave from the Total petrol station on Moi Hwy.

Buses to Nairobi (KSh600, 4½ hours) are quite frequent, as are matatus to Kisumu (KSh250, 1½ hours), Kisii (KSh300, two hours), Eldoret (KSh400 to KSh500, 3½ hours) and Nakuru (KSh300, two hours). The odd Peugeot also serves these destinations, but costs about 25% more.

Kakamega

☎056 / POP 73,600

There is no real reason to stay in this small agricultural town, but if you arrive late in the day it can be convenient to sleep over and stock up with supplies before heading to nearby Kakamega Forest Reserve.

Look out for the **Crying Stone of Ilesi** (Map p151), a local curiosity perched on a ridge 3km south of town. The formation, looking like a solemn head resting on weary shoulders, consists of a large boulder balanced atop a huge column of rock, down which tears flow. There are two legends regarding the reason for this. The first is that the stone is that of a girl who continues to cry after she fell in love with a man her father didn't approve of and, as punishment, the father turned her to stone. The second is that the stones weep for the state

WESTERN BULL FIGHTING

Bull fighting (between two bulls) is the fastest growing sport in Western Kenya, and Khayega (Map p151, 6km south of Kakamega) has Friday and Saturday showdowns. They start early at 7am (the whole thing wraps up at around 8am), with a whole lot of horn blowing, drumming, chanting and stick waving.

The purpose-bred bulls are fed on molasses-spiked grass and, to help them preserve their energy, isolated from heifers, making them understandably tetchy. Then the bulls are fed secret concoctions guaranteed to make them even more aggressive.

When the bulls meet, they'll lock horns and fight until one submits and turns tail. Besides a bruised ego or two, no bulls are injured during the show of strength (cattle are valued too highly for owners to put them at risk). There are no safety barriers, so spectators should keep their distance and be prepared to run or climb a tree should a bull break away.

The winning bull (and all of the crowd) then race to the next venue, usually about 1km to 2km away, where they meet up with a similar winner and the whole performance is repeated.

Bull fighting is practised mostly by the Isukha and Idako peoples.

of humanity in general. A far less romantic explanation is offered by science; a hidden reservoir at the top of the formation fills will rain water and, as the water escapes via hairline cracks, it produces the weeping effect.

The town's municipal **market** is worth poking your nose into. It operates every day but is at its loudest on Saturday and Wednesday mornings when, as if by magic, people appear from all over the surrounding countryside.

Sleeping & Eating

While there are lots of local eateries, there are few to get excited about. Seemingly, without exception, they serve chicken, fish or beef; fried or 'wet fried' (which means it comes with gravy).

Franka Hotel HOTEL $
(Mumias Rd; r excl breakfast KSh800) A maze of dark and dastardly rooms sit above what is arguably the town's best eating and drinking hole (meals KSh250 to KSh300). Rooms all have bathrooms and come with nets and noise – some of it road-produced, some bar-produced and some of the baby-making variety. The **Western Grill Guesthouse** next door has a similar set up with similar prices.

Friends Hotel HOTEL $
(☎31716; Mumias Rd; s excl breakfast KSh1500-1800, d KSh1800-2200) Friends has comfortable rooms that are pleasing to the eye and come in two sizes, both with 24-hour hot water, but both a little overpriced for what you get. The larger 'deluxe' rooms also include breakfast in the well-regarded restaurant (mains KSh300 to KSh400) downstairs.

Nakumart SUPERMARKET $
(Holden Mall; meals KSh200-300; ⏲breakfast, lunch & dinner) The best stocked supermarket in town. The attached Kula Korner restaurant has good pizzas, disappointing smoothies and OK burgers.

Information

Barclays Bank (A1 Hwy) With ATM.

KWS Area Headquarters (☎30603; 1½km from town centre) Kakamega Forest information.

Post office (A1 Hwy)

Telkom Kenya (A1 Hwy) Calling cards and cardphones.

Getting There & Around

Easy Coach (off Mumias Rd) serves Nairobi (KSh1200, seven hours) at 8.30am and 8pm, via Kisumu (KSh300, one hour), Kericho (KSh600, 3½ hours) and Nakuru (KSh800, five hours). Nearby, **Akamba** (off Mumias Rd) services the same route at slightly cheaper rates with 7.30am and 8pm departures.

Kitale (KSh 300, three hours), Eldoret (KSh250, two hours) and Shinyalu (KSh70, 30 minutes) matatus leave from the main stage behind the market. Kisumu (KSh250, 1¾ hours) bound matatus can be caught near the Total petrol station on the northern edge of town.

Kakamega Forest

☎056

Not so long ago much of western Kenya was hidden under a dark veil of jungle and formed a part of the mighty Guineo-Congolian forest ecosystem – even gorillas are rumoured to have once played in the mists here. However, the British soon did their best to turn all that lovely virgin forest into tea estates. Now all that's left is this slab of tropical rainforest surrounding Kakamega.

Though seriously degraded, this forest is unique in Kenya and contains plants, animals and birds that occur nowhere else in the country. It's so wild here trees actually kill each other – seriously! Parasitic fig trees grow on top of unsuspecting trees and strangle their hosts to death.

Sights & Activities

Walking Trails HIKING
The best way, indeed the only real way, to appreciate the forest is to walk, and trails radiate from Buyangu and Isecheno areas.

While guides are not compulsory, they are well worth the extra expense. Not only do they prevent you from getting lost, but most are walking encyclopaedias and will reel off both the Latin and common name of almost any plant or insect you care to point out, along with any of its medicinal properties. They are also able to recognise and imitate birdcalls so effectively that you wouldn't be surprised if they suddenly sprouted wings and flew off.

As ever, the early morning and late afternoon are the best times to view birds, but night walks can also be a fantastic experience. Though the forest is crawling with life, this isn't the Masai Mara and sightings of animals are fleeting at best (except for the primates, which are normally easy to find).

Rather than expecting to see leopards, forest hogs and the like it's better to think small. Concentrate on the birds and the bees – the insect life here is phenomenal (it's said that if you spend one hour rummaging through the leaf litter of a tropical rainforest then you will discover a new species of insect!). However, it's the birds that really steal the show and Kakamega, with its unique collection of species, more common to the forests of the Congo, is easily one of the top birding destinations in Kenya.

Buyangu Area

Rangers state that trails vary in length from 1km to 7km. Of the longer walks, **Isiukhu Trail**, which connects Isecheno to the small **Isiukhu Falls**, is one of the most popular and takes a minimum of half a day. The 4km drive or walk to **Buyangu Hill** allows for uninterrupted views east to the Nandi Escarpment.

Isecheno Area

The five-hour return hike to **Lirhanda Hill** for sunrise or sunset is highly recommended, as too are the night walks, which occasionally turn up slow-moving pottos (an insanely cute, furry primate). An interesting short walk (2.6km) to a 35m-high **watchtower** affords views over the forest canopy and small grassland.

Sleeping & Eating

BUYANGU AREA

If you're staying at either of the KWS-managed options, you will have to pay park entry fees for each night you're there.

Isikuti Guesthouse GUESTHOUSE $$

(☎30603, 0727415828, www.kws.go.ke; cottage US$50) Hidden in a pretty forest glade close to Udo's are four massive KWS cottages (sleeping up to four), with equipped kitchens and bathrooms.

De Brazza's Campsite CAMPSITE $

(☎0721628343, camping KSh400, bandas per person KSh600) Just before the park gates, this simple campsite is as basic as basic gets. There's no electricity and the toilets are the kind where the long-drops aren't long enough.

Udo's Bandas & Camping BANDA $

(☎30603, 0727415828, www.kws.go.ke; camping US$15, bandas per person US$30) Named after Udo Savalli, a well-known ornithologist, this lovely KWS site is tidy, well maintained and has seven simple thatched *bandas*; nets are provided, but you will need your own sleeping bag and other supplies. There are long-drop toilets, bucket showers, and a communal cooking and dining shelter.

Kakamega Forest

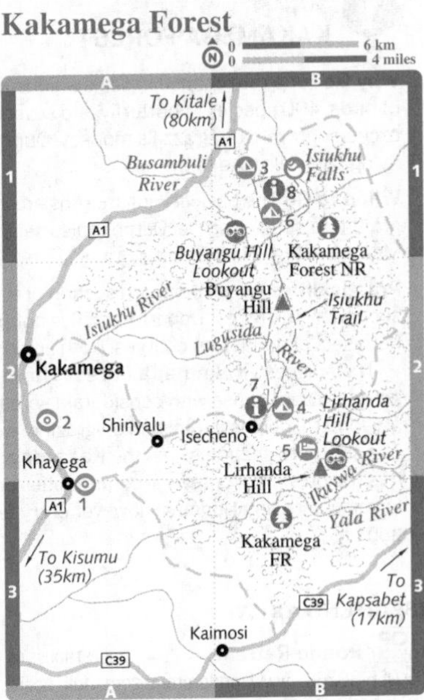

Kakamega Forest

Sights

1 Bull Fighting Grounds....A3
2 Crying Stone of Ilesi....A2

Sleeping

3 De Brazza's Campsite....B1
4 Forest Rest House....B2
Isikuti Guesthouse....(see 6)
KEEP Bandas....(see 7)
5 Rondo Retreat....B2
6 Udo's Bandas & Campsite....B1

Information

Kakamega Forest Guide Association....(see 8)
7 Kakamega Forest Reserve Office....B2
Kakamega Rainforest Tour Guides....(see 7)
8 KWS Office....B1

KAKAMEGA FOREST

Why Go For a rare chance to see a unique rainforest ecosystem with over 330 species of birds, 400 species of butterfly and seven different primate species, one being the exceedingly rare de Brazza's monkey. During darkness, hammer-headed fruit bats and flying squirrels take to the air.

When to Go The best viewing months are June, August and October, when many migrant bird species arrive. October also sees many wildflowers bloom, while December to March are the driest months.

Practicalities As the northern section of the forest is managed by KWS and the southern section by the Forest Department, it is not possible to visit the whole park without paying both sets of admission charges. Both areas have their pros and cons.

The northern **Kakamega Forest National Reserve** has a variety of habitats but is generally very dense with considerable areas of primary forest and regenerating secondary forest. There is a total ban on grazing, wood collection and cultivation in this zone. The southern section forms the **Kakamega Forest Reserve**. Predominantly forested, this region supports several communities and is under considerable pressure from both farming and illegal logging, however entry fees are lower and there is better accommodation here.

ISECHENO AREA

TOP CHOICE **Rondo Retreat** GUESTHOUSE **$$**
(☎056-30268; www.rondoretreat.com; full board adult/child KSh7400/5400) To arrive at the Rondo Retreat is to be whisked back to 1922 and the height of British rule. Consisting of a series of wooden bungalows filled with a family's clutter, this gorgeous and eccentric place is a wonderful retreat from modern Kenya. The gardens are absolutely stunning and worth visiting even if you're not staying – don't miss the secluded garden by the pond, or the afternoon tea and cake on the veranda. Dinner is a formal affair: you should dress smart (no shorts) and expect old-fashioned English meat-and-two-veg. Profits go to a Christian charity.

Forest Rest House HUT **$**
(☎0727486747; camping KSh650, r per person KSh500) The four rooms of this wooden house, perched on stilts 2m above the ground and with views straight onto a mass of impenetrable jungle, might be as basic as it gets (no electricity, no bedding and cold-water baths that look like they'd crash through the floor boards if you tried to fill one), but it's guaranteed to bring out the inner Tarzan in even the most obstinate city-slicker.

KEEP Bandas BANDA **$**
(☎0729258205; per person shared bathroom KSh700) The five small *bandas* here are almost swallowed up by jungle and are a little overpriced, considering all you get is a small hut with no electricity and communal cold-water showers. Still, it's very atmospheric and you're in the jungle – life isn't supposed to be easy. Meals (KSh270 to KSh400) can be arranged with the caretaker if you don't wish to self-cater in the basic kitchen.

Information

Kakamega Forest National Reserve (www.kws.go.ke; park entrance adult/child US$20/10, vehicles KSh300) in the north is under the stewardship of KWS. Ranger guides cost the standard KSh1500 for up to six hours and can be arranged at the park gates. Alternatively, guides from the **Kakamega Forest Guide Association** (per person per hr KSh400) are also on hand to offer their services.

Kakamega Forest Reserve (park entrance adult/child KSh600/150) in the southern Isecheno area is managed by the Forest Department, which maintains a small office with friendly staff next to the just-as-friendly **Kakamega Rainforest Tour Guides** (☎0729911386, kakamegaforestguides@yahoo.com; per person short/long walk KSh500/800).

Getting There & Away

Buyangu Area

Matatus heading north towards Kitale can drop you at the access road about 18km north of Kakamega town (KSh70). It is a well-signposted 2km walk from there to the park office and Udo's.

Isecheno Area

Regular matatus link Kakamega with Shinyalu (KSh70), but few go on to Isecheno. Shinyalu is also accessed by a rare matatu service from Khayega. From Shinyalu you will probably need to take a *boda-boda* for KSh100 to Isecheno.

The improved roads are still treacherous after rain and you may prefer to walk once you've seen the trouble vehicles can have. To Shinyalu it's about 7km from Khayega and 10km from Kakamega. From Shinyalu it is 5km to Isecheno.

The dirt road from the Isecheno continues east to Kapsabet, but transport is rare.

Eldoret

053 / POP 167,000

The Maasai originally referred to this area as *eldore* (stony river) after the nearby Sosiani River, but this proved too linguistically challenging for the South African Voortrekkers who settled here in 1910 and they named their settlement Eldoret instead.

In 2008 Eldoret achieved notoriety when 35 people (mostly Kikuyus) were burnt alive in a church on the outskirts of town. This incident was the largest single loss of life during the 2007 post-election violence.

Today, Eldoret is a thriving service town straddling the Kenya–Uganda highway. It's the principal economic hub of Western Kenya but for the traveller, there is little to see, and even less to do. The highlight is a visit to the **Doinyo Lessos Creameries Cheese Factory** (Kenyatta St; 8am-6pm) to stock up on any one of 20 different varies of cheese. Enjoy.

Sleeping

TOP CHOICE **White Castle Motel** HOTEL $

(62773; whitecastle@deepafrica.com Uganda Rd; s KSh1500-1800, tw KSh3000) While it has little in the ways of frills or personality, the White Castle is a sound choice. It's centrally located, comparatively clean, the security is top-notch and the staff delightful. The street-level restaurant is similarly reliable and surprisingly, most things on its menu are actually available. Its basement disco only opens on weekends, when the air becomes thick with the adolescent hormones of the students it attracts.

White Highlands Inn HOTEL $

(0734818955; Elgeyo St; s/d KSh1800/2500; P) In a quiet corner on the edge of town, this place offers good value. Its spacious rooms were so spotless that we actually lay in the bathtub as opposed to just looking at it wistfully. The whole complex is a bit rambling but retains a certain old-fashioned charm, and has a popular bar and less-popular restaurant.

Aya Inn HOTEL $

(2062259; Oginga Odinga St; r excl breakfast KSh650, r excl breakfast without bathroom KSh550) The staff will think you're off your head wanting to look at the rooms before handing over your cash – as if you can't trust them when they say it's like the Hilton! Alas, it's not, but it's also a lot cheaper and for the money it's probably better value. Opt for one of the quieter, secluded rooms with hot water.

WHERE BOYS BECOME MEN

The Bungoma/Trans-Nzoia district goes wild in August with the sights and sounds of the Bukusu Circumcision Festival, an annual jamboree dedicated to the initiation of local young boys into manhood.

The tradition was apparently passed to the Bukusu by the Sabaot tribe in the 19th century, when a young hunter cut the head off a troublesome serpent to earn the coveted operation.

The evening before the ceremony is devoted to substance abuse and sex; in the morning the youngsters are trimmed with a traditional knife in front of their entire village.

Unsurprisingly, this practice has attracted a certain amount of controversy in recent years. Health concerns are prevalent, as the same knife can be used for up to 10 boys, posing a risk of HIV/AIDS and other infections. The associated debauchery also brings a seasonal rush of underage pregnancies and family rifts that seriously affect local communities.

Education and experience now mean that fewer boys undergo the old method, preferring to take the safe option at local hospitals. However, those wielding the knife are less likely to let go of their heritage. To quote one prominent circumciser: 'Every year at this time it's like a fever grips me, and I can't rest until I've cut a boy'.

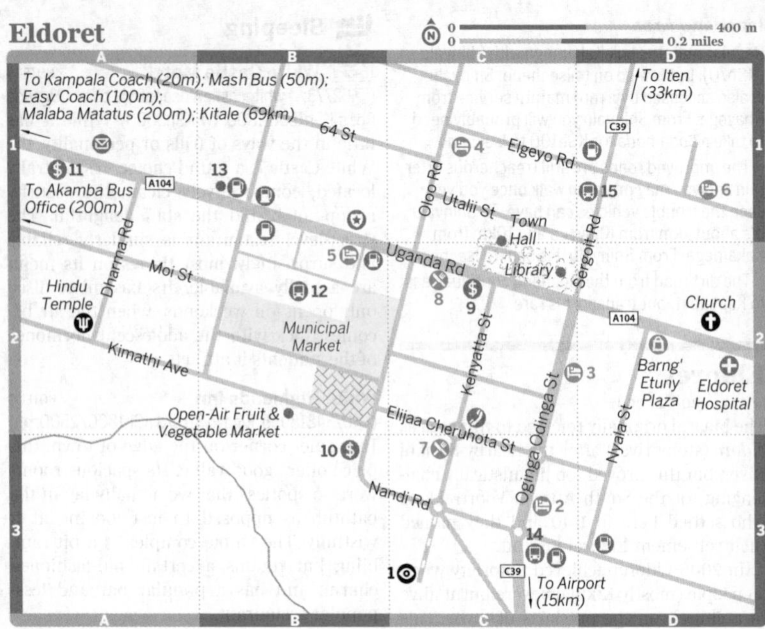

Eldoret

Sights

1 Doinyo Lessos Creameries Cheese Factory C3

Sleeping

2 Aya Inn C3
3 Klique Hotel C2
4 Sirikwa Hotel C1
5 White Castle Hotel B2
6 White Highlands Inn D1

Eating

Klique Hotel .... (see 3)
7 Sunjeel Palace C3
8 Will's Pub & Restaurant C2

Information

9 Barclays Bank C2
Consani .... (see 8)
10 Postbank B3
11 Postbank A1

Transport

12 Bus & Matatu Stand B2
13 Elgeyo Travel & Tours B1
14 Local Matatus C3
15 Matatus to Iten & Kabarnet D1

Klique Hotel HOTEL $$
(☎0732060903; www.kliquehotel.com; Oginga Odinga St; s/d excl breakfast US$40/50) A modern and comfortable high-rise with brightly (sometimes garishly) painted rooms and the best bathrooms in all of Eldoret. Non-resident rates are a bit steep but if they automatically assume you're a resident you could just go with the flow...

Sirikwa Hotel HOTEL $$
(☎2063614; sirikwahotel@yahoo.com Elgeyo Rd; s from US$75, d/tw from US$90, f from US$165; P🛜≋) Screams 1977 through and through, and Prince Charles would fall into a faint if he saw how ugly the building is. Its day might be done, but everyone continues to insist it's the top hotel in town; by which they probably mean it's the most expensive. If you ask for the resident rates you'll only pay KSh3500/4500 for a single/double, which is what they are worth.

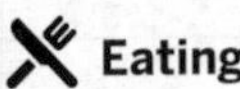

Eating

TOP CHOICE Sunjeel Palace INDIAN $$
(Kenyatta St; mains KSh450-600; ⏲lunch & dinner; ✎) This formal, dark and spicy Indian restaurant serves superb, real-deal curries. Portion sizes are decent and if you mop up all the gravy with a freshly baked butter *naan*, you'll be as rotund as Ganesh himself.

Klique Hotel INTERNATIONAL $
(Oginga Odinga St; mains KSh400-500; ⏲breakfast, lunch & dinner) Head upstairs to the enclosed terrace for some swanky dining and a fine view of the street life below. The menu offers some good steak and chicken options that are a bit tastier than all the other steak and chicken options (of which there are many) around town.

Will's Pub & Restaurant INTERNATIONAL $
(Uganda Rd; mains KSh300-450; ⏲breakfast, lunch & dinner) Looks and feels like an English pub, with similarly heavyweight food – salads, pasta, steak and fried breakfasts. The big-screen TV makes it a great place for a cold beer, and the low-key vibe makes it a safe spot for solo female travellers.

Information

Barclays Bank (Uganda Rd) With ATM.

Consani (Uganda Rd; per hr KSh60) Besides reliable internet, it can burn images to CD and has VOIP and scanning facilities.

Eldoret Hospital One of Kenya's best hospitals, with 24-hour emergency. It's off Uganda Rd.

Post office (Uganda Rd)

Telkom Kenya (cnr Kenyatta St & Elijaa Cheruhota St) Calling cards and cardphones.

Getting There & Away

Air

There are morning and afternoon flights between Eldoret and Nairobi (from KSh4940, one hour) with either **Jetlink** (www.jetlink.co.ke) or **Fly540.com** (www.fly540.com). Bookings can be handled online or through **Elgeyo Travel & Tours** (✆20 733557798; info@elgeyotravel.com; Uganda Rd).

Matatu

The main matatu stand is in the centre of town by the municipal market although some local matatus and more Kericho services leave from Nandi Rd. Irregular matatus to Iten and Kabarnet leave from Sergoit Rd. Further west on Uganda Rd, matatus leave for Malaba on the Uganda border.

MATATUS FROM ELDORET

DESTINATION	FARE	DURATION
Iten	KSh100	1 hour
Kabarnet	KSh300	2 hours
Kakamega	KSh250	2 hours
Kericho	KSh350-400	3 hours
Kisumu	KSh350-400	3 hours
Kitale	KSh200	1¼ hours
Nairobi	KSh700	6 hours
Nakuru	KSh300	2¾ hours
Nyahururu	KSh450	3½ hours

Bus

A string of bus companies line Uganda Rd west of the Postbank. Most service Nairobi via Nakuru. Some reliable operators include:

Akamba (Moi St) 10pm buses to Nairobi (KSh800, five hours) via Nakuru (KSh400, 2¾ hours) and a 1am service to Kampala (KSh1500, six hours).

Easy Coach (Uganda Rd) 10am and 9.30pm buses to Nairobi (KSh1100) via Nakuru (KSh600).

Mash Bus (Uganda Rd) Direct bus to Mombasa (KSh1600, 12 hours, 5pm).

Kampala Coach (Uganda Rd) Noon and midnight buses to Kampala (KSh1800) and a 6pm coach to Kigali (KSh3300, 14 hours).

Getting Around

A matatu to or from the airport costs KSh70, and a taxi will cost around KSh1000-1500. *Boda-bodas* (especially the motorised variety) can be found on most street corners.

Kitale

✆054 / POP 86,100

Agricultural Kitale is a small and friendly market town with a couple of interesting museums and a bustling market. It makes an ideal base for explorations of Mt Elgon and Saiwa Swamp National Parks. It also serves as the take-off point for a trip up to the western side of Lake Turkana.

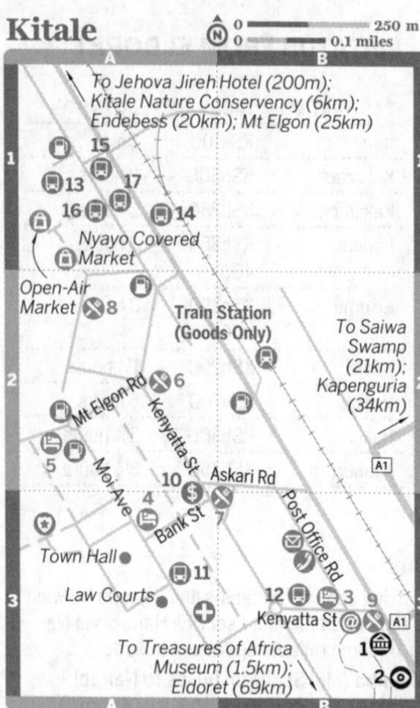

Kitale

Sights
- 1 Kitale Museum ... B3
- 2 Olof Palme Agroforestry Centre ... B3

Sleeping
- 3 Alakara Hotel ... B3
- 4 Bongo Lodge ... A3
- 5 Kahuruko Bar & Lodge ... A2

Eating
- 6 Corner Café ... A2
- 7 Iroko Boulevard Restaurant ... B3
- 8 Khetia's Gigamart ... A2
- 9 The Coffee Shop ... B3

Information
- 10 Barclays Bank ... A3

Transport
- 11 Akamba ... A3
- 12 Easy Coach ... B3
- 13 Main Bus & Matatu Park ... A1
- 14 Matatus to Eldoret and Nairobi ... A1
- 15 Matatus to Kapenguria ... A1
- 16 Matatus to Kisumu & Kakamega ... A1
- 17 Matatus to Marich Pass ... A1

Sights & Activities

Kitale Museum MUSEUM
(☎30996; A1 Hwy; adult/child KSh500/250; ⊙8am-6pm) Founded on the collection of butterflies, birds and ethnographic memorabilia left to the nation in 1967 by the late Lieutenant Colonel Stoneham, this museum has an interesting range of ethnographic displays of the Pokot, Akamba, Marakwet and Turkana peoples. There is also any number of stuffed dead things shot by various colonial types. The outdoor exhibits include some traditional tribal homesteads and a collection of snakes, tortoises and crocodiles, plus an interesting 'Hutchinson Biogas Unit'.

The best thing here is the small nature trail that leads through some not-quite-virgin rainforest at the back of the museum.

Kitale Nature Conservancy ZOO
(Ndura; ☎0722370803; www.kitalenature.or.ke; A1 Hwy; admission KSh800; ⊙8am-7pm) Self-described as 'a sanctuary for animal mutants' this place looks as if it was designed by Frankenstein after he converted to Christianity and dropped acid. While there is an incredibly kitsch portrayal of biblical scenes in the form of life-sized concrete statues and a rather boring nature trail, the real reason people visit is to gawk at deformed animals, the star of which is a three-eyed, five-horned cow.

Treasures of Africa Museum MUSEUM
(☎30867; http://treasuresofafricamuseum.blogspot.com; A1 Hwy; admission KSh250; ⊙9am-noon & 2-5.30pm Mon-Sat) This private museum is the personal collection of Mr Wilson, a former colonial officer in Uganda. Based mainly on his experiences with the Karamojong people of northern Uganda, Mr Wilson's small museum illustrates his theory that a universal worldwide agricultural culture existed as far back as the last Ice Age.

FREE **Olof Palme Agroforestry Centre** GARDENS
(A1 Hwy; ⊙8am-5pm) The Olof Palme Agroforestry Centre is a Swedish-funded program aimed at educating local people about the protection and rehabilitation of the environment by integrating trees into farming

systems. The project includes a small demonstration farm and agroforestry plot, an information centre and an arboretum.

Sleeping

Bongo Lodge HOTEL $
(☎32520593; Moi Ave; s & d excl breakfast KSh800, tw excl breakfast KSh900) Stop wasting time and come straight here if you want to get your hands on the best budget beds in town. All rooms have bathrooms and are scrupulously clean (well at least by Kenyan standards).

Jehova Jireh Hotel HOTEL $$
(☎31752; s excl breakfast KSh1500, tw excl breakfast KSh2200-3500) A solid midrange choice that boasts twin rooms that are spacious, quiet and clean and, don't worry, it's not as God-fearing as it sounds. There's an excellent downstairs restaurant that serves food later than most.

Kahuruko Bar & Lodge HOTEL $
(☎0750107384; kahurukoh@yahoo.com; Mt Elgon Rd; s excl breakfast KSh600) These small but spiffy rooms are a bargain and well suited to solo travellers and feuding couples as they only have singles. You can sink your teeth into some decent dead cow at the *nyama choma* (barbecued meat) restaurant downstairs (half a kilo KSh260).

Alakara Hotel HOTEL $
(☎31554; Kenyatta St; r without bathroom KSh1000, d/tw KSh1800/1300; P) The rooms with shared bathrooms are over-priced, but the others are fair value with comfortable beds, reliable hot water and friendly staff. It also has a good bar, restaurant and TV room.

Eating & Drinking

TOP CHOICE **The Coffee Shop** INTERNATIONAL $
(A1 Hwy; mains KSh200-400; ⏰breakfast & lunch) While it may not be the first choice for many locals, the Coffee Shop provides welcome relief from the chicken and chips menus found elsewhere. Some of the tempting treats include Mexican-style fajitas and enchiladas, European desserts (including a warm chocolate brownie with ice cream), cheeseburgers, filtered coffee and sweet honey *lassis* (an Indian yoghurt drink). You'll also find a curio shop selling local handicrafts and a small book exchange. Keep an eye on its noticeboard for announcements on upcoming pizza nights and special Sunday night buffets (KSh600).

Iroko Boulevard Restaurant KENYAN $
(Askari Rd; mains KSh170-250; ⏰breakfast, lunch & dinner) It's got style, it's got glamour, it's got big-city aspirations and it's totally unexpected in Kitale. With cheap dishes that include a different African special every day and an old Morris car hanging from the ceiling, this is the most popular place to eat in town.

Corner Café KENYAN $
(Kenyatta St; mains KSh110-180; ⏰breakfast & lunch) This cheap and cheerful local eatery is located inside an old colonial building and attracts a steady stream of locals after no-nonsense African staples at low prices.

Khetia's Gigamart SUPERMARKET $
(⏰7.30am-7pm) Stock up at this massive supermarket.

Information

Barclays Bank (Bank St) With ATM. Other banks are next door.
Cyber Cafe (Kenyatta St; internet per hr KSh60)
Post office (Post Office Rd)
Telkom Kenya (Post Office Rd) Calling cards and cardphones.

Getting There & Away

Matatus, buses and Peugeots are grouped by destination, and spread in and around the main bus and matatu park.

Regular matatus run to Endebess (KSh70, 45 minutes, change here for Mt Elgon National Park), Kapenguria (KSh120, 45 minutes, change here to continue north to Marich), Eldoret (KSh200 to KSh230, 1¼ hours), Kakamega (KSh250, 2½hours) and Kisumu (KSh450, four hours).

Most bus companies have offices around the bus station and serve Eldoret (KSh200, one hour), Nakuru (KSh600, 3½ hours), Nairobi (KSh700, seven hours) and Lodwar (KSh800, 8½ hours) each day.

Akamba (Moi Ave) runs buses from outside its office to Nairobi at 8pm (KSh1000, seven hours).

Easy Coach (Kenyatta St) does the same (Nairobi, KSh1200) but besides its 8pm departure there is also an 8.30am departure that calls into Nakuru (KSh900, 3½ hours).

MT ELGON NATIONAL PARK

Why Go Some superb overnight treks along with some interesting half-day options to caves occasionally visited by salt-loving elephants.

When to Go It's extremely wet most of the year; serious trekkers should visit between December and February when it is at its driest.

Practicalities The easiest section of the park to visit is the area accessed via Chorlim Gate, from where you can walk or drive to the caves and surrounding forest. Waterproof gear and warm clothing is essential, as the Mt Elgon area is as chilly as it is wet. Altitude may also be a problem for some people.

Check out the security situation with **KWS headquarters** Nairobi (☎020-600800; kws@kws.org; PO Box 40241, Nairobi); Mt Elgon National Park (☎0538005393; park gate) before you plan anything. Crossing into Uganda wasn't permitted at the time of research, but ask for the latest at the gate.

Mt Elgon National Park

Straddling the Ugandan border and peaking with Koitoboss (4187m), Kenya's second-highest peak, and Uganda's Wagagai (4321m), the mist-shrouded slopes of Mt Elgon are a sight indeed.

With rainforest at the base, the vegetation changes as you ascend to bamboo jungle and finally alpine moorland featuring the giant groundsel and giant lobelia plants.

Common animals include buffaloes, bushbucks (usually grazing on the airstrip near Cholim gate), olive baboons, giant forest hogs and duikers. The lower forests are the habitat of the black-and-white colobus, and blue and de Brazza's monkeys.

There are more than 240 species of birds here, including red-fronted parrots, Ross's turacos and casqued hornbills. On the peaks you may even see a lammergeier raptor gliding through the thin air.

Sights & Activities

Elkony Caves CAVE

Four main lava tubes (caves) are open to visitors: **Kitum**, **Chepnyalil**, **Mackingeny** and **Rongai**.

While rarely seen, elephants are known to 'mine' for salt from the walls of the caves. Kitum holds your best hope for glimpsing them (particularly before dawn in the dry season), but sadly the number of these saline-loving creatures has declined over the years, mainly due to incursions by Ugandan poachers. Nonetheless, a torchlight inspection will soon reveal their handiwork in the form of tusking – the groves and gouges made by their tusks during the digging process.

Mackingeny, with a waterfall cascading across the entrance, is the most spectacular of the caves and has colonies of large fruit bats and smaller horseshoe bats towards the rear. If you plan on visiting the bats, be sure to bring whatever kind of footwear you feel will cope well with 100 years of accumulated dusty bat shit.

The caves are a 6km drive or walk (one way) from Chorlim Gate.

Koitoboss Trek HIKING

Allow at least four days for any round-trips, and two or three days for any direct ascent of Koitoboss from the Chorlim Gate. Once you reach the summit, there are a number of interesting options for the descent. You can descend northwest into the crater to **Suam Hot Springs**. Alternatively you could go east around the crater rim and descend the Masara Route, which leads to the small village of Masara on the eastern slopes of the mountain (about 25km) and then returns to Endebess. Or you can head southwest around the rim of the crater (some very hard walking) to **Lower Elgon Tarn**, where you can camp before ascending **Lower Elgon Peak** (4301m).

If all of this sounds too tiring, you'll be pleased to know that it's possible to get within 4km of the summit with a 4WD in decent weather.

Sleeping

Camping CAMPGROUND $

(www.kws.go.ke; camping US$15) If you're trekking, your only option is to camp. The fee

Mt Elgon National Park

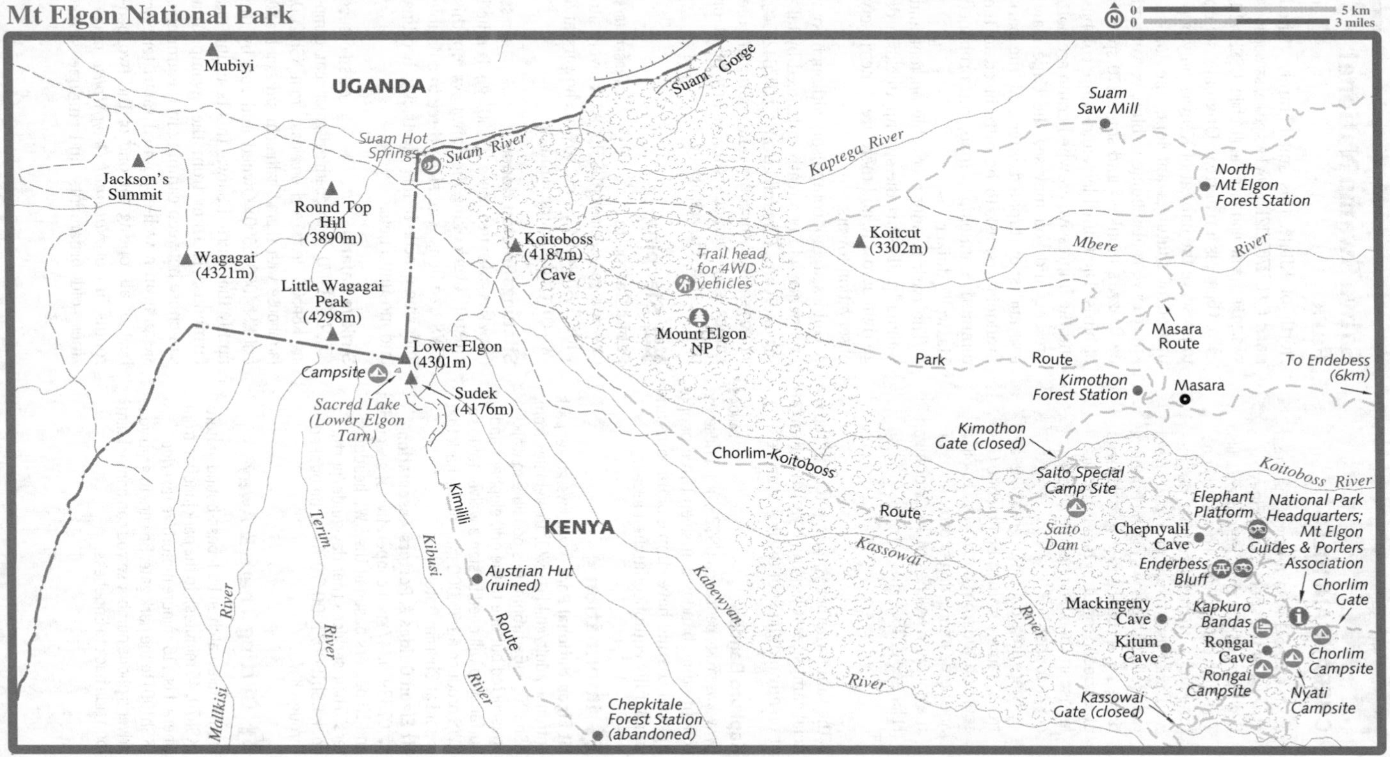

0 5 km
0 3 miles

Mubiyi
UGANDA
Suam Gorge
Suam Hot Springs
Suam River
Jackson's Summit
Round Top Hill (3890m)
Wagagai (4321m)
Little Wagagai Peak (4298m)
Koitoboss (4187m)
Cave
Kaptega River
Suam Saw Mill
North Mt Elgon Forest Station
Koitcut (3302m)
Trail head for 4WD vehicles
Mount Elgon NP
Mbere River
Masara Route
Lower Elgon (4301m)
Campsite
Sudek (4176m)
Sacred Lake (Lower Elgon Tarn)
Park Route
To Endebess (6km)
Kimothon Forest Station
Masara
Kimothon Gate (closed)
Chorlim-Koitoboss Route
Koitoboss River
Saito Special Camp Site
Saito Dam
Elephant Platform
National Park Headquarters; Mt Elgon Guides & Porters Association
Chepnyalil Cave
Enderbess Bluff
Chorlim Gate
Mackingeny Cave
Kapkuro Bandas
Kitum Cave
Rongai Cave
Chorlim Campsite
Rongai Campsite
Nyati Campsite
Kassowai Gate (closed)
Kassowai River
Kabewyan River
KENYA
Kimilili Route
Austrian Hut (ruined)
Kibusi River
Terim River
Mallkisi River
Chepkitale Forest Station (abandoned)

WORTH A TRIP

CHERANGANI HILLS

Northeast of Kitale, forming the western wall of the spectacular Elgeyo Escarpment, are the Cherangani Hills. This high plateau has a distinctly pastoral feel, with thatched huts, patchwork *shambas* (small farm plots) and wide rolling meadows cut by babbling brooks. You could easily spend weeks absorbed in the utter beauty of this landscape and never come across a single tourist.

There are a couple of great five-day treks, namely from Kabichbich to Chesengoch and from Kapcherop to Sigor, and some interesting shorter hikes in the northern reaches of the Cherangani Hills, see p218.

is the same whether you drop tent in the official campsites (Chorlim, Nyati and Rongai) or on any old flat spot during your trek.

Kapkuro Bandas BANDA $
(www.kws.go.ke; per banda US$25; P) These excellent stone bandas can sleep three people in two beds and have simple bathrooms and small, fully equipped kitchen areas.

Information

Mt Elgon National Park (www.kws.go.ke; park entrance adult/child US$25/15, vehicles from KSh300; 6am-6pm) It is possible to walk unescorted but due to the odd elephant and buffalo you will need to sign a waiver to do so. KWS produce a 1:35,000 map of the park that is sold at Chorlim Gate.

Mt Elgon Guides & Porters Association (0733919347) is a cooperative of six guides and 10 porters based at the KWS headquarters. Their services (per day guide/porter/cook KSh1500/1000/700) can be booked through KWS.

Getting There & Away

From Kitale, catch an Endebess-bound matatu (KSh70, 45 minutes), to the park junction from where it is a 15-minute motorbike taxi ride (KSh100) to the park gate. Be sure to grab your driver's phone number so you can contact him for a ride back to Endebess.

Saiwa Swamp National Park

North of Kitale, this small, rarely visited **park** (0717672121; www.kws.go.ke, saiwapark@kws.go.ke; park entrance adult/child US$20/10; 6am-6pm), is a real treat. Originally set up to preserve the habitat of Kenya's only population of sitatunga antelope, the 15.5-sq-km reserve is also home to blue, vervet and de Brazza's monkeys and some 370 species of birds. The fluffy black-and-white colobus and the impressive crowned crane are both present, and you may see the Cape clawless and spot-throated otters. At the park headquarters, ask to be introduced to the diminutive antelope, Ippo, an orphaned Maxwell's duiker.

The park is only accessible on foot and walking trails skirt the swamp, duckboards go right across it, and there are some rickety observation towers.

Guides are not compulsory although your experience will be greatly enhanced by taking one. Ours, **Chesoli Lutah** (0726427040; lutahchesoli@yahoo.com), could rattle off the names and characteristics of any plant or bird we cared to ask about.

Sleeping

Public Campsite CAMPGROUND $
(www.kws.go.ke; camping US$15; P) A lovely site with flush toilets, lock boxes, showers and two covered cooking bandas.

Sitatunga Treetop House HUT $$
(www.kws.go.ke; tree house US$50; P) Perched on stilts overlooking the Saiwa swamp, this KWS tree house can sleep three in a double and single bed. It has electricity, bedding and mosquito nets.

Sirikwa Safaris GUESTHOUSE $$
(0737133170; sirikwabarnley@gmail.com; camping KSh500, tents excl breakfast from KSh1200, farmhouse with shared bathroom s/d excl breakfast KSh4000/5600) Owned and run by the family that started Saiwa, this beautiful old farmhouse is 11km from the swamp. You can chose between camping in the grounds, sleeping in a well-appointed safari tent or, best of all, opting for one of the two bedrooms full of *National Geographic* magazines, old ornaments and antique sinks.

WEST TO UGANDA

There are two main border crossing points into Uganda: **Malaba** and **Busia**. Both are generally pain-free as Ugandan (or Kenyan) visas are available on arrival (see p370 for further information on visa requirements).

Both towns have a couple of banks where you can exchange cash but unless you're a fan of bureaucracy, it is easier to use one of the numerous moneychangers prowling around. Just make sure you know the exchange rate beforehand and count your money carefully.

The Kenyan border is open 24 hours, but we've heard the Ugandan one runs to a somewhat more 'flexible' timetable, so try and arrive in daylight hours. Also it is prudent to keep an eye on your bus. Nothing irritates the drivers more than someone who hasn't the sense to take note of where they park.

If you get stuck in either town for the night then you'll find a couple of ropy places to put your head down for the night. Thankfully onward matatus are fairly easy to come by on both sides of both borders.

The mother and son who run it will entertain you for hours with stories from their more than 70 years in Kenya. Wholesome, though fairly expensive, home-cooked food and excursions, including ornithological tours of the Cherangani Hills and Saiwa Swamp, can all be arranged here.

Getting There & Away

The park is 18km northeast of Kitale; take a matatu towards Kapenguria (KSh120, 30 minutes) and get out at the second signposted turn-off (KSh70, 15 minutes), from where it is a 5km walk or KSh70 *moto-taxi* (motorcycle taxi) ride.

Central Highlands

Includes »

Best of Nature

» Meru National Park (p189)
» Mt Kenya National Park (p172)
» Solio Game Reserve (p165)
» Laikipia plateau (p183)

Best of Culture

» Chewing *miraa* (boxed text, p186)
» Kikuyu cultural shows (p179)

Why Go?

The Central Highlands are the fertile, mist- and rain-fattened breadbasket of the nation and the green-girt, red-dirt spiritual heartland of Kenya's largest tribe, the Kikuyu. This is the land the Mau Mau fought for, the land the colonists coveted and the land whose natural, cyclical patterns define the lives of the country's largest rural population as they tend their *shambas* (small plots) in its valleys.

The prime attraction here is Kirinyaga, the Mountain of Mysteries (or Ostriches, depending on who's translating). Better known as Mt Kenya, this icy massif dominates the small towns scattered in its shadow and looms large near some of the nation's most stunning, and least visited, national parks.

Southwest of Mt Kenya, some of the oldest mountains on the continent, the dramatic Aberdare Range, help bolster the region's reputation as Kenya's premier trekking destination.

When to Go

Nanyuki

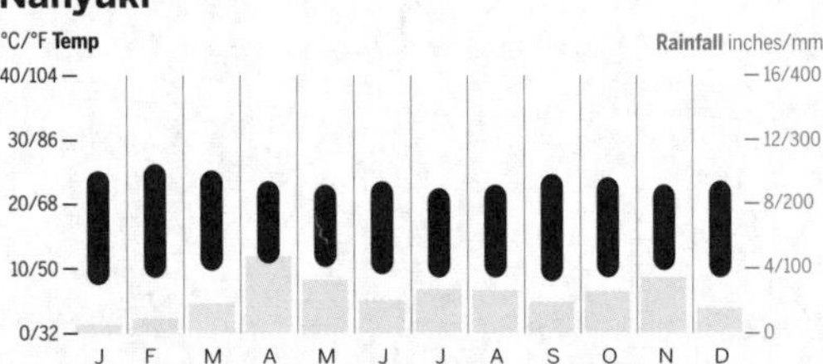

Mid-Jan–Feb & mid-Jul–Aug Your best chance of favourable weather to bag Mt Kenya.

Mar–early Jun The long rains fall everywhere – even in the dry zones near Thika and Kamburu Dam.

Oct & Nov The short rains make a brief appearance.

THE NINE-MONTH COUP

During the colonial period, the appointed leaders of tribal Africa were headmen and, by and large, men they were (and, usually, remain). But there's one exception from the history books, a woman who both reversed the constraints of her sex and, if the unusual story behind her removal from power is to be believed, fell prey to the pitfalls of gender in a way only a woman could appreciate.

These are the facts as we know them: Wangu wa Makeri was a Kikuyu, born in the second half of the 19th century. In 1901 she was appointed headman of Weithaga, becoming the only female ruler in colonial Kenya. Accounts agree she was a rigid and authoritarian ruler, but whether or not this was a good thing seems to have been a matter of opinion. Wangu made a point of literally using men as furniture, discarding traditional Kikuyu stools for the backs of Kikuyu males. Perhaps unsurprisingly, stories suggest her rule was warmly approved of by Kikuyu women.

And so the wily (and, more pertinently, fertile) men of the Kikuyu tribe hatched a plot, one of the most unique coups in history (disclaimer: we are now leaving the realm of history and entering the more entertaining, if less reliable, space of tribal folklore). They all did their husbandly duty and impregnated their wives, including Wangu, more or less simultaneously. This ensured that in nine months, the chief and her supporters were either in labour, nursing or too heavily pregnant to prevent the re-ascendancy of male Kikuyu-dom.

History

After most likely arriving from West or central Africa, the ancestors of the Kikuyu, like the *wazungu* (white) settlers who arrived in the 19th century, recognised a good thing when they saw it: the incredibly fertile soil of the slopes of Mt Kenya. Hunter-gathers and pastoralists became farmers who lived fat off the land.

Said land became the ripest plum for col onial picking when European newcomers filtered into East Africa. Failing farms in other parts of Kenya magnetised *wazungu* into the highlands, and in the 1880s the Kikuyu were displaced from their homes to make way for white agriculture and the Mombasa–Uganda railway.

Having borne the brunt of colonialism's abuses, the Kikuyu shouldered much of the burden of nationalism's struggle and formed the core of the Mau Mau rebellion in the 1950s (see p296). That struggle was largely fought in highland valleys, and the abuses of the anti-insurgency campaign were largely felt by highland civilians. While even the staunchest patriot cannot claim the Mau Mau won the uprising, the movement, combined with the general dismantling of the British Empire, forced colonial authorities to reassess their position and eventually abandon Kenya.

It was a Kikuyu, Jomo Kenyatta, who assumed presidency of the new country, and the Kikuyu, widely recognised (even by grudging rivals) as one of the hardest-working, most business-savvy tribes in Kenya, who assumed control of the nation's economy. Incidentally, they also reclaimed their rich fields in the Central Highlands, a move that has been a source of tension in Kenya to this day. Many *wazungu* farmers remain, and their huge plots can be seen stretching all along the highways between Timau, Meru and Nanyuki.

ABERDARES

The cloud-kissed contours of the brown-and-grey slopes of the Aberdare Range, dubbed Nyandarua (Drying Hide) by the Kikuyu, are deceptively round and inviting. But with an average elevation of 3350m, the Aberdares are no soft foothills. Stretching 160km from South Kinangop, east of Naivasha, up to the Laikipia Escarpment northwest of Nyahururu, the Aberdares form the solid spine of western Central Province, and were a popular base for Mau Mau fighters during the independence struggle.

The tallest regions of this range can claim some of Kenya's most dramatic up-country scenery, packed with 300m waterfalls, dense forests and serious trekking potential. The fuzzy moors in particular possess a stark, wind-carved beauty, wholly unexpected after driving up from the richly cultivated plots of the eastern Aberdares. In contrast, the western high country has been left to leopards, buffaloes, warthogs, lions and elephants, and remains one of Kenya's best places to spot black rhinos.

European settlers established coffee and tea plantations on the eastern side of the Aberdares and wheat and pyrethrum (chrysanthemum) farms on the western slopes.

Nyeri & Around

☎061 / POP 98,910

Nyeri is a welcoming and bustling Kikuyu market town. It's as busy as the Central Highlands get, but unless you have a thing for chaotic open-air bazaars and the mad energy of Kikuyu and white Kenyans

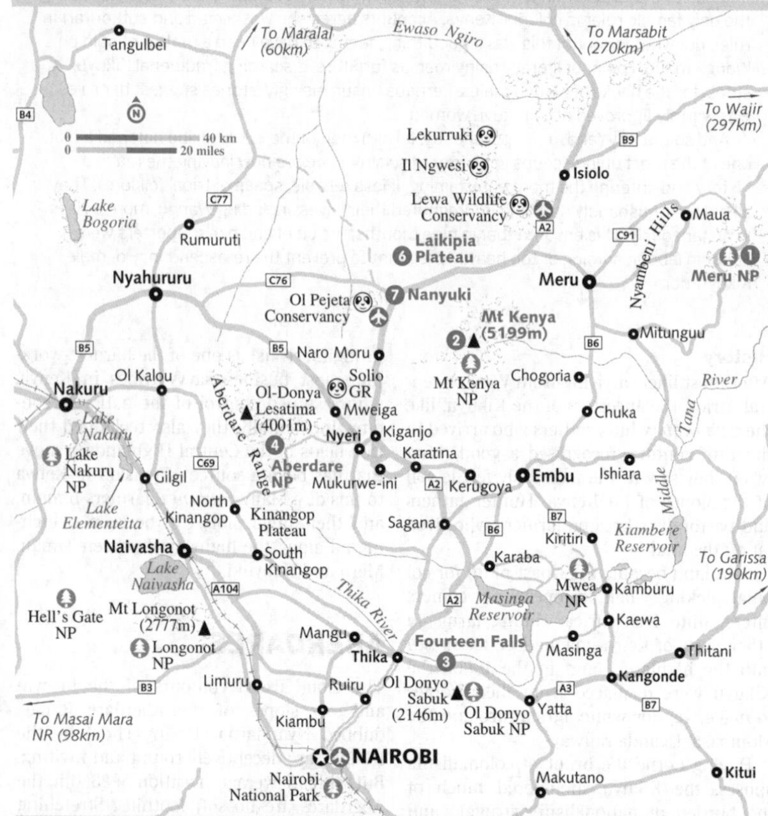

Central Highlands Highlights

1 Braking suddenly when confronted by a one-tonne rhino during a safari in **Meru National Park** (p189).

2 Holding a frozen Kenyan flag in your frozen hands atop the frozen summit of Point Lenana on **Mt Kenya** (p172), 16km from the equator.

3 Questioning your sanity as you find yourself scrambling across the lip of **Fourteen Falls** (p192).

4 Playing 'dodge the elephant' with the megafauna of **Aberdare National Park** (p168).

5 Eating *githeri* (beans, corn and meat) with the Kikuyu in their homeland.

6 Saddling up for a horseback safari across the **Laikipia plateau** (p183), then unwinding afterwards at an exclusive, privately owned wildlife conservancy.

7 Watching the kids squeal in delight when a monkey at the **Mt Kenya Wildlife Conservancy Animal Orphanage** (p182) bounds onto their head.

WILDLIFE IN THE CENTRAL HIGHLANDS

Much of the Central Highlands' best game viewing can be found in privately owned reserves including the Solio Game Reserve (p165) and Ol Pejeta Conservancy (p183) in the Laikipia Plateau. Both have great success in breeding black and white rhinos and animals born here are regularly moved to restock other parks.

Meru National Park (p189), which contains both riverine jungle and open savannah, is one of Kenya Wildlife Services' best-kept (or perhaps worst-publicised) secrets. Carnivores are hard to spot but zebras, waterbucks, buffaloes, giraffes, hippos and elephants are easily seen.

Aberdare National Park's (p168) landscape veers between dark, clotted jungle and wind-blown moors. The jungle supports rare bongo antelope, elephants and black rhinos although the thick cover makes sightings infrequent. Like Mt Kenya National Park (p172) the Afro-alpine moorlands in Aberdare National Park offer exceptional walking and the real stars here are the flora. Much of it, like the giant groundsel, ostrich plume plant and giant lobelia would not look out of place on another planet. Rock hyraxes and duiker antelope also live comfortably at these higher altitudes.

selling maize, bananas, arrowroot, coffee and macadamia nuts, there's not much reason to linger for more than a day or two. Boy Scout Association founder Lord Baden-Powell, who died here in 1941, might beg to differ. He once wrote, 'The nearer to Nyeri, the nearer to bliss.'

Sights & Activities

TOP CHOICE Solio Game Reserve WILDLIFE RESERVE
(Map p169; ☎55271; B5 Hwy; adult/child/guide/vehicle KSh2000/1000/500/500) This family-run, private 17,000-acre reserve, 22km north of Nyeri, is an important breeding centre for **black rhinos**, and many of the horned beasts you see wandering national parks were actually born here. Sadly, rhinos are popular poacher fare; their horns are used in Eastern medicines and for Arabic dagger hilts, but here they thrive, along with oryxes, gazelles, hartebeests, giraffes, lions, hyenas and buffaloes. The physical contours of the park, which run between clumps of yellow-fever acacia, wide skies and wild marsh, are lovely in and of themselves. Self-drive safaris are permitted but you will need to be accompanied by a Solio guide (KSh500).

Baden-Powell Museum MUSEUM
(admission KSh250; ⌚opened on request) Lord Baden-Powell, the founder of the Boy Scout Association, spent his last three years at Paxtu cottage in the Outspan Hotel. The ultimate scoutmaster's retirement was somewhat poetic: to 'outspan' is to unhook your oxen at the end of a long journey, and, as Baden-Powell's former home was named 'Pax' (peace) in honour of Armistice Day after WWI, it made sense to dub his second digs 'Paxtu'.

Paxtu is now a museum filled with scouting scarfs and paraphernalia. The young woman next to Baden-Powell in the photographs isn't his granddaughter but his wife. Famed tiger-hunter Jim Corbett later occupied the grounds The museum is a short (1km) walk west from the town centre, in the grounds of the Outspan Hotel.

Baden-Powell's Grave CEMETERY
(B5 Hwy; admission Ksh250; ⌚8.30am-5pm) The scoutmaster's grave is tucked behind **St Peter's Church**, facing Mt Kenya and marked with the Scouts trail sign for 'I have gone home'. His more famous Westminster Abbey tomb is empty.

Tours

Bongo Asili Travel TOUR
(☎0700391203, 2030884; www.bongoasilitravel.com; Kanisa Rd; ⌚9am-5pm Mon-Sat) The only locally based tour operator, Bongo Asili can arrange safaris to Solio Game Reserve, Aberdare National Park and multiday excursions further abroad. It can also book hotels throughout Kenya and coordinate airline ticketing.

Sleeping

There's plenty of budget accommodation in Nyeri and a stroll around town will turn up half a dozen options in addition to those mentioned here. In truth, there is little to recommend one budget option over the

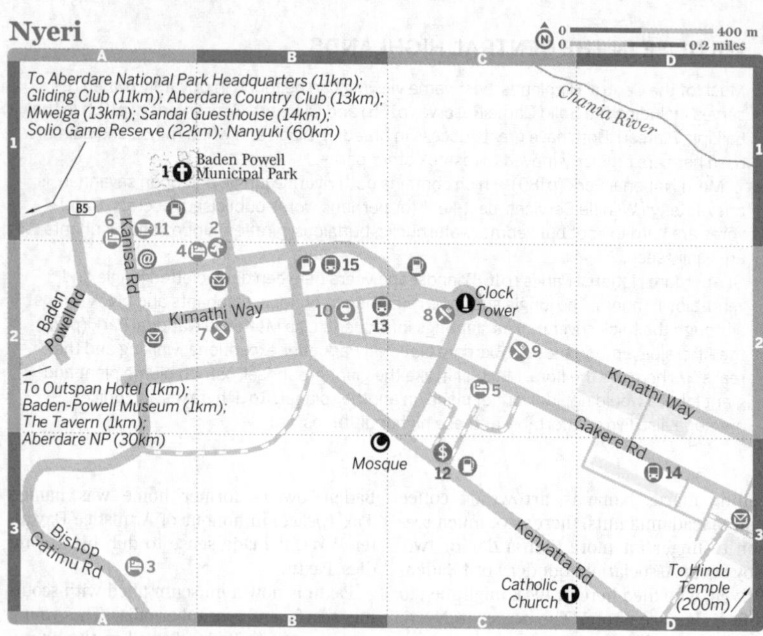

Nyeri

Sights

Baden-Powell's Grave ....(see 1)
1 St Peter's Church A1

Activities, Courses & Tours

2 Bongo Asili Travel................................B2

Sleeping

3 Green Hills Hotel....................................A3
4 Ibis Hotel B2
5 Nyama Choma Village Accommodation C2
6 White Rhino Hotel...................................A1

Eating

Green Hills Hotel...........................(see 3)
7 Raybells...B2
8 Rayjo's Café..C2
9 Samrat Supermarket...............................C2

Drinking

10 Green Oaks B2
11 Julie's Coffee Shop A1
Kifaru..(see 6)

Information

12 Barclays Bank...C3

Transport

13 Local Matatus B2
14 Lower Bus Stand......................................D3
15 Upper Bus Stand.......................................B2

next; most come with a desultory on-site restaurant and an occasional harmless drunk.

TOP CHOICE **Sandai Guesthouse** GUESTHOUSE **$$$**
(☎0721656699; www.africanfootprints.de; camping KSh500, s/d/tw full board US$130/220/220, cottages US$80; Ⓟ) Fourteen kilometres northwest from town (ask locals for directions), Sandai is run by the effervescent Petra Allmendinger, whose enthusiasm and warm welcome make this a great weekend escape from Nairobi's bustle or for those looking for something a little more personal than what is on offer elsewhere. Accommodation is either in the extremely cosy lodge, where you will feel like part of the family, or in self-contained cottages that can accommodate up to six. Both are pleasantly eccentric. Horse riding, nature walks (the guesthouse's guide, Sammy, is an excellent

birdwatcher) and wildlife drives can all be organised here.

Green Hills Hotel HOTEL $$
(☎2030604; www.greenhills.co.ke; Bishop Gatimu Rd; s KSh4500-5600, d KSh6900-9100, ste KSh18,000; P 📶 🏊) The best deal in town is actually a little way out of Nyeri. The small drive is worth it for the palm-lined, poolside ambience (nonguests KSh300) and general sense of serenity.

Ibis Hotel HOTEL $
(☎2034858; kihuria@ibishotel.co.ke; Kanisa Rd; s/d/tw excl breakfast KSh1000/1200/1600) Located in a building with a surprisingly grand facade (it's not that opulent on the inside), Ibis has comfortable and clean rooms with brilliant power showers.

Nyama Choma Village Accommodation HOTEL $
(☎0788174384; Gakere Rd; r excl breakfast KSh800) With its light-blue walls and blue-linoleum showers, Nyama Choma is as colourful as it is cheap. And as you'd expect with a name like Nyama Choma (barbecued meat), meat-eaters will love this place.

White Rhino Hotel HOTEL $$
(☎0726967315; www.whiterhinohotel.com; Kanisa Rd; s/d/tw KSh9600/10,800/14,000; P 📶) The White Rhino had fallen into disrepair, but since its remodelling in 2011 now boasts smart rooms that are polished to an inch of their lives, and swanky, tiled bathrooms. With three bars and two restaurants, this is the top hotel in the city centre.

Outspan Hotel HOTEL $$$
(☎2032424, Nairobi 020-4452095; www.aberdaresafarihotels.com; s full board US$220-275, d full board $299-432, cottages US$464; P 📶 🏊) This rather gorgeous lodge was last decorated in the 1950s, when wood panelling was the height of interior design. The dining room is a cross between the Hogwarts School hall (from the Harry Potter films) and a colonial retreat. Nineteen of the 34 standard rooms have cosy fireplaces, and all have a whiff of historical class. A Kikuya cultural group performs here daily at 1.45pm daily (nonguests adult/child US$10/5).

Aberdare Country Club HOTEL $$$
(Map p169; ☎Nairobi 0737799990; s/d/tr excl breakfast US$210/288/340, day entry adult/child KSh500/300; P 🏊) This stately stone club acts as the staging post for those going to the Ark in Nairobi.

Solio Game Reserve Lodge LODGE $$$
(Map p169; ☎Nairobi 020-2513166; www.tamimiea.com; ste full board US$1240; P 📶) The ultimate safari lodge, with a price tag to match.

Eating

All the hotels listed above have decent restaurants and lively bars (more often than not, these are one and the same).

Green Hills Hotel INTERNATIONAL $
(Bishop Gatimu Rd; mains/buffets KSh600/650; ⌚breakfast, lunch & dinner) As with accommodation, so with food: Green Hills dominates again. The full buffet (when numbers permit) is an impressive piece of work, with some tasty mixed-grill options done up in a satisfyingly fancy fashion. Steaks are tender and come sizzling on a platter with a good mix of vegies.

ANIMALS ON THE MOVE

In 2008 the Kenyan government bought 15,000 acres of Solio Ranch as part of a scheme to provide homes to the landless 'roadside squatters' of the area. As plans were made to build seven new villages to home the roughly 3000 people, plans were also hastily made to relocate an equal number of animals. Fearing they would otherwise be poached for bushmeat, more than 3000 animals (mainly zebras, hartebeests and various species of gazelle) were helicopter-shepherded into curtained traps, funnelled onto trucks and shipped to various conservancies and national parks throughout the Central Highlands.

While this may be the biggest such operation to date, Kenya is no stranger to this Noah's Ark–like approach to conservation. Usually done to allow failing populations a second chance in more-favourable habitats, it also allows the gene pool to be thoroughly stirred.

In 2011, 18 hippos that had been happily wallowing in Nairobi's Ruai Sewer had to be moved to Nairobi National Park and 200 elephants that were having a fine time creating havoc and destroying crops near Narok were relocated to the Masai Mara National Reserve, from which they had been cut off.

Rayjo's Café KENYAN $
(Kimathi Way; meals KSh50-140; ⌚lunch & dinner) This tiny canteen is usually packed with customers, including bus and matatu (minibus transport) drivers, notoriously good judges of cheap places to eat.

Raybells INTERNATIONAL $
(Kimathi Way; meals KSh120-400; ⌚breakfast, lunch & dinner) Pretty much anything you want to eat (well, anything Kenyan or Western), from pizza to *nyama choma*, is available and cooked passably well here. You may want to avoid the fresh juice as it has tap water added to it.

Samrat Supermarket SUPERMARKET $
Off Kimathi Way, this is the best-stocked supermarket in town.

Drinking

Green Oaks PUB
The friendliest bar in town. There's usually European football on the box, but like every other joint, it gets rowdy as the night wears on. Teetotallers will appreciate the balcony's fine view over the taxi stands and the warming chai (tea) on any of Nyeri's many rainy days. It's off Kimathi Way.

Julie's Coffee Shop CAFE $
(Kanisa Rd; snacks KSh35-80; ⌚breakfast & lunch; wi-fi) The best (and by best, we mean only) place in town for genuine espresso coffee and free wi-fi.

Tavern BAR
(Kirinyaga Club; Outspan Hotel; ⌚11am-1am) Located behind the posh Outspan Hotel's gates, the Tavern has a bonfire and traditional dancing on Saturday nights and is a good spot for those seeking a little upmarket atmosphere with their Tusker.

Kifaru BAR
(White Rhino; Kenyatta Rd, ⌚11am-3am) The largest of White Rhino's three bars, Kifaru doubles as a spacious, open-air restaurant and late nightclub. The nightly DJ plays an eclectic mix of African and Western pop. For something quieter and more intimate, check out the Marura Bar with its open fire and safari club vibe.

Information

There are three post offices: two in the centre of town and one near the lower bus stand.

Barclays Bank (Kenyatta Rd) One of several banks around town with an ATM and which will exchange cash.

Villa Cyber (Kanisa Rd; per hr KSh30) Decent, fast connection.

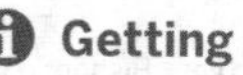

Getting There & Away

The **upper bus stand** deals with sporadic buses and a plethora of matatus to destinations north and west and of Nyeri including Nanyuki (KSh150, one hour), Nyahururu (KSh280, 1¼ hours) and Nakuru (KSh450, 2½ hours).

From the **lower bus stand** matatus head in all directions south and east including Thika (KSh250, two hours) and Nairobi (KSh350, 2½ hours).

Some **local matatus** are also found on Kimathi Way.

Aberdare National Park

While there's plenty of reason to wax rhapsodic over herds of wildlife thundering over an open African horizon, there's also something to be said for the soil-your-pants shock of seeing an elephant thunder out of bush that was, minutes before, just plants.

And that's why people love Aberdare National Park. Camera reflexes are tested as the abundant wildlife pops unexpectedly out of bushes, including elephants, buffaloes, black rhinos, spotted hyenas, bongo antelope, bush pigs, black servals and rare black leopards.

And baboons. Lots and lots of baboons.

The park has two major environments: an eastern hedge of thick rainforest and

ABERDARE NATIONAL PARK

Why Go Two interesting ecosystems to explore: a dense rainforest and high, Afro-alpine moorlands with great trekking possibilities and some spectacular waterfalls.

When to Go Although close to the equator, the park receives plenty of rain year-round and is cooler and mistier than you would expect. The driest months are January to February and June to September.

Practicalities During the rains, roads are impassable, and the numbered navigation posts in the Salient are often difficult to follow. With several possible points of access, the most straightforward visit is to drive between the Ruhuruini and Mutubio West gates.

Aberdare National Park

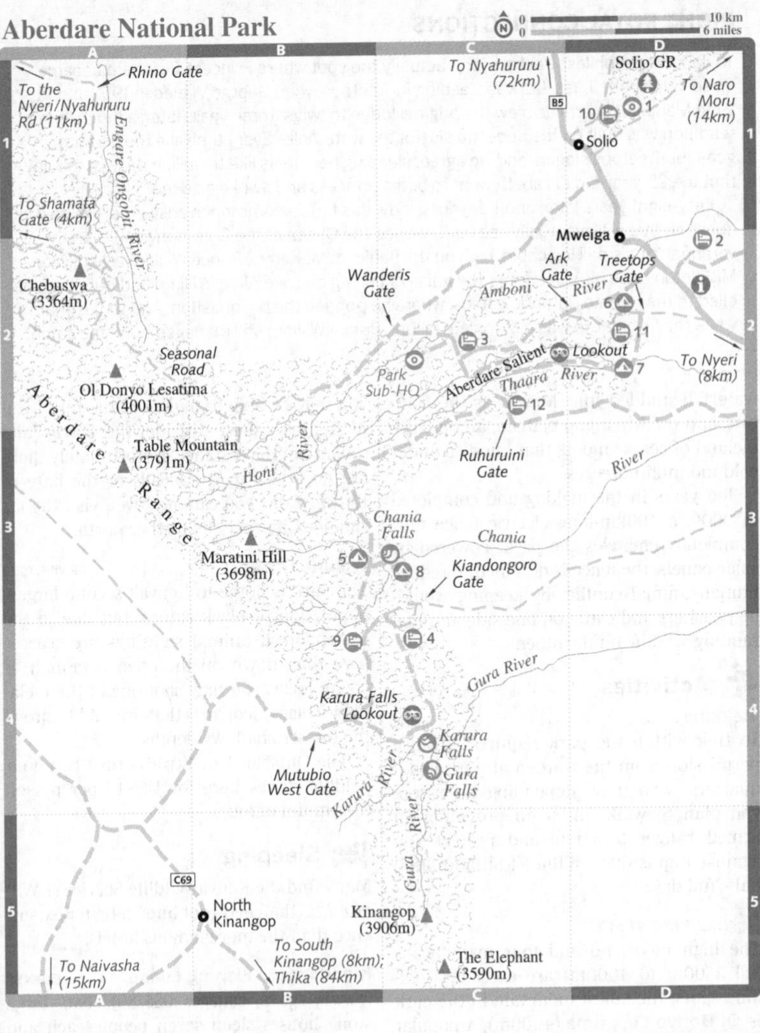

Aberdare National Park

Sights

1 Solio Game Reserve D1

Sleeping

2 Aberdare Country Club D2
3 Ark C2
4 Kiandongoro Fishing Lodge C4
5 Public Campsite B3
6 Public Campsite D2
7 Public Campsite D2
8 Public Campsite C3
9 Sapper Hut B4
10 Solio Game Reserve Lodge D1
11 Treetops D2
12 Tusk Camp C2

RIGHT ROYAL CONNECTIONS

Trivia for royal-philes: Treetops isn't actually the spot where Princess Elizabeth became Queen Elizabeth II. Yes, Liz was sleeping in Treetops when George VI died in 1952, but in 1954 Mau Mau guerrillas blew the original lodge to twigs; three years later, a much larger rendition was built on the opposite side of the waterhole. 'Every time like the first time', goes the Treetops slogan, and we agree: sleeping here feels like travelling back to the day that the 25-year-old Elizabeth went to bed a princess and awoke a queen.

Fifty-eight years later, another young lady, this time a commoner, answered 'yes' to a question that will eventually see her crowned the Queen of the Commonwealth. On the verandah of a small log cabin, high on the flanks of Mt Kenya, Prince William asked Kate Middleton to be his wife. Under the guise of fishing on Lake Alice, William and Kate travelled to the remote Rutundu cabins, where he popped the big question. And so it is that while the fishing trip was a complete failure, Prince William still managed quite the catch.

waterfall-studded hills known as the **Salient**, and the Kinangop plateau, an open tableland of coarse moors that huddles under cold mountain breezes.

Ten years in the making and completed in 2009, a 400km-long electric fence now completely encircles the park. Powered by solar panels, the fence is designed to reduce human–animal conflict by keeping would-be poachers and cattle on one side and marauding wildlife on the other.

Activities

Trekking HIKING

To trek within the park requires advance permission from the warden at park headquarters, who may (depending on where you plan to walk) insist on providing an armed ranger to guide and protect you against inquisitive wildlife (KSh1500/3000 half-/full day).

Northern Moorland

The high moorland and four main peaks (all 3500m to 4000m) are excellent trekking spots; the tallest mountain in the park is **Ol Donyo Lesatima** (4000m), a popular bag for those on the East African mountain circuit. Between Honi Campsite and Elephant Ridge is the site of the **hideout** of Mau Mau leader Dedan Kimathi, who used these mountains as a base; many of his companions learned the ropes of jungle warfare fighting in Burma in WWII.

Kinangop Plateau

From the dirt track that connects the Ruhuruini and Mutubio West gates, it is possible to walk to the top of **Karura Falls** and watch Karura Stream slide over the rocky lip into the 272m abyss. Weather permitting, you may be able to make out the misty veil of Kenya's tallest cascade, the **Gura Falls** (305m), in the distance. Unfortunately there are no tracks to Gura Falls or the base of Karura Falls. You can, however, visit the far smaller **Chania Falls** further north.

Wildlife Drives DRIVING TOUR

The park is home to Kenya's second-largest population of black rhinos, but due to the dense forest, animal sightings are scarcer here than down on the open savannah. If you're lucky, you may spot one of the melanistic (black) leopards that are said to prowl the forest's shadowy depths.

The Outspan Hotel (p167) runs two-hour wildlife drives here for US$45 per person (minimum of four).

Sleeping

Many find the Kenya Wildlife Service (KWS) *bandas* (thatched-roof huts) a better experience than the more famous hotels.

Kiandongoro Fishing Lodge CABIN **$$**

(www.kws.go.ke; cottages US$180) Two large stone houses sleep seven people each and command a good view of the moors that sweep into the Gura River. There are two bathrooms in each house. All utensils and linens are provided, along with gas-powered kitchens, paraffin cookers and fireplaces.

Tusk Camp CABIN **$$**

(www.kws.go.ke; cottages US$120) Two dark and cosy alpine cottages located near Ruhuruini gate sleep four people each. The lounge area is comfy, with great views (if the fog hasn't rolled in), and plenty of rhinos around to boot. Hot water, blankets, kerosene lamps, a gas cooker and some utensils are provided.

Ark HOTEL $$$

(☎Nairobi 0737799990; www.arkkenya.com; s/d/tr US$210/288/340) The Ark is more modern (1960s as opposed to 1950s chic) and roomier than Treetops, and has a lounge that overlooks a waterhole. Watch buffalo as you sip wine in a moulded chair lifted from *Austin Powers* and you'll have an idea of the ambience. An excellent walkway leads over a particularly dense stretch of the Salient, and from here and the waterhole lounge you can spot elephants, rhinos, buffaloes and hyenas. Sold as an overnight excursion from the Aberdare Country Club in Nyeri.

Sapper Hut BANDA $

(www.kws.go.ke; bandas US$50) A simple *banda,* with an open fire, two beds and a hot-water boiler, overlooking a lovely waterfall on the Upper Magura River. It's best to bring your own gear.

Public Campsites CAMPGROUND $

(www.kws.go.ke; camping US$15) Basic sites with minimal facilities – some have water.

Treetops HISTORIC HOTEL $$$

(☎Nairobi 020-4452095; www.aberdaresafarihotels.com; s/tw without bathroom full board US$328/415; @) Treetops is sold as part of a package with the Outspan Hotel in Nyeri. Guests are given lunch at the Outspan, transported to Treetops, where they dine and sleep before being returned to the Outspan the following morning for breakfast.

Rooms are small and decorated in mid-20th-century wood-panelling and floral linen chic, but there is excellent wildlife viewing and a sense of rusticity (and a little neglect) pervades. High rollers can splurge for the Queen Elizabeth 'suite', which has a picture of the monarch and – wait for it – a *double bed!*

Information

To enter the **park** (www.kws.go.ke; adult/child US$50/25) through the Treetops or Ark gates, ask permission at **national park headquarters** (☎061-202379409; Mweiga; ⏲6am-6pm). Excellent 1:25,000 maps, which are essential if you are on a self-drive safari, are available at the gates.

Getting There & Away

Access roads from the B5 Hwy to the Wanderis, Ark, Treetops and Ruhuruini gates are in decent shape. Keep in mind that it takes a few hours to get from the Salient to the moorlands and vice versa.

Nyahururu (Thomson's Falls)

☎065 / POP 24,750

This unexpectedly attractive town leaps out of the northwest corner of the highlands and makes a decent base for exploring the western edge of the Aberdares.

Its former namesake, Thomson's Falls, are beautiful in their own right and offer excellent trekking options on small forested tracks that lead to friendly farming villages.

At 2360m, this is Kenya's highest major town, with a cool and invigorating climate.

Sights & Activities

Thomson's Falls WATERFALL

(adult/child KSh200/100) Set back in an evergreen river valley and studded with sharp

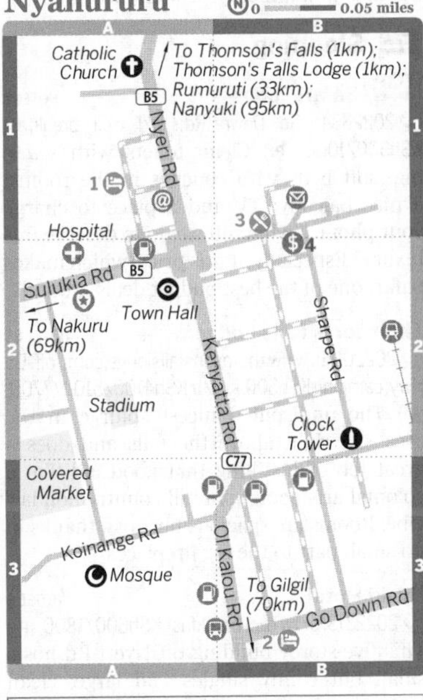

Nyahururu

Sleeping

1 Nyaki Hotel A1

2 Safari Lodge B3

Eating

Nyaki Hotel .... (see 1)

3 Savannah Green Hotel B1

Information

4 Barclays Bank B2

rocks and screaming baboons, the white cataracts that plummet over 72m are Nyahururu's undeniable main attraction. A fairly straight path approaches the falls over a series of stone steps and leads to the bottom of the ravine. The dramatic sight of looking up at the falls as baboons pad over the surrounding cliffs is worth the drenching you get from the fall's spray.

There are some fantastic **walks** downstream through the forested valley of the Ewaso Narok River and upstream a couple of kilometres to one of the highest **hippo pools** in Kenya.

Don't sweat finding a guide. They, along with locals in traditional Kikuyu attire, souvenir sellers, camel wranglers and other enterprising locals, will find you. To walk (1km) to the falls, follow Nyeri Rd, which swings east soon after leaving town. If the ticket booth is unmanned, just walk in.

Sleeping

TOP CHOICE Safari Lodge HOTEL $

(☎2022334; Go Down Rd; s/d excl breakfast KSh500/1000; P) Clean toilets with *seats;* big, soft beds with couches in the rooms; a nice balcony; TV and a place to charge your phone – what did we do to deserve this luxury? Especially at this price, which makes Safari one of the best budget deals around.

Thomson's Falls Lodge HOTEL $$

(☎2022006; www.thomsonsfallslodge.com; off B5 Hwy; camping KSh500, s/d/tr KSh4100/5100/7700; P) The undisputed nicest splurge in the area sits right above the falls and does a great job of instilling that good old 'I'm a colonial aristocrat on a hill-country holiday' vibe. Rooms are spacious but cosy, thanks in no small part to the log fireplaces.

Nyaki Hotel HOTEL $

(☎2022313; s/tw excl breakfast KSh600/1800; P) This five-storey building off Nyeri Rd hosts small but comfy singles and large, clean twins that have small separate lounges and reliable hot-water showers.

Eating & Drinking

It's best to eat early in Nyahururu; for reasons we couldn't fathom, most eateries were shutting shop by 7pm.

Thomson's Falls Lodge BUFFET $$

(breakfast/lunch/dinner buffets KSh455/850/900; ⏱breakfast, lunch & dinner) This is the best (and only) place in town to go for a fancy feast. There's a set buffet for each of the day's three meals, and while they're pricey for this area, you'll walk away well stuffed and satisfied. It's located off the B5 Hwy.

Savannah Green Hotel KENYAN $

(Sulukia Rd; mains KSh150-300; ⏱breakfast, lunch & dinner) There may not be any rooms at this 'hotel' but there's a decent restaurant with outdoor seating and a fine selection of all things fried or stewed. With huge portions and tempting, freshly squeezed juice, bring an appetite.

Nyaki Hotel KENYAN $

(mains KSh250-280; ⏱breakfast, lunch & dinner) Serves standard Kenyan fare in a standard Kenyan setting: bare-bones, smiling service and about 100 watts away from being well lit. Off Nyeri Rd.

Information

Barclays Bank (cnr Sulukia & Sharpe Rds) With ATM.

Clicks Cyber Cafe (Mimi Centre, Nyeri Rd; per hr KSh60)

Post office (Sulukia Rd)

Getting There & Away

There are numerous matatus that run to Nakuru (KSh150, 1¼ hours) and Nyeri (KSh280, 1¾ hours) until late afternoon. Less plentiful are services to Naivasha (KSh300, two hours), Nanyuki (KSh330, three hours) and Nairobi (KSh400, 31/2 hours). The odd morning matatu reaches Maralal (KSh500, four hours).

Several early-morning buses also serve Nairobi (KsH350, three hours).

MT KENYA NATIONAL PARK

Africa's second-highest mountain attracts spry trekkers, long, dramatic cloud cover and all the eccentricities of its mother continent in equal measure. Here, mere minutes from the equator, glaciers carve out the throne of Ngai, the old high god of the Kikuyu. To this day the tribe keeps its doors open to the face of the sacred mountain, and some still come to its lower slopes to offer prayers and the foreskins of their young men – this was the traditional place for holding circumcision ceremonies. Besides being venerated by the Kikuyu, Mt Kenya has the rare honour of being both a Unesco World Heritage Site and a Unesco Biosphere Reserve.

Mt Kenya National Park

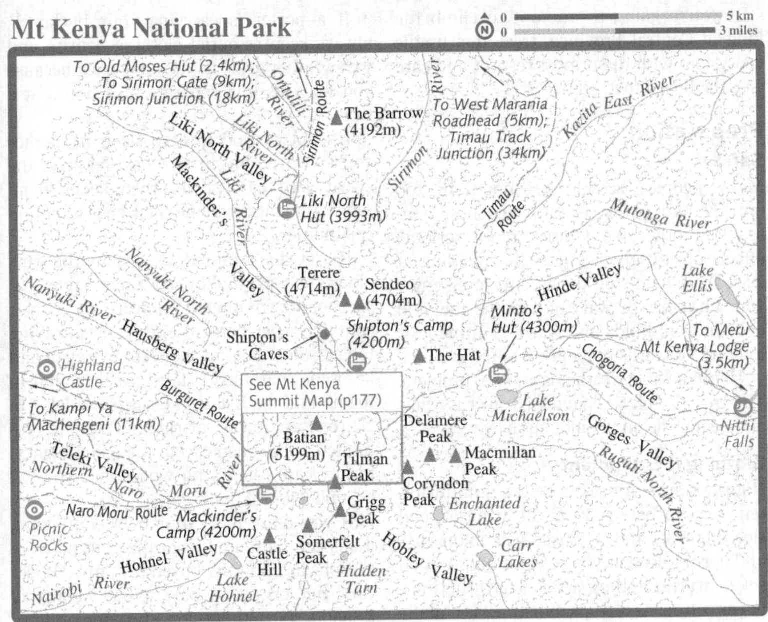

In the past, 12 glaciers wore Mt Kenya down to 5199m worth of dramatic remnants, but today it is the ice itself that is under threat, disappearing under increased temperatures and taking with them crystalline caves and snowy crevasses. That means the climb up the mountain is easier than it has ever been – but by no means does it mean the ascent is easy.

The highest peaks of Batian (5199m) and Nelion (5188m) can only be reached by mountaineers with technical skills, but Point Lenana (4985m), the third-highest peak, can be reached by trekkers and is the usual goal for most mortals. The views are awe-inspiring – when they're not hemmed in by opaque mist.

Environment

There are flora, fauna and ecosystems on the slopes of Mt Kenya that cannot be found anywhere else in the country.

This extinct volcano hosts, at various elevations, upland forest, bamboo forest (2500m), high-altitude equatorial heath (3000m to 3500m) and lower alpine moorland (3400m to 3800m), which includes several species of bright everlasting flowers. Some truly surreal plant life grows in the Afro-alpine zone (above 3500m) and the upper alpine zone (3800m to 4500m), including hairy carpets of tussock grass, the brushlike giant lobelias, or rosette plants, and the sci-fi-worthy *Senecio Brassica,* or giant groundsel, which looks like a cross between an aloe, a cactus and a dwarf. At the summit it's all rock and ice, a landscape that possesses its own stark beauty, especially this close to the equator.

Unfortunately, there's more rock than ice these days. 'In 15 years I've seen all the glaciers move. I don't need crampons any more', one guide told us. Warmer weather has led to disappearing glaciers, and ice climbing in Mt Kenya is largely finished. We've heard these conditions have led to drier rivers in the region, which makes sense, as Mt Kenya is the country's most important permanent watershed.

In lower elevations large wildlife are around; you may need to clap and hoot as you trudge to stave off elephants and buffaloes. Rock hyraxes are common, as are, rather annoyingly, bees. There are also Sykes's monkeys, Mackinder's eagle owls, waterbucks, and (very rarely spotted) leopards, hyenas and servals, but these animals tend to stay hidden in the thick brush of the lower forests.

If you're going to attempt to climb the king of Central Province, treat this fragile ecosystem with the utmost respect and care (see the boxed text, p39).

Preparation

Safety

Many people ascend the mountain too quickly and suffer from headaches, nausea and other (sometimes more serious) effects of altitude sickness. By spending at least three nights on the ascent, you'll enjoy yourself more. Be wary of hypothermia and dehydration; fluids and warm clothing go a long way towards preventing both.

Unpredictable weather is another problem. The trek to Point Lenana isn't an easy hike and people die on the mountain every year.

Clothing & Equipment

Nightly temperatures near the summit often drop to below -10°C, so bring a good sleeping bag and a closed-cell foam mat or Therm-a-Rest if you're camping. A good set of warm clothes (wool or synthetics – never cotton, as it traps moisture) is equally important. As it can rain heavily any time of year, you'll need waterproof clothing (breathable fabric like Gore-Tex is best). A decent pair of boots and sandals or light shoes (for the evening when your boots get wet) are a great idea. At this altitude the sun can do some serious damage to your skin and eyes, so sunblock and sunglasses are also crucial items.

If a porter is carrying your backpack, always keep essential clothing (warm- and wet-weather gear) in your day pack because you may become separated for hours at a time.

It's not a good idea to sleep in clothes you've worn during the day because the sweat your clothes absorbed keeps them moist at night, reducing their heat-retention capabilities.

If you don't intend to stay in the huts along the way, you'll need a tent, stove, basic cooking equipment, utensils, a 3L water container (per person) and water-purifying tablets. Stove fuel in the form of petrol and kerosene (paraffin) is fairly easily found in towns, and methylated spirits is available in Nairobi, as are gas cartridges. Fires are prohibited in the open except in an emergency; in any case, there's no wood once you get beyond 3300m.

If you don't have your own equipment, items can be rented from the guiding associations listed in the boxed text, p175. Prices vary, but expect to pay in the vicinity of KSh500/200/150/300 for a two-person tent/sleeping bag/pair of boots/stove per day.

If you have a mobile phone, take it along; reception on the mountain's higher reaches is actually very good, and a link to the outside world is invaluable during emergencies.

Guides, Cooks & Porters

Having a porter for your gear is like travelling in a chauffeured Mercedes instead of a matatu. A good guide will help set a sustainable pace and hopefully dispense interesting information about Mt Kenya and its flora, fauna and wildlife. With both on your team, your appreciation of this mountain will be enhanced a hundredfold. If you hire a guide or porter who can also cook, you won't regret it.

Considerable effort has been made in recent years to regulate guides and porters operating on the mountain. The KWS now issues vouchers to all registered guides and porters, who should also hold identity cards; they won't be allowed into the park without them.

COSTS

The cost of guides varies depending on the qualifications of the guide, whatever the last party paid and your own negotiating skills. You should expect to pay a minimum of US$20/18/15 per day for a guide/cook/porter.

MT KENYA NATIONAL PARK

Why Go Awe-inspiring views from Africa's second-highest mountain; and unlike Mt Kilimanjaro, it's possible to take different routes up and down, with arguably better scenery.

When to Go Unsurprisingly, the climbing seasons are during the driest months – mid-January to late February and late August to September.

Practicalities Don't underestimate the difficulty of this trek. Unless you're a seasoned trekker with high-altitude experience and a good knowledge of reading maps and using a compass, you'd be flirting with death by not taking a guide.

ORGANISED TREKS

If you bargain hard, a package trek may end up costing only a little more than organising each logistical element of the trip separately. If you are keen to save money, think like a wildebeest and join a herd – the larger the group, the cheaper the per-person rate becomes. All prices listed here are per person in a three-person group and tours generally include guides, cooks and porters, park fees, meals and accommodation. Solo trekkers can expect to pay double these prices.

EWP (Executive Wilderness Programmes; ☎UK 1550-721319; www.ewpnet.com/kenya) Employs knowledgeable local guides; three-day trips cost US$645 per person.

IntoAfrica (☎UK 0114-255 5610, Nairobi 722511752; www.intoafrica.co.uk) An environmentally and culturally sensitive company offering both scheduled (US$1495 per person) and exclusive seven-day trips ascending Sirimon route and descending Chogoria.

KG Mountain Expeditions (☎721604930, 722261028; www.kenyaexpeditions.com) Run by a highly experienced mountaineer, KG offers all-inclusive scheduled four-day treks (US$550 per person).

Montana Trek & Information Centre (Map p182; ☎062-32731; www.montanatrekks.com; Nanyuki) This community-based association has friendly and knowledgeable guides. Four-day trips start at US$440 per person but vary depending on where you exit. The centre is particularly useful for Sirimon trekkers.

Mountain Rock Safaris Resorts & Trekking Services (Bantu Mountain Lodge; ☎Nairobi 020-242133; www.mountainrockkenya.com; Naro Moru) Runs the Mountain Rock Lodge (p181) near Naro Moru. Its popular four-day Naro Moru–Sirimon crossover trek costs US$650 per person.

Mt Kenya Guides & Porters Safari Club (Map p180; ☎020-3524393; www.mtkenyaguides.com; Naro Moru) The most organised association of guides, cooks and porters in Naro Moru. Expect to pay around US$120 per person per day for an all-inclusive package.

Mt Kenya Chogoria Guides & Porters Association (Map p180; ☎733676970; anthonytreks@yahoo.com; Chogoria) A small association of guides, cooks and porters based in Chogoria's Transit Motel, specialising in the Chogoria route up the mountain. An all-inclusive trip will cost around US$120 per person per day.

Mountain View Tour Trekking Safaris (☎722249439; mountainviewt@yahoo.com; Naro Moru) A new association of seven local guides working together who often approach independent travellers as they arrive in Naro Moru. Rates are around US$120 per person per day.

Naro Moru River Lodge (Map p180; ☎724082754, Nairobi 020-4443357; www.naromoruriverlodge.com; Naro Moru) Runs a range of all-inclusive trips (four-day treks start at US$609 per person) and operates Met Station Hut and Mackinder's Camp on the Naro Moru route.

Sana Highlands Trekking Expeditions (Map p60; ☎Nairobi 020-227820; www.sanatrekkingkenya.com; Nairobi) Operates five-day all-inclusive treks on the Sirimon and Chogoria routes that start at US$550 per person.

These fees don't include park entry fees and tips, and the latter should only be paid for good service.

Eating

In an attempt to reduce luggage, many trekkers exist entirely on canned and dried foods. You can do this by keeping up your fluid intake, but it's not a good idea. Keep in mind that your appetite for 'heavy' meals (ie lots of big solids) drops considerably at high altitudes.

Increased altitude creates unique cooking conditions. The major consideration is that the boiling point of water is considerably reduced. At 4500m, for example, water boils at 85°C; this is too low to sufficiently cook rice or lentils (pasta is better) and you won't be able to brew a good cup of tea (instant coffee is the answer). Cooking times and fuel usage are considerably increased as a result, so plan accordingly.

Take plenty of citrus fruits and/or citrus drinks as well as chocolate, sweets or dried fruit to keep your blood-sugar level up.

To avoid severe headaches caused by dehydration or altitude sickness, drink at least 3L of fluid per day and bring rehydration sachets. Water-purification tablets, available at most chemists, aren't a bad idea either.

The Routes

There are at least seven different routes up Mt Kenya. Of those, we cover Naro Moru, the easiest and most popular, as well as Sirimon and Chogoria, which are excellent alternatives, and the exciting but demanding Summit Circuit, which circles Batian and Nelion, thus enabling you to mix and match ascending and descending routes.

As well as the sleeping options given for each route it is possible to **camp** (www.kws.go.ke; camping US$15) anywhere on the mountain; the nightly fee is payable to KWS at any gate. Most people camp near the huts or bunk-houses, as there are often toilets and water nearby.

NARO MORU ROUTE

Although the least scenic, this is the most straightforward and popular route and is still spectacular.

Starting in Naro Moru town, the first part of the route takes you along a gravel road through farmlands for some 13km (all the junctions are signposted) to the start of the forest. Another 5km brings you to the park entry gate (2400m), from where it's 8km to the road head and the Met Station Hut (3000m), where you stay for the night and acclimatise.

On the second day, set off through the forest (at about 3200m) and Teleki Valley to the moorland around so-called **Vertical Bog**; expect the going here to be, well, boggy. At a ridge the route divides into two. You can either take the higher path, which gives better views but is often wet, or the lower, which crosses the Naro Moru River and continues gently up to Mackinder's Camp (4200m). This part of the trek should take about 4½ hours. Here you can stay in the dormitories or camp.

On the third day you can either rest at Mackinder's Camp to acclimatise or aim for **Point Lenana** (Map p177; 4895m). This stretch takes three to six hours, so it is common to leave around 2am to reach the summit in time for sunrise. From the bunk-house, continue past the ranger station to a fork. Keep right, and go across a swampy area, followed by a moraine, and then up a long scree slope – this is a long, hard slog. The KWS Austrian Hut (4790m) is three to four hours from Mackinder's and about one hour below the summit of Lenana, so it's a good place to rest before the final push.

The section of the trek from Austrian Hut up to Point Lenana takes you up a narrow rocky path that traverses the south-west ridge parallel to the Lewis Glacier, which has shrunk more than 100m since the 1960s. Be careful, as the shrinkage has created serious danger of slippage along the path. A final climb or scramble brings you up onto the peak. In good weather it's fairly straightforward, but in bad weather you shouldn't attempt the summit unless you're experienced in mountain conditions or have a guide.

Sleeping

There are three good bunk-houses along this route: **Met Station Hut** (Map p180; dm US$12) is at 3000m, **Mackinder's Camp** (Map p173; dm US$15) is at 4200m and **Austrian Hut** (Map p177; dm KSh500) is at 4790m. Beds in Met Station and Mackinder's are harder to find, as they're booked through Naro Moru River Lodge (p179). If you're denied beds, you can still climb this route if you camp and carry all the appropriate equipment.

Those needing more luxury can doss in lovely, KWS-run **Batian Guest House** (Map p180; www.kws.go.ke; cottages US$180), which sleeps eight and is a kilometre from the Naro Moru gate.

SIRIMON ROUTE

A popular alternative to Naro Moru, Sirimon has better scenery, greater flexibility and a gentler rate of ascent but takes a day longer. It's well worth considering combining it with the Chogoria route for a six- to seven-day traverse that really brings out the best of Mt Kenya.

The trek begins at the Sirimon gate, 23km from Nanyuki, from where it's about a 9km walk through forest to Old Moses Hut (3300m), where you spend the first night.

On the second day you could head straight through the moorland for Shipton's Camp,

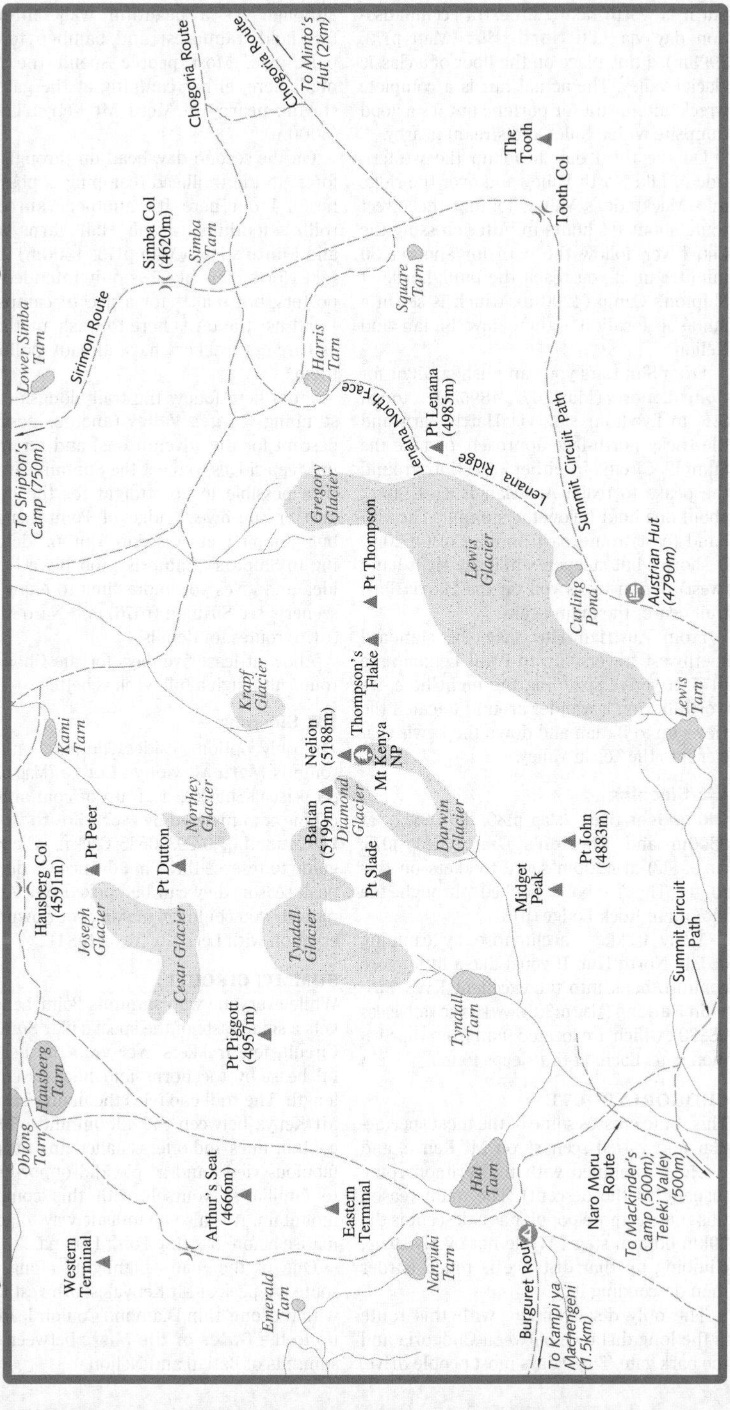

Mt Kenya Summit

Oblong Tarn
Hausberg Tarn
Hausberg Col (4591m)
Western Terminal
Joseph Glacier
Pt Peter
Kami Tarn
To Shipton's Camp (750m)
Lower Simba Tarn
Sirimon Route
Simba Col (4620m)
Pt Dutton
Cesar Glacier
Northey Glacier
Arthur's Seat (4666m)
Pt Piggott (4957m)
Simba Tarn
Chogoria Route
Krapf Glacier
Chogoria Route
To Minto's Hut (2km)
Emerald Tarn
Tyndall Glacier
Batian (5199m)
Nelion (5188m)
Gregory Glacier
Harris Tarn
Diamond Glacier
Eastern Terminal
Thompson's Flake
Pt Thompson
Pt Slade
Mt Kenya NP
Lenana North Face
Square Tarn
Nanyuki Tarn
Darwin Glacier
Pt Lenana (4985m)
Tyndall Tarn
Lewis Glacier
Hut Tarn
Lenana Ridge
The Tooth
Burguret Route
Midget Peak
Tooth Col
To Kampi ya Machengeni (1.5km)
Pt John (4883m)
Curling Pond
Summit Circuit Path
Naro Moru Route
To Mackinder's Camp (500m); Teleki Valley (500m)
Austrian Hut (4790m)
Summit Circuit Path
Lewis Tarn
0 500 m
0 0.3 miles

but it is worth taking an extra acclimatisation day via **Liki North Hut** (Map p173; 3993m), a tiny place on the floor of a classic glacial valley. The actual hut is a complete wreck and meant for porters, but it's a good campsite with a toilet and stream nearby.

On the third day, head up the western side of Liki North Valley and over the ridge into Mackinder's Valley, joining the direct route about 1½ hours in. After crossing the Liki River, follow the path for another 30 minutes until you reach the bunk-house at Shipton's Camp (4200m), which is set in a fantastic location right below Batian and Nelion.

From Shipton's you can push straight for **Point Lenana** (Map p177; 4895m), a tough 3½- to five-hour slog via Harris Tarn and the tricky north-face approach, or take the Summit Circuit in either direction around the peaks to reach Austrian Hut (4790m), about one hour below the summit. The left-hand (east) route past Simba Col (4620m) is shorter but steeper, while the right-hand (west) option takes you on the Harris Tarn trail nearer the main peaks.

From Austrian Hut take the standard southwest traverse up to Point Lenana; see p176. If you're spending the night here, it's worth having a wander around to catch the views up to Batian and down the Lewis Glacier into the Teleki Valley.

Sleeping

Old Moses Hut (Map p180; dm US$12) at 3300m and **Shipton's Camp** (Map p173; dm US$12) at 4200m serve trekkers on this route. They're both booked through the Mountain Rock Lodge (p181).

Many trekkers acclimatise by camping at Liki North Hut. If you'd like a little more comfort, book into the excellent KWS **Sirimon Bandas** (Map p180; www.kws.go.ke; bandas US$80), which are located 9km from the Sirimon gate. Each *banda* sleeps four.

CHOGORIA ROUTE

This route crosses some of the most spectacular and varied scenery on Mt Kenya, and is often combined with the Sirimon route (usually as the descent). The main reason this route is more popular as a descent is the 29km bottom stage. While not overly steep, climbing up that distance is much harder than descending it.

The only disadvantage with this route is the long distance between Chogoria and the park gate. These days most people drive, although it's a beautiful walk through farmland, rainforest and bamboo to the park gate. Most people spend the first night here, either camping at the gate or staying nearby in Meru Mt Kenya Lodge (3000m).

On the second day, head up through the forest to the trailhead (camping is possible here). From here it's another 7km over rolling foothills to the Hall Tarns area and **Minto's Hut** (Map p173; 4300m). Like Liki North, this place is only intended for porters, but makes for a decent campsite. Don't use the tarns here to wash anything, as careless trekkers have already polluted them.

From here follow the trail alongside the stunning **Gorges Valley** (another possible descent for the adventurous) and scramble up steep ridges to meet the Summit Circuit. It is possible to go straight for the north face or southwest ridge of Point Lenana, but stopping at Austrian Hut or detouring to Shipton's Camp is probably a better idea and gives you more time to enjoy the scenery; see Sirimon (p176) and Naro Moru (p176) routes for details.

Allow at least five days for the Chogoria route, although a full week is better.

Sleeping

The only option besides camping on this route is **Meru Mt Kenya Lodge** (Map p180; per person KSh1500), a group of comfortable cabins administered by **Meru South County Council** (☎0729390686; Chuka). Ask your guide to reserve these in advance, as during peak season they can be booked out. Alternatively you could try making your own reservation with Let's Go Travel (p84).

SUMMIT CIRCUIT

While everyone who summits Point Lenana gets a small taste of the spectacular Summit Circuit, few trekkers ever grab the beautiful beast by the horns and hike its entire length. The trail encircles the main peaks of Mt Kenya between the 4300m and 4800m contour lines and offers challenging terrain, fabulous views and a splendid opportunity to familiarise yourself with this complex mountain. It is also a fantastic way to acclimatise before bagging Point Lenana.

One of the many highlights along the route is a peek at Mt Kenya's southwest face, with the long, thin Diamond Couloir leading up to the **Gates of the Mists** between the summits of Batian and Nelion.

Depending on your level of fitness, this route can take between four and nine hours. Some fit souls can bag Point Lenana (from Austrian Hut or Shipton's Camp) and complete the Summit Circuit in the same day.

The trail can be deceptive at times, especially when fog rolls in, and some trekkers have become seriously lost between Tooth Col and Austrian Hut. It is imperative to take a guide.

Information

The daily fees for the **national park** (www.kws.go.ke; adult/child US$55/25, 3-day package adult/child US$150/70) are charged upon entry, so you must estimate the length of your stay. If you overstay, you pay the difference when leaving.

Technical climbers and mountaineers should get a copy of the **Mountain Club of Kenya** (MCK; ☎Nairobi 020-602330; www.mck.or.ke) *Guide to Mt Kenya & Kilimanjaro*. This substantial and comprehensive guide is available in bookshops or from the MCK offices (p67); MCK also has reasonably up-to-date mountain information posted on its website.

AROUND MT KENYA

Mt Kenya forms the hub of a wheel of communities that live, literally and figuratively, in the shadow of its snow-covered bulk, which looms over the land, starkly dark and visible on clear days.

Most of the area is given over to agriculture and the cultivation of staples of both the Kenyan plate and Somali and Yemeni addicts, the latter living for the fields of *miraa* (twigs and shoots that are chewed as a stimulant) grown near Meru, to the northeast.

Naro Moru

☎062 / POP 9880

Naro Moru may be little more than a string of shops and houses, with a couple of very basic hotels and a market, but it's the most popular starting point for treks up Mt Kenya. There's a post office, and internet is available above Nice and Spice Cafe. There are no banks.

Sights & Activities

In addition to gawking at Mt Kenya (best before 6.30am, after which it is obscured by clouds) and starting the Naro Moru route up to its summit, there are a number of interesting day excursions. Either of the guide associations listed in the boxed text, p175, can organise **nature walks** on Mt Kenya and hikes to the **Mau Mau caves**, which are impressive from both a physical and historical perspective. Mountain Rock Lodge and Naro Moru River Lodge also run similar trips, as well as offering **horse riding**, **fishing** and **wildlife drives** to Aberdare National Park, Solio Game Reserve or Ol Pejeta Conservancy.

KIKUYU CULTURAL SHOWS

Once famed for their elaborate dress of white body paint, impressive ostrich feather headdress and animal-skin tunics, most Kikuyu now forego traditional attire for Western clothes. Sadly your only real opportunity of meeting a tribesperson in full tribal regalia is at a hotel cultural performance or someone posing for photographs at Thomson's Falls.

While there is something undeniably contrived about meeting locals this way, cultural performances are one of the few ways that old customs can be a source of new pride. Recommended shows include those at Nyeri's Outspan Hotel (p167) and Mountain Rock Lodge (p181) in Naro Moru.

Sleeping & Eating

All of the basic hotels are to be found in the town, while the more tourist-oriented options are in the surrounding countryside, particularly on the bumpy road between Naro Moru and the park gates. Eating options in town are slim, but you won't starve if you like greasy chips and dining on goats who have lived long and eventful lives.

TOP CHOICE **Naro Moru River Lodge** LODGE $$
(Map p180; ☎31047, 0724082754, Nairobi 020-4443357; www.naromoruriverlodge.com; Naro Moru; camping/dm US$11/15, s full board US$142-201, d & tw full board US$204-309; P 📶 🏊) A bit like a Swiss chalet, the River Lodge is a lovely collection of dark, cosy cottages and rooms embedded into a sloping hillside that overlooks the rushing Naro Moru River 3km from town. All three classes of room are lovely, but the middle-of-the-road

Around Mt Kenya

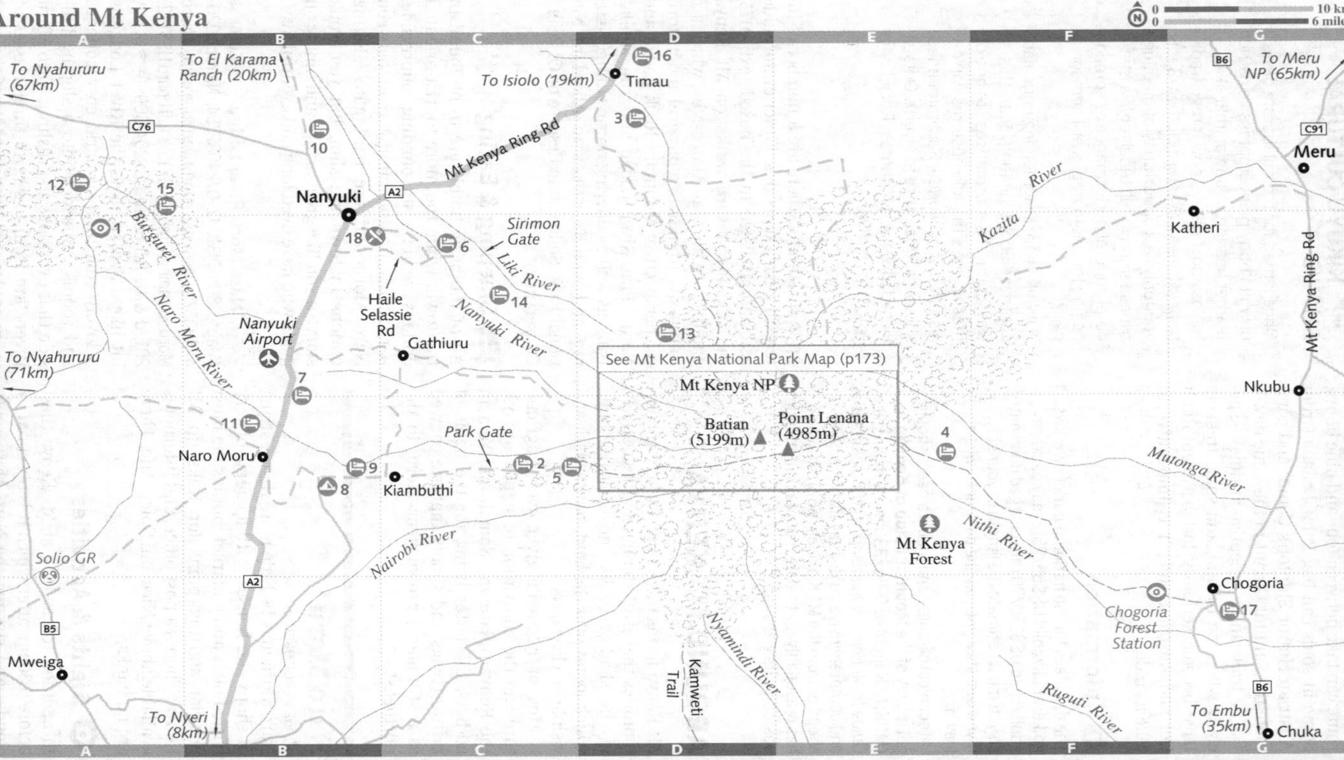

Around Mt Kenya

'superior' option seemed the best of the lot. Backpackers may consider camping here or staying in the dorm, which allows them access to the pool, squash and tennis courts. The restaurants here are the best in town.

Timberland Hotel HOTEL **$**
(Naro Moru; s/d excl breakfast KSh350/500) It doesn't get much cheaper or more basic than this. If you don't mind squat toilets, the odd bug and a little late-night noise, you can save a packet.

Mt Kenya Guides & Porters Safari Club BANDA **$**
(Map p180; ☎020-3524393; www.mtkenyaguides.com; per person KSh1500) Principally in the business of supplying guides and porters, this association has branched out with a couple of excellent-value cottages with open fires. Meals can be arranged on request and, obviously, organising a trek here is a breeze.

Mountain Rock Lodge HOTEL **$$**
(Bantu Mountain Lodge; Map p180; ☎020-8097157, Nairobi 020-242133; www.mountainrockkenya.com; camping KSh550, s/d/tw full board US$95/140/140; P ᯤ) This is one of the major bases for Mt Kenya climbers and the operators of Old Moses Hut and Shipton's Camp on the mountain. There are three classes of rooms and the prices quoted here are for the better-value, midrange 'superior' rooms. Like most hotels in this price bracket, the rooms are serviceable enough but in need of refurbishment. It's located 9km north of Naro Moru, tucked away in woods that are occasionally frequented by elephants.

Mt Kenya Leisure Lodge HOTEL **$$**
(Map p180; ☎0715724381; www.mtkenyaleisurelodge.com; camping US$70, s/d/tw US$95/130/130; P ᯤ) Built in 2008 and already showing signs of wear, the spacious rooms are in a large lodge reminiscent of an old English manor. It's a bit of rabbit warren inside but when you find it, there is a communal lounge with an open fire to fend off the chilly night air. Seventy dollars for camping – really?

Getting There & Away

There are plenty of buses and matatus heading to Nanyuki (KSh50, 30 minutes), Nyeri (KSh120, 45 minutes) and Nairobi (KSh400, three hours) from either the northbound or southbound 'stages'.

Nanyuki

☎062 / POP 31,580

This small but bustling mountain town makes a living off sales, be it of treks to climbers, curios to soldiers of the British Army (which has a training facility nearby) or drinks to pilots of the Kenyan Air Force (this is the site of its main airbase). For all that mercantilism, it's laid-back for a market town. Nanyuki also serves as a gateway to the Laikipia plateau, one of Africa's most important wildlife conservation sites.

Nanyuki

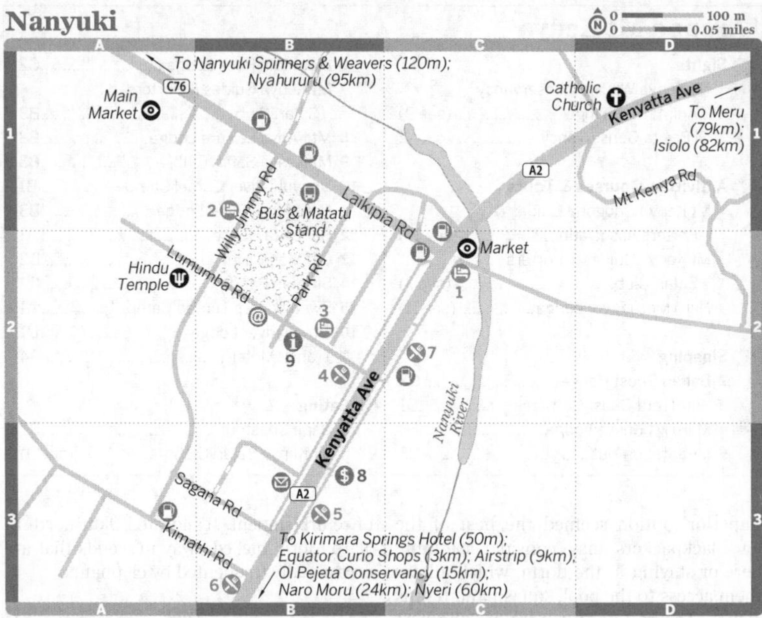

Nanyuki

Sleeping

1	Equator Chalet	C2
2	Ibis Hotel	B1
3	Joskaki Hotel	B2

Eating

4	Eatery	B2
5	Marina Grill & Restaurant	B3
6	Nakumart Supermarket	B3
7	Walkers Kikwetu	C2

Information

8	Barclays Bank	B3
	Boma Holidays	(see 6)
9	Montana Trek & Information Centre	B2

Sights & Activities

Besides tackling Mt Kenya's Sirimon (p176) or Burguret routes, you should stroll 3km south to the **equator** (there's a sign) and get a lesson from the men who make a living giving demonstrations of the Coriolis force (see p184). 'Graduates' of the course can buy a 'diploma' for KSh300.

Mt Kenya Wildlife Conservancy Animal Orphanage ZOO
(Map p180; Mount Kenya Safari Club; per person KSh1500; ⊙8am-12.30pm & 1.30-5.30pm) It may come off a little zoolike at first but this orphanage is one of the few places in the world to have successfully bred the rare mountain bongo. Its success is such that there are now plans to release some of the captivate-bred antelope into the Mt Kenya forests to bolster the current population of around 70. Children, and anyone who wants to have a baby monkey scramble over their head, will love this place.

Sleeping

TOP CHOICE **Kirimara Springs Hotel** HOTEL $
(☎0726370191; www.kirimaraspringshotel.com; Kenyatta Ave; s/d/tw KSh2300/3000/3500; P ⓦ) While Kirimara isn't going to win any architecture awards, its friendly staff and spacious and bright rooms were cleaner and cheaper than others in this price bracket. The rooms on the western side of the building catch less traffic noise, while those on the east get glimpses of Mt Kenya.

WORTH A TRIP

LAIKIPIA PLATEAU

Set against the backdrop of Mt Kenya, the **Laikipia plateau** (www.laikipia.org) extends over 9500 sq km (roughly the size of Wales) of semi-arid plains, dramatic gouges and acacia-thicket-covered hills. Conceived in 1992, this patchwork of privately owned ranches, wildlife conservancies and small-scale farms has become one of the most important areas for biodiversity in the country. It boasts wildlife densities second only to those found in the Masai Mara and is the last refuge of Kenya's African wild dogs. Indeed, these vast plains home some of Kenya's highest populations of endangered species, including half of the country's black rhinos and half of the world's Grevy's zebras.

In late 2011, after six years of difficult negotiations, the African Wildlife Foundation (www.awf.org) and Nature Conservancy (www.nature.org) gifted 17,000 acres to the Kenya Wildlife Service, which was then gazetted as Laikipia National Park. Kenya's newest park, and the first to be established in 20 years, lies in the heart of the plateau and allows for unimpeded wildlife movement between the privately owned conservancies.

Ol Pejeta Conservancy

Ol Pejeta Conservancy (Map p180; www.olpejetaconservancy.org; adult/child US$65/32, vehicle from KSh300; ⏲7am-7pm) was once one of the largest cattle ranches in Kenya, but is now a 90,000-acre, privately owned wildlife reserve. It possesses a full palette of African plains wildlife, including the Big Five, massive eland and a healthy population of rhinos (including a blind and tame orphan named Barrack). The on-site **chimpanzee sanctuary** (⏲9-10.30am & 3-4.30pm) is less inspiring, in no small part because many of the orphaned chimps show signs of psychological damage (presumably from before they were rescued and brought here). Accommodation options include **Sweetwaters Tented Camp** (Map p180; www.serenahotels.com) beside a floodlit waterhole and **Ol Pejeta House** (Map p180; www.serenahotels.com), a massive bush villa that was once home to Lord Delamere.

Visiting Laikipia

Even though Laikipia now boasts a brand-new national park, the vast majority of protected lands are owned by private conservatories and their efforts have helped to create one of Kenya's foremost safari destinations.

Virtually all of the lodges and camps (now numbering over 40) fall squarely into the luxurious bracket and cater to the well-heeled who visit as part of prepackaged tours. The Laikipia plateau website listed above is the obvious place to start when researching accommodation options and the properties listed below are by no means the only gems in the Laikipia crown.

El Karama Ranch (☎0720386616; www.horsebackinkenya.com) Affordable horseback safaris.

Sanctuary at Ol-Lentille (www.ol-lentille.com) Packages start at over US$1000 and are the ultimate in luxury safaris.

Il Ngwesi Eco Lodge (☎020-2033122; www.ilngwesi.com) A Maasai-owned ecolodge with exceptional wildlife viewing.

Tassia Lodge (☎0725972923; www.tassiasafaris.com) Beautifully sited on the edge of a rocky bluff with sweeping views.

Borana Lodge (www.borana.com) One of two lodges on the Borana Ranch – both overlooking waterholes.

Bobong Campsite (☎062-32718; olmaisor@africaonline.co.ke) Self-catering *bandas* and camping at a child-friendly farm.

Ol Malo (☎062-32715; www.olmalo.com) Posh rock and olive-wood cottages in an equally stunning setting.

Tharua Safaris (☎0721638337; www.tharua-safaris.info) Affordable homestays and horseback safaris.

LOCAL KNOWLEDGE

PETER MUTUNGA: PROFESSOR OF THE CORIOLIS FORCE

'Hello sir. Welcome to the equator! Would you like a demonstration of the Coriolis force?'

'Hello. Sure.'

'Now we are at the centre. On either side is the northern [gestures north] and southern [gestures south] hemisphere. If I pour water from this pitcher into this bowl with a hole inside it [holds up bowl] 20m to the north, it will drain clockwise. Observe!'

He does so, dropping a stick in the water to demonstrate its draining direction.

'Wow.'

'Now, if we go 20m to the south, it will go out in an anticlockwise direction.' He repeats the procedure.

'OK.'

'This whole effect is known as the Coriolis force. It was described by Gaspard de Coriolis in 1835 and is based off Newton's second law of motion. Now, here at zero degrees, when I pour out the water, it will drain out in a straight line. Watch!' (The water drains out in a straight line.)

'Wow! That's pretty impressive, Peter.'

'Thank you. I am the professor of the Coriolis force. I am also an entrepreneur. Would you like to give me a tip?'

Author's note: while the demonstration seems to work, scientists say the Coriolis force doesn't actually cause water to drain in the manner Mutunga depicted.

TOP CHOICE Mount Kenya Safari Club LUXURY HOTEL $$$
(Map p180; ☎Nairobi 020-2265000; www.fairmont.com; d US$329-479; P 🛜 ≋) For our money this is *the* top-end resort in the Central Highlands – it's the kind of place that makes you want to grow a moustache, kick back and smoke a pipe. The rooms are safari-chic and decorated to a sumptuous standard, all with their own open fires and exquisite bathrooms. The whole shebang overlooks the Mt Kenya Wildlife Conservancy and there are more facilities here than you can shake a Maasai throwing-stick at (including a heated pool, clay tennis court, topiary maze, wedding chapel and art gallery). This once-exclusive club now welcomes day visitors, although you will need to validate your entry ticket by buying at least one drink at the bar. Keep an eye on its website as special rates are sometimes promoted there.

Ibis Hotel HOTEL $
(☎0714420888; http://nanyuki@ibishotels.co.ke; Willy Jimmy Rd; s/d/tw excl breakfast KSh1000/1200/1800; 🛜) A little smarter than nearby Joskaki; the few extra shillings buy you a little more cheer and a slightly larger bathroom. This multilevel building encloses a covered courtyard restaurant that is better than most. Angle for a room with Mt Kenya views.

Joskaki Hotel HOTEL $
(☎31403; Lumumba Rd; s/tw/d excl breakfast KSh600/700/900) This enormous option is the best of the budget sleeps, offering clean rooms with nice views over town (and Mt Kenya, if you're lucky). Some of the self-contained toilets even have seats (gasp!). The on-site bar and restaurant and early morning traffic can make this a little noisy.

Kongoni Camp BANDA $
(☎702868888; www.kongonicamp.com; camping KSh600, bandas per person KSh3200, d KSh5400; P 🛜) Founded by a friendly local-turned-Londoner-turned-local-again, Kongoni has five, concrete circular *bandas*. Each contains a double and single bed. The large barnlike restaurant-cum-bar comes as a refreshing dash of hip after the many spartan budget digs around town. Kongoni Camp is located just off the A2, 4km east of town.

Nanyuki River Camel Camp HUT $
(Map p180; ☎0722-361642; www.fieldoutdoor.com; camping KSh1000, huts without bathroom half/full board KSh4500) The most innovative sleep in town (well, 4km outside of it, off the C76 Hwy) is this ecocamp, set in a dry swab of scrub. The camp offers lodging in genuine Somali grass-and-camelskin huts imported from Mandera. A series of pleasant paths, picnic areas and a tree house are all situated on the nearby Nanyuki River.

Best known for its camel treks (half-/full day KSh3500/5000), it's a good idea to give them at least 48 hours advance notice as the camels are often grazed many kilometres away. Somalian food such as *nyiri nyiri* (fried camel jerky with cardamom) is a house speciality but also requires advance notice.

Equator Chalet HOTEL $
(☎31480; Kenyatta Ave; theequatorchalet@yahoo.com; s/tw/d KSh1500/2300/2300; @) The Equator is welcoming and comfortable with some fairly decent rooms that boast tea- and coffee-making facilities. The hotel surrounds a breezy internal courtyard with two balconies and a roof terrace.

Nanyuki Simbas Lodge HOTEL $
(☎0711784552; nanyukisimbalodge@gmail.com; off Simba Rd; s/d/tw excl breakfast KSh800/1500/1800; P) Despite being a rather foreboding, medieval-keep-like structure, with all the personality of a concrete block, this hotel has some of the cleanest rooms in town. It's a 10-minute walk from town. Follow the main drag northeast to Simba Rd just before a Catholic Church. The lodge is a further 200m up Simba Rd down a small side street.

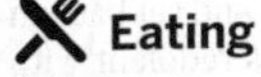

Eating

Eatery INTERNATIONAL $
(Kenyatta Ave; mains KSh500-900; ⏲breakfast, lunch & early dinner) Bridging the gap between *nyama choma* butcheries and the plush lodges, this place specialises in decent Western favourites such as burgers, sandwiches, chips and pizza. If you are heading here for dinner, be aware that it closes at 6pm.

Mount Kenya Safari Club INTERNATIONAL, BUFFET $$$
(Map p180; meals KSh850-1000, buffets KSh4300; ⏲breakfast, lunch & dinner) If you are looking to splurge then this is the place to do it. Sink back into a sofa in the drawing room or saunter over to the pool and take in the vista. The buffet is only served at breakfast and lunch and includes all kinds of delectable yummies. Feeling romantic? Order your beau a gemstone martini (one with blue topaz costs a mere KSh32,650) – just be sure they don't accidentally swallow it (the gemstone that is, not the martini).

Marina Grill & Restaurant INTERNATIONAL $
(Kenyatta Ave; mains KSh140-420; ⏲lunch & dinner) Popular with trekking groups, British soldiers and Kenyan Air Force officers (the odd cross-section that is Nanyuki), this place does good burgers and pizza and has a nice rooftop eating area for those needing fresh air.

Walkers Kikwetu BUFFET $
(Kenyatta Ave; mains KSh200-350; ⏲breakfast, lunch & dinner Mon-Sat) *Kikwetu* means 'ours' in Kikuyu and provides the inspiration behind the menu. Several African dishes from various tribes are brought together and served buffet style (but charged according to the dishes you select). If you haven't tried *matoke* (cooked plantains), pilau (Swahili curried rice) or *mukimo* (mashed beans and vegetables), here is your big chance.

Cape Chestnut INTERNATIONAL $
(Map p180; mains KSh350-550; ⏲breakfast & lunch Mon-Sat; 📶) This coffee garden caters mostly to white farmers and expats, although all are welcome. The blackboard menu changes daily but features mostly Western-style home-cooked fare. Tuesday night is tapas night (KSh600 to KSh800), and the only day it stays open late. It's off Kenyatta Ave, 1km south of town.

Nakumart Supermarket SUPERMARKET $
(Kenyatta Ave) The best supermarket in town.

Shopping

There are a number of souvenir stalls and shops around town, catering mostly to the British army. Eatery (p185) runs a two-for-one book exchange.

Nanyuki Spinners & Weavers CLOTHING
(Laikipia Rd) For something less tacky, try this women's craft cooperative that specialises in high-quality woven woollen goods. The store is a short walk past the main market on Laikipia Rd.

Equator Curio Shops SOUVENIRS
(Kenyatta Ave) The equator just wouldn't be the same without the 30 or so shops that cluster around its sign. Each shop owner takes a turn at being the first to approach arriving tourists. After that, it's game on.

Information

Barclays Bank (Kenyatta Ave) Reliable ATMs.

Boma Holidays (☎020 269194; pamela@bomaadventures.com; 2nd fl, Nakumart Centre, Kenyatta Ave) Travel agency that can arrange airline ticketing, car hire, airport transfers, hotel reservations and local safaris.

'YOU WILL BUILD CASTLES'

'What does this stuff do?' we ask our driver.

'It gives you energy. When you chew this thing, you will build castles.'

That was our introduction to *miraa*, the small shoots and leaves that are chewed throughout the Mt Kenya area and Muslim parts of the country.

Some of the best *miraa* in the world is grown around Meru. Much of the demand is from Somalia and, since *miraa*'s potency is diminished 48 hours after picking, massively overladen pick-up trucks race nightly to Wilson Airport in Nairobi for the morning flight to Mogadishu.

Chewing *miraa* pre-dates coffee drinking and is deeply rooted in the cultural traditions of some societies, especially in Muslim countries. It's usually chewed in company to encourage confidence, contentment and a flow of ideas. The active ingredient, cathinone, is closely related to amphetamine, and the euphoric effects can last for up to 24 hours, depending on how much is chewed.

Chewing too much can be habit-forming and has serious consequences, known as 'khat syndrome'. Aggressive behaviour, nightmares and hallucinations are common mental side effects, while reduced appetite, malnourishment, constipation and brown teeth are common physical consequences.

Meru is a good place for curious travellers to give *miraa* a go. It's bitter and gives a brief high, followed by a long come-down. Note that *miraa* is illegal in neighbouring Tanzania, so best leave it out of the suitcase if you're heading that way.

Montana Trek & Information Centre (☎062-32731; www.montanatrekks.com; Nanyuki) As well as supplying guides for Mt Kenya treks, this place is an excellent source of local information.

Peak Cyber (2nd fl, Bidhaa Bora Bldg, Lumumba Rd; per hr KSh60) Internet and CD burning services.

Post office (Kenyatta Ave)

Getting There & Away

Airkenya (☎020-391 6000; www.airkenya.com) and **Safarilink** (☎020-600777; www.flysafarilink.com) fly daily from Wilson Airport in Nairobi to Nanyuki. A return trip on Airkenya/Safarilink costs US$200/220. **Tropic Air** (☎020-2033032; www.tropicairkenya.com) operates its charter-helicopter and light-aircraft services from here.

Nanyuki is well connected to all points north and south, as well as most major Rift Valley towns. Sample matatu fares include Nyeri (KSh150, one hour), Isiolo (KSh200, 1½ hours), Meru (KSh150, 1½ hours), Nakuru (KSh500, three hours) and Nairobi (KSh400, three hours).

Timau

Sky-kissed fields of flowers and grain roll in enormous waves all the way to the border of the northern frontiers. This is another major artery in Kenya's agricultural heartland but wouldn't warrant a stop if it weren't for the two terrific diversions listed below.

Sleeping & Eating

Ken Trout Guest Cottages BANDA $

(Map p180; ☎0720804751; camping KSh300, cottages half board per person KSh2500) This fishing lodge, located off the A2 Hwy and set back in a pine-clad riverine retreat, is redolent with pastoral isolation and wood smoke. Needless to say, some fine fish is whipped up at the restaurant and there is some good angling about, although you pay for everything you catch.

Timau River Lodge BANDA $

(Map p180; ☎0721331098; timauriverlodge@hotmail.com; camping KSh500, cottages per person incl breakfast/half board/full board KSh1500/2000/2500) Nestled in a skein of cold streams and grassy fields off the A2 Hwy, this beautiful little compound of offbeat log cabins is scattered with wandering chickens, ducks and a few tortoises. The thatched accommodation is warm, slightly funky and enlivened by bouts of electricity in the evening, although it's magic enough to watch the stars with the lights out.

Getting There & Away

Any matatu running between Nanyuki and Isiolo, or Nanyuki and Meru, will drop you in Timau (KSh120, around one hour) or at the turn-off to either sleeping option.

Meru

☎064 / POP 126,430

Meru is the largest municipality in the Central Highlands and the epicentre of Kenyan production of *miraa* (see p186), a mild, leafy stimulant more widely known outside of Kenya as khat. The town itself is like a shot of the stuff: a briefly invigorating, slightly confusing head rush.

The obvious base for exploring Meru National Park, Meru is worth a day visit in its own right and is a focal point for the Meru people (see p303).

Sights

Meru National Museum MUSEUM

(adult/child KSh500/200; ⏲9am-6pm) There's a series of faded exhibits, desultory stuffed and mounted wildlife and a small but informative section concerning the clothing, weapons, and agricultural and initiation practices (including clitoridectomies) of the Meru people. Out back is a small menagerie of disheartened animals that have had the misfortune of ending up here. It's off Kenyatta Hwy.

Meru

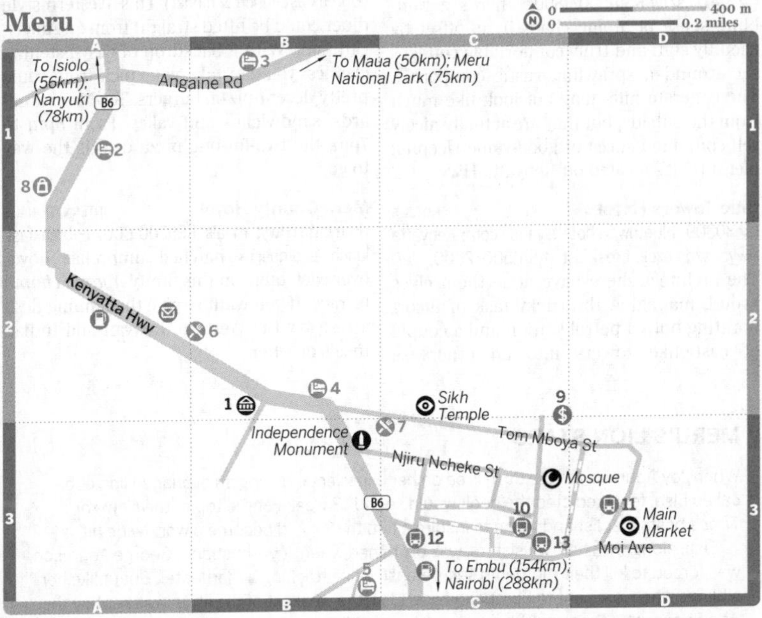

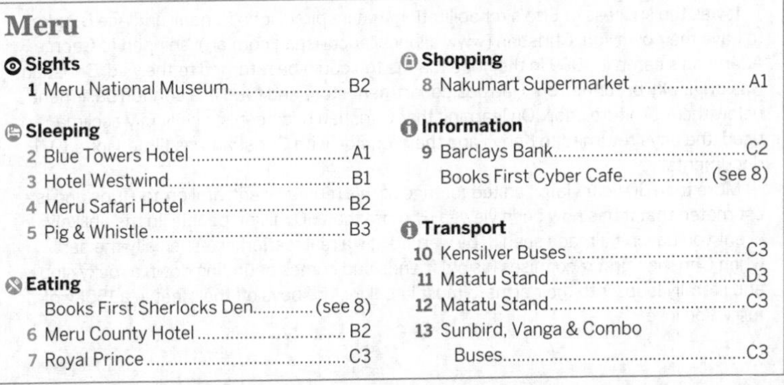

Meru

Sights

1 Meru National Museum B2

Sleeping

2 Blue Towers Hotel A1
3 Hotel Westwind B1
4 Meru Safari Hotel B2
5 Pig & Whistle B3

Eating

Books First Sherlocks Den .... (see 8)
6 Meru County Hotel B2
7 Royal Prince C3

Shopping

8 Nakumart Supermarket A1

Information

9 Barclays Bank C2
Books First Cyber Cafe .... (see 8)

Transport

10 Kensilver Buses C3
11 Matatu Stand D3
12 Matatu Stand C3
13 Sunbird, Vanga & Combo Buses C3

Sleeping

Hotel Westwind HOTEL $

(☎31890; westwindhotelmeru@gmail.com; Angaine Rd; s KSh1800-2500, d KSh2500-3000; P) Catering to the business elite, this is Meru's accommodation at its finest. Service here is friendly and comes from the heart; the decor, however, comes from the '80s. Some rooms are surprisingly small. Follow Kenyatta Rd uphill past the Nakumart supermarket and turn right onto Angaine Rd at the major intersection. Hotel Westwind is 500m along this road on the left.

Pig & Whistle BANDA $

(☎31411; s/tw KSh1500/1800) There's a rambling sense of alpine chaos here, offset by friendly staff and truly comfortable cottages set around a sprawling rustic compound. The concrete huts may not look like much from the outside, but they are actually nicely self-contained slices of good-value sleeping pleasure. It's located off Kenyatta Hwy.

Blue Towers Hotel HOTEL $

(☎30309; bluetowershotel@yahoo.com; Kenyatta Hwy; s/d excl breakfast KSh1500/2000; P) The architects here have done themselves proud, managing the tricky task of incorporating both a petrol station and a couple of castlelike towers into an otherwise unmemorable building. Not to be outdone on the peculiarity stakes, the rooms all have windows facing the hall.

Meru Safari Hotel HOTEL $

(☎31500, 0725259852; merusafari@yahoo.com; Kenyatta Hwy; s/d/tw/tr excl breakfast KSh1300/2000/2000/2400) Clean and adequate if somewhat soulless, it's a step up from the rock-bottom hotels, with friendly staff, but there is little memorable about this place.

Eating & Drinking

Books First Sherlocks Den CAFE $

(Nakumart, Kenyatta Hwy; mains KSh350-700; ⏰breakfast, lunch & dinner) This Western-style diner could be lifted straight from an American mall. With a backdrop of easy-listening classics, you can take your pick from some pretty decent pizza, burgers, Tex-Mex standards, sandwiches and cakes. From 5pm to 7pm, the two-for-one pizza deal is the way to go.

Meru County Hotel INTERNATIONAL $

(Kenyatta Hwy; meals KSh300-600; ⏰breakfast, lunch & dinner) Thatched umbrellas hover over each table on this pretty *nyama choma* terrace. If you want to give the flaming flesh a rest, try the Western, Kenyan and Indian meals on offer.

MERU'S LION STARS

When Joy Adamson wrote *Born Free* on her experience raising an orphaned lion cub called Elsa, few predicted the book would spend 13 weeks at the top of the *New York Times* bestseller list and go on to inspire a film that would become a worldwide hit.

Elsa, along with her two sisters, was orphaned when Joy's husband, George Adamson, was forced to kill their mother in self-defense while tracking a man-eater. But unlike her siblings who were sent to European zoos, Elsa, the weakest of the litter, was kept by the Adamsons, who then spent two years educating her in the ways of lions before successfully releasing her into the wilds of what is today Meru National Park.

It was the success of Elsa's rehabilitation that inspired John Rendall and Ace Bourke to have their own lion, Christian (www.alioncalledchristian.com.au), shipped to George Adamson's camp in 1969 in the hope that he too could be returned to the wild. Christian was originally brought from Harrods department store and lived in a London basement below their furniture shop. On learning that Christian had been successfully acclimatised, the boys returned to Kenya and their reunion with Christian was filmed for a 1971 documentary.

More than 30 years later, edited footage of this reunion went viral on YouTube and is estimated that it has now been viewed by more than 60 million people. In the unlikely event you haven't already seen it, be warned: it's a real tearjerker, especially the part when Christian first recognises his old friends and comes bounding down a rocky slope and literally leaps into their arms, almost knocking the boys off their feet in a 150kg of furry, lion love.

Royal Prince KENYAN $
(Tom Mboya St; mains KSh200-350; ⏲lunch & dinner) There are two stories of bustling eating goodness at this cheap hotel. The downstairs restaurant specialises in all things fried, while upstairs houses the '*choma* zone', where half a kilo of grilled flesh costs KSh350.

Nakumart Supermarket SUPERMARKET $
(Kenyatta Hwy; ⏲8.30am-8.30pm Mon-Sat, 10am-8pm Sun) The best-stocked supermarket in town.

Information

Barclays Bank (Tom Mboya St) Reliable ATM.

Books First Cyber Cafe (Nakumart, Kenyatta Hwy; per hr KSh120)

Post office (Kenyatta Hwy)

Getting There & Away

Kensilver (Mosque Hill Rd) and **Sunbird** (Mosque Hill Rd) have 15 daily departures between them from 6.45am onwards, covering Embu (KSh300, two hours), Thika (KSh300, 3½ hours) and Nairobi (KSh400, five hours).

Vanga (Mosque Hill Rd) and **Combo** (Mosque Hill Rd) run daily buses at 6.30pm and 5.30pm to 5pm respectively to Mombasa (KSh1300, 12 hours). The Vanga bus is the more comfy.

Regular matatus also serve Nairobi (KSh650, four hours), Thika (KSh550, 3½ hours), Embu (KSh300, two hours), Nanyuki (KSh250, 1½ hours) and Isiolo (KSh200, 1½ hours). Long-distance matatus leave from the 'stage' near the main market.

Meru National Park

Marred by a decade of poaching in the 1980s and the subsequent murder of George Adamson (of *Born Free* fame) in 1989, Meru fell off the tourist map and has never quite managed to struggle back on despite recent massive investment by the KWS. This is a pity, because with wildlife numbers on the rise, Hemingway-esque green hills and fast-flowing streams bordered by riverine forests, baobab trees and doum palms, Meru is one of Kenya's best-kept secrets.

Sights & Activities

Walking within the park is not permitted, so without your own 4WD you will need to join an organised tour to see the **zebras**, **waterbucks**, **buffaloes**, **giraffes** and **elephants** the park is renowned for. Thanks to the cover afforded by the long grass and thickets of acacia bushes, animals are not seen as readily here as they are in the more open parks. Consequently, it is not uncommon to turn a corner and find yourself practically bumper-to-snout with some large and threatening herbivore.

MERU NATIONAL PARK

Why Go A pristine, seldom-visited park where you will be guaranteed a 'congestion-free' experience.

When to Go Although falling within Mt Kenya's eastern rain shadow, the park is accessible year-round with a 4WD.

Practicalities There is no public transport within the park but self-drive safaris are possible as park road junctions are numbered on the ground and labelled on park maps.

The park's relative obscurity also means that **wildlife drives** are a far more personal experience here than elsewhere – you'll often feel as if you have the whole place to yourself.

Most safaris enter the park at Murera gate and head for the **rhino sanctuary**, a fenced portion of the park that's home to both black and white rhinos reintroduced here from Lake Nakuru National Park after the disastrous poaching of the '80s.

The park's most significant waterway, **Rojewero River**, is a reliable place to view **hippos** and **crocodiles**. To the south you may want to check out **Elsa's Grave**, a stone memorial to the Adamson's star lioness. Access to the adjacent **Kora National Park** is via the bridge near **Adamson's Falls**.

Sleeping

Kinna Bandas BANDA $$
(www.kws.go.ke; bandas US$100;) These four *bandas* each sleep two and are stocked with kerosene lanterns that add the right romanticism to a star-studded bush night. Located in the heart of the park, you can't get closer to the wildlife without the risk of being eaten by it.

Elsa's Kopje BANDA $$$
(020-6003090; www.elsaskopje.com; d full board from US$1190;) Plenty of hotels claim to blend into their environment, but Elsa's did so in such a seamless manner that the bar on chic ecosuites was permanently raised. Carved into Mughwango Hill, these

Meru National Park

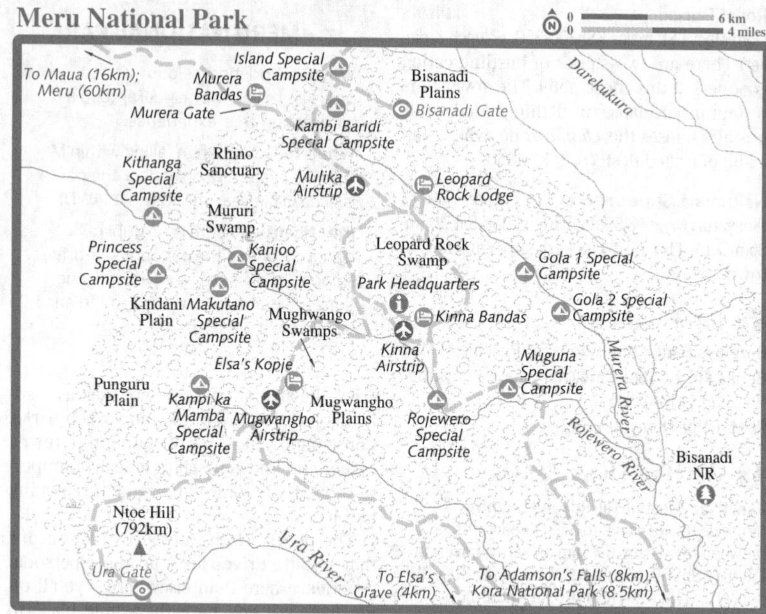

highly individualised 'three-walled' rooms open out onto views *The Lion King* animators would have killed for. Stone-hewn infinity pools plunge over the clifftops, while rock hyraxes play tag in your private garden. These features come with intense luxury pampering, wildlife drives, walking safaris and transfers.

Leopard Rock Lodge LODGE $$$
(☎020-600031, Nairobi 0733333100; www.leopardmico.com; per person full board US$240; ☒) This beautiful unfenced lodge lets the wildlife right in; keep an eye on your possessions, as the baboons and/or Sykes's monkeys will nick your stuff. Due to recent competition, prices here have fallen considerably and while it may not be in the class of Elsa's Kopje, it's a great deal cheaper.

Murera Bandas BANDA $$
(www.kws.go.ke; bandas US$50-70) The Murera camp, overflowing with plain wooden cottages and huts, isn't as charming as Kinna's, but it's a fine place to doss if everything is booked up. Each *banda* sleeps three.

Special Campsites CAMPGROUND $
(www.kws.go.ke; camping US$30, reservation fee KSh7500) There are about a dozen of these bush campsites (no facilities) located throughout the park. The gate will let you know which are currently open.

Information

Entrance to **Meru National Park** (☎020-2109508; www.kws.go.ke; adult/child US$60/30, vehicles from KSh300; ⏲6am-7pm) also entitles you to enter the adjacent **Kora National Park**, although visits into Kora must be prearranged with Meru's warden at the park headquarters.

The KWS *Meru National Park* map (KSh450), sold at the park gates, is essential if you want to find your way around. Even so you may want to hire a guide (six-hour/full-day tour KSh1500/3000).

Getting There & Away

There's no point reaching the park without a vehicle, as although the rangers can sometimes arrange 4WDs, they'll need plenty of advance notice to do so.

Without your own wheels, your best option is to contact John Kirimi of **J Kirimi Safaris** (☎0721683700; www.jkirimisafaris.com), a small safari operator who has a 4WD based in Maua (a small town 31km from the main gate). A full-day safari, including pick-up and drop-off at Meru town, costs around US$135 for the whole 4WD.

Airkenya (www.airkenya.com) has daily flights connecting Meru to Nairobi (return US$449).

Chogoria

064 / POP 3020

This town shares its name with the most difficult route up Mt Kenya (p178). It's a friendly enough place but unless you're trekking, there's no reason to stop here.

You can probably arrange local accommodation with one of the many touts offering Mt Kenya climbs; otherwise, head to **Transit Motel** (Map p180; 0725609151; www.transitmotelchogoria.com; camping per tent KSh500, s/d/tw/tr KSh1200/1900/1900/2600), 2km south of town. This is a large, friendly lodge with pleasant rooms (some with small balconies) and a decent restaurant (meals KSh350 to KSh500). Mt Kenya Chogoria Guides and Porters Association (boxed text, p175) are also based here.

Chogoria is 3km off the main B6 drag to which it is connected by two roads that radiate out from it. In all likelihood an express matatu will drop you at either the Kiriani (southern) junction or the Kirurumwe (northern) junction, from where you will have to catch a *boda-boda* (motorcycle taxi) to town. When leaving it is best to use the town's matatu stand rather than head back to the B6 and rely on a passing vehicle to have an empty seat. Sample fares include Meru (KSh150, one hour), Embu (KSh220, 1½ hours) and Nairobi (KSh400, four hours).

Embu

068 / POP 31,500

This sleepy town is the unlikely capital of Eastern Province, but despite its local significance there's not a lot to do, and it's a long way from the mountain. The town is at its best around October/November, when the local jacaranda trees are in full, purple bloom.

Sleeping & Eating

Panesic Hotel HOTEL $
(0722533442; panesichotel@yahoo.com; s/d/tw KSh2500/3000/3500; P) Off the B6 Hwy, this is currently Embu's finest hotel. The rooms are spotless, with flat-screen TVs, modern bathrooms (or what passes as modern in these parts) and beds boasting the most impressive mosquito nets we've ever seen.

Canan Guest House GUESTHOUSE $
(0723285517; s/d/tw KSh800/1000/1200) These green-and-white rooms set off from the main road are good value for money, although if you plan to swing a cat, it could get messy. This place also has a no-smoking, -toking or -boozing policy (this includes *miraa*).

Valley View Lodge HOTEL $
(0720757921; s/d/tw excl breakfast from KSh900/1100/1400) Painted in pea-soup shades of institutional green, this is a decent

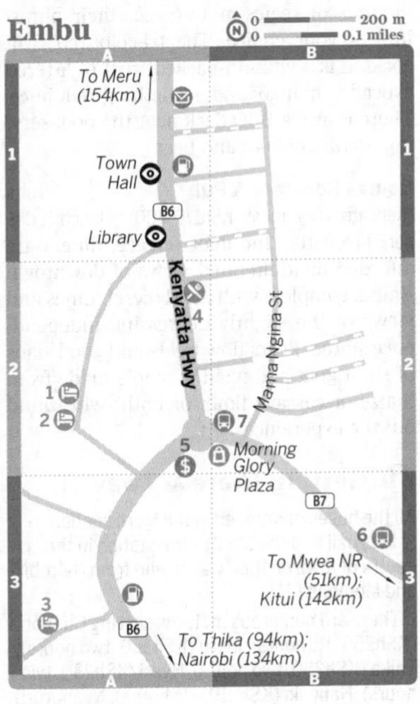

Embu

Sleeping
1 Canan Guest House A2
2 Panesic Hotel A2
3 Valley View Lodge A3

Eating
4 Bomas Roasters & Pub A2
Panesic Hotel .... (see 2)

Information
5 Barclays Bank A2

Transport
6 Bus & Matatu Stand B3
7 Buses B2
Shell Petrol Station .... (see 7)

sleep with clean if faded rooms. The restaurant here has a pool table and large verandah and consequently is more popular as a watering hole than a dining establishment. It's located off the B6 Hwy.

Eating & Drinking

TOP CHOICE Panesic Hotel INTERNATIONAL $
(mains KSh400-600; ⌚breakfast, lunch & dinner) The food here is great value and only a few shillings more than the town's cheap eateries. The steaks come with a soup starter, mounds of vegies and *starch* (their phrasing) of your choice. The tri-coloured fruit cocktail is a vitamin-packed treat of layered avocado, mango and something-red juice. There is also a BBQ deck near the pool serving *nyama choma* and beer.

Bomas Roasters & Pub PUB $
(Kenyatta Hwy; meals KSh170-400; ⌚lunch & dinner) From the 2nd-floor terrace, diners are afforded unadulterated views of downtown Embu, complete with acrid diesel fumes and views of the slightly depressing independence statue. Beers flow freely and good slabs of roast goat and ugali (a staple made from maize or cassava flour, or both) will round out the experience.

Getting There & Away

All the buses mentioned in the Meru section (p192) call into the Shell petrol station in the centre of town on their way to and from Nairobi and Mombasa.

There are numerous matatus serving Chogoria (KSh250, 1½ hours), Meru (KSh350, two hours), Thika (KSh250, two hours), Nyeri (KSh230, two hours), Nanyuki (KSh310, 3½ hours), Nyahururu (KSh510, five hours), Nairobi (KSh300, three hours) and Nakuru (KSh630, six hours).

Mwea National Reserve

In contrast to the rich greens that characterise so much of the highlands, this reserve is set in a dry depression that is nonetheless beautiful in a stony-scarp, thorn bush and aloe-field kind of way. Kamburu Dam, at the meeting point of the Tana and Thiba Rivers, forms the focus for the 48-sq-km **reserve** (www.kws.go.ke; adult/child US$20/10; ⌚6am-7pm). Enclosed by an electric fence, elephants, hippos, buffaloes, lesser kudu and myriad birdlife are present here.

There's a **campsite** (adult/child US$15/10) with basic facilities (no water) close to the reserve headquarters and another site with similar facilities close to Hippo Point.

Mwea is best accessed from the 11km dirt road that's signposted off the B7 Hwy some 40km south of Embu. There's a signposted 27km dirt track to the park that's 14km south of Embu, but the going is very rough. A 4WD is essential to get to Mwea and around the park.

Thika & Around

☎067 / POP 82,665

Flame trees may have put Thika on the map but it is pineapples that keep her there and Del Monte is a big player in these parts. The famous flame trees may be gone, but Thika is known as the cleanest town in Kenya. In truth, there seemed little evidence to substantiate that claim.

Sights & Activities

TOP CHOICE Fourteen Falls WATERFALL
(adult/child KSh350/160; ⌚9am-5pm) It may not be the scenic highlight of the Central Highlands but clambering along the waterfall's rim as 14 cataracts (or one huge waterfall after rain) topple 10m to the rocks below is a lot of fun. Obviously you'll need a guide (KSh400 after bargaining) to show you how, as the rocks are slippery, slimy and submerged under fast-flowing water. We obviously don't recommend this when river levels are high or for those wobbly on their feet. A more sedate five-minute amble upstream will bring you to a placid pool and a pod of resident **hippos**.

The easiest way to reach the falls, which are 25km southeast of Thika, is to catch a matatu from St Patrick's School (KSh80, 40 minutes) and let the driver know your destination.

FREE Thika & Chania Falls WATERFALL
(Muranga Rd) Both children of the Aberdare Range, the Chania and Thika Rivers finally meet 2km north of town, where they tumble over a rocky, tree-lined cliff. The scene is delightfully appreciated from the porch of the Blue Post Hotel with a stiff drink in one hand and a book in the other.

Sleeping

Blue Post Hotel HISTORIC HOTEL $$
(☎0721578245; blueposthotel@africaonline; Muranga Rd; s/d/tr excl breakfast KSh3850/4200/5550;

(@P) With a history that outdates the town itself, the Blue Post still retains a faint whiff of the colonial. Undoubtedly it was the prime location, opposite Thika's waterfalls, that first attracted its original proprietors in 1908. Today the beautifully maintained grounds attract Kenyan couples intent on tying the knot in all their polyester glory. Our tip: insist on the 'Chania Wing' as these rooms have views to the falls. Also located within the hotel grounds is a small and surprisingly well-stocked craft village and an equally surprising, but hardly stocked at all, zoo.

Stadview Apartments HOTEL $
(☎0727401127; Commercial St; r/tw/ste excl breakfast KSh1300/1500/3000) Virtually next door to the more prominently signposted December Hotel, the Stadview represents better value in its cheery but dated rooms in the centre of town.

Samann Guest House HOTEL $
(Bamboo Bar, Anger Guest Restaurant; ☎072233956; Kenyatta Hwy; r excl breakfast KSh500) These reasonably clean rooms have decent hot showers from 8.30pm (once the boiler has had time to do its thing). At this price don't expect any frills – and by frills we mean toilet seats.

Eating & Drinking

Dining out in Thika requires commitment. It is not uncommon to wait an hour for your meal to arrive.

TOP CHOICE **Raheels Cafe Pan House** INDIAN $
(Section 9; meals KSh350; ⌚dinner, closed Tue) There is only one reason to come to this unassuming takeout place and that reason is chicken tikka. Be sure to order some naan to mop up the gravy and finish off with a paan parcel – a concoction of sugar syrup, dates, herbs and spices wrapped in a betel leaf specially imported from India.

Coconut Grill EUROPEAN, CHINESE $
(Kenyatta Hwy; meals KSh250-350; ⌚breakfast, lunch & dinner; 📶) A local favourite, particularly with those eager to impress first dates, the Coconut Grill is the lightest and brightest restaurant in town thanks to a high ceiling and some large windows. Our only gripe: the staff tend to miscalculate the bill for out-of-towners.

Porkies Garden BEER GARDEN
(Uhuru St; admission free Mon-Thu, KSh100 Fri & Sat; ⌚10am-late) Besides serving the best chicken stew in town and having a huge TV screen for sports fans, Porkies really comes into its fore when the place turns into a nightclub for some hot-and-heavy, bump-and-grind Kenyan-style dancing. The ante is raised on Thursdays when 'bend-over' night attracts couples whose motto is 'a good dance is a dirty dance', to compete for prize money.

Getting There & Away

Thika's steady stream of matatus leave from the 'main stage' in the centre of town. Destinations include Nairobi (KSh100, one hour), Sagana (KSh140, one hour), Nyeri (KSh200, two hours) and Embu (KSh200, 1½ hours).

Ol Donyo Sabuk National Park

This tiny **park** (www.kws.go.ke; adult/child US$20/10; ⌚6am-7pm) is built around the summit and slopes of **Ol Donyo Sabuk** (2146m), known by the Kikuyu as Kilimambongo (Buffalo Mountain). The name fits, as buffaloes are one of the few animals that you may actually encounter here.

Because of the death-by-buffalo-attack threat, it is only possible to explore on foot if accompanied by a ranger (per half-/full day KSh1500/3000). We found its signature 9km hike (three or four hours) to the summit on a dirt road to be disappointing and the views, while impressive, are slowly getting obscured by mobile-phone towers. More interesting was the weird Afro-alpine fauna that crowns the summit you'd otherwise have to climb Mt Kenya to see.

There's a pretty **campsite** (www.kws.go.ke; camping US$15) just before the main gate. Facilities include one long-drop toilet, a rusty tap and free firewood. If you want a bit more comfort, **Sabuk House** (www.kws.go.ke; US$300) is a lovely lodge that comes at a bargain rate compared with similar KWS *bandas* when you consider that it sleeps 10.

From Thika, take the same matatu you would for Fourteen Falls but continue to the village of Ol Donyo Sabuk (KSh100, 50 minutes), from where it's a 2km walk along a straight dirt road to the gate.

Northern Kenya

Includes »

Best of Nature

» Lewa Wildlife Conservancy (p199)

» Samburu, Buffalo Springs & Shaba National Reserves (p201)

» Matthews Range (p204)

» Il Ngwesi (p200)

Best of Culture

» Loyangalani (p216)

» Marsabit (p205)

» South Horr (p215)

» Moyale (p209)

Why Go?

Calling all explorers! We dare you to challenge yourself against some of the most exciting wilderness in Africa. Step forward only if you're able to withstand appalling roads, searing heat, clouds of dust torn up by relentless winds, primitive food and accommodation, vast distances and more than a hint of danger (see p210).

The rewards include memories of vast shattered lava deserts, camel herders walking their animals to lost oases, fog-shrouded mountains full of mysterious creatures, prehistoric islands crawling with massive reptiles and jokes shared with traditionally dressed warriors. Additional perks include camel trekking through piles of peachy dunes, elephant encounters in scrubby acacia woodlands and the chance to walk barefoot along the fabled shores of a sea of jade.

In our 21st-century world of wireless internet and dumbed-down TV, northern Kenya is an opportunity to leave behind all that is familiar and to fall completely off the radar.

When to Go

Loyangalani

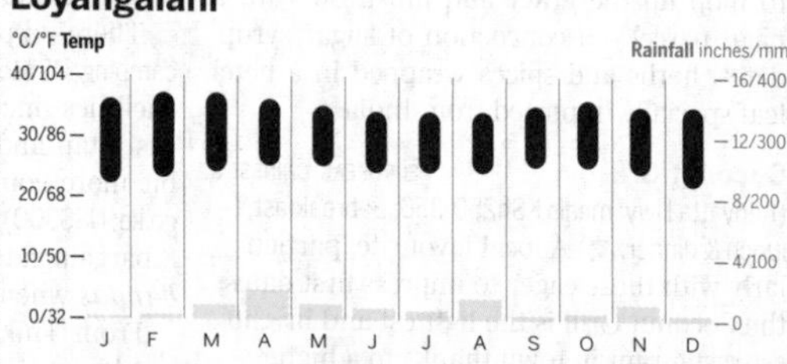

Jun–Jul Work up a sweat running from rhinos during the Lewa Safaricom Marathon.

Aug Saddle up a camel and race through the Maralal International Camel Derby.

Nov–Dec It's marginally cooler in the northern deserts.

ISIOLO TO ETHIOPIA

For most people this route means two things: the wildlife riches of the Samburu ecosystem or the road to the cultural riches of Ethiopia. But in between and beyond, this area has much more to offer. You can drink tea and track game with the Samburu people, climb mist-shrouded volcanoes in the desert, blaze trails in untrammelled mountains and get so far off the beaten track you'll start to wonder whether you're still on the same planet. All told, this massive wilderness offers something to everyone whose heart sings with adventure.

Isiolo

☎064

Isiolo is where anticipation and excitement first start to send your heart a-flutter. This vital pit stop on the long road north is a true frontier town, a place on the edge, torn between the cool, verdant highlands just to the south and the scorching badlands, home of nomads and explorers, to the north. On a more practical note it's also the last place with decent facilities until Maralal or Marsabit.

One of the first things you'll undoubtedly notice is the large Somali population (descendants of WWI veterans who settled here) and the striking faces of Boran, Samburu and Turkana people walking the streets. It's this mix of people, cultures and religions that is the most interesting thing about Isiolo. Nowhere is this mixture better illustrated than in the hectic market.

Sleeping

Isiolo has happy homes for budget and midrange travellers, but desperately lacks decent top-end options.

Range Land Hotel COTTAGES $$

(☎0721434353; A2 Hwy; camping KSh500, tw cottages KSh2500; P) About 8km south of town, this is a nice option for those with their own set of wheels. The sunny campsite has bickering weaver birds in abundance, as well as neat and tidy stone bungalows with hot showers. Many people come to laze around in the gardens at weekends, but during the week it's quiet. Excellent meals are available and the house special is rabbit (KSh1200), a delicious rarity in Kenyan cuisine.

Josera Guest House HOTEL $

(☎0725228482; r with breakfast KSh800-1500) Excellent value sky-blue rooms that range from tiny cubes to those large enough to swing a backpack. All have hot showers and there's a decent in-house restaurant.

Gaddisa Lodge LODGE $$

(☎0724201115; www.gaddisa.com; camping KSh 400; s/tw with breakfast KSh3000/4000; P) Around 3km northeast of town is this spotlessly clean Dutch-run lodge, where peaceful cottages overlook the fringes of the northern savannah country. There's an occasionally full pool to wallow like a hippo in.

Moti Peal Hotel HOTEL $$

(☎52400; s/d KSh2500/3500; wi-fi) This brand spanking new place markets itself as the 'Pearl of Isiolo'. This actually says more about the state of Isiolo than the quality of the hotel, but even so its shockingly clean, well run and has friendly management. It's squat toilets only, though.

Bomen Hotel HOTEL $$

(☎52389; www.bomenhotel.com; s/tw KSh2500/3500; P) The NGOs' favourite home, the Bomen Hotel has the town's most toe-curlingly frilly pink bed sheets! It also has TVs and shared terraces with views.

WILDLIFE IN NORTHERN KENYA

Northern Kenya is one vast wilderness and one of the few areas in East Africa where close encounters with large mammals outside the protected areas are almost a given. The north contains a full hand of almost all of Kenya's animals, but many that you know and love from elsewhere take on slightly different forms up here, where the climate is harsher. Zebras become elegant Grevy's zebras, giraffes turn into beautifully blotchy versions of those down south and then there's all the creatures that occur only in Kenya's dry north. The gerenuk, a type of long-necked antelope, and the beisa oryx are only the most obvious. The bird life, with numerous species not found elsewhere in Kenya, is possibly even more impressive than the roll call of large mammals.

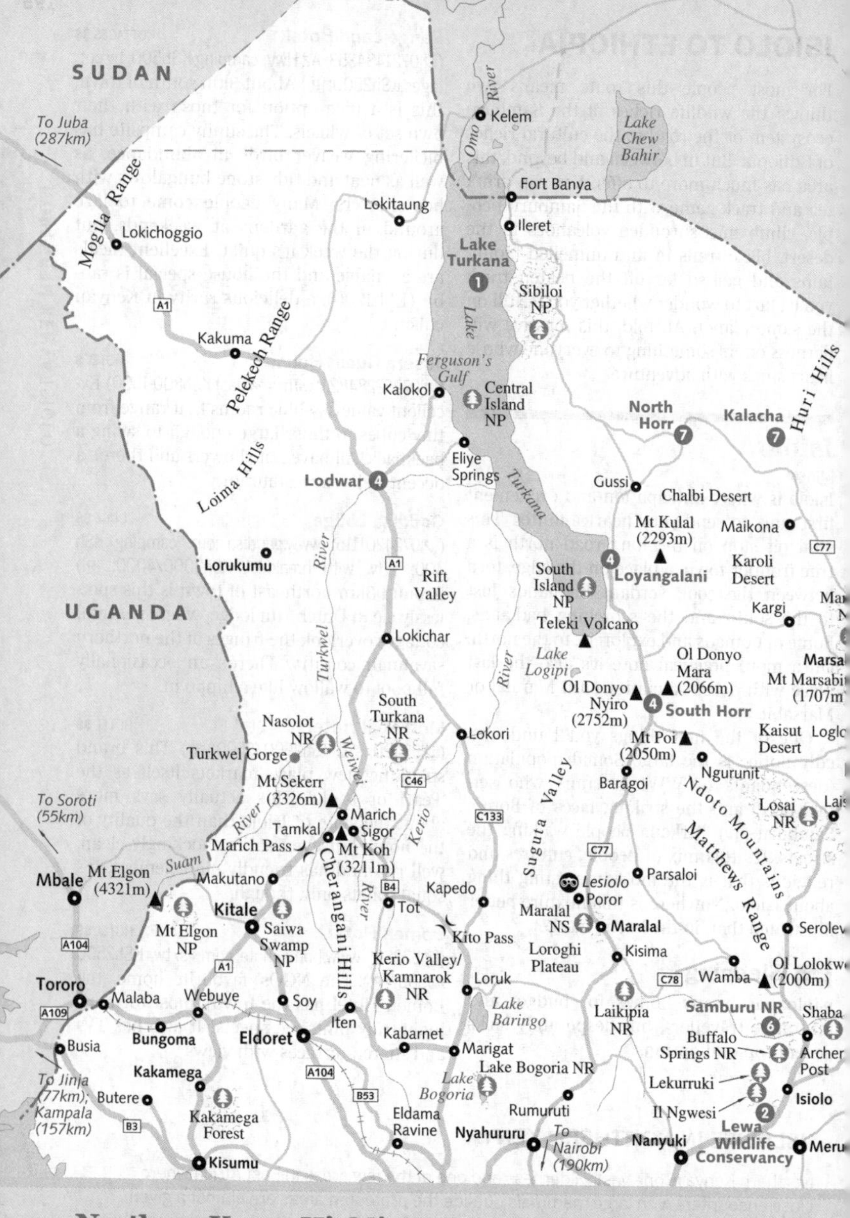

Northern Kenya Highlights

1 Blasting over the plains of darkness destined for a sea of jade, **Lake Turkana** (p215).

2 Experiencing the incredible wildlife and luxurious accommodation of **Lewa Wildlife Conservancy** (p199).

3 Searching for forest elephants lost in an ocean of sand in **Marsabit National Park** (p208).

4 Shaking hands with the Samburu, crocodile fishing with the El Molo and passing the time of day with the Turkana in **South Horr** (p215).

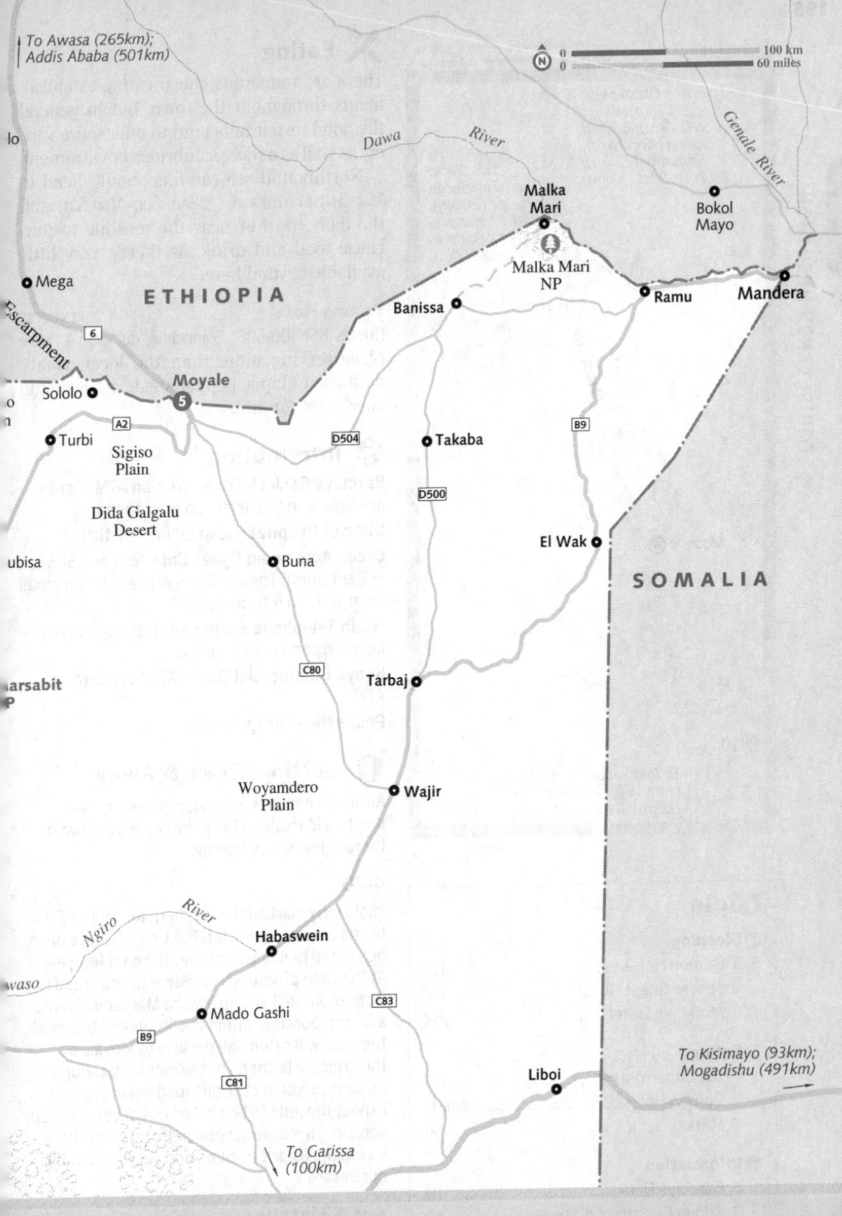

Loyangalani (p216) and **Lodwar** (p221).

5 Getting your first taste of *injera* and *wat* and washing it down with an espresso in **Moyale** (p209).

6 Realising that not only do zebras change their stripes in **Samburu National Reserve** (p201), but that giraffes change their spots and ostriches their legs.

7 Leading your camels to water in the remote oases villages of **Kalacha** (p217) and **North Horr** (p217).

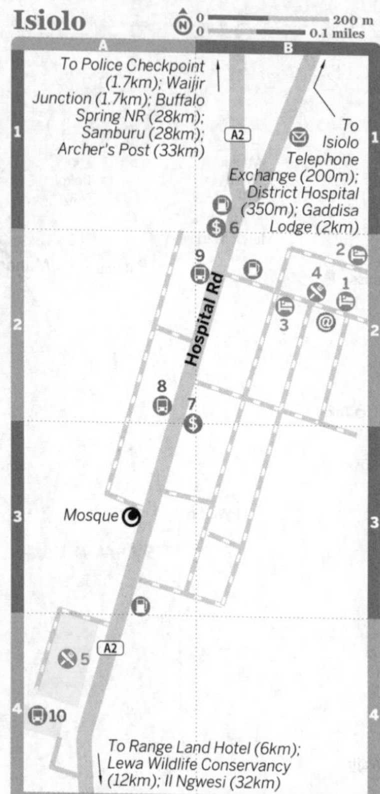

Isiolo

Sleeping

1	Bomen Hotel	B2
2	Josera Guest House	B2
3	Moti Peal Hotel	B2

Eating

4	101 Supermarket	B2
	Bomen Hotel	(see 1)
5	Market	A4

Information

6	Barclays Bank	B1
7	Kenya Commercial Bank	A2

Transport

8	Bus Offices for Nairobi	A2
9	Liban Buses	B2
10	Matatu & Bus Stand	A4
	Trucks to Marsabit & Moyale	(see 8)

Eating

There are numerous cheap eating establishments throughout the town, but in general the hotel restaurants tend to offer more variety as well as a more salubrious environment.

Northbound self-caterers should head to **101 Supermarket** (8am-6pm Mon-Sat) and the daily **market** near the mosque to purchase food and drink, as there's very little available beyond here.

Bomen Hotel KENYAN **$$**
(meals KSh300-500; lunch & dinner) A rare place serving more than the local usuals, with fried tilapia, pepper steak, goulash and curries up for grabs.

Information

Barclays Bank (A2 Hwy) With an ATM. Banks are scarce in the north, so plan ahead.

District Hospital (Hospital Rd; 24hr)

Green Acres.com Cyber Cafe (per hr KSh60; 8am-9pm). The world eagerly awaits an email from you. Do it from here.

Isiolo Telephone Exchange (Hospital Rd) Calling cards and card phones.

Kenya Commercial Bank (A2 Hwy) With an ATM.

Post office (Hospital Rd)

Getting There & Away

Although convoys are no longer being used north to Marsabit, check the security situation thoroughly before leaving.

4WD

Isiolo long marked the northern terminus of the tarmac road system, but the Chinese have been busy road building here over the past few years. At the time of writing, a pristine tarmac road now runs about halfway up toward Marsabit. Eventually, and possibly within the lifetime of this book, the road will extend all the way to Moyale on the Ethiopia border. For the moment, though, as soon as you hit the dirt road again you can expect the guts to be shaken out of you and your vehicle. There are several petrol stations here, so top up, as prices climb and supplies diminish northward.

Bus & Matatu

A couple of bus companies serve Nairobi with most buses leaving between 6am and 6.30am (KSh600, 4½ hours) from the main road through town and also stopping at the matatu and bus stand just south of the market. Nightly buses operated by **Liban Buses** creep north to Marsabit (KSh700, six hours) where you can change for Moyale.

For Maralal take an early-morning matatu to Wamba (KSh350, 2½ hours), and then a Maralal-bound matatu (KSh400, 2½ hours) from there. Regular matatus leave from a chaotic stand around the market and also serve Archer's Post (KSh100, 25 minutes), Meru (KSh150, 1½ hours) and Nanyuki (KSh250, 1¾ hours).

Hitching

Trucks are filthy and uncomfortable but a viable option for the northbound adventurous. Although they pick up passengers at the police checkpoint north of town, better seats are available if you board when they stop near bus offices. Drain your bladder, purchase enough food, water and sunscreen, and hop aboard. Prices are negotiable but if you sit atop the load reckon on KSh400 to Marsabit and KSh1000 to Moyale. Double these prices for a seat in the cab.

Lewa Wildlife Conservancy

Falling away from the Mt Kenya highlands is a vast region of open savannah grasslands that make up some of the most incredible wildlife-viewing territory in Kenya.

TOP CHOICE **Lewa Wildlife Conservancy** WILDLIFE RESERVE
(LWC; ☎064-31405; www.lewa.org; admission US $90) While the massive 222-sq-km conservancy, just south of Isiolo, could boast about their luxury lodges, stunning scenery, astounding wildlife activities and having hosted Prince William, they'd rather talk about their community and conservation projects. Founded in 1995, LWC is a non-profit organisation that invests around 70% of its annual US$2.5 million-plus budget into health care, education and various community projects for surrounding villages, while the rest of the funds further conservation and security projects. To help raise awareness and funds they host one of the world's most rewarding and exhausting marathons (see boxed text, p200).

The conservation effort has been astounding and 20% of the world's Grevy's zebras, 12% of Kenya's black rhinos, a rare population of aquatic sitatunga antelope (though many of these have recently been eaten by lions!) and sizeable populations of white rhinos, elephants and buffaloes call the reserve home. Of the predators there are small, but growing, populations of leopards, lions and cheetahs. All of this makes Lewa not just a flagship model for private conservation but one of the finest wildlife viewing areas in all of Kenya – and there's no minibus circus to contend with. A plethora of activities, ranging from drives (day and night) and walks to horse riding and camel rides, are available at most lodges.

However, visiting this Kenyan Garden of Eden doesn't come easily – nor cheaply. Wildlife drives in private vehicles aren't permitted, only guests of the LWC's lodges are allowed into the conservancy and the accommodation here is for the very well-heeled only.

LEWA WILDLIFE CONSERVANCY

Why Go For some of the finest game-viewing in Kenya; almost guaranteed sightings of all the Big Five; walking safaris and night safaris. Strictly limited visitor numbers means there is no minibus circus.

When to Go Year-round, but the dry season between November to March is best.

Practicalities Lewa is closed to casual visitors: you must be staying at one of the (very expensive) lodges in order to enter. Most visitors fly in from Nairobi but road access is easy from Isiolo or the Central Highlands.

Sleeping & Eating

There are a number of very exclusive places to stay inside the wildlife conservancy. These include the beautiful **Lewa House** (www.lewa.org), **Wilderness Trails** (www.lewa.org) and **Sirikoi** (www.sirikoi.com).

Lewa Safari Camp TENTED CAMP $$$
(☎Nairobi 020-6003090; www.lewasafaricamp.com; s/d full board US$640/1060;) This is about the only camp vaguely accessible to mere mortals. Its safari tents have that whole chic-bush-living thing down to a tee and nothing beats an evening gin and tonic by the roaring log fire of the main building in the company of the delightful English managers. Prices include all safaris and activities.

DON'T MISS

RUNNING FOR YOUR LIFE

It's one thing to run a marathon to the encouraging screams of people, it's entirely another to run it sharing the course with elephants, rhinos and the odd lion! Established in 2000 to raise funds for wildlife conservation and community development, the Safaricom Marathon, run within the Lewa Wildlife Conservancy in late June/early July, attracts world-record holders and is renowned worldwide as one of the planet's toughest marathons. Thanks to experienced rangers, helicopters and spotter planes, your only worry should be the heat and the 1700m average elevation. Visit www.tusk.org for more information and registration details.

 Getting There & Away

The turn-off to LWC is only 12km south of Isiolo (the entrance gate is another 5km on) and is well signposted on the A2 Hwy. **Airkenya** (www.airkenya.com) as well as **Safarilink** (www.safarilink-kenya.com) have daily flights to LWC from Nairobi.

Private vehicles are not generally allowed into Lewa. Those arriving by private vehicle will have to leave their car at the entrance gate and change to a lodge-provided jeep.

Around Lewa Wildlife Conservancy

IL NGWESI

Il Ngwesi is another fine example of a private conservation project linking wildlife conservation and community development. The Maasai of Il Ngwesi, with help from neighbour LWC, have transformed this undeveloped land, previously used for subsistence pastoralism, into a prime wildlife conservation area hosting white and black rhinos, waterbucks, giraffes and other plains animals. It's truly fitting that Il Ngwesi translates to 'people of wildlife'.

The community now supplements its herding income with tourist dollars gained from their award-winning ecolodge, **Il Ngwesi Group Ranch** (Nairobi 020-2033122; www.ilngwesi.com; s/d all incl US$485/770;). The divine open-fronted thatched cottages here boast views over the dramatic escarpment, and at night the beds can be pulled out onto the private 'terraces' allowing you to snooze under the Milky Way. The best part is that profits go straight to the Maasai community. Il Ngwesi is north of Lewa and accessed off the main Isiolo to Nairobi Rd.

Archer's Post

With the recent arrival of the tarmac road, the ramshackle village of Archer's Post, 33km north of Isiolo, has started to expand rapidly and the once forgotten-world feel of the place has disappeared with the dust of the dying dirt road. Despite this loss of charm the village still makes an excellent base for budget travellers searching for elephants and lions in the neighbouring Samburu, Buffalo Springs and Shaba national reserves.

There are a number of Samburu villages in the area that welcome paying guests. Probably the best one is **Umoja village**, which was originally founded as a refuge for abused women and has now budded into a viable village in its own right. Admission is KSh500. It's located next to the Umoja campsite.

About 30km north of town and shrouded in Samburu folklore is the massive mesa of **Ol Lolokwe**. It's a great day hike (five hours just to climb up it) and, at sunset, light radiating off its rusty bluffs is seen for miles around. The mountain is renowned for its raptors and has the highest population of

STALL TACTICS

In 1990, 15 women who'd suffered too long from violent husbands abandoned their homes and started the village of Umoja (meaning 'unity' in Kiswahili), just outside Archer's Post. They hoped to survive together by producing and selling traditional Samburu jewellery to tourists. It all proved rather successful and Umoja thrived, even opening a campsite a few years later. Boosted by its success, dozens more women left unhappy situations and now call the women-only village home.

However, things aren't quite perfect in this female paradise and the success of Umoja has spawned jealousy and even reports of violence directed at Umoja from local men. Find out more about them at www.umojawomen.org.

KALAMA

Eight kilometres north of Archer's Post, and abutting the northern boundary of Samburu National Reserve, is the immense 384-sq-km **Kalama Community Wildlife Conservancy** (admission incl camping US$40), which opened in 2004. It hosts wildlife, including Grevy's zebras, elephants and reticulated giraffes, and acts as a vital wildlife corridor for animals migrating between the Samburu and Marsabit areas. The road network is still undeveloped, but the sheer dearth of other visitors means that you generally have the place to yourself. One big attraction of a visit here over Samburu reserve is that walking is allowed and local Samburu guides lead morning bush walks (US$10). It's also easy enough to base yourself here and do game drives in neighbouring Samburu (though you'll need to pay entrance fees).

If you want to linger in this magnificent slab of wild Africa then you can either camp in one of the three pleasant shady sites or you can go to the opposite extreme and stay in one of the most spectacular lodges in Kenya. So perfectly designed is the Italian-run **Saruni Samburu Lodge** (www.sarunisamburu.com; s/d full board US$770/1300;) that its 'tents' virtually melt into the rocky bluff on which it's located. When we say tents we don't of course mean the sort of tents you used on cub scouts camping weekends. Oh no, we mean tents with stone bath tubs, open-air showers, terraces, designer-chic furnishings, heavenly beds and views, overlooking the northern savannah lands, that are quite simply out of this world. Throw in an infinity pool, superb Italian–Kenyan fusion cooking and attentive staff and you get a place to stay that gives any hotel in the world a run for its money.

Ruppell's vultures in Kenya. It's now managed by the **Namunyak Wildlife Conservation Trust**, a locally run community-based conservation effort. It charges US$20 to climb it and US$50 for a guide.

A number of locals can take you on wildlife-tracking walks in the surrounding wilderness. **Mohamed Leeresh** (0724143080; leeresh@yahoo.com) is recommended. He charges US$50 per day, per group and he can organise jeep rental for US$100 per half-day.

Sleeping & Eating

Don't want to camp with the lions and leopards in the national reserves? Want to save some moolah? Archer's Post can sort you out.

TOP CHOICE **Umoja Campsite** CABINS $$
(Map p202; 0721659717; www.umojawomen.org; camping KSh500, bandas KSh2500) Sitting on the Ewaso Ngiro's banks between town and Archer's Post gate, this fantastic option has clean and comfortable *bandas*, great camping, a chilled cafe (meals available on request) and frequent big-nosed, big-eared visitors coming in from the reserves.

Samamani Lodge HOTEL $
(Map p202; 0720979315; r KSh1500) The newest, brightest and cleanest of several cheap and cheerful options in the village and the only one with attached bathrooms.

Getting There & Away

Matatus from Isiolo stop here en route to Wamba (KSh300, 1¾ hours), and those coming from Wamba also pick up for Isiolo (KSh100, 25 minutes). Expensive fuel is available by the jerry can from several shops in town.

Samburu, Buffalo Springs & Shaba National Reserves

Blistered with termite skyscrapers, shot through with the muddy Ewaso Ngiro River and heaving with heavyweight animals, the three national reserves of Samburu, Buffalo Springs and Shaba are not as famous as some others, but they have a beauty that is unsurpassed, as well as a population of creatures that occur in no other major Kenyan park. These include the blue-legged Somali ostrich, super-stripy Grevy's zebras, unicorn-like beisa oryxes, ravishing reticulated giraffes and the gerenuk – a gazelle that dearly wishes to be a giraffe. Despite comprising just 300 sq km, the variety of vegetation and landscapes here is amazing. Shaba, with its great rocky *kopjes* (isolated hills), natural springs and doum palms, is the most physically beautiful, as well as the least visited (but it should be pointed out that it often has a lot less wildlife than the other two reserves). Meanwhile the open savannahs,

Samburu & Buffalo Springs National Reserves

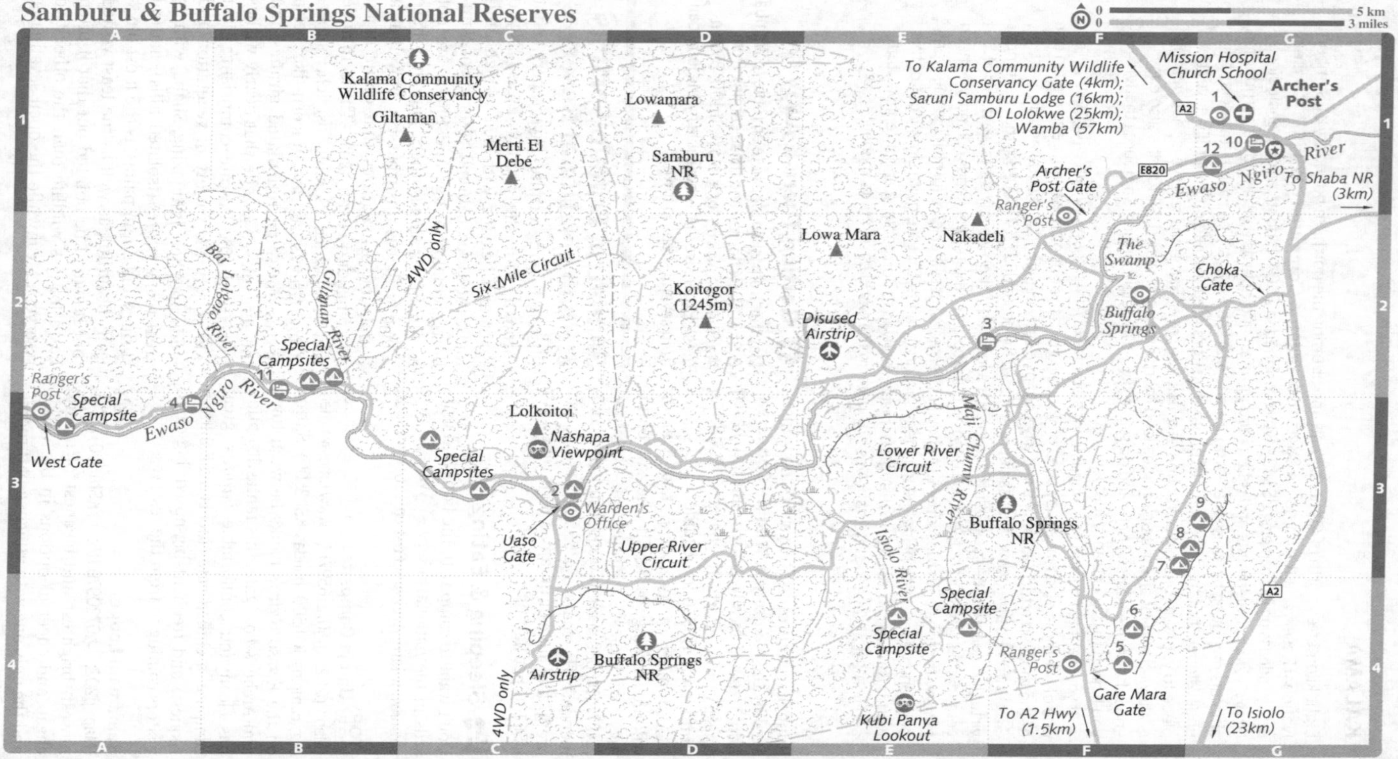

0 5 km
0 3 miles

Kalama Community Wildlife Conservancy
Giltaman
Merti El Debe
Lowamara
Samburu NR
To Kalama Community Wildlife Conservancy Gate (4km); Saruni Samburu Lodge (16km); Ol Lolokwe (25km); Wamba (57km)
Mission Hospital
Church School
Archer's Post
A2
1
10
12
River
E820
Ewaso Ngiro
To Shaba NR (3km)
Archer's Post Gate
Ranger's Post
Nakadeli
Lowa Mara
4WD only
Six-Mile Circuit
Bar Lolgoto River
Giltaman River
The Swamp
Choka Gate
Koitogor (1245m)
Buffalo Springs
Disused Airstrip
3
Special Campsites
11
Ranger's Post
Special Campsite
4
Ewaso Ngiro River
West Gate
Lolkoitoi
Nashapa Viewpoint
Special Campsites
2
Warden's Office
Uaso Gate
Lower River Circuit
Maji Chumvi River
Buffalo Springs NR
Upper River Circuit
Isiolo River
9
8
7
A2
Special Campsite
Special Campsite
6
5
Ranger's Post
Airstrip
Buffalo Springs NR
4WD only
Kubi Panya Lookout
To A2 Hwy (1.5km)
Gare Mara Gate
To Isiolo (23km)

Samburu & Buffalo Springs National Reserves

Sights
1 Market G1

Sleeping
2 Beach Camp C3
3 Elephant Bedroom E2
4 Elephant Watch Camp A3
5 Public Campsite 1 .... F4
6 Public Campsite 2 .... F4
7 Public Campsite 3 .... F3
8 Public Campsite 4 .... F3
9 Public Campsite 5 .... G3
10 Samamani Lodge G1
11 Samburu Intrepids Club B2
Samburu Public Campsite .... (see 2)
12 Umoja Campsite G1

Eating
Sundowner Restaurant .... (see 10)

scrub desert and verdant river foliage in Samburu and Buffalo Springs virtually guarantee close encounters with elephants and all the others.

Archer's Post has a bustling little daily **market** filled with Samburu peoples.

Sleeping & Eating

Each reserve is blessed with at least two luxury lodges and several campsites. For campers and day visitors, all the luxury lodges have buffet meals (US$25).

BUFFALO SPRINGS NATIONAL RESERVE

The five **public campsites** (camping US$10) close to Gare Mara gate are overgrown, hard to find and have absolutely no facilities or water. For toilets, showers and less solitude, camp in Samburu.

Special Campsites CAMPGROUND $
(camping US$15) While scenically located by freshwater springs along the Isiolo and Maji ya Chumvi Rivers, there are no facilities here.

SAMBURU NATIONAL RESERVE

TOP CHOICE **Elephant Watch Camp** TENTED CAMP $$$
(Nairobi 020-8048602; www.elephantwatchsafaris.com; s/d full board incl guided walks US$800/1360, plus per person US$25 service charge; closed Apr & Nov) Undoubtedly the most unique and memorable place to stay in Samburu. Massive thatched roofs cling to crooked acacia branches and tower over cosy, palatial, eight-sided tents and large grass-mat-clad terraces. Natural materials dominate and the bathrooms are stunning. Owners Iain and Oria Douglas-Hamilton are renowned elephant experts.

Elephant Bedroom TENTED CAMP $$$
(Nairobi 020-4450035; www.atua-enkop.com; full board s/d US$250/500;) Twelve absolutely superb riverfront tents that are so luxurious that even budding princesses will feel a little overwhelmed by the surroundings. Exactly how luxurious are we talking? Well, when was the last time you saw a tent that came with a private plunge pool?

Beach Camp TENTED CAMP $
(0721252737, 0711565156; per person KSh1500) On the banks of the Ewaso Ngiro River's northern bank, the scrappy (and hot) dark canvas safari tents here might not climb as high in the luxury stakes as some of the big-boy lodges but, let's face it, this is much more authentic Africa. Meals can be prepared on request. Vervet monkeys and baboons can be a menace, though.

Samburu Intrepids Club TENTED CAMP $$$
(Nairobi 020-446651; full board s/d KSh12,450/16,800; @) Owned by Kenya's very own 'Royal Family', the Kenyattas, the 28 tightly packed tents here are sited along a gorgeous stretch of river, but the dark decor makes it all feel a little gloomy. Despite this, it's one of the cheaper and better value luxury options in the reserve. Game drives cost US$55 per person.

Samburu Public Campsite CAMPGROUND $
(camping US$10) Several public campsites can be found close to the Beach Camp, though most lack even basic amenities (you could pop around to Beach Camp for a meal, though).

Special Campsites CAMPGROUND $
(camping US$15) Special they're not – bush sites with no facilities or water. They're further west and tricky to find.

SHABA NATIONAL RESERVE

TOP CHOICE **Joy's Camp** TENTED CAMP $$$
(☎Nairobi 020-6003090; www.joyscamp.com; s/d full board US$700/1180;) Once the home of Joy Adamson, this is now an outrageously luxurious camp in the remotest corner of Shaba. The accommodation here is in 'tents', but we use the word in the loosest possible way. These tents come with underfloor lighting, lots of stained glass and giant, walk-in rain showers – now if only all tents came like this then camping would be fun! Oh, you can also throw in a swamp filled with wallowing buffaloes overlooked by an infinity pool full of wallowing guests.

Special Campsites CAMPGROUND $
(camping US$15) Of the several sites (no facilities), Funan, set in Shaba's core, takes the cake. Shaded by acacias, it's next to a semi-permanent spring, which provides water for visitors and wildlife. A ranger must accompany you to these sites; the cost is included in the fee but a tip is appropriate.

Shaba Sarova Lodge LODGE $$$
(☎32030; www.sarovahotels.com; s/d full board from US$184/246;) Water, water everywhere and not a drop to drink. This place nestles on the Ewaso Ngiro River and its pathways intertwine with frog-filled streams and ponds. There's a large pool and natural springs flow through the gorgeous open-air bar. The rooms are very comfortable in a formal, business-like way. The lodge leaves bait out to attract local animals. There have been reports that, once the hotel was constructed, the springs became inaccessible to local Samburu herders, who used to water their flocks there.

SAMBURU, BUFFALO SPRINGS & SHABA NATIONAL RESERVES

Why Go To see the unusual dry country and northern versions of all the animals you've seen elsewhere in Kenya, as well as fantastic birdwatching with many species that cannot be seen in southern Kenya. Visitor numbers are low.

When to Go There's little rain in these parts so it's possible to visit year-round, but between November and March animals congregate near the Ewaso Ngiro river.

Practicalities Isiolo is the main gateway town. The best wildlife-spotting is generally in Samburu, but Shaba is the most beautiful and you'll have it almost to yourself. Tickets are valid for all three parks but you must buy your ticket at the gate to the park in which you're staying.

Information

Conveniently, **Buffalo Springs**, **Shaba** and **Samburu** (adult/child US$70/20) entries are interchangeable, so you only pay once, even if you're visiting all three in one day.

Petrol is available at Sarova Shaba Lodge and Samburu Game Lodge, but stock up in Isiolo.

Getting There & Away

The vehicle-less can wrangle a 4WD and driver in Archer's Post for about US$100 per half-day. **Airkenya** (www.airkenya.com) and **Safarilink** (www.safarilink-kenya.com) have frequent flights from Nairobi to Samburu and Shaba.

Matthews Range

West of the remarkable flat-topped mountain Ol Lolokwe and north of Wamba is the Matthews Range. The name might sound tame enough, but rest assured that this is real-wilderness Africa, full of a thousand forest-clad adventures. These forests and dramatic slopes support a wealth of wildlife, including elephants, lions, buffaloes and Kenya's most important wild-dog population. With few roads and almost no facilities, only those willing to go the extra mile on foot will be rewarded with the spoils.

In 1995 the local Samburu communities collectively formed the **Namunyak Wildlife Conservation Trust**, now one of Kenya's most successful community conservation programs. The trust is unique as it's run by a democratically elected board, each community having one trustee. Now endorsed by the Kenya Wildlife Service (KWS), it oversees 750 sq km and has substantially increased animal populations by successfully combating poaching.

The launch pad for the mountains is the one-street town of **Wamba**, remarkable only for the amount of drunks that roam around. If you're a budget traveller intending to explore the mountains independently and on foot then you will need a guide, but

WORTH A TRIP

NDOTO MOUNTAINS

Climbing from the Korante Plain's sands are the magnificent rusty bluffs and ridges of the Ndoto Mountains. Kept a virtual secret from the travelling world by their remote location, the Ndotos abound with hiking, climbing and bouldering potential. **Mt Poi** (2050m), which resembles the world's largest bread loaf from some angles, is a technical climber's dream, its sheer 800m north face begging to be bagged. If you're fit and have a whole day to spare, it's a great hike to the summit and the views are extraordinary.

The tiny village of **Ngurunit** is the best base for your adventures and is interesting in its own right, with captivating, traditionally dressed Samburu people living in simple, yet elegantly woven, grass huts. Ngurunit is best accessed from Loglogo, 47km south of Marsabit and 233km north of Archer's Post. From Loglogo it's a tricky 79km drive with many forks; offer a lift to someone in Loglogo who can then act as a guide. You can also get there from Baragoi.

no matter what the guides might tell you, to really get into the heart of the mountains you either need your own transport, be patient enough to wait for very rare trucks heading to remote Samburu villages deep in the mountains or be prepared for a couple of days of hot, hard walking to even reach the foot of the mountains proper (the mountain overlooking Wamba is merely an outlying chunk of the range). Unfortunately, most of the self-appointed guides are in fact the aforementioned drunks, and none of them can really be recommended.

Sleeping & Eating

There are a couple of unappealing places to stay in Wamba itself, but most appear to be permanently full.

TOP CHOICE **Kitich Camp** TENTED CAMP **$$$**
(Nairobi 020-6003090; www.kitichcamp.com; s/d full board US$480/800; closed Apr–mid-Jun & Nov–mid-Dec) Arguably the remotest camp in Kenya, this place falls squarely into the luxury tented-camp category, but staying here is unquestionably a 100% wild Africa experience. Elephants pass through almost daily and at night they can come so close to your tent that you can hear them breathing (you can also hear your own heartbeat racing wildly at such times!) and passing lions aren't unknown either. The managers, Patrick and Meriem, run the place with a cool efficiency and treat their guests as friends rather than customers.

Getting There & Away

Matatus run from Isiolo (KSh350; p198) and Maralal (KSh400; p214) to Wamba, but from there to Kitich Camp you'll need your own transport. Once at Kitich the dense vegetation makes only walking safaris possible; which means fewer animals sightings – but when they come they're much more exciting!

Marsabit

069

Marsabit is a long way from anywhere. The road from Isiolo is now smooth tarmac for about half the distance (and it's likely that during the lifetime of this book the road will be surfaced all the way) but even so, for hour after scorching hour, you'll pass an almost unchanging monoscape of scrubby bush, where encounters with wildlife are common and elegant Samburu walk their herds of camels and goats. As the afternoon heats up and your brain starts to cook, you'll find the world around you sliding in and out of focus, as mirages flicker on the horizon. Then, as evening comes, one final mirage appears: a massive wall of forested mountains providing an unlikely home to mammoth tusked elephants. But this is no mirage, this is Marsabit.

The small town sits on the side of a 6300-sq-km shield volcano, whose surface is peppered with 180 cinder cones and 22 volcanic craters (*gofs* or *maars*), many of which house lakes – or at least they did until very recently. The drought that began in 2009 and has brought such misery to much of north Kenya has hit Marsabit very hard. At the time of research there had been no rain at all for three years and Marsabit, which just a couple of years earlier had been relatively lush and green, was utterly parched and covered in dust.

Marsabit

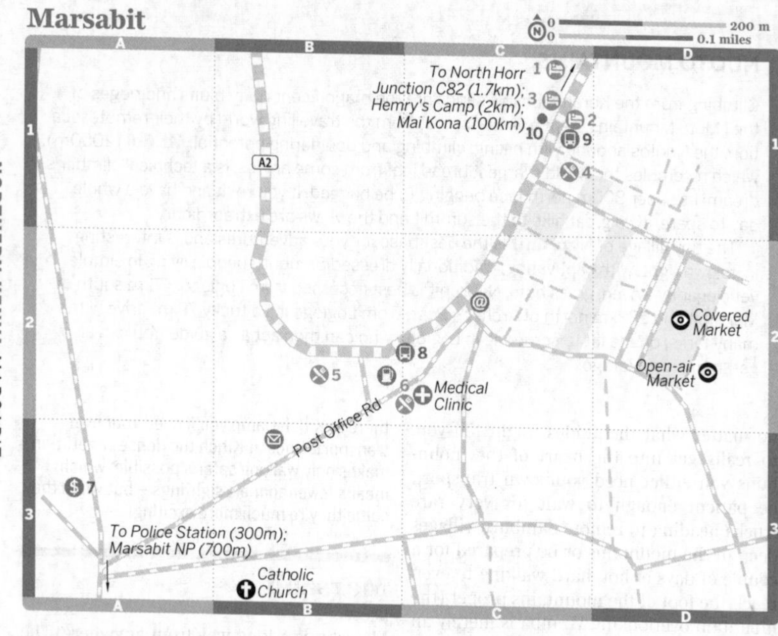

Marsabit

Sleeping
1 Horr House C1
2 JeyJey Centre C1
3 Nomads Trail Hotel C1

Eating
4 Al-Subra Modern Hotel C1
5 Five Steers Hotel B2
JeyJey Centre .... (see 2)
6 Nomads Shopping Store C2

Information
7 Kenya Commercial Bank A3

Transport
8 Local Matatus C2
9 Moyale Raha Buses C1
10 Truck Pick-up Area C1

While the town is less attractive than its surrounds, which comprise the enormous 1500-sq-km **Marsabit National Reserve**, it's an interesting and lively place, thanks to a colourful migrant population of passing nomads. The best place to take in the cornucopia of culture is the lively **market**.

Sleeping

Water is a very scarce commodity in Marsabit and all the guesthouses have to truck it in from more H2O-blessed parts of the country. Use it sparingly.

JeyJey Centre HOTEL $
(☎0717383883; A2 Hwy; r KSh750, s/tw with shared bathroom KSh400/600) This mud-brick castle bedecked in flowers is something of a travellers' centre and is always bursting with road-hardened souls. Basic rooms with mosquito nets surround a courtyard, and bathrooms (even shared ones) sport on-demand hot water. There's also an unattractive campsite (per person KSh250).

Nomads Trail Hotel HOTEL $
(☎0722259699; A2 Hwy; r incl breakfast KSh1200-1500) The smartest accommodation in town, though not necessarily the best value, are the prim and proper rooms on offer here. All rooms have attached bathrooms that come with, wait for it, real hot water from a real shower!

Henry's Camp CAMPGROUND $
(☎0717766145; camping per person KSh300, dm KSh500) The only real option for campers

is this sun-blasted campsite a couple of kilometres out of town. There's a barbecue, fire pit, shady dining area and, for those who've had enough of camping, a mud-walled cabin with six dorm beds.

Horr House HOTEL $
(☎0726147226; A2 Hwy; s/d with shared bathroom KSh500-800) Alright, so we have a juvenile sense of humour, but honestly how could we not include a place with a name like this?! Despite the name, ladies of the night are not a part of the furniture and it's actually one of the better maintained cheapies in town.

Eating & Drinking

While not having as many Michelin stars as Paris, you at least won't go to bed hungry here.

Five Steers Hotel KENYAN $
(A2 Hwy; meals KSh70-130; ⏲lunch & dinner) With a wooden fenced-off terrace, this place is the height of Marsabit style. The '½ Federation' meal (a bulging pile of rice, spaghetti, beef, vegetables and chapatti) is filling and tasty. The owner is a good source of information on onward transport.

Al-Subra Modern Hotel KENYAN, ETHIOPIAN $
(meals KSh70-150; ⏲lunch & dinner) As well as all the Kenyan staples, this place also presents the first flavours of Ethiopia with its *injera* (Ethiopian sour pancake-like staple) and *wat* (spicy stew). It has two TVs, one blasting out Kenyan programs, the other Ethiopian, making either impossible to watch.

JeyJey Centre KENYAN $
(A2 Hwy; meals KSh120-250; ⏲lunch & dinner) Inside the popular hotel, JeyJey serves local favourites as well as the odd curry. Take a good book to read while you wait if you order anything out of the ordinary.

If you're short of food or supplies check out the market and **Nomads Shopping Store** (Post Office Rd; ⏲Mon-Sat).

Information

Cyber Wireless Internet World (per hr KSh60; ⏲8am-7pm Mon-Sat, until 5pm Sun) Opening hours aren't always what they're supposed to be.

Kenya Commercial Bank (off Post Office Rd) With ATM.

Medical clinic (Post Office Rd; ⏲8am-7pm Mon-Sat, noon-7pm Sun)

Post office (Post Office Rd)

GETTING AROUND NORTH KENYA

4WD Having your own 4WD gives you flexibility but comes with its own challenges, thanks to wide-ranging road conditions. For starters you'll need a large 4WD (a Toyota RAV4 or Suzuki won't do) with high ground clearance and a skid plate to protect the undercarriage. You should have a high-rise jack, sand ladders, a shovel, a long, strong rope or chain (to hitch up to camels or other vehicles) plus enough fuel, water and spare tyres (one is rarely enough). A compass and good map are also invaluable.

Do not underestimate how bad the roads are up here – during a month's research in the far north we ploughed through three large 4WDs. Many car rental companies simply will not allow their vehicles to be taken north of Samburu. If you do come up here it's sensible to take an experienced driver and, if possible, travel in company with another jeep.

Road conditions between destinations are discussed in each town's Getting There & Away section.

Bus & Matatu There's regular public transport as far north as Kalokol and Lokichoggio on Turkana's west side, but it's more limited up the lake's east side, only reaching Maralal via Nyahururu or Isiolo. With improved security, buses now run from Isiolo to Moyale on the Ethiopian border via Marsabit.

Hitching For the ultimate Kenyan adventure, hop aboard a dusty transport truck with the locals. It's an uncomfortable and dirty, but utterly enchanting, way to travel around northern Kenya. However, improved bus services mean that Loyangalani is the only major destination that still requires hitching.

Safaris A few organised safaris and overland trucks now go to Lake Turkana's west, but most still stick to the lake's east side. Average trips are seven to 10 days long and they typically follow the same route. See p35 for details and operators.

Getting There & Away

Although improved security meant convoys and armed guards weren't being used to Moyale or Isiolo during our research, it's still wise to get the latest security and Ethiopian border information from locals and the police station before leaving town.

4WD

One day the road to Moyale will be surfaced, but at the time of research it still remained a rutted, dusty, car-destroying mess. The only fuel north is in Moyale, so stock up in Marsabit. As a rule, if buses and trucks travel in a convoy or take armed soldiers on board, you should too! For advice on travel to Loyangalani, see p217.

Bus

Moyale Raha Buses connect Marsabit to Moyale daily at 8.30am (KSh1000, 8½ hours). Calling it a bus is something of a misnomer: instead try and picture the offspring of a truck that slept with a bus! Heading south **Liban Buses** run boringly normal buses to Isiolo (KSh700, six hours) at 8am. Journey times will fall as the tarmac road grows.

Hitching

Trucks regularly ply the bus routes for about KSh100 less, but balancing on a metal bar above discontented cows for eight hours, while simultaneously battling the sun, wind and dust, is one tricky, tiring act. On the flip side, you'll have a lifetime of memories. There are also some very rare trucks to Loyangalani (very negotiable KSh1000, hours and hours) travelling either the northern route via Kalacha and North Horr or the southern one via Kargai. Most trucks pick up opposite JeyJey Centre.

Marsabit National Park

Within the larger national reserve, this small **park** (adult/child US$20/10), nestled on Mt Marsabit's upper slopes, is coated in thick forests and contains a wide variety of wildlife, including lions, leopards, elephants (some with huge tusks) and buffaloes. The dense forest makes spotting wildlife very difficult, but fortunately help is at hand in the form of a couple of natural clearings (that become lakes after rainfall – something that hasn't happened in a while) where animal sightings are almost guaranteed.

It used to be possible to walk in the park, but at the time of writing this had been suspended due to a shortage of rangers and widespread encroachment by local herders with animals to feed. It's worth asking if walking safaris are again possible.

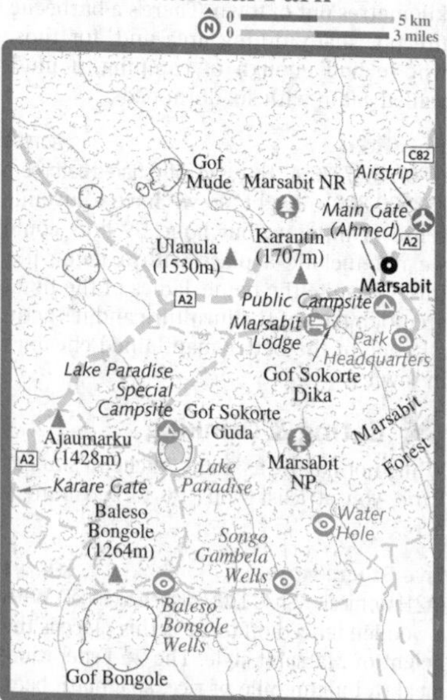

Sleeping & Eating

At the time of research KWS were in the process of constructing some bungalow-style accommodation.

Lake Paradise Special Campsite CAMPGROUND $
(camping adult/child US$30/15, plus set-up fee KSh5000) Although there's nothing except a dried-up lake bed and firewood, this picturesque site is the best place to stay in the park. Due to roaming buffaloes and elephants, a ranger must be present when you camp here.

Marsabit Lodge LODGE $$
(Nairobi 020-604781; www.marsabitlodge.com; s/tw incl breakfast US$83/106) Judging by the drab 1970s decor, mouldy bathrooms and not-quite-clean surfaces, you'd never know that this place has been recently renovated. Still, the location, on the edge of the (now largely dry) lake occupying Gof Sokorte Dika, is spectacular and it's about as cheap a national-park lodge as you'll find.

Public Campsite CAMPGROUND $
(camping adult/child US$15/10) This site, which is next to the main gate, has water and firewood. The shower and toilet facilities were undergoing a much needed facelift at the time of research.

Moyale

Let's be honest, nobody comes to Moyale to see Moyale; people come because it's the gateway to one of the world's most fascinating countries – Ethiopia. The drive from Marsabit is long and hard, but immensely rewarding. Leaving the misty highlands of Marsabit, you drop onto the bleak by name, bleak by nature **Dida Galgalu Desert** (Plains of Darkness) and trundle for endless hours through a magnificent monotony of black, sunburnt lava rock. The only sign of life, aside from the odd nomad and his camels, is the hamlet of **Bubisa**, a fly-blown place marked on few maps, where bored-looking Gabbra, Somali and Ethiopians sit day after day chewing *miraa* (leaves and shoots that are chewed as a stimulant; see boxed text, p186). Then it's onwards over an empty landscape until you reach the tiny village of **Turbi**, sheltered by two small, forested peaks. These can be climbed in half a day, but take a guide as there are a lot of wildlife and wild people in these parts. If you were to get stuck here for the night there are a couple of very meagre places to stay. For security's sake, however, it's best to push onto Moyale. After Turbi, scrubby thorn bushes replace lava desert and, in the distance, the mountain fastness of Ethiopia springs up and tantalises.

In stark contrast to the solitary journey here, Moyale's small, sandy streets burst with activity. The town's Ethiopian half is more developed, complete with sealed roads, and there's a palpable difference in its atmosphere. You will find a small *miraa* market halfway up the main drag on the Ethiopian side.

Sleeping & Eating

For years the hardy few travellers that passed through Moyale have had to put up with some truly nasty accommodation. While 99% of places to stay on both sides of the border maintain this tradition, there is one new option that seems keen to break this mould. Be aware that prostitution here is almost unavoidable as most cheap hotels and bars in this region double as brothels.

KENYA

Al-Yusra Hotel HOTEL **$$**

(0722257028; r from KSh2500) Big news, folks! Kenyan Moyale finally has a decent place to stay! OK, let's not go overboard, it's hardly

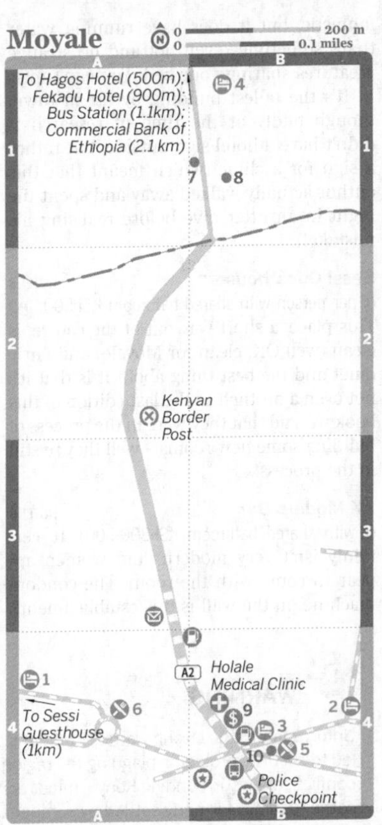

Moyale

Sleeping
1 AK Modern Bar A4
2 Al-Yusra Hotel B4
3 Sherif Guest House B4
4 Tourist Hotel B1

Eating
5 Baghdad Hotel II B4
6 Prison Canteen A4

Information
7 Ethiopian Customs B1
8 Ethiopian Immigration Post B1
9 Kenya Commercial Bank B4

Transport
Moyale Raha Buses .... (see 5)
10 Truck Pick-up Area B4

fantastic, but it does have running water that's sometimes even hot and no strange creatures sharing your bed. You can't miss it. It's the tallest building by far in town, though oddly at the time of research it didn't have a hotel sign outside, but rather a sign for a clinic (which meant that this author actually walked away and spent the night in an utter dive before realising his mistake!).

Sessi Guesthouse HOTEL $

(r per person with shared bathroom KSh500; P) This place, a short way out of the centre, is clean (well OK, clean for Moyale) and fairly quiet and the best thing about it is that it's not even a brothel! In the last edition of this book we said that they were in the process of building some new rooms – well they're still in the process…

AK Modern Bar HOTEL $

(r with shared bathroom KSh300-500) It certainly isn't very modern, and women appear to come with the room. The condom machine on the wall is this establishment's only nodto hygiene and cleanliness. A new accommodation block was in the process of being built over the road.

Sherif Guest House HOTEL $

(r with shared bathroom KSh300) Sitting above the bank, this guesthouse has vaguely clean rooms, some with mosquito nets. The communal toilet is memorable for all the wrong reasons.

Prison Canteen KENYAN $

(meals KSh150-200; ⌚lunch & dinner) It says a lot about the quality of life up here when the best place to eat, drink and party is inside the town jail. Not only do you get a great atmosphere and an excellent *nyama choma* (barbecued meat), but you also get to tell your friends that you went to prison on the Ethiopia–Kenya border!

Baghdad Hotel II KENYAN $

(meals KSh80-150; ⌚lunch & dinner) This is the most popular local restaurant – sit down, swipe some flies and get stuffed.

WARNING

Unfortunately, the strong warrior traditions of northern Kenya's nomadic peoples have led to security problems plaguing the region for years. With an influx of cheap guns from conflict zones surrounding Kenya, minor conflicts stemming from grazing rights and cattle rustling (formerly settled by compensation rather than violence) have quickly escalated into ongoing gun battles that the authorities struggle to contain.

While travellers, who rarely witness any intertribal conflict, may consider the issue exaggerated, the scale of the problem is enormous and growing. Over the past decade hundreds of people are thought to have been killed and more than 160,000 displaced by intertribal conflicts. The serious drought of the past few years has dramatically reduced grazing land, dried up water supplies and had a huge impact on traditional nomadic social structures. This has led in turn to a major escalation in intertribal fighting and cattle rustling. Fortunately, security on the main routes in the north, and anywhere a tourist is likely to be, is generally good (though a group of tourists were attacked in 2011 on the Moyale to Isiolo road and, for a few days in October 2011, the Isiolo to Samburu National Reserve road was cut due to tribal violence). For the moment, though, convoys and armed guards are no longer used between Marich and Lodwar or between Isiolo and Moyale, on the Ethiopian border.

Sadly, not everything is on the mend and bloody conflict continues in large parts of the north. The whole northeastern region around Garsen, Wajir and Mandera is still unstable and you should avoid travelling there.

Incidentally, travelling up towards the Somali border (which is currently closed) has been dangerous for years, but with a full-scale Kenyan military invasion and renewed fighting in that blood-saturated country, only the most foolhardy would attempt to travel up there.

Improvements or not, security in northern Kenya is a fluid entity. Travellers should seek local advice about the latest developments before travelling and never take unnecessary risks.

ETHIOPIA

Since prices in the area are quoted in Ethiopian Birr, we've done the same here. The exchange rate is around US$1 to Birr17.

Tourist Hotel HOTEL $

(☎046-440513; s/d with shared toilet Birr22/44) Sheltered behind its cool Rasta- inspired bar, this sleeping option has colourful rooms that include private showers. The shared toilets are nothing to sing about, but thankfully they're nothing to scream about either.

Fekadu Hotel HOTEL $

(s/d Birr70/100) Simple, somewhat overpriced self-contained rooms set around an excellent courtyard restaurant and a decent bar.

Hagos Hotel ETHIOPIAN $

(meals Birr20; ⏲lunch & dinner) Dig into some *injera* or spice-laden roasted meat. There's a terrace out the back and some shady seating below a flowering tree. It's just up from the border and the Tourist Hotel.

ℹ Information

If you've traipsed all the way up here then presumably you're heading to Ethiopia; in which case make sure you've already got an Ethiopian visa because they're not available on the border. It used to be possible for those without a visa to at least cross into Ethiopian Moyale for a few hours to see what they were missing. This is now only possible if you really sweet talk the Ethiopian officials on the border. For those sensible enough to have a visa and to be continuing to Addis Ababa, see p374 for more information on crossing this border. If you're coming the other way, three month Kenyan tourist visas are available on the border for most western nationalities for US$50. The border is open from 6am-6pm daily. Onward transport from either side of the border leaves before the border opens, so if you arrive in town early enough, cross straight to the other side, thus allowing you to get out of Moyale the next morning. Otherwise you'll get stuck here for an extra day. The Commercial Bank of Ethiopia, 2km from the border, changes travellers cheques as well as US dollars and euros. While it doesn't exchange Kenyan shillings, the Tourist Hotel will swap them for Ethiopian Birr.

Holale Medical Clinic (A2 Hwy)

Kenya Commercial Bank (A2 Hwy) With ATM.

ℹ Getting There & Away

Moyale Raha Buses leave town daily at 6am for Marsabit (KSh1000, 8½ hours). Trucks for Marsabit (KSh800 to KSh1000) pick up passengers near the main intersection in town. More details about hitching and driving between Moyale and Marsabit are found on p208. Drivers should note that petrol on the Ethiopian side of Moyale is half the cost of that in Kenya.

On the Ethiopian side, a bus leaves for Addis Ababa (Birr200) each morning at around 5am. The two-day journey is broken with a night's sleep at either Awasa or Shashemene. A minibus from the border to the bus station is Birr2.

> ℹ At the time of writing the Ethiopian embassy in Nairobi had stopped issuing tourist visas, which means that if you're intending to cross this border you'll need to plan ahead and arrive in Kenya with a shiny new Ethiopian visa already stamped in your passport.

MARALAL TO TURKANA'S EASTERN SHORE

Journeying to a sea of jade shouldn't be something that is easy to do and this route, the ultimate Kenyan adventure, is certainly not easy. But for the battering you'll take you'll be rewarded a thousand times over with memories of vibrant tribes, camel caravans running into a red sunset, mesmerising volcanic landscapes and, of course, the north's greatest jewel, the Jade Sea – Lake Turkana.

North to Maralal

The 130km drive from Nyahururu to Maralal along the C77 is bumpy but straightforward, despite the tarmac running out at Rumuruti (we do hope you said goodbye, because you won't see it again any time soon). Punctures on this route are common. While the scenery isn't special, the wildlife is. Don't be at all surprised to see large groups of elephants, giraffes and zebras racing your bus or truck along the edge of the road.

The Kenyan-/English-run **Bobong Camp** and **Treefrog Cottage** (☎0735243075; olmaisor@africaonline.co.ke; camping per person KSh500, bandas KSh4000), perched on a hill with grand views of the plains below, offers basic (and overpriced) *bandas* that will house a family of four, but you need to be fully self-sufficient. Camping is also possible. They also offer some of the cheapest **camel treks** (per day incl guide KSh2000) in the north.

You must provide all your own camping equipment and food.

At the very western edge of the Laikipia plateau, the **Mugie Ranch** (☎062-2031235; www.mugieranch.com; wildlife drives adult/child US$25/12), is a 200-sq-km working ranch and private game reserve, and is crawling with heavyweight animals. It's one of Kenya's newest rhino sanctuaries (26 rhinos are present) and also plays host to all the rest of the Big Five, as well as Grevy's zebras and endangered Jackson's hartebeest.

Maralal

☎065

Walking down Maralal's dusty streets, it wouldn't come as much of a surprise to see Clint Eastwood stride slowly from a bar and proclaim the town not big enough for the two of you. With its swinging cowboy doors and camels tied up outside colourful wooden shopfronts, it's impossible not to think that you've somehow been transported to the Wild West.

Maralal has gained an international reputation for its fantastically frenetic **International Camel Derby** (see the boxed text, p214) and a visit over its duration is truly unforgettable. Less crazy, but almost as memorable, are the year-round camel safaris and treks that are offered here.

Sadly, most visitors don't delve into Maralal, stopping only for a night en route to Lake Turkana. The opposite is true for independent travellers, who often end up spending more time here than planned, simply because transport north is erratic at best. Take it all in your stride: you're an explorer and Maralal is the kind of place where you should spend some time. After all, the town's most famous former resident was one of the greatest explorers of the 20th century, Wilfred Thesiger, and if he decided that Maralal was the perfect place for retirement, then it must be doing something right.

Sights & Activities

Trekking WALKING

The **Loroghi Hills Circuit**, which takes in one of Kenya's most astounding vistas, Lesiolo (p214), is a rewarding five days and 78km. This trek is detailed in Lonely Planet's *Trekking in East Africa*. Somewhat shorter walks are possible by just strolling aimlessly around the high country and down the paths linking *shambas* that surround the town.

Yare Camel Club & Camp CAMEL SAFARI

(☎62295, Nairobi ☎020-2101137) Organises guides and camels for independent camel safaris in the region. Self-catered day/overnight trips cost US$15/30 per person.

Maralal National Sanctuary WILDLIFE RESERVE

(admission free) Surrounding the town is the sanctuary, home to zebras, impalas, hyenas, elephants and all the rest. There is no entry fee and you'll probably have the place much to yourself. One of the best ways to take in the animals is with a cold beverage in hand at Maralal Safari Lodge's bar, which also attracts animals after a thirst-quencher from the waterhole just in front.

Sleeping

Advance booking is absolutely essential in Maralal during the derby.

TOP CHOICE **Sunbird Guest House** GUESTHOUSE $

(☎0720654567; s/d KSh700/1000; P) This shiny and very friendly place has quiet, clean and comfortable rooms with nice linen, mosquito nets, sparkling bathrooms, 24-hour hot water and good security. The courtyard has a sunny, garden vibe, there's a pleasant attached restaurant and, if you've been naughty, you'll find a Bible in each room.

Samburu Guest House HOTEL $

(☎0729733435; s/d KSh700/1300; P) Only a month old at the time of our visit, this large pink cube of a building has spacious rooms that still retain their sparkling just-out-of-the-wrapper look – of course, whether it manages to maintain these lofty standards remains to be seen. It's a bit of a walk into the town centre.

Maralal Safari Lodge LODGE $$

(☎0727373406, Nairobi 020-211124; www.angelfire.com/jazz/maralal; camping KSh500, s/d/tw with breakfast Ksh4950/7000/7000; P ✻) The wooden cottages are starting to show their age, but the low lighting helps hide the worst of it and, as discounts are as common as impala at the waterhole right outside your window, you can't really moan. The open fireplaces in each room and the views over animal-filled plains provide a romantic atmosphere.

Yare Camel Club & Camp CAMPGROUND $

(☎62295, Nairobi 020-2101137; www.yaresafaris.co.ke; camping KSh300, s/tw/tr US$32/48/55; @) This long-standing favourite, 3km south of town, is under new management, and

Maralal

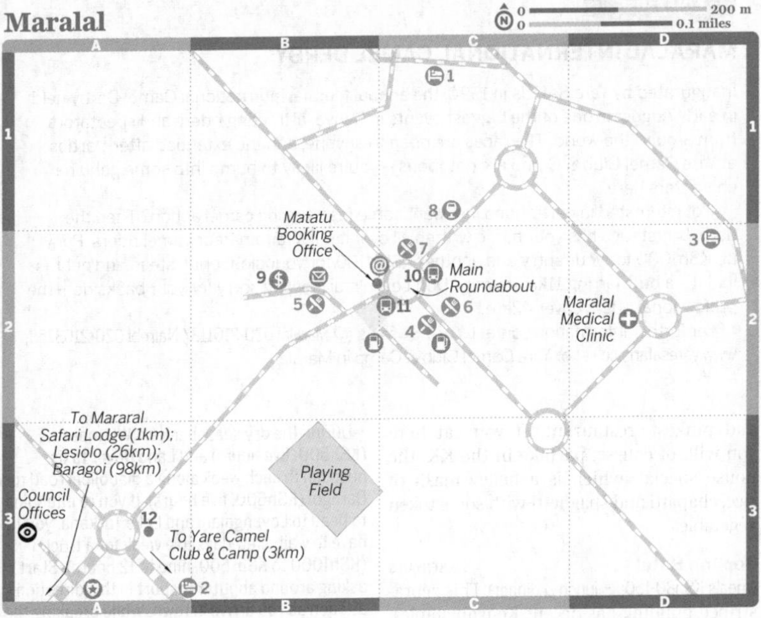

0 — 200 m
0 — 0.1 miles

Matatu Booking Office
Main Roundabout
Maralal Medical Clinic
Playing Field
To Mararal Safari Lodge (1km); Lesiolo (26km); Baragoi (98km)
Council Offices
To Yare Camel Club & Camp (3km)

Maralal

Sleeping

1 Jadana Guest House C1
2 Samburu Guest House A3
3 Sunbird Guest House D2

Eating

4 Hard Rock Café C2
5 Market B2
6 Pop Inn Hotel C2
Samburu Guest House .... (see 2)
Sunbird Guest House .... (see 3)
7 Sunguia Supermarket C2

Drinking

8 Buffalo House Hotel C1

Information

9 Kenya Commercial Bank B2

Transport

10 4WD Matatus & Land Rover Taxis C2
BP Petrol Station .... (see 12)
11 Matatus C2
12 Truck Pick-up Area A3

although the dreary cabins, which have seen recent price hikes, are now laughably poor value, it's still a good spot for overlanders thanks to grassy lawns perfect for camping on.

Jadana Guest House HOTEL $
(s/tw KSh300/500; P) First impressions don't bode well but in fact the rooms at this really cheap place aren't all that bad.

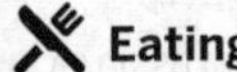

Eating

Unless you've got the *ugali* (a staple made from maize or cassava flour, or both) or *nyama choma* itch, few of your taste buds will be scratched here. That said, a few places hammer out quality local eats, or check out the restaurants of the Sunbird and Samburu Guest Houses, both of which have menus that, for Maralal, are positively cosmopolitan. Stock up at the market or the Sunguia Supermarket if you're heading north.

Hard Rock Café KENYAN $
(meals KSh60-170; ⏲lunch & dinner) While the Hard Rock Café chain would probably cringe at the use of their name, this Somali-run restaurant is the town centre's best,

DON'T MISS

MARALAL INTERNATIONAL CAMEL DERBY

Inaugurated by Yare Safaris in 1990, the annual Maralal International Camel Derby held in early August is one of the biggest events in Kenya, attracting riders and spectators from around the world. The races are open to anyone, and the extended after-parties at Yare Camel Club & Camp are notorious – you're likely to bump into some genuine characters here.

Not interested in parties and just want some fast-moving camel action? Then the derby's first race has your name written all over it – it's for amateur camel riders. Pony up KSh1000 for your entry and another KSh3000 for your slobbering steed and get racing! It's a butt-jarring 11km journey. Don't even start feeling sorry for your backside – the professional riders cover 42km.

For further information contact **Yare Safaris** (☎Maralal 020-2101137, Nairobi 020-2163758; www.yaresafaris.co.ke) or Yare Camel Club & Camp in Maralal.

and pinkest, restaurant. If you eat here you will, of course, partake in the KK, the house special, which is a heavy mash of rice, chapatti and spaghetti with some token vegetables.

Pop Inn Hotel KENYAN $
(meals KSh80-150; ⊙lunch & dinner) This zebra-striped building has decent Kenyan staples, but its claim to have the 'best food south of the Sahara' might be pushing it a tad – south of the roundabout seems more realistic.

Drinking

The Buffalo House Hotel used to be a legendary drinking and partying spot, but not so much these days. Even so, the sight of a Samburu Moran in full regalia propping up the bar isn't something you'll forget in a hurry. The bars at Yare Camel Club & Camp and Maralal Safari Lodge are nicer, but if you're staying in town transport back may pose a problem.

Information

Kenya Commercial Bank Behind the market, with an ATM (the last one going north).

Links Cyber Café (per hr KSh120; ⊙8am-8pm Mon-Sat, 2-8pm Sun)

Maralal Medical Clinic (⊙Mon-Sat)

Post office Next to the market.

Getting There & Away

Matatus serve Nyahururu (KSh500, three to four hours), Rumuruti (KSh500, 2½ hours) and Wamba (KSh400, 3½ hours). For Nairobi you need to change in Nyahururu. Reaching Isiolo involves staying overnight in Wamba to catch the early-morning southbound matatu.

During the dry season a few 4WD matatus (KSh500, five hours) and Land Rover taxis head north each week along a diabolical road to Baragoi (KSh600, five hours). If you're intending to head to Loyangalani and Lake Turkana, you'll have to wait a few days to a week for a truck (KSh1000 to KSh1500, nine to 12 hours). Start asking around about transport in this direction as soon as you arrive in town. While breaking the truck journey in Baragoi or South Horr may seem like a good idea, remember that you may have to wait there for a week before another truck trundles through. After rain you can expect prices of all transport to rise.

Most transport leaves from the main roundabout, while trucks usually pick up passengers at the former BP station.

Around Maralal

There are views and then there are views. **Lesiolo** (meaning 'World's View'), which perches atop an escarpment marking the Loroghi Plateau's dramatic end, offers an outrageous 120km panoramic view over the Rift Valley and serrated Tiati Hills. Lesiolo is part of the Malasso Ecotourism Project and a viewing fee (KSh350) is now charged – pricey, but worth every penny.

The **Lesiolo Loop** is a spectacular and gruelling 12km trek (four to five hours) that takes you down the escarpment to the Rift Valley floor and then slowly brings you back up again. A local guide (Malasso Ecotourism Project guides cost KSh1000 per day) is essential for this trek.

Sleeping & Eating

It's possible to **camp** (adult/child US$10/5) at Lesiolo and the viewing fee is waived if you do so. There's water (collected rain), crude toilets and a whole lot of cow patties to go with the astounding view.

Dri Camping CAMPGROUND, BUNGALOW $
(☎0729733438; tent per person KSh500; cottage KSh3000) This Dutch-owned property, around 20km north of town near the village of Poror, also offers camping emplacements with views that are defeated only by Lesiolo itself. If camping is just too rough and dirty for you, then the fully furnished cottage with exposed stone walls and utter privacy should do very nicely indeed. You'll need to bring your own food and have private transport.

Getting There & Away

To get here, head north from the town, towards Baragoi; the Malasso Ecotourism Project sign marks the turn-off about 17km from Maralal. Several more signs and helpful locals will point you the rest of the way. Patience and erratic transport can get you to the village of Poror, an easy 9km walk (two to three hours) from Lesiolo. You'll need a 4WD if driving in the wet season. A motorbike taxi from town to Lesiolo is around KSh1000 with bargaining and another KSh123 per hour that they wait for you.

Baragoi

The long descent off the Loroghi Plateau towards Baragoi serves up some sweet vistas, and for mile after gorgeous mile you'll literally see nothing but tree-studded grasslands alive with wildlife. Reaching Baragoi is a bit of an anticlimax though, as the dusty, diminutive town is clearly outdone by its surroundings.

The Star Station Filling sells pricey petrol and the bougainvillea-dressed Morning Star Guest House (r with shared bathroom KSh300) provides for a night's kip – though they don't supply the peg you'll need to place over your nose before entering the communal toilets.

Getting There & Away

The dirt track from Maralal to Baragoi is very rocky in places. If there has been any rain it becomes treacherous. The drive takes a minimum of four or five hours.

South Horr

South Horr, surrounded by flowering trees, is the next village north and sits in an acacia-paved valley beneath the towering peaks of **Ol Donyo Nyiro** (2752m) and **Ol Donyo Mara** (2066m). Despite the delightful craggy scenery, your eyes will rarely look up from the enchanting Samburu herders who gather in the wavering trees' shadows.

This is fantastic walking country – easy hikes are possible on the valley's forested lower slopes, while more motivated souls can try to bag Ol Donyo Nyiro's peak. In either case take a guide (around KSh1000 per day), because these woodlands are haunted by all manner of large, toothy creatures who'd love to have a passing *mzungu* (white person) for lunch.

Sleeping & Eating

There are several camping 'sites' around the village, all of which consist of nothing but a patch of ground with the odd tap. All charge between KSh250 and KSh300 per person. There are a couple of basic snack joints; Gunners fans will obviously pick the **Arsenal Inn** (meals KSh40-80).

Samburu Sports Centre Guesthouse BANDAS $
(☎0720334561; stockwellee@yahoo.com; tent per person KSh300, s/d KSh1000/2000; wi-fi) If we told you there was a place to stay in South Horr with plush *banda*-style accommodation complete with art on the walls and twisted-branch bookcases and wardrobes, great traditional food and wireless internet you wouldn't believe us would you? Well prepare to be surprised!

Getting There & Away

The road between Baragoi and South Horr is described as being in reasonable shape – what they mean is it's in reasonable shape for northern Kenya.

North to Lake Turkana

Travelling north from South Horr, the scrub desert suddenly scatters and you'll be greeted by vast volcanic armies of shimmering bowling-ball-sized boulders, cinder cones and reddish-purple hues. If this arresting and barren Martian landscape doesn't take your breath away, the first sight of the sparkling Jade Sea a few kilometres north certainly will.

DID YOU KNOW?

» Lake Turkana, which is the world's largest permanent desert lake, has a shoreline that's longer than Kenya's entire Indian Ocean coast.

» The lake's water level was over 100m higher some 10,000 years ago and used to feed the mighty Nile. If the Gibe 3 Dam in Ethiopia is completed then the lake's waters may drop a further 10m.

» The first Europeans to reach the lake were Austrian explorers Teleki and von Höhnel in 1888. They proudly named it Lake Rudolf, after the Austrian Crown Prince at the time. It wasn't until the 1970s that the Kiswahili name Turkana was adopted.

As you descend to the lake, South Island stands proudly before you, while Teleki Volcano's geometrically perfect cone lurks on Turkana's southern shore. Since most of you have probably pulled over for the moment, looking for your swimming kit, we thought we'd warn you that Turkana has the world's largest crocodile population.

Loyangalani

Standing in utter contrast to the dour desert shades surrounding it, tiny Loyangalani assaults all your senses in one crazy explosion of clashing colours, feather headdresses and blood-red robes. Overlooking Lake Turkana and surrounded by small ridges of pillow lava (evidence that this area used to be underwater), the sandy streets of this one-camel town are a meeting point of the great northern tribes: Turkana and Samburu, Gabbra and El Molo. It's easily the most exotic corner of Kenya and a fitting reward after the hard journey here.

Sights & Activities

South Island National Park WILDLIFE RESERVE

(adult/child US$20/10) Opened as a public reserve in 1983 and made a World Heritage site by Unesco in 1997, this tiny 39-sq-km purplish volcanic island is completely barren and uninhabited, apart from large populations of crocodiles, poisonous snakes and feral goats. Spending the night at a **special campsite** (camping adult/child US$15/10) makes for an even eerier trip.

In calm weather a speedboat can reach the island in 30 minutes and circumnavigate it in another hour. If winds crop up, trip times can easily double. As speedboats are somewhat limited in number, you will probably end up in something much more sedate: reckon on a six-hour return trip, for which you will pay about KSh4000 per hour. Ask at either the KWS office in town or the Oasis Lodge about hiring boats.

Mt Kulal MOUNTAIN

Mt Kulal dominates Lake Turkana's eastern horizon, and its forested volcanic flanks offer up some serious hiking possibilities. This fertile lost world in the middle of the desert is home to some unique creatures, including the Mt Kulal Chameleon, a beautiful lizard first recorded in only 2003.

No matter what the local guides tell you, trekking up to the summit (2293m) from Loyangalani in a day isn't feasible. Plan on several days for a return trip; guides (KSh1000 per day) and donkeys (KSh500 per day) to carry your gear can be hired in Loyangalani, or you can part with substantial sums of cash (KSh8000 to KSh12,000) for a lift up Mt Kulal to the villages of **Arapal** or **Gatab**. From there you can head for the summit and spend a long day (eight to 10 hours) hiking back down to the base of the mountain.

If you pass by Arapal be sure to whistle a tune at the **singing wells** from where the Samburu gather water (and sing while doing so – hence the name).

El Molo Villages VILLAGE

The El Molo tribe (see p307), which is one of Africa's smallest, lives on the lake shore just north of here in the villages of **Layeni** and **Komote**. Although outwardly similar to the Turkana, the El Molo are linguistically linked to the Somali and Rendille people. Unfortunately, the last speaker of their traditional language died before the turn of the millennium. Visiting their villages (per person KSh700 to KSh1000) is something of a circus.

Loyangalani Desert Museum MUSEUM

(adult/child KSh500/250; 9am-6pm) Standing on a bluff above the lake several kilometres north of town, this museum contains lots of photo-heavy displays, but it's seriously overpriced.

Sleeping & Eating

Let's face it; you came north for adventure, not comfort. If you're camping, remember to tie down your tent, as early evening winds pick up tremendously and can be blowing at 60km per hour by 8pm.

TOP CHOICE **Palm Shade Camp** BANDAS $

(0726714768; camping KSh500, s/tw bandas with shared bathroom KSh750/1500) Drop your tent on the grass beneath acacias and doum palms or crash in the tidy domed rondavels. The huts have simple wood beds with foam mattresses and unique walls with meshed cut-outs that let light and heavenly evening breezes in. Throw in the town's best toilets and showers, a cooking shelter and electricity until 10pm and your decision is an easy one.

Oasis Lodge LODGE $$$

(s/tw US$220/350;) This place is in a dreadful condition and the prices are hugely inflated. The best asset is the pool, which non-guests are allowed to use for KSh500.

Cold Drink Hotel KENYAN $

(meals KSh100-150; lunch & dinner) Not just cold drinks but also, according to locals, the finest eating experience in all of Turkana country. Well, OK, maybe in Loyangalani.

Information

Other than the post office and the Catholic mission occasionally selling petrol out of the barrel at exorbitant prices, there's nothing in the way of services.

Getting There & Away

Trucks loaded with fish (and soon-to-be-smelly passengers) leave Loyangalani for Maralal (KSh1000 to KSh1500, nine to 12 hours) around once or twice a week at best. Trucks heading in any other direction are even rarer and locals talk of waits of between a week and a month for transport to Marsabit (when trucks do travel this route they tend to take the slightly easier southern route via Kargi and charge a flexible KSh1000).

If you're travelling in your own vehicle, you have two options to reach Marsabit: continue northeast from Loyangalani across the dark stones of the Chalbi Desert towards North Horr, or head 67km south towards South Horr and take the eastern turn-off via Kargai. The 270km Chalbi route (10 to 12 hours) is hard in the dry season and impossible after rain. It's also wise to ask for directions every chance you get, otherwise it's easy to take the wrong track and not realise until hours later. The 241km southern route (six to seven hours) via the Karoli Desert and Kargi is composed of compacted sands and is marginally less difficult in the rainy season.

North Horr

On the map, North Horr stands out like a beacon from all that surrounding desert, but once you finally drag your weary and battered self onto its sand-washed streets the reality of this drab town is a little disappointing. Don't miss the **water source** on the edge of town, where hundreds of camels, goats and weathered nomadic faces come to water each day. Photos not appreciated.

There are two places to stay, **Manzigar Lodge** (s/tw KSh150/200) and the neighbouring **Northern Palm Shades** (banda KSh200). Luxury they are not, authentic they are.

For food you'll find a couple of bare-bones *dukas* (small shops) and cafes in the town including the **Mandera Hotel** (meals KSh80-120), which is also the best place to enquire about onward transport.

Trucks and 4WDs run with some frequency to **Marsabit** (KSh400-700) via Kalacha, but only very rarely does anything venture onward to Loyangalani. There is no set price for the Loyangalani leg. Whichever way you're heading, don't be at all surprised if you get stuck here for anything between a couple of days and a couple of weeks. Even in the dry season the 'roads' are often impassable and after rain it's completely out of the question. Whichever way you're heading it's a road to adventure; blasting over the plains of darkness destined for a sea of jade is nothing short of magical.

Kalacha

Huddled around a permanent watery oasis in the middle of the Chalbi Desert, the acacia- and doum-palm-pocked village of Kalacha is home to the fascinating Gabbra people. There's little to see and do, but the sense of isolation is magnificent and the sight of camels, released from their night corrals and kicking up the dust on the way to the grazing grounds, will remain with you forever. Don't miss the cartoonlike biblical murals in the church, a prelude for those of you heading northward to Ethiopia. Some **rock paintings** and **carvings** can be found

DON'T MISS

SIBILOI NATIONAL PARK

A Unesco World Heritage site and probably Kenya's most remote national park, **Sibiloi** (www.sibiloi.com; adult/child US$20/10) is located up the eastern shore of Lake Turkana and covers 1570 sq km. It was here that Dr Richard Leakey discovered the skull of a *Homo habilis* believed to be 2½ million years old, and where others have unearthed evidence of *H erectus*. Despite the area's fascinating prehistory, fossil sites and wonderful arid ecosystem, the difficulties involved in getting this far north tend to discourage visitors, which is a real shame. It seems slightly ironic that the so-called 'Cradle of Mankind' is now almost entirely unpopulated.

The National Museums of Kenya (NMK) maintain a small museum and **Koobi Fora** (www.kfrp.com), a research base. It's usually possible to sleep in one of the base's **bandas** (per person KSh1000) or to pitch a tent in one of the **campsites** (camping per person KSh200). At the time of research a member of the Leakey family was in the process of constructing a lodge here.

Contact both the staff of the Loyangalani Desert Museum, the **KWS** (kws@kws.org) and **NMK** (☎Nairobi 020-3742131; www.museums.or.ke) before venturing in this direction.

In the dry season it's a tricky seven-hour drive north from Loyangalani to Sibiloi. You will need a guide from either KWS or the Loyangalani Desert Museum. Hiring a jeep in Loyangalani will work out at around KSh15,000 per day. It's also possible to hire a boat (KSh22,000 to KSh30,000 return with an overnight stop) from Fergusons Gulf (see p221) on the western side of the lake.

near the **Afgaba** waterhole not far from Kalacha – take a guide.

Chalbi Safari Resort Kalacha (☎0727218566; camping KSh400, tw bandas per person KSh5000; 🅿), managed by the friendly Abdul, is an excellent choice with several immaculate *bandas* and a sun-battered camping area. With notice they will prepare meals.

The town's other sleeping option, the Kalacha Camp, was closed for 'renovations' at the time of research, but we'd be surprised if it ever reopens.

Coming from Marsabit the road winds down off the mountains and sinks into a mass of black lava rocks. Slowly the land becomes ever more barren until finally you hit the blank expanse of the Chalbi Desert, featureless, sandy and blisteringly hot. It's a spectacular ride through a clutter-free world, where the only signs of life are occasional camels heading to the wells in the bustling village of **Maikona**. Don't drive this route without a heavy-duty 4WD and an experienced local guide – that GPS unit you confidently bought before you came to Kenya, and which cannot hope to tell you which is good or bad sand to drive on, or which is currently the best track to use, is worthless here. Good luck if you're travelling by public transport – you'll need it. Trucks might or might not pass by, bound for either Marsabit (KSh500) or North Horr a couple of times a week.

MARICH TO TURKANA'S WESTERN SHORE

Despite boasting some of northern Kenya's greatest attributes, such as copious kilometres of Jade Sea shoreline, striking volcanic landscapes, ample wildlife and vivid Turkana tribes, this remote corner of the country has seen relatively few visitors. With fairly reliable public transport, this is definitely the easier side of the lake in which to grab a taste of the northern badlands.

Marich to Lodwar

The spectacular descent from Marich Pass through the lush, cultivated Cherangani Hills leads to arid surroundings, with sisal plants, cactus trees and acacias lining both the road and the chocolate-brown Morun River. Just north, the minuscule village of Marich marks your entrance into northern Kenya. Welcome to adventure!

Sights & Activities

Trekking WALKING

Although the northern plains may beckon, it's worth heading into the hills for some eye-popping and leg-loving trekking action. **Mt Sekerr** (3326m) is a few kilometres northwest of Marich and can be climbed comfortably in a three-day round trip via the agricultural plots of the Pokot tribe, passing through forest and open moors.

The **Cherangani Hills**, the green and lush chalk next to the northern desert's baked cheese, sit immediately south and are also ripe with superb trekking options. In fact, many people consider these intensely farmed and deeply forested hills to be one of the most beautiful corners of the country.

Reaching the dome of **Mt Koh** (3211m), which soars some 1524m above the adjacent plains, is a hard but rewarding two-day slog. A more horizontally endowed (13km one way) and vertically challenged (only 300m elevation gain) trek is possible up the **Weiwei Valley** from **Sigor** to **Tamkal**. See p160 for more Cherangani Hills trekking options.

The **Marich Pass Field Studies Centre** offers English-speaking Pokot and Turkana guides for half-day (KSh550), full-day (KSh750) and overnight (KSh1000) treks.

Sleeping & Eating

Marich Pass Field Studies Centre CAMPGROUND, BANDAS $

(www.gg.rhul.ac.uk/MarichPass; camping KSh360, dm KSh420, s/tw KSh1450/1950, with shared bathroom KSh900/1240) Just north of Marich village, this is essentially a residential facility for visiting student groups, but it also makes a great base for independent travellers. The centre occupies a beautiful site alongside the misty Morun River and is surrounded by dense bush and woodland. Facilities include a secure campsite with drinking water, toilets, showers and firewood, as well as a tatty dorm and simple, comfortable *bandas*.

Getting There & Away

The road from Kitale via Makutano is the oh-so-scenic A1 Hwy, which is often described as 'Kenya's most spectacular tarmac road'. The buses plying the A1 between Kitale and Lodwar

THE WINDS OF CHANGE

North Kenya has long been ignored by Kenya's rulers. Today, though, black gold, a new nation and Turkana's relentless winds are on the cusp of changing life in these parts forever – perhaps...

When South Sudan became the worlds newest nation in July 2011, it faced a problem. It had oil and natural gas, but no reliable way of getting it out of the country (all the current oil pipelines head north to the Red Sea via its former overlord Sudan, but relations between Juba and Khartoum are so tense that access cannot be guaranteed). The solution is to build a new set of pipelines from South Sudan to Lamu down on the Kenyan coast. Riding on the back of this pipeline will be a major new port and oil refinery in Lamu, surfaced two-lane highways linking all the main towns of the north, new airports and tourist resorts in Lamu, Isiolo and on the shores of Lake Turkana. The cherry on the pie though is the new rail system which will stretch from Lamu to South Sudan, with another line to Ethiopia, along which dozens of daily trains will hurtle along at up to 160km/h! It's certainly an ambitious project. Some would say it's so ambitious that it's nothing but a white elephant. And as if to prove the sceptics right, in October 2011 it was announced by the European Coalition on Oil in Sudan that the pipeline project was unviable due to insufficient oil-reserve estimates in South Sudan and general insecurity.

So that leaves just the one thing north Kenya does have no shortage of – wind – and that leads us to the biggest wind farm in Africa. The Dutch consortium behind the proposed Lake Turkana Wind Power project aims to build 365 giant wind turbines on the southeast corner of Lake Turkana, which will generate 300MW, or a quarter of Kenya's current installed power. Although less ambitious than the other projects, the wind farm project came to a grinding halt in 2010 due to financial reasons. However, by the middle of 2011 things started moving again and the people behind the project now say that the first stage will be completed by 2013.

Meanwhile, over the border in Ethiopia, a massive dam project, Gibe 3, is underway on the Omo river. Opponents say this could lower Turkana's waters by up to 10m when completed.

can drop you anywhere along the route, whether at Marich, the field studies centre or at the turn-off to Nasolot National Reserve. You may be asked to pay the full fare to Lodwar (KSh1000), but a smile and some patient negotiating should reduce the cost.

Between Marich and Lokichar the A1 is a bumpy mess of corrugated dirt and lonely islands of tarmac. The first 40km north of Lokichar is better, but you'll still spend more time on the shoulder than on the road. The opposite is true for the remaining 60km to Lodwar, where patches outnumber potholes and driving is straightforward.

The security situation is in a constant state of flux in this area. At the time of research convoys were not required, but there had been numerous incidents of cattle rustling as well as tribal clashes. This is most prevalent in the area between Marich and Lokichar.

Lodwar

☎054

Besides Lokichoggio near the South Sudan border, Lodwar is the only town of any size in the northwest. Barren volcanic hills skirted by traditional Turkana dwellings sit north of town and make for impressive early-morning sunrise spots. Lodwar has outgrown its days as just an isolated administrative outpost of the Northern Frontier District and has now become the major service centre for the region. If you're visiting Lake Turkana, you'll find it convenient to stay here for at least one night.

Sleeping

Nawoitorong Guest House HOTEL $

(☎0722938814; camping KSh300, s/tw with shared bathroom KSh500/800, cottages KSh800-2000) Built entirely out of local materials and run by a local women's group, Nawoitorong is an excellent option and the only one for campers. Thatched roofs alleviate the need for fans and all rooms have mosquito nets.

Lodwar Lodge HOTEL $

(☎0728007512; r with breakfast KSh850-1350; P) Smart concrete cottages that are quiet and secure. It's the best of several town centre options.

Eating

Nawoitorong Guest House KENYAN $

(meals KSh150-225; lunch & dinner) Burgers and toasted sandwiches join local curries and various meaty fries on the menu. It offers the most pleasant dining experience in the region but give them time – lots of it – to prepare dinner!

Salama Hotel KENYAN $

(meals KSh80-150; lunch & dinner) The most popular place in the town centre. The culinary highlight of the Salama has to be its giant bowl of pilau (curried rice with meat, KSh100). There's always a crowd of people here waiting for buses to depart.

If you're self-catering, there's a well-stocked Naipa Supermarket next to the Kobil petrol station.

Information

The **Kenya Commercial Bank** (with ATM) changes cash and travellers cheques. For internet, surf on over to **Maxtech Computer Solutions & Cyber Café** (per hr KSh60; 7am-7pm Mon-Sun).

Getting There & Away

Fly540 (www.fly540.com) runs daily flights from Nairobi to Lodwar via Kitale for around US$150.

A couple of different bus companies operate along the route to Kitale (KSh1000, 8½ hours). Most depart nightly at 5.30pm or 6pm from outside the Salama Hotel. Erratic matatus serve Kalokol (KSh250, one hour) and Lokichoggio (KSh600 to KSh800, three hours).

Eliye Springs

Spring water percolates out of crumbling bluffs and oodles of palms bring a taste of the tropics to the remote sandy shores of Lake Turkana. Down on the slippery shore children play in the lake's warm waters, while Central Island lurks magically on the distant horizon.

Besides the spring water there are no facilities, bar the skeleton of an old resort which locals may allow you to camp in.

Getting There & Away

The turn-off for Eliye Springs is signposted a short way along the Lodwar–Kalokol road. The gravel is easy to follow until it suddenly peters out and you're faced with a fork in the road – stay left. The rest of the way is a mix of gravel, deep sand and even deeper sand, which can turn into a muddy nightmare in the wet season. Over the really bad sections locals have constructed a 'road' out of palm fronds, which means that on a good day normal saloon cars can even make it here (though expect to do a bit of pushing and shoving).

DON'T MISS

CENTRAL ISLAND NATIONAL PARK

Bursting from the depths of Lake Turkana and home to thousands of living dinosaurs is the Jurassic world of Central Island Volcano, last seen belching molten sulphur and steam just over three decades ago. It is one of the most otherworldly places in Kenya. Quiet today, its stormy volcanic history is told by the numerous craters scarring its weathered facade. Several craters have coalesced to form two sizeable lakes, one of which is home to thousands of fish that occur nowhere else.

Both a **national park** (adult/child US$20/10) and Unesco World Heritage site, Central Island is an intriguing place to visit. Budding Crocodile Dundee types will love the 14,000 or so Nile crocodiles, some of which are massive in proportion, who flock here at certain times of year (May is the most crocodile-friendly month, but there are some crocs here year-round). The most northerly crater lake, which is saline, attracts blushing pink flocks of flamingos.

Camping (adult/child US$15/10) is possible and, unlike South Island National Park, there are trees to tie your tent to. But there's no water or any other facilities, so come prepared.

Hiring a boat from Ferguson's Gulf is the only option to get here. Depending on what you drive up in, locals can ask anywhere from KSh8000 to KSh20,000 for the trip. A fair price is KSh8000-9000 for a motorboat – don't ever think about being cheap and taking a sailboat. The 10km trip and sudden squalls that terrorise the lake's waters aren't to be taken lightly. You should also visit the KWS office, a couple of kilometres out of Kalokol towards Ferguson's Gulf, to pay your entrance fees and get the latest lowdown on the island.

If you don't have your own vehicle, you can usually arrange a car and driver in Lodwar for about KSh5000 including waiting time. Very occasionally you might find a truck travelling there, for which a seat on top of the load will set you back about KSh150 to KSh200, but be prepared for a long wait back out again!

Ferguson's Gulf

Ferguson's Gulf, while more accessible than Eliye Springs, has none of its southern neighbour's charm. Fishing boats in various states of disrepair litter its grubby western beach and a definite feeling of bleakness pervades.

If you're planning on visiting Central Island National Park or Sibiloi National Park (p218), this is the best place to arrange a boat.

If you want to stay, the nearby village of **Kalokol** contains the **Starehe Lodge** (s/d Ksh250/400) which claims to offer the 'best accommodation in town', though we think it's only fair to point out that this is because it's the only accommodation in town.

Getting There & Away

Few people in Lodwar have heard of Ferguson's Gulf so you need to ask around for transport to nearby Kalokol, which is 75km along a good stretch of tarmac. Ferguson's Gulf is only a few kilometres from there. Matatus to Kalokol cost KSh250 or a taxi direct to Ferguson's Gulf will be around KSh4000 to KSh5000 with waiting time.

Mombasa & the South Coast

Includes »

Best of Nature

- Shimba Hills National Reserve (p239)
- Mwaluganje Elephant Sanctuary (p241)
- Kisite Marine National Park (p249)
- Haller Park (p253)
- Colobus Trust (p242)

Best of Culture

- Mombasa (p225)
- Wasini Island (p248)
- Jumba la Mtwana (p255)
- Kaya Kinondo (p244)

Why Go?

There's something in the air here.

It's the smell of salt and spice on the streets of Mombasa (*Kisiwa Cha Mvita* in Swahili – the Island of War). It's muttered chants echoing over the flagstones of a Jain temple, and the ecstatic passion of the call to prayer. It's the sun's glint off coral castles, it's ribbons of white sand, it's the teal break of a vanishing wave and it's the sight of a Zanzibar-bound dhow slipping over the horizon.

Thanks to the long interplay of Africa, India and Arabia, the coast feels wildly different from the rest of Kenya. Its people, the Swahili, have created a distinctive Indian Ocean society – built on the scent of trade with distant shores – that lends real romance to the coasts sugar-white beaches and to a city that poets have embraced for as long as ivory has been traded for iron.

When to Go

Mombasa

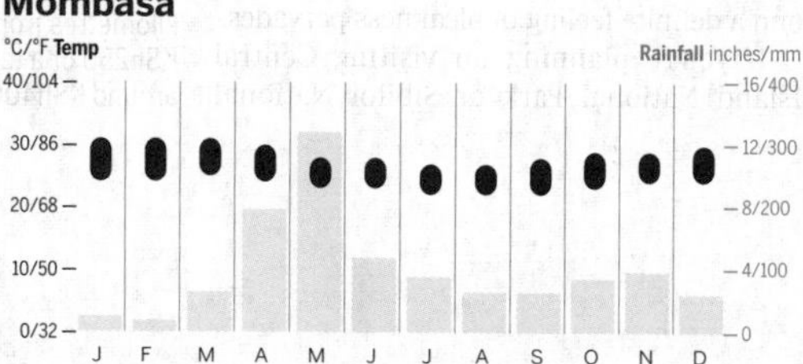

Jan–Mar Dolphins (and the occasional whale-shark) fill the ocean and diving is at its best.

Apr–Aug The rainy season is the coolest time of year.

Sep School-holiday crowds are gone; accommodation is cheaper and beaches are quieter.

History

The coast's written history stretches much further back than the history of the interior, and is essentially a tale of trade and conquest with outside forces. By the 1st century, Yemeni traders were in East Africa, prompting one unidentified Greek observer to write about 'Arab captains and agents, who are familiar with the natives and intermarry with them, and who know the whole coast and understand the language'. Merchants traded spices, timber, gold, ivory, tortoise shell and rhinoceros horn, as well as slaves.

The admixture of Arabs, local Africans and Persian traders gave birth to the Swahili culture and language. But the Swahili were not the only inhabitants of the coast. Of particular note were the Mijikenda, or 'Nine Homesteads', a Bantu tribe whose homeland, according to oral history, was located somewhere in southern Somalia. Six hundred years ago they began filtering into the coast and established themselves in *kayas* (sacred forests), which are dotted from the Tanzanian border to Malindi.

The riches of this region never failed to attract attention, and in the early 16th century it was the Portuguese who took their turn at conquest. The Swahilis did not take kindly to becoming slaves (even if they traded them), and rebellions were common throughout the 16th and 17th centuries. It's fashionable to portray the Portuguese as villains, but their replacements, the sultans of Oman, were no more popular. Despite their shared faith, the natives of this ribbon of land staged countless rebellions, and passed Mombasa into British hands from 1824 to 1826 to keep it from the sultans. Things only really quietened down after Sultan Seyyid Said moved his capital from Muscat to Zanzibar in 1832.

Said's huge coastal clove plantations created a massive need for labour, and the slave caravans of the 19th century marked the peak of the trade in human cargo. News of massacres and human-rights abuses reached Europe, galvanising the British public to demand an end to slavery. Through a mixture of political savvy and implied force, the British government pressured Said's son Barghash to ban the slave trade, marking the beginning of the end of Arab rule here.

Of course, this 'reform' didn't hurt British interests: as part of the treaty, the British East Africa Company took over administration of the Kenyan interior, taking the opportunity to start construction of the East African Railway. A 16km-wide coastal strip was recognised as the territory of the sultan and leased by the British from 1887. Upon independence in 1963, the last sultan of Zanzibar gifted this land to the new Kenyan government.

The coast remains culturally and religiously distinctive (most coastal people are Muslim) and there are calls by some coastal politicians for some kind of autonomy from the rest of Kenya.

MOMBASA

☎041 / POP 939,000

Mombasa, like the coast it dominates, is both quintessentially African and somehow...not.

If your idea of Africa is roasted meat, toasted maize, beer and cattle, and farms and friendliness, those things are here (well, maybe not the cows). But it's all interwoven into the humid peel of plaster from Hindu warehouses, filigreed porches that lost their way in a Moroccan *riad* (traditional town house), spice markets that escaped India's Keralan coast, sailors chewing *miraa* (shoots chewed as a stimulant) next to boats bound for Yemen, and a giant coral castle built by invading Portuguese sailors. Thus, while the city sits perfectly at home in Africa, it could be plopped anywhere on the coast of the Indian Ocean without too many moving pains.

Therein lies Mombasa's considerable charm. But said seduction doesn't hide this town's warts, which include a sleazy underbelly, bad traffic and ethnic tension, the last of which ebbs and flows and is smoothed by the unifying faith of Islam, but it's not entirely sublimated. Overlaying everything is the sweating, tropical lunacy you tend to get in the world's hot zones (and it gets *hot* here). But what would you expect from East Africa's largest port? Cities by the docks always attract mad characters, and Mombasa's come from all over the world.

Perhaps though it's best to let the Swahili people themselves describe their city in their native tongue with an old line of poetry and proverb: *Kongowea nda mvumo, maji maangavu. Male!* ('Mombasa is famous, but its waters are dangerously deep. Beware!').

History

Unlike Nairobi, Mombasa, which sits over the best deep-water harbour in East Africa, has always been an important town.

Travellers who come here are walking in the footsteps of Ibn Battuta, Marco Polo and Zhang He, which says something of this town's importance to trade rather than tourism. Modern Mombasa traces its heritage back to the Thenashara Taifa (Twelve Nations), a Swahili clan that maintains a contiguous chain of traditions and customs stretching from the city's founding to this day. The date of when those customs began – ie when Mombasa was born – is a little muddy, although it was already a thriving port by the 12th century. Early in its life, Mombasa became a key link on Indian Ocean trade routes.

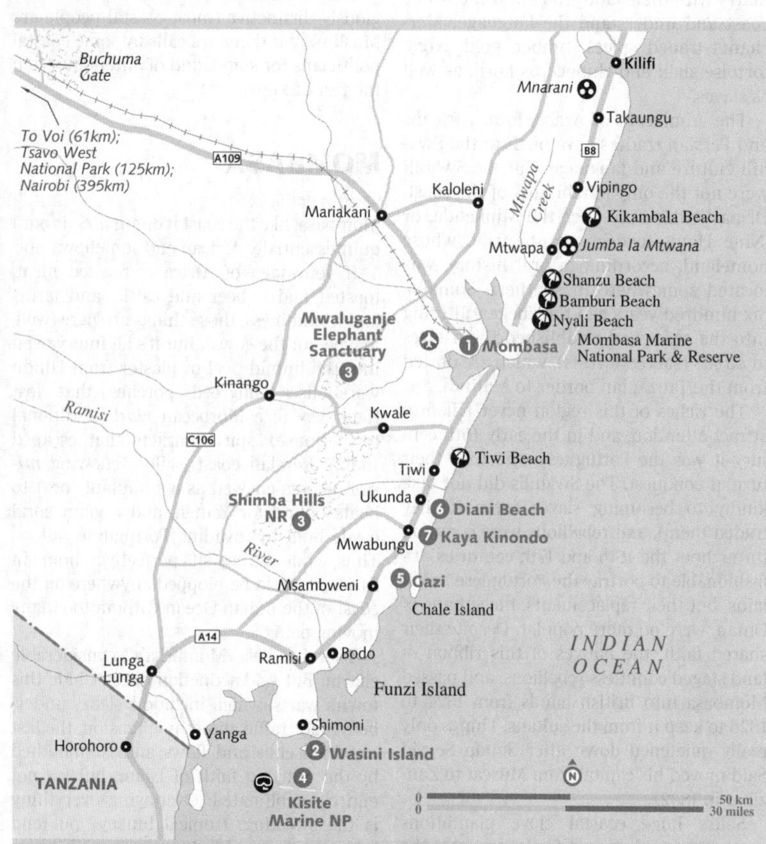

Mombasa & the South Coast Highlights

1 Discovering Indian sweets and narrow streets in **Mombasa Old Town** (p232).

2 Taking a dhow to go-slow **Wasini Island** (p249) and soaking up the Swahili spirit.

3 Tracking down tuskers and sable antelope in **Shimba Hills National Reserve** (p239) and **Mwaluganje Elephant Sanctuary** (p241).

4 Diving head first into beautiful waters alive with rainbow-coloured fish and playful dolphins in the **Kisite Marine National Park** (p249).

5 Birdwatching and strolling the mangrove boardwalk of **Gazi** (p248).

6 Spending some one-on-one time with a baby colobus monkey at the **Colobus Trust** (p242) .

7 Finding god in the greenery in a **kaya** (p244).

In 1498, Vasco da Gama became the first Portuguese visitor here. Two years later his countrymen returned and sacked the town, a habit they repeated in 1505 and 1528, when Nuña da Cunha captured Mombasa using what would become a time-honoured tactic: slick 'em up with diplomacy (offering to act as an ally in disputes with Malindi, Pemba and Zanzibar), then slap 'em down by force. Once again Mombasa was burnt to the ground.

In 1593, the Portuguese constructed the coral edifice of Fort Jesus as a way of saying, 'We're staying'. This act of architectural hubris led to frequent attacks by rebel forces and the ultimate expulsion of the Portuguese by Omani Arabs in 1698. But the Omanis were never that popular either, and the British, using a series of shifting alliances and brute force, turfed them out in 1870. All these power struggles, by the way, are the source of Mombasa's Swahili nickname: the Island of War.

Mombasa subsequently became the railhead for the Uganda railway and the most important city in British East Africa. In 1920, when Kenya became a fully fledged British colony, Mombasa was made capital of the separate British Coast Protectorate. Following Kenyan independence in 1963 the city fell into a torpor; it was the most important city in the region and the second-largest in the country, but it was removed from the cut and thrust of Kenyan politics, whose focus had turned inland.

Between independence and today the city has drifted along in a quiet daze. It's status as the chief port in East Africa was largely superseded by Dar es Salaam in Tanzania. In the early 1990s violence briefly engulfed the city as supporters and opponents of the Islamic Party of Kenya clashed, but this has long since died down. During the 2007 elections, the coast, and Mombasa in particular, provided a rare peek into the policy platforms, rather than communal politics, of Raila Odinga and Mwai Kibaki. Neither politician could rely on a Kikuyu or Luo base here, and both campaigned on ideas, rather than appeals to tribalism. Odinga won the province by promising, in effect, a form of limited federation, which remains a hope of many Mombasan politicians who consider the coast culturally, economically and religiously distinct enough to warrant some form of self-governance.

Sights

Fort Jesus FORTRESS

(Map p226; adult/child KSh800/400; ⏲8am-6pm)

All along the coast you'll spot castles and mosques carved out of coral, but the exemplar of the genre is Fort Jesus: Mombasa's most visited site, Unesco World Heritage site, anchor of Old Town and dominant structure of the city's harbour. The metre-thick walls, frescoed interiors, traces of European graffiti, Arabic inscriptions and Swahili embellishment aren't just evocative – they're a record of the history of Mombasa, and the coast, writ in stone.

The fort was built by the Portuguese in 1593 to serve as both symbol and headquarters of their permanent presence in this corner of the Indian Ocean. So it's ironic that the construction of the fort marked the beginning of the end of local Portuguese hegemony. Between Portuguese sailors, Omani soldiers and Swahili rebellions, the fort changed hands at least nine times between 1631 and 1875, when it finally fell under British control and was used as a jail.

The fort was the final project completed by Joao Batista Cairato, whose buildings can be found throughout Portugal's Eastern colonies, from Old Goa to Old Mombasa. The building is an opus of period military design; assuming the structure was well-manned, it would have been impossible to approach its walls without falling under the cone of interlocking fields of fire.

These days the fort houses a **museum** built over the former barracks. The exhibits should give a good insight into Swahili life and culture, but, like with the rest of the complex, it's all poorly labelled and woefully displayed, which, considering it's the city's number-one tourist attraction, is fairly scandalous.

Elsewhere within the fort compound, the **Mazrui Hall**, where flowery spirals fade across a wall topped with wooden lintels left by the Omani Arabs, is worthy of note. In another room, Portuguese sailors scratched graffiti that illustrates the multicultural naval identity of the Indian Ocean, leaving walls covered with four-pointed European frigates, three-pointed Arabic dhows and the coir-sewn 'camels of the ocean', the elegant Swahili *mtepe* (traditional sailing vessel). Nearby, a pair of whale bones serves in the undignified role of children's see-saw. The **Omani house**, in the San Felipe bastion in the northwestern corner of the fort, was

Mombasa

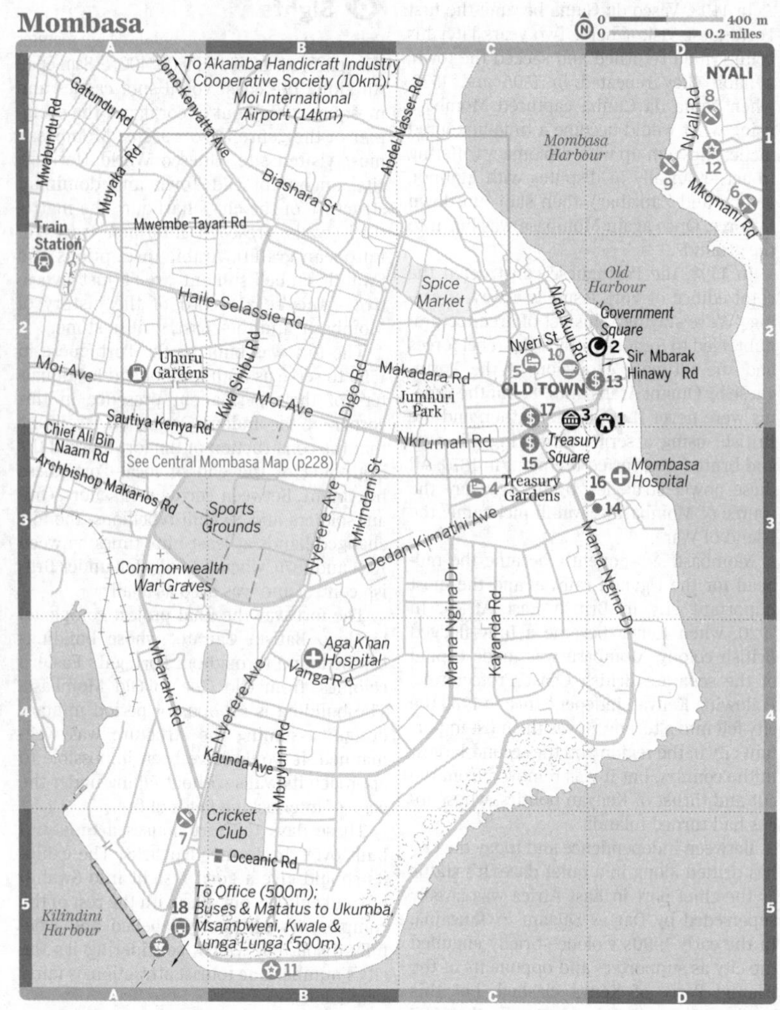

built in the late 18th century. It was closed at the time of research, but used to house a small exhibition of Omani jewellery and artefacts. The **eastern wall** includes an Omani audience hall and the **Passage of the Arches**, which leads under the pinkish-brown coral onto a double-azure vista of sea floating under sky.

If you arrive early in the day you may avoid group tours, but the same can't be said of extremely persistent guides, official and unofficial, who will swarm you the minute you approach the fort. Some of them can be quite useful and some can be duds. Unfortunately, you'll have to use your best judgement to suss out which is which. Official guides charge KSh500 for a tour of Fort Jesus or the Old Town; unofficial guides charge whatever they can. If you don't want a tour, shake off your guide with a firm but polite no; otherwise they'll launch into their spiel and expect a tip at the end. Alternatively, you can buy the *Fort Jesus* guide booklet from the ticket desk and go it alone.

Mombasa

Sights

1 Fort Jesus........D2
2 Mandhry Mosque........D2
3 Old Law Courts Gallery........C2

Activities, Courses & Tours

Tamarind Dhow........(see 9)

Sleeping

4 Lotus Hotel........C3
5 Royal Palace Hotel........C2
Tamarind Village........(see 9)

Eating

6 Hunter's Steak House........D1
7 Nakumatt Supermarket........A5
8 Ooh! Ice Cream........D1
Roberto's........(see 12)
9 Tamarind Restaurant........D1

Drinking

Cafe Mocha........(see 12)
10 Jahazi Coffee House........C2

Entertainment

Hollywood Bowl........(see 12)
11 New Florida Nightclub........B5
12 Nyali Cinemax........D1

Shopping

Books First........(see 7)

Information

13 Fort Jesus Forex Bureau........D2
14 Immigration Office........D3
15 Kenya Commercial Bank........C3
16 KWS Office........D3
17 Standard Chartered Bank........C2

Transport

18 Local Bus & Matatu Stand........A5

Religious Buildings RELIGIOUS

In this city of almost one million inhabitants, 70% of whom are Muslim, there are a lot of mosques. Unfortunately, non-Muslims are usually not allowed to enter them, although you can have a look from the outside. **Mandhry Mosque** (Map p226; Sir Mbarak Hinawy Rd) in Old Town is an excellent example of Swahili architecture, which combines the elegant flourishes of Arabic style with the comforting, geometric patterns of African design; note, for example, the gently rounded minaret.

More modern examples include the **Sheikh Nurein Islamic Centre** (Map p228; opposite Uhuru Gardens) and the **Khonzi Mosque** (Map p228; Digo Rd).

Mombasa's large Hindu (and smaller Jain) population doesn't lack for places of worship. The enormous **Lord Shiva Temple** (Map p228; Mwinyi Ab Rd) is airy, open and set off by an interesting sculpture garden, while the **Swaminarayan Temple** (Map p228; Haile Selassie Rd) is stuffed with highlighter-bright murals that'll make you feel as if you've been transported to Mumbai. For even more esoteric design, there's a **Sikh Temple** (Map p228; Mwembe Tayari Rd), a **Hare Krishna Temple** (Map p228; Sautiya Kenya Rd) and a lovely **Jain Temple** (Map p228; Langoni Rd).

The two main Christian churches are also worth seeing, for rather different reasons. The **Holy Ghost Cathedral** (Map p228; Nyerere Ave) is a very European hunk of neo-Gothic buttressed architecture, with massive fans in the walls to cool its former colonial congregations. The **Mombasa Memorial Cathedral** (Map p228; Nkrumah Rd), on the other hand, tries almost too hard to fit in, resembling a mosque with its white walls, arches and cupola.

Spice Market MARKET

(Map p228; Langoni Rd; ⏲to sunset) This market, which stretches along Nehru and Langoni Rds west of Old Town, is an evocative, sensory overload; expect lots of jostling, yelling, wheeling, dealing and of course the exotic scent of stall upon stall of cardamom, pepper, turmeric, curry powders and everything else that makes eating enjoyable.

Old Law Courts ART GALLERY

(Map p226; Nkrumah Rd; admission free; ⏲8am-6pm) Dating from 1902, the old law courts on Nkrumah Rd have been converted into an informal gallery, with regularly changing displays of local art, Kenyan crafts, school competition pieces and votive objects from various tribal groups.

Central Mombasa

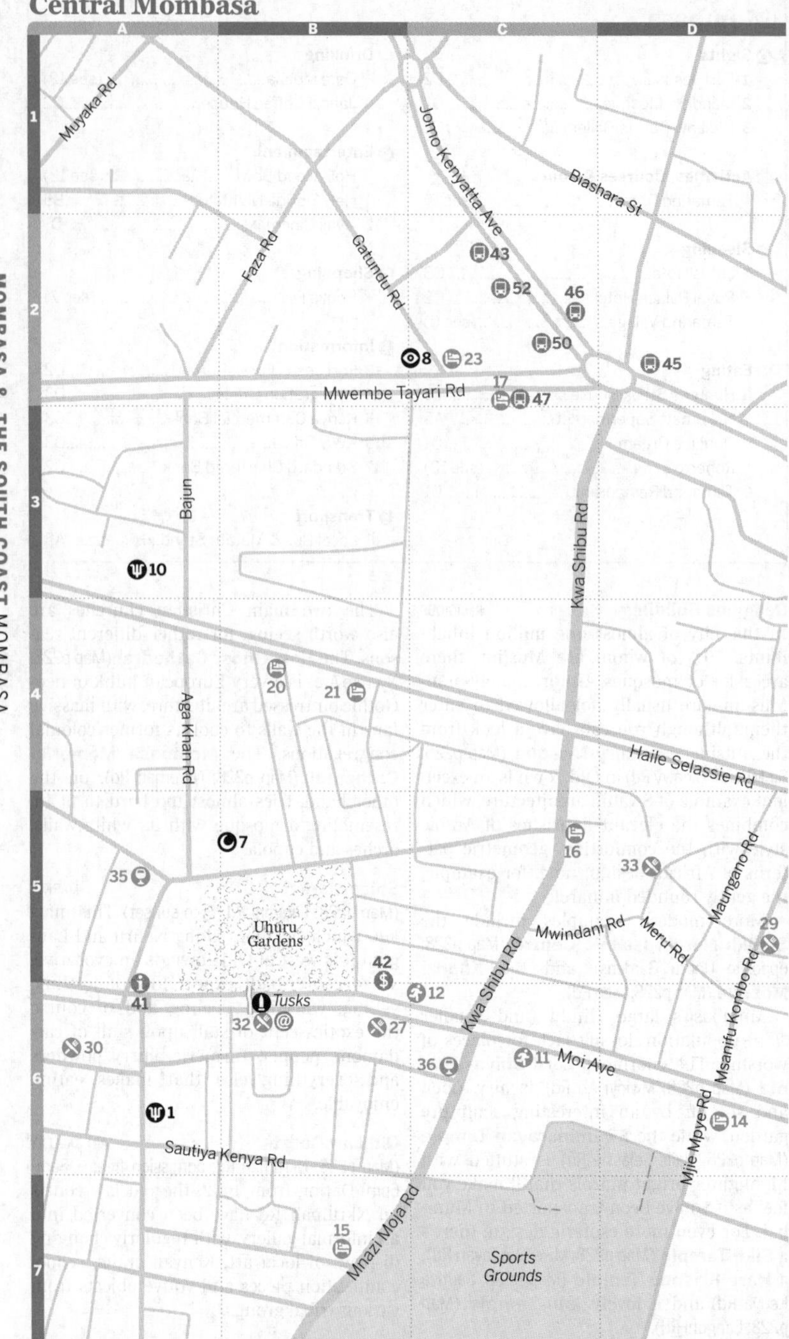

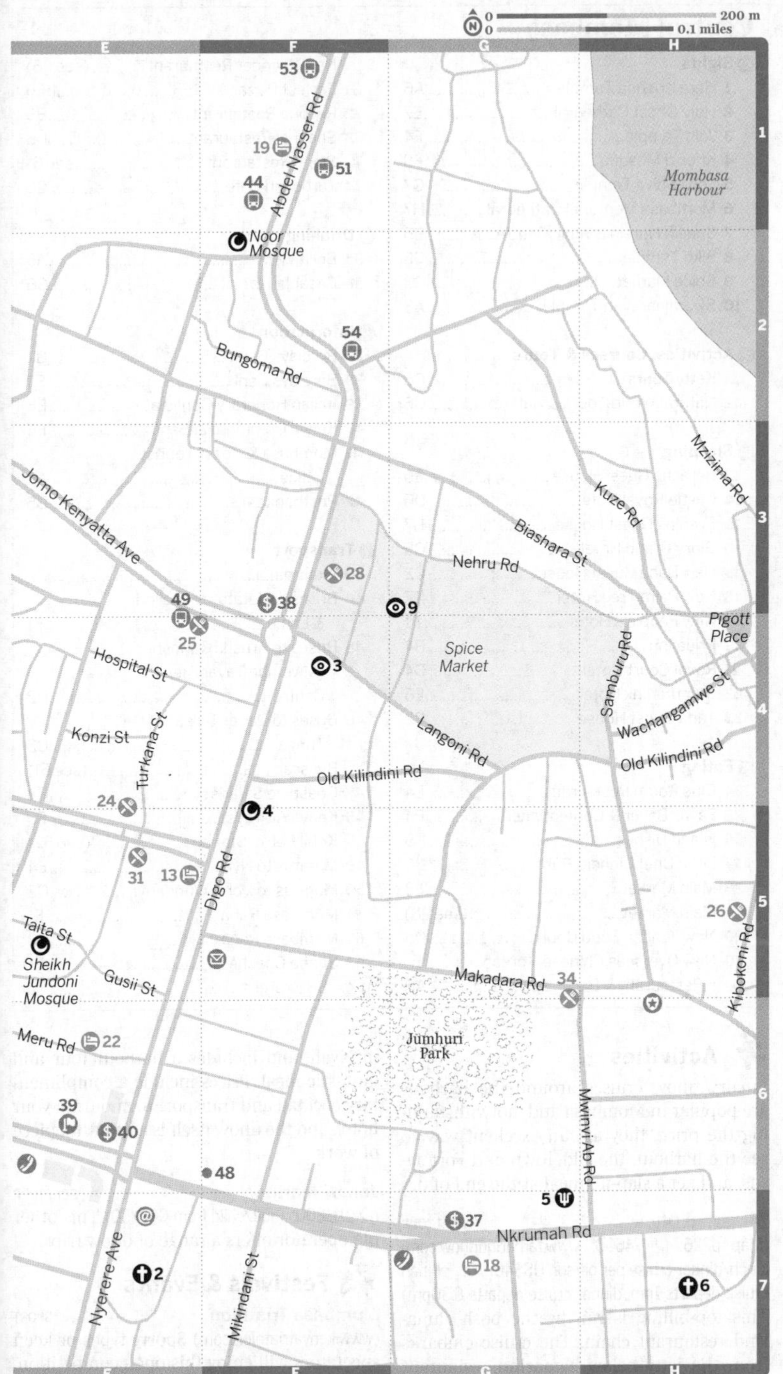

0 200 m
0 0.1 miles
Mombasa Harbour
Abdel Nasser Rd
Noor Mosque
Bungoma Rd
Jomo Kenyatta Ave
Mzizima Rd
Kuze Rd
Biashara St
Nehru Rd
Pigott Place
Spice Market
Hospital St
Samburu Rd
Wachangamwe St
Langoni Rd
Konzi St
Turkana St
Old Kilindini Rd
Old Kilindini Rd
Digo Rd
Taita St
Sheikh Jundoni Mosque
Gusii St
Makadara Rd
Kibokoni Rd
Meru Rd
Jumhuri Park
Mwinyi Ab Rd
Nkrumah Rd
Nyerere Ave
Mikindani St

Central Mombasa

Sights

1	Hare Krishna Temple	A6
2	Holy Ghost Cathedral	E7
3	Jain Temple	F4
4	Khonzi Mosque	F5
5	Lord Shiva Temple	G7
6	Mombasa Memorial Cathedral	H7
7	Sheikh Nurein Islamic Centre	B5
8	Sikh Temple	C2
9	Spice Market	G3
10	Swaminarayan Temple	A3

Activities, Courses & Tours

11	Ketty Tours	C6
12	Natural World Tours & Safaris	C6

Sleeping

13	Beracha Guest House	E5
14	Castle Royal Hotel	D6
15	Evening Guest House	B7
16	Glory Grand Hotel	C5
17	New Daba Guest House	C2
18	New Palm Tree Hotel	G7
19	New People's Hotel	F1
20	Pride Inn	B4
21	Royal Court Hotel	B4
22	Summerlink Hotel	E6
23	Tana Guest House	C2

Eating

24	Blue Room Restaurant	E4
25	Fayaz Baker & Confectioners	E4
26	Island Dishes	H5
27	Little Chef Dinners Pub	B6
28	Main Market	F3
	Main Market	(see 28)
29	New Jundan Food Court	D5
30	New Overseas Chinese-Korean Restaurant & Bar	A6
	New Recoder Restaurant	(see 26)
31	Perfect Pizza	E5
32	Recoda Restaurant	B6
33	Shehnai Restaurant	D5
	Singh Restaurant	(see 8)
34	Tarboush Cafe	G5

Drinking

35	Bella Vista	A5
36	Casablanca	C6

Information

37	Barclays Bank	G7
38	Barclays Bank	F3
39	Italian Honorary Consulate	E6
40	Kenya Commercial Bank	E6
41	Mombasa & Coast Tourist Office	A6
42	Postbank	B5

Transport

43	Akamba	C2
44	Buses & Matatus to Malindi & Lamu	F1
45	Buses to Arusha & Moshi (Mwembe Tayari Health Centre)	D2
46	Buses to Dar es Salaam & Tanga	C2
	Busscar	(see 51)
47	Coastline Safaris	C2
48	Kenya Airways	F6
	Kobil Petrol Station	(see 52)
49	Matatus to Nyali	E4
50	Matatus to Voi & Wundanyi	C2
51	Mombasa Raha	F1
52	Mombasa Raha	C2
53	Simba Coaches	F1
54	TSS Express	F2

Activities

Luxury dhow cruises around the harbour are popular in Mombasa and, notwithstanding the price, they are an excellent way to see the harbour, the Old Town and Fort Jesus, and get a slap-up meal at the end of it.

Tamarind Dhow BOAT TOUR
(Map p226; ☎474600; www.tamarinddhow.com; lunch/dinner cruise per person US$40/70; ⏲lunch cruise departs 1pm, dinner cruise departs 6.30pm) This top-billing is run by the posh Tamarind restaurant chain. The cruise embarks from the jetty below Tamarind restaurant in Nyali, and includes a harbour tour and fantastic meal. Prices include a complimentary cocktail and transport to and from your hotel, and the dhow itself is a beautiful piece of work.

Jahazi Marine BOAT TOUR
(☎2111800; adult/child from €60/30) This other big operator offers a range of dhow trips.

Festivals & Events

Mombasa Triathlon SPORT
(www.kenyatriathlon.com) Sporty types or keen spectators will enjoy this open competition,

with men's, women's and children's races. It's held in November.

Sleeping

Many people choose to skip Mombasa and head straight for the beaches to the south and north, but we'd suggest spending at least one night in town. It's difficult to appreciate Mombasa's energy without waking up to the call to prayer and the honk of a tuk-tuk (minitaxi). All the places listed here have fans and mosquito nets as a minimum requirement.

Dirt-cheap choices are in the busy area close to the bus stations on Abdel Nasser Rd and Jomo Kenyatta Ave. Lone female travellers might want to opt for something a little further up the price scale.

Castle Royal Hotel HISTORIC HOTEL **$$**
(Map p228; 2228780; www.castlemsa.com; Moi Ave; s/d US$90/125;) A creaky, old-fashioned place full of the ghosts of colonial days, this charming institution offers great service, comfortable rooms with modern facilities and a primo (free) breakfast: coconut beans and *mandazi* (semisweet doughnuts), or bacon and croissants. The streetside terrace is grade A people-watching territory.

Tamarind Village RESORT **$$$**
(Map p226; 474600; www.tamarind.co.ke; Silos Rd, Nyali; apt from KSh13,000;) This is the plushest hotel in town, bar none. Located in a modern (and quite elegantly executed) take on a Swahili castle overlooking the blue waters of the harbour, the Tamarind offers crisp rooms with satellite TV, DVD players, palm-lined balconies and a general sense of white-washed, sun-lathered luxury.

Glory Grand Hotel BUSINESS HOTEL **$**
(Map p228; 2228202; Kwa Shibu Rd; s/d from KSh2500/3500) The recently renovated Glory offers top-notch value for money. The rooms are cool, quiet and pleasantly furnished, and all up it's a great retreat from the noise and heat of the big city outside.

Beracha Guest House HOTEL **$**
(Map p228; 0725006228; Haile Selassie Rd; s/d without breakfast KSh1200/1350) This popular central choice is located in the heart of Mombasa's best eat-streets. It has variable but clean rooms in a range of unusual shapes. It's on the 2nd floor of the building it occupies – on the stair landing, turn right into the hotel, and not left into the evangelical church. It's probably the most backpacker-friendly of the city centre options.

THE SLAVE TRADE

One of the most important, controversial, hotly contested and silently-dealt-with topics in African history is the slave trade of the Swahili coast, better known as the East African slave trade. Between the 7th and 19th centuries, Arab and Swahili traders kidnapped some four million slaves from East Africa, and sold them for work in households and plantations across the Middle East and Arab-controlled African coastal states. The legacy of the trade is seen today in the chain motifs carved into doors (representing homes of slave traders) in Mombasa Old Town.

The East African slave trade both predated and exceeded the Atlantic Triangle Trade. Slave uprisings in southern Iraqi sugar plantations are reported from the 9th century, while Qatari royalty kept African slaves in their retinue at the coronation of Queen Elizabeth in 1953.

At first, slaves were obtained through trade with inland tribes, but as the 'industry' developed, caravans set off into the African interior, bringing back plundered ivory and tens of thousands of captured men, women and children. Of these, fewer than one in five survived the forced march to the coast, most either dying of disease or being executed for showing weakness along the way.

Although some slaves married their owners and gained freedom, the experience for the majority was much harsher. Thousands of African boys were surgically transformed into eunuchs to provide servants for Arabic households, and an estimated 2.5 million young African women were sold as concubines.

After the trade was brought to a close in the 1870s, the Swahili communities along the coast went into steady decline, although illicit trading continued right up until the 1960s, when slavery was finally outlawed in Oman. These days this dark chapter of African history is seldom discussed by Kenyans.

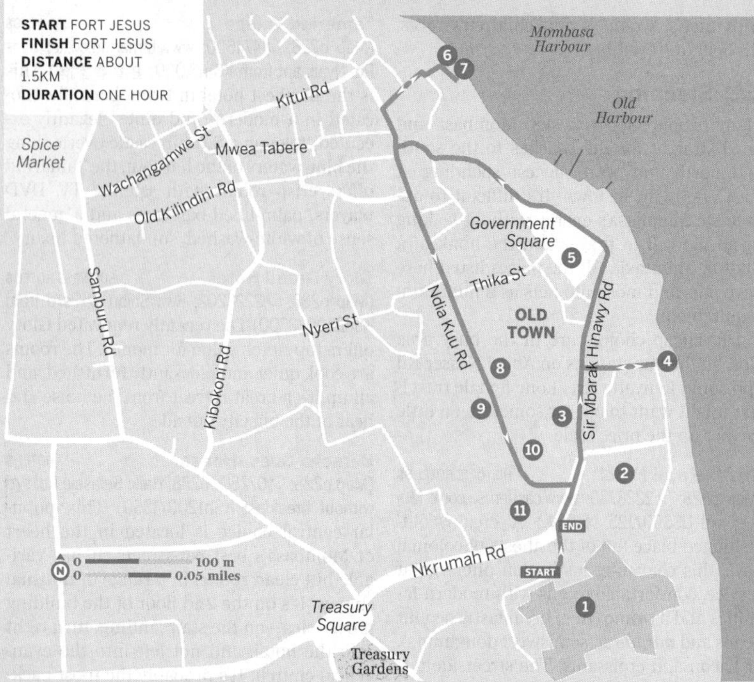

Walking Tour
Mombasa Old Town

Mombasa may not have the medieval charm of Lamu or Zanzibar, but the Old Town is a unique architectural blend of all who have influenced Swahili history and culture.

Start at 1 **Fort Jesus**. From here head past the colonial 2 **Mombasa Club** onto Sir Mbarak Hinawy Rd, once the main access road to the port and still a lively thoroughfare.

On the left, 3 **Africa Hotel** was one of only three hotels in the city at the turn of the 20th century. If you take a quick jaunt to your right you'll hit the water and see the restored facades of 4 **old houses**.

Turn the corner at the end of the street and you'll enter 5 **Government Square**, the largest open space in the Old Town. The buildings lining the square used to hold some of the city's key administrative offices.

Heading out of the square you'll need to bang a right towards the harbour; here you'll find the 6 **Leven Steps** which lead down past a great view of the ships docking in the harbour to 7 **Vasco da Gama's Well**, a reservoir that supposedly never dries.

Returning to Ndia Kuu Rd, the final stages of your route can be as direct or as tangential as you wish – diverting into side streets is highly recommended. The winding alleyways linking Old Town to Digo Rd are lively with market traders. Or you can light out west, which will eventually land you in the city spice market.

If you do stick to Ndia Kuu Rd, you'll see a lot of nicely restored traditional buildings, including the 8 **Balcony House**, so-named for obvious reasons; 9 **Edward St Rose**, the former chemist, which retains its original engraved glass panel; and 10 **Ali's Curio Market**, one of the better-preserved balcony houses. Pass the Muslim 11 **cemetery** and you're back at Fort Jesus.

New Palm Tree Hotel HOTEL $
(Map p228; ☎8025682; newpalmtreehotel@hotmail.com; Nkrumah Rd; s/d KSh2500/3500; @📶) This sociable option has rooms set around a terraced roof, and while the amenities (like hot water) aren't always reliable, the service is fine, it's generally well-cared-for and there's a good vibe about the place.

Royal Palace Hotel HISTORIC HOTEL $
(Map p226; ☎0717620602; cnr Old Kilindini & Kibokoni Rds; s/d from KSh1300/2500) This is an interesting new budget hotel, and the only place to stay within the exotic tangled streets of the Old Town. The rooms are so colourful it looks rather like a group of children have gone on a rampage with tins of paint. Our favourite is the 'Honeymoon' room, covered in, you guessed it, hundreds upon hundreds of bright red hearts! Sadly, despite being fairly new, it was already starting to look a little run-down when we visited.

Royal Court Hotel BUSINESS HOTEL $$
(Map p228; ☎223379; www.royalcourtmombasa.co.ke; Haile Selassie Rd; s/d KSh5350/6550; ❄@📶🏊) The swish lobby is the highlight of this stylish business hotel. Still, service and facilities are good, disabled access is a breeze, and you get great views and great food at the Tawa Terrace restaurant on the roof, which also has a pool. It wins points for charging tourists and residents (expatriates) the same, but looses points for charging KSh1100 to use the wi-fi.

Pride Inn BUSINESS HOTEL $$
(Map p228; ☎2317895; kohinoor@africaonline.co.ke; Haile Selassie Rd; s/d KSh4500/5700; ❄@📶) With art on the walls and friendly folk behind the reception, this business hotel offers value that, despite the odd bit of peeling paint, is pretty hard to beat. What it can be beaten on though is location – it's on a busy and noisy road.

Summerlink Hotel HOTEL $
(Map p228; ☎2226178; Meru Rd; s/d KSh1700/2300; ❄🏊) If you can't quite bump up your budget to that next level of comfort, the Summerlink, which hovers (price-wise) at the bottom of the midrange choices, might be your best option. It's a clean place with excellent security, good service and loads of Kenyan businessmen. There's also an on-site gym and karate classes, which is obviously what you came here for.

New People's Hotel HOTEL $
(Map p228; ☎0722471032; Abdel Nasser Rd; s/d without breakfast from KSh600/700) At this hotel near the 'Ideal Chicks' poultry building ('Because Chicks is the Boss'), you'll get loads of noise from traffic and the Noor Mosque next door, but rooms are cleanish and security is good. There's a nice, cheap restaurant downstairs and it's very convenient for buses to Lamu and Malindi.

New Daba Guest House HOTEL $
(Map p228; Mwembe Tayari Rd; r without breakfast KSh800) The distinctly functional (ie ugly) New Daba is nonetheless one of the cleaner options you could go for if you're either on a budget, or have just arrived on a night bus and need a place to crash.

Evening Guest House HOTEL $
(Map p228; ☎221380; Mnazi Moja Rd; s with shared bathroom KSh700, d KSh1500) If you need a budget doss set off from the bus-stand chaos, this is a good option. The doubles are decent value, the singles a bit less so, service is friendly and you'll get a good night's sleep. All rooms have power points 'for mobile phones only'. There's a cheap restaurant attached.

Tana Guest House HOTEL $
(Map p228; ☎490550; cnr Mwembe Tayari & Gatundu Rds; s/d/tr without breakfast KSh400/600/800) A simple but friendly place; rooms are small, tidy and pretty much what you'd expect for the price.

Eating

If a never-ending parade of chicken, chips, meat and corn roasted beyond palatability, and starch that tastes like...well, nothing, doesn't do it for you, well here comes the coast. Flavours! Fresh seafood! Spice! Anything but more *ugali* (maize- or cassava-based staple).

Explore the Old Town for cheap, authentic Swahili cuisine; if in doubt, follow the locals to find the best deals. Most places are Muslim-run, so no alcoholic drinks are sold and they're closed until after sunset during Ramadan.

Mombasa's good for street food: stalls sell cassava, samosas, bhajis, kebabs and the local take on pizza (meat and onions wrapped in soft dough and fried). A few dish out stew and *ugali*. For dessert, vendors ply you with *haluwa* (an Omani version of Turkish delight), fried taro root, sweet baobab seeds and sugared doughnuts.

TOURS & SAFARIS FROM MOMBASA

A number of tour companies offer standard tours of the Old Town and Fort Jesus (per person from US$45), plus safaris to Shimba Hills National Reserve and Tsavo East and Tsavo West National Parks. Most safaris are expensive lodge-based affairs, but there are a few camping safaris to Tsavo East and West.

The most popular safari is an overnight tour to Tsavo, and though most people enjoy these be warned that a typical two-day, one-night safari barely gives you time to get there and back, and that your animal-spotting time will be very limited. It's much better to add in at least one extra night.

We receive a constant stream of emails from travellers who feel that their promised safari has not lived up to expectations, but the following two companies have received positive feedback.

Ketty Tours (Map p228; ☎2315178; www.kettysafari.com; Ketty Plaza, Moi Av) Organised and reliable.

Natural World Tours & Safaris (Map p228; ☎2226715; www.naturaltoursandsafaris.com; Jeneby House, Moi Av) The hard-sell prattled out by the company 'representatives' on the street can quickly put you off, but otherwise it has a reputation for delivering what it promises.

TOP CHOICE Shehnai Restaurant INDIAN $$
(Map p228; ☎222847; Fatemi House, Maungano Rd; mains from KSh300; ⊙noon-2pm & 7.30-10.30pm Tue-Sun) Mombasa's classiest curry-house specialises in tandoori and rich *mughlai* (North Indian) cuisine complemented by nice decor that's been copied from Indian restaurants the world over (pumped-in sitar music thrown in for free). It's very popular with well-heeled Indian families, probably because the food is authentic and very good. Add 25% in various taxes to all prices.

TOP CHOICE New Jundan Food Court KENYAN $
(Map p228; Gussi St; mains KSh100-200; ⊙lunch) You'll need to kick and shove your way through crowds of locals to get to this excellent 2nd-floor restaurant that backs onto the Sheikh Jundoni Mosque. It's Swahili food through and through and the special is a stunning pilau.

Tamarind Restaurant KENYAN $$$
(Map p226; ☎474600; Silos Rd, Nyali; mains KSh1100-1800) If you're entertaining an 'I'm a Swahili sultan overlooking my coastal kingdom with a giant plate of chilli crab' fantasy, can we recommend the Tamarind? Big Moorish-palace exterior, big jewellery-box dining room, big keyboard music (ugh) and a big menu that concentrates on seafood (but does everything well) equals big satisfaction (and, yeah, a big bill). If you're staying elsewhere they'll collect you from your hotel.

Roberto's ITALIAN $$$
(Map p226; ☎476559; Nyali Centre, Nyali Rd, Nyali; mains KSh800-1600) As you've probably guessed, Roberto's is a true-blue Italian restaurant and many Italian expats will tell you it does the best old-country cooking in town. It might not be cheap but it really is worth every shilling.

Tarboush Cafe INTERNATIONAL $
(Map p228; Makadara Rd; mains KSh70-250) Most people come to this open-air, park-side restaurant for the chicken tikka, and rightfully so. Eat it with lovely soft naan bread, rice or chips. There's also a good range of Swahili staples and some curries. Despite being packed at all hours the service remains fast and friendly.

Hunter's Steak House STEAKHOUSE $$
(Map p226; 'Königsallee', Mkomani Rd, Nyali; mains KSh450-2000; ⊙Wed-Mon) Where's *die* beef? Here, *meine Freunde,* at this German-run steakhouse, generally regarded as the best purveyor of cooked cow in town (by tourists and expats – Kenyans generally prefer their *choma*). It's aimed mainly at visitors, and is often closed for a month or so in June.

Recoda Restaurant KENYAN $
(Map p228; Moi Ave; mains around KSh120; ⊙lunch & dinner) This Muslim eatery is packed in the evenings with locals clamouring for their version of kebabs, which are grilled to fat-dripping perfection. Service is a bit sharp, but take it with a spoonful of sugar, because the food is worth your patience.

Island Dishes KENYAN $
(Map p228; Kibokoni Rd; mains KSh80-220) Once your eyes have adjusted to the dazzling strip-lights, feast them on the tasty menu at this very popular Swahili restaurant. *Mishikaki* (marinated, grilled meat kebabs), chicken tikka, fish, fresh juices and all the usual favourites are on offer to eat in or take away, though the biryani (rice with meat or seafood) is only available at lunchtime.

Singh Restaurant INDIAN $
(Map p228; Mwembe Tayari Rd; mains KSh250-320) This used to be a very simple cafeteria, but it has received an extensive makeover and now looks like your standard dark-wood and Mughal painting–bedecked classy Indian restaurant. With that said, the food is excellent and, thanks to the nearby Sikh temple, this spot serves vegetarians, and well.

New Recoder Restaurant KENYAN $
(Map p228; Kibokoni Rd; mains KSh50-180) This is a local favourite, slightly tattier than Island Dishes, but with much the same coast cuisine.

New Overseas Chinese-Korean Restaurant & Bar CHINESE $
(Map p228; ☎230729; Moi Ave; mains KSh220-480; ⊙lunch & dinner) Despite the overblown name and the hilariously clichéd interior design, the New Overseas does actually deliver on its oriental promises, and its seafood dishes are particularly good.

Blue Room Restaurant INTERNATIONAL $
(Map p228; Haile Selassie Rd; mains KSh170-380; ⊙lunch & dinner; @) It's not blue, but between the steaks, pizzas, curries and…internet access (no, really), the Blue Room has basically been constructed to serve the needs of every traveller anywhere.

Little Chef Dinners Pub KENYAN $
(Map p228; Moi Ave; mains KSh120-300; ⊙lunch & dinner) This funky, green-hued pub-restaurant has no relation to the British motorway diners of the same name. Little Chef dishes up big, tasty portions of Kenyan and international dishes (as long as those dishes are fried, anyway). There are a couple more outlets in the area, but this is by far the nicest.

Perfect Pizza FAST FOOD $
(Map p228; Haile Selassie Rd; pizzas from KSh549; ⊙lunch & dinner) 'Perfect' might be pushing it, but this is surprisingly good pizza (of the greasy American sort) considering you're in East Africa. There are plenty of topping options, including make-your-own pizzas.

Ooh! Ice-Cream ICE CREAM $
(Map p226; Nyali Rd, Nyali; ice cream KSh60-100) Even if this glossy, air-conditioned place didn't serve fantastic ice creams, cakes and snacks, we'd still consider including it just because of the name!

Fayaz Baker & Confectioners BAKERY $
(Map p228; Jomo Kenyatta Ave) Mombasa's 'Master Baker' cooks up excellent cakes and muffins in several locations around town.

Nakumatt Supermarket SUPERMARKET $
(Map p226; Nyerere Ave) Close to the Likoni ferry jetty, this place has a good selection of provisions, drinks and hardware items – just in case you need a TV, bicycle or lawnmower to take on safari.

Main market MARKET $
(Map p228; Digo Rd) Mombasa's dilapidated 'covered' market is packed with stalls selling fresh fruit and vegetables. Roaming produce carts also congregate in the surrounding streets, and dozens of *miraa* sellers join the fray when the regular deliveries come in. Remember, if you're chewing you chew the peeled stalks and not the leaves like in Ethiopia and Yemen.

Drinking

There are plenty of good drinking holes in Mombasa, and many restaurants cater primarily to drinkers in the evening.

Jahazi Coffee House CAFE
(Map p226; Ndia Kuu Rd; ⊙8am-8pm) Bringing a touch of cosmopolitan style to Mombasa Old Town, this classy Swahili boutique cafe is a superb place to wile away a few hours playing cards over a steaming pot of tea in the front room or lounging like Persian royalty on the pompous cushions with a fruit juice or snack in the back room. A percentage of profits goes toward local development projects.

Cafe Mocha CAFE
(Map p226; Nyali Centre, Nyali Rd, Nyali; ⊙8am-9pm) Mocha is usually brimming with well-heeled Mombasan teeny- and tweeny-boppers and their parents enjoying the good coffee, air-conditioning, and lovely cakes and pastries.

Office BAR
(off Map p226; Shelly Beach Rd, Likoni; ⏲11am-late) Perched above the Likoni ferry jetty and matatu stand, the entirely unaptly named Office is a real locals' hang-out, with regular massive reggae and dub nights shaking the thatched rafters. Any business that goes on here is definitely not the executive kind.

Bella Vista BAR
(Map p228; west of Uhuru Gardens; ⏲midday-late) This two-storey beer-fest is plenty of fun for those who feel the need to kick back with a cold one, some sports on the tube, a few rounds of pool and a great view of Mombasa's nightlife action unfolding in all it's storied, slightly sleazy, glory.

Casablanca BAR
(Map p228; Mnazi Moja Rd; ⏲midday-late) This legendary-for-all-the-wrong-reasons, giant two-storey bar in the town centre gets full to bursting point with all the sleazy characters Mombasa can muster (which is quite a lot) as well as loads of prostitutes. In the daytime it calms down considerably and is a fairly pleasant place for a drink.

☆ Entertainment

New Florida Nightclub CLUB
(off Map p226; Mama Ngina Dr; entry after 7.30pm KSh500; ⏲6pm-6am; 🏊) This vast seafront complex houses Mombasa's liveliest nightclub, which boasts its own open-air swimming pool. It's owned by the same people as the infamous Florida clubs in Nairobi and offers the same atmosphere, clientele and Las Vegas–style floorshows, with the bonus of outdoor bars, table football and German *Currywurst* (curry sausage)! Friday, Saturday and Sunday are the big party nights. A taxi fare here from central Mombasa is around KSh400 to KSh500.

Nyali Cinemax CINEMA
(Map p226; www.nyalicinemax.com; Nyali Centre, Nyali Rd, Nyali; tickets KSh300-550) A multiscreen, modern Cineplex with 3D capabilities. Primarily screens big name Holly- and Bollywood films.

Hollywood Bowl BOWLING
(Map p226; Nyali Centre, Nyali Rd, Nyali; games KSh250-350; ⏲4pm-midnight) A typical American-style bowling alley.

Shopping

Biashara St (Map p228), west of its Digo Rd intersection (just north of the spice market), is Kenya's main centre for *kikoi* (brightly coloured woven sarongs for men) and *kangas* (printed wraps worn by women). *Kangas* come as a pair, one for the top half of the body and one for the bottom, and are marked with Swahili proverbs. You may need to bargain, but what you get is generally what you pay for; bank on about KSh500 for a pair of cheap *kangas* or a *kikoi*. *Kofia*, the handmade caps worn by Muslim men, are also crafted here; a really excellent one can cost up to KSh2500.

Mombasa has an incredible number of skilled tailors and you can have a safari suit or shirt custom-made in a day or two for no more than US$20. There are numerous choices on Nehru Rd (Map p228), behind the spice market.

Moi Ave (Map p228) has loads of souvenir shops, but prices are high and every shop seems to stock exactly the same stuff. There are stalls selling sisal baskets and spices in and around the main market, but you'll rarely pay fair prices as touts loiter here and 'accompany' tourists for a commission.

Akamba Handicraft Industry Cooperative Society HANDICRAFTS
(off Map p226; www.akambahandicraftcoop.com; Port Reitz Rd; ⏲8am-5pm Mon-Fri, to noon Sun) This cooperative employs an incredible 10,000 people from the local area. It's also a non-profit organisation and produces fine woodcarvings. Kwa Hola/Magongo matatus run right past the gates from the Kobil petrol station on Jomo Kenyatta Ave. Many coach tours from Mombasa also stop here.

Books First BOOKS
(Map p226; Nyerere Ave; @) Well-stocked bookshop with separate cafe, in the Nakumatt supermarket.

Information

Dangers & Annoyances

Mombasa isn't Nairobi, but the streets still clear pretty rapidly after dark so it's a good idea to take taxis rather than walk alone at night. The Likoni ferry is a bag-snatching hot spot.

Emergency

AAR Health Services (Lulu Centre, Machakos St, off Moi Av; ⏲24hr)

Central Police Station (Map p228; ☎999; Makadara Rd)

Internet Access

All of the following charge KSh60 per hour.

SWA-WHO-LI?

'So you are a Swahili?' we ask the Mombasa shop owner, who is dressed like all the Swahili in the street and shares their caramel skin colour. 'No! No, I am Kenyan, but my roots are in Gujarat,' he says.

In the village, watching a man walk by, we turn to our guide: 'He's a Digo, right?'

'No!' says the guide. 'His father and his mother are Digo. His mother is so traditional she won't wear shoes. But he was sent to work in a Swahili house when he was young and converted to Islam, married a Muslim girl, made the haj (pilgrimage to Mecca) and would be insulted to be called anything but Swahili.'

Just who the Swahili are is a complex question, and not just for anthropologists. For many people on the Kenyan coast, being Swahili is the most important marker of their identity. This is not a unique set of affairs – the same emphasis on tribe can be noted in many groups in Kenya – but what sets the Swahili apart is their connection to the Muslim, particularly Arab, world.

To put it plainly: there are Swahili who believe the presence, real or imagined, of Arab and Persian blood sets them apart – and above – 'black' Africans (this despite the fact many Swahili are as black as any inland Kenyans). This attitude is not shared by all Swahili by any stretch, but it is present. It stems from both good-old racism and a sense of superiority engendered by, among other things, Swahili cosmopolitanism, the Kiswahili language (generally considered to be spoken at its 'purest' on the coast), and the fact the Swahili were the area's original converts to Islam. A stronger link to the Arab world (which may be arbitrarily measured or fancifully concocted, much like white Americans claiming descent from European nobility) is often taken to mean a weaker tie to black Africa, and by extension, a stronger tie to Islam.

Due to its mixed nature, Swahili identity has been, and remains, in some ways, a malleable thing. At its uglier edges, it still draws influence from the Arab imperialism that once dominated the coast. With that said, many thousands of Swahili cheerfully acknowledge they are black and something else – something quintessentially 'coast'.

Blue Room Cyber Café (Map p228; Haile Selassie Rd; ⏲9am-10pm)

Cyber Dome (Map p228;Moi Ave; ⏲8am-9pm Mon-Sat, 9am-6pm Sun)

FOTech (Map p228; ☎225123; Ambalal House, Nkrumah Rd; ⏲9am-7.30pm)

Internet Resources

TOMASI Holidays Africa (www.hotelsmombasa.com) Good for booking online and checking current contact details.

MombasaInfo.com (www.mombasainfo.com) Descriptive tourist information.

Mombasa North Coast (www.mombasanorthcoast.com) More tourist-info goodness.

Media

Coastweek (www.coastweek.com) Weekly news and features from the coast province.

Medical Services

All services and medication must be paid for upfront, so have travel insurance details handy.

Aga Khan Hospital (Map p226; ☎2227710; www.agakhanhospitals.org; Vanga Rd)

Mombasa Hospital (Map p226; ☎2312191, 2312099, 2228010; www.mombasahosptial.com; off Mama Ngina Dr)

Money

Outside business hours you can change money at most major hotels, although rates are usually poor. Exchange rates are generally slightly lower here than in Nairobi, especially if you're changing travellers cheques.

Barclays Bank Nkrumah Rd (Map p228); Digo Rd (Map p228) Both with ATMs.

Fort Jesus Forex Bureau (Map p226; Ndia Kuu Rd)

Kenya Commercial Bank Nkrumah Rd (Map p226); Moi Ave (Map p228) With ATMs.

Postbank (Map p228; Moi Ave) Western Union money transfers.

Standard Chartered Bank (Map p226; Treasury Square, Nkrumah Rd) With ATM.

Post

Post office (Map p228; Digo Rd)

Telephone

Telkom Kenya (Map p228) Locations on Nkrumah Rd and Moi Ave.

WORTH A TRIP

LUNATIC LINE: THE MOMBASA–NAIROBI RAILWAY

Few subjects divide our readers' letters more fiercely than the train from Nairobi to Mombasa. Once one of the most famous rail lines in Africa, the train is today, depending on whom you speak to, either a sociable way of avoiding the rutted highway and spotting wildlife from the clackety comfort of a sleeping car, or a ratty, tatty overrated waste of time. The truth lies somewhere in the middle. The train's state could be described as 'faded glory', occasionally bumping up to 'romantically dishevelled', or slipping into 'frustrating mediocrity'. The latter isn't helped by spotty scheduling and lax timetable enforcement. However, all this might be due to change thanks to a major investment in new trains and lines, although none of this will happen immediately.

Currently then, the 'iron snake' departs Mombasa train station (Map p226) at 7pm on Tuesday, Thursday and Sunday, arriving in Nairobi the next day somewhere between 8.30am and 11am. Fares are US$65 for 1st class and US$55 for 2nd class, including bed and breakfast (you get dinner with 1st class) – reserve as far in advance as possible. The booking office, open 8am to 5pm, is at the station in Mombasa.

Tourist Information

Mombasa & Coast Tourist Office (Map p228; Moi Ave; ⏲8am- 4.30pm) Provides information and can organise accommodation, tours, guides and transport.

 Getting There & Away

Air

Airkenya (☎0727131977; Moi International Airport; www.airkenya.com) No ticket office in Mombasa city centre (you can book online or head out to the airport office), but flies between Nairobi and Diani Beach (45 minutes away) once a day (one way US$152, one hour).

Fly540 (☎3434821; www.fly540.com; Moi International Airport) Flies between Nairobi and Mombasa at least five times daily (one way from US$69, one hour) as well as Malindi (one way from US$40, 20 minutes), Lamu (one way from US$55, 45 minutes) and Zanzibar (one way from US$80, 40 minutes).

Kenya Airways (Map p228; ☎2125000; www.kenya-airways.com; TSS Towers, Nkrumah Rd) Flies between Nairobi and Mombasa at least 10 times daily (one way US$200, one hour).

Mombasa Air Safari (☎0734400400; www.mombasaairsafari.com; Moi International Airport) Flies to Amboseli (US$315, one hour), Tsavo (US$315, one hour and 45 minutes) and Masai Mara (US$305, two hours and 45 minutes) National Parks among other destinations; it can also arrange complete safari packages.

Bus & Matatu

Most bus offices are on either Jomo Kenyatta Ave or Abdel Nasser Rd. Services to Malindi and Lamu leave from Abdel Nasser Rd, while buses to destinations in Tanzania leave from the junction of Jomo Kenyatta Ave and Mwembe Tayari Rd.

For buses and matatus to the beaches and towns south of Mombasa, you first need to get off the island via the Likoni ferry. Frequent matatus run from Nyerere Ave to the transport stand by the ferry terminal.

Note that as with most bus and matatu fares in Kenya, fares vary depending on demand (and fuel prices).

NAIROBI There are dozens of daily departures in both directions (mostly in the early morning and late evening). Companies include the following:

Akamba (Map p228; ☎490269; Jomo Kenyatta Ave)

Busscar (Map p228; ☎222854; Abdel Nasser Rd)

Coastline Safaris (Map p228; ☎220158; Mwembe Tayari St)

Mombasa Raha (Map p228; ☎225716) Offices on Abdel Nasser Rd and Jomo Kenyatta Ave.

Simba Coaches (Map p228; Abdel Nasser Rd)

Daytime services take at least six hours, and overnight trips eight to 10 hours and include a meal/smoking break about halfway. The trip isn't particularly comfortable, although it's not bad for an African bus ride. Fares vary from KSh800 to KSh1300. Most companies have at least four departures daily.

All buses to Nairobi travel via Voi (KSh300 to KSh500), which is also served by frequent matatus from the Kobil petrol station on Jomo Kenyatta Ave (KSh200). Several companies go to Kisumu and Lake Victoria, but all go via Nairobi.

HEADING NORTH There are numerous daily buses and matatus up the coast to Malindi, leaving from in front of the Noor Mosque on Abdel Nasser Rd. Buses take up to 2½ hours (around KSh300), matatus take about two hours (KSh350 rising to KSh600 during holidays and very busy periods).

Tawakal, Simba, Mombasa Raha and TSS Express have buses to Lamu, most leaving at around 7am (report 30 minutes early) from their offices on Abdel Nasser Rd. Buses take around seven hours to reach the Lamu ferry at Mokoke (KSh600 to KSh800) and travel via Malindi.

HEADING SOUTH Regular buses and matatus leave from the Likoni ferry terminal and travel along the southern coast.

For Tanzania, Simba and a handful of other companies have daily departures to Dar es Salaam (KSh1200 to KSh1600, eight hours) via Tanga from their offices on Jomo Kenyatta Ave, near the junction with Mwembe Tayari Rd. Dubious-looking buses to Moshi and Arusha leave from in front of the Mwembe Tayari Health Centre in the morning or evening.

Getting Around

To/From the Airport

There is currently no public transport to or from the airport, so you'll need to hop in a taxi. The fare to central Mombasa is around KSh1200.

Boat

The two Likoni ferries connect Mombasa island with the southern mainland. There's a crossing roughly every 20 minutes between 5am and 12.30am, less frequently outside these times. It's free for pedestrians, KSh75 per small car and KSh165 for a safari jeep. To get to the jetty from the centre of town, take a Likoni matatu from Digo Rd.

Matatu, Taxi & Tuk-tuk

Matatus charge between KSh20 and KSh30 for short trips. Mombasa taxis are as expensive as those in Nairobi, and harder to find; a good place to look is in front of Express Travel on Nkrumah Rd. Assume it'll cost KSh250 to KSh400 from the train station to the city centre. There are also plenty of three-wheeled tuk-tuks about, which run to about KSh70 to KSh150 for a bit of open-air transit.

SOUTH OF MOMBASA

Why do folks head south of Mombasa? For most people it's all wrapped up in a word: beaches.

And yet there's so much more. We're not saying the sand isn't gorgeous or the ocean isn't lovely, because they are. But in some places there's a depressing amount of package tourists opting for high-end resorts that only access the above.

Slip into the sea and lay out under those coconut fronds, but, while you're at it, try walking through the groves of a 600-year-old sacred forest, scouting for mudskippers in a forest of mangroves, snorkelling in the jewel-box waters of a marine park or feeling the salt wind curl off a dhow's prow as you head out to a new island.

Shimba Hills National Reserve

If you're in need of traditional African landscapes of the rolling hills variety, this 320-sq-km **reserve** (adult/child US$20/10; 6am-6pm) is just 30km from Mombasa, directly inland from Diani Beach. It's often overlooked, and is one of the most underrated parks in the country – as well as one of the easiest to visit. The park's gentle grassy hills are interspersed with patches of forest which together provide a home to elephants, leopards, warthogs, buffaloes, baboons, a variety of antelope species and a small population of masai giraffes (which have been introduced), but the park is best known for its population of magnificent sable antelope, which occur in no other Kenyan park. The sable antelope have made a stunning recovery after their numbers dropped to less than 120 in 1970.

WILDLIFE ON THE SOUTH COAST

While you wouldn't come to the south Kenyan coastline in search of the Big Five, it doesn't mean that bringing a pair of binoculars is a waste of time. Quite the contrary. If you want to see elephants, giraffes, buffaloes and more, then **Shimba Hills National Reserve** and the neighbouring **Mwaluganje Elephant Sanctuary** (p241) should put a smile on your face. Diani Beach has a unique subspecies of beautiful **colobus monkeys** (p242), and coral reefs everywhere are alive with fish big and small, some of them really big: **dolphins** are common and **whale sharks** occasionally cruise by. But it's the **birds** that are the real standout wildlife event. The Kenyan coast features many birds that cannot be seen anywhere else in the country, and from October to March it also plays host to thousands of **winter migrants** escaping the cold of northern latitudes. Pack those binoculars!

SHIMBA HILLS NATIONAL RESERVE

Why Go It's an easy day trip from the coast, has excellent elephant-spotting, and is the only Kenyan home of the sable antelope.

When to Go Year-round, but the dry season from November to March is best.

Practicalities Diani Beach, just 45 minutes away, is the most popular base, and numerous safari companies and hotels there offer safaris to Shimba Hills. With good roads, short distances and ease of access, this is a perfect 'family-friendly' park.

In 2005, the elephant population reached an amazing 600 – far too many for this tiny space. Instead of culling the herds, Kenya Wildlife Service (KWS) organised an unprecedented US$3.2 million translocation operation to reduce the pressure on the habitat, capturing no fewer than 400 elephants and moving them to Tsavo East National Park.

There are over 150km of 4WD tracks that criss-cross the reserve; Marere Dam and the forest of Mwele Mdogo Hill are good spots for seeing bird life. Highly recommended guided forest walks are run by the KWS from the Sheldrick Falls ranger post. The walk down to Sheldrick Falls, a fairly gentle up-and-down climb through the forest (a couple of hours roundtrip) is free, but a tip is appropriate. Walks normally take place at 10am and 2pm.

Sleeping

The public campsite (per person KSh300) and *bandas* (per person US$25) are basic and have cold-water-only bathrooms, but they're superbly located on the edge of an escarpment close to the main gate. Monkeys sit in the trees around the camp, birds sing in the mornings and a campfire can be lit at night. You must be self-sufficient.

Kwale Golden Guest House HOTEL $
(☎0722326758; Kwale town; r KSh600-1200) In the regional 'capital' of Kwale and just a couple of kilometres from the park entrance, this typical small-town boarding house has two classes of room: one with hot showers and sit-down toilets and the other with cold showers and squat toilets.

Shimba Rainforest Lodge LODGE $$$
(☎0722200952; www.aberdaresafarihotels.com; Kinango Rd; full board with shared bathroom per person US$277) Let's start with the good news. This place has a fantastic setting deep in the forest and next to a waterhole that attracts lots of wildlife. Now for the bad news. The tiny rooms are drab and overpriced. Many safari companies will try to persuade you to come and eat lunch here, but the meal we had was unpleasant and overpriced. Bring a packed lunch instead.

Getting There & Away

You'll need a 4WD to enter the reserve, but hitching may be possible at the main gate. From Likoni, small lorry-buses to Kwale pass the main gate (KSh80).

Every safari company in Mombasa and at Diani Beach offers safaris to Shimba Hills. A half-day tour costs a standard US$80 per person.

Tiwi Beach

☎040

The sleepy sister to manic Diani is a string of blissed-out resorts, accessible by dirt tracks, about 20km south of Likoni. It's good for a quiet, cottage-style escape by the sand. One of the best features of Tiwi is Diani reef (which, funnily enough, isn't as evident in Diani), creating a stable, pool-like area between the shore and the coral that's great for swimming.

To get to Tiwi, turn left off the main highway (A14) about 18km south of Mombasa; follow the track until it terminates in a north–south T-intersection.

Sleeping & Eating

With a few exceptions, Tiwi doesn't provide the all-in-one package experience of the high-end resorts to the south. The name of the game here is small, self-catered cottages, which can be a real joy for couples and groups. All of these places are located off the unnamed dirt track that runs parallel to the main highway and the beach.

TOP CHOICE **Sand Island Beach Cottages** COTTAGES $$
(Map p242; ☎0722395005; www.sandislandbeach.com; cottages from KSh6000) A bunch of friendly dogs greet you as you enter this

gardenlike strip of lovely cottages, fronting a beach that the owners claim is the 'best beach in East Africa'. Now that is a mighty big claim, but when you see for yourself how sublime this patch of paradise is, with its shimmering-white desert island poking out of a turquoise lagoon, you probably won't argue. The cottages are a pretty fine example of the perfect paradise pad as well.

Coral Cove Cottages COTTAGES $$
(Map p242; ☎3300010; www.coralcove.tiwibeach.com; cottages from KSh4800) When Doctor Doolittle goes on vacation, he looks no further than this awesome beachfront option. There are dogs, roosters, monkeys, geese, ducks and other fluffy denizens scattered throughout, and they're all tame. The self-catering cottages are as full of colour and character as the rest of the place.

Twiga Lodge HOTEL $
(Map p242; ☎0721577614; twigakenya@gmail.com; camping KSh300, s/d KSh1500/2500, new wing s/d KSh3000/4800) Twiga is great fun when there's a crowd staying, with the palpable sense of isolation alleviated by the sheer tropical exuberance of the place. The older rooms are set off from the beach and are slightly grotty, while the newer wing is crisper. The on-site restaurant is OK, but having a drink under thatch while stars spill over the sea is as perfect as moments come.

Maweni & Capricho Beach Cottages RESORT $$
(Map p242; ☎3300012; www.mawenibeach.com; s/d from KSh5000/8000, cottages from KSh4500;) This large resort is actually three similar groupings of huts (Maweni, Capricho and Moonlight Bay) under the umbrella of one property. All of the options include nicely thatched tropical huts and cottages, and share a lovely restaurant and pretty pool.

Getting There & Away

Buses and matatus on the Likoni–Ukunda road can drop you at the start of either track down to Tiwi (KSh50) – keep an eye out for the signs to Capricho Beach Cottages or Tiwi Beach Resort. The southern turn-off, known locally as Tiwi 'spot', is much easier to find.

Although it's only 3.5km to the beach, both access roads are notorious for muggings so take a taxi or hang around for a lift. If you're heading back to the highway, any of the places listed can call ahead for a taxi.

DON'T MISS

MWALUGANJE ELEPHANT SANCTUARY

This **sanctuary** (☎040-41121; adult/child US$15/2, vehicles KSh150-500; ⊙6am-6pm) is a good example of community-based conservation with local people acting as stakeholders in the project. It was opened in October 1995 to create a corridor along an elephant migration route between Shimba Hills and Mwaluganje Forest Reserve, and comprises 2400 hectares of rugged, beautiful country along the valley of the Cha Shimba River.

Other than the 150 or so elephants, the big-ticket wildlife can be a little limited. However, you're likely to have the place to yourself, the scenery is almost a cliché of what East Africa should look like, and there's plenty of little stuff to see. All this makes Mwaluganje more suitable for those who've done a few safaris elsewhere and are after a wilder, more pristine experience. The drier country means that the wildlife in Mwaluganje differs slightly from that of wetter and greener Shimba Hills. This is especially noticeable when it comes to the birds, with many species found here that aren't to be seen anywhere else on the coast.

Mwaluganje Elephant Camp (☎Mombasa 011-5486121; s/d US$160/225) is a rather fine place to stay, with very plush safari tents overlooking a waterhole. Unless your stay happens to coincide with that of a tour group then you're likely to be the only person staying – peace indeed! If you can't afford the fancy-pants tents then camping in your own tent is possible at the **campsite** (per person KSh300), located near the main gate. The setting is sublime (though the rock surface makes things tricky for tent pegs!). It's as genuine an African wilderness experience as you can ask for.

The main entrance to the sanctuary is about 13km northeast of Shimba Hills National Reserve, on the road to Kinango. A shorter route runs from Kwale to the Golini gate, passing the Mwaluganje ticket office. It's only 5km but the track is 4WD only. The roads inside the park are pretty rough and a 4WD is the way to go.

Diani Beach

☎040

Diani, the biggest resort town on the Kenyan coast, is a mixed bag. It's an undeniably stunning swath of white-sand perfection, and if you're looking to party, you're in the right spot. On the other hand, it's rife with the sort of uniform uber-resorts that could be plopped anywhere in the world. We've tried to review the more distinctive places.

There's a lot beyond the stale blocks of hotel overdevelopment. You can visit coral mosques with archways that overlook the open ocean and sky; go to sacred forests where guides hug trees that speak in their ancestors' voices; and (well, why not) head to a monkey sanctuary – all good ways of experiencing more of the coast than the considerable charms of sun and sand.

The town of Ukunda, which is basically a traffic junction on the main Mombasa–Tanzania road, is the turn-off point for Diani Beach. There are all sorts of essentials here including post offices and banks. From here a sealed road runs about 2.5km to a T-junction with the beach road, where you'll find everything Diani has to offer.

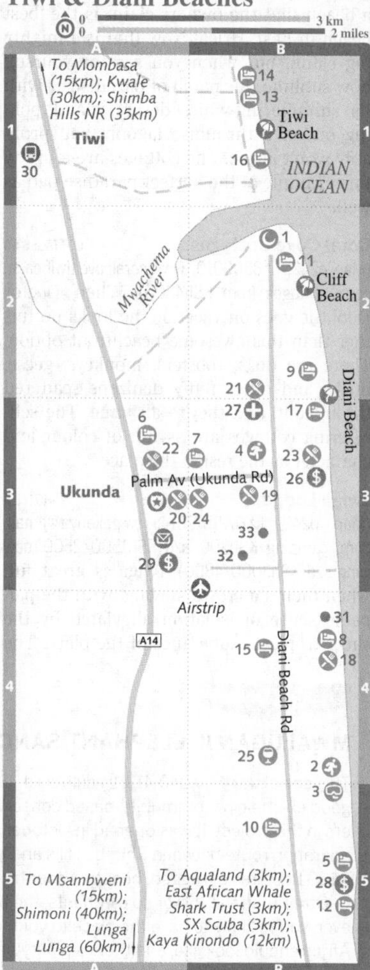

Sights & Activities

Package-holiday tat seems ubiquitous in Diani, but there's far more waiting to be discovered by independent travellers.

TOP CHOICE Colobus Trust WILDLIFE RESERVE

(☎0711479453; www.colobustrust.org; Diani Beach Rd; tours KSh500; ⏱8am-5pm Mon-Sat) Notice the monkeys clambering on rope ladders over the road? The ladders are the work of the Colobus Trust, which aims to protect the Angolan black-and-white colobus monkey *(Colobus angolensis palliatus),* a once-common species now restricted to a few isolated pockets of forest south of Mombasa. Besides being vulnerable to traffic, the monkeys only eat the leaves of certain coastal trees and are particularly vulnerable to habitat destruction, a big problem in this area. The monkeys are also at risk from power lines and poaching. The Trust works to insulate power lines and reduce poaching.

It runs excellent tours of its headquarters, where you'll likely get to see a few orphaned or injured colobus and other monkeys undergoing the process of rehabilitation to the wild. With advance notice it can organise **forest walks** (per person KSh1000) in search of wilder primates and other creatures.

Kongo Mosque MOSQUE

At the far northern end of the beach road (turn right at the three-way intersection where the sealed road ends) is the 16th-century Kongo Mosque – Diani's last surviving relic of the ancient Swahili civilisations that once controlled the coast, and one of a tiny handful of coral mosques still in use in Kenya.

Tiwi & Diani Beaches

Watersports

All the big resorts either have their own dive schools or work with a local operator. Rates run around €75 to €90 for a reef dive. Most dive sites are under 29m, including the purpose-sunk 15m-MFV *Alpha Funguo* at 28m.

If you prefer to be above water than below it then Diani, with its near-constant trade winds, is rapidly gaining a name for itself as a kitesurfing hot spot.

Diani Marine DIVING
(☎3202367; www.dianimarine.com; Diani Marine Village) This German-run centre provides its own accommodation (see p245). Open-water diving courses cost €495.

Diving the Crab DIVING
(☎0723108108; www.divingthecrab.com; Sands at Nomad) The most popular diving outfit used by the big hotels. Open-water courses cost €480.

H_2O Extreme KITESURFING
(☎0721495876; www.h2o-extreme.com) The best regarded kitesurfing outfit in Diani offers half-day beginner courses for €100. It has locations at Sands at Nomad, Kenyaways Kite Village and Forty Thieves Beach Bar.

SX Scuba DIVING
(☎3202720, 0734601221; www.southerncrossscuba.com; Aqualand) Does open-water diving courses for €470.

Festivals & Events

Diani Rules SPORTS
(www.dianirules.com) This entertaining charity sports tournament in aid of the Kwale District Eye Centre is held at Diani Sea Lodge around the first weekend of June. It's more of an expat event than a tourist attraction, but if you're staying locally there's every chance you'll be invited to watch or asked to

DON'T MISS

ENTERING THE SACRED FOREST

Entering the *kaya* (sacred forests) of the Mijikenda can be one of the crowning experiences of a visit to the coast. Visiting these groves has elements of nature walk, historical journey and cultural experience.

Currently, the most visited and accessible *kaya* is **Kaya Kinondo** (off Map p242; www.kaya-kinondo-kenya.com, admission KSh700), near Diani Beach.

Before entering the Kaya Kinondo you have to remove headwear, promise not to kiss anyone inside the grove, wrap a black *kaniki* (sarong) around your waist and go with a guide; ours was Juma Harry, a local *askari* (security guard) and member of the Digo tribe.

The Mijikenda (Nine Homesteads) are actually nine subtribes united, to a degree, by culture, history and language. Yet each of the tribes – Chonyi, Digo, Duruma, Giriama, Jibana, Kambe, Kauma, Rabai and Ribe – remains distinct and speaks its own dialect of the Mijikenda language. Still, there is a binding similarity between the Nine Homesteads, and between the modern Mijikenda and their ancestors: their shared veneration of the *kaya*.

This historical connection becomes concrete when you enter the woods and realise – and there's no other word that fits here – they simply feel *old*.

Many trees are 600 years old, which corresponds to the arrival of the first Mijikenda from Singwaya, their semi-legendary homeland in southern Somalia. Cutting vegetation within the *kaya* is strictly prohibited, to the degree that visitors may not even take a stray twig or leaf from the forest.

Harry explains: 'When we are near the trees, we feel close to our ancestors. I know my father, and my grandfather, and his grandfather and so on, all cared for this tree.' Here Harry, who is a tough-looking character (and decidedly not a hippie), hugs a tree so large his arms cannot encircle it.

'We feel if the tree is old, it is talking. If you hold it and hear the wind,' and there is a pause for breezy effect, 'you can hear it talking.'

The preserved forests do not just facilitate dialogue with the ancestors; they provide a direct link to ecosystems that have been clear-felled out of existence elsewhere. A single *kaya* like Kinondo contains five possible endemic species within its 30 hectares. That's five endemic species – ie trees that only grow here – and 140 tree species classified as 'rare' within the space of a suburban residential block.

The main purpose of the *kaya* was to house the villages of the Mijikenda, which were located in a large central clearing. Entering the centre of a *kaya* required ritual knowledge to proceed through concentric circles of sacredness surrounding the node of the village; sacred talismans and spells were supposed to cause hallucinations that disoriented enemies who attacked the forest.

The *kaya* were largely abandoned in the 1940s, and conservative strains of Islam and Christianity have denigrated their value to the Mijikenda, but World Heritage status and a resurgence of interest in the forests will hopefully preserve them for future visitors. The *kaya* have lasted 600 years; with luck, the wind will speak through their branches for much longer.

Hopefully, more *kaya* will become the focus of responsible tourism initiatives by the time you read this: 11 of the forests were inscribed together as Kenya's fourth World Heritage site in July 2008.

join a team. Games include football (played with a rugby ball) and blindfold target-throwing, but the real endurance event is the three days of partying that accompanies proceedings.

Sleeping

Diani is largely known for its 20-odd high-end resorts, strung out all along the beach. Those listed here are among the best of the bunch, but don't expect a particularly 'authentic Africa' experience. Note that many of these places close for renovation between May and June, and most increase rates during the Christmas holiday up to mid-January.

Beach access can be a problem – your best bet is the path by Diani Beach Campsite or through Forty Thieves.

TOP CHOICE Kenyaways Kite Village BOUTIQUE HOTEL $$
(☎0728886821; www.thekenyaway.com; Diani Beach Rd; s/d from UK£30/50; wifi) This small and casual beachside hotel has a handful of brightly painted and funkily decorated rooms that come with a dollop of bohemian surf attitude. It's primarily a kitesurfers camp (it's the main base for H_2O Extreme; see p243), but is open to anyone. Easily one of the better value places in Diani.

TOP CHOICE Diani Marine Village BOUTIQUE HOTEL $$
(☎3202367; www.dianimarine.com; Diani Beach Rd; s/d from €49/78; pool wifi) The huge guest rooms at this dive resort are more than just a little bit appealing; with stone floors, a modern Swahili style, and a beautiful pool and gardens, this place represents superb value for money. The complimentary breakfast is fit for a king.

Stilts Eco-Lodge HUTS $
(☎0722523278; www.stiltsdiani.com; Diani Beach Rd; s/d KSh1500/2400) The only dedicated backpacker lodgings at the time of research, Stilts offers seven charming stilted tree houses set back in a sandy swathe of coastal forest. It attracts a young, fun-seeking crowd, has its own thatched lounge-bar area and is all-round enjoyable. It's located across the street from Forty Thieves. Book ahead.

Forest Dream Cottages COTTAGES $$
(☎3300220; www.forestdreamkenya.com; Diani Beach Rd; cottages from €89; air-con pool) This fantastic choice is set in an actual forest reserve. The thatched cottages are slightly kooky but always plush, and the little open-air rooftop lounge areas are great. Fish ponds, jacuzzis and fully fitted kitchens round out this secluded, tree-clad escape.

Flamboyant Beach Houses BOUTIQUE HOTEL $$$
(☎0722917013; www.dianibeachkenya.com; Diani Beach Rd; r/ste €145/245; air-con @ wifi pool) This intimate boutique hotel has breathtaking beach views, subtly decorated rooms with some of the nicest bathrooms this side of the Indian Ocean and a fantastic pool complex.

Warandale Cottages COTTAGES $$
(☎3202186; www.warandale.com; Diani Beach Rd; cottages from KSh7000; pool) These excellent cottages are strung along a pleasant garden-like retreat that is utterly Edenesque. The rooms are tastefully done in an understated Swahili style, with the right amount of dark wood and white walls to evoke Africa without a steaming surfeit of safari tat. Our picks of the litter are the Mlima and Kipepeo cottages.

Indian Ocean Beach Club RESORT $$$
(☎3203730; www.jacarandahotels.com; Diani Beach Rd; s/d full board KSh1740/2480; air-con @ wifi pool family) If you're going down the resort road then this is a good bet. The Beach Club consists of a series of pearl-bright Moorish-style houses along a long, low lawn that slopes into the lovely ocean. Inside, rooms are decorated in a breezy but luxurious spread of polished wood and ornate Swahili details. There are innumerable activities on offer.

Diani Reef Beach Resort RESORT $$$
(☎3202723; www.dianireef.com; Diani Beach Rd; s/d half board from €165/270; air-con @ pool family) Let's face it: when the floor of the lobby is a big aquarium, you know some crazy pampering and spoiling is going to ensue. This is as over-the-top as high-end luxury gets on the coast, stuffed with spas, bars, and restaurants, but for some it just might not be intimate enough.

DON'T MISS

BEST BEACHES

Beaches, beaches everywhere, but which is the best? We think you'll never want to stop building sandcastles on the following beaches:

Tiwi Beach (p240) Sunny, sandy and empty.

Diani Beach (p242) Despite the tourist resorts and the crowds, Diani Beach is stunning.

Takaungu (p257) The very definition of a perfect beach.

IT'S A SAILOR'S LIFE

The salty breeze and the high seas, it's a sailor's life for you and me. There's no more romantic a way to explore the Kenyan coast than sailing by dhow (a traditional sailing boat that has been used here for centuries) past slivers of sand, offshore coral islands and reefs bubbling with colourful fish. Several companies offer dhow trips down the coast to Funzi and Wasini Islands. **Pilli Pipa** (Map p242; ☎3203559; www.pillipipa.com; Colliers Centre, Diani Beach Rd, per person US$130) is probably the best known, but there are several other operators in Diani.

The **East African Whale Shark Trust** (off Map p242; ☎0720293156; www.giantsharks.org; Aqualand) is an excellent conservation body monitoring populations of the worlds largest fish – the harmless, plankton-feeding whale shark. In February and March (the busiest time for whale sharks) it occasionally opens survey and shark-tagging expeditions to paying guests. Trip costs vary depending on how much sponsorship money has been raised but averages US$150 per person, with a minimum of six people needed for a trip. Its offices are located in the Aqualand centre, about 4km south of Diani.

Diani Beachlets COTTAGES $
(☎2170209; www.dianibeachalets.com; Diani Beach Rd; cottages KSh2500) About the only beachside budget accommodation in Diani, this friendly, but somewhat ramshackle, place has cottages that are bright white on the outside but a little dingy on the inside. However, as you'll be spending all day on the equally bright white beach this isn't a problem.

Diani Classic Guest House HOTEL $
(☎0729643547; Ukunda; s/d KSh1000/1300) The cheapest budget option in town is, thankfully, excellent: sparkling clean and quite sizeable rooms, en-suite toilets with seats (we can't stress how rare this is for the price!), even balconies. Some of which, OK, look out onto Ukunda junction, but whatever. There are two branches – one just on Ukunda junction and the other a little way down the beach access road – and both offer the same experience. The only real drawback is the distance to the beach, and road noise.

Eating

All of the top-end hotels have on-site restaurants that tend to be pricey and fairly dull. Otherwise, you're spoilt for choice.

Self-caterers can stock up at the supermarkets in Diani's shopping centres, or in Ukunda.

Swahili Pot Restaurant KENYAN $
(☎3203890; Coral Beach Cottages; mains KSh150-230; ⊙lunch & dinner) This place and its culinary siblings (there are two other branches, one about halfway down the beach access road and another at Ukunda junction) do excellent traditional African and Swahili dishes. The title comes from the gimmick of selecting a meat and having it cooked in a variety of sauces and marinades, all of which are highly rated. Note that the three branches are also trading under their old name of African Pot Restaurant.

Coast Dishes KENYAN $
(Palm Ave, Ukunda; mains KSh300; ⊙lunch & dinner) Want to give the overpriced tourist restaurants a miss? Want to eat where the locals eat? Coast Dishes ticks both of these criteria and if you're sensible you'll opt for a steaming great bowl of biryani, the house special.

Shan-e-Punjab Restaurant INDIAN $
(☎3202116; Diani Complex; mains KSh350-800; ⊙lunch & dinner) One of the only dedicated Indian options in town, this restaurant could easily hold its own against any high-class curry house in the world. The food is well-spiced, rich and delicious. It often closes in the low season.

Aniello's ITALIAN $$
(☎0733740408; Colliers Centre; mains KSh300-850; ⊙lunch & dinner) It (kind of) looks like an Italian street cafe, it's filled with Italians and it's run by an Italian; what we're not-so-subtly saying is Aniello's is the place to pop in for pastas, pizzas and osso-bucco goodness.

Ali Barbour's Cave Restaurant SEAFOOD $$
(☎3202033; Diani Beach Rd; mains KSh550-1200; ⊙from 7pm) Well, they've got coral mosques and palaces on the coast – why not a restaurant set in a coral cave? The focus here is seafood, cooked up poshly and generally quite tasty. It's served under the stars, jagged rocks and fairy lights.

Rongai Fast Food KENYAN $
(Palm Ave, Ukunda; mains KSh200; ⊙lunch & dinner) This rowdy joint is a popular place for *nyama choma* (barbecued meat); if you've been missing your roast meat and boiled maize, Rongai's here for you.

Drinking & Entertainment

Be aware that there are many prostitutes and gigolos in the bars in Diani.

Forty Thieves Beach Bar BAR $
(Diani Beach Rd) Of all the phrases you'll hear in Diani, 'Meet you at Forty's?' is probably the most common, and the most welcome. This is easily the best bar on the strip. It has movie nights and live bands, there's a pub quiz at least once a week and it's open until the last guest leaves. It's a very popular place to eat as well, but in truth the food is highly overpriced and bland in the extreme.

Shakatak CLUB $
(Diani Beach Rd) The only full-on nightclub in Diani not attached to a hotel is Shakatak; it's quite hilariously seedy, but can be fun once you know what to expect. Like most big Kenyan clubs, food is served at all hours.

Kim4Love DJ $
(www.kim4love.com) Not a venue but a person, this local DJ and musician puts on regular summer concerts and events to promote tourism. They're usually held at Kim's beach bar, by the former Two Fishes hotel – look out for the sign along Diani Beach Rd.

ℹ Information

Dangers & Annoyances

Take taxis at night and try not to be on the beach by yourself after dark. Souvenir sellers are an everyday nuisance, sex tourism is pretty evident and beach boys are a hassle; you will hear a lot of, 'Hey, one love one love' Rasta-speak spouted by guys trying to sell you drugs or scam you into supporting fake charities for 'local schools'. Yes, very 'one love'.

Emergency

Diani Beach Hospital (☎3202435; www.dianibeachhospital.com; Diani Beach Rd; ⊙24hr)
Police (☎3202229; Ukunda)

Internet Access

Baba's Bistro & Cyber Cafe (Forty Thieves Beach Bar; per hr KSh60; ⊙from 9am)

Internet resources

Diani Beach (www.dianibeach.com) Includes information on Tiwi and Funzi Island.

Money

Barclays Bank (Barclays Centre) With ATM.
Kenya Commercial Bank (Ukunda) With ATM.

Post

Diani Beach post office (Diani Beach Rd)
Ukunda post office (Ukunda)

Tourist Information

i-Point (Barclays Centre; ⊙8.30am-6pm Mon-Fri, 9am-4pm Sat) Private information office with plenty of brochures.

ℹ Getting There & Around

Bus & Matatu

Numerous matatus run south from the Likoni ferry directly to Ukunda (KSh70, 30 minutes) and onwards to Msambweni and Lunga Lunga. From the Diani junction in Ukunda, matatus run down to the beach all day for KSh40; check before boarding to see if it's a Reef service (heading north along the strip, then south) or a Neptune one (south beach only).

Car & Motorcycle

Motorcycles can be hired from **Fredlink Tours** (Map p242; ☎3300253; www.motorbike-safari.com; Diani Plaza). A full motorcycle licence, passport and credit card or cash deposit are required for rental. The company also arranges motorcycle safaris.

You can rent cars from **Glory Car Hire** (Map p242; ☎3203076; Diani Beach shopping centre) and **Ketty Tours** (Map p242; ☎23203582; www.kettysafari.com; Diani Beach Rd).

Taxi

Taxis hang around Ukunda junction and all the main shopping centres; most hotels and restaurants will also have a couple waiting at night. Fares should be between KSh150 and KSh800, depending on the distance.

Gazi Island

About 20km south of Diani (and a world away from its international resort scene), is Gazi, where you'll find a village of friendly Digo Mijikenda folk, a big dollop of African rural life and an excellent **mangrove boardwalk** (KSh150) run by a local women's group. The boardwalk is a sun-blanched, pleasantly rickety affair that winds back into a wine-dark lagoon webbed over by red, orange, green and grey mangrove plants; nearby, the husks of old dhows bake into driftwood on the sand. Previously, the mangroves were cut for timber, which led to extreme beach erosion; today both the shore and the mangroves are being restored, and a glut of entrepreneurial activities has grown around the boardwalk including oyster farming and bee-keeping. The fare for the walk goes into improving the boardwalk, buying school textbooks and paying teachers at local schools.

Homestay-style accommodation is available in Gazi in the house just behind the telephone mast (ask around – everyone knows it). We were told the price was KSh1200 with breakfast, but much confusion ensued when we asked if that was per person or per room. The accommodation is much more swish than you'd expect from muddy old Gazi.

Shimoni & Wasini Island

☎040

The final pearls in the tropical beach necklace that stretches south of Mombasa are the mainland village of Shimoni and the idyllic island of Wasini, located about 76km south of Likoni.

Shimoni and Wasini (the name of the island's main village and the island) are usually visited as part of a package tour that includes a dhow trip to Kisite Marine National Park. Every morning in high season a convoy of coaches arrives carrying tourists from Diani Beach; independent travellers are still fairly rare in these parts. This is something of a surprise because excursions to the marine park are easy to organise directly with the local boatmen. Wasini in particular is ripe with the ingredients required for a perfect backpacker beach-side hideaway; it has that sit-under-a-mango-tree-and-do-nothing-all-day vibe, a coastline licked with pockets of white sand and cultural and natural world interest. In fact the only things it doesn't have are banana-pancake traveller cafes and backpacker hostels, and it's all the better for it. Although you wouldn't know it by looking at the group tours, this is a fairly conservative Muslim area, and women travelling independently may want to cover up their legs and shoulders.

WORTH A TRIP

FUNZI ISLAND

Funzi is a small mangrove island about 35km south of Diani that tends to be visited as part of package tours organised through agencies and hotels to the north. The main attraction (besides the beaches and palm trees) is birdwatching and croc-spotting.

Arranging your own boat trip is easy if you're in a group: boatmen in the mainland village of **Bodo**, west of Funzi, ask around KSh2500 to KSh3000 per person with a minimum of three people required (or one person with a really big wallet!), or you can negotiate individual dolphin- and crocodile-spotting trips up the Ramisi River.

If you arrive independently, you can generally count on the permanent presence of an accompanying guide from the moment you land, which is actually no bad thing, as they'll show you around the island and can arrange accommodation in the village for around KSh500 to KSh800, with meals available for a further KSh500 (all negotiable).

You can also stay in the **Funzi Keys Lodge** (☎0733900446; www.thefunzikeys.com; s/d from US$450/680; ⏲Jul-Mar; ❄🏊), which is a series of exclusive Swahili villas. The property may not seamlessly blend into the beach, but it does manage to strike a harmonious (and luxurious) Zen note with its surroundings.

To get here, take a matatu from Ukunda towards Lunga Lunga and ask for the Bodo turn-off (KSh100). The village is another 1.5km along a sandy track – you can take a *boda-boda* (bicycle taxi), though they'll try and charge you KSh150, or get someone to show you the way.

TAG & BRAG

While the idea of wrestling a huge marlin on the open sea has macho allure, catches of billfish in the Indian Ocean are getting smaller all the time. The biggest threat to game fish is overfishing by commercial tuna companies, who routinely hook other pelagic fish as so-called 'bycatch'. Pollution and falling stocks of prey are also having a serious knock-on effect. Some large species are believed to have declined by as much as 80% since the 1970s; sharks are particularly vulnerable.

You can do your bit to help sustain shark and billfish populations by tagging your catch and releasing it back into the ocean. Most deep-sea fishing companies provide anglers with a souvenir photo and official recognition of their catch, then release the fish to fight another day, carrying tags that will allow scientists to discover more about these magnificent predators.

SHIMONI

The mainland village of Shimoni is the departure point for boats to Wasini, and can be a bit of a circus when the tour buses rock up. But after sunset, when the day trippers go home, a tranquil Swahili vibe returns.

Sights & Activities

Slave Caves HISTORICAL SITE
(KSh400; ⌚8.30-10.30am & 1.30-6pm) These caves, where slaves were supposedly kept before being loaded onto boats, are the main attraction in Shimoni. A custodian takes you around the dank caverns to illustrate this little-discussed part of East African history. Actual evidence that slaves were kept here is a little thin, but as piles of empty votive rosewater bottles indicate, the site definitely has significance for believing locals.

Shimoni Reef FISHING
(☎041-4473969; www.shimonireeflodge.com; Shimoni; trips per day from US$700) The Pemba Channel is famous for deep-sea fishing, and Shimoni Reef can arrange a variety of different offshore fishing trips.

WASINI ISLAND

Wasini Island is a slowly decaying delight of coral houses and sticky alleyways. There are no roads or running water, and the only electricity comes from generators. Long ago Lamu and Zanzibar must have felt a little like this. It's worth poking about the ancient **Swahili ruins** and the **coral gardens** (KSh200), a bizarre landscape of exposed coral reefs with a boardwalk for viewing, on the edge of Wasini village.

Sights & Activities

Kisite Marine National Park WILDLIFE RESERVE
(adult/child US$20/10) Off the south coast of Wasini, this marine park, which also incorporates the Mpunguti Marine National Reserve, is one of the best in Kenya. The park covers 28 sq km of pristine coral reefs and offers excellent diving and snorkelling. You have a reasonable chance of seeing dolphins in the Shimoni Channel, and humpback whales are sometimes spotted between August and October.

There are various organised trips to the marine park but these tend to be outside ventures and don't always contribute a great deal to the local communities. It's easy to organise your own boat trip with a local captain – the going rate is KSh2500 per person for a group (or KSh10,000 per boat), including lunch and a walk in the coral gardens on Wasini Island. Masks and snorkels can be hired for KSh200 (fins are discouraged as they may damage the reef).

The best time to dive and snorkel is between October and March. Avoid diving in June, July and August because of rough seas, silt and poor visibility. During the monsoon season you can snorkel over the **coral gardens** (adult/child US$5/3) just opposite the pier in Wasini. Although the marine life can't compare with that of the national park, it's completely sheltered from the worst of the monsoon weather. It gets busy with tour boats, but if you're a sailor without a ship you can dive in straight off Wasini village.

Mkwiro Village VILLAGE
Mkwiro is a small village on the unvisited end of Wasini Island. There are few facilities here and there's not a lot to do, but the gorgeous hour-long walk from Wasini village, through woodlands, past tiny hamlets and along the edge of mangrove forests, is more than reason enough to visit.

WASINI TOURS

Various companies offer organised dhow tours for snorkelling, and there are loads of private operators hanging out around the piers at either Shimoni or Wasini. Hotels can normally recommend someone reliable as well. Tours generally follow the same pattern: leave Shimoni pier at 9am, travel through Kisite Marine National Park, stop for snorkelling and beach time, head for Wasini for a seafood lunch, visit the coral gardens and return to Shimoni around 3pm or 4pm.

Charlie Claw's (Map p242; ☎040-3203154, 0722410599; www.wasini.com; office Jadini Beach Hotel, Diani Beach) and **Pilli Pipa** (Map p242; ☎3203559; www.pillipipa.com; office Colliers Centre, Diani Beach) are good outfits offering well-managed dhow trips. Trips cost from US$130 to US$150 per person.

There are some wonderful, calm swimming spots around the village. Local children are sure to take you by the hand and show you the best places to dive in.

The Mkwiro Youth Group can help you dig a little deeper into village life by organising village tours and cooking classes. It's all a little vague and prices are highly flexible, but the man you need to speak to about organising these is **Shafii Vuyaa** (☎0728741098).

You can arrange homestays in Mkwiro for roughly KSh650, which should include a nice home-cooked coastal dinner.

Sleeping & Eating

Mpunguti Lodge HOTEL $
(☎0710562494; Wasini Island; r per person KSh1850, with shared bathroom KSh950) The rooms here, which overlook the delicious turquoise ocean, are uncomplicated, with mosquito nets and small verandahs. Running water is collected in rain barrels and doesn't always look pleasant! The food is excellent (ask for the seagrass starter, possibly the nicest thing we ate on the Kenyan coast), and it's a common lunch stop for boat trips. It's on the edge of Wasini village.

Shimoni Reef LODGE $$$
(041-4473969, 020-2327669; www.shimonireeflodge.com; Shimoni; s/d US$180/300; ❄) This waterfront fishing camp has a pleasant series of white-washed cottages, but considering the price we'd have hoped for more of a 'wow' factor. Fortunately, walk-in guests are normally assumed to be residents and thus are offered massive discounts which make it much more worthwhile.

KWS Bandas & Camping BANDAS $
(☎0728854118; Shimoni; camping KSh200, bandas US$25) The reasonably well-maintained *bandas* are set in monkey-infested forest on the edge of the KWS grounds. They'd be great if you were in a group but it'd be a bit spooky staying here alone.

Shimoni Gardens BANDAS $
(☎0712023216; Shimoni; banda KSh4000) The unkempt *bandas* at this place, 2.5km west of Shimoni, would be overpriced for anywhere else in Kenya, but in expensive Shimoni they come out at quite good value. If the *bandas* themselves can be faulted, the peaceful setting certainly can't.

Getting There & Around

There are matatus every hour or so between Likoni and Shimoni (KSh300, 1½ hours) until about 6pm. It's best to be at Likoni by 6.30am if you want to get to Shimoni in time to catch one of the dhow sailings.

Getting to Wasini island is easy enough. 'Matatu' boats charge KSh50 per person, although frankly the only way you'd ever get to pay this is if you get yourself reincarnated as a Kenyan. Otherwise you're looking at KSh250 to KSh300 for the crossing.

Lunga Lunga

There isn't much at Lunga Lunga apart from the Tanzanian border crossing, which is open 24 hours. It's 6.5km from the Kenyan border post to the Tanzanian border post at Horohoro – *boda-bodas* (bicycle taxis) run between the two border posts throughout the day (KSh50). From Horohoro, there are numerous matatus and buses to Tanga (matatu/bus KSh1500/2000). Matatus to Likoni cost KSh250.

NORTH OF MOMBASA

From Nyali to Shanzu, it's all big-box beach resorts, highway junctions, bottle-green palms and acres of sisal. But there are sights of interest for independent

North of Mombasa

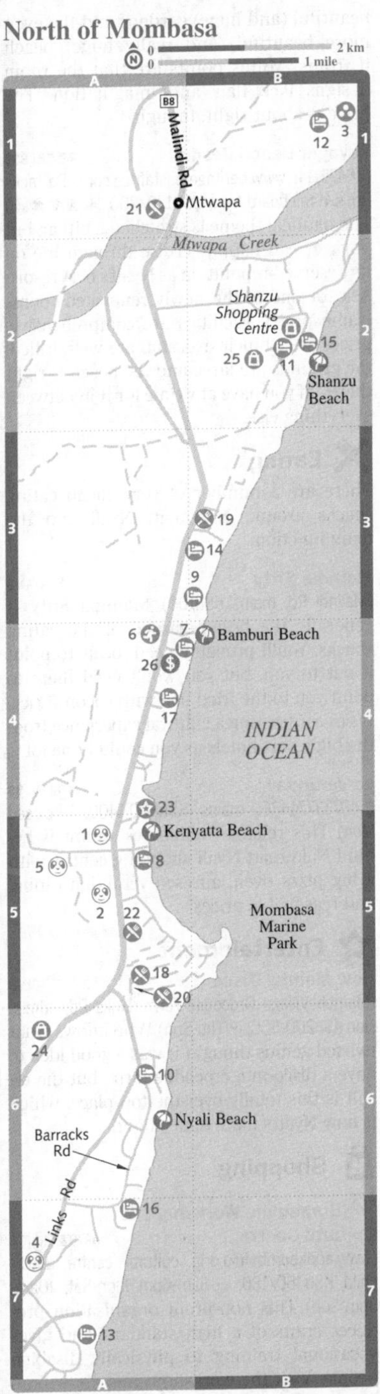

North of Mombasa

Sights

1 Baobab Adventure ... A5
2 Haller Park ... A5
3 Jumba la Mtwana ... B1
4 Mamba Village Crocodile Farm ... A7
Ngomongo Villages ... (see 25)
5 Nguuni Wildlife Sanctuary ... A5

Activities, Courses & Tours

6 Bamburi Forest Trails ... A4
Prosurf Extreme ... (see 13)

Sleeping

7 Bamburi Beach Hotel ... A4
8 Camper's Haven Beach Resort ... A5
9 Kahama Hotel ... B3
10 Mombasa Backpackers ... A6
11 Mombasa Safari Inn ... B2
12 Mtwapa Beach Villas ... B1
13 Nyali Beach Hotel ... A7
14 Papillon ... B3
15 Serena Beach Hotel & Spa Kenya ... B2
16 Voyager Beach Resort ... A7
17 Whitesands Sarova Hotel ... A4

Eating

18 La Veranda ... A5
19 Maharajah Restaurant ... B3
20 Mamma Sitty ... A5
21 Moorings Restaurant ... A1
22 Splendid View Restaurant ... A5
Yul's Beach Bar ... (see 7)

Entertainment

New Mamba Disco ... (see 4)
23 Pirates ... A4

Shopping

24 Bombolulu Workshops & Cultural Centre ... A6
25 Shanzu Transitional Workshop ... B2

Information

26 Barclays Bank ... A4

travellers. These include the stunning Swahili ruins of Jumba la Mtwana, the raucous fishing village of Mtwapa and some nice nature parks. Beyond that, the high-end resorts are hardly the 'real Kenya' and from December to April, seaweed often clogs the sand. Still, for most of the year this is tropical pleasantness, if not paradise. Expect lots of *makuti* (thatch) chic.

Nyali Beach

041

You won't be on the road for long before the first string of resorts looms off the highway. Nyali Beach (Map p251) is within the orbit of Mombasa's northern suburbs, and it's quite easy to access the city if you're staying here.

Sights & Activities

Mamba Village Crocodile Farm ZOO
(Links Rd; adult/child KSh650/350; 8.30am-7pm) This is the largest reptile farm in Kenya, but be aware that some of the crocodiles here become handbags and fried reptile bites. Crocodile feeding time is at 5pm.

Prosurf Extreme WINDSURFING
(0733622882; www.prosurfkenya.com; Nyali Beach Hotel) Nyali Beach has world-class wind- and kitesurfing conditions. Prosurf Extreme, one of the best-known schools on this part of the Kenyan coast, charges KSh6500 for a two-hour kitesurf lesson, and from KSh2500 for windsurf lessons. Sadly, though, the staff could be more helpful.

Sleeping

Hotels are clearly signposted from relevant roundabouts on Links Rd.

TOP CHOICE **Mombasa Backpackers** BACKPACKERS $
(0701561233; www.mombasabackpackers.com; Mwamba Drive 69, Nyali; dm/s/d without breakfast KSh800/1200/2000;) If you thought backpacker hostels had to be cramped and grimy places, be prepared for a surprise. This is a huge white mansion surrounded by lush, coconut busy gardens (with camping areas). The spacious rooms and dorms are well-maintained and there's a decent swimming pool. There are frequent party nights and the staff can organise all manner of activities. Anyone over the age of about 23 might find the 'student halls of residence' atmosphere off-putting. Note that there have been some muggings in the vicinity of the hostel (which is a couple of kilometres north of the centre in Nyali).

Nyali Beach Hotel RESORT $$
(474640; Beach Rd; s/tw half board from US$84/100;) At the southern end of the beach is the oldest resort in Nyali. If you like small and intimate then you'll hate this place – it's HUGE. Plus points are the beautiful (and yes, huge) pool, the equally beautiful (and huge) gardens and the even more beautiful (and really huge) beach it fronts. Minus points are that the room designs lack flair and imagination. The price is about right, though.

Voyager Beach Resort RESORT $$$
(475114; www.heritage-eastafrica.com; Barracks Rd; s/d full board from US$130/200;) The nautical theme is stretched a bit far, but Voyager can happily cruise through life on its deserved reputation as Nyali's best resort. Ask for one of the newly renovated rooms (same price). Facilities are comprehensive, prices are all-inclusive, staff are well drilled, the grounds are large and the beach is right there – if you have any time for it in between everything else.

Eating

There are a number of very cheap eating shacks around Nakumatt Nyali and the main junction.

Mamma Sitty KENYAN $
(Malindi Rd; mains KSh100) Mamma Sitty is generally the best regarded of the eating shacks. You'll probably need locals to point it out to you, but you won't need them to point you to the fried fish with coconut rice. It's as contrasting a cultural experience from the big resort hotels as you could hope for.

La Veranda ITALIAN $$
(0733774436; mains KSh800-1400; closed Mon) This reliable Italian restaurant is behind Nakumatt Nyali shopping centre, with a big pizza oven, alfresco verandah dining and reasonable prices.

Entertainment

New Mamba Disco CLUB
(Mamba Village Crocodile Farm, Links Rd; admission KSh200-500; Thu-Sun) Who knows what twisted genius thought it was a good idea to have a disco in a crocodile farm, but the result is this totally over-the-top place, which is now Nyali's main dance floor.

Shopping

Bombolulu Workshops & Cultural Centre ARTS & CRAFTS
(www.apdkbombolulu.org; cultural centre adult/child KSh360/180; 8am-6pm Mon-Sat, 10am-3pm Sun) This non-profit organisation produces crafts of a high standard and gives vocational training to physically disabled people. Visit the workshops and showroom

for free to buy jewellery, clothes, carvings and other crafts, or enter the cultural centre to tour mock-ups of traditional homesteads. The turn-off for the centre is on the left about 3km north of Nyali Bridge. Bombolulu matatus run here from Msanifu Kombo Rd, and Bamburi services also pass the centre.

Getting There & Away

From Mombasa, Nyali Beach is reached via Nyali Rd, which branches off the main road north just after Nyali Bridge. There are regular matatus to and from Mombasa (KSh30).

Bamburi Beach

☎041

Bamburi (Map p251) is a bit of a rarity in these parts, in that it's just as popular with Africans as it is with Europeans. The top hotels tend to attract a foreign crowd, while Kenyatta Beach, near the south end of Bamburi, thumps to the beat of hundreds of holidaying Kenyans.

Sights & Activities

TOP CHOICE **Baobab Adventure** WILDLIFE RESERVE
(www.bamburicement.com; Malindi Rd) Funnily enough, one of the prettiest nature reserves on the Mombasa north coast has been carved out by a cement company. In a nice example of environmentalism and entrepreneurship finding common ground, Baobab Adventure is the child of seemingly unlikely parents: Bamburi Cement and a group of conservationists. The pair has worked hand-in-hand to convert industrial slag into a forested sanctuary cut through with animal parks and nature trails.

The main attraction is **Haller Park** (adult/child KSh800/400; ⏲8am-5pm), a genuinely lovely escape from the crass commercialism of the resorts. There's a fish farm, reptile park, wildlife sanctuary (in a rehabilitated quarry!) and other green goodness. Guided walks around the park last about 1½ hours.

A couple of kilometres up the road (opposite the Bamburi Beach Hotel) are the **Bamburi Forest Trails** (adult/child KSh300/150; ⏲7am-6pm), a network of walking and cycling trails through reforested cement workings, with a butterfly pavilion and terrace (it's also known as the Butterfly Pavilion) from which to catch the sunset. North of the main cement plant is **Nguuni Wildlife Sanctuary**, where herds of ostriches, elands and oryxes are farmed. Tours here must be booked in advance through Baobab Adventure.

The various parts of the Baobab Adventure are well signposted from the highway north of Mombasa and have well-marked bus stops.

SEX ON THE BEACH

Visitors to Kenya will soon notice that sex tourism is very common on parts of the coast, and occurs in different contexts, from petrol stations to high-end restaurants.

There is a sizeable number of Western men with younger Kenyan boys and girls, and older Western women with younger Kenyan boys. Assuming nobody is actually underage (which does happen) then there's nothing illegal in this. Sometimes romance is sparked, though some beach boys proudly display long lists of girlfriends on their mobile phones. It's difficult to judge how many Westerners visit Kenya to seek brief, beachside affairs; one Reuter's article quotes the figure as one in five Western women who visit the coast.

Many Kenyans are scandalised by the sight of both older Western men with teenage Kenyans and the sight of Western women with significantly younger Kenyan men. While they may recognise these relationships are legal, many also find them extremely distasteful and feel that sex tourism destroys the fabric of their society.

It's often assumed by both foreign tourists and Kenyans that it's the Westerner who is in the wrong, but of course nothing is clear cut. A major exposé in a big Kenyan newspaper a couple of years ago revealed that some married Kenyan couples in Malindi actually choose to 'break up' during the tourist season and seek foreign 'lovers' for financial gain.

Areas like Bamburi, Shanzu, Malindi and Mtwapa attract the largest number of sex tourists.

Mombasa Marine National Park & Reserve WILDLIFE RESERVE
(adult/child US$15/10) The offshore Mombasa Marine National Park has impressive marine life, although it cops some pollution from industry in the area.

You can hire glass-bottomed boats for a couple of hours for around KSh2000 (excluding park fees), but you need to be seriously silver tongued to whittle the price down to that.

Sleeping

TOP CHOICE **Kahama Hotel** HOTEL $
(Nairobi 020-3507205; www.kahamahotel.co.ke; s/d from KSh3150/3350;) Thank you, thank you. At last a Kenyan hotelier has realised that charging the earth and delivering rubbish doesn't equal happy repeat-customers. Instead, what the Kahama hotel delivers is nothing short of fantastic value for money. The rooms are modern, spotless and stylishly decorated with lots of natural lines and driftwood furnishings. Throw in free wi-fi, a huge pool and a cool cafe next door and the result is a lot of happy guests. The only real downside is that it's not overlooking the beach (which is a two-minute walk away).

Papillon HOTEL $
(5487493; Malindi Rd; r from KSh3500;) We know folks here like their *makuti* (thatched roof of palm leaves), but this is just ridiculous. The lobby is like thatch taken to post-modern heights of hugeness, overlooking an equally enormous restaurant stuffed with all manner of Africana. The beach is 100m beyond the compound, and rooms are good, although toilets are occasionally wanting. It offers great value for this area.

Whitesands Sarova Hotel RESORT $$$
(5485926; www.sarovahotels.com; s/d half board from US$180/260;) The Whitesands is beautiful: a seafront Swahili castle of airy corridors, marble accents and wooden detailing uplifted by every flash, modern amenity you can imagine. It's considered one of the best high-end resorts on the coast, and with good reason. It's also big. Really big.

Bamburi Beach Hotel RESORT $$
(5485611; www.bamburibeachkenya.com; s/d half board €130/170;) This tidy little complex has direct access to the beach, and a choice of appealing bamboo-finished hotel rooms and self-catering rooms (with outdoor kitchens). There's a nice beachfront bar with a big shaggy *makuti* thatch.

Camper's Haven Beach Resort HOTEL $$
(0720240991; campers_haven@yahoo.com; camping per tent KSh400-800, s/d KSh3600/5400) About the closest the Bamburi strip gets to a cheap beach hotel. The rooms are pleasant, but nothing more, and be warned that this place has a disco, and it is loud. We're not sure how anyone can sleep in the rooms, let alone the tents, given the party raging outside. All that said, if you're looking for fun, it's a good party to join.

Eating

Splendid View Restaurant INDIAN $$
(Malindi Rd; mains KSh300-600; lunch & dinner, closed Mon) Sister to the original branch in Mombasa, this is the more attractive sibling and has a wider menu, serving customary Indian cuisine and a handful of Western dishes. Ironically, the views aren't all that splendid.

Yul's Beach Bar INTERNATIONAL $$
(Bamburi Beach Hotel; mains KSh 400-700; 9am-11pm) Few places in Bamburi have received such enthusiastic recommendations from locals and tourists alike who swear that this is the best Bamburi has to offer. The menu runs the gamut from burgers to pizzas to pastas to curries, and it apparently makes 60 flavours of ice cream.

Maharajah Restaurant INDIAN $$
(Indiana Beach Hotel; mains KSh350-600; dinner Wed-Mon, plus lunch Sat & Sun) A stylish Indian restaurant with good veg and nonveg food.

Entertainment

From here to Malindi, the nightlife can be dodgy with lots of sex tourism evident.

Pirates CLUB
(Kenyatta Beach; Fri & Sat KSh200; Wed-Sat) A huge complex of water slides and bars transforms into the strip's rowdiest nightclub from Wednesday to Saturday in high season, blazing into the small hours. During the day it's surprisingly wholesome, with family 'fun shows' every Saturday.

Getting There & Away

Matatus run from Mombasa to Bamburi for KSh70. If you're driving yourself, be aware that the roads near Kenyatta Beach can get *insane* with a combination of matatus and drunk holiday-makers – never a good mix.

Shanzu Beach

Just north of Bamburi is Shanzu Beach (Map p251). The coastline here is beautiful, but it's dominated by all-inclusive resorts. Outside of these areas, Shanzu is not much more than a highway fuel stop and string of seedy bars.

Sights & Activities

Ngomongo Villages CULTURAL VILLAGE
(adult/child KSh850/425; ⌚9am-5pm Tue-Sun) Maybe best described as a 'tribal theme park', this place attempts to give visitors a glimpse of eight of Kenya's different tribal groups in one place. Although it's touristy, the tours are good fun and you can try your hand at various tribal activities such as dancing, archery and pounding maize.

Sleeping & Eating

Most visitors eat at their hotel, but there are several restaurants in the Shanzu Shopping Centre offering almost identical menus of pizzas and other European favourites for between KSh350 and KSh700.

Serena Beach Hotel & Spa Kenya RESORT **$$$**
(☎Nairobi 020-3548771; www.serenahotels.com; s/d from US$160/235; ❄@☎≋♿) Serena's only Kenyan beach resort is so extensive that it's styled on a traditional Swahili village – the pathways around the tree-filled complex even have street names. The split-level rooms are equally impressive, and the design lends an incongruous intimacy.

Mombasa Safari Inn HOTEL **$**
(☎0736417575; s/d KSh950/1450) This small, cheerful and authentically Kenyan place has a few dark, basic but adequate rooms set behind a busy bar that may as well be sponsored by Tusker, so many advertising posters does it have.

Shopping

Shanzu Transitional Workshop ARTS & CRAFTS
(shanzuworkshop@yahoo.com; ⌚8am-12.30pm & 2-5.30pm Mon-Fri, 8am-12.30pm Sat) Run by the Girl Guides Association, this centre provides training for handicapped women and sells their crafts for them.

Getting There & Away

Public transport plying the route between Mombasa and Malindi or Mtwapa pass the turn-off to Shanzu (KSh30), where a crowd of *boda-bodas* tout for rides to the hotels (KSh10). Hourly matatus from Mtwapa stop at the resorts (KSh30) before heading to Mombasa. The Metro Mombasa bus 31 to Mtwapa also comes through here; look out for the yellow 'Via Serena' sign in the windscreen.

Mtwapa

☎041

At first glance, Mtwapa (Map p251) just looks like a busy roadside service town, but the small fishing village at its heart has a lovely setting with fine views of Mtwapa Creek, and makes a great stop for a scenic supper.

Several companies based in Mtwapa offer deep-sea fishing for marlin and other large billfish. The fishing trips organised by **Howard Lawrence-Brown** (☎0722831464) receive good feedback.

Sights

Jumba la Mtwana RUINS
(adult/child KSh500/100; ⌚8am-6pm) These Swahili ruins, just north of Mtwapa Creek, are easily comparable in terms of archaeological grandeur to the more famous Gede Ruins (p263), but unlike at those, you're likely to have Jumba la Mtwana largely to yourself. In the dying evening light, your imagination will be able to run riot with thoughts of lost treasures, ghosts, pirates and abandoned cities. The remains of buildings, with their exposed foundations for mangrove beam poles; ablution tanks; floors caked with millipedes and swarms of safari ants; and the twisting arms of 600-year-old trees – leftover from what may have been a nearby *kaya* – are quite magical. Jumba la Mtwana means 'Big House of Slaves', and while there is no hard historical evidence to back the theory, locals believe the town was once an important slave port.

Slaves may or may not have been traded here, but turtle shell, rhino horn and ambergris (sperm-whale intestinal secretions, used for perfume – mmm) all were. In return, Jumba received goods like Chinese dishes, the fragments of which can be seen in the floors of some buildings today. While here, keep your eyes peeled for the upper-wall holes that mark where mangrove support beams were affixed; the House of Many Doors, which is believed to have been a guesthouse (no breakfast included); and dried out, 40m-deep wells. You'd be remiss to miss the Mosque by the Sea, which overlooks a crystal-sharp vista of the Indian

Ocean (and don't forget your swimmers for a splash in the empty waters here).

Notice the Arabic inscription on the stela adjacent to the nearby graveyard: 'Every Soul Shall Taste Death'. Underneath is a small hole representing the opening all humans must pass through on the way to paradise. There are three other mosques on the site, and evidence of extensive sanitation facilities in all the main buildings. A handy guidebook may be available, and the custodian gives excellent tours for a small gratuity.

Sleeping & Eating

Should you want to stay in Mtwapa, there are several cheap and noisy hotels in the town centre – none of which are the sort of places where you'd want to spend an extended holiday.

Moorings Restaurant SEAFOOD $$
(☎5485260; mains KSh500-1000) This popular expat hang-out is on a floating pontoon on the north shore of Mtwapa Creek. It's a fine place for a beer and serves great seafood with a view. The turn-off is just after the Mtwapa bridge – follow the signs down to the water's edge.

Getting There & Away

Regular matatus and buses run from Mtwapa to Mombasa (KSh50) and Malindi (KSh80).

Kilifi

☎041

Like Mtwapa to its south, Kilifi is a gorgeous river estuary with effortlessly picture-perfect views from its massive road bridge. Many white Kenyans have yachts moored in the creek and there are numerous beach houses belonging to artists, writers and adventurers from around the globe.

The main reasons that most travellers come here are to stay at one of the pleasant beach resorts at the mouth of the creek or to visit the ruins of Mnarani, high on a bluff on the south bank of the creek.

The town centre has the full range of traveller facilities.

Sights

Mnarani RUINS
(adult/child KSh500/250; ⏲7am-6pm) The partly-excavated atmospheric and deliciously peaceful ruins of the Swahili city of Mnarani are high on a bluff just west of the old ferry landing-stage on the southern bank of Kilifi Creek. The site was occupied from the end of the 14th century to around the first half of the 17th century, when it was abandoned following sieges by Galla tribespeople from Somalia and the failure of the water supply.

The best preserved ruin is the Great Mosque, with its finely carved inscription around the mihrab (prayer niche showing the direction of Mecca). Under the minaret lies the skeleton of the supposed founder of the town. A group of carved tombs (including a restored pillar tomb), a small mosque dating back to the 16th century and parts of the town wall are also preserved.

Don't miss the monstrous old baobab trees just beyond the walls of the main complex. The largest, a right royal 900-year-old beauty, is the site of frequent religious offerings by the local (Muslim) community – a throw back to pre-Islamic times.

An informative guide is normally available to show you around the ruins (tip expected).

Kilifi Creek BEACH
The beach on either side of the creek is lovely and doesn't suffer the seaweed problems of the beaches further south, but most of the frontage is private property. Hotels and local boatmen can arrange sailing trips around the creek for about KSh500 per person.

Reptile Rescue Park ZOO
(admission incl in Mnarani ticket; ⏲7am-6pm) Next to the entrance to the Mnarani ruins, the Reptile Rescue Park houses a fascinating collection of snakes and other slithery reptiles rescued at Kenya's international airports from the clutches of smugglers or retrieved from the houses of nervous villagers. The snakes are later released back into the wild. Although admission is free with entrance to the Mnarani ruins, it's actually a privately run affair and relies entirely on donations.

Sleeping & Eating

TOP CHOICE **Dhows Inn** HOTEL $
(☎0722375214; dhowsinn_kilifi@yahoo.com; Malindi Rd; s/d KSh1200/1800) On the main road south of Kilifi Creek, this small hostelry is well-maintained and is a real travellers institution. It has simple but comfortable and immaculate rooms around a garden, and offers exceptional value for the coast. The Mnarani ruins are within walking distance, and it has a popular bar and restaurant.

WORTH A TRIP

TAKAUNGU

If you want breathtaking Indian Ocean beaches and utter tranquillity, then Takaungu fits the bill. The creek here, with its luxurious blue waters framed by an explosion of greenery and pockets of golden cove beaches, will do the aforementioned breath-stealing. And for seclusion, the exposed ocean-facing beaches (1km east of the village) are unlikely to contain a single other footprint.

The village of Takaungu is a real Swahili fishing village that is absolutely untouched by tourism. This of course means there are no facilities whatsoever, but it's easy to find a very basic room in someone's house for around KSh1000, including meals.

Takaungu is just south of Kilifi and any bus or matatu between there and Mombasa can drop you at the junction from which it's a pleasant (but hot) 3km walk to the village, or you can grab a ride on the back of a motorbike.

Kilifi Bay Beach Resort RESORT **$$$**
(☎522511; www.madahotels.com; s/d full board €135/190;) About 5km north of Kilifi on the coast road, this small resort has a Swahili palace exterior and rooms that are just as swanky. There are lots of facilities, although at high-tide the beach almost disappears under the waves.

Baobab Sea Lodge RESORT **$$$**
(☎522570; www.madahotels.com; s/d full board €115/155;) This very low-key resort, a few kilometres north of Kilifi on the coast road, overlooks a mighty fine stretch of sand and has spacious rooms in individual cottages.

Kilifi Members Club KENYAN
(mains KSh150-400) This is a fantastic spot to watch the sunset, perched on the northern cliff edge with breathtaking views over the creek to the Mediterranean-like beaches lining the opposite bank (and the Hollywood-like houses beyond). There's a good menu with lots of *nyama choma,* seafood and beer. Despite the name, you don't have to be a member.

Village Dishes KENYAN
(mains KSh200) Inside the petrol station (of all places) in the centre of town, this is the popular cheap cafe in town. It does a tasty fried fish with coconut rice.

Getting There & Away

All buses and matatus travelling between Mombasa (matatu KSh100 to KHs130, bus KSh100, up to 1½ hours) and Malindi (matatu/bus KSh150/100, 1¼ hours) stop at Kilifi.

The North Coast

Includes »

Best of Nature

- » Arabuko Sokoke Forest Reserve (p263)
- » Mida Creek (p260)
- » Malindi Marine National Park (p265)
- » Tana River (p271)
- » Watamu Marine National Park (p260).

Best of Culture

- » Lamu (p272)
- » Paté Island (p284)
- » Gede (p263)
- » Maulidi Festival (p275)

Why Go?

The exotic. It permeates everything here, blending spice and soul and cramming your head with the accents that equal adventure. Here you'll find honey-gathering crocodile hunters; ghost crabs, tree crabs and elephant shrews; the Vain Island and the Island of Wailing; and a stone city divided into two halves, the Beauteous and the Fortunate.

The inhabitants of this mythic land are, as everywhere on the edges of the Indian Ocean, a blend: Cushitic Somalis, Bantu-speaking Mijikenda, cattle-herding Orma, the Bajun, who once sewed their boats together with coconut fibre, and, of course, the Swahili.

It's these people who inspire the poetry of the place. Their muddy intermingling makes this a shore where people meet and move and leave stories; so come and be part of an adventure that's been writ since the first dhow sailed under the sunset.

When to Go

Lamu

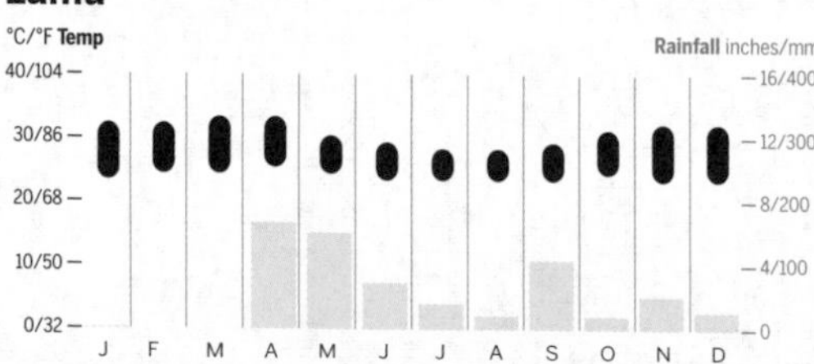

Jan & Feb The Maulidi Festival adds spice to Lamu.

Feb & Mar Superb diving with tropical fish in the reefs of the marine parks.

Nov & Dec Migrating birds flock to Tana River and Mida Creek.

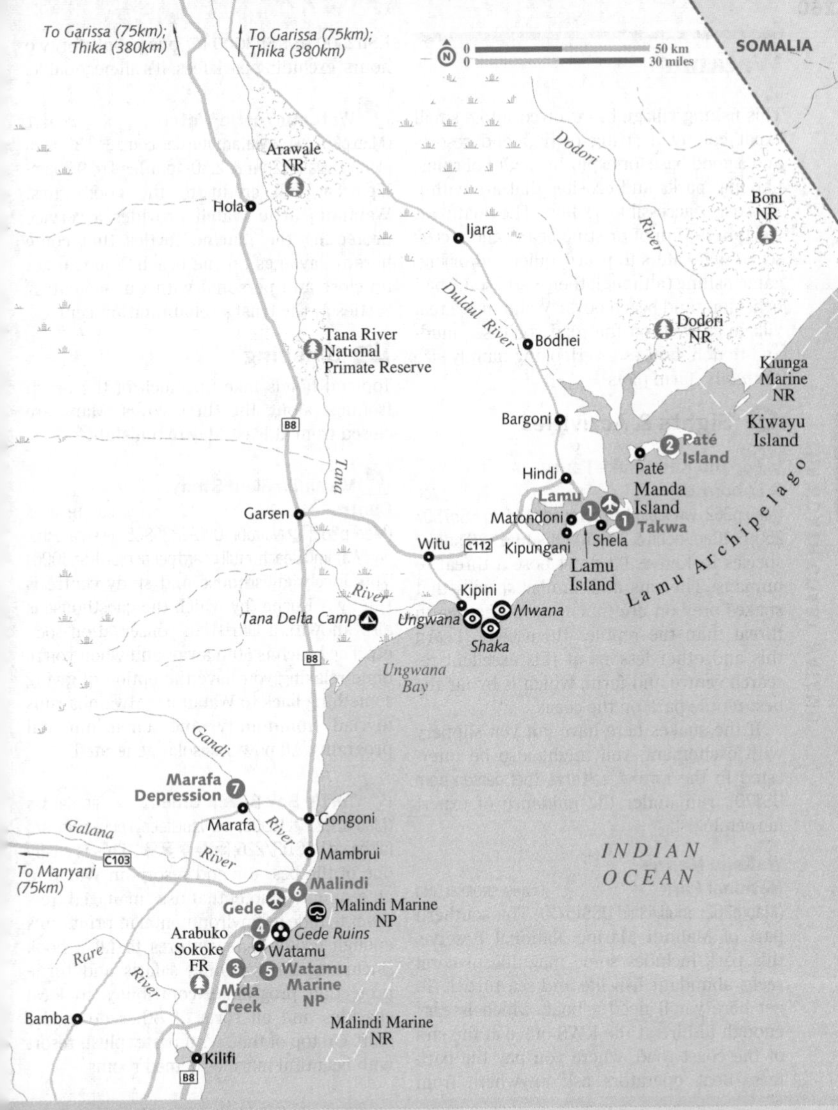

The North Coast Highlights

1. Sailing from **Lamu** (p272) to the coral ruins of once-mighty **Takwa** (p284) on Manda Island.
2. Having no electricity, no cars and no worries on **Paté Island** (p284).
3. Watching shooting stars tear the sky open while camping at **Mida Creek** (p260).
4. Exploring the ruined city of **Gede** (p263).
5. Slapping a mask on and peering at the underwater world of **Watamu Marine National Park** (p260).
6. Finding a slice of pizza even Italians appreciate, eaten by starlight in **Malindi** (p265).
7. Discovering the jagged Marscape of the **Marafa Depression** (p269).

Watamu

042

This fishing village has evolved into a small expat colony, a string of high-end resorts and a good base for exploring a glut of ruins, national parks and ecosites that are within an easily accessible radius. The main attraction is 7km of pristine beach and a cosy scene that caters to peace, quiet and/or big-game fishing (although there's still some bad behaviour and beach boys). Watamu is a real village as well; on the road you'll see mud-and-thatch houses overlooking family-size *shambas* (farm plots).

Sights & Activities

TOP CHOICE **Bio Ken Snake Farm & Laboratory** ZOO

(Map p262; www.bio-ken.com; adult/child KSh750/250; 10am-noon & 2-5pm) Of some 126 snake species in Kenya, 93 don't pose a threat to humans. The rats and similar species that snakes prey on are much more of a health threat than the reptiles themselves. Learn this and other lessons at this excellent research centre and farm, which is by far the best reptile park on the coast.

If the snakes here have got you slippery with excitement, you might also be interested in the **snake safaris** (per person from US$70), run under the guidance of expert herpetologists.

Watamu Marine National Park DIVING, SNORKELLING

(Map p262; adult/child US$15/10) The southern part of Malindi Marine National Reserve, this park includes some magnificent coral reefs, abundant fish life and sea turtles. To get here you'll need a boat, which is easy enough to hire at the KWS office at the end of the coast road, where you pay the park fees. Boat operators ask anywhere from KSh2500 to KSh3000 for two people for two hours, excluding park fees; it's all negotiable.

Watamu Turtle Watch WILDLIFE

(Map p262; www.watamuturtles.com; 2.30-4pm Mon, 9.30am-12pm & 2.30-4pm Tue-Fri, 9.30am-12pm Sat) All credit to the good guys: Watamu Turtle Watch provides a service protecting the marine turtles that come here to lay eggs on the beach. You can get up close and personal with various cutesy turtles at the trust's rehabilitation centre.

Sleeping

Top-end hotels take up much of the beach frontage along the three coves. Many are closed from at least May to mid-July.

Mwamba Field Study Centre GUESTHOUSE $

(Map p262; Nairobi 020-2335865; www.arocha.org; Watamu Beach; r full board per person KSh3000) This lovely guesthouse and study centre is run by A Rocha (by which the guesthouse is also known), a Christian conservation society. The beach is 50m away, and when you're done relaxing you have the option of giving something back to Watamu – Mwamba runs myriad community and environmental programs. All power is solar generated.

Turtle Bay Beach Club RESORT $$$

(Map p262; 32003; www.turtlebaykenya.com; s/d full board US$113/226;) This is easily one of the best top-end resorts in Watamu: an ecominded hotel that uses managed tree-cover to hide its environmental imprint, runs enough ecotourism ventures to fill a book (including birdwatching safaris and turtle protection programs), contributes to local charities and all sorts of other do-gooder stuff. On top of that, it's a pretty plush resort with beautiful marine-themed rooms.

WILDLIFE ON THE NORTH COAST

The wildlife story on the north Kenyan coast is very similar to that of the south coast; put simply it's not grade A safari country. The underwater life, though, is very impressive and the marine parks of Watamu and Malindi offer world-class diving and snorkelling. The most noteworthy terrestrial protected area is the **Arabuko Sokoke Forest Reserve** (p263), a rare slab of coastal forest filled with endemic bird species, a few elephants and the much smaller, but equally impressive, golden-rumped elephant shrew. The **Tana river** estuary (p271) offers adventurous canoe safaris in search of hippos and crocodiles. But just like the south coast it's the birds that rule the roost and **Mida Creek** (p260) offers outstanding birdwatching.

Villa Veronika GUESTHOUSE $
(Map p261; ☎0728155613; Beach Way Rd; r KSh800-1000) Colourful walls, flowery murals and well-maintained rooms (they were even renovating some rooms when we went past) set around a shady courtyard garden make this cheapie hard to beat.

Marijani Holiday Resort GUESTHOUSE $
(Map p261; ☎32510; www.marijani-holiday-resort.com; r from KSh3000) Best described as a coral villa, Marijani is a friendly, German-owned place on the edge of the village. Rooms are airy and elegant and the grounds are home to several parrots, curious house cats and chillin' tortoises.

Ocean Sports RESORT $$
(Map p262; ☎32288; www.oceansports.net; s/d KSh6900/11,200;) Smart rooms combining whitewash Swahili designs with colourful Indian textiles make this one of the better value places in the area. Most rooms command a stellar view all the way down to the beach. It's very popular with young, white Anglo-Kenyans.

Malob Guest House GUESTHOUSE $
(Map p261; ☎0714048140; Beach Way Rd; r KSh800) This is a cute option: a series of simple rooms set around an open courtyard, comfy and friendly and, for this area, incredibly cheap.

Eating

The better hotels cater for their clients. For local cuisine, try the several tiny stalls lining Beach Way Rd, selling kebabs, chicken, chips, samosas, chapatis and the like.

Bistro Coffee Shop CAFE $
(Map p261; ⏰until 5pm) Quick, run away from Africa! Sometimes you just need to escape to a relaxed Western-style cafe and this is the place in Watamu to do so. Great juices, tea, coffee and homemade cakes – lemon tart or apple pie? Oh what a decision!

Savannah INTERNATIONAL $$
(Map p261; KSh550-700; ⏰dinner Tue-Sat, lunch & dinner Sun) This pleasant garden restaurant doesn't have the worlds most imaginative menu, but it's burgers and pasta are decent enough and it's a great place for an evening beer. It's signed down a dirt track just off the main road into town.

Ascot Pizzeria ITALIAN $$
(Map p261; Ascot Hotel, Beach Way Rd; mains KSh300-750) Many places on the coast hide good Italian joints, and the Ascot is Watamu's noteworthy contribution to the cause.

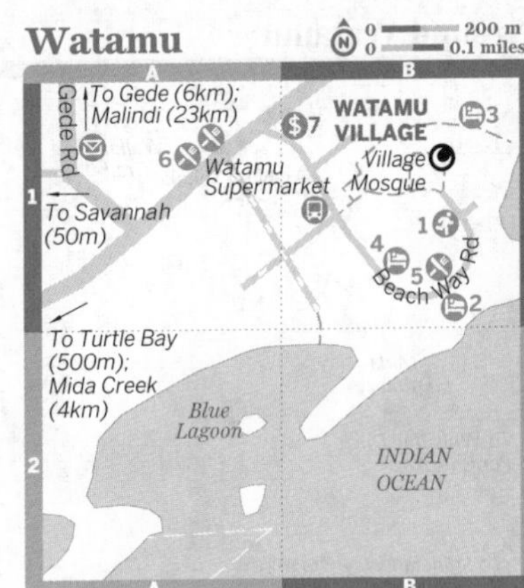

Watamu

Activities, Courses & Tours
1 Tunda Tours ... B1

Sleeping
2 Malob Guest House ... B1
3 Marijani Holiday Resort ... B1
4 Villa Veronika ... B1

Eating
5 Ascot Pizzeria ... B1
6 Bistro Coffee Shop ... A1

Information
7 KCB ... B1

Information

There's a KCB with an ATM on Beach Way Rd. The post office is on Gede Rd.

Getting There & Around

There are matatus between Malindi and Watamu throughout the day (KSh80 to KSh100, one hour). All matatus pass the turn-off to the Gede ruins (KSh40). For Mombasa (KSh250), the easiest option is to take a matatu to Gede and flag down a bus or matatu. A handful of motorised rickshaws ply the village and beach road; a ride to the KWS office should cost around KSh200.

Bicycles can be hired from most hotels or guesthouses for around KSh100 per hour.

Around Watamu

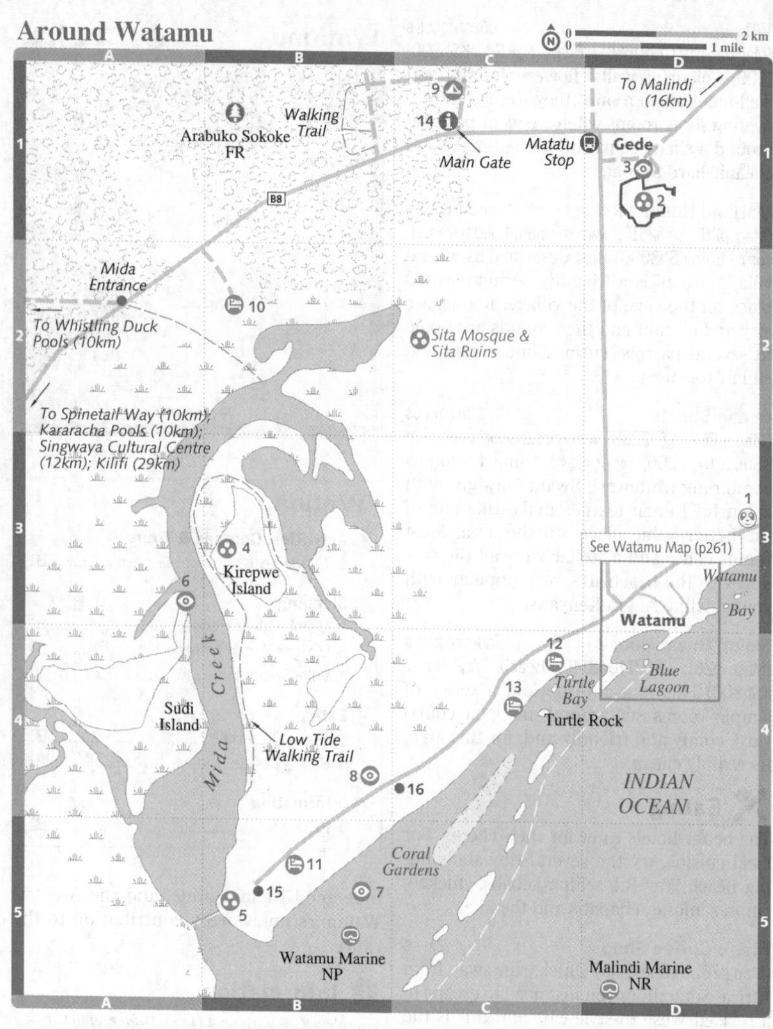

Around Watamu

Sights

1	Bio Ken Snake Farm & Laboratory	D3
2	Gede Ruins	D1
3	Kipepeo Butterfly Farm	D1
4	Ruins of Old Mosque	B3
5	Ruins of Old Mosque	B5
6	Walkway	A3
7	Watamu Marine National Park	B5
8	Watamu Turtle Watch	B4

Activities, Courses & Tours

	Aqua Ventures	(see 12)

Sleeping

9	Campsite	C1
10	Mida Ecocamp	B2
11	Mwamba Field Study Centre	B5
12	Ocean Sports	C4
13	Turtle Bay Beach Club	C4

Information

14	Arabuko Sokoke Visitor Centre	C1
	Gede Forest Station	(see 14)
15	KWS Office	B5
16	Mwamba Field Study Centre	C4

DON'T MISS

DIVING, FISHING & WINDSURFING

There are plenty of waterborne activities on offer at Watamu including diving, deep-sea fishing and windsurfing.

Aqua Ventures (Map p262; ☎32420, 0703628102; www.diveinkenya.com), at Ocean Sports resort, offers guided dives in the marine park for €32 and a PADI course for €320; they're also good for diving expeditions around Malindi.

Tunda Tours (Map p261; ☎0733952383; www.tundatourssafaris.com; Beach Way Rd) runs fishing safaris (half-/full day UK£250/350).

Oceansports (Map p262; ☎2332288; www.oceansports.net) based inside the hotel of the same name, offers windsurfing courses from €20, which is about as cheap as you'll find in Kenya.

Arabuko Sokoke Forest Reserve

Elephants are such an indelibly African image, but what about the elephant shrew? Specifically, the golden-rumped elephant shrew, which is about the size of a rabbit and cute as a kitten?

They're only found here, in **Arabuko Sokoke Forest Reserve** (Map p262; adult/child US$20/10; ⌚6am-6pm), the largest tract of indigenous coastal forest remaining in East Africa. But with 240 bird species, including the endemic Clarke's weaver, Sokoke scops owl (only 15cm tall) and Sokoke pipit, as well as other creatures such as forest elephants, baboons, Syke's monkey and 260 species of butterfly, there's a lot more to Arabuko Sokoke than just shrews.

The **Arabuko Sokoke Visitor Centre** (Map p262; Malindi Rd; ⌚8am-4pm) is very helpful; it's at Gede Forest Station, with displays on the various species found here.

From the visitors centre, nature trails and 4WD paths cut through the forest. There are more bird trails at **Whistling Duck Pools**, **Kararacha Pools** and **Spinetail Way**, located 16km further south. Near Kararacha is **Singwaya Cultural Centre**, where you can arrange to see traditional dance performances.

There are basic **campsites** (adult/child US$15/10) close to the visitors centre and further south near Spinetail Way.

The forest is just off the main Malindi–Mombasa road. The main gate to the forest and visitors centre is about 1.5km west of the turn-off to Gede and Watamu, while the Mida entrance is about 3km further south. All buses and matatus between Mombasa and Malindi can drop you at either entrance. From Watamu, matatus to Malindi can drop you at the main junction.

Gede Ruins

If you thought Kenya was all about nature, you're missing an important component of its charm: lost cities. The remains of medieval Swahili towns dot the coast, and many would say the most impressive of the bunch are the **Gede ruins** (Map p262; adult/child KSh500/250; ⌚7am-6pm).

This series of coral palaces, mosques and townhouses lies quietly in the jungle's green grip, but excavation has unearthed many structures. Within Gede (or Gedi) archaeologists found evidence of the cosmopolitan nature of Swahili society: silver necklaces decorated with Maria Teresa coins (from Europe) and Arabic calligraphy (from the Middle East), vermicelli makers from Asia that would become pasta moulds in the Mediterranean, Persian sabres, Arab coffeepots, Indian lamps, Egyptian or Syrian cobalt glass, Spanish scissors and Ming porcelain.

But the good times were not to last. Gede, which reached its peak in the 15th century, was inexplicably abandoned in the 17th or 18th century. Some theories point to disease and famine; others blame guerrilla attacks by Somalian Gallas and cannibalistic Zimba from near Malawi, or punitive expeditions from Mombasa. Or Gede ran out of water – at some stage the water table here dropped rapidly and the 40m wells dried up.

Other Attractions

Kipepeo Butterfly Farm FARM
(☎32380; nonresident adult/child KSh100/50; ⌚8am-5pm), Right by the entrance to the Gede complex, this centre pays locals to collect live pupae from Arabuko Sokoke, which

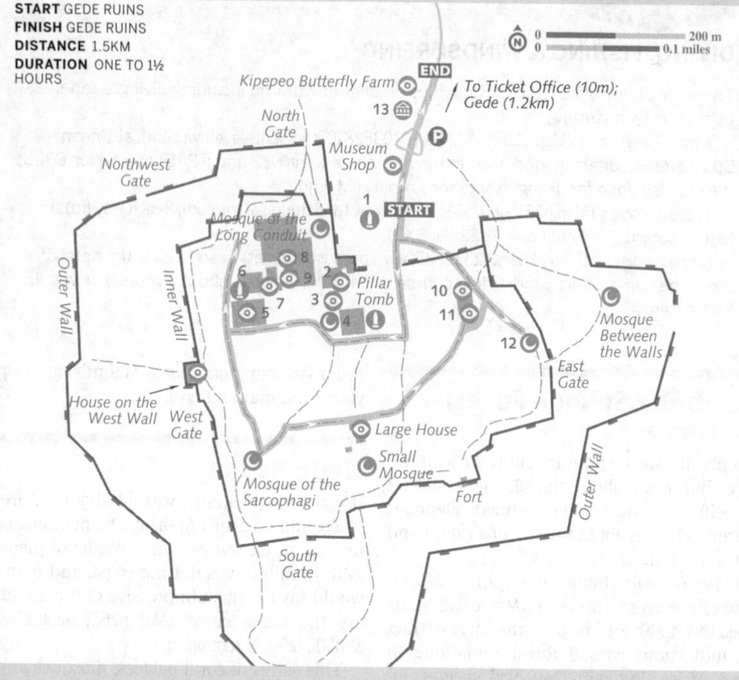

Walking Tour
Gede Ruins

Gede is the most visitor-friendly archaeological site in Kenya. Most of the excavated buildings are concentrated near the entrance, but there are dozens of other ruins scattered through the forest. Guides are available for KSh300.

On your right as you enter the compound is the ❶ **Dated Tomb**, so called because of the inscription on the wall, featuring the Muslim date corresponding to 1399. Near it, inside the wall, is the ❷ **Tomb of the Fluted Pillar**, which is characteristic of such pillar designs found along the East African coast.

Past the tomb, next to the ❸ **House of the Long Court**, the ❹ **Great Mosque** is one of Gede's most significant buildings. The entranceway was on the side of a long rectangular prayer hall, with the mihrab (prayer niche that faces Mecca) obscured behind rows of stone pillars.

Behind the mosque are the ruins of an extensive ❺ **palace**. One of the most interesting things found within the ruins was an earthenware jar containing a *fingo* (charm), thought to attract *djinns* (guardian spirits) who would drive trespassers insane. The palace also has a particularly fine ❻ **pillar tomb**; its hexagonal shape is unique to East Africa.

Just off to the right from the palace is a ❼ **tree** with steps leading high up into its canopy for a bird's-eye view of the site.

Along the path past the tomb are around 11 old ❽ **Swahili houses**. They're each named after particular features of their design or objects found in them by archaeologists, such as the House of Scissors and the House of the Iron Lamp. The ❾ **House of the Cistern** is particularly interesting, with ancient illustrations incised into the plaster walls.

The other excavations include the ❿ **House of the Dhow**, the ⓫ **House of the Double Court** and the nearby ⓬ **Mosque of the Three Aisles**, which has the largest well at Gede. On the way out you'll find an excellent little ⓭ **museum**.

ALL ALONE AT GEDE?

Come to Gede very early in the day or late in the evening when nobody else is around and as you poke about the site you may well get an overwhelming sensation that you're being watched.

All manner of ghost stories are associated with Gede and many local villagers, who talk about being followed around the ruins by a strange creature, regard the place with a certain amount of dread. James Kirkman, the archaeologist who first worked at the site back in the late 1940s, wrote, "When I first started to work at Gedi I had the feeling that something or somebody was looking out from behind the walls, neither hostile nor friendly, but waiting for what he knew was going to happen".

Some years ago, this author, who at the time didn't know about Gede's spooky reputation, was walking alone one wet, dimly lit evening back from the House of the Dhow to the main site, when he had such a powerful sense of being watched that all the hairs on the back of his head stood up on end. The man at the ticket office later said that he himself never walked around Gede alone due to experiencing the same sensation many times himself.

are hatched into butterflies and sold to collectors and live exhibits in the UK and USA. The money is then ploughed back into conservation of the forests. The price includes a (brief) guided tour.

Getting There & Away

The ruins lie off the main highway on the access road to Watamu. The easiest way here is via any matatu plying the main highway between Mombasa and Malindi. Get off at the village of Gede and follow the well-signposted dirt road from there – it's about a 10-minute walk.

Malindi

042

Malindi is lot nicer than it's detractors realise, and probably not quite as nice as it's advocates insist. It's easy to bash the place as an Italian beach resort – which it is. But you can't deny it's got a *bella spiaggia* (beautiful beach) and, excuse the stereotype, all those Italians have brought some high gastronomic standards with them. Did we mention a fascinating history that speaks to the great narrative of exploration, Malindi Marine Park and the twisty warren of thatch and whitewash that is Old Town? Throw it all together and you get a lot more character than the beach bums let on.

Sights & Activities

Malindi Marine National Park WILDLIFE RESERVE

(off Map p266; adult/child US$15/10; 7am-7pm)

The oldest marine park in Kenya covers 213 sq km of rainbow clouds of powder-blue fish, organ-pipe coral, green sea-turtles and beds of *Thalassia* seagrass. If you're extremely lucky, you may spot mako and whale sharks. Unfortunately, these reefs have suffered (and continue to suffer) extensive damage, evidenced by the piles of seashells on sale in Malindi. Note that silt from the Galana River reduces underwater visibility between March and June and the monsoon-generated waves can make visibility very low from June to September.

You're likely to come here on a snorkelling or glass-bottom-boat tour, which can be arranged at the KWS office on the coast road south of Malindi. Boats only go out at low tide, so it's a good idea to call in advance to check times (your hotel can help with this). The going rate is around KSh5000 per boat (five to 10 people) for a two-hour trip.

Most hotels offer diving excursions. Or try **Blue-Fin-Diving** (www.bluefindiving.com), which operates out of several Malindi resorts. Charges €95 for a Discover Scuba course and €360 for the PADI Open Water course.

Malindi Historic Circuit HISTORIC BUILDINGS

National Museums of Kenya has smartly grouped the three major cultural sites of Malindi under the one general ticket of this **circuit** (adult/child KSh500/250; 8am-6pm).

The most compelling attraction covered in the Malindi Historic Circuit is the **House of Columns** (Mama Ngina Rd). The structure itself is a good example of traditional Swahili architecture and, more pertinently, contains great exhibits of all sorts of archaeological finds dug up around the coast.

Malindi

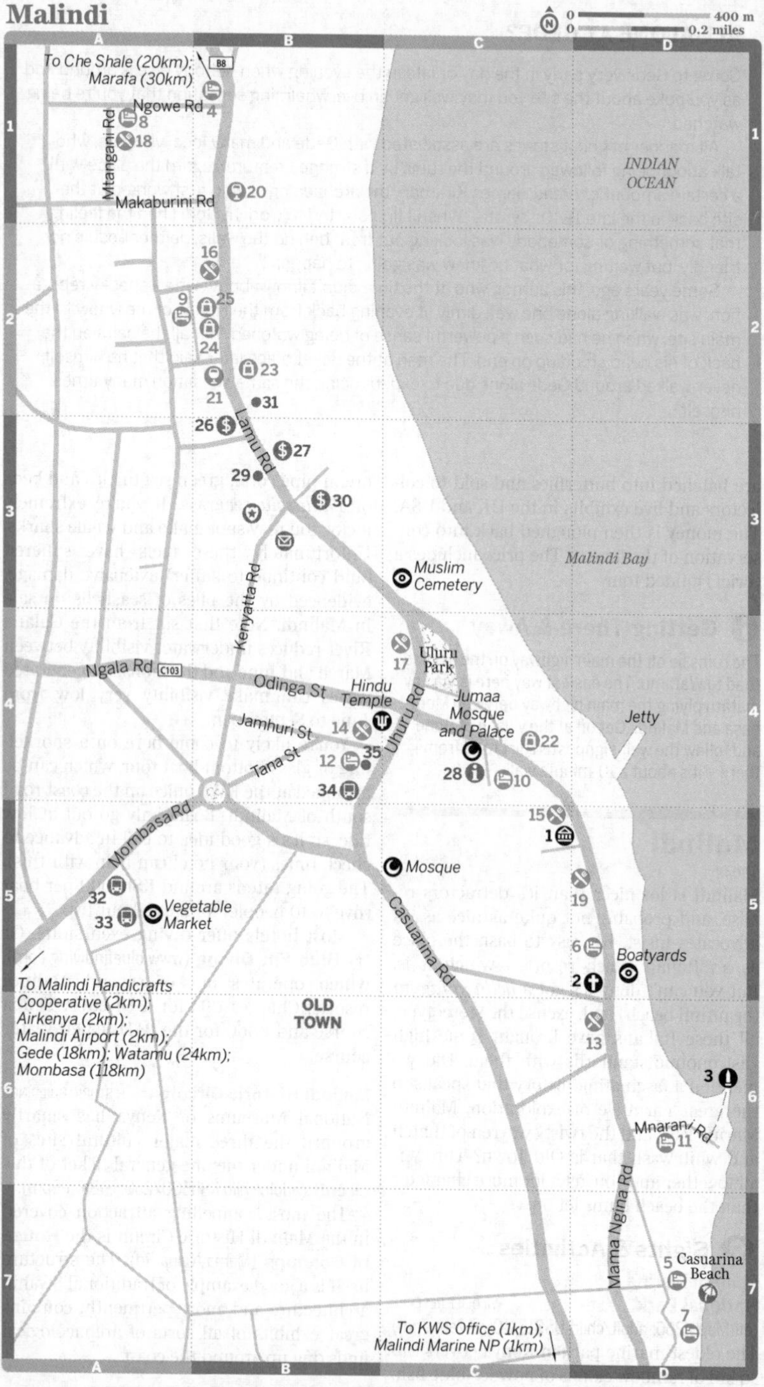

0 400 m
0 0.2 miles

A B C D
1 2 3 4 5 6 7

To Che Shale (20km); Marafa (30km)
B8
Ngowe Rd
4
8
18
Mtangani Rd
20
Makaburini Rd
INDIAN OCEAN
16
9
25
24
23
21
31
26
Lamu Rd
27
29
30
Kenyatta Rd
Muslim Cemetery
Malindi Bay
17
Uluru Park
Ngala Rd
C103
Odinga St
Hindu Temple
Uhuru Rd
Jumaa Mosque and Palace
Jetty
Jamhuri St
14
22
12
35
Tana St
28
10
34
Mombasa Rd
15
1
Mosque
32
Vegetable Market
33
19
Casuarina Rd
6
Boatyards
2
To Malindi Handicrafts Cooperative (2km); Airkenya (2km); Malindi Airport (2km); Gede (18km); Watamu (24km); Mombasa (118km)
OLD TOWN
13
3
Mnarani Rd
11
Mama Ngina Rd
5
Casuarina Beach
7
To KWS Office (1km); Malindi Marine NP (1km)

Malindi

Sights
1 Malindi Museum/House of Columns... C5
2 Portuguese Church ... D5
3 Vasco da Gama Pillar ... D6

Sleeping
4 African Pearl Hotel ... B1
5 Coral Key Beach Resort ... D7
6 Da Gama's Inn ... D5
7 Driftwood Beach Club ... D7
8 Jardin Lorna ... A1
9 Lutheran Guest House ... A2
10 Ozi's Guest House ... C4
11 Scorpio Villas ... D6
12 Tana Guest House ... B4

Eating
13 Baby Marrow ... D6
14 Barani Dishes ... B4
Chariba ... (see 31)
Da Gama's Inn ... (see 6)
15 I Love Pizza ... C5
16 Il Fornado Italian Supermarket ... B2
17 Izzipoint Supermarket ... C4
Jardin Lorna Restaurant ... (see 8)
18 La Malindina ... A1
19 Old Man and the Sea ... D5
Scorpio Villas ... (see 11)

Drinking
20 Club 28 ... B1
Fermento Piano Bar ... (see 23)
Karen Blixen Restaurant & Coffee Shop ... (see 23)
21 Star Dust ... B2

Shopping
22 Curio Market ... C4
23 Galana Centre ... B2
24 Malindi Centre ... B2
25 Sabaki Centre ... B2

Information
26 Barclays Bank ... B3
27 Dollar Forex Bureau ... B3
28 Immigration Office ... C4
Italian Consulate ... (see 25)
29 North Coast Travel Services ... B3
30 Standard Chartered Bank ... B3
Tourist Office ... (see 24)

Transport
Buses to Lamu ... (see 34)
31 Kenya Airways ... B2
32 Matatus to Mombasa & Nairobi ... A5
33 New Malindi Bus Station ... A5
Simba Coaches ... (see 12)
Simba Coaches ... (see 34)
Southern Sky Safaris ... (see 24)
34 Starways Express ... B4
35 Tawakal Office ... B4
TSS Office ... (see 34)

The **Vasco da Gama pillar** is admittedly more impressive for what it represents (the genesis of the Age of Exploration) than the edifice itself. Erected by da Gama as a navigational aid in 1498, the coral column is topped by a cross made of Lisbon stone, which almost certainly dates from the explorer's time. There are good views from here down the coast and out, thousands of kilometres east, to India, where Portugal and eventually Europe would extend its political control. To get here turn off Mama Ngina Rd, by Scorpio Villas.

The tiny thatched **Portuguese church** (Mama Ngina Rd) is so called because Vasco da Gama is reputed to have erected it, and two of his crew are supposedly buried here. It's certainly true that St Francis Xavier visited on his way to India.

Sleeping

Note that most of the top-end places close or scale down operations between April and June or July.

TOP CHOICE **Scorpio Villas** RESORT $$
(☎20194; www.scorpio-villas.com; Mnarani Rd; s/d KSh4800/7600;) Every once in a while Kenya throws a hotel at you that is so much better value than anything else in its class that it leaves you wondering if you misheard the price. The Italian-run Scorpio Villas is one such place. Its 40-odd rooms are whitewashed and art-bedecked, with wooden roof beams. Step into the bathroom and you'll find huge walk-in rain showers. When you're feeling sleepy, dive into the giant four-poster beds. Throw in gardens heavy with foliage, a fantastic pool complex and a restaurant with excellent Italian food

DON'T MISS

MIDA CREEK

Mida Creek is a different world from that of the all-inclusive tourist resorts of nearby Watamu and Malindi. It's a quiet and gentle place hugged by silver-tinged mudflats flowing with ghost crabs and long tides, it's a place where the creeping marriage of land and water is epitomised by a mangrove forest and the salty, fresh scent of wind over an estuary. Mida Creek saves its real appeal for evening, when the stars simply rain down on you.

There's no shortage of activities on offer either. Excellent Giriama guides will take you through the water-laced landscape of the creek and through the mangroves on a rickety **walkway** (adult/child KSh250/150, guides per hr KSh300). At the end of the walkway a bird hide looks out over the surrounding wetlands. Of all the mangrove walkways on the Kenyan coast this one is by far the best and has the most knowledgeable guides. You can also organise **canoe trips** (3hr KSh700) from here. Best of all, as this is a community project, visiting here helps the local Giriama people.

If you want to savour the peace a little longer (and you will), the **Mida Ecocamp** (Map p262; ☎0729213042; www.midaecocamp.com; huts per person KSh800-1400, camping KSh200), located just off the coast highway (B8) about 6km south of Watamu, has three huts for rent – Giriama, Swahili and Zanzibari. All of them, in their own sweet way, are lovely – the Giriama is 'rustic' Africa, while the Zanzibari house is an enjoyable Lamu-style cottage with a rooftop bed-lounge for catching cool breezes. There's also a laid-back **restaurant** (meals KSh650) with tasty local meals, a wind-conditioned *makuti*-topped (palm-thatched) bar and the opportunity to venture into nearby villages on culture tours (your money goes to local schools).

Any bus travelling between Mombasa and Malindi can drop you on the main road near Mida Creek from where it's a pleasent 20-minute walk to the camp.

(four-course evening meal KSh1200) and you get a place that's hard to beat. However, we have heard rumours that prostitutes are allowed into the hotel, although we saw no evidence whatsoever of this during our stay.

Jardin Lorna GUESTHOUSE **$$**
(☎30658; harry@swiftmalindi.com; Mtangani Rd; s with/without bathroom KSh2500/1500, d with/without bathroom KSh5000/3000; ❄≋) Lorna is very unpretentious, providing accommodation mainly for students of the Hospitality Training and Management Institute. Rooms are endearingly quirky with zebra rugs and local art punctuating the interior. Outside are some very peaceful gardens.

African Pearl Hotel HOTEL **$**
(☎0725131956; www.africanpearlhotel.com; Lamu Rd; d/tw from KSh2500/3500; ❄wifi≋) This complex is done up with Africana accents, dark-wood sculptures, safari-themed souvenirs and a (murky) pool and lounge area that connects the scattered corners of this large resort.

Driftwood Beach Club RESORT **$$$**
(☎20155; www.driftwoodclub.com; Mama Ngina Rd; s/d KSh10,560/15,070; ❄wifi≋👪) One of the best-known resorts in Malindi, and a key expat and Anglo-Kenyan hang-out, Driftwood prides itself on an informal atmosphere and attracts a more independent clientele than many of its peers. The ambience is closer to palm-breezed serenity than the party atmosphere at similar hotels.

Lutheran Guest House GUESTHOUSE **$**
(☎30098; s/d KSh1000/1800) If you need quiet, this religious centre (which accepts guests of all stripes) is a nice option. Like most church-run places in Kenya, everything here is a little cleaner, staff are earnestly friendly and alcohol is strictly prohibited.

Ozi's Guest House HOTEL **$**
(☎20218; ozi@swiftmalindi.com; Mama Ngina Rd; s/d KSh900/1800) Popular with backpackers, probably because it perches on the attractive edge of Old Town (next to a mosque – a very noisy mosque), Ozi's runs good tours and has friendly service that knows the needs of independent travellers. Rooms share bathrooms.

Coral Key Beach Resort RESORT **$$**
(☎30717; Mama Ngina Rd; s/d from €70/140; ❄@wifi≋👪) It's a bit bling and full of, well, we're not really sure what they are; possibly swimming pools, or maybe ponds or

perhaps water features? Whatever, they're certainly memorable. The rooms though are comfortable, clean and good bang for your Shillings.

Tana Guest House HOTEL $
(☎0733243020; Jamhuri St; s/d without breakfast, with shared bathroom KSh550/650, d KSh1100) If you're scraping the budget barrel, you probably can't come up with a better price and location than this place, right by the bus stops. Rooms are passably clean, with mosquito nets, squat toilets and other joys of budget-travel life.

Da Gama's Inn HOTEL $
(☎0722357591; Mama Ngina Rd; s/d without breakfast KSh800/1000) Big, bare doubles and smaller singles share this modern block, with a decent Indian restaurant downstairs. If you can get hot water out of those rusty water storage tanks then you're a better person than we are.

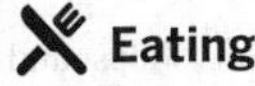

Eating

Many cheaper Swahili places close during the month of Ramadan. Of the hotel restaurants open to nonguests, those of the Scorpio Villas (see p267) and the Driftwood offer the best meals. Self-caterers can stock up in the **Izzipoint Supermarket** (Uhuru Rd) and **Il Fornado Italian Supermarket** (Lamu Rd).

La Malindina ITALIAN $$$
(☎31449; Mtangani Rd; meals around KSh2000-2500; ⊙late Jul–mid-Apr dinner only) This extremely upmarket Italian seafood place serves locally caught, fantastically fresh seafood and is regarded by all and sundry as the best place in town to eat.

I Love Pizza ITALIAN $
(☎20672; Mama Ngina Rd; pizzas around KSh900, pastas around KSh400-600) We do too, and the pizza is done really well here – way better than you might expect this far from Naples. No matter how good the pizza, many people come instead for the seafood and pastas. The porch-front and Mediterranean atmosphere top off this excellent place.

Old Man and the Sea SEAFOOD $$
(☎31106; Mama Ngina Rd; mains KSh400-750, seafood KSh550-1100; ✎) This Old Man's been serving elegant, excellent seafood using a combination of local ingredients and fresh recipes for years. The classy waitstaff and wicker-chic ambience all combine for some nice colonial-style, candlelit meals under the stars. The menu also contains a small selection of vegetarian options.

DON'T MISS

DON'T MISS MARAFA!

Away from the hedonistic delights of sun and sand, one of the more intriguing sights along the north Kenyan coast is the **Marafa Depression** (Map p260), also known as Hell's Kitchen or Nyari ('the place broken by itself'). It's an eroded sandstone gorge where jungle, red rock and cliffs upheave themselves into a single stunning Marscape.

About 30km northeast of Malindi, the Depression is currently managed as a local tourism concern by **Marafa village**. It costs a steep KSh600 (that goes into village programs) to walk around the lip of the gorge, and KSh400 for a guide who can walk you into the sandstone heart of the ridges and tell Hell's Kitchen's story. Which goes like so: a rich family was so careless with their wealth that they bathed themselves in the valuable milk of their cattle. God became angry with this excess and sank the family homestead into the earth. The white and red walls of the Depression mark the milk and blood of the family painted over the gorge walls. The more mundane explanation? The Depression is a chunk of sandstone that is geologically distinct from the surrounding rock and more susceptible to wind and rain erosion.

Most people visit here on organised tours, with a self-drive car or by taxi (KSh7000). Alternatively, there are one or two morning matatus from Mombasa Rd in Malindi to Marafa village (KSh150, three hours) and from there it's a 20-minute walk to Hell's Kitchen. There are two very basic places to stay if needed.

If you come by private transport it's worth making a day trip of it and enjoying the beautiful African countryside, stopping for a chat in any one of the numerous little villages that line the route.

WORTH A TRIP

LET'S GO SURF A KITE

There are plenty of beach resorts offering kitesurfing classes, but maybe the best place to pick up this pastime and experience utter tropical escapism is at **Che Shale/Kajama Beach Bandas** (☎0722230931; www.cheshale.com; Kajama s/d €35/70, Che Shale s/d from €80/160), one of the best-executed sandy retreats we've stumbled across. It manages to blend Swahili aesthetics with contemporary flash in a luxurious and tasteful way. There's a huge thatched bar and playfully irreverent riffs on the 'coconut-chic' thing. For those with smaller wallets, the Kajama Beach Bandas (same location) offers a very comfortable budget equivalent. To top it off, Che Shale's instructors and isolated location make for some of the best kitesurfing on the coast; a full course for beginners runs to €315.

It's located at the end of a long dirt track (you'll need a 4WD, or arrange a pick-up with the hotel) about 30 minutes north of Malindi.

Baby Marrow ITALIAN, SEAFOOD $$$
(Mama Ngina Rd; mains KSh500-2000) Everything about this place is quirkily stylish, from the thatched verandah and plant-horse to the Italian-based menu and tasty seafood. The quiet garden setting also adds to the relaxed vibe.

Barani Dishes KENYAN $
(Jamhuri St; meals KSh80-220) If you ask a local where they think the best cheap local food comes from chances are they'll point you towards this packed town-centre place. It's clean, bright and has all the Kenyan staples you must surely be missing so much!

Chariba KENYAN $
(Lamu Rd; meals KSh80-220) This is a top African option, and by African we mean interior cuisine like grilled meat with *githeri*, *mukimo* and other variations on mashed corn and beans.

Drinking

Karen Blixen Restaurant & Coffee Shop CAFE $
(Lamu Rd; coffee KSh90-400, snacks KSh500-900) Despite being outrageously pretentious, this Italian-style pavement cafe is a fine place to escape the hubbub of the street outside. As befits an Italian cafe, it's Italian coffees and snacks all the way, and lots and lots of Italians who think they're in Milan. It's open for breakfast as well.

Fermento Piano Bar LOUNGE $
(☎31780; Galana Centre, Lamu Rd; admission KSh200; ⊙from 10pm Wed, Fri & Sat; ❄) Fermento has the town's hippest dance floor, apparently once frequented by Naomi Campbell. It's young and trendy, so try to look so yourself if you show up here.

The main nightclubs outside the resorts are **Star Dust** (Lamu Rd) and **Club 28** (Lamu Rd), which open erratically out of season but are generally rammed when they do. Expect lots of working-girl and beach-boy attention.

Shopping

There are numerous souvenir shops and a large curio market along Uhuru Rd and Mama Ngina Rd near the Old Town – bargain hard and walk away with the *bao* set (African board game) of your dreams. Avoid shell vendors – the shells are mostly plundered from the national park.

Another good place to buy handicrafts is Malindi Handicrafts Cooperative. This community project employs local artisans and the woodcarvings are of high quality. To get there, turn off the main road to Mombasa near the BP petrol station; the centre is 2km along a dirt road, just opposite the community clinic.

Information

Dangers & Annoyances

Being on the beach alone at night is asking for trouble, as is walking along any quiet beach back roads at night. Also, avoid the far northern end of the beach or any deserted patches of sand, as muggings are common. There are lots of guys selling drugs, so remember: everything from marijuana on up is illegal. Sales of drugs often turn into stings, with the collusive druggie getting a cut of whatever fee police demand from you (if they don't throw you in jail). There's also a lot of prostitution here, unfortunately.

Emergency

Ambulance (☎30575, 041-3432411, 999)
Police (☎20485, 999; Kenyatta Rd)

Money

Barclays Bank (Lamu Rd) With ATM.

Dollar Forex Bureau (Lamu Rd)

Standard Chartered Bank (Stanchart Arcade, Lamu Rd) With ATM.

Post

Post office (Kenyatta Rd)

Tourist Information

Italian Consulate (20502; Sabaki Centre, Lamu Rd)

Tourist office (20689; Malindi Complex, Lamu Rd; 8am-12.30pm & 2-4.30pm Mon-Fri)

Travel Agencies

North Coast Travel Services (20370; Lamu Rd) Agent for Fly540.

Southern Sky Safaris (20493; www.southernskysafaris.com; Lamu Rd) Has a good reputation.

Getting There & Away

Air

Airkenya (30646; Malindi Airport) Has daily afternoon/evening flights to Nairobi (US$100, two hours).

Kenya Airways (20237; Lamu Rd) Flies the same route at least once a day (US$134).

Bus & Matatu

LAMU

There are usually at least six buses a day to Lamu (KSh600 but can rise in periods of high demand, four to five hours). Most leave around 9am. TSS Buses and Tawakal are the biggest operators.

MOMBASA

There are numerous daily buses and matatus to Mombasa (bus/matatu KSh300/350, two hours). Bus company offices are found opposite the old market in the centre of Malindi. Note that during periods of high demand fares can rise up to KSh600.

NAIROBI

All the main bus companies have daily departures to Nairobi at around 7am and/or 7pm (KSh110 to KSh1200, 10 to 12 hours), via Mombasa. Starways Express is one of the bigger operators.

WATAMU

Matatus to Watamu (KSh80 to KSh100, one hour) leave from the not very new New Malindi Bus Station on the edge of town.

Getting Around

You can rent bicycles from most hotels or the KWS for KSh200 to KSh500 per day. Cycling at night is not permitted. Tuk-tuks (minitaxis) are ubiquitous – a trip from town to the KWS office should cost around KSh150 to KSh200. A taxi to the airport is at least KSh150 and a tuk-tuk is KSh50. However, these are official prices and you'll need the gift of the gab to actually bargain them down to this.

Tana River

The Tana River delta is regarded by most travellers as an inconvenient stretch of road between Malindi and Lamu. It's true that the delta marks the fall line, as it were, of resorts; past here, David Attenborough might say, the hotels simply cannot survive (well, until Lamu).

But there are some fantastic areas of exploration here for intrepid travellers. The delta country is a long, low marshland dotted with domes of jungle sprouting over a wet prairie. Cooking smoke from the thin houses of the Orma people and mud-and-thatch huts of the Pokomo floats over the sedge, while black herons dinosaur-flap over the slow water and, in the tall grass, hippos and crocodiles warily circle one another. This is one of those parts of Kenya where hippos are a viable traffic hazard!

If you'd like to explore this region on your own, disembark Lamu–Malindi buses at little Witu and catch a bus or matatu (bus/matatu KSh70/100) to smaller Kipini, at the mouth of the delta (when you're ready to leave, you can board Lamu–Malindi buses in Witu up to about 2.30pm).

Sights & Activities

There was no formal tour structure when we arrived in Kipini and nobody really seems to know what to do with foreign tourists, but those willing to put up with some discomfort and misunderstandings will find plenty of opportunity for adventure here.

The **Kipini Wildlife Conservancy** (www.kipiniconservancy.org) was being established at the time of research. It's trying to model itself on private conservancies such as Lewa (p199). For the moment there are few facilities.

Boat Safari BOAT TOUR

The most obvious thing to do is a **boat safari** onto the great, greasy, green Tana River. There's no thrill like that of being in a small boat, looking at a tree, then watching said tree slide into the water and realising 'that's a crocodile!'. The guides are utterly unfazed by the crocs but terrified of the local hippos, which are ubiquitous and actually far more dangerous than the crocs. Canoe safaris are about KSh2000 for the day, but the problem is that most of the crocs and hippos are a fair way upriver and you won't get very far very quickly in a canoe. Therefore it's better to hire a motor boat, but that's going to cost you. We were quoted KSh6000 per hour with fuel and you'd best allow three hours to make it worthwhile.

Sleeping & Eating

Delta Dunes LODGE **$$$**
(☎0718139359; www.deltadunes.co.ke; s/d full board US$590/1000, plus conservation fee per person US$60;). This remote, exclusive lodge sits at the scenic mouth of the Tana River and offers walking and canoe safaris (included in the price) amid the marshes. It's at least three hours from Malindi by road and canoe, but if you can afford the sky-high rates then you can also afford the private helicopter transfer.

Mamba Campsite & Lodging COTTAGES **$**
(Kipini; cottage without breakfast KSh500). Very basic cottages with smelly shared toilets, but it's about the only 'formal' accommodation in Kipini village. If it happens to be full then you'll find a couple of other really quite rank places for around KSh400.

LAMU ARCHIPELAGO

The Arabs called them 'The Seven Isles of Eryaya', while sailors called them a welcome port of call when en route to, or from, India. Hundreds of expats who have fallen irrevocably in love with these islands call them home, as do the Swahili, who trace the deepest roots of their culture here.

Few would dispute the Lamu archipelago forms the most evocative destination on the Kenyan coast. In travelling terms, it's the best of several possible worlds: medieval stone towns of narrow streets *and* charming architecture *and* tropical island paradise *and* delicious local cuisine *and* star-heavy nights that are pregnant with the smell of spice and possibility.

Lamu

☎042

Lamu town has that quality of immediately standing out as you approach it from the water (and let's face it – everything is better when approached from water). The shopfronts and mosques, faded under the relentless kiss of the salt wind, creep out from behind a forest of dhow masts. Then you take to the streets, or more accurately, the labyrinth: donkey-wide alleyways from which children grin; women whispering by in full-length *bui-bui* (black cover-all worn by some Islamic women outside the home); cats casually ruling the rooftops; blue smoke from meat grilling over open fires and the organic, biting scent of the cured wooden shutters on houses built of stone and coral. Many visitors call this town – the oldest living town in East Africa, a Unesco World Heritage site and arguably the most complete Swahili town in existence – the highlight of their trip to Kenya. Residents call it *Kiwa Ndeo* – The Vain Island – and, to be fair, there's plenty for them to be vain about.

History

In pre-Arab times the islands were home to the Bajun, but their traditions vanished almost entirely with the arrival of the Arabs.

In the 19th century, the soldiers of Lamu caught the warriors of Paté on open mud at low tide and slaughtered them. This victory, plus the cash cows of ivory and slavery, made Lamu a splendidly wealthy place, and most of the fine Swahili houses that survive today were built during this period.

It all came to an end in 1873, when the British forced Sultan Barghash of Zanzibar to close down the slave markets. With the abolition of slavery, the economy went into rapid decline. The city-state was incorporated into the British Protectorate from 1890, and became part of Kenya with independence in 1963.

Until it was 'rediscovered' by travellers in the 1970s, Lamu existed in a state of humble obscurity – which has allowed it to remain well preserved for tourists today.

Sights

Lamu is one of those places where the real attraction is just the overall feel of the place and there actually aren't all that many 'sights' to tick off. Having said that there are a couple of museums; all of which are open from 8am to 6pm daily. Admission to each is a much overpriced KSh500 for a nonresident adult, KSh250 for a child.

Lamu Museum MUSEUM
(Harambee Ave) The best museum in town is housed in a grand Swahili warehouse on

Lamu Archipelago

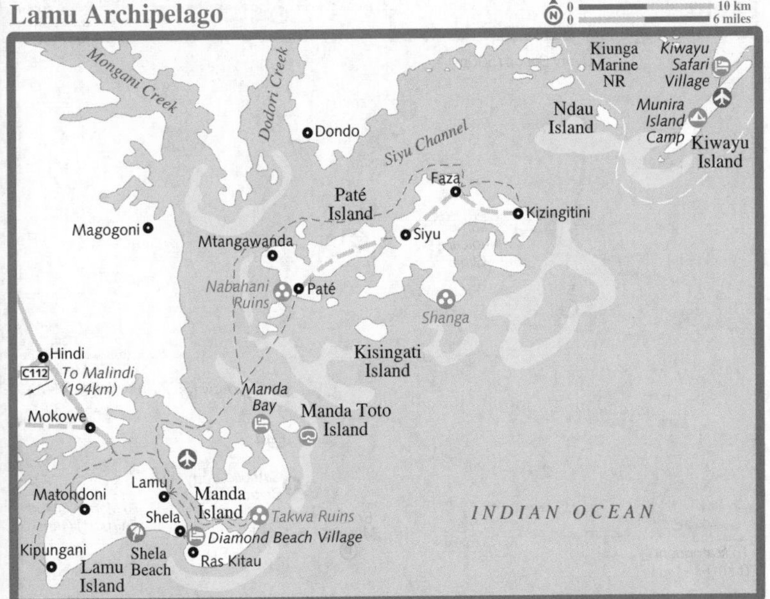

the waterfront. This is as good a gateway as you'll get into Swahili culture and that of the archipelago in particular. Of note are the displays of traditional women's dress – those who consider the head-to-toe *bui-bui* restrictive might be interested to see the *shiraa* – a tentlike garment (complete with wooden frame to be held over the head), once the respectable dress of local ladies. There are also exhibits dedicated to artefacts from Swahili ruins, the bric-a-brac of local tribes and the nautical heritage of the coast (including the *mtepe,* a traditional coir-sewn boat meant to resemble the Prophet Mohammed's camel – hence the nickname: 'camels of the sea'). Guides are available to show you around.

Lamu Fort FORTRESS

(Kenyatta Rd) This squat castle was built by the sultan of Paté in 1810 and completed in 1823. From 1910 right up to 1984 it was used as a prison. It now houses the island's library, which holds one of the best collections of Swahili poetry and Lamu reference work in Kenya. Entrance is free with a ticket to the Lamu Museum.

Swahili House Museum MUSEUM

This preserved Swahili house, tucked away to the side of Yumbe House hotel, is beautiful, but the KSh500 entry fee is very hard to justify, especially as half the hotels in Lamu are as well preserved as this small house.

German Post Office Museum MUSEUM

(Kenyatta Rd) In the late 1800s, before the British decided to nip German expansion into Tanganyika in the bud, the Germans regarded Lamu as an ideal base from which to exploit the interior. As part of their efforts, the German East Africa Company set up a post office, and the old building is now a museum exhibiting photographs and memorabilia from that fleeting period when Lamu had the chance of being spelt with umlauts.

Donkey Sanctuary ZOO

(Harambee Ave; admission free; ⌚9am-1pm Mon-Fri)

> A man without a donkey, *is* a donkey.
>
> *Swahili proverb*

Or, as the staff of this sanctuary might tell you, a man who doesn't look after his donkey *is* a donkey. With around 3000 donkeys (and a couple of cars) active on Lamu, *Equus asinus* is the main form of transport here. This sanctuary was established by the International Donkey Protection Trust of Sidmouth, UK, to improve the lot of the island's hard-working beasts of burden.

Lamu

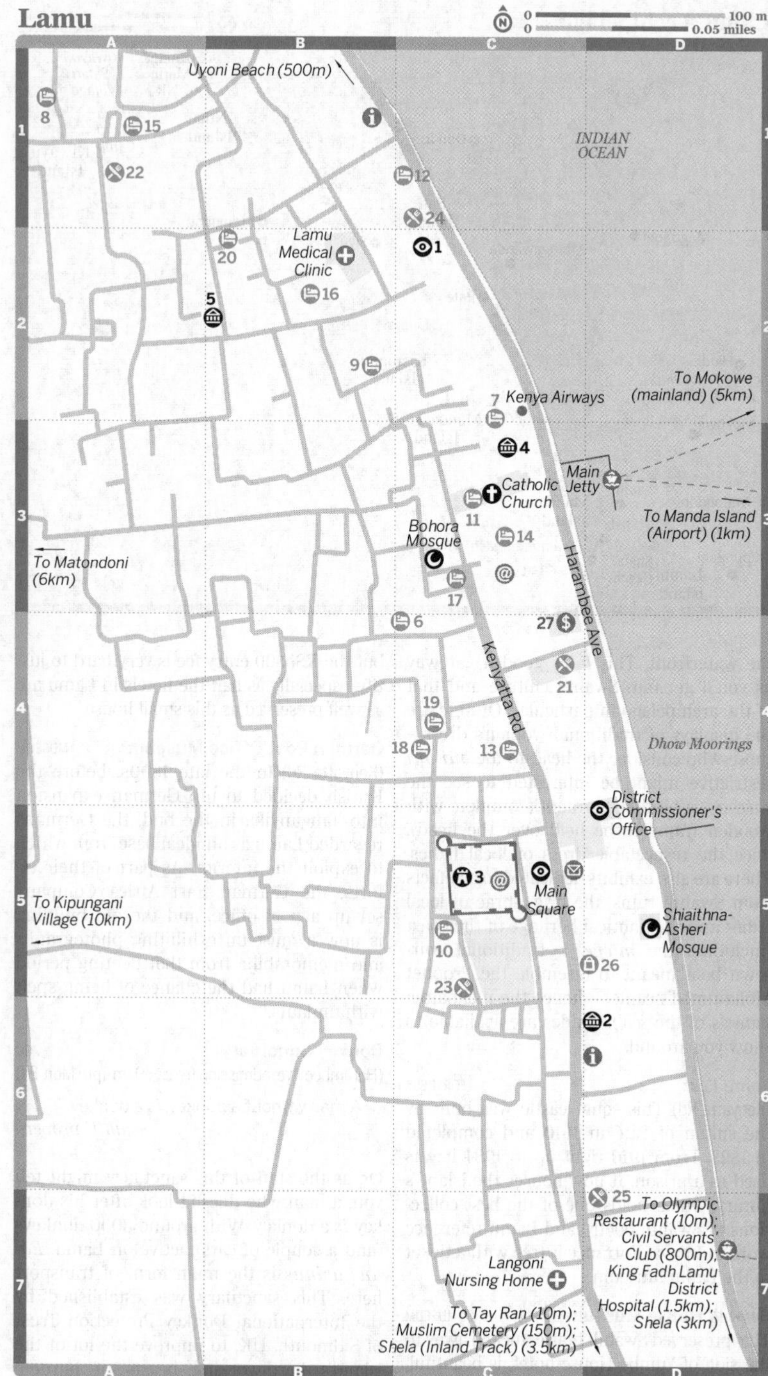

0 100 m
0 0.05 miles
Uyoni Beach (500m)
INDIAN OCEAN
Lamu Medical Clinic
To Mokowe (mainland) (5km)
Kenya Airways
Main Jetty
Catholic Church
To Manda Island (Airport) (1km)
Bohora Mosque
To Matondoni (6km)
Harambee Ave
Kenyatta Rd
Dhow Moorings
District Commissioner's Office
Main Square
To Kipungani Village (10km)
Shiaithna-Asheri Mosque
To Olympic Restaurant (10m); Civil Servants' Club (800m); King Fadh Lamu District Hospital (1.5km); Shela (3km)
Langoni Nursing Home
To Tay Ran (10m); Muslim Cemetery (150m); Shela (Inland Track) (3.5km)

Lamu

Sights

1	Donkey Sanctuary	C2
2	German Post Office Museum	D6
3	Lamu Fort	C5
4	Lamu Museum	C3
5	Swahili House Museum	B2

Sleeping

6	Amu House	C4
7	Casuarina Rest House	C2
8	Jannat House	A1
9	Kilimanjaro House	B2
10	Lamu Castle Hotel	C5
11	Lamu Guest House	C3
12	Lamu House	C1
13	New Mahrus Hotel	C4
14	Petley's Inn	C3
15	Pole Pole Guest House	A1
16	Stone House Hotel	B2
17	Sultan Palace Hotel	C3
18	Wildebeeste 1	C4
19	Wildebeeste 2	C4
20	Yumbe House	B2

Eating

21	Bush Gardens Restaurant	C4
22	Bustani Cafe	A1
	Lamu House	(see 12)
23	Main Market	C5
24	Mwana Arafa Restaurant Gardens	C1
	Stone House Hotel	(see 16)
25	Whispers Coffeeshop	D7

Drinking

	Lamu House	(see 12)
	Petley's Inn	(see 14)

Shopping

	Baraka Gallery	(see 25)
	Black & White Gallery	(see 6)
	Lamu Museum Shop	(see 4)
26	Mani Books & Stationers	D5

Information

27	Kenya Commercial Bank	C4

Transport

	Airkenya	(see 25)

Visitors are free to visit the sanctuary and learn about their work – donations appreciated.

Beaches BEACH

If you want to hit the beach, you've got the choice of a 40-minute walk (or quick KSh150 dhow ride) to Shela (p281) or you can catch some rays on the newly constructed **Uyoni Beach**, a manmade beach just a few minutes walk to the north of Lamu town. Being so new, it still feels very sterile (and a little like a building site), but give it a couple of years and some backing vegetation and it'll probably be quite pleasant.

Festivals & Events

Maulidi Festival ISLAMIC

The Maulidi Festival celebrates the birth of the Prophet Mohammed. Its date shifts according to the Muslim calendar; during the lifetime of this book it will fall sometime between January and February. The festival has been celebrated on the island for over 100 years and much singing, dancing and general jollity takes place around this time. On the final day a procession heads down to the tomb of the man who started it all, Ali Habib Swaleh.

Lamu Cultural Festival CULTURAL FESTIVAL

The Lamu Cultural Festival is another colourful carnival, exact dates vary each year but in 2011 it was held in November.

Sleeping

The alleyways of Lamu are absolutely rammed with places to stay and competition means that prices are often lower than in other parts of Kenya. There's always scope for price negotiation, especially if you plan to stay for over a day or two. Touts will invariably try and accompany you to get commission; the best way to avoid this is to book at least one night in advance, so you know what you'll be paying.

TOP CHOICE **Stone House Hotel** BOUTIQUE HOTEL $$

(☎633544; www.stonehousehotellamu.com; s/d with breakfast from US$40/60) This Swahili mansion is set into a tourist-free back street and is notable for its fine, whitewashed walls and fantastic rooftop, which includes a superb restaurant (no alcohol) with excellent views over the town and waterfront. The rooms are spacious and nicely decorated and it's easily one of the better value midrange options in town.

START LAMU MAIN JETTY
FINISH SHIAITHNA-ASHERI MOSQUE
DISTANCE ABOUT 1KM
DURATION 45 MINUTES TO ONE HOUR

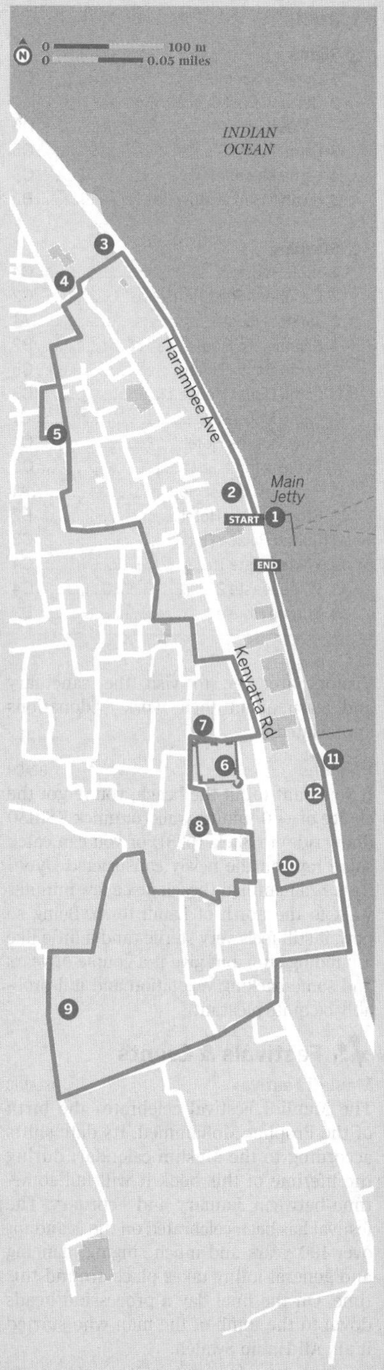

Walking Tour
Lamu Town

The best, indeed only, way to see Lamu town is on foot. Few experiences compare with exploring the far back streets, where you can wander amid wafts of cardamom and carbolic and watch the town's agile cats scaling the coral walls. There are so many wonderful Swahili houses that it's pointless for us to recommend specific examples – keep your eyes open wherever you go, and don't forget to look up.

Starting at the 1 **main jetty**, head north past the 2 **Lamu Museum** and along the waterfront until you reach the 3 **door-carving workshops**.

From here head onto Kenyatta Rd, passing an original Swahili 4 **well**, and into the alleys towards the 5 **Swahili House Museum**. Once you've had your fill of domestic insights, take any route back towards the main street.

Once you've hit the main square and the 6 **fort**, take a right to see the crumbled remains of the 14th-century 7 **Pwani Mosque**, one of Lamu's oldest buildings – an Arabic inscription is still visible on the wall. From here you can head round and browse the covered 8 **market**, then negotiate your way towards the bright Saudi-funded 9 **Riyadha Mosque**, the centre of Lamu's religious scene.

Now you can take as long or as short a route as you like back to the waterfront. Stroll along the promenade, diverting for the 10 **German Post Office Museum** if you haven't already seen it – the door is another amazing example of Swahili carving. If you're feeling the pace, take a rest and shoot the breeze on the 11 **baraza ya wazee** ('old men's bench') outside the stucco minarets of the 12 **Shiaithna-Asheri Mosque**.

Carrying on up Harambee Ave will bring you back to the main jetty.

TOP CHOICE Lamu House BOUTIQUE HOTEL $$$
(☎633491; www.lamuhouse.com; Harambee Ave; s/d €190/235; @☎✱) In a city where every building wants to top the preservation stakes, Lamu House stands out as the leader of the pack. It looks like an old Swahili villa, but it feels like a contemporarily decked out boutique hotel, where they've blended the pale, breezy romance of the Greek islands into an African palace, with predictably awesome results. In short it's one of the best hotels on the coast of Kenya.

Jambo House BOUTIQUE HOTEL $
(☎0713411714; www.jambohouse.com; s/d KSh2100/2500, with shared bathroom KSh1800/2200; ☎) The new star on the Lamu hotel scene, this highly regarded budget hotel has small but immaculate rooms in terracotta colours with electric-blue bathrooms. There's a fantastic rooftop terrace and a breakfast to rave about, but it's the owner, Arnold, who really makes the place stand out.

Yumbe House BOUTIQUE HOTEL $
(☎633101; lamuoldtown@africaonline.co.ke; s/d KSh2200/3000) As coral castles go, Yumbe's pretty good…wait a minute, did we say coral castle? Yes, it's a coral castle! With spacious rooms decorated with pleasant Swahili accents, verandahs that are open to the stars and the breeze, and a ridiculously romantic top-floor suite that's perfect for couples needing a palace tower retreat, Yumbe's a well-priced winner in a field of standouts.

Kilimanjaro House BOUTIQUE HOTEL $
(☎0721141924; www.kilimanjaro-lamu.com; town centre; s/d KSh2000/3000) Another nicely restored Swahili house, this is a smallish place, but friendly and cosy. It's across from the Stone House Hotel on a pleasantly quiet side street. We can't help feeling that it's a little overpriced though.

Pole Pole Guest House HOTEL $
(☎0722736768, 0715259139; s/d KSh800/1600) Pole Pole, set some way back from the waterfront, is one of the tallest buildings in Lamu and has bright doubles with fans and nets. Bathrooms, though, are a bit mouldy. There's a spacious *makuti*-roofed terrace area with great views and its own mini 'tower'.

Casuarina Rest House HOTEL $
(☎633123; r KSh1500) Some of the rooms (notably the triples) are a bit worse for wear, but this is still a budget bargain: a tilted palace with a social lounge rooftop, fun staff and a general sense of that feel-good backpacker-style camaraderie you'd have to be an ogre not to love. Sadly, recent price rises have made it much less of a bargain than it used to be.

Jannat House HOTEL $$
(☎633414; s/d from KSh3500/5000; ✱) The architects clearly had a field day designing

LAMU'S LAYOUT

Lamu town realises Swahili urban-planning conventions like few other places in the world. Within the seemingly random conglomeration of streets are a patchwork of neighbourhoods and districts divided by family hierarchy, social standing and profession.

There are 28 *mitaa* (districts) in Lamu, with names that range from the functional, such as *Madukani* (Place of Shopping), to the esoteric, such as *Makadara* (Eternal Destiny), to the funny, like *Kivundoni* (Smelly Place). In addition, the town is divided into two halves; the north, *Zena* (Beauteous) and the south, *Suudi* (Fortunate).

This division stems from the traditional contempt of the *Zijoho* (Arab-Swahili elite) for trade. The *Zena* half of town is, to this day, where the grandest houses are to be found, while the main markets, noisy activity and, to be frank, poorer, blacker faces are generally on the *Suudi* side of the tracks. Note that the construction/restoration of grand houses by foreigners has disrupted this dynamic, but it's still present; you'll notice most of these new villas are on the *Zena* side of town.

Also note how the 'front' of a house tends to face north. This may be because of the Muslim concept of kiblah, the direction towards Mecca in which Muslims are supposed to pray (a Swahili term for north is *upande ya kibla*). Or it may be for sunlight protection.

Like most Swahili houses, Lamu homes were built around courtyards. The town's sanitation system was once an engineering marvel, but today it is overtaxed by overpopulation. This can make for some hairy, stinky times of overflow (especially given all the donkey crap lying around) – watch your step here after it rains.

Jannat: it's essentially two houses spliced together around a courtyard, with several levels and multiple terraces. Sadly, though, nobody has remembered to maintain it and so it's starting to look a little rundown and a little overpriced. Rooms on the upper floors are much better than those lower down. The pool is a rare refresher in these parts.

Petley's Inn HOTEL $
(☎0726275438; Harambee Ave; r KSh3500) With the prime waterfront location right in front of the main jetty and with views to kill for, you might well expect Petley's to be vastly overpriced, but its spacious rooms are some of the better value ones in town. It had just been taken over by new management when we last passed by, so expect some changes to have taken place by the time you get there (including even the name).

Sultan Palace Hotel APARTMENT $
(☎0723593292; Kenyatta Rd; apt per person KSh3000) Central lodging house with a handful of impressive apartment-style rooms in sunny Mediterranean colours and with creaky Swahili four-poster beds. It's a good value option for single travellers but kind of overpriced for couples.

Wildebeeste 1 & 2 APARTMENTS $
(☎0712851499; apt KSh2500-3000) Well it's certainly the most memorable place to stay in Lamu, but depending on your mood it will either come across as dusty and neglected or eccentric and arty. The truth lies somewhere in between (though it probably leans more towards the former). The compound is divided into apartments, which sleep from two to six people.

THE NEW FACE OF LAMU

Lamu is often touted as an isolated island community untouched by the rest of the world. This, of course, is sheer fantasy, but today Lamu is at the centre of a massive new development project for North Kenya that will see life change dramatically and forever in Lamu. The proposed project envisions the archipelago hosting one of the biggest ports in East Africa, an oil pipeline from South Sudan, a US naval base, a series of new resorts, a new airport and a train line and multi-lane highways that will link Lamu to the rest of the country. For more on this see the box on p219.

Amu House APARTMENT $
(☎0718196286; apt without breakfast KSh2000) Above the Black & White Gallery (see p280) there is only one huge apartment available here. It's fairly simple, but is airy and cool and would be a good bet for long-stay families.

Lamu Guest House HOTEL $
(☎633338; Kenyatta Rd; s/d without breakfast KSh1000/1750, with shared bathroom KSh800/1600) The basic rooms here are very plain, but the upper-floor ones are better and catch the sea breeze. The 'official' rates quoted here are a good KSh500 more than you'll end up paying. Abdul, the boss, is a real character – check out his shell-picture collection.

They're both mega tatty, but the **Lamu Castle Hotel** (behind the main market), and **New Mahrus Hotel** (Kenyatta Rd) have rooms for as low as KSh600 if you're truly budget-conscious.

Eating

It's important to know all the cheap places to eat, and that many of the more expensive restaurants are closed until after sunset during Ramadan.

Lamu's fruit juices, which almost every restaurant sells, are worth drawing attention to. They're good. They're really, really good.

As well as the restaurants listed here it's worth checking out the very up-market dining on offer at Lamu House (p277) or the slightly less refined rooftop restaurant inside the Stone House Hotel (p275).

At some point most travellers will come across Ali Hippy, who offers meals at his house (price dependent on number of people and weight of fish bought) and will almost certainly point out his presence in this book. The whole family entertains you while you eat and some people come away quite satisfied, but plenty are put off instantly by the sales pitch!

Self-caterers should head to the main market next to the fort.

TOP CHOICE **Mwana Arafa Restaurant Gardens** SEAFOOD $$
(Harambee Ave; meals KSh350-800; ⊙lunch & dinner) One of the more up-market restaurants in Lamu; it has a perfect combination of garden seating and views over the dhows bobbing about under the moonlight. With barbequed giant prawns, grilled calamari,

SAFETY ON LAMU

In September 2011 an English couple staying on the island of Kiwayu, north of Lamu, were attacked by Somali pirates/militants. One person died and one was kidnapped and taken to Somalia. It was widely thought that this was a one-off attack and that Lamu itself was not at risk. However, despite a massive beefing up of security, just over two weeks later another attack occurred. This time a French woman was kidnapped from her home on Manda Island and taken to Somalia (where she later died); with Manda being almost within swimming distance of Lamu it suddenly seemed as if anywhere within the archipelago was at risk. Because of this, at the time of writing, most Western governments were advising against all but essential travel to coastal areas within 150km of the Somalia border, which includes the entire Lamu archipelago. In addition, the Kenyan government had announced that all fishing boats and their crews along the entire Kenyan coast were to report to police before and after each fishing trip and that all boats were to be inspected. Fishing was banned altogether in the waters between Kiwayu Island and the Somali border.

Such statements mean that most tour operators will pull out of Lamu and the effects on the local tourist industry are likely to be enormous. Many locals and tourists will see such warnings as being unnecessarily cautious and they may well be right, but there are a couple of points to bear in mind.

Firstly, as long as the government travel warnings remain in force, many insurance companies will not cover you for trips to Lamu. This means that if, for example, you were hospitalised in Lamu then your insurance company is not obliged to pay out.

In October 2011 the Kenyan military invaded southern Somalia in an effort to push militants and criminal gangs away from the common border. In response, al-Shahab threatened to launch attacks on Kenya. Once again Lamu, with its combination of Western tourists, a US naval base, the construction of a huge oil pipeline to South Sudan and ease of access via sea or land from Somalia, will be a prime target for terrorist attacks. Sadly this is a threat that is unlikely to decrease until the conflicts of Somalia are solved.

The above information is likely to change within the lifetime of this book and we would urge you to check the latest on the security situation before venturing to Lamu, although at the time of going to print there had been no further attacks and independent travellers were starting to return to these otherwise blessed isles.

lobster or a seafood platter, we guess you'll be eating the fruits of the sea tonight.

Bustani Café CAFE $

(meals KSh120-300) This is a very enjoyable garden cafe where the tables are set about a lily-bedecked pond. The small menu includes lots of healthy salads and various snack foods. The cafe also contains a decent bookshop and an evening-only internet cafe (KSh240 per hour).

Olympic Restaurant KENYAN $

(Harambee Ave; mains KSh250-700; ⌚lunch & dinner) The family that runs the Olympic makes you feel as if you've come home every time you enter, and their food, particularly the curries and biriyani, is excellent. There are few better ways to spend a Lamu night than with a cold mug of passionfruit juice and the noir-ish view of the docks you get here, at the ramshackle end of town.

Bush Gardens Restaurant INTERNATIONAL $$

(Harambee Ave; mains KSh180-800; ⌚breakfast, lunch & dinner) Bush Gardens is the template for a whole set of restaurants along the waterfront, offering breakfasts, seafood (including 'monster crab' and the inevitable lobster in Swahili sauce) and superb juices and shakes mixed up in panelled British pint mugs.

Whispers Coffeeshop CAFE $$

(Kenyatta Rd; mains KSh240-750; ⌚9am-9pm) You know how sometimes you just need that escape into the world of magazines and fresh pastries? Welcome to Whispers. For a fresh pizza, real cappuccino or the best desserts in town, this garden cafe, set in the same building as the Baraka Gallery, is highly recommended.

Tay Ran KENYAN $

(Kenyatta Rd; mains KSh100) This very basic place, which doesn't even have a sign board

DON'T MISS

DHOW TRIPS

More than the bustle of markets or the call to prayer, the pitch of, 'We take dhow trip, see mangroves, eat fish and coconut rice', is the unyielding chorus Lamu's voices offer up when you first arrive. With that said, taking a dhow trip (and seeing the mangroves and eating fish and coconut rice) is almost obligatory and generally fun besides, although this depends to a large degree on your captain.

Incompetent crews will lead you on a dreary day of nonstop tacking up Manda Channel and give you disastrously false information about local sites. Good ones are competent seamen and knowledgeable of the area. And the good is, frankly, great. There's a real joy to kicking it on the boards under the sunny sky, with the mangroves drifting by in island time while snacking on spiced fish.

Prices vary depending on where you want to go and how long you go for; with bargaining you could pay around KSh1000 per person in a group of four or five people. Make sure you know exactly how much you'll be paying and what that will include. Don't hand over any money until the day of departure, except perhaps a small advance for food. On long trips, it's best to organise your own drinks. A hat and sunscreen are essential.

(and which might be spelt Tehran – no one behind the counter seemed to know or care) serves dirt-cheap meals of fish, beans done in several ways (the best is *maharagwe ya chumvi* – with coconut milk) and chapattis. It's consistently packed with locals and is pretty much open all the time.

Drinking & Entertainment

As a Muslim town, Lamu has few options for drinkers and local sensibilities should be respected. **Full moon parties** sometimes take place in season over on Manda Island. The local beach boys should be able to advise. **Petley's Inn** (Harambee Ave) and **Lamu House** (Harambee Ave) both have nice bars where you can sink a cold beer. Petley's has the edge as it gets much livelier, the pool table is well used and it has a ridiculous glitter ball–lit dance floor.

Civil Servants' Club CLUB
(admission KSh100) Even bureaucrats need to let their hair down and the Civil Servants' Club, along the waterfront towards Shela village, is virtually the only reliable spot for a drink and a dance on weekends. It's small, loud and rowdy. Lone women should run for cover, lone men should expect working-girl attention and the harbour wall outside is a potential death-trap after a few Tuskers.

Shopping

There's a huge international market for traditional doors, furniture and window frames and many families have actually sold off their doors and other furnishings. If you want something custom-made, carvers tend to concentrate on the north side of the waterfront. Woodwork that's slightly more friendly to your airline baggage allowance includes picture frames, *bao* sets, Quran stands and *ito* – round painted 'eyes' from Swahili dhows, originally used as talismans to avoid underwater obstacles and protect against the evil eye.

Lamu is also a good place to buy *kikois*, the patterned wraps traditionally worn by Swahili men. The standard price is around KSh350, more for the heavier Somali style.

Baraka Gallery CRAFTS
(Kenyatta Rd) For upmarket Africana, Baraka Gallery has a fine selection, but stratospheric prices.

Black & White Gallery CRAFTS
Spanish-run art shop with some beautiful tribal-inspired crafts and paintings.

Lamu Museum Shop BOOKSHOP
(Harambee Ave) Specialists in Lamu and Swahili cultural books.

Mani Books & Stationers BOOKSHOP
(Kenyatta Rd) A very meagre collection of novels and other books.

Information

Dangers & Annoyances

Most Western governments were advising against all travel to Lamu and the remainder of the archipelago at the time of writing. See the box on p279.

When times are normal the biggest real issue are the beach boys. They'll come at you the minute you step off the boat, offering drugs, tours and hotel bookings (the last can be useful if you're disoriented).

Lamu has long been popular for its relaxed, tolerant atmosphere, but it does have Muslim views of what is acceptable behaviour. In 1999, a gay couple who planned a public wedding here had to be evacuated under police custody. Whatever your sexuality, it's best to keep public displays of affection to a minimum and respect local attitudes to modesty.

Internet Access

Cyberwings (across from Petley's Inn; per hr KSh40; ⏲8am-8pm)

Real Tyme Cyber Cafe (per min KSh1; ⏲8am-10pm) Inside Lamu Fort.

Medical Services

King Fadh Lamu District Hospital (☎633075) One of the most modern and well-equipped hospitals on the coast.

Lamu Medical Clinic (Kenyatta Rd; ⏲8am-9pm)

Langoni Nursing Home (☎633349; Kenyatta Rd; ⏲24hr) Offers clinic services.

Money

Local shopkeepers may be able to help with changing money.

Kenya Commercial Bank (Harambee Ave) The only bank on Lamu has an ATM (Visa only).

Post

Post office (Harambee Ave)

Tourist Information

Tourist information office (☎633132; Harambee Ave; lamu@tourism.go.ke; ⏲9am-1pm & 2-4pm)

 Getting There & Away

Air

Airkenya (☎633445; www.airkenya.com; Baraka House, Kenyatta Rd) offers daily afternoon flights between Lamu and Wilson Airport in Nairobi (US$195, 1¾ hours).

Fly540 (☎632054; www.fly540.com) offers twice-daily flights to Malindi (around US$45) and Nairobi (around US$170).

Safarilink (www.flysafarilink.com) offers daily flights to Nairobi Wilson airport (around US$185).

The airport at Lamu is on Manda Island, and the ferry across the channel to Lamu costs KSh150. You will be met by 'guides' at the airport who will offer to carry your bags to the hotel of your choice for a small consideration (about KSh200). Many double as touts, so be cautious about accepting the first price you are quoted when you get to your hotel.

Bus

There are booking offices for several bus companies on Kenyatta Rd. The going rate for a trip to Mombasa is KSh600 to KSh700 and to Malindi it's KSh500; most buses leave between 7am and 8am, so you'll need to be at the jetty at 6.30am to catch the boat to the mainland. It takes at least four hours to get from Lamu to Malindi, plus another two hours to Mombasa. Book early.

 Getting Around

There are ferries (KSh50) between Lamu and the bus station on the mainland (near Mokowe). Boats leave when the buses arrive at Mokowe; in the reverse direction, they leave at around 6.30am to meet the departing buses. Private charters cost KSh1500. Ferries between the airstrip on Manda Island and Lamu cost KSh150 and leave about half an hour before the flights leave (yes, in case you're wondering, all the airline companies are aware of this and so that's sufficient time). Expect to pay KSh200 for a custom trip if you miss either of these boats.

Between Lamu village and Shela there are plenty of motorised dhows throughout the day until around sunset; these cost about KSh150 per person and leave when full.

There are also regular ferries between Lamu and Paté Island (see p286).

Around Lamu

SHELA

Shela has undergone a severe case of gentrification and is sort of like Lamu put through a high-end wringer. It's cleaner, more sterile, has less character and a lot more expats. On the plus side, there's a long, lovely stretch of beach and a link to a specific slice of coast culture – the locals speak a distinct dialect, which they're quite proud of.

Sights & Activities

Beach BEACH

Most people are here for the beach – a 12km-long sweep of sand where you're guaranteed an isolated spot (at least if you're prepared to walk some way!) to pitch your kit and catch some rays. But as locals say, *Yana vuta kwa kasi* – 'There is a violent current there'. And no lifeguards. Tourists drown every year, so don't swim out too far. It should be pointed out that, beautiful as Shela beach is, it's more of a wild, windy and empty kind of beauty rather than an intimate palm-tree-backed tropical beauty.

DON'T MISS

BEST BEACHES

Lay a towel down on one of these beauties and feel the smile spread over your face.

» **Manda Island** It's a desert island in the Indian Ocean. Of course it's good.

» **Shela Beach** Vast, wild and empty (if you walk a bit).

» **Watamu** (p260) Turquoise waters, laid-back vibe, great snorkelling.

Water Sports WATER SPORTS

There's reasonable **windsurfing** in the channel between Shela and Manda Island.

The **water-sports centre** at Peponi Hotel runs all kinds of activities of the damp sort, including diving, snorkelling, windsurfing and kayaking.

Sleeping

All room rates include breakfast. You can negotiate all these prices when business is slow.

As so many houses in Shela are owned by expats who only live here part-time, there's a huge amount of accommodation available, very little of which is widely advertised outside the island. The best place to check these out and book ahead of time is through **Lamu Retreats** (www.lamuretreats.com), which will help you into 11 posh houses situated between Shela and Lamu town.

TOP CHOICE **Stopover Guest House** GUESTHOUSE $

(☎0720127222; s/d KSh4500-5000) The first place you come to on the waterfront is this simply beautiful guesthouse of pure white unfussy lines. Rooms are spacious, airy, bright and crisp, and a salt wind through your carved window-shutters is the best alarm clock we can think of. It's above the popular restaurant of the same name.

Kijani House Hotel BOUTIQUE HOTEL $$$

(☎Nairobi 020-243700; www.kijani-lamu.com; s/d €125-180; ⊙closed May & Jun; @📶🏊) This villa complex is enormous, yet the design is elegantly understated, achieving a sort of Zen or Swahili aesthetic even as it spoils you with luxuriant tropical gardens, the nicest pool in Lamu and palatial-sized, and equally palatially decorated, rooms. It's one of the best top-end deals on the island.

White House HOTEL $

(☎0734183500; www.shelalamu.com; d from KSh3500) With rooms that look like they could fit in a Swahili cultural museum, a great roof lounge and breeze-laced views, this is one of the better deals in Shela. It's located a little way north of Peponi.

Peponi Hotel HOTEL $$$

(☎Nairobi 020-2435033; www.peponi-lamu.com; s/d from €175/215; ⊙closed May & Jun; @📶🏊) If there were a capital of Shela it would be located here: this top-end resort has a grip on everything in this village, from tours to water sports to whatever else you can imagine. Sleeping-wise it's a winner, but then for the price they're charging you'd hope so! The fairly lavish rooms are decorated in the usual Swahili styles of light colours set off by dark embellishments.

Shella Pwani Guest House HOTEL $

(☎0712506778; r from KSh3500) This lovely Swahili house, located a little east of Stopover Guest House in town, is all decked out with carved plasterwork and pastel accents. Some rooms have fine sea views, as does the airy roof terrace, and some of the bathrooms are modelled to look like kiblahs (mosque prayer niches). The Muslim owners of the hotel don't seem to find this offensive, if you were wondering.

Jannataan Hotel HOTEL $

(☎0722729219; www.shelalamu.com; d with breakfast from KSh2500; 🏊) Ever wonder what a Swahili-run Holiday Inn would look like? How about a pretty compound of soft yellow stone rooms, arranged in big boxy fashion around a pretty pool? Sadly, the interior of the rooms is a little uninspiring.

Eating & Drinking

TOP CHOICE **Stopover Restaurant** SEAFOOD $$

(Stopover Guest House; mains KSh350-1200) There are waterfront restaurants all over the place here, but the Stopover's friendly staff and excellent grub (of the spicy Swahili seafood sort) make it a cut above the competition. Oh, and it's a big call, but its fruit juices might just be the best around…

Rangaleni Café KENYAN $

(meals KSh60-100) Hidden away in the alleys behind the shorefront mosque is this tiny greeny-turquoise cafe, which does the usual stews and *ugali* (staple made from maize or cassava flour or both).

Peponi's Bar BAR

(Peponi's Hotel) Naturally, the bar at a Swiss-owned Kenyan hotel with an Italian name has to resemble an English pub. Pretty much everyone on Shela comes to this terrace for a (ridiculously expensive) sundowner as evening sets in.

Getting There & Away

You can take a motorised dhow here from the moorings in Lamu for KSh150 per person. Alternatively, you can walk it in about 40 minutes. The easiest way is to take Harambee Ave (the waterfront road) and follow the shoreline, though this may be partly flooded at high tide. If that's the case, wade through the sunken bits or cut across to the inland track, which starts near the Muslim cemetery in Lamu. If you need to get back to Lamu (or Shela) after dark, find someone to walk with (restaurant staff are often happy to accompany solo travellers once they get off their shift) and bring a torch as the tides are unpredictable and there have been muggings in the past, especially on the inland track. Boat captains, for all their 'brother, we are one' prattle, will rip you off if you want a ride back at night.

MATONDONI & KIPUNGANI

The best place to see dhows being built is the village of **Matondoni**, in the northwest of the island. It's a peaceful little fishing village that receives few visitors so the welcome is always warm. To get there from Lamu town you have a choice of walking (6km, or about two hours – ask for directions from the back of town and follow the telephone poles), hiring a donkey or taking an organised dhow trip (which normally continues onto Kipungani for a swim and, sea conditions depending, then loops around the entire island and back to Lamu town via Shela).

Kipungani, 'the place of fresh air', is a small village at the southwest tip of Lamu Island where locals make straw mats, baskets, hats and *kifumbu,* used to squeeze milk from mashed coconut. Tea and snacks can be arranged and there's a beautiful empty beach nearby, but it's a long, hot walk to get here from Lamu or Shela and the path is very hard to find.

Sleeping

Kipungani Explorer RESORT **$$$**

(Nairobi 020-4446651; www.heritage-eastafrica.com; s/d full board from US$247/380; closed Apr-Jun). The only accommodation here is at this exclusive resort. It's quite luxurious, in a rustic, end-of-the-world, *banda*-on-the-beach kind of way, which is probably what you're looking for if you come out this far. The resort deserves a shout-out for employing local villagers as staff, funding school projects, experimenting with solar and wind power and sourcing food from village fishermen.

Manda Island

Manda is a quiet lattice of dune and mangroves a short hop and jump (OK, a 30-minute boat ride) from Lamu. The island has just started to feel the claws of development, and the shoreline facing Lamu is now backed by a couple of places to stay and

SWAHILI ARCHITECTURE

The Swahili culture has produced one of the most distinctive architectures in Africa, if not the world. Once considered a stepchild of Arabic building styles, Swahili architecture, while owing some of its aesthetic to the Middle East, is more accurately a reflection of African design partly influenced by the Arab (and Persian, Indian and even Mediterranean) worlds.

One of the most important concepts of Swahili space is marking the line between the public and private, while also occasionally blurring those borders. So, for example, you'll see Lamu stoops (semi-covered doorway areas or porches) that exist both in the public arena of the street yet serve as a pathway into the private realm of the home. The use of stoops as a place for conversation further blends these inner and outer worlds. Inside the home, the emphasis is on creating an airy, natural interior that contrasts with the exterior constricting network of narrow streets. The use of open space also facilitates breezes that serve as natural air-conditioning.

You will find large courtyards, day beds placed on balconies and porches that all provide a sense of horizon within a town where the streets can only accommodate a single donkey. Other elements include *dakas* (verandahs), which again sit in the transitional zone between the street and home and also provide open areas; *vidaka,* wall niches that either contain a small decorative curio or serve a decorative purpose in their own right and *mambrui* (pillars), which are used extensively in Swahili mosques.

several huge private villas. Away from here, though, the island quickly starts to feel like a deserted fleck – an impression that extends with the shadows as they grow with the setting sun in the thornbush-lined alleyways of the once great city of Takwa.

Sights & Activities

Takwa Ruins RUINS

(adult/child KSh500/250; 6.30am-6pm) What sets the Takwa ruins, the remains of a city that existed between the 15th and 17th centuries, apart from other archaeological sites on the coast? Quiet. When you're here and the light shatters in the trees, which have grown over some 100 ruined Mecca-aligned houses, you feel as if the ruins are speaking to you in the breeze. As you're likely to have Takwa to yourself, it's a good spot to enter an abandoned home and ponder the lives of whoever inhabited it without the buzz of a guide. The seminal structure here is the **Jamaa mosque**, with its unusually tall pillar facade. You can arrange camping here for about US$10; it's a supremely peaceful way to spend a star-heavy evening.

Beaches BEACH

The island is ringed by beaches (and in places mangrove swamps and mud flats) and it's easy to find a quiet patch of sand on which to lay your towel. The most popular beach (but still virtually deserted) is the one facing Lamu.

Manda Toto Island SNORKELLING

Just off the northeast coast of Manda is Manda Toto Island, which offers some of the best snorkelling possibilities in the archipelago. The only way to get here is by dhow, a full day (there and back) from Lamu.

Sleeping & Eating

All places to stay have in-house restaurants, which is handy because there aren't any other eating options.

TOP CHOICE **Diamond Beach Village** HUT $$

(0720915001; www.diamondbeachvillage.com; s/d with breakfast from UK£45/90;) This is one of those Robinson Crusoe–style beach-shack hideouts; but don't worry, that doesn't mean it's basic. The thatched huts stand out thanks to the judicious use of driftwood and shell art and there are lots of cosy nooks and crannies. If you want a different view of the world, opt for the eccentric tree house perched up in the branches of an old baobab tree. The beach out the front is glorious. We can't help feeling that it's a little overpriced though.

Manda Bay RESORT $$$

(Nairobi 020-2115453; www.mandabay.com) This was, and hopefully in the future will again become, a luxury top-end resort sitting on the northern end of the island. However, due to the attacks around Lamu by Somali pirates/militias, at the time of writing it was closed. You should note that none of the attacks took place here, but that it had been closed just as a precaution.

Getting There & Away

The trip across to Manda from Lamu takes about half an hour by boat (to the beach opposite Lamu). Once in a blue moon a boat man will take you for just KSh350, but somewhere between KSh450 to KSh600 is much more realistic. It can sometimes be cheaper if you take a boat to Shela first and then another from there across the channel. To the Takwa ruins takes around 1½ hours and can only be done at high tide. Since you have to catch the outgoing tide, your time at Takwa will probably be an hour or less.

Paté Island

Paté is a low island of green brush, silver tidal flats, coconut trees like thin legs dancing in the wind, and a red track slithering over dust-embedded ridges and rivers. And it is quiet. Not like 'small town quiet', but 'utter auditory void' quiet. You can walk over the island in about seven hours (excluding lots of stopping time for chats and cups of tea with locals) or ride across in one of the jeeps that act as an informal bus service.

As isolated from the modern world as Paté is, this was once the dominant island of the archipelago. 'None who go to Paté returns; what returns is wailing', goes one archipelago song. Whether this refers to military battles or the slave trade that was conducted through here is unknown, but the warning certainly doesn't apply now. Most people return from Paté with a peaceful smile these days.

You're likely to experience great hospitality here – residents are either not used to tourists and consider them a happy novelty, or work in the tourism industry in Lamu and appreciate your making the effort to come all the way out here.

Sights and Activities

Siyu & Shanga VILLAGE, RUINS

It's hard to believe today that Siyu was once the major city of the Lamu archipelago, with 30,000 inhabitants and several major universities. The only remnant of this glory is an enormous **fort**, which, given its emergence from the abandoned mangrove and coconut forest, is quite dramatic. Today Siyu is a small village with a whole lot of donkeys; locals will happily put you up with a meal for about KSh400 to KSh600.

South of Siyu is **Shanga**, arguably the oldest archaeological site on the Kenyan coast. Legend says it was originally settled by stranded Chinese traders (the name being a corruption of 'China'), but this version of events is disputed. We can say this for sure, though: getting here requires a rewarding slog through a mangrove swamp and under swaying palm-groves and, once you arrive, there's a real feeling of discovery. That's probably because Shanga is, despite its obscurity, the most complete example of a medieval Swahili town in the world. You may be able to hire a guide in Siyu (several men here helped dig out Shanga in the 1980s), but otherwise you're on your own and, if you have any sense of imagination, feeling very Indiana Jones.

Be on the lookout for a 21-sided pillar tomb topped by a 15th-century celadon bowl, five town gates, 'Lamu' arches constructed of sandstone bedrock, coral ragstone and sand gathered from the nearby dunes, tablets marked with Arabic inscriptions and the ruins or foundations of some 130 houses and 300 tombs. There is no official Museums of Kenya presence here so your visit is free, but remember *not to remove anything* from the site.

Faza VILLAGE, RUINS

The biggest settlement on the island has a chequered history. Faza was almost totally destroyed by Paté in the 13th century, then again by the Portuguese in 1586 or 1587 (accounts differ but it is known that the Portuguese chopped off the local sheik's head and preserved it in salt). With the demise of slavery, Faza faded away, but its new status as an administrative centre is breathing some life back into the place.

The modern town is quite extensive, if not terribly interesting. A major fire in 2010 largely gutted the town and destroyed what old buildings there were (amazingly nobody died). Today the town has been totally rebuilt and you'd hardly know that a fire had taken place. The only remaining historical relics are rotting Portuguese offices on the waterfront, the ruined **Kunjanja Mosque** on the creek next to the district headquarters and the **Mbwarashally Mosque**, also ruined, with a mihrab containing beautiful heart motifs, including the *shahada* (Muslim declaration of faith) written in an inverted heart pattern. Outside town is the **tomb of Amir Hamad**, commander of the sultan of Zanzibar's forces, who was killed here in 1844 while campaigning against Siyu and Paté.

A GUIDE TO PATÉ

To get the most out of a trip to Paté Island it's well worth having a little local help. **Mansur Ile** (0717165311) is a top guide to the island's historical sites. He worked on many of the original excavations, knows the island intimately and speaks superb English.

Paté Town VILLAGE, RUINS

Paté town, on the west side of the island, is a functioning village carved out of orange and brown coral ragstone. The **Nabahani ruins**, which are slowly vanishing under a riot of tropical vegetation and banana plantations, are just outside town. They've never been seriously excavated, yet National Museums of Kenya still manages to charge you KSh500 to enter! A lot of locals will tell you to go after sunset for free – we plead silence on passing moral judgement on this activity.

The modern village itself is almost identical in design and construction to the ruins and in fact the two merge almost seamlessly into one another. Paté, with its tall coral-ragstone houses and narrow streets leading to a small port among the mangroves, is a fascinating place to wander around.

Sleeping & Eating

Accommodation and food are easy to arrange with local families, and there are one or two simple restaurants offering basic meals and tea. The only formal accommodation is in Faza Town.

Peponi Hotel HOTEL $

(r without breakfast KSh500) You know the Hilton and Sheraton hotel chains? Well, this is nothing like those. Not even slightly.

SAFETY ON KIWAYU

In September 2011 an English couple staying at the Kiwayu Safari Village were attacked by Somali pirates/militants. The man was shot and killed and the woman was kidnapped and taken to Somalia. At the time of writing all accommodation on the island was closed, all foreign embassies were advising against travel to Kiwayu, and the Kenyan government had even banned all fishing by locals (and any other nautical activities) in the vicinity of the island. Unless things change dramatically during the lifetime of this book you should stay away from Kiwayu.

It is a bed for the night though, and the family who runs it (and can provide meals) are lovely. It's also known as the Thuerya Hotel.

Getting There & Away

A motor launch leaves Lamu more or less daily for Mtangawanda (diesel/petrol boat KSh250/350, about two hours). Boats continue to Faza (KSh150, about another two hours) and Kizingitini (an additional KSh150, another one hour), also stopping at the mouth of the channel to Siyu (KSh100), where small boats transfer passengers to shore. Boats leave from the main jetty in Lamu town; times depend on the tides, but it can be tricky finding out when they go, as everyone you ask will tell you something different! It's normally around one or two hours before high tide. Note that the boats can't always get very close to shore so you might need to wade ashore.

Coming back from Paté, ask to make sure the boat will be calling at Mtangawanda on the return trip. If not, you may have to wait an extra day.

A bunch of landrover taxis meet the boats and link the three main settlements on the island together. Taxi fares from Mtangawanda:

Paté Town KSh50
Siyu KSh150
Faza KSh200

Kiwayu Island

At the far northeast of the Lamu archipelago, Kiwayu Island has a population of just a few hundred people and is part of the **Kiunga Marine National Reserve** (adult/child US$15/10). Gloriously remote, it's a long, narrow ridge of sand and trees surrounded by reefs, with a long beach stretching all down the eastern side of the island. Standing at the tallest point and surveying your surroundings at sunset will probably be one of the defining experiences of your time on the coast.

The main reason to come here is for the three-day dhow trip itself, and to explore the coral reefs off the eastern side of the island, rated as some of the best along the Kenyan coast.

The village on the western side of the island where the dhows drop anchor is very small, but it does have a general store with a few basics.

Sleeping & Eating

Following the attack on Kiwayu Safari Village all accommodation was closed. The following reviews are based on pre-September 2011 information. It's unknown if these resorts will ever reopen.

Munira Island Camp RESORT **$$$**
(www.mikescampkiwayu.com) Seven glorious *bandas*. Also known as Mike's Camp.

Kiwayu Safari Village RESORT **$$$**
(www.kiwayu.com) An exclusive collection of open luxury *bandas*.

Getting There & Away

The most interesting trip to Kiwayu used to be by dhow. The island formed part of a three- or five-day dhow trip from Lamu, usually with stops along the way. At the time of writing all dhow trips to the island had ceased.

If you'd rather spend more time on the island and less on the boat, you used to be able to take the public ferry to Kizingitini on Paté and catch a dhow from there. However, at the time of writing it was unlikely that anyone on Paté would be willing to take you across.

Understand Kenya

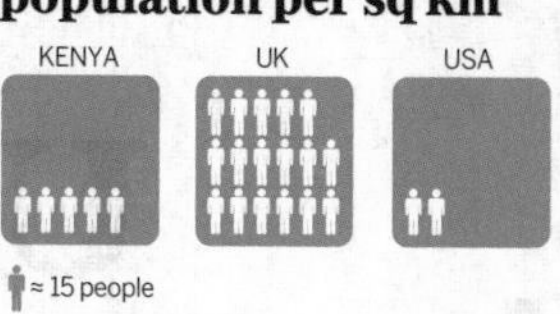

Kenya Today

» Population: 41.07 million

» Total fertility rate: 4.19 children per woman

» Population growth rate: 2.46%

» Average age: 18.9

» Life expectancy: 59.48 years

» Urban population as % of total: 75%

Cementing Democracy

Depending on how you look at it, Kenya's democracy is either extremely robust or in a permanent state of peril. After the horrendous violence that followed the disputed elections of 2007 – violence that resulted in 1000 deaths, 600,000 Kenyans displaced from their homes and six senior Kenyan public figures forced to appear before the International Criminal Court – the country is holding its breath in advance of the 2012 poll. The surprising stability with which the government of erstwhile foes President Mwai Kibaki (who will be standing down after two terms) and Prime Minister Raila Odinga (a leading candidate for the presidency) has ruled Kenya (since being forced into a marriage of convenience) has restored considerable faith in the country's democratic institutions. Cynicism, however, remains high among ordinary Kenyans when it comes to their political class. More than that, the underlying suspicions between various tribal groupings, poverty, and the increasing competition for scarce resources, which lay behind the violence, remain unresolved.

Climbing Out of Poverty

Kenya's economy is booming, and neither natural disasters, post-election violence or war with Somalia can shake the country's confidence that Kenya is on the up. There's just one problem: only a small percentage of Kenyans see the benefits of the growing prosperity. Unemployment sits at around 40%, a staggering 50% of Kenyans live below the poverty line and the prices of basic foodstuffs are soaring. By one estimate, Kenya would require an annual growth rate of 11% for the prosperity gains to even begin to trickle down to poorer sectors of Kenyan society. Although Kenya has shown some gains in recent years, the Human Development

Top Books

A Primate's Memoir: Love, Death and Baboons in East Africa (Robert M Sapolsky) Funny, poignant account by a young primatologist in Kenya.

No Man's Land: An Investigative Journey Through Kenya and Tanzania (George Monbiot) The modern struggle of the region's nomadic tribes.

Out of Africa (Karen Blixen, aka Isak Dinesen) The definitive account of colonial Kenya.

The Flame Trees of Thika (Elspeth Huxley) A marvellously told colonial memoir.

The Tree Where Man Was Born (Peter Matthiessen) Classic of African nature writing.

Dreams in a Time of War (Ngũgĩ wa Thiong'o) Kenya's premier writer looks back at his early life.

Petals of Blood (Ngũgĩ wa Thiong'o) Perhaps Kenya's finest novel.

belief systems

(% of population)

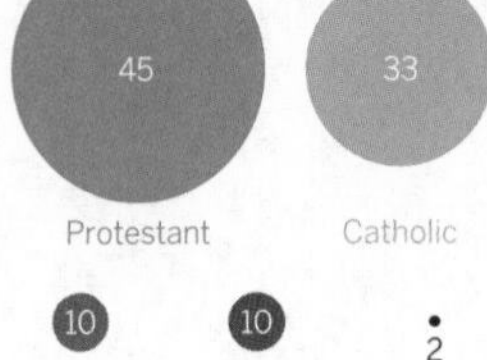

if Kenya were 100 people

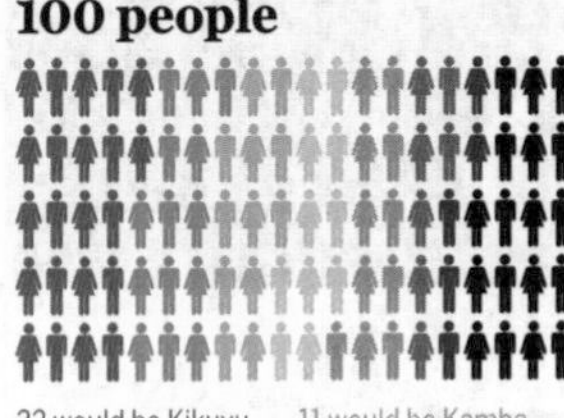

Report Index (which measures the well-being of a country, taking into account life expectancy, education and standard of living) ranked Kenya at a fairly dismal 143 out of 187 countries in 2011, while the country's income gap between rich and poor remains within the 10 worst in the world. Climbing up the world rankings in a range of indicators is a major long-term goal of the government, and few have disputed the worthy aims that lie behind the 'Vision 2030' blueprint for dragging the country out of poverty. Much, however, remains to be done.

» Land area: 580,367 sq km

» Highest point: Mt Kenya 5199m

» Lowest point: Indian Ocean 0m

» Land boundaries: 3477km

» Length of coastline: 536km

Kenya at War

In October 2011, for the first time in its independent history, Kenya went to war. The spark for such a drastic move was a series of cross-border raids allegedly carried out by al-Shabaab, an al-Qaeda-affiliated Somali group who stood accused of kidnapping foreign-aid workers and tourists from inside Kenya. Aware that its lucrative tourism industry could be at risk, Kenya's military launched a large-scale invasion of Somalia, claiming that it was acting in self-defence; most Western governments agreed. Whatever the outcome of the war (which remained ongoing at the time of writing), two consequences seemed clear. First, Kenya's decision to flex its muscles reflected the country's growing confidence as East Africa's most important regional powerhouse. Equally significant was the strain the conflict placed on Kenya's relations with its large Somali population. This was particularly true in Nairobi where the Muslim community as a whole came under suspicion for its supposed support for Somalia's Islamic groups. Although the initial hysteria soon subsided, the episode served as a reminder that Kenya's future as a multicultural, multi-faith state is always going to be complicated.

Top Docos

The Great Rift: Africa's Greatest Story (BBC) Fabulous 2010 study of the Rift Valley.

Big Cat Diary (BBC) Masai Mara leopards, lions and cheetahs.

Echo of the Elephants (BBC) The elephants of Amboseli National Park.

Dos & Don'ts

» **Do** take the time to talk with older Kenyans – it's amazing how far this country has come.

» **Do** learn a few words in Kiswahili – everyone speaks English, but Kenyans really appreciate the gesture.

» **Don't** eat with your left hand.

» **Don't** take the last food from the communal bowl – your hosts may worry that you're still hungry.

» **Do** eat with your hands if others are doing so, even if cutlery has been provided.

History

Africa's Great Rift Valley, including parts of Kenya, is where human beings first walked upright upon the earth, and Kenyan soil has yielded some of the most significant remains of humankind's forerunners.

Millions of years later, the ancestors of modern Kenyans began arriving in the country. While most of these peoples in the Kenyan interior went quietly about their business, coastal Kenya was increasingly connected with the outside world in the form of Indian Ocean trade with the Arabs, whose culture fused with that of the East African coast to form the hybrid Swahili people. Over time, trade yielded to coercion and exploitation, beginning with the Portuguese, then becoming a European free-for-all from 1500 until the late 19th century when at least two million East Africans were sold into exile and slavery.

The British appeared on the scene, also late in the 19th century, with grand notions of civilisation and profit. Choosing the best land for themselves, denying political participation to Kenyans and later co-opting many to fight in far-distant WWII all proved to be a recipe for disaster, prompting the devastating Mau Mau rebellion in the 1950s.

With independence won in 1963, Kenyans were once again let down by their rulers. After a promising start, Jomo Kenyatta and especially Daniel arap Moi (from 1978) ruled Kenya as their personal fiefdoms, institutionalising corruption, cracking down on the merest hint of dissent and pursuing self-aggrandising but ultimately disastrous economic policies. Deeply troubled elections throughout the 1990s hardly inspired confidence in Kenya's democratic process, but President Mwai Kibaki was finally sworn in on 30 December 2002 following free elections. Disillusionment over the pace of reform, coupled with the divisive politics of ethnicity, led to widespread ethnic violence following the disputed elections of 2007.

Somehow, the country has emerged once again at peace, with a new constitution and with Kenyans cautiously optimistic that the worst is behind them.

TIMELINE

3,700,000 BC

A group of early hominids walk across the Laetoli pan, moving away from the volcano. Their footsteps take them to the grasslands of the Serengeti plains.

1,760,000 BC

In 2011, archaeologists announce the discovery at Lake Turkana of a four-sided hand axe dubbed by scientists the 'Swiss army knife' of the Stone Age.

1,600,000 BC

In 1984, Kamoya Kimeu discovers the Turkana Boy, a nearly complete skeleton of an 11- or 12-year-old hominid boy who died 1.6 million years ago near Lake Turkana.

The First Kenyans

The Tugen Hills

Following the Leakey discoveries of hominid fossils at Olduvai Gorge in Tanzania in 1959, palaeontologists digging in the Tugen Hills, west of Lake Baringo, unearthed one of the most diverse and densely packed accumulations of fossil bone in Africa. Bedded down in lava flows and representing a unique archaeological record in Africa, the fossil beds incorporate that most elusive period of human history between 14 and 4 million years ago when the largely primate *Kenyapithecus* evolved into our earliest bipedal ancestor *Australopithecus afarensis*.

In the sandy clay, seven of the 18 hominoid specimens known from that period were found. The jaw fragment at 5 million years old represents the closest ancestor of *A afarensis,* that family band that left their footprints on the Laetoli mud pan (Tanzania), while a fragment of skull, dating from 2.4 million years ago, represents the earliest-known specimen of our own genus, *Homo*.

Prehistoric Sites

- Cradle of Humankind exhibit, National Museum, Nairobi
- Sibiloi National Park
- Olorgasailie Prehistoric Site
- Hyrax Hill Prehistoric Site
- Kariandusi Prehistoric Site

Lake Turkana

Richard Leakey – son of veteran archaeologists Louis and Mary – began digging in the Tugen Hills in 1967, but shifted to Lake Turkana in Kenya's north in 1969; he turned up dozens of fossil sites. Discoveries here were to turn accepted archaeological thought on its head with the surprise find of a completely new hominid specimen – *Homo habilis* (able man).

Prior to the Leakey discovery it was thought that there were only two species of proto-humans: the 'robust' hominids and the 'gracile' hominids, which eventually gave rise to modern humans. However, the Turkana finds demonstrated that the different species lived at the same time and even shared resources – advancing the Leakey theory that evolution was more complex than a simple linear progression.

For more on Kenya's fossil finds look up www.leakeyfoundation.org. Members can even sign up for trips with the Leakeys themselves.

In 1984, Kamoya Kimeu (a member of the Leakey expedition) uncovered the spectacular remains of a young boy's skeleton dating back 1.6 million years. Standing at a height of 1.6m tall, the boy was appreciably bigger than his *H habilis* contemporary. His longer limbs and striding gait were also more characteristic of modern human physiology, and his larger brain suggested greater cognitive ability. *H erectus* was the biggest and brainiest hominid to date and was the longest surviving and most widely dispersed of all the ancestral toolmakers, disappearing from the fossil records a mere 70,000 years ago.

From these remarkable evolutionary leaps it was but a small step to our closest ancestors, *H sapiens,* who made an appearance around 130,000 years ago.

100,000 BC

Homo sapiens strike out to colonise the world, moving into the eastern Mediterranean. By 40,000 years ago they reach Asia and Australia and 10,000 years later are settled across Europe.

2000–1000 BC

Immigrant groups colonise sub-Saharan Africa. First Cushites from Ethiopia move into central Kenya, followed by Nilote-speakers from Sudan. Finally, they're joined by Bantu-speakers from Nigeria and Cameroon.

400 BC

Azania (as the East African coast was then known) is known to the peoples of the Mediterranean and becomes an important trading post for the Greeks.

AD 200

It's estimated that by the year 200 there are 20 million people living in Africa. More than half live in North Africa, leaving only 10 million people in sub-Saharan Africa.

Kenya's Ancestors

Ten thousand years ago, Africa was unrecognisable: the Sahara was a green and pleasant land, and much of Kenya was uninhabitable because its tropical forests and swamps were inhabited by the deadly tsetse fly, which is fatal to cattle and people.

Over the five millennia that followed, a changing climate saw the tsetse belt drop south, Kenya's grasslands began to spread and migrating peoples from the north began to populate what we now know as Kenya. Soon, the peoples of the continent began to converge on East Africa.

The first arrivals of peoples from the north in East Africa were a Cushitic-speaking population, who moved south with their domestic stock from Ethiopia. At the same time a population of Nilote-speakers from the Sudan moved into the western highlands of the Rift Valley (the Maasai, Luo, Samburu and Turkana tribes are their modern-day descendants). These pastoralists shared the region with the indigenous Khoikhoi (ancestors of the modern-day San), who had occupied the land for thousands of years.

Africa's fourth linguistic family, the Bantu-speakers, arrived from the Niger Delta around 1000 BC. Soon they became East Africa's largest ethnolinguistic family, which they remain today. Kenya's largest tribe, the Kikuyu, along with the Gusii, Akamba and Meru tribes, are all descended from them.

Most of Kenya's peoples had arrived.

SWAHILI ORIGINS

The word *Swahili* originates from the Arabic word *sawahil*, which means 'of the coast'. It refers both to the Swahili language as well as the Islamic people of the coast.

Arabs, Swahili & Portuguese

The Land of Zanj

It was in the 8th century that Arab dhows began docking regularly in East African ports as part of their annual trade migration. In their wake, Arabs set up trading posts along the seaboard, intermarrying with Africans and creating a cosmopolitan culture that became known as Swahili. Before long there were Arab-Swahili city states all along the coast from Somalia to Mozambique; the remains of many of these settlements can still be seen, most notably at Gede (p263).

By the 10th century the 'Land of Zanj' (the present-day coastal region of Kenya and Tanzania) was exporting leopard skins, tortoiseshell, rhino horns, ivory and, most importantly, slaves and gold to Arabia and India. Ports included Shanga, Gede, Lamu and Mombasa as well as Zanzibar (Tanzania). Kilwa, 300km south of Zanzibar, marked the southernmost limit of travel for Arab dhows. For over 700 years, up to 1450, the Islamic world was virtually the only external influence on sub-Saharan Africa.

200–300

With the introduction of the camel, trans-Saharan journeys become practicable and profitable. The news of large gold deposits undoubtedly spur Arab ambitions and interests in the continent.

800

Muslims from Arabia and Persia begin to dock in East African ports. Soon they establish Arab-Swahili states and trading depots along the coast from Somalia to Mozambique.

10th century

The 'Land of Zanj' along East Africa's coast becomes known for its exotic export goods, including leopard skins, tortoiseshell, rhino horns, ivory, slaves and gold, predominantly to Arabia and India.

1415

Chinese fleets visit East Africa in the early 15th century. In 1415 a giraffe is transported to Beijing and presented by Malindi envoys to the emperor himself.

Portuguese East Africa

Arab-Swahili domination on the coast received its first serious challenge with the arrival of the Portuguese in the 15th century, spurred by the tales of gold and riches that traders brought back from their travels. In 1497, for example, while on his pioneering voyage along the coastline of South and East Africa, Vasco da Gama found Arab dhows at the Zambezi delta loaded with gold dust. During the same period Europe was desperately short of labour as it struggled to recover from the effects of the Black Death (1347–51). The plantations of southern Europe were initially worked by captive Muslims and Slavic peoples (hence the word 'slaves'), but with access to Africa a whole new labour market opened up.

The Portuguese consolidated their position on the East African coast through blatant force and terror, justifying their actions as battles in a Christian war against Islam. They sailed their heavily armed vessels into the harbours of important Swahili towns, demanding submission to the rule of Portugal and payment of large annual tributes. Towns that refused were attacked, their possessions seized and resisters killed. Zanzibar was the first Swahili town to be taken in this manner (in 1503). Malindi formed an alliance with the Portuguese, which hastened the fall of Mombasa in 1505.

For a more detailed look at the history of Kenya's coastal regions, see p224.

EAST AFRICAN SLAVES

Slaves left Africa via the Sahara, the Red Sea, the Atlantic and the East African coast. The total estimated number of slaves exported from tropical Africa between 1500 and the late 1800s is put at 18 million; two million from East Africa. By the height of the slave trade in the 18th century, the slave trade had touched every region on the continent.

In East Africa, around 50,000 slaves passed through the markets every year – nearly 44% of the total population of the coast. Overall, close to 600,000 slaves were sold through the Zanzibar market between 1830 and 1873, when a treaty with Britain paved the way for the end of the trade. It's true that slavery was already an established fact of African life before the advent of the slave trade. But enslavement for sale, the importation of foreign goods and the sheer scale of Europe's involvement were radical departures from everything that had gone before. The social, psychological and economic impact changed the fate of the continent forever.

For more details on the slave trade in Kenya, see p231.

1441–46

By the 15th century Portuguese caravels begin exploring West Africa. They look for gold, but find slaves. Between 1441 and 1446 the first 1000 slaves were shipped to Portugal.

1492–1505

Dom Francisco de Almeida's armada begins the Portuguese conquest of Kenya. Mombasa falls in 1505, followed by towns like Barawa (Somalia), Kilwa, Moçambique and Sofala, up and down the coast.

1593

The Portuguese construct the coral Fort Jesus in Mombasa. Accounts from the garrison at Mombasa record the first evidence of maize production in Africa.

» Fort Jesus, Mombasa

British East Africa

Securing Control

In 1884 European powers met in Germany for the Berlin conference. Here behind closed doors they decided the fate of the African continent. No African leaders were invited to attend, nor were they consulted. What's more, the new national terrain may have satisfied political ambitions but it hid a multitude of potential problems; the newly defined nation states cut through at least 177 ethnic 'culture areas', while some new countries were hardly viable economic units.

The colonial settlement of Kenya dates from 1885, when Germany established a protectorate over the sultan of Zanzibar's coastal possessions. In 1888 Sir William Mackinnon received a royal charter and concessionary rights to develop trade in the region under the aegis of the British East Africa Company (BEAC). Seeking to consolidate its East African territories, Germany traded its coastal holdings in return for sole rights over Tanganyika (Tanzania) in 1890. Still, it was only when the BEAC ran into financial difficulties in 1895 that the British government finally stepped in to establish formal control through the East African Protectorate.

Swahili Ruins

- Gede, North Coast
- Jumba la Mtwana, south of Mombasa
- Mnarani, south of Mombasa
- Takwa, North Coast
- Shanga, North Coast
- Wasini Island, south of Mombasa
- Faza, North Coast

British Kenya

Initially, British influence was confined to the coastal area. Large parts of the interior were inaccessible due to the presence of warrior tribes such as the Maasai. However, the Maasai front began to crack following a brutal civil war between the Ilmaasai and Iloikop groups and the simultaneous arrival of rinderpest (a cattle disease), cholera, smallpox and famine. The British were able to negotiate a treaty with the Maasai, allowing the British to drive the Mombasa–Uganda railway line through the heart of Maasai grazing lands.

The completion of the railway enabled the British administration to relocate from Mombasa to more temperate Nairobi. Although the Maasai suffered the worst annexations of land, being restricted to designated reserves, the Kikuyu from Mt Kenya and the Aberdares (areas of white settlement), came to nurse a particular grievance about their alienation from the land.

In order to force the indigenous population into the labour market, the British introduced a hut tax in 1901. This could only be paid in cash, so Africans had to seek paid work.

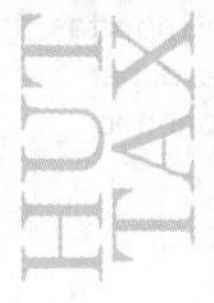

By 1912, settlers had established themselves in the highlands and set up mixed agricultural farms, turning a profit for the colony for the first time. These first outposts, Naivasha and the Ngong Hills, are still heavily white-settled areas today.

The colonial process was interrupted by WWI, when two-thirds of the 3000 white settlers in Kenya formed impromptu cavalry units and marched against Germans in neighbouring Tanganyika. Colonisation resumed after the war, under a scheme by which white veterans of

1729

The Portuguese grip on East Africa ends in 1698, when Mombasa falls to Baluchi Arabs from Oman after a 33-month siege. In 1729 the Portuguese leave the Kenyan coast for good.

1807–73

Legislation abolishing the slave trade is enacted in Britain in 1807. Another 65 years pass before Sultan Barghash of Zanzibar bans the slave trade on the East African coast.

1884–85

The Berlin Conference convenes and Africa is divided into colonial territories. Today the continent is divided into 54 states; more than four times the number in South America.

1888

Sir William Mackinnon establishes the British East Africa Company (BEAC) in Mombasa. Its focus is the exportation of goods and agriculture and the construction of the East African Railway.

THE LORD OF HAPPY VALLEY

During the colonial heyday, Happy Valley (the highland area outside Nairobi) played host to an eccentric cast of British elites with a reputation for fondness of drinking, drug abuse and wife swapping. However, few can rival Hugh Cholmondeley (1870–1931), third Baron of Delamere.

Lord Delamere first set foot on the African continent in 1891 to hunt lion in then British Somaliland; he is widely credited with coining the term 'white hunter'. Five years later, he led an expedition across the deserts of southern Somaliland into the verdant highlands of what is now central Kenya. By the early 1900s, Lord Delamere owned more than 300,000 acres of land, and was one of Kenya's most influential colonists.

For more than 20 years, he doggedly farmed his vast country estates by mere trial and error, experimenting with various crop strains from around the British Empire. Lord Delamere was also active in recruiting English landed gentry to buy up holdings in British East Africa, and helped put Happy Valley on the map. At the Norfolk Hotel, which still bears a restaurant named in his honour (p74), Lord Delamere once rode his horse through the dining room, wooing dinner guests with his ability to leap over banquet tables.

In his later years, Lord Delamere became fully convinced of white supremacy, and established himself as a firebrand politician determined to protect British holdings in Africa. Often described as the 'Cecil Rhodes of Kenya', he once wrote of his support for the 'extension of European civilisation', stating that the British were 'superior to heterogeneous African races only now emerging from centuries of relative barbarism'.

In 2005, charges were dropped against Lord Delamere's great-grandson, Baron Thomas Cholmondeley, who was suspected of shooting a Maasai game warden. One year later, a poacher was shot on Cholmondeley's property and in 2009 Cholmondeley was sentenced to eight months' imprisonment for manslaughter. The police spokesman on the case was reported as saying, 'The Delameres used to be untouchable. But that's all changed now.'

the European campaign were offered subsidised land in the highlands around Nairobi. The net effect was a huge upsurge in the white Kenyan population, from 9000 in 1920 to 80,000 in the 1950s.

The Road to Independence

Nationalist Stirrings

Although largely peaceful and a period of economic growth, the interwar years were to see the fomenting of early nationalist aspirations. Grievances over land appropriation and displacement were only exacerbated in 1920, when, after considerable lobbying from white settlers, Kenya was transformed into a Crown Colony. A Legislative Council was

1895
After experiencing serious financial difficulties, BEAC hands over to the British government, which becomes responsible for Kenya through the East African Protectorate.

1901
The East African Railway links the coast with Uganda. The construction of the line sees a huge influx of Indians, who provide the bulk of skilled manpower.

1890
Waiyaki Wa Henya, a Kikuyu chief who signed a treaty with Frederick Lugard of the BEAC under pressure, burns down Lugard's Fort. Waiyaki is abducted two years later and murdered.

1918–39
The interwar period facilitates economic activity. Famine relief and campaigns against epidemic diseases are established in the colonies stimulating a 37.5% increase in Africa's population.

established but Africans were barred from political participation (right up until 1944). In reaction to their exclusion, the Kikuyu tribe, who were under the greatest pressure from European settlers, founded the Young Kikuyu Association, led by Harry Thuku. This was to become the Kenya African Union (KAU), a nationalist organisation demanding access to white-owned land.

Red Strangers: The White Tribe of Kenya (CS Nicholls) has a different, unusually sympathetic perspective on colonialism, examining the history of Kenya's white settler population before and after independence.

One passionate advocate for the movement was a young man called Johnstone Kamau, later known as Jomo Kenyatta. When this early activism fell on deaf ears he joined the more outspoken Kikuyu Central Association; the association was promptly banned.

In 1929, with money supplied by Indian communists, Kenyatta sailed for London to plead the Kikuyu case with the British colonial secretary, who declined to meet with him. While in London, Kenyatta met with a group called the League Against Imperialism, which took him to Moscow and Berlin, back to Nairobi and then back to London, where he stayed for the next 15 years. During this time, he studied revolutionary tactics in Moscow and built up the Pan-African Federation with Hastings Banda (who later became the president of Malawi) and Kwame Nkrumah (later president of Ghana).

The War Years

Africans played a key role in WWII. The East African Carrier Corps consisted of over 400,000 men, and the development of the atom bomb was utterly dependent on uranium from the Congo.

WWII

Although African nationalists made impressive headway, it was the advent of WWII that was to ultimately bring about the rapid demise of colonialism in Africa. The war demonstrated that Africa was an invaluable member of the world community, contributing significant numbers of men and indispensable mineral resources to the war effort.

In 1941, in a desperate bid for survival, British premier Winston Churchill crossed the Atlantic to plead for American aid. The resulting Atlantic Charter (1942), which Churchill negotiated with President Roosevelt, enshrined the end of colonialism in the third clause, which stated self-determination for all colonies as one of the postwar objectives.

In October 1945 the sixth Pan-African Congress was convened in Manchester, England. For the first time this was predominantly a congress of Africa's young leaders. Kwame Nkrumah and Jomo Kenyatta were there, along with trade unionists, lawyers, teachers and writers from all over Africa. By the time Kenyatta returned to Kenya in 1946, he was the leader of a bona fide Kenyan liberation movement. Using his influence as leader, he quickly assumed the top spot of the pro-independence KAU, a group with considerable support from African war veterans.

Mau Mau

Although Kenyatta appeared willing to act as the British government's accredited Kenyan representative within a developing constitutional

1920

Kenya is declared a Crown Colony. Africans are barred from the Legislative Council. The next year the first nationalist organisation, the Kenya African Union (KAU), is established and presses for land rights.

1929

Jomo Kenyatta sails for London, beginning 15 years of travels in his bid to drum up support for Kenyan independence. During this period, he helps build up the Pan-African Federation.

1931

Lord Delamere dies at the age of 61. He had helped to lay the foundations for Kenya's agricultural economy, but personified the deeply resented policies of the British colonial government.

1930s

Thousands of European settlers occupy the Central Highlands, farming tea and coffee. The land claims of the area's million-plus members of the Kikuyu tribe are not recognised in European terms.

framework, militant factions among the KAU had a more radical agenda. When in 1951 Ghana became the first African country to achieve independence, it raised the stakes even higher.

Starting with small-scale terror operations, bands of guerrillas began to intimidate white settlers, threaten their farms and anyone deemed to be a collaborator. Their aim: to drive white settlers from the land and reclaim it. Kenyatta's role in the Mau Mau rebellion, as it came to be known, was equivocal. At a public meeting in 1952, he denounced the movement. But he was arrested along with other Kikuyu politicians and sentenced to seven years' hard labour for 'masterminding' the plot.

Four years of intense military operations ensued. The various Mau Mau units came together under the umbrella of the Kenya Land Freedom Army, led by Dedan Kimathi, and outright guerrilla warfare followed, with the British declaring a state of emergency in 1952.

By 1956, the Mau Mau had been quelled and Dedan Kimathi was publicly hanged on the orders of Colonel Henderson (who was later deported from Kenya for crimes against humanity). But Kenyatta was to continue the struggle following his release in 1959. Soon even white Kenyans began to feel the winds of change, and in 1960 the British government officially announced its plan to transfer power to a democratically elected African government. Independence was scheduled for December 1963, accompanied by grants and loans of US$100 million to enable the Kenyan assembly to buy out European farmers in the highlands and restore the land to local tribes.

It had been a long time coming, but Kenya finally became independent on 12 December 1963.

The first major Kenyan film to tackle the thorny subject of the Mau Mau uprising, Kibaara Kaugi's *Enough is Enough* is a fictionalised biopic of Wamuyu wa Gakuru, a Kikuyu woman who became a famed guerrilla fighter.

Independent Kenya

Harambee

The political handover had begun in earnest in 1962 with Kenyatta's election to a newly constituted parliament. To ensure a smooth transition of power, Kenyatta's party, the Kenya African National Union (KANU), which advocated a unitary, centralised government, joined forces with the Kenya African Democratic Union (KADU), which favoured *majimbo,* a federal set-up. *Harambee,* meaning 'pulling together', was seen as more important than political factionalism, and KADU voluntarily dissolved in 1964, leaving Kenyatta and KANU in full control.

It is difficult to overstate the optimism that accompanied those early days of postcolonial independence. Kenyatta took pains to allay the fears of white settlers, declaring 'I have suffered imprisonment and detention; but that is gone, and I am not going to remember it. Let us join hands and work for the benefit of Kenya'. But the nascent economy

Weep Not, Child, by Kenya's most famous novelist, Ngũgĩ wa Thiong'o, tells the story of British occupation and the effects of the Mau Mau on the lives of black Kenyans. His 2010 memoir *Dreams in a Time of War* is a patiently told chronicle of his childhood in colonial Kenya.

DAVID WALL/LONELY PLANET IMAGES ©

» Kikuyu witchdoctor

1942

The Atlantic Charter, signed by Winston Churchill and President Roosevelt, guarantees self-determination for the colonies as a postwar objective. The charter also gives America access to African markets.

1946

Jomo Kenyatta completes his anthropology degree and returns to Kenya as head of the KAU. The British government views him as its accredited representative in the independence handover.

was vulnerable and the political landscape was barely developed. As a result the consolidation of power by the new ruling elite nurtured an authoritarian regime.

One-Party State

Although considered an African success story, the Kenyatta regime failed to undertake the essential task of deconstructing the colonial state in favour of a system with greater relevance to the aspirations of the average Kenyan. The *majimbo* (regionalist) system – advocated by KADU and agreed upon in the run-up to independence – was such a system. But with their dissolution in 1964 it was abandoned. It would not be until the 2010 constitution that the idea of a federalist system would be revived.

Power was not only being centralised in Nairobi, but increasingly also in the hands of the president. The consolidation of presidential power was buttressed by a series of constitutional amendments, culminating in the Constitutional Amendment Act No 16 of 1969, which empowered the president to control the civil service. The effects were disastrous. Subsequent years saw widespread discrimination in favour of Kenyatta's own tribe, the Kikuyu. The Trade Union Disputes Act illegalised industrial action and when KADU tried to reassemble as the Kenya People's Union (KPU) it was banned. Corruption soon became a problem at all levels of the power structure and the political arena contracted.

TORTURE

In July 2011, Britain's High Court ruled that four elderly Kenyans could sue the British government for alleged torture suffered in detention camps set up by the colonial authorities during the Mau Mau rebellion in the 1950s.

The Moi Years

Kenyatta was succeeded in 1978 by his vice-president, Daniel arap Moi. A Kalenjin, Moi was regarded by establishment power brokers as a suitable front man for their interests, as his tribe was relatively small and beholden to the Kikuyu.

On assumption of power, Moi sought to consolidate his regime by marginalising those who had campaigned to stop him from succeeding Kenyatta. Lacking a capital base of his own upon which he could build and maintain a patron-client network, and faced with shrinking economic opportunities, Moi resorted to the politics of exclusion. He reconfigured the financial, legal, political and administrative institutions. For instance, a constitutional amendment in 1982 made Kenya a de jure one-party state, while another in 1986 removed the security of tenure for the attorney-general, comptroller, auditor general and High Court judges, making all these positions personally beholden to the president. These developments had the effect of transforming Kenya from an 'imperial state' under Kenyatta to a 'personal state' under Moi.

1952–56

The British declare a state of emergency during the Mau Mau rebellion. By 1956 nearly 2000 Kikuyu loyalists and 11,500 Mau Mau have been killed. Thirty-two white settlers die.

1963

Kenya gains independence; Jomo Kenyatta becomes president. In the same year the Organisation of African Unity is established, aimed at providing Africa with an independent voice in world affairs.

1966

The Kenya People's Union is formed by Jaramogi Oginga Odinga. Following unrest at a presidential visit to Nyanza Province the party is banned; Kenya becomes a de facto one-party state.

1978

Kenyatta is succeeded by his vice-president, Daniel arap Moi, who goes on to become one of the most enduring 'Big Men' of Africa, ruling for the next 25 years.

Winds of Change

By the late 1980s, most Kenyans had had enough. Following the widely contested 1988 elections, Charles Rubia and Kenneth Matiba joined forces to call for the freedom to form alternative political parties and stated their plan to hold a political rally in Nairobi on 7 July without a licence. Though the duo was detained prior to their intended meeting, people turned out anyway, only to be met with brutal police retaliation. Twenty people were killed and police arrested a slew of politicians, human-rights activists and journalists.

The rally, known thereafter as *Saba Saba* ('seven seven' in Kiswahili), was a pivotal event in the push for a multiparty Kenya. The following year, the Forum for the Restoration of Democracy (FORD) was formed, led by Jaramogi Oginga Odinga, a powerful Luo politician who had been vice-president under Jomo Kenyatta, and had played an important role in the independence movement – first as a member of KANU and then, after an ideological split, as leader of his own party, the KPU. FORD was initially banned and Odinga was arrested, but the resulting outcry led to his release and, finally, a change in the constitution that allowed opposition parties to register for the first time.

Faced with a foreign debt of nearly US$9 billion and blanket suspension of foreign aid, Moi was pressured into holding multiparty elections in early 1992, but independent observers reported a litany of electoral inconsistencies. Just as worrying, about 2000 people were killed during ethnic clashes in the Rift Valley, widely believed to have been triggered by government agitation. Nonetheless, Moi was overwhelmingly re-elected.

In 1992 Moi secured only 37% of the votes cast against a combined opposition tally of 63%. The same results were replicated in the 1997 elections, when Moi once again secured victory with 40% of the votes cast against 60% of the combined opposition. After the 1997 elections, KANU was forced to bow to mounting pressure and initiate some changes: some Draconian colonial laws were repealed, as well as the requirement for licences to hold political rallies.

But Kenya was about to enter a difficult period. On 7 August 1998, Islamic extremists bombed the US embassies in Nairobi and Dar es Salaam in Tanzania, killing more than 200 people and bringing al-Qaeda and Osama bin Laden to international attention for the first time. The effect on the Kenyan economy was devastating. It would take four years to rebuild the shattered tourism industry.

1982

The Universities Academic Staff Union (UASU), one of the few credible opposition groups remaining, is banned. This leads to a short-lived coup by the airforce.

1984

The medical community learns of the first reported case of AIDS in East Africa. By 2005 the estimated number of people living with HIV/AIDS in Kenya is 1.3 million.

1991

The collapse of the Soviet Union changes the face of African politics with foreign pressure on one-party states. In 1991 parliament repeals the one-party state section of the constitution.

1993

In August 1993 inflation reaches a record 100% and the government's budget deficit is over 10% of GDP. Donors suspend aid to Kenya and insist on wide-ranging economic reforms.

The Kibaki Years

Democratic Kenya

Having been beaten twice in the 1992 and 1997 elections, 12 opposition groups united to form the National Alliance Rainbow Coalition (NARC). With Moi's presidency due to end in 2002, many feared that he would alter the constitution again to retain his position. This time, though, he announced his intention to retire.

Moi put his weight firmly behind Uhuru Kenyatta, the son of Jomo Kenyatta, as his successor, but the support garnered by NARC ensured a resounding victory for the party, with 62% of the vote. Mwai Kibaki was inaugurated as Kenya's third president on 30 December 2002.

When Kibaki assumed office in January 2003, donors were highly supportive of the new government. During its honeymoon period, the Kibaki administration won praise for a number of policy initiatives, especially a crackdown on corruption. In 2003–04, donors contributed billions of dollars to the fight against corruption, including support for the office of a newly appointed anticorruption 'czar', and the International Monetary Fund resumed lending in November 2003.

JOHN GITHONGO

Michela Wrong's *It's Our Turn to Eat: The Story of a Kenyan Whistle-blower* (2009) is a searing insight into Kenya's battle against corruption. Taking centre stage is John Githongo, the anticorruption 'czar' who fled into exile after unearthing corruption at the highest level.

Corruption Continues

Despite initially positive signs, it became clear by mid-2004 that large-scale corruption was still a considerable problem in Kenya. Western diplomats alleged that corruption had cost the treasury US$1 billion since Kibaki took office. In February 2005, the British High Commissioner Sir Edward Clay denounced the 'massive looting' of state resources by senior government politicians, including sitting cabinet ministers. Within days, Kibaki's anticorruption 'czar', John Githongo, resigned and went into exile amid rumours of death threats related to his investigation of high-level politicians. The UK, the US and Germany rapidly suspended their anticorruption lending. With Githongo's release of a damning detailed dossier on corruption in the Kibaki regime in February 2006, Kibaki was forced to relieve three ministers of their cabinet positions.

At the root of the difficulties of fighting corruption were the conditions that brought Kibaki to power. To maximise his electoral chances his coalition included a number of KANU officials who were deeply implicated in the worst abuses of the Moi regime. Indebted to such people for power, Kibaki was only ever able to affect a half-hearted reshuffle of his cabinet. He also allowed his ministers a wide margin of manoeuvre to guarantee their continued support.

The slow march to democratisation in Kenya has been attributed to the personalised nature of politics, where focus is placed on individuals with ethnic support bases rather than institutions.

1998

Terrorist attacks shake US embassies in Nairobi and Dar es Salaam, killing more than 200 people. The effect on the Kenyan economy is devastating.

2002

Mwai Kibaki wins the 2002 election as leader of the National Alliance Rainbow Coalition (NARC). For the first time in Kenya the ballot box elects a president by popular vote.

2006

Chinese President Hu Jintao signs an oil exploration contract with Kenya; the deal allows China to prospect for oil on the borders of Sudan and Somalia and in coastal waters.

2007

Kenyans go to the polls again. The outcome is contested amid bloody clashes. International mediation finally brings about a power-sharing agreement in April 2008.

But it hasn't all been bad news. The Kibaki government has succeeded in making primary and secondary education more accessible for ordinary Kenyans, while state control over the economy has been loosened.

Things Fall Apart

On 27 December 2007, Kenya held presidential, parliamentary and local elections. While the parliamentary and local government elections were largely considered credible, the presidential elections were marred by serious irregularities, reported by both Kenyan and international election monitors, and by independent nongovernmental observers. Nonetheless, the Electoral Commission declared Mwai Kibaki the winner, triggering a wave of violence across the country.

The Rift Valley, Western Highlands, Nyanza Province and Mombasa – areas afflicted by years of political machination, previous election violence and large-scale displacement – exploded in ugly ethnic confrontations. The violence left more than 1000 people dead and over 600,000 people homeless.

Fearing the stability of the most stable linchpin of East Africa, former UN Secretary-General Kofi Annan and a panel of 'Eminent African Persons' flew to Kenya to mediate talks. A power-sharing agreement was signed on 28 February 2008 between President Kibaki and Raila Odinga, the leader of the ODM opposition. The coalition provided for the establishment of a prime ministerial position (to be filled by Raila Odinga), as well as a division of cabinet posts according to the parties' representation in parliament.

2007 ELECTION

The most up-to-date history of Kenya, *Kenya: Between Hope & Despair, 1963-2011*, by Daniel Branch, covers the 2007 election and its aftermath in searing detail.

Rebuilding Confidence

Despite some difficult moments, the fragile coalition government has stood the test of time, thereby going some way towards reassuring Kenyans and the international community that the violence was a one-off, rather than a vision of Kenya's future. The government has also begun the complex (and long-overdue) task of long-term reform. Arguably its most important success has been the 2010 constitution, which was passed in a referendum by 67% of Kenya's voters. Among the key elements of this new constitution are the devolution of powers to Kenya's regions, the introduction of a bill of rights and the separation of judicial, executive and legislative powers.

Much more remains to be done, not least in addressing the inequality that plagues the country; local economists also estimate that Kenya needs to achieve growth of at least 12% if the country is to achieve any trickle-down effect. The challenge is huge. Inflation is on the rise, fuel and food price rises are cutting deep. But the government has taken some hugely significant first steps that can only stand the country in good stead over the coming years.

2008

Former anticorruption 'czar' John Githongo returns to Kenya. Three years later, he launches Kenya Ni Yetu (Kenya is Ours), aimed at mobilising ordinary people to speak up against corruption.

2010

67% of Kenya's voters approve the radically overhauled constitution that provides for judicial independence, devolves powers to the regions and incorporates a bill of rights.

ZHAO YINGQUAN/XINHUA PRESS/CORBIS ©

»President Mwai Kibaki

October 2011

Kenya's army crosses the border into Somalia in an attempt to clear the border areas of al-Shabab militants blamed for recent kidnappings of tourists and aid workers in Kenya.

Tribes of Kenya

The tribe remains an important aspect of a Kenyan's identity: upon meeting a fellow Kenyan, the first question on anyone's mind is, 'What tribe do you come from?'

Although we have divided Kenya's tribes into geographical areas, this is a guide only, as you'll find Kenyans from most tribal groupings well beyond their traditional lands. In the same way, distinctions between many tribal groups are slowly being eroded as people move to major cities for work, and intermarry.

Rift Valley & Central Kenya

Kikuyu (also Gikikuyu)

22% of population

The Kikuyu are Kenya's largest and most influential tribe, and contributed the country's first president, Jomo Kenyatta, and its current one, Mwai Kibaki. Famously warlike, the Kikuyu overran the lands of the Athi and Gumba tribes, becoming hugely populous in the process. Now their heartland surrounds Mt Kenya, although they also represent the largest proportion of people living in Kenya's major cities. With territory bordering that of the Maasai, the tribes share many cultural similarities due to intermarriage. The administration of the *mwaki* (clans) was originally taken care of by a council of elders, with a good deal of importance being placed on the role of the witchdoctor, the medicine man and the blacksmith. Initiation rites for both boys and girls consist of ritual circumcision for boys and genital mutilation for girls (although the latter is slowly becoming less common). Each group of youths of the same age belongs to a *riikaan* (age-set) and passes through the various stages of life, and their associated rituals, together. Subgroups of the Kikuyu include the Embu, Ndia and Mbeere.

The Kikuyu are renowned for their entrepreneurial skills and for popping up everywhere in Kenya (the Kikuyu name Kamau is as common as Smith is in Britain).

Kalenjin

11% of population

The Kalenjin comprise the Nandi, Kipsigis, Eleyo, Marakwet, Pokot and Tugen (former president Daniel arap Moi's people) and occupy the western edge of the central Rift Valley area. They first migrated to the area west of Lake Turkana from southern Sudan around 2000 years ago, but gradually filtered south as the climate became harsher. More recent times have seen them band together to form a larger power base, although frictions still exist. For example, the Kipsigis have a love of cattle rustling. which continues to cause strife between them and neighbouring tribes. However, the tribe is most famous for producing Kenya's Olympic runners (75% of all the top runners in Kenya are Kalenjin). As with most tribes, the Kalenjin are organised into age-sets. Administration of the law is carried out at the *kok* (an informal court led by the clan's elders).

Meru

5% of population

Originally from the coast, the Meru now occupy the northeastern slopes of Mt Kenya. Up until 1974 the Meru were led by a chief (the *mogwe*), but upon his death the last incumbent converted to Christianity. Strangely, many of their tribal stories mirror the traditional tales of the Old Testament, which has led some to theorise that the Meru might be a lost tribe of Israel. The practice of ancestor worship, however, is still widespread. They have long been governed by an elected council of elders *(njuuri)*, making them the only tribe practising a structured form of democratic governance prior to colonialism. The Meru now live on some of the most fertile farmland in Kenya and grow numerous cash crops. Subgroups of the Meru include the Chuka, Igembe, Igoji, Tharaka, Muthambi, Tigania and Imenti.

The Meru are active in the cultivation of *miraa*, the stems of which contain a stimulant similar to amphetamines and are exported to Somalia and Yemen.

Samburu

0.5% of population

Closely related to the Maasai, and speaking the same language, the Samburu occupy an arid area directly north of Mt Kenya. It seems that when the Maasai migrated to the area from Sudan, some headed east and became the Samburu. Like the Maasai, they too have retained their traditional way of life as nomadic pastoralists, depending for their survival on their livestock. They live in small villages of five to eight families, divided into age-sets, and they continue to practise traditional rites like male and female circumcision and polygamy. After marriage, women traditionally leave their clan, so their social status is much lower than that of men. Samburu women wear similar colourful bead necklaces to the Maasai. Like the Maasai and Rendille, Samburu warriors paste their hair with red ochre to create a visor to shield their eyes from the sun. Due to conflicts with the Somalis, they regard Islam with great suspicion and some Samburu have converted to Christianity.

Pokot

less than 0.1% of population

The pastoral Pokot (who are Kalenjin by language and tradition but less urbanised than other Kalenjin groups) herd their cattle and goats across the waterless scrub north of Lake Baringo and the Cherangani Hills. Cattle-raiding, and the search for water and grazing, has often brought them into conflict with the Turkana, Samburu and the Ugandan Karamojong. Pokot warriors wear distinctive headdresses of painted clay and feathers. Flat, aluminium nose ornaments shaped like leaves and lower-lip plugs are common among men. Circumcision is part of the initiation of men and many Pokot women undergo female genital mutilation at around age 12. Pokot hill farmers are a separate and distinct group who grow tobacco and keep cattle, sheep and goats in the hills north of Kitale, on the approaches to Marich Pass. These hill farmers have a strong craft tradition, producing pottery and metalwork, as well as snuff boxes from calabashes or horns.

Western Kenya

Luhya

14% of population

Made up of 18 different groups (the largest being the Bukusu), the Bantu-speaking Luhya are the second-largest group in Kenya. They occupy a relatively small, high-density area of the country in the Western Highlands centred on Kakamega. In the past, the Luhya were skilled metal workers, forging knives and tools that were traded with other groups, but today most Luhya are agriculturists, farming groundnuts, sesame and maize. Smallholders also grow large amounts of cash crops such as cotton and sugar cane. Many Luhya are superstitious and still have a strong belief in witchcraft, although to the passing traveller this is rarely obvious. Traditional costume and rituals are becoming less common, due mostly to the pressures of the soaring Luhya population.

Luo

12% of population

The tribe of US president Barack Obama's father, the Luo live on the shores of Lake Victoria and are Kenya's third-largest tribal group. Though originally a cattle-herding people like the Maasai, their herds suffered terribly from the rinderpest outbreak in the 1890s so they switched to fishing and subsistence agriculture. During the struggle for independence, many of the country's leading politicians and trade unionists were Luo, including Tom Mboya (assassinated in 1969) and the former vice-president Oginga Odinga, who later spearheaded the opposition to President Moi. Kenya's current prime minister, Raila Odinga, is also a Luo. Socially, the Luo are unusual among Kenya's tribes in that they don't practise circumcision for either sex. The family unit is part of a larger grouping of *dhoot* (families), several of which in turn make up an *ogandi* (group of geographically related people), each led by a *ruoth* (chief). The Luo, like the Luhya, have two major recreational passions, soccer and music, and there are many distinctive Luo instruments made from gourds and gut or wire strings.

HERITAGE LIBRARY

The Rosen Publishing Group (www.rosenpublishing.com) publishes the Heritage Library of African Peoples, aimed at late-primary and early-secondary school students. Although the entire East Africa set is available, individual titles (such as *Luo, Kikuyu, Maasai* and *Samburu*) are also easy to track down.

Gusii (also Kisii)

7% of population

The Gusii occupy the Western Highlands, east of Lake Victoria, forming a small Bantu-speaking island in a mainly Nilotic-speaking area. Primarily cattle-herders and crop-cultivators, they farm Kenya's cash crops – tea, coffee and pyrethrum – as well as market vegetables. They are also well known for their basketry and distinctive, rounded soapstone carvings, which have a cubist air about them. (In fact, Picasso was heavily influenced by African art during his cubist period.) Like many other tribal groups, Gusii society is clan based, with everyone organised into age-sets. Medicine men *(abanyamorigo),* in particular, hold a highly respected and privileged position, performing the role of doctor and social worker. One of their more peculiar practices is trepanning: the removal of sections of the skull or spine to aid maladies such as backache or concussion.

Southern Kenya

Akamba (also Kamba)

11% of population

The region east of Nairobi towards Tsavo National Park is the traditional homeland of the Bantu-speaking Akamba. Great traders in ivory, beer, honey, iron weapons and ornaments, they traditionally plied their trade between Lake Victoria and the coast, and north to Lake Turkana. In particular, they traded with the Maasai and Kikuyu for food stocks. Highly regarded by the British for their fighting ability, they were drafted in large numbers into the British Army. After WWI the British tried to limit their cattle stocks and settled more Europeans in their tribal territories. In response, the Akamba marched en masse to Nairobi to squat peacefully at Kariokor Market in protest, forcing the administration to relent. Nowadays, they are more famous for their elegant *makonde*-style (ebony) carving. Akamba society is clan-based with all adolescents going through initiation rites at about the age of 12. Subgroups of the Akamba include the Kitui, Masaku and Mumoni.

Maasai

2% of population

Despite representing only a small proportion of the total population, the Maasai are, for many, the definitive symbol of Kenya. With a reputation (often exaggerated) as fierce warriors, the tribe has largely managed to stay outside the mainstream of development in Kenya and still maintains large cattle herds along the Tanzanian border. The British gazetted the Masai Mara National Reserve in the early 1960s, displacing the Maasai, and they slowly continued to annexe more and more Maasai land. Resettlement programs have met with limited success as the Maasai scorn agriculture and land ownership. The Maasai still have a distinctive style and traditional age-grade social structure, and circumcision is still widely practised for both men and women. Women typically wear large platelike bead necklaces, while the men typically wear a red-checked *shuka* (blanket) and carry a distinctive ball-ended club. Blood and milk is the mainstay of the Maasai diet, supplemented by a drink called *mursik,* made from milk fermented with cow's urine and ashes, which has been shown to lower cholesterol.

MAASAI WORLDS

The Worlds of a Maasai Warrior: An Autobiography, by Tepilit Ole Saitoti, presents an intriguing perspective on the juxtaposition of traditional and modern in East Africa.

Maasai warriors in the Masai Mara National Reserve (p129)

THE MAASAI & THEIR CATTLE

The Maasai tell the following story. One of the Maasai gods, Naiteru-Kop, was wandering the earth at the beginning of time and there he found a Dorobo man – 'Dorobo' is a derogatory Maasai word used to describe hunter-gatherer groups – who lived with a snake, a cow and an elephant. The man killed the snake and the elephant, but the elephant calf escaped and came upon Le-eyo, a Maasai man to whom he told the story of the Dorobo.

The elephant calf took Le-eyo to the Dorobo man's compound, where Le-eyo heard Naiteru-Kop, the Maasai god, calling out to the Dorobo man and telling him to come out the next morning. Having heard this, it was Le-eyo who emerged first the following morning and asked Naiteru-Kop what to do next. Following the god's instructions, Le-eyo built a large enclosure, with a little hut of branches and grasses on one side. He then slaughtered a thin calf, but did not eat it, instead laying out the calf's hide, and piling the meat high on top. He then built a large fire, and threw the meat upon it.

A great storm swept over the land. With the storm clouds overhead, a leather cord dropped from the sky into Le-eyo's compound, and down the cord came cattle until Le-eyo's compound was full of cattle. One of the cattle stuck its hoof through the hut's wall, and Le-eyo called out, frightened. Upon Le-eyo's cry, the cattle stopped falling from the sky. Naiteru-Kop called out to Le-eyo: 'These are all the cattle you will receive, because your cry stopped them coming. But they are yours to look after, and you will live with them.'

Since that day, the Dorobo have been hunters and the Maasai have herded their cattle, convinced that all the cattle in the world belong to them.

Taita

0.1% of population

The Taita people came originally from what is now Tanzania, and first settled in the region around Voi and Taveta in Kenya's far southeast around ten centuries ago. The Taita language belongs to the Bantu group of languages and is similar to Swahili, although such is their interaction with other tribes that their language has imported many words from neighbouring tribes, including the Kikuyu. Taita social life was traditionally dispersed and strongly territorial, with each clan inhabiting a discrete area of the Taita Hills, south of what are now the Tsavo National Parks. It was only after colonialism that a collective sense of Taita identity developed in earnest, a process accelerated by the intrusion of the railway through Taita lands; Mwangeka, a Taita hero, was lauded for his resistance to colonial rule. Taita religion was largely animist in nature with sacred meeting places and elaborate burial rituals defining features, although few Taita now live according to traditional ways. Taita subgroups include the Wadawida, Wasagalla and Wakasighau.

Northern Kenya

Turkana

1.5% of population

Originally from Karamojong in northeastern Uganda, the Turkana live in the virtual desert country of Kenya's northwest. Like the Samburu and the Maasai (with whom they are linguistically linked), the Turkana are primarily cattle herders, although fishing on the waters of Lake Turkana and small-scale farming is on the increase. Traditional costume and practices are still commonplace, although the Turkana are one of the few tribes to have voluntarily given up the practice of circumcision. Men typically cover part of their hair with mud, which is then painted blue and decorated with ostrich and other feathers and, despite the intense heat, their main garment is a woollen blanket. A woman's attire is dictated by her marital and maternal status; the marriage ritual itself is quite unusual and involves kidnapping the bride. Tattooing is also common. Men were traditionally tattooed on the shoulders for killing an enemy – the right shoulder for killing a man, the left for a woman. Witchdoctors and prophets are held in high regard and scars on someone's lower stomach are usually a sign of a witchdoctor's attempt to cast out an undesirable spirit using incisions.

TRIBAL MARKINGS

A surprising number of Turkana men still wear markings on their shoulders to indicate they have killed another man.

Borana

less than 0.1% of population

The Borana are one of the cattle-herding Oromo peoples, indigenous to Ethiopia, who migrated south into northern Kenya. They are now concentrated around Marsabit and Isiolo. The Borana observe strict role segregation between men and women – men being responsible for care of the herds while women are in charge of children and day-to-day life. Borana groups may pack up camp and move up to four times a year, depending on weather conditions and available grazing land. As a nomadic group their reliance on oral history is strong, with many traditions passed on through song.

El Molo

less than 0.1% of population

This tiny tribal group has strong links with the Rendille, their close neighbours. The El Molo rely on Lake Turkana for their existence, living on a diet mainly of fish and occasionally crocodiles, turtles and other wildlife. Hippos are hunted from doum-palm rafts, and great social status is given to the warrior who kills a hippo. An ill-balanced, protein-rich diet and the effects of too much fluoride found in local water sources have taken their toll on the tribe. Intermarriage with other tribes and abandonment of the nomadic lifestyle has helped to raise their numbers to about 4000, who now live on the mainland near Loyangalani.

Gabbra

less than 0.1% of population

This small pastoral tribe lives in the far north of Kenya, from the eastern shore of Lake Turkana up into Ethiopia. Many Gabbra converted to Islam during the time of slavery. Traditional beliefs include the appointment of an *abba-olla* (father of the village), who oversees the moral and physical well-being of the tribe. Fathers and sons form strong relationships, and marriage provides a lasting bond between clans. Polygamy is still practised by the Gabbra, although it is becoming less common. Gabbra men usually wear turbans and white cotton robes, while women wear *kangas*, thin pieces of brightly coloured cotton. The Gabbra are famous for their bravery, hunting lions, rhino and elephants.

Rendille

less than 0.1% of population

The Rendille are pastoralists who live in small nomadic communities in the rocky Kaisut Desert in Kenya's northeast. They have strong economic and kinship links with the Samburu and rely heavily on camels for many of their daily needs, including food, milk, clothing, trade and transport. The camels are bled by opening a vein in the neck with a blunt arrow or knife. The blood is then drunk on its own or mixed with milk. Rendille society is strongly bound by family ties centred on monogamous couples. Mothers have high status and the eldest son inherits the family wealth. It is dishonourable for a Rendille to refuse to grant a loan, so even the poorest Rendille often has claims to at least a few camels and goats. Rendille warriors often sport a distinctive visorlike hairstyle, dyed with red ochre, while women may wear several kilos of beads.

TRIBAL DRESS

After giving birth to their first child, Rendille women adopt a clay head-decoration known as a *doko*, resembling a rooster's comb.

Coastal Kenya

Swahili

0.6% of population

Although the people of the coast do not have a common heritage, they do have a linguistic link: Kiswahili (commonly referred to as Swahili), a Bantu-based language that evolved as a means of communication between Africans and the Arabs, Persians and Portuguese who colonised the East African coast; the word *swahili* is a derivative of the Arabic word for coast – *sawahil*. The cultural origins of the Swahili come from intermarriage between the Arabs and Persians with African slaves from the 7th century onwards. In fact, many anthropologists consider the Swahili a cultural tribe brought together by trade routes rather than a tribe of distinct biological lineage. A largely urban tribe, they occupy coastal cities like Mombasa, Malindi, Lamu and Stone Town (Zanzibar); and given the historical Arab influence, the Swahili largely practise Islam. Swahili subgroups include Bajun, Siyu, Pate, Mvita, Fundi, Shela, Ozi, Vumba and Amu (residents of Lamu).

Daily Life

Traditional Cultures, Modern Country

Traditional cultures are what hold Kenya together. Respect for one's elders, firmly held religious beliefs, traditional gender roles and the tradition of *ujamaa* (familyhood) create a well-defined social structure with stiff moral mores at its core.

Extended family provides a further layer of support, which is increasingly important as parents migrate to cities for lucrative work, leaving their children with grandparents or aunts and uncles to be cared for. This fluid system has also enabled many to deal with the devastation wrought by the HIV/AIDS epidemic.

Historically, the majority of Kenyans were either farmers or cattle herders with family clans based in small interconnected villages. Even today, as traditional rural life gives way to a frenetic urban pace, this strong sense of community remains and the importance of social interactions such as greetings should never be underestimated.

An estimated 1.2 million Kenyan children have lost one or both parents to HIV/AIDS, and an estimated 180,000 children are living with HIV/AIDS.

Education, too, is critical to understanding modern Kenya. Kenya sends more students to the US to study than any other African country and literacy stands at an impressive 85%. The positive effects of a generation of educated Kenyans who came of age in the 1980s are now everywhere to be seen: Kenyans abroad have started to invest seriously in the country, Nairobi's business landscape is changing rapidly and a new middle class is demanding new apartment blocks and cars.

One Country, Many Tribes

Kenya is home to more than 40 tribal groups (for more information, see p302). Although most tribal groups have coexisted quite peacefully since independence, the ethnocentric bias of government and civil service appointments has led to escalating unrest and disaffection. During

THE INDIAN INFLUENCE

Kenya's first permanent settlers from the Indian subcontinent were indentured workers, brought here from Gujarat and the Punjab by the British to build the Uganda Railway. After the railway was finished, the British allowed many workers to stay and start up businesses, and hundreds of *dukas* (small shops) were set up across the country.

After WWII, the Indian community came to control large sectors of the East African economy, and still does to some degree. However, few gave their active support to the black nationalist movements in the run-up to independence, despite being urged to do so by India's prime minister, and many were hesitant to accept local citizenship after independence. This earned the distrust of the African community, who felt the Indians were simply there to exploit African labour. Thankfully, however, Kenya escaped the anti-Asian pogroms that plagued Uganda.

the hotly contested elections of 1992, 1997 and 2007, clashes between two major tribes, the Kikuyu and Luo, bolstered by allegiances with other smaller tribes like the Kalenjin, resulted in death and mass displacement (see p301).

This has led to an increasing anxiety among the middle and upper classes that the country may be riven along ethnic lines if something isn't done to address major inequalities. Local analysts point out that election violence is more to do with economic inequality than with tribalism – they insist that there are only two tribes in Kenya: the rich and the poor.

In Ngũgĩ wa Thiong'o's *Petals of Blood*, Wanja the barmaid sums up the situation for women in newly independent Kenya: '...with us girls the future seemed vague... as if we knew that no matter what efforts we put into our studies, our road led to the kitchen or the bedroom'.

Christian Interior, Muslim Coast

As a result of intense missionary activity, the majority of Kenyans outside the coastal and eastern provinces are Christians (including some home-grown African Christian groups that do not owe any allegiance to the major Western groups). Street preachers are common throughout the country, and their fire-and-brimstone sermons normally attract a large crowd. Hard-core evangelism has made some significant inroads and many TV-style groups from the US have a strong following.

In the country's east, the majority of Kenyans are Sunni Muslims. They make up about 10% of the population.

Women in Kenya

During Kenya's struggle for independence, many women fought alongside the men, but their sacrifice was largely forgotten when independence came. At the Lancaster House conference, where Kenya's independence constitution was negotiated, just one out of around 70 Kenyan delegates was a woman and the resulting constitution made no mention of women's rights.

I Laugh So I Won't Cry: Kenya's Women Tell the Stories of Their Lives, edited by Helena Halperin, offers fascinating glimpses into the lives of Kenyan women.

Under the new 2010 constitution, things improved, at least on paper: women are described as a disadvantaged group, and the bill guarantees equal treatment for men and women, protects against discrimination on the basis of gender, calls on the state to undertake affirmative action policies and sets aside 47 special seats for women in parliament.

Even so, major discrepancies remain in the ways in which women and men have access to essential services and resources such as land and credit, while traditional gender roles still largely prevail. Only around 10% of Kenya's MPs are women.

FEMALE GENITAL MUTILATION

Female genital mutilation (FGM), often termed 'female circumcision', is still widespread across Africa, including throughout Kenya. In some parts of tribal Kenya more than 90% of women and girls are subjected to FGM in some form.

The term FGM covers a wide range of procedures from a small, mainly symbolic cut, to the total removal of the clitoris and external genitalia (known as infibulation). The effects of FGM can be fatal. Other side effects, including chronic infections, the spread of HIV, infertility, severe bleeding and lifelong pain during sex, are not uncommon.

FGM is now banned in Kenya for girls under 17, but the ritual still has widespread support in some communities and continues clandestinely; attempts to stamp out FGM are widely perceived as part of a Western conspiracy to undermine African cultural identity. Many local women's groups, such as the community project Ntanira na Mugambo (Circumcision Through Words), are working towards preserving the rite-of-passage aspect of FGM without any surgery. It seems likely that it will be African initiatives such as this, rather than Western criticism, that will put an end to FGM.

Busy street, Malindi (p265)

Kenyan women are increasingly able to access educational opportunities and, particularly in the cities, are coming to play a more prominent role in business and politics. In rural areas typical gender roles are observed, although women are accorded status and respect in their capacity as mothers, wives, healers, teachers and members of extended lineages. The majority of small-scale farming in Kenya is undertaken by women.

The Arts

Kenya has a dynamic and burgeoning arts scene, with Kenyan musicians, writers and filmmakers particularly worth watching out for. Often these arts provide not only a powerful medium for expressing African culture but also a means for expressing the dreams and frustrations of the poor and disenfranchised.

For coverage of Swahili architecture, see the boxed text, p283.

Music

With its diversity of indigenous languages and culture, Kenya has a rich and exciting music scene. Influences, most notably from the nearby Democratic Republic of Congo and Tanzania, have helped to diversify the sounds. More recently reggae and hip hop have permeated the pop scene.

The live-music scene in Nairobi is fluid and a variety of clubs cater for traditional and contemporary musical tastes. A good reference is the *Daily Nation,* which publishes weekly top-10 African, international and gospel charts and countrywide gig listings on Saturday. Live-music venues are listed under Entertainment headings throughout this book.

Outside Influences

www.artmatters.info is a fabulous resource covering many aspects of the arts scene throughout Kenya and the rest of Africa.

The Congolese styles of rumba and soukous, known collectively as *lingala,* were first introduced into Kenya by artists such as Samba Mapangala (who is still playing) in the 1960s and have come to dominate most of East Africa. This upbeat party music is characterised by clean guitar licks and a driving *cavacha* drum rhythm.

Music from Tanzania was influential in the early 1970s, when the band Simba Wanyika helped create Swahili rumba, which was taken up by bands such as the Maroon Commandos and Les Wanyika.

Popular bands today are heavily influenced by benga, soukous and also Western music, with lyrics generally in Kiswahili. These include bands such as Them Mushrooms (now reinvented as Uyoya) and Safari Sound. For upbeat dance tunes, Ogopa DJs, Nameless, Redsan and Deux Vultures are recommended acts.

Home-Grown Styles

Kenyan bands were also active during the 1960s, producing some of the most popular songs in Africa, including Fadhili William's famous *Malaika* (Angel), and *Jambo Bwana,* Kenya's unofficial anthem, written and recorded by the hugely influential Them Mushrooms.

Benga is the contemporary dance music of Kenya. It refers to the dominant style of Luo pop music, which originated in western Kenya, and spread throughout the country in the 1960s being taken up by Akamba and Kikuyu musicians. The music is characterised by clear electric guitar licks and a bounding bass rhythm. Some well-known exponents of benga include DO Misiani (a Luo) and his group Shirati

PLAYLIST

» *Amigo* – classic Swahili rumba from one of Kenya's most influential bands, Les Wanyika

» *Guitar Paradise of East Africa* – ranges through Kenya's musical styles including the classic hit 'Shauri Yako'

» *Journey* – Jabali Afrika's stirring acoustic sounds complete with drums, congas, shakers and bells

» *Kenyan: The First Chapter* – Kenya's home-grown blend of African lyrics with R&B, house, reggae and dancehall genres

» *Mama Africa* – Suzanna Owiyo, the Tracy Chapman of Kenya, with acoustic Afropop

» *Nuting but de Stone* – phenomenally popular compilation combining African lyrics with American urban sounds and Caribbean *ragga*

» *Rumba is Rumba* – infectious Congolese soukous with Swahili lyrics

» *Nairobi Beat: Kenyan Pop Music Today* – regional sounds including Luo, Kikuyu, Kamba, Luhya, Swahili and Congolese

» *Virunga Volcano* – from Orchestre Virunga, with samba, sublime guitar licks, a bubbling bass and rich vocals

Jazz, which has been around since the 1960s and is still churning out the hits. You should also look out for Globestyle, Victoria Kings and Ambira Boys.

Contemporary Kikuyu music often borrows from benga. Stars include Sam Chege, Francis Rugwiti and Daniel 'Councillor' Kamau, who was popular in the 1970s and is still going strong.

Taarab, the music of the East African coast, originally only played at Swahili weddings and other special occasions, has been given a new lease of life by coastal pop singer Malika.

Rap, Hip Hop & Other Styles

American-influenced gangster rap and hip hop are also on the rise, including such acts as Necessary Noize, Poxi Presha and Hardstone. Admiration for big American names has translated into a home-grown industry and the slums of Nairobi have proved to be particularly fertile for local rap music. In 2004, Dutch producer Nynke Nauta gathered rappers from the Eastlands slums of Nairobi and formed a collective, Nairobi Yetu. The resultant album, *Kilio Cha Haki* (A Cry for Justice), featuring raps in Sheng (a mix of Kiswahili, English and ethnic languages), has been internationally recognised as a poignant fusion of ghetto angst and the joy of making music.

Kenya pioneered the African version of the reggaeton style (a blend of reggae, hip hop and traditional music), which is now popular in the US and UK. Dancehall is also huge here.

Other names to keep an eye or ear out for include Prezzo (Kenya's king of bling), Nonini (a controversial women-and-booze rapper), Nazizi (female MC from Necessary Noize) and Mercy Myra (Kenya's biggest female R&B artist).

Literature

There are plenty of novels, plays and biographies by contemporary Kenyan authors, but they can be hard to find outside the country. The Heinemann African Writers Series (www.africanwriters.com) offers an accessible collection of such works.

Ngũgĩ wa Thiong'o

Ngũgĩ is uncompromisingly radical, and his harrowing criticism of the neocolonialist politics of the Kenyan establishment landed him in jail for a year (described in his *Detained: A Prison Writer's Diary*), lost him his job at Nairobi University and forced him into exile.

His works include *Petals of Blood, Matigari, The River Between, A Grain of Wheat, Devil on the Cross* and *Wizard of the Crow,* which was shortlisted for the 2007 Commonwealth Writers' Prize. His latest work is the 2010 memoir *Dreams in a Time of War*. All offer insightful portraits of Kenyan life and will give you an understanding of the daily concerns of modern Kenyans. He has also written extensively in his native language, Gikuyu.

Nairobi Art Galleries

- » Gallery Watatu
- » Rahimtulla Museum of Modern Art
- » Go-Down Arts Centre

Meja Mwangi

Meja Mwangi sticks more to social issues and urban dislocation, but has a mischievous sense of humour that threads its way right through his books. Notable titles include *The Return of Shaka, Weapon of Hunger, The Cockroach Dance, The Last Plague* and *The Big Chiefs*. His *Mzungu Boy,* winner of the Children's Africana Book Award in 2006, depicts the friendship of white and black Kenyan boys at the time of the Mau Mau uprising.

Binyavanga Wainaina

One of Kenya's rising stars on the literary front is Binyavanga Wainaina, who won the Caine Prize for African Writing in July 2002. The award-winning piece was the short story *Discovering Home,* about a young Kenyan working in Cape Town who returns to his parents' village in Kenya for a year.

More recently, Wainaina helped form the Concerned Kenyan Writers (CKW) group in the aftermath of the 2008 post-election crisis. CKW aims to inspire and unite Kenyans and show them that there is a pay-off in peace and nationhood; it also seeks to counter the 'Dark Continent' reporting by the international media in the wake of the violence.

To follow the work of contemporary writers, look out for *Kwani?,* Kenya's first literary journal, established by Wainaina in 2003. Nairobi based, it facilitates the production and distribution of Kenyan literature and hosts an annual literary festival that attracts a growing number of international names. Their website (http://kwani.org) is a great way to stay up to date with the contemporary scene.

Facing the Lion is Joseph Lekuton's beautifully crafted memoir of how he grew up as a poor Maasai boy, who, through a series of incredible twists and turns, ends up in the US studying for an MBA.

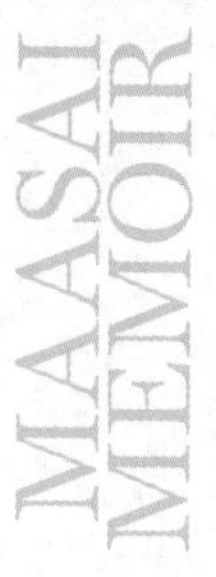

Contemporary Women Writers

The first female Kenyan writer of note is Grace Ogot, the first woman to have her work published by the East African Publishing House. Her work includes *Land Without Thunder, The Strange Bride, The Graduate* and *The Island of Tears*. Born in Nyanza Province, she sets many of her stories against the scenic background of Lake Victoria, and offers an insight into Luo culture in pre-colonial Kenya.

Another interesting writer is Margaret Atieno Ogola, the author of the celebrated novel *The River and the Source* and its sequel, *I Swear by Apollo,* which follow the lives of four generations of Kenyan women in a rapidly evolving country.

Other books of note are Marjorie Magoye's *The Present Moment,* which follows the life of a group of elderly women in a Christian refuge, and *The Man from Pretoria* by Kenyan conservationist and journalist Hilary Ngweno.

Cinema

Kenya's underfunded film industry has struggled to establish itself, but the Zanzibar International Film Festival (ZIFF), one of the region's premier cultural events, has helped to bring East African filmmakers to the fore. One such auteur is Kibaara Kaugi, whose *Enough is Enough* (2004), a brave exploration of the Mau Mau uprising, garnered critical praise.

In 2005, the government established the **Kenya Film Commission** (KFC; www.kenyafilmcommission.com) which aims to support and promote the Kenyan film industry. One notable success since its inception is *Kibera Kid,* a short film set in the Kibera slum, written and directed by Nathan Collett. It tells the story of 12-year-old Otieno, an orphan living with a gang of thieves, who must make a choice between gang life and redemption. Featuring a cast of children, all of whom live in Kibera, the film played at film festivals worldwide.

Filmed in Kenya

» *King Solomon's Mines* (1950)

» *The Snows of Kilimanjaro* (1952)

» *Mogambo* (1953)

» *Born Free* (1966)

» *Out of Africa* (1985)

» *Mountains of the Moon* (1990)

» *Nowhere in Africa* (2001)

» *The Constant Gardener* (2005)

Painting

Kenya has a diverse artistic heritage, and there is a wealth of artistic talent in the country, practising both traditional painting and all manner of sculpture, printing, mixed media and graffiti. For an overview of the local scene, visit Gallery Watatu and the Go-Down Arts Centre (see the boxed text, p68), both in Nairobi.

Textiles & Jewellery

Women throughout East Africa wear brightly coloured lengths of printed cotton cloth, typically with Swahili sayings printed along the edge, known as *kanga*. Many of the sayings are social commentary or messages, often indirectly worded, or containing puns and double meanings. Others are a local form of advertising, such as the logo of political parties.

In coastal areas, you'll also see the *kikoi*, which is made of a more thickly textured cotton, usually featuring striped or plaid patterns, and traditionally worn by men. Also common are batik-print cottons depicting everyday scenes, animal motifs or geometrical patterns.

Jewellery, especially beaded jewellery, is particularly beautiful among the Maasai and the Turkana. It is used in ceremonies as well as in everyday life, and often indicates the wearer's wealth and marital status.

Woodcarving & Sculpture

Woodcarving was only introduced into Kenya in the early 20th century. Mutisya Munge, an Akamba man, is considered the father of Kenyan woodcarving, having brought the tradition from Tanzania's Makonde people to Kenya following World War I. Kenya's woodcarving industry has grown exponentially in the century since, although recent shortages of increasingly endangered hardwoods have presented major challenges to the industry. While woodcarvings from Kenya may lack the sophistication and cultural resonance of those from Central and West Africa, the carvings' subjects range from representations of the spirit and animal worlds to stylised human figures.

Carvings rendered in soapstone from the village of Tabaka, close to Kisii in the Western Highlands, are among the most attractive of Kenyan handicrafts. These sculptures take on numerous forms, but the abstract figures of embracing couples are the genre's undoubted highpoint. See p146 for more information.

Kenyan Cuisine

The Kenyan culinary tradition has generally emphasised feeding the masses as efficiently as possible, with little room for flair or innovation. Most meals are centred on ugali, a thick, doughlike mass made from maize and/or cassava flour – an acquired taste for foreigners. While traditional fare may be bland but filling, there are some treats to be found.

Many of your most memorable eating experiences in Kenya are likely to revolve around dining alfresco in a safari camp, surrounded by the sights and sounds of the African bush. Sadly, on such occasions the only thing African about these meals is often the setting, with the food usually international in inspiration.

Cooking the East African Way, by Constance Nabwire and Bertha Vining Montgomery, combines easy-to-follow recipes from across the region with interesting text on culinary and cultural traditions in Kenya and elsewhere.

Staples & Specialities

Counting Carbs

Kenyan cuisine has few culinary masterpieces and is mainly survival food, offering the maximum opportunity to fill up at minimum cost. Most meals in Kenya largely consist of heavy starches.

In addition to ugali, Kenyans rely on potatoes, rice, chapatti and *matoke.* The rice-based dishes, biriani and pilau, are clearly derived from Persia – they should be delicately spiced with saffron and star anise and liberally sprinkled with carrot and raisins. The chapatti is identical to its Indian predecessor, while *matoke* is mashed green plantains, which when well prepared can taste like buttery, lightly whipped mashed potato. Also look out for *irio* (or *kienyeji),* made from mashed greens, potato and boiled corn or beans; *mukimo,* a kind of hash made from sweet potatoes, corn, beans and plantains; and *githeri,* a mix of beans and corn.

Pilau flavoured with spices and stock is the signature dish at traditional Swahili weddings. The expression 'going to eat pilau' means to go to a wedding.

Flesh & Bone

Kenyans are enthusiastic carnivores and their unofficial national dish, *nyama choma* (barbecued meat), is a red-blooded, hands-on affair. Most

THE ART OF EATING UGALI

A meal wouldn't be a meal in Kenya without ugali. Ugali is made from boiled grains cooked into a thick porridge until it sets hard, then served up in flat (and rather dense) slabs. It's incredibly stodgy and tends to sit in the stomach like a brick, but most Kenyans swear by it – it will fill you up after a long day's safari, but it won't set your taste buds atingle.

In general, good ugali should be neither too dry nor too sticky, which makes it easy to enjoy as a finger food. Take some with the right hand from the communal pot (your left hand is used for wiping – and we don't mean your mouth!), roll it into a small ball with the fingers, making an indentation with your thumb, and dip it into the accompanying sauce. Eating with your hand is a bit of an art, but after a few tries it starts to feel natural. Don't soak the ugali too long (to avoid it breaking up in the sauce), and keep your hand lower than your elbow (except when actually eating) so the sauce doesn't drip down your forearm.

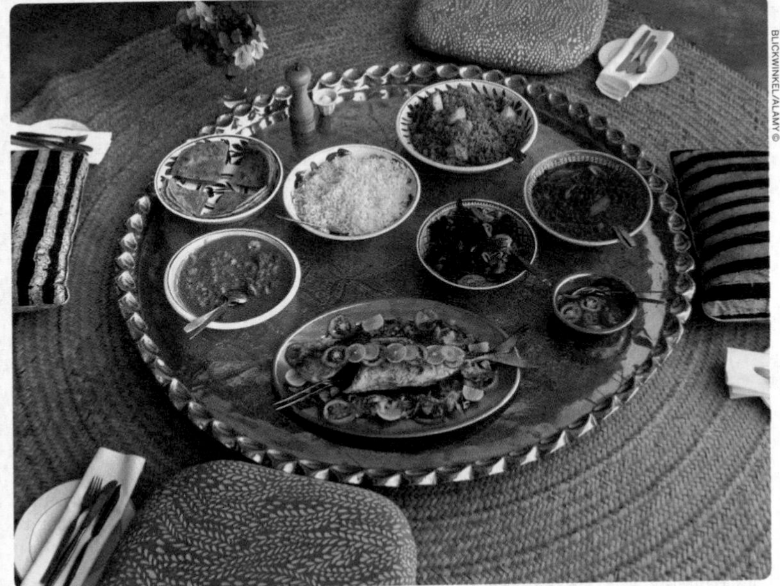

BLICKWINKEL/ALAMY ©

Traditional Swahili meal of fish, rice, curry, beans and vegetables

places have their own on-site butchery, and *nyama choma* is usually purchased by weight, often as a single hunk of meat. Half a kilogram is usually enough for one person (taking into account bone and gristle). It'll be brought out to you chopped into small bite-sized bits with vegetable mash and greens.

Goat is the most common meat, but you'll see chicken, beef and some game animals (ostrich and crocodile) in up-market places. Don't expect *nyama choma* to melt in the mouth – its chewiness is probably indicative of the long and eventful life of the animal you're consuming and you'll need a good half-hour at the end of the meal to work over your gums with a toothpick. We find that copious quantities of Tusker beer also tend to help it go down.

In addition to *nyama choma*, Kenyans are fond of meat-based stews, which help make their carb-rich diet more palatable. Again, goat, chicken and beef, as well as mutton, are the most common cuts on the menu, though they tend to be pretty tough, despite being cooked for hours on end.

Nyama Choma

- Kikopey Nyama Choma Centre, Rift Valley
- Hygienic Butchery, Nakuru
- *Nyama choma* stalls, Nairobi
- Carnivore, Nairobi
- The Grill, Kisimu
- Rongai Fast Food, Diani Beach

Fruit & Vegetables

Ugali (and most Kenyan dishes for that matter) is usually served with *sukuma wiki* (braised or stewed spinach). *Sukuma wiki* in Kiswahili means, literally, 'stretch the week', the implication being that it's so cheap it allows the householder to stretch the budget until the next weekly pay cheque. Despite its widespread availability, a dish of well-cooked *sukuma wiki* with tomatoes, stock and capsicum makes a refreshing change from the abundance of meat in other recipes.

Depending on the place and the season, you can buy mangoes, pawpaws, pineapples, passionfruit, guavas, oranges, custard apples, bananas (of many varieties), tree tomatoes and coconuts. Chewing on a piece of sugar cane is also a great way to end a meal.

DOS & DON'TS

For Kenyans, a shared meal and eating out of a communal dish are expressions of solidarity between hosts and guests: here are a few tips to help you get into the spirit of things.

» If you're invited to eat and aren't hungry, it's OK to say that you've just eaten, but try to share a few bites of the meal in recognition of the bond with your hosts.

» Leave a small amount on your plate to show your hosts that you've been satisfied.

» Don't take the last bit of food from the communal bowl – your hosts may worry that they haven't provided enough.

» Never, *ever* handle food with the left hand!

» If others are eating with their hands, do the same, even if cutlery is provided.

» Defer to your hosts for customs that you aren't sure about.

Kenyan Classics

Breakfast in Kenya is generally a simple affair consisting of chai accompanied by a *mandazi* (semisweet doughnut). *Mandazi* are best in the morning when they're freshly made – they become ever more rubbery and less appetising as the day goes on. Another traditional breakfast dish is *uji* (a thin, sweet porridge made from bean, millet or other flour); it's similar to ugali and best served warm, with lashings of milk and brown sugar.

PORTUGUESE

The most long-lasting impact that Portuguese explorers had on Kenya was in the culinary field. Portuguese travellers introduced maize, cassava, potatoes and chillies from South America – all of which are now staples of the Kenyan diet.

On the coast, Swahili dishes reflect the history of contact with Arabs and other Indian Ocean traders, and incorporate the produce of the region; the results can be excellent. Grilled fish or octopus will be a highlight of any menu, while coconut and spices such as cloves and cinnamon feature prominently.

The large South Asian presence in East Africa means that Indian food commonly appears on menus throughout Kenya. Most restaurants serve curries and Indian-inspired dishes such as masala chips (ie chips with a curry sauce), while authentic Indian restaurants along the coast and elsewhere serve up traditional dishes from the subcontinent.

Drinks

Tea & Coffee

Despite the fact that Kenya grows some excellent tea and coffee, getting a decent cup of either can be difficult. Quite simply, the best stuff is exported.

Chai is the national obsession, and although it's drunk in large quantities, it bears little resemblance to what you might be used to. As in India, the tea, milk and masses of sugar are boiled together and stewed for ages and the result is milky and very sweet – it may be too sickly for some, but the brew might just grow on you. Spiced masala chai with cardamom and cinnamon is very pleasant and rejuvenating. For tea without milk ask for chai *kavu*.

As for coffee, it's often sweet, milky and made with a bare minimum of instant coffee. However, in Nairobi and in other larger towns, there is a steadily increasing number of coffee houses serving very good Kenyan coffee, and you can usually get a good filter coffee at the big hotels. With all the Italian tourists who visit the coast, you can now get a decent cappuccino or espresso pretty much anywhere between Diani Beach and Lamu.

Fruit Juices

With all the fresh fruit that's available in Kenya, the juices on offer are breathtakingly good. All are made using modern blenders, so there's no point asking for a fruit juice during a power cut. Although you can get juices made from almost any fruit, the nation's favourite is passionfruit. It is known locally just as 'passion', although it seems a little odd asking a waiter or waitress whether they have passion and how much it costs! On a more serious note, be wary of fruit juices watered down with tap water. Either watch them prepare it or stick with bottled fruit juices instead.

Beer

Kenya has a thriving local brewing industry, and formidable quantities of beer are consumed day and night. You'll usually be given a choice of 'warm' or 'cold' beer. 'Why warm?', you might well ask. Curiously, most Kenyans appear to prefer it that way, despite the fact that room temperature in Kenya is a lot hotter than room temperature in the USA or Europe.

The local beers are Tusker, Pilsner and White Cap, all manufactured by Kenya Breweries and sold in 500mL bottles. Tusker comes in three varieties: Tusker Export, Tusker Malt Lager and just plain Tusker. Tusker Export is a stronger version of ordinary Tusker, while Tusker Malt has a fuller taste, for more discerning palates. Locally produced foreign labels include Castle (a South African beer) and Guinness, though the Kenyan version is nothing like the genuine Irish article.

Wine

Kenya has a fledgling wine industry, and the Lake Naivasha Colombard wines are generally quite good. This is something that cannot be said about the most commonly encountered Kenyan wine – pawpaw wine. Quite how anyone came up with the idea of trying to reproduce a drink made from grapes using pawpaw is a mystery, but the result tastes foul and smells unbearable. On the other hand, you can get cheap South African, European and even Australian wine by the glass in up-market restaurants in major cities and tourist areas.

Cocktails

A popular Kenyan cocktail is *dawa,* which translates from the Kiswahili as 'medicine'. Clearly based on the Brazilian caipirinha, it's made with vodka, lime and honey. We suggest you enjoy a tipple at sunset in a bar overlooking the coast, which can certainly have a therapeutic effect on mind and body.

Home Brew

Although it is strictly illegal for the public to brew or distil liquor, it remains a way of life for many Kenyans. *Pombe* is the local beer, usually a fermented brew made with bananas or millet and sugar. It shouldn't do you any harm. The same cannot be said for the distilled drinks known locally as *chang'a,* which are laced with genuine poisons. In 2005, 48 people died near Machakos after drinking a bad batch of *chang'a*. A further 84 were hospitalised and treated with vodka to reduce the effect of methyl alcohol poisoning – such events are not uncommon. Perhaps the

WE DARE YOU

If you're lucky (!) and game (more to the point), you may be able to try various cattle-derived products beloved of the pastoral tribes of Kenya. Samburu, Pokot and Maasai warriors have a taste for cattle blood. The blood is taken straight from the jugular, which does no permanent damage to the cattle, but it's certainly an acquired taste. *Mursik* is made from milk fermented with grass ash, and is served in smoked gourds. It tastes and smells pungent, but it contains compounds that reduce cholesterol, enabling the Maasai to live quite healthily on a diet of red meat, milk and blood. You may be able to sample it at villages in the Masai Mara National Reserve or near Amboseli National Park.

KENYA'S TOP FIVE EATERIES

- **Carnivore** (see the boxed text, p75), Nairobi
- **Ali Barbour's Cave Restaurant** (p247), Diani Beach
- **Railway Beach** (p140), Kisumu
- **Tamarind Restaurant** (p234), Mombasa
- **Haandi Restaurant** (p76), Nairobi

most dangerous *chang'a* comes from Kisii, and is fermented with marijuana twigs, cactus mash, battery alkaline and formalin. Don't touch it.

Where to Eat & Drink

'Hotels' & Restaurants

The most basic local eateries are usually known as 'hotels' or *hotelis,* and they often open only during the daytime. You may find yourself having dinner at 5pm if you rely on eating at these places. However, even in smaller towns it's usually possible to find a restaurant that offers a more varied menu at a higher price. Often these places are affiliated with the town's midrange and top-end hotels, and are usually open in the evening. You'll find that many of the big nightclubs also serve food until late into the night. Menus, where they exist in the cheaper places, are usually just a chalked list on a board. In more up-market restaurants, they're usually written only in English.

RECIPES

For the low-down on various Kenyan recipes, including the ubiquitous ugali and *sukuma wiki,* check out www.blissites.com/kenya/culture/recipes.html.

Quick Eats

Eating fast food has taken off in a big way and virtually every town has a place serving greasy-but-cheap chips, burgers, sausages, pizzas and fried chicken. Lashings of tomato and chilli sauces are present to help lubricate things. A number of South African fast-food chains have taken hold in Nairobi, such as the ubiquitous Steers.

On the streets in Kenya, you may encounter roasted corn cobs and deep-fried yams, which are eaten hot with a squeeze of lemon juice and a sprinkling of chilli powder. *Sambusas,* deep-fried pastry triangles stuffed with spiced mincemeat, are good for snacking on the run, and are obvious descendants of the Indian samosa.

Something you don't come across often, but which is an excellent snack, is *mkate mayai* (literally 'bread eggs'), a wheat dough pancake, filled with minced meat and egg and fried on a hotplate.

On the coast street food is more common and you will find cassava chips, chapattis and *mishikaki* (marinated grilled meat kebabs, usually beef).

Vegetarians & Vegans

Vegetarian visitors are likely to struggle, as meat features in most meals and many vegetable dishes are cooked in meat stock. But, with a bit of scouting around, you should be able to find something. You may find yourself eating a lot of *sukuma wiki* (p317), while other traditional dishes such as *githeri* are hearty, if not particularly inspiring, options. Beans and avocado will also figure prominently in any vegetarian's culinary encounters in Kenya. Many Indian restaurants will provide a vegetarian thali (an all-you-can-eat meal) that will certainly fill you up. Buying fresh fruit and vegetables in local markets can help relieve the tedium of trying to order around the meat on restaurant menus.

Note that most tour operators are willing to cater to special dietary requests, such as vegetarian, vegan, kosher or halal, with advance notice.

Environment

The Land

Kenya, as the cliché goes, is Africa in microcosm, and in the case of Kenya's landscapes, the cliché happens to be true. Within Kenya's borders you'll find astonishing variety, from deserts to tropical coast and snow-capped mountains, from sweeping savannah grasslands to dense forests. And running through the heart of it all is the Great Rift Valley.

Great Rift Valley

Africa's Great Rift Valley is one of Africa's defining landforms and this great gouge in the planet cuts a swath through the heart of Kenya. It was formed some eight million years ago, when Mother Earth tried to rip Africa in two. Africa bent, Africa buckled, but Africa never gave in.

The Rift Valley is part of the Afro-Arabian rift system that stretches 5500km from the salty shores of the Dead Sea to the palm trees of Mozambique, passing through the Red Sea, Ethiopia, Kenya, Tanzania and Malawi en route. A western branch forms a string of lakes in the centre of the continent (Albert, Edward, Kivu and Tanganyika), joining the main system at the tip of Lake Malawi. The East African section of the rift 'failed' and now only the Red Sea rift continues, slowly separating Africa from the Middle East. The Rift's path through Kenya can be traced through Lake Turkana, the Cherangani Hills and Lakes Baringo, Bogoria, Nakuru, Elmenteita, Naivasha and Magadi.

For an evocative and beautifully written picture of Kenya's physical, environmental and cultural make-up, track down Peter Matthiessen's classic, *The Tree Where Man Was Born*, an account of the author's epic journey through East Africa in the 1960s.

The Rift created Africa's highest mountains – including Mt Kenya, Mt Elgon, Mt Kilimanjaro (across the border in Tanzania) and the Virunga Range (in the Democratic Republic of the Congo; DRC, formerly Zaïre) – most of which began as volcanoes. Most of the volcanoes that line the valley are now extinct, but no fewer than 30 remain active and, according to local legend, Mt Longonot erupted as recently as the 1860s. This continuing activity supports a considerable number of hot springs, and provides ideal conditions for geothermal power plants (in Hell's Gate National Park and the Menengai Crater, for example), which are increasingly important for Kenya's energy supply.

Besides providing fertile soil, the volcanic deposits have created alkaline waters in most Rift Valley lakes. For information on these lakes, see p323.

The Savannah

The African savannah is a quintessentially African landform, so much so that it covers an estimated two-thirds of the African land mass. In Kenya, the most famous sweeps of savannah are found in the country's west (particularly in the Masai Mara National Reserve) and south.

Savannah is usually located in a broad swath surrounding tropical rainforest and its sweeping plains are home to some of the richest concentrations of wildlife on earth. The term itself refers to a grasslands

IGNACIO PALACIOS/LONELY PLANET IMAGES ©

Sunset over acacia trees in the Masai Mara (p129)

ecosystem. While trees may be (and usually are) present, such trees do not, under the strict definition of the term, form a closed canopy, while wet and dry seasons (the latter often with regenerating and/or devastating wildfires) are also typical of Africa's savannah regions.

The Coast

Along the coast of East Africa, warm currents in the Indian Ocean provide perfect conditions for coral growth, resulting in beautiful underwater coral reefs.

Coral reefs are the most biologically diverse marine ecosystems on earth, rivalled only by tropical rainforests on land. Corals grow over geologic time – ie over millennia rather than the decades that mammals etc live – and have been in existence for about 200 million years. The delicately balanced marine environment of the coral reef relies on the interaction of hard and soft corals, sponges, fish, turtles, dolphins and other marine life forms.

Coral reefs also rely on mangroves, the salt-tolerant trees with submerged roots that form a nursery and breeding ground for birds and most of the marine life that migrates to the reef. Mangroves trap and produce nutrients for food and habitat, stabilise the shoreline, and filter pollutants from the land base. Both coral reefs and the mangrove colonies that support them are under threat from factors such as oil exploration and extraction, coastal degradation, deforestation and global warming.

For information on how to explore Kenya's offshore reefs, see p40.

Forests

Kenya's forests border the great rainforest systems of central Africa, and western Kenya once formed part of the mighty Guineo-Congolian forest ecosystem. Few vestiges remain and just 6.2% of Kenyan territory is now covered by forest. The process of clearing these forests began with Kenya's colonial rulers, who saw in the land's fertility great potential for the vast tea plantations that now provide critical export revenue to Kenya. It has continued apace ever since as Kenya's population soars and the need for land given over to agriculture has increased. The Kakamega Forest has been protected just in time and shows what most of western Kenya must have once looked like. Other important forest areas include the forests (including the Kamweti Forest) that cover 2000 sq km of the slopes of Mt Kenya; the Arabuko Sokoke Forest Reserve, the largest surviving tract of coastal forest in East Africa; Mt Elgon National Park; and Aberdare National Park.

Mangroves

- Wasini Island
- Funzi Island
- Gazi Island
- Mida Creek

Deserts

Much of northern Kenya is extremely arid, with rainfall of less than 100mm a year. A number of contiguous deserts occupy the territory between Lake Turkana's eastern shore and the Ethiopian and Somali borders. The largest and best known of these is the Chalbi Desert, centred on North Horr and Kalacha, and formed by an ancient lake bed. Other deserts of northern Kenya include the Kaisut Desert (between Marsabit and South Horr) and the Dida Galgalu Desert (close to the Ethiopian border, near Moyale).

Parts of southern Kenya are also considered arid or semiarid, thanks largely to the looming hulk of Mt Kilimanjaro, which diverts rain elsewhere. One of these is the Nyiri Desert, which lies between Lake Magadi and Amboseli National Park.

Lakes & Wetlands

Lake Victoria, which is shared between Uganda, Tanzania and Kenya, is Africa's largest freshwater lake (and the second-largest by area in the world after the USA's Lake Superior). Its surface covers an area of over 68,000 sq km, with only 20% of the lake lying within Kenyan territory. Water levels fluctuate widely, depending largely on the rains, with depths never more than 80m and more often lower than 10m.

Most of Kenya's section of Lake Victoria is taken over by the Winam Gulf, a 100km-long, 50km-wide arm of the lake with a shoreline of almost 550km and an average depth of 6m. A fast-growing population around the gulf's shoreline has caused massive environmental problems such as siltation, sedimentation and toxic pollution (primarily pesticides and untreated sewage), although the major issue has been the invasion of water hyacinth since the late 1980s. The millions of dollars ploughed into solving the problem largely rid the gulf of hyacinth by 2005, although heavy rains in 2006, and the subsequent return of hyacinth, showed that the gulf is still highly susceptible to the hyacinth's clutches.

RIVERS

Four rivers – the Sondu-Miriu, Kibos, Nyando and Kisat – send an average 231 cu metres of water into the Winam Gulf on Kenya's stretch of Lake Victoria every second.

Aside from Lake Victoria in the west, Kenya has numerous small volcanic lakes, as well as a sea of jade, otherwise known by the more boring name of Lake Turkana, which straddles the Ethiopian border in the north. The main alkaline lakes in the Rift Valley include Bogoria, Nakuru, Elmenteita, Magadi and Oloiden. These shallow soda lakes, formed by the valley's lack of decent drainage, experience high evaporation rates, which further concentrates the alkalinity. The strangely soapy and smelly waters are, however, the perfect environment for the growth of microscopic blue-green algae, which in turn feed lesser flamingos, tiny crustaceans (food for greater flamingos) and insect larvae (food for soda-resistant fish). In 2011, the global significance of Kenya's Rift Valley lake system (primarily Lakes Nakuru, Elmenteita and Bogoria) was recognised when it was inscribed on Unesco's list of World Heritage sites.

Not all of the Rift Valley's lakes are alkaline; freshwater lakes include Baringo and Naivasha.

Five of the Rift Valley's lakes – Baringo, Bogoria, Elmenteita, Naivasha and Nakuru – have also been listed on the Ramsar List of Wetlands of

International Importance, and represent important habitats for wintering waterbirds from the north.

For a look at the threats to the ecosystems of the Rift Valley lakes, see the boxed text on p127.

UNESCO

Five sites in Kenya are included on the Unesco World Heritage list: Mt Kenya, the Lake Turkana national parks, Lamu's Old Town, the Mijikenda *kayas* (sacred forests) and the lake system in the Great Rift Valley.

Rivers

One of Kenya's most important rivers is the Athi/Galana River system. The Athi River passes east of Nairobi, joins the Tsavo River (which passes through the Tsavo West National Park), and the two then feed into the Galana River which cuts Tsavo East National Park in two. The Athi/Galana River then empties into the Indian Ocean close to Malindi. The Tana River is the country's other major river, rising northeast of Nairobi and emptying into the Indian Ocean between Malindi and Lamu.

Environmental Issues

Kenya faces a daunting slew of environmental issues, among them deforestation, desertification, threats to endangered species and the impacts of tourism. The ongoing debate over whether conservation should be in public or private hands is also a hot topic in Kenya.

Deforestation

More than half of Africa's forests have been destroyed over the last century, and forest destruction continues on a large scale in parts of Kenya – today, less than 3% of the country's original forest cover remains. Land grabbing, charcoal burning, agricultural encroachment, the spiralling use of firewood, and illegal logging have all taken their toll over the years. However, millions of Kenyans (and the majority of hotels, lodges and restaurants) still rely on wood and charcoal for cooking fuel, so travellers to the country will almost certainly contribute to this deforestation, whether they like it or not.

WANGARI MAATHAI, NOBEL LAUREATE

On Earth Day in 1977 Professor Wangari Maathai planted seven trees in her backyard, setting in motion the grassroots environmental campaign that later came to be known as the Green Belt Movement. Since then more than 40 million trees have been planted throughout Kenya and the movement has expanded to more than 30 other African countries. The core aim of this campaign is to educate women – who make up some 70% of farmers in Africa – about the link between soil erosion, undernourishment and poor health, and to encourage individuals to protect their immediate environment and guard against soil erosion by planting 'green belts' of trees and establishing tree nurseries.

For decades, Maathai's activism came at a cost. The Moi regime consistently vilified her as a 'threat to the order and security of the country', due to her demands for free and fair multiparty elections, and throughout the years her public demonstrations have been met with acts of violence and she has spoken of receiving death threats. She also won few friends in powerful circles for working extensively with various international organisations to exert leverage on the Kenyan government. Later, however, Maathai served as Assistant Minister for the Environment between 2003 and 2005, and was awarded the Nobel Peace Prize in 2004 (the first African woman to receive one) for her tireless campaigning on environmental issues.

In addition, she was also heavily involved in women's rights (her first husband divorced her because she was 'too strong-minded for a woman'; the judge in the divorce case agreed and then had her imprisoned for speaking out against him!), and in 2006 she was one of the founders of the Nobel Women's Initiative, which aims to bring justice, peace and equality to women.

Maathai died of cancer in a Nairobi Hospital in 2011 at the age of 71, but the Green Belt Movement she founded is still one of the most significant environmental organisations in Kenya. Maathai's book *Unbowed: One Woman's Story* was published in 2006.

The de-gazetting of protected forests is another contentious issue, sparking widespread protests and preservation campaigns. On the flip-side, locals in forest areas can find themselves homeless if the government does enforce protection orders.

Native hardwood such as ebony and mahogany is often used to make the popular carved wooden statue souvenirs sold in Kenya. Though this industry supports thousands of local families who may otherwise be without an income, it also consumes an estimated 80,000 trees annually. The WWF and Unesco campaigned to promote the use of common, faster-growing trees, and many handicraft cooperatives now use wood taken from forests managed by the Forest Stewardship Council. If you buy a carving, ask if the wood is sourced from managed forests.

Desertification

Northern and eastern Kenya are home to some of the most marginal lands in East Africa. Pastoralists have eked out a similarly marginal existence here for centuries, but recurring droughts have seriously degraded the land, making it increasingly susceptible to creeping desertification and erosion. As a consequence, the UN estimates that the livelihoods of around 3.5 million herders may be under medium- to long-term threat.

And desertification, at least in its early stages, may even soon begin to encroach upon the most unlikely places. The fertile lands of Kenya's Central Highlands rank among Africa's most agriculturally productive, but therein lies their peril: here, around three-quarters of Kenya's population crowds into just 12% of the land, with the result that soils are being rapidly depleted through overexploitation – one of the early warning signs of desertification.

Endangered Species

Many of Kenya's major predators and herbivores have become endangered over the past few decades, because of poisoning, the ongoing destruction of their natural habitat and merciless poaching for ivory, skins, horn and bushmeat.

For a full-colour exploration of Kenya's wildlife, see p335.

Elephants

The African elephant, the largest living land animal, is for many travellers the continent's most charismatic mammal. Elephants are plentiful in many areas of Kenya, but it hasn't always been so and their survival is one of world conservation's most enduring success stories.

In the 1970s and 1980s, the numbers of African elephants plummeted from an estimated 1.3 million to around 500,000 thanks to widespread poaching. In Kenya, elephant numbers fell from 45,000 in 1976 to just 5400 in 1988. The slaughter ended only in 1989 when the trade in ivory was banned under the Convention for International Trade in Endangered Species (Cites). When the ban was established, world raw ivory prices plummeted by 90%, and the market for poaching and smuggling was radically reduced. The same year, Kenyan President Daniel arap Moi dramatically burned 12 tons of ivory in Nairobi National Park as a symbol of Kenya's resolve in the battle against poachers.

Illegal poaching continues to feed demand in Asia, and may even be on the rise, and poaching continues (albeit much reduced) in Kenya's parks and beyond. Even so, the ivory ban remains an overwhelming success, so much so that in some areas elephant populations have grown to unsustainable levels – in Amboseli National Park, for example, numbers have doubled in the past decade alone. Indeed, Kenya's elephant numbers have now largely recovered overall, with an estimated 32,000 elephants calling Kenya home at last count.

Game Changer: Animal Rights & the Fate of Africa's Wildlife, by Glen Martin, is a provocative look at wildlife conservation in 2012, covering Kenya, Tanzania and Namibia.

POACHING & CULLING DEBATE

Poaching is one of the most notorious environmental issues in Kenya and although much reduced since the 1980s, it still occurs throughout the country. But just as poaching has diminished, a whole new set of problems has arisen.

After the excesses of the 1970s and '80s, elephant populations recovered in most areas, but as human populations continued to grow, another problem surfaced – elephants eat huge quantities of foliage, but in the past, herds would eat their fill then migrate to another area, allowing time for vegetation to regenerate. However, an increasing human population pressed the elephants into smaller and smaller areas and the herds were forced to eat everything available.

Increasingly, park authorities are facing elephant overpopulation. Proposed solutions include relocation (where herds are permanently transplanted to other areas) and contraception. The only other alternative is to cull herds, sometimes in large numbers. In the West, people generally hold a preservationist viewpoint, that elephant herds should be protected for their own sake or for aesthetic reasons. While there are exceptions, the general local sentiment maintains that the elephant must justify its existence on long-term economic grounds for the benefit of local people, or for the country as a whole.

Proponents of culling cite the health of the parks and wildlife, including the elephants themselves, while organisations such as the International Fund for Animal Welfare (IFAW) are appalled at such a solution, which they claim is cruel, unethical and scientifically unsound. IFAW believes aerial surveys of elephant numbers are inaccurate, population growth has not been accurately surveyed, and other solutions have not been looked at carefully enough.

Furthermore, there is much dispute about whether controlled ivory sales should be reintroduced. In 2010, Tanzania and Zambia petitioned the Convention on the International Trade in Endangered Species (Cites) for a downgrading of the elephant's endangered status to allow these countries to sell their large stockpiles of ivory. Kenya lobbied against the move and the ivory ban was upheld, although some see the debate as a precursor to future attempts to legalise the ivory trade.

For more information on the fight to save elephants in Kenya and further afield, contact **Save the Elephants** (www.savetheelephants.org).

For the best places to see elephants, see p18. And to visit one of the most distinguished elephant research programs in Kenya, see p93.

White rhinos aren't white at all – the name comes from the Dutch word *wijd*, which means wide and refers to the white rhino's wide lip (the black rhino has a pointed lip).

Rhinoceros

These inoffensive vegetarians are armed with impressive horns that have made them the target of both white hunters and poachers; rhino numbers plummeted to the brink of extinction during the 20th century and the illegal trade in rhino horns is still driven by their use in traditional medicines in Asian countries. Despite having turned the situation around from the desperate lows of the 1980s, wildlife authorities in Kenya and elsewhere are battling a recent upsurge in rhino poaching again.

There are two species of rhino – black and white – both of which are predominantly found in savannah regions. The black rhino is probably Kenya's most endangered large mammal. Pursued by heavily armed gangs, the black rhino's numbers fell from an estimated 20,000 in the 1970s to barely 300 a decade later. Numbers are slowly recovering (rhinos are notoriously slow breeders), with an estimated 630 black rhinos surviving in the wild in Kenya, which represents around one-sixth of Africa's total.

Although numbers are quite small in Kenya, the survival of the white rhino is an environmental conservation success story, having been brought back from the brink of extinction in South Africa through captive breeding. As a result, the white rhino is now off the endangered list.

The Kenya Wildlife Service estimated in late 2010 that Kenya was home to 350 white rhinos in the wild.

Rhino Ark (☎020-2136010; www.rhinoark.org) is one organisation that raises funds to create rhino sanctuaries, and donations are always appreciated. Sanctuaries already in existence include the Ngulia Rhino Sanctuary in Tsavo West National Park, and the privately run Solio Game Reserve and Ol Pejeta Conservancy. Lake Nakuru National Park also has a large population of black rhinos, which has grown to the extent that there are plans to relocate 10 to Tsavo National Park.

Rhino Hot Spots

- Lake Nakuru National Park
- Tsavo West National Park
- Nairobi National Park
- Masai Mara National Reserve
- Solio Game Reserve
- Aberdare National Park
- Laikipia plateau

Lions

Lions may be the easiest of Kenya's big cats to spot – leopards are notoriously secretive and largely keep to the undergrowth, while cheetahs live in similarly low-density populations and can also prove elusive. But don't let appearances fool you: the lion is the most endangered of Africa's three big cats.

Fewer than 30,000 lions are thought to remain in Africa (there is a tiny, highly inbred population of Asian lions in the Gir Forest in Gujarat state in India), although most conservationists agree that the number is most likely considerably below that figure. In Kenya, fewer than 2000 are thought to survive, although this, too, is feared to be an overestimate. Although there are small, scattered prides around the country, including in Lake Nakuru National Park and northern Kenya, the only viable lion populations in the long term are those in Laikipia, Meru National Park and Maasailand (which stretches across southern Kenya from the Masai Mara National Reserve to Tsavo East National Park).

And numbers are falling alarmingly, possibly by as many as 100 lions per year, thanks primarily to human encroachment and habitat loss. The poisoning of lions (as well as scavengers and other predators), either in retaliation for lions killing livestock or encroaching onto farming lands, has also reached dangerous levels, to the extent that some lion conservationists predict that the lion could become extinct in Kenya within 20 years.

Living with Lions (www.livingwithlions.org) is one organisation fighting to protect Kenya's lions and is an important source of information. **Wildlife Direct** (wildlifedirect.org) is another useful source of information, particularly on the threat posed by poisoning. For a fascinating insight into an innovative approach to lion conservation in the Amboseli region, see the boxed text, p95.

For some of the best places to see lions, leopards and cheetahs, see p18.

Having trouble telling your dik-dik from your klipspringer? Try the hand-illustrated *Kingdon Field Guide to African Mammals* (Jonathon Kingdon), widely considered to be the definitive guide to the continent's fauna. It's also available in a pocket edition.

Grevy's Zebra

Kenya (along with neighbouring Ethiopia) is home to the last surviving wild populations of Grevy's zebra. Distinguished from other zebra species by having narrow stripes and bellies free from stripes, the Grevy's zebra is found in the Lewa Wildlife Conservancy, Ol Pejeta Conservancy and the Samburu, Buffalo Springs and Shaba national reserves.

In the 1970s, approximately 15,000 Grevy's zebras were thought to survive in the wild. Just 2500 are estimated to remain and less than 1% of the Grevy zebra's historical range lies within protected areas.

Rothschild's Giraffe

The most endangered of the nine giraffe subspecies, the Rothschild's giraffe has recently been hauled back from the brink of extinction. At the forefront of the fight to save the Rothschild's giraffe (which, unlike other subspecies, has distinctive white 'stockings' with no orange-and-black markings below the knee) has been the Giraffe Centre in

Nairobi – visiting here is a fascinating experience, and helps further the attempts to save the giraffes and facilitate their return to the wild. Rothschild's giraffes are making a comeback, with populations having been reintroduced into the wild at Lake Nakuru National Park.

Invasive Plant Species

There are many well-known threats to the ecosystem of Kenya's iconic Masai Mara National Reserve – poaching, overdevelopment and growing human populations. But one of the most dangerous threats comes in the form of a simple plant: a foreign weed called parthenium *(Parthenium hysterophorus)*. The toxic weed, which is not native to Kenya, first appeared around Nairobi, the Athi River, Naivasha and Busia, but its rapid growth in the Mara has led to it being designated a noxious weed by Kenya's government. Known to grow along the banks of the Mara River and some tracks through the reserve, parthenium (which is unpalatable to the Mara's herbivores) is spreading at an alarming rate, and in some areas is even replacing the fabled grasslands of the Mara. A single parthenium plant can produce up to 25,000 seeds and its chemical composition is such that it inhibits the growth of other plants, prompting concerns that the weed could pose a long-term threat to the Mara.

In a related issue, many lodges in the Mara and elsewhere also have gardens filled with beautiful, but non-native, plants, which can cause devastation to the local environment.

For information on the problem of highly invasive water hyacinth in Lake Victoria, see p323.

Private versus Public Conservation

Kenya Wildlife Service (KWS)

Conservation in Kenya has, for over two decades, been in the hands of the government-run **Kenya Wildlife Service** (www.kws.org) and few would dispute that it has done a pretty impressive job. In the dark years of the 1970s and '80s when poaching was rampant, a staggering number of Kenya's rhinos and elephants were slaughtered and many KWS officers were in league with poachers. It all changed after the famous palaeontologist Dr Richard Leakey cleaned up the organisation in the 1980s and '90s. A core part of his policy was arming KWS rangers with modern weapons and high-speed vehicles and allowing them to shoot poachers on sight, which seems to have dramatically reduced the problem.

The East African Wildlife Society (www.eawildlife.org), based in Nairobi, is the most prominent conservation body in the region and a good source of information.

However, there have been several raids on elephant and rhino populations over the past decade and KWS rangers continue to lose their lives every year in battles with poachers. As a result, there is now open talk of abandoning some of the more remote parks (such as those parks that are close to the Ethiopian or Somali borders) and concentrating resources in the parks that receive most visitors and where results can be achieved. In times of shrinking government revenues, funding also remains a major issue in how well the KWS can fulfil its mandate.

Private Conservation

For all the success of KWS, it has been claimed that more than 75% of Kenya's wildlife lies outside the country's national parks and reserves, and there seems to be little doubt that the future of conservation in Kenya lies in private hands. Private wildlife reserves often have the resources to work more intensively on specific conservation issues than national parks and reserves can.

Lewa Wildlife Conservancy, near Isiolo, is probably the best known, and most successful, private reserve. The private conservancies of the

Laikipia plateau have also produced some startling results – without a single national park or reserve in the area, Laikipia has become a major safari destination, and is proving to be a particularly important area for viable populations of endangered black rhinos, Grevy's zebras, African wild dogs and lions. Ranches in this area – many of which are affiliated with the umbrella **Laikipia Wildlife Forum** (LWF; ☎0726500260; www.laikipia.org) – are particularly active in wildlife conservation, and the LWF is a good source of up-to-date information about projects and accommodation in the region.

Other private game ranches and conservation areas (some of which we've covered throughout the book) can be found across the country, particularly close to Tsavo (East and West, though mainly West) and Amboseli national parks, and the Masai Mara National Reserve. One of these is the **Mara Conservancy** (www.maratriangle.org), a nonprofit organisation that manages the Mara Triangle sector of the Masai Mara National Reserve. The first such project of its kind in the Mara region, it is considered a significant example of how locals communities can work with conservation groups for the benefit of both traditional peoples and wildlife.

Renewable Energy

The use of renewable energy has been slow to catch on in Kenya. Many top-end lodges attempt to pursue sound environmental practices – the use of solar energy is increasingly widespread – but these remain very much in the minority. And many of these top-end lodges suggest that you travel to them by air, which surely cancels out any gains of having solar-powered hot water in your shower.

Ecotourism Kenya (www.ecotourismkenya.org) lists only 56 establishments as having been awarded an ecofriendly status (although a business does have to request that they are assessed) ranked gold, silver or bronze. In practice, you'll find that very few lodges and camps have recycling systems, alternative energy sources or other environmental initiatives in place. The KWS now insists that every new lodge and camp be designed in an ecofriendly manner, but existing lodges are yet to be called to account.

PREDATORS

If predators get your heart racing, track down a copy of Dr Luke Hunter's outstanding *A Field Guide to the Carnivores of the World,* which was released in late 2011.

COMMUNITY-RUN CONSERVANCIES

While other countries have been fighting a losing battle to preserve wildlife by separating animals and humans, local communities in parts of northern Kenya, like the Maasai of Il Ngwesi, Laikipia Maasai of Lekurruki and the Samburu within the Matthews Range, are actually increasing animal populations (and their own standard of living) by embracing peaceful cohabitation.

These communities treat wildlife as a natural resource and take serious action to protect the animals' well-being, whether by combating poaching with increased security or by modifying their herding activities to minimise human–animal conflict and environmental damage. With financial and logistical support from many sources, including Lewa Wildlife Conservancy (LWC), Laikipia Wildlife Forum (LWF) and the Northern Ranchlands Trust (NRT), these communities have built the magical ecolodges whose income now provides much-needed funds for their education, health and humanitarian projects.

The pioneering doesn't stop there. The LWF and NRT also coordinate wildlife conservancy on large private ranches and small farms (in northern Kenya and on the Laikipia plateau), hoping to spark more sustainable development projects and further improve local standards of living. If these brave projects continue to prove that humans and wildlife can not only live in the same environment but actually thrive from the mutual relationship, an amazing precedent will be set.

CATTLE-FREE NATIONAL PARKS?

Nothing seems to disappoint visitors to Kenya's national parks more than the sight of herders shepherding their livestock to water sources within park boundaries. In the words of former Kenya Wildlife Service head Dr Richard Leakey: 'People don't pay a lot of money to see cattle'. The issue is, however, a complicated one.

On the one hand, what you are seeing is far from a natural African environment. For thousands of years people, and their herds of cattle, lived happily (and sustainably) alongside the wildlife, and their actions helped to shape the landscapes of East Africa. But with the advent of conservation and national parks, many of Kenya's tribal peoples, particularly pastoralists such as the Maasai and Samburu, have found themselves and their cattle excluded from their ancestral lands, often with little or no compensation or alternative incomes provided (although of course some do now make a living through tourism and conservation). Having been pushed onto marginal lands and with limited access to alternative water sources in times of drought, many have been forced to forgo their traditional livelihoods and have taken to leading sedentary lifestyles. Those that continue as herders have little choice but to overgraze their lands. This position is passionately argued in the excellent (if slightly dated) book *No Man's Land: An Investigative Journey Through Kenya & Tanzania* (2003) by George Monbiot.

At the same time, tourism is a major (and much-needed) source of revenue for Kenya and most visitors to Kenya want to experience a natural wilderness – on the surface at least, the national parks, reserves and private conservancies appear to provide this Eden-esque slice of Africa. And even where the parks have been artificially carved out at the expense of tribal peoples, Kenya's population numbers are such that it remains questionable whether allowing herders and their livestock to graze within park boundaries would alleviate the pressures on overexploited land and traditional cultures, or would instead simply lead to the degradation of Kenya's last remaining areas of relatively pristine wilderness.

Plans are well developed for the Lake Turkana Wind Power project to begin operations in 2013. When completed, the project is expected to provide the equivalent of 25% of Kenya's current power needs. For more information on this project, see the boxed text, p219. In the meantime, expect fossil fuels to continue to drive Kenya's economy.

Tourism

The tourist industry, as well as being a saviour of Kenya's animals, is also the cause of some pretty major environmental problems, most notably the heavy use of firewood by tourist lodges and erosion caused by safari minibuses, which creates virtual dust bowls in parks and reserves such as Amboseli, Samburu and the Mara. A number of operators have been banned from the Mara in recent years for misdemeanours ranging from nonpayment of rent for tented camps to harassment of wildlife, but there are few signs that the ban is being enforced.

As a visitor, the best way to help combat these problems is to be very selective about who you do business with and very vocal about the kind of standards you expect. The more that tourists insist on responsible practices, the more safari operators and hotels will take notice, and, while you may end up paying more for an ecofriendly trip, in the long term you'll be investing in a sustainable tourist industry and the preservation of Kenya's delicate environment.

National Parks & Reserves

Kenya's national parks and reserves rate among the best in Africa. Around 10% of the country's land area is protected by law – that means, at least in theory, no human habitation, no grazing and no hunting within park boundaries. The parks range from the 15.5-sq-km Saiwa Swamp National Park to the massive, almost 21,000-sq-km Tsavo East and West National Parks. Together they embrace a wide range of habitats and ecosystems and contain an extraordinary repository of Africa's wildlife. These parks are home to some of the most beautiful corners of Africa.

History

The idea of setting aside protected areas began during colonial times, and in many cases this meant authorities forcibly evicting the local peoples from their traditional lands. Local anger was fuelled by the fact that many parks were set aside as hunting reserves for white hunters with anything but conservation on their minds.

Many of these hunters, having pushed some species to the brink of extinction, later became conservationists and by the middle of the 20th century the push was on to establish the national parks and reserves of today. In 1946 Nairobi National Park became the first park in British

NATIONAL PARKS VERSUS RESERVES

If you go onto the website of the **Kenya Wildlife Service** (KWS; www.kws.org) looking for information on the Masai Mara National Reserve, you'll be disappointed. That's because Kenya's parks and reserves are divided into those that are administered by the national government (this includes all national parks and some national reserves) and those administered by local communities (such as the Masai Mara and Lake Bogoria national reserves).

The difference is significant from a local perspective, less so in terms of your experience on safari. It all comes down to revenues. The entry fees for parks administered by the KWS go directly into the coffers of the national government, with a proportion, in theory at least, returned to the local communities. In the case of the locally administered reserves, revenues go to the local county council, which forwards some revenue on to the national government and, again in theory, uses the money for the benefit of local communities.

The whole issue came to national and international attention in 2005 when President Kibaki announced plans to de-gazette Amboseli National Park and turn it into a reserve administered by the Maasai-dominated Kajiado County Council. His motives remained unclear, although cynics suggested it may have been a ploy to win over the Maasai vote in advance of a crucial national referendum on constitutional reform. The move was declared illegal by Kenya's High Court in 2011.

MAJOR NATIONAL PARKS & RESERVES

PARK/RESERVE	HABITATS	WILDLIFE	ACTIVITIES	BEST TIME TO VISIT
Aberdare National Park (p168)	dramatic highlands, waterfalls & rainforest	elephants, black rhinos, bongo antelope, black leopards, black servals	trekking, fishing, gliding	year-round
Amboseli National Park (p92)	dry plains & scrub forest	elephants, buffaloes, lions, antelope, birds	wildlife drives	Jun-Oct
Arabuko Sokoke Forest Reserve (p263)	coastal forest	Sokoke scops owls, Clarke's weavers, birds, elephant shrews, elephants	bird tours, walking, cycling	year-round
Hell's Gate National Park (p116)	dramatic rocky outcrops & gorges	eland, giraffes, lions, birds of prey	cycling, walking	year-round
Kakamega Forest Reserve (p150)	virgin tropical rainforest	de Brazza's monkey, red-tailed monkeys, flying squirrels, 330 bird species	walking, birdwatching	year-round
Lake Bogoria National Reserve (p124)	scenic soda lake	flamingos, greater kudu, leopards	birdwatching, walking, hot springs	year-round
Lake Nakuru National Park (p122)	hilly grassland & alkaline lakeland	flamingos, black & white rhinos, lions, leopards, over 400 bird species	wildlife drives	year-round
Masai Mara National Reserve (p129)	savannah & grassland	Big Five, antelope, cheetahs, hyenas, wildebeest migration	wildlife drives, ballooning	Jul-Oct
Meru National Park (p189)	rainforest, swamplands & grasslands	white rhinos, elephants, lions, cheetahs, lesser kudu	wildlife drives, fishing	year-round
Mt Elgon National Park (p158)	extinct volcano & rainforest	elephants, black-and-white-colobus, de Brazza's monkey, >240 bird species	walking, trekking, fishing	Dec-Feb
Mt Kenya National Park (p172)	rainforest, moorland & glacial mountain	elephants, buffaloes, mountain flora	trekking, climbing	Jan & Feb, Aug & Sep
Nairobi National Park (p58)	open plains with urban backdrop	black rhinos, lions, leopards, cheetahs, giraffes, >400 bird species	wildlife drives	year-round
Saiwa Swamp National Park (p160)	swamplands & riverine forest	sitatunga antelope, otters, black-and-white colobus, >370 bird species	walking, birdwatching	year-round
Samburu, Buffalo Springs & Shaba National Reserves (p201)	semiarid open savannah	elephants, leopards, gerenuks, crocodiles, Grevy's zebras	wildlife drives	year-round
Shimba Hills National Reserve (p239)	densely forested hills	elephants, sable antelope, leopards	walking, forest tours	year-round
Tsavo West & East National Parks (p97 & p102)	sweeping plains & ancient volcanic cones	Big Five, cheetahs, giraffes, hippos, crocodiles, around 500 bird species	rock climbing, wildlife drives	year-round

NATIONAL PARKS & RESERVES CATEGORIES

CATEGORY	PARK
Masai Mara	Masai Mara
Premium	Amboseli, Lake Nakuru
Wilderness	Meru, Tsavo East & Tsavo West
Aberdare National Park	Aberdare
Urban Safari	Nairobi
Mountain Climbing	Mt Kenya day trip
Mt Kenya National Park (3-day package)	Mt Kenya
Scenic & Special Interest 1	Hell's Gate & Mt Elgon
Scenic & Special Interest 2	Chyulu, Marsabit, Arabuko Sokoke, Kakamega, Shimba Hills & all other parks
Marine Parks	Kisite & Mpunguti
Other Marine Parks	Kiunga, Malindi, Mombasa & Watamu

East Africa. Now, there are 22 national parks, plus numerous marine parks and national reserves.

Many of the parks came under siege in the 1970s and 1980s when poaching became endemic. Tsavo East and Tsavo West National Parks were the epicentre of the poaching storm, with an estimated 5000 elephants and similar numbers of rhinos killed annually in these two parks alone. In response, President Moi grabbed international headlines when, in 1989, he set fire to a stockpile of 12 tons of ivory in Nairobi National Park and appointed Richard Leakey to the head of the Wildlife Conservation and Management Department (WMCD), which became the Kenya Wildlife Service (KWS) a year later. Leakey is largely credited with saving Kenya's wildlife, but his methods were hugely controversial: he declared war on poachers by forming elite and well-armed anti-poaching units with orders to shoot on sight.

Things are much quieter these days in the national parks, although poaching on a smaller scale remains a problem.

POACHING

Wildlife Wars: My Battle to Save Kenya's Elephants (2001) is Dr Richard Leakey's fascinating account of his years at the forefront of the fight against ivory poaching in Kenya.

Visiting National Parks & Reserves

Going on safari is an integral part of the Kenyan experience, and the wildlife and scenery can be extraordinary. Even in more popular parks such as Masai Mara National Reserve and Amboseli National Park, which can become massively overcrowded in high season (July to October and January to February, although KWS maintains high-season prices into March), this natural splendour is likely to be your most enduring memory.

Throughout this book, we have covered the parks and reserves in detail. In the case of the major parks and reserves, we've also included a quick-reference box, summing up practical details from the wildlife you're likely to see to the best gates by which to enter. We've also covered many of the parks and reserves in this chapter, to help with planning.

Park & Reserve Entry

KWS now accepts euros and UK pounds, but you're still better off paying in Kenyan shillings or US dollars, as KWS exchange rates are punitive.

SAFARICARDS

Entry fees to national parks are controlled by the **KWS** (Kenya Wildlife Service; ☎020-6000800; www.kws.org; Nairobi National Park) and admission

NATIONAL PARKS & RESERVES FEES

CATEGORY	NONRESIDENT ADULT/CHILD (US$) HIGH SEASON	NONRESIDENT ADULT/CHILD (US$) NORMAL SEASON	CAMPING NONRESIDENT ADULT/CHILD (US$)
Masai Mara	70-80	40-45	30-40
Premium	70/40	60/30	25/20
Wilderness	60/30	50/25	15/10
Aberdare National Park	50/25	50/25	15/10
Urban Safari	40/20	40/20	15/10
Mountain Climbing	55/25	55/25	15/10
Mt Kenya (3-day package)	150/70	150/70	15/10
Scenic & Special Interest 1	25/15	25/15	15/10
Scenic & Special Interest 2	20/10	20/10	15/10
Marine Parks	20/10	20/10	n/a
Other Marine Parks	15/10	15/10	n/a

Marine Parks

» Kisite Marine National Park

» Kiunga Marine National Reserve

» Malindi Marine National Park

» Mombasa Marine National Park & Reserve

» Watamu Marine National Park

to parks in Kenya is being converted to a 'safaricard' system for payment of fees. The cards must be charged with credit in advance and can be topped up at certain locations (usually the parks' main gates only, which can be inconvenient). Remaining credit is not refundable.

At the time of writing the safaricard system was in use at Nairobi, Lake Nakuru, Aberdare, Amboseli and Tsavo national parks. The other parks still work on a cash system.

Currently, safaricards are only available at the KWS headquarters in Nairobi and Mombasa, at the main gates of the participating parks, and at the Malindi Marine National Park office.

What if you don't have a safaricard? It is still possible to purchase a temporary entry card at the main gates of most national parks, although we recommend purchasing a safaricard in advance where possible.

ENTRY FEES

The KWS has a number of categories for parks and reserves. See the table on p333. In the table on this page you'll find the various entry fees for nonresidents during high season (January to March and July to October) and 'normal' season (April to June, November and December) and year-round camping fees for nonresidents. Rates for Kenyan citizens and residents are available from the KWS website.

For non-KWS reserves such as the Masai Mara (see p129), Buffalo Springs (p201) and Lake Bogoria (p124), see the individual park reviews.

Although the changes had not yet come into effect at the time of writing, there are plans to raise the entry for Premium parks to US$80 per adult regardless of the season.

Further costs in the land-based parks and reserves include KSh300 for vehicles with fewer than six seats and KSh1000 for vehicles seating six to 12. For details on camping inside national parks and reserves, see p361.

It's important to remember that the entry fees for parks and reserves only entitle you to stay for a 24-hour period, and you pay an additional fee of the same amount for each day you are inside the park, even if you don't leave the park during that period. Not all parks allow you to leave the park and re-enter under the same ticket – Lake Nakuru National Park, for example – so always check the situation and be sure of your plans before you pay for a multiday ticket.

Wildlife & Habitat

David Lukas

East Africa is synonymous with safaris – and Kenya is where it all began. From the year-long safari undertaken by US President Theodore Roosevelt in 1909, to Joy Adamson's portrayal of the lioness Elsa in *Born Free*, to Karen Blixen's sweeping tale *Out of Africa*, Kenya forms the centrepiece of our popular image of Africa. And for good reason – it is one of the best places in the world to see wildlife. You will never forget the shimmering carpets of zebras and wildebeest, or the spine-tingling roars of lions at night. Even better, Kenya offers unlimited opportunities for independent travellers.

Elephants in Amboseli National Park (p92)

DOUGLAS STEAKLEY/LONELY PLANET IMAGES ©

Big Cats

In terms of behaviour, the six common cats of Kenya are little more than souped-up housecats; it's just that some weigh half as much as a horse and others travel as fast as a speeding car. With their excellent vision and keen hearing, cats are superb hunters. And some of the most stunning scenes in Africa are the images of big cats making their kills. You won't easily forget the energy and ferocity of these life-and-death struggles.

Leopard

1 *Weight 30-60kg (female), 40-90kg (male); length 170-300cm* More common than you realise, the leopard relies on expert camouflage to stay hidden. During the day you might only spot one reclining in a tree after it twitches its tail, but at night there is no mistaking their bone-chilling groans.

Lion

2 *Weight 120-150kg (female), 150-225kg (male); length 210-275cm (female), 240-350cm (male)* Those lions sprawled lazily in the shade are actually Africa's most feared predators. Equipped with teeth that tear effortlessly through bone and tendon, they can take down an animal as large as a bull giraffe. Each group of adults (a pride) is based around generations of females who do all the hunting; the swaggering males fight among themselves and eat what the females catch.

Cheetah

3 *Weight 40-60kg; length 200-220cm* The cheetah is a world-class sprinter. Although it reaches speeds of 112km/h, the cheetah runs out of steam after 300m and must cool down for 30 minutes before hunting again. This speed comes at another cost – the cheetah is so well adapted for running that it lacks the strength and teeth to defend its food or cubs from attack by other large predators.

1

3

IGNACIO PALACIOS/LONELY PLANET IMAGES ©

2

MITCH REARDON/LONELY PLANET IMAGES ©

1

3

2

IGNACIO PALACIOS/LONELY PLANET IMAGES ©

ARIADNE VAN ZANDBERGEN/LONELY PLANET IMAGES ©

Small Cats

While big cats get the lion's share of attention from tourists, Kenya's small cats are equally interesting though much harder to spot. You won't find these cats chasing down gazelles or wildebeest, instead look for them slinking around in search of rodents or making incredible leaps to snatch birds out of the air.

Wildcat

1 *Weight 3-6.5kg; length 65-100cm* If you see what looks like a tabby wandering the plains of Kenya you're probably seeing a wildcat, the direct ancestor of our domesticated housecat. Occurring wherever there are abundant mice and rats, the wildcat is readily found on the outskirts of villages, where it can be best identified by its unmarked rufous ears and longish legs.

Caracal

2 *Weight 8-19kg; length 80-120cm* The caracal is a gorgeous tawny cat with long, pointy ears. This African version of the northern lynx has jacked-up hind legs like a feline dragster. These beanpole kickers enable this slender cat to make vertical leaps of 3m and swat birds in flight.

Serval

3 *Weight 6-18kg; length 90-130cm* Twice as large as a housecat but with long legs and large ears, the beautifully spotted serval is adapted for walking in tall grass and making prodigious leaps to catch rodents and birds. More diurnal than most cats, it may be seen tossing food in the air and playing with it.

Savannah Primates

East Africa is the evolutionary cradle of primate diversity, giving rise to more than 30 species of monkeys, apes and prosimians (the 'primitive' ancestors of modern primates), all of which have dextrous hands and feet. Several species have evolved to living on the ground where they are vulnerable to lions and hyenas.

Patas Monkey

1 *Weight 7-25kg; length 110-160cm* A unique subspecies of this widespread West African monkey lives on the Serengeti Plains. Russet-backed and slender bodied with lanky legs, this remarkable monkey is the fastest primate in the world — able to sprint 55km/h as it races towards the nearest trees. Still, quite a few adults are eaten by carnivores so Patas monkeys have a very high reproductive rate.

Olive Baboon

2 *Weight 11-30kg (female), 22-50kg (male); length 95-180cm* Although the formidable olive baboon has 5cm-long fangs and can kill a leopard, its best defence may consist of running up trees and showering intruders with liquid excrement. Intelligent and opportunistic, troops of these greenish baboons are common in western Kenya, while much paler yellow baboons range over the eastern half of the country.

Vervet Monkey

3 *Weight 4-8kg; length 90-140cm* Each troop of vervets is composed of females who defend a home range passed down from generation to generation, while males fight each other for bragging rights and access to females. Check out the extraordinary blue and scarlet colours of their sexual organs when aroused.

2

ARIADNE VAN ZANDBERGEN/LONELY PLANET IMAGES ©

JOHN EARNSHAW/ALAMY ©

1

3

ARIADNE VAN ZANDBERGEN/LONELY PLANET IMAGES ©

Forest Primates

Forest primates are a diverse group that live entirely in trees. These agile, long-limbed primates generally stay in the upper canopy where they search for leaves and arboreal fruits. It might take the expert eyes of a professional guide to help you find some of these species.

Black-and-White Colobus

1 *Weight 10-23kg; length 115-165cm* Also known as the guereza, the black-and-white colobus is one of Kenya's most popular primates due to the flowing white frills of hair arrayed across its black body. Like all colobus, this agile primate has a hook-shaped hand, so it can swing through the trees with the greatest of ease. When two troops run into each other expect to see a real show.

2

OCEAN/CORBIS ©

Lesser Galago

2 *Weight 100-300g; length 40cm* A squirrel-sized nocturnal creature with a doglike face and huge eyes, the lesser galago belongs to a group of prosimians that have changed little in 60 million years. Best known for its frequent bawling cries (hence the common name 'bushbaby'), the galago would be rarely seen except that it readily visits feeding stations at many popular safari lodges. Living in a world of darkness, galagos communicate with each other through scent and sound.

De Brazza's Monkey

3 *Weight 4-8kg; length 90-135cm* Riverside forests of west-central Kenya are home to this rare and colourful monkey. Despite glaring red eyebrows and big bushy white beards, de Brazza's monkeys are surprisingly inconspicuous due to their grizzled upperparts and habit of sitting motionless for up to eight hours. In the early morning and late afternoon they ascend to higher branches to eat fruit and sunbathe.

Cud-Chewing Mammals

Africa is arguably most famous for its astounding variety of ungulates – hoofed mammals that include everything from buffaloes to giraffes. In this large family cud-chewing antelopes are particularly numerous, with 40 different species in East Africa alone.

1

Gerenuk

1 *Weight 30-50kg; length 160-200cm* Adapted for life in semiarid brush, the gerenuk stands on its hind legs to reach 2m-high branches with its giraffelike neck.

Wildebeest

2 *Weight 140-290kg; length 230-340cm* Few animals evoke the spirit of the African plain as much as the wildebeest. Over a million gather on the Masai Mara alone, where they form vast, constantly moving herds.

Thomson's Gazelle

3 *Weight 15-35kg; length 95-150cm* This long-legged antelope is built for speed. In southern Kenya an estimated 400,000 migrate in great herds, along with zebras and wildebeest.

Waterbuck

4 *Weight 160-300kg; length 210-275cm* If you're going to see any antelope on safari, it's likely to be the big, shaggy and, some say, smelly waterbuck. However, their numbers fluctuate dramatically between wet and dry years.

African Buffalo

5 *Weight 250-850kg; length 220-420cm* Imagine a cow on steroids then add a particularly fearsome set of curling horns and you get the massive African buffalo. Thank goodness they're usually docile.

4

2

ADRIAN BAILEY/LONELY PLANET IMAGES ©

3

ALEX DISSANAYAKE/LONELY PLANET IMAGES ©

1

ARIADNE VAN ZANDBERGEN/LONELY PLANET IMAGES ©

4

IGNACIO PALACIOS/LONELY PLANET IMAGES ©

DAN HERRICK/LONELY PLANET IMAGES ©

DLILLC/CORBIS ©

Hoofed Mammals

The continent has a surprising diversity of hoofed animals. Those that don't chew cuds occur over a much broader range of habitats than the cud-chewing antelope. They have been at home in Africa for millions of years. Without human intervention, Africa would be ruled by elephants, zebras, hippos and warthogs.

Plains Zebra

1 *Weight 175-320kg; length 260-300cm* My oh my, those plains zebras sure have some wicked stripes. Although each animal is as distinctly marked as a fingerprint, scientists still aren't sure what function these patterns serve. Do they help zebras recognise each other?

African Elephant

2 *Weight 2200-3500kg (female), 4000-6300kg (male); height 2.4-3.4m (female), 3-4m (male)* No one stands around to argue when a bull elephant rumbles out of the brush. Though the elephant is commonly referred to as 'the king of beasts', elephant society is ruled by a lineage of elder females.

Grevy's Zebra

3 *Weight 350-450kg; length 290-375cm* This large and distinctive zebra is restricted to the semiarid plains of northern Kenya, where it mingles with the plains zebra. Look for the thinner black stripes that do not extend down onto its white belly.

Giraffe

4 *Weight 450-1200kg (female), 1800-2000kg (male); height 3.5-5.2m* The 5m-tall giraffe does such a good job of reaching up to grab high branches that stretching down to get a simple drink of water is difficult. Though they stroll along casually, a healthy giraffe can outrun any predator.

More Hoofed Mammals

This sampling of miscellaneous hoofed animals highlights the astonishing diversity in this major group of African wildlife. Every visitor wants to see elephants and giraffes, but don't pass up a chance to watch hyraxes or warthogs.

1

Rock Hyrax

1 *Weight 1.8-5.5kg; length 40-60cm* It doesn't seem like it, but those funny tail-less squirrels you see lounging around on rocks are an ancient cousin to the elephant. You won't see some of the features that rock hyraxes share with their larger kin, but look for tusks when one yawns.

Black Rhinoceros

2 *Weight 700-1400kg; length 350-450cm* Pity the black rhinoceros for having a horn worth more than gold. Once widespread and abundant south of the Sahara, the rhino has been poached to the brink of extinction. Unfortunately, females may only give birth every five years.

Hippopotamus

3 *Weight 510-3200kg; length 320-400cm* The hippopotamus is one strange creature. Designed like a floating beanbag with tiny legs, the 3000kg hippo spends its time in or very near water chowing down on aquatic plants. Placid? No way! Hippos have tremendous ferocity and strength when provoked.

Warthog

4 *Weight 45-75kg (female), 60-150kg (male); length 140-200cm* Despite their fearsome appearance and sinister tusks, only the big males are safe from lions, cheetahs and hyenas. To protect themselves when attacked, warthogs run for burrows and reverse backside in while slashing wildly with their tusks.

4

2

MITCH REARDON/LONELY PLANET IMAGES ©

3

ARIADNE VAN ZANDBERGEN/LONELY PLANET IMAGES ©

PETER MALSBURY/ISTOCK ©

ANUP SHAH/CORBIS ©

Carnivores

It is a sign of Africa's ecological richness that the continent supports a remarkable variety of predators. Expect the unexpected and you'll return home with a lifetime of memories!

Spotted Hyena

1 *Weight 40-90kg; length 125-215cm* Living in packs ruled by females that grow penislike sexual organs, hyenas are savage fighters that use their bone-crushing jaws to disembowel terrified prey on the run or battle with lions.

Golden Jackal

2 *Weight 6-15kg; length 85-130cm* Despite its trim, diminutive form, the jackal fearlessly stakes a claim at the dining table of the African plain while holding hungry vultures and much stronger hyenas at bay.

Banded Mongoose

3 *Weight 1.5-2kg; length 45-75cm* Bounding across the savannah on their morning foraging excursions, a family of mongooses is a delightful sight. Not particularly speedy, they find delicious snacks such as toads, scorpions and slugs.

Hunting Dog

4 *Weight 20-35kg; length 100-150cm* Organised in complex hierarchies with strict rules of conduct, these social canids are incredibly efficient hunters. They run in packs of 20 to 60 to chase down antelopes and other animals.

Common Genet

5 *Weight 1-2kg; length 80-100cm* Though nocturnal, these slender, agile hunters are readily observed slinking along roadsides or scrambling among the rafters of safari lodges. They look like a cross between a cat and a raccoon, but are easily recognised by their cream-coloured bodies and leopardlike spotting.

Birds of Prey

Kenya has nearly 100 species of hawks, eagles, vultures and owls. With a range from the songbird-sized pygmy kestrel to the massive lammergeier, this is one of the best places in the world to see an incredible variety of birds of prey.

Lappet-Faced Vulture

1 *Length 115cm* It's not a pretty sight when gore-encrusted vultures take over a rotting carcass that no other scavenger wants, but it's the way nature works. The monstrous lappet-faced vulture, a giant among vultures, gets its fill before other vultures move in.

Secretary Bird

2 *Length 100cm* With the body of an eagle and the legs of a crane, the secretary bird stands 1.3m tall and walks up to 20km a day in search of vipers, cobras and other snakes.

African Fish Eagle

3 *Length 75cm* With a wingspan over 2m, this replica of the American bald eagle is most familiar for its loud ringing vocalisations, which have become known as 'the voice of Africa'.

Bateleur

4 *Length 60cm* French for 'tightrope-walker', this eagle's name refers to its distinctive low-flying aerial acrobatics. At close hand, look for its bold colour pattern and scarlet face.

Augur Buzzard

5 *Length 55cm* Perhaps Kenya's most common raptor, the augur buzzard occupies a wide range of wild and cultivated habitats. One of their hunting strategies is to float motionless in the air by riding the wind then swooping down quickly to catch unwary critters.

1

4

2

JOHANNES SWANEPOEL/ALAMY ©

3

ADRIAN BAILEY/LONELY PLANET IMAGES ©

1

IGNACIO PALACIOS/LONELY PLANET IMAGES ©

4

DAVE LEWIS/LONELY PLANET IMAGES ©

ARIADNE VAN ZANDBERGEN/LONELY PLANET IMAGES ©

MITCH REARDON/LONELY PLANET IMAGES ©

Other Birds

Birdwatchers from all over the world travel to Kenya in search of the country's 1100 species of bird, an astounding number by any measure, including every shape and colour imaginable.

Lesser Flamingo

1 *Length 1m* Coloured deep rose-pink and gathering by the hundreds of thousands on shimmering salt lakes, lesser flamingos create some of the most dramatic wildlife spectacles found in Africa, especially when they all fly at once or perform synchronised courtship displays.

Saddle-Billed Stork

2 *Height 150cm; wingspan 270cm* The saddle-billed stork is one of the more remarkably coloured of Kenya's birds. As if the 270cm wingspan wasn't impressive enough, check out its brilliant-red-coloured kneecaps and bill.

Lilac-Breasted Roller

3 *Length 40cm* Nearly everyone on safari gets to know the gorgeously coloured lilac-breasted roller. The roller gets its name from its tendency to 'roll' from side to side in flight as a way of showing off its iridescent blues, purples and greens.

Ostrich

4 *Height 200-270cm* Standing 270cm and weighing upwards of 130kg, these ancient flightless birds escape predators by running away at 70km/h or lying flat on the ground to resemble a pile of dirt.

Vulturine Guineafowl

5 *Length 71cm* Take an electric-blue chicken, drape black-and-white speckled feathers over its body and place an elegant ruff around its neck and you have a pretty flamboyant bird. Look for guineafowl walking around in groups in semiarid areas.

Habitats

Nearly all of Kenya's wildlife occupies a specific type of habitat. You will hear rangers and fellow travellers refer to these habitats repeatedly as they describe where to search for animals. If this is your first time in Kenya, some of these habitats and their seasonal rhythms take some getting used to, but your wildlife-viewing experience will be greatly enhanced if you learn how to recognise these habitats and the animals you might expect to find in each one.

Semiarid Desert

1 Much of eastern and northern Kenya sees so little rainfall that shrubs and hardy grasses, rather than trees, are the dominant vegetation. This is not the classic landscape that many visitors come to see and it doesn't seem like a great place for wildlife, but the patient observer will be richly rewarded. While it's true that the lack of water restricts larger animals such as zebras, gazelles and antelopes to areas around waterholes, this habitat explodes with plant and animal life whenever it rains. During the dry season many plants shed their leaves to conserve water and grazing animals move on in search of food and water.

High Mountains

2 Kenya is remarkable for having extensive high-mountain habitats, including unexpected snowy crags and glaciers that are located right on the equator, a habitat that is very rare anywhere else in East Africa. The massive extinct volcanoes of Mt Elgon and Mt Kenya are islands of montane forests, bogs, giant heathers and moorlands that are perched high above the surrounding lowlands. The few animals that survive here are uniquely adapted to these bizarre landscapes.

DOUG MCKINLAY/LONELY PLANET IMAGES ©

Savannah

3 Savannah is *the* classic East African landscape – broad rolling grasslands dotted with lone acacia trees. The openness and vastness of this landscape make it a perfect home for large herds of grazing zebras and wildebeest, in addition to fast-sprinting predators like cheetahs, and it's the best habitat for seeing large numbers of animals. Savannah develops in areas where there are long wet seasons alternating with long dry seasons, creating ideal conditions for the growth of dense, nutritious grasses. Shaped by fire and grazing animals, savannah is a dynamic habitat in constant flux with adjacent woodlands.

Rivers & Lakes

4 Since vast areas of Kenya are extremely dry, at least on a seasonal basis, any source of water is a mecca for wildlife. Everything from slow-moving rivers to shallow lakes and muddy wallows attract steady streams of birds and mammals; one of the best ways to watch wildlife is to sit quietly near watering holes. Some of the highly saline and alkaline lakes of the Rift Valley, such as Lake Nakuru and Lake Bogoria, attract fantastic numbers of birds, including African fish eagles, shorebirds and ducks, as well as flocks of over a million flamingos.

ARIADNE VAN ZANDBERGEN/LONELY PLANET IMAGES ©

1. Gazelles, Samburu National Reserve (p201) **2.** Mt Kenya National Park (p172) **3.** Safari van, Masai Mara (p129) **4.** Flamingo, Lake Nakuru National Park (p122)

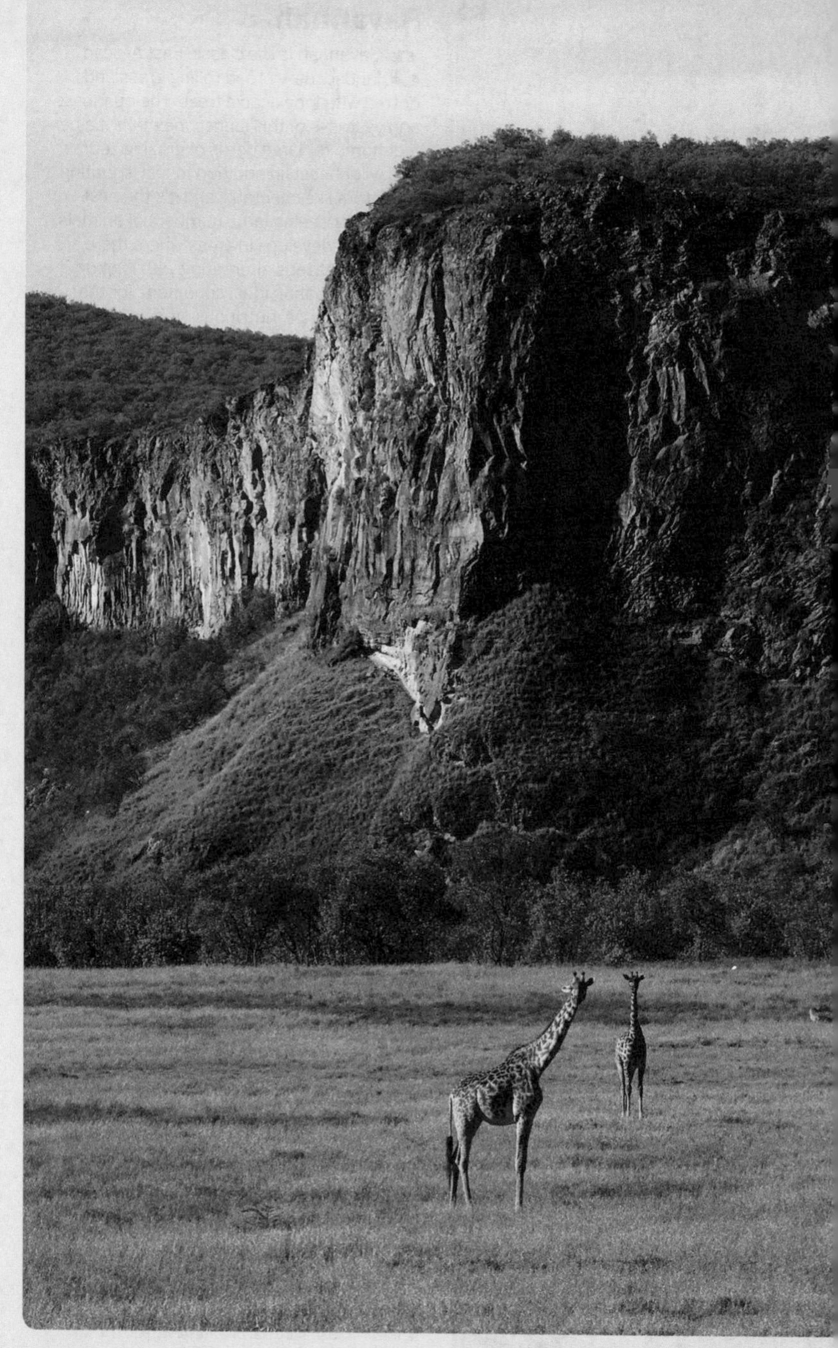

Giraffes, Hell's Gate National Park (p116)

Survival Guide

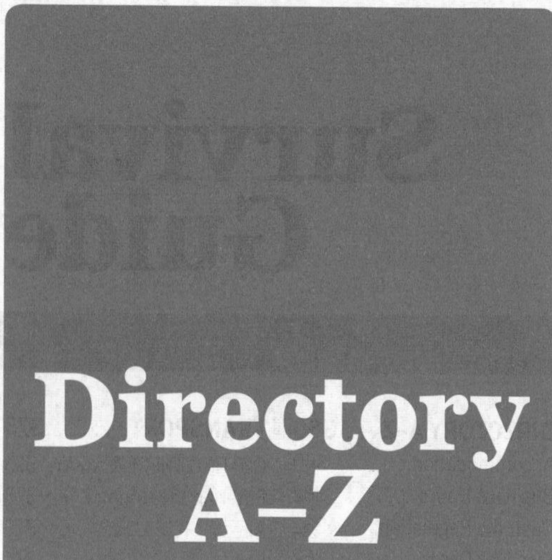

Directory A–Z

Accommodation

Kenya has a wide range of accommodation options, from basic cubicle hotels overlooking city bus stands to luxury tented camps hidden away in remote corners of national parks. There are also all kinds of campsites, budget tented camps, *bandas* (thatched-roof wood or stone huts) and cottages scattered around the parks and rural areas.

Seasons

High-season prices usually run from June to October, from January until early March, and include Easter and Christmas, although there may be slight variations in some regions. Sometimes high season is also referred to as peak season. Low season usually covers the rest of the year, although some lodges and top-end hotels also have intermediate shoulder seasons.

On the coast, peak times tend to be July, August and December to March, and a range of lower rates can apply for the rest of the year.

During the low season many companies offer excellent deals on accommodation on the coast and in the main wildlife parks, often working with airlines to create packages aimed at the local and expat market.

Prices

Throughout this guidebook, the order of accommodation listings is by author preference, and each place to stay is accompanied by one of the following budget-category symbols (the price relates to a high-season double room with private bathroom and, unless stated otherwise, includes breakfast):

$	less than US$50
$$	US$50 to US$150
$$$	more than US$150

It's worth remembering that many places, particularly places in national parks or other remote areas, offer full-board-only rates – prices may, therefore, seem higher than you'd expect, but less so once you factor in three meals a day.

Kenya also operates on a dual pricing system, particularly in midrange and top-end places – nonresidents pay significantly more (often double or triple the price) than Kenyan (or other East African) residents. When things are quiet, you may be able to get the residents' rate if you ask, but don't count on it. Prices quoted throughout this book are nonresident rates, unless otherwise stated.

One final thing: hotels and other places to stay in Kenya quote their prices in a variety of currencies, usually US dollars or Kenyan shillings (KSh). Throughout this book, we quoted the price preferred by the place in question, although in almost all cases you can pay in dollars, shillings, euros and (sometimes) other foreign currencies.

Accommodation Types

The website of **Uniglobe Let's Go Travel** (www.uniglobeletsgotravel.com) displays almost all the major hotels and lodges in Kenya, giving price ranges and descriptions.

BANDAS

These are Kenyan-style huts and cottages, usually with some kind of kitchen and bathroom, which offer excellent value. There are Kenya Wildlife Service (KWS) *bandas* at some national parks – some are wooden huts, some are thatched stone huts and some are small brick bungalows with solar-powered lights. Facilities range from basic dorms

> **BOOK YOUR STAY ONLINE**
>
> For more accommodation reviews by Lonely Planet authors, check out http://hotels.lonelyplanet.com. You'll find independent reviews, as well as recommendations on the best places to stay. Best of all, you can book online.

and squat toilets to kitchens and hot water provided by wood-burning stoves. In such places, you'll need to bring all your own food, drinking water, bedding and firewood.

Although originally aimed at budget travellers, an increasing variety of places are calling *bandas* huts, which are decidedly midrange in price and quality.

PRACTICALITIES

» Newspapers & Magazines: the *Daily Nation*, the *East African Standard*, the *East African*, the *Weekly Review* and the *New African*.

» TV: KBC and NTV, formerly KTN, are the main national TV stations. CNN, Sky and BBC networks are also widely available on satellite or cable (DSTV).

» Radio: KBC Radio broadcasts across the country on various FM frequencies. BBC World Service is easily accessible.

» Weights & Measures: metric.

» Smoking: banned in restaurants, bars and enclosed public areas, with expensive fines for breaches.

BEACH RESORTS

Much of the coast, from Diani Beach to Malindi, is taken up by huge luxury beach resorts. Most offer a fairly similar experience, with swimming pools, water sports, bars, restaurants, mobs of souvenir vendors on the beach and 'tribal' dance shows in the evening. They aren't all bad, especially if you want good children's facilities, and a handful of them have been very sensitively designed. Note that many of these places will close in early summer, generally from May to mid-June or July.

CAMPING

There are many opportunities for camping in Kenya, and although gear can be hired in Nairobi and around Mt Kenya it's worth considering bringing a tent with you. There are KWS campsites in just about every national park or reserve. These are usually very basic, with a toilet block with a couple of pit toilets, a water tap, perhaps public showers, and very little else. They cost US$25/20 per adult/child in Amboseli and Lake Nakuru National Parks, US$30 to US$40 in Masai Mara National Reserve and US$15/10 in all other parks.

As well as these permanent campsites, KWS also runs so-called 'special' campsites in most national parks. These sites move every year and have even fewer facilities than the standard camps, but cost more because of their wilder locations and set-up costs. They cost US$40/20 per adult/child in Amboseli and Lake Nakuru, US$30/15 elsewhere; a reservation fee of KSh7500 per week is payable on top of the relevant camping fee.

Private sites are rare, but they offer more facilities and may hire out tents if you don't have your own. It's sometimes possible to camp in the grounds of some hotels in rural towns, and Nairobi has some good private campsites. Camping in the bush is possible but unless you're doing it with an organised trip or a guide, security is a major concern – don't even think about it on the coast.

All camping prices in this book are per person unless otherwise specified.

HOSTELS

The only youth hostel affiliated with Hostelling International (HI) is in Nairobi. It has good basic facilities and is a pleasant enough place to stay, but there are plenty of other cheaper choices that are just as good. Other places that call themselves 'youth hostels' are not members of HI, and standards are variable.

HOTELS & GUESTHOUSES

Real bottom-end hotels (often known as 'board and lodgings' to distinguish them from *hotelis*, which are often only restaurants) are widely used as brothels, and tend to be very rundown. Security at these places is virtually nonexistent, though the better ones are set around courtyards, and are clean if not exactly comfortable.

Proper hotels and guesthouses come in many different shapes and sizes. As well as the top-end Western companies, there are a number of small Kenyan chains offering reliable standards across a handful of properties in particular towns or regions, and also plenty of private family-run establishments.

Self-catering options are common on the coast, where they're often the only midpriced alternative to the top-end resorts, but not so much in other parts of the country. A few fancier places offer modern kitchens, but more often than not the so-called kitchenettes will be a side room with a small fridge and portable gas stove.

Terms you will come across in Kenya include 'self-contained', which just means a room with its own private bathroom, and 'all-inclusive' (called 'full board' in this book), which generally means all meals, certain drinks and possibly some activities should be included. 'Half board' generally means breakfast and dinner or lunch are included.

RENTAL HOUSES

Renting a private house is a popular option on the coast, particularly for groups on longer stays, and many expats let out their holiday homes when they're not using them. Properties range from restored Swahili houses on the northern islands to luxurious colonial mansions inland, and while they're seldom cheap, the experience will often be something pretty special. Papers and noticeboards in Nairobi and along the coast are good places to find out about rentals, as is the internet and old-fashioned word of mouth.

SAFARI LODGES

Hidden away inside or on the edges of national parks are some fantastic safari lodges. These are usually visited as part of organised safaris, and you'll pay much more if you just turn up and ask for a room. Some of the older places trade heavily on their more glorious past, but the best places feature five-star rooms, soaring *makuti*-roofed bars (with a thatched roof of palm leaves) and restaurants overlooking waterholes full of wildlife. Staying in at least one good safari lodge while you're in Kenya is recommended. Rates tend to fall significantly in low season.

TENTED CAMPS

As well as lodges, many parks contain some fantastic luxury tented camps. These places tend to occupy wonderfully remote settings, usually by rivers or other natural locations, and feature large, comfortable, semipermanent safari tents with beds, furniture, bathrooms (usually with hot running water) and often some kind of external roof thatch to keep the rain out; you sleep surrounded by the sounds of the African bush. Most of the camps are very up-market and the tents are pretty much hotel rooms under canvas. The really exclusive properties occupy locations so isolated that guests fly in and out on charter planes.

Business Hours

Reviews in this guidebook won't list business hours unless they differ significantly from the following standards.

Banks 9am-3pm Mon-Fri; 9am-11am Sat

Post Offices 8.30am-5pm Mon-Fri, 9am-noon Sat

Restaurants 11am-2pm, 5-9pm

Shops 9am-3pm Mon-Fri; 9-11am Sat

Supermarkets 8.30am-8.30pm Mon-Sat; 10am-8pm Sat

Customs Regulations

There are strict laws about taking wildlife products out of Kenya. The export of products made from elephant, rhino and sea turtle are prohibited. The collection of coral is also not allowed. Ostrich eggs will also be confiscated unless you can prove you bought them from a certified ostrich farm. Always check to see what permits are required, especially for the export of any plants, insects and shells.

You are allowed to take up to KSh100,000 out of the country.

Otherwise, allowable quantities you can bring into Kenya include the following:

Cigars 50

Cigarettes 200

Pipe tobacco 250g

Alcohol 1L

Perfume 250ml

Discount Cards

Residence permits Very favourable admission fees and accommodation rates around the country.

Seniors No concessions.

Student cards Concession rates at museums and some other attractions; the international ISIC card should be widely recognised.

Electricity

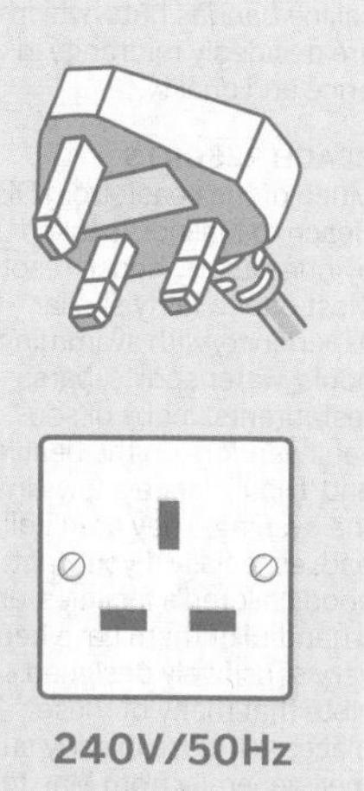

Embassies & Consulates

Missions are located in Nairobi (area code ☎020) unless otherwise stated.

Australia High Commission (Map p56; ☎4277100; www.kenya.embassy.gov.au; Riverside Dr, off Chiromo Rd)

Canada High Commission (off Map p56; ☎3663000; www.canadainternational.gc.ca/kenya/index.aspx; Limuru Rd, Gigiri)

Ethiopia (Map p56; ☎2732050; off State House Rd)

France (Map p60; ☎2778000; www.ambafrance-ke.org; Barclays Plaza Bldg, Loita St)

Germany (off Map p56; ☎4262100; www.nairobi.diplo.de; 113 Riverside Dr)

Netherlands (off Map p56; ☎4288000; http://kenia.nlembassy.org; Riverside Lane)

South Sudan (Map p56; ☎2356542; 6th fl Bishops Gate House, 5th Ngong Ave)

Tanzania High Commission (Map p60; ☎2311948; 9th fl, Reinsurance Plaza, Aga Khan Walk)

Uganda High Commission (off Map p56; ☎4445420; Riverside Paddocks); Consular section (Map p60; ☎2217447; 1st fl, Uganda House, Kenyatta Ave)

UK High Commission (Map p56; ☎2844000; http://ukinkenya.fco.gov.uk/en/; Upper Hill Rd)

USA (off Map p56; ☎3636000; http://nairobi.usembassy.gov; United Nations Ave)

Food

Throughout this guidebook, the order of restaurant listings follows the author's preference, and each place to eat is accompanied by one of the following budget-category symbols (price per main dish):

$	less than US$5
$$	US$5 to US$10
$$$	more than US$10

For comprehensive coverage of Kenya's cuisine, see p316.

Gay & Lesbian Travellers

Negativity towards homosexuality is still widespread in Kenya and recent events ensure that it's a brave gay or lesbian Kenyan who comes out of the closet. In a 2007 poll, 96% of Kenyans surveyed stated that homosexuality should be rejected by society. Then, in early 2010, mob violence rocked a health centre where suspected homosexuals were targeted. In November 2010, Prime Minister Raila Odinga described homosexuality as 'unnatural' and called for gays and lesbians to be arrested. And when British PM David Cameron threatened in November 2011 to withdraw aid to some African countries if they did not improve their record on gay and lesbian rights, there was a vociferous public outcry in Kenya. Underlying all of this is a penal code that states that homosexual (and attempted homosexual behaviour) behaviour is punishable by up to 14 years in prison.

Awareness is increasing in Kenya, but with the vast majority of churches and mosques maintaining a traditional, conservative position, homosexuality continues to be frowned upon.

Of course, people do live homosexual lifestyles covertly, particularly along the coast. There are very few prosecutions under the law, but it's certainly better to be extremely discreet – some local con artists do a good line in blackmail, picking up foreigners then threatening to expose them to the police.

Although there are probably more gays and lesbians in Nairobi, the coast is more tolerant of gay relationships, at least privately. There is now a Swahili word for gay: *msenge*. Lamu has long been considered a paradise getaway for gay couples, but it's not as tolerant as it once was. Memories still linger from 1999, when a couple was taken into protective custody in Lamu to shield them from an angry mob of locals opposed to their plans for a gay wedding.

USEFUL RESOURCES

Afriboyz (www.afriboyz.com/Homosexuality-in-Africa.html) Links to gay topics in an African context.

David Tours (www.davidtravel.com) Can arrange anything from balloon safaris to luxurious coastal hideaways, all with a gay focus.

Gay Kenya (www.gaykenya.com) Organises discreet gay events.

Global Gayz (www.globalgayz.com) Links to country-by-country gay issues, including Kenya.

Purple Roofs (www.purpleroofs.com/africa/kenyata.html) Lists a number of gay or gay-friendly tour companies in Kenya that may be able to help you plan your trip.

Insurance

Two words: get some! A travel-insurance policy to cover theft, loss and medical problems is a very sensible precaution. Worldwide travel insurance is available at www.lonelyplanet.com/travel_services. You can buy, extend and claim online anytime – even if you're already on the road.

Medical cover is the most vital element of any policy, but make sure you check the small print:

» Some policies specifically exclude 'dangerous activities', which can even include motorcycling, scuba-diving and trekking. If such activities are on your agenda you'll need a fully comprehensive policy, which may be more expensive. Using a locally acquired motorcycle licence may not be valid under your policy.

» You may prefer a policy that pays doctors or hospitals directly rather than you having to pay on the spot and claim later. If you have to claim later, make sure you keep all documentation.

» Some policies ask you to call back (reverse charges) to a centre in your home country where an immediate assessment of your problem is made. Be aware that reverse-charge calls are only possible to certain countries from Kenya (see p368).

» Check that the policy covers ambulances or an emergency flight home.

Local Agencies

If you're travelling through Africa for some time or heading to more remote corners of the country, consider signing up with either of the following services. Check with your insurance company that you can contact these services direct in the event of a serious emergency without having to confirm it with your company at home first.

AAR Health Services (Map p56; ☎020-2895000, emergency 0725225225; www.aarhealth.com; 2nd fl, Williamson House, Fourth Ngong Ave, Nairobi) Comprehensive medical network that covers Kenya, Tanzania and Uganda and offers a road and local service as well as emergency air evacuation to any suitable medical facility in East Africa.

Flying Doctors Service (☎020-6993000, emergency 020-315454, 6992000; www.amref.org) Part of the African Medical and Research Foundation (AMREF), with a 24-hour air-ambulance service out of Nairobi's Wilson Airport.

Internet Access

Establishments with internet access are identified in this book with a computer icon (@), while those with wireless sport the wireless icon.

Internet cafes Common in large and medium-sized Kenyan towns; connection speeds fluctuate wildly and prices range from KSh1 to KSh10 per minute; we even came across places charging KSh30 per hour.

Post offices Internet at almost every main post office in the country; prepaid cards with PIN are valid at any branch around Kenya.

Wireless Increasingly common in midrange and top-end hotels; often available in up-market safari lodges, less common in midrange places in remote areas.

Local networks Both Safari.com and Airtel have dongles/modems that you plug into your laptop, giving you wireless access anywhere that there's mobile coverage. Rates start at KSh1999 for the dongle; credit costs extra and you top up using scratchcards.

Language Courses

Taking a language course (or any course) entitles you to a 'Pupil's Pass', an immigration permit allowing continuous stays of up to 12 months. You may have to battle with bureaucracy and the process may take months, but it can be worth it, especially as you will then have resident status in Kenya during your stay. For more information, see p371.

Recommended places:

ACK Language & Orientation School (Map p56; ☎020-2721893; www.ackenya.org/institutions/language_school.html; Bishops Rd, Upper Hill, Nairobi) The Anglican Church runs full-time courses of varying levels lasting 14 weeks and taking up to five hours a day. Private tuition is available on a flexible part-time schedule.

Language Center Ltd (Map p64; ☎020-3870610; www.language-cntr.com/welcome.shtml; Ndemi Close, off Ngong Rd, Nairobi) Another good centre offering a variety of study options ranging from private hourly lessons to daily group courses.

Legal Matters

All drugs except *miraa* (a leafy shoot chewed as a stimulant) are illegal in Kenya. Marijuana (commonly called *bhang*) is widely available but illegal; possession carries a penalty of up to 10 years in prison. Dealers are common on the beaches north and south of Mombasa and frequently set up travellers for sting operations for real or phoney cops to extort money.

African prisons are unbelievably harsh places – don't take the risk! Note that *miraa* is illegal in Tanzania, so if you do develop a taste for the stuff in Kenya you should leave it behind when heading south.

Maps

Country Maps

The *Tourist Map of Kenya* gives good detail, as does the *Kenya Route Map;* both cost around KSh250. Otherwise, Marco Polo's 1:1,000,000 *Shell Euro Karte Kenya*, Geocenter's *Kenya* (1:1,000,000) and IGN's *Carte Touristique: Kenya* (1:1,000,000) are useful overview maps that are widely available in Europe. The scale and clarity are very good, but the locations of some minor features are inaccurate.

For those planning a longer trip in southern and East Africa, Michelin's 1:4,000,000 *Map 955 (Africa Central and South)* is very useful.

National Park Maps

Most maps to Kenya's national parks might look a bit flimsy on detail (you won't get much in the way of topographical detail), but they include the numbered junctions in the national parks.

Macmillan publishes a series of maps to the wildlife parks and these are not bad value at around KSh250 each (three are available in Europe: *Amboseli*, *Masai Mara* and *Tsavo East & West*). Tourist Maps also publishes a national-park series for roughly the same price. The maps by the KWS are similar.

The most detailed and thorough maps are published by the Survey of Kenya, but the majority are out of date and many are also out of print. The better bookshops in Nairobi usually have copies of the most important maps, including *Amboseli National Park* (SK 87), *Masai Mara Game Reserve* (SK 86), *Meru National Park* (SK 65), *Tsavo East National Park* (SK 82) and *Tsavo West National Park* (SK 78). It may be worth a visit to the **Kenya Institute of Surveying & Mapping** (☎020-8561484; Thika Rd,

Nairobi), but this can take all day and there's no guarantee it will have any more stock than the bookshops.

Money

The unit of currency is the Kenyan shilling (KSh), which is made up of 100 cents. Notes in circulation are KSh1000, 500, 200, 100, 50 and 20, and there are also coins of KSh40, 20, 10, five and one in circulation. Locally, the shilling is commonly known as a 'bob', after the old English term for a one-shilling coin.

The shilling has been relatively stable over the last few years, maintaining fairly constant rates against a falling US dollar and a strong British pound. Both these currencies are easy to change throughout the country, as is the euro, which is rapidly replacing the dollar as the currency quoted for hotel prices on the coast.

The most convenient way to bring your money is in a mixture of cash and a debit or credit card. See p17 for information on exchange rates and costs.

ATMs

Virtually all banks in Kenya now have ATMs at most branches, but their usefulness to travellers varies widely. Barclays Bank has easily the most reliable machines for international withdrawals, with a large network of ATMs covering most major Kenyan towns. They support MasterCard, Visa, Plus and Cirrus international networks.

Standard Chartered and Kenya Commercial Bank ATMs also accept Visa but not the other major providers, and are more likely to decline transactions. Whichever bank you use, the international data link still goes down occasionally, so don't rely on being able to withdraw money whenever you need it.

Black Market

With deregulation, the black market has almost vanished, and the handful of moneychangers who still wander the streets offering 'good rates' are usually involved in scams. The exception is at land border crossings, where moneychangers are often the only option. Most offer reasonable rates, although you should be careful not to get short-changed or scammed during any transaction.

Cash

While most major currencies are accepted in Nairobi and Mombasa, once away from these two centres you'll run into problems with currencies other than US dollars, pounds sterling and euros.

Credit Cards

Credit cards are becoming increasingly popular, although the connections fail with tedious regularity. Visa and MasterCard are now widely accepted in midrange and top-end hotels, top-end restaurants and some shops.

Moneychangers

The best places to change money are foreign exchange or 'forex' bureaus, which can be found everywhere and usually don't charge commission. The rates for the main bureaus in Nairobi are published in the *Daily Nation* newspaper. Watch out for differing small bill (US$10) and large bill (US$100) rates; the larger bills usually get the better rates.

International Transfers

Postbank, a branch of the Kenyan Post Office, is the regional agent for Western Union, the global money-transfer company. Using its service is an easy way (if the phones are working) of receiving money in Kenya. Handily, the sender pays all the charges and there's a Postbank in most towns, often in the post office or close by. Senders should contact **Western Union** (USA ☎1800-3256000, Australia ☎1800-501500, New Zealand ☎0800-270000, UK ☎0800-833833; www.westernunion.com) to find the location of their nearest agency.

Tipping

Tipping is not common practice among Kenyans, but there's no harm in rounding up the bill by a few shillings if you're pleased with the service.

Hotel porters Tips expected in up-market hotels.

Restaurants A service charge of 10% is often added to the bill along with the 16% VAT and 2% catering levy.

Taxi drivers As fares are negotiated in advance, no need to tip unless they provide you with exceptional service.

Tour guides, safari drivers and cooks Will expect some kind of gratuity at the end of your tour or trip – see p31.

Travellers Cheques

Travellers cheques are next to useless in Kenya – very few banks or foreign exchange bureaus accept them and those that do, do so reluctantly and charge high commissions.

Photography

Photographing people remains a sensitive issue in Kenya – it is advisable to ask permission first. Some ethnic groups including the Maasai request money for you to take their photo.

You should never get your camera out at border crossings or near government or army buildings – even bridges can sometimes be classed as sensitive areas.

Taking Pictures

As the natural light in Kenya can be extremely strong, morning and evening are the best times to take photos. A plain UV filter can also be a good idea to take the harshness out of daylight pictures.

SLR cameras and zoom lenses are best for serious wildlife photography. When using long lenses you'll find that a tripod can be extremely useful.

If in a safari minibus, ask your driver to switch off the engine to avoid vibrations affecting your photo.

Post

The Kenyan postal system is run by the government **Posta** (www.posta.co.ke). Letters sent from Kenya rarely go astray but can take up to two weeks to reach Australia or the USA.

If sent by surface mail, parcels take three to six months to reach Europe, while airmail parcels take around a week.

Most things arrive eventually, although there is still a problem with theft within the system. Curios, clothes and textiles will be OK, but if your parcel contains anything of obvious value, send it by courier. Posta has its own courier service, EMS, which is considerably cheaper than the big international courier companies. The best place to send parcels from is the main post office in Nairobi.

Public Holidays

For more on festivals and other events, see p21.

National Holidays

1 January New Year's Day
March/April Good Friday and Easter Monday
1 May Labour Day
1 June Madaraka Day
10 October Moi Day
20 October Kenyatta Day
12 December Independence Day
25 December Christmas Day
26 December Boxing Day

HOLIDAY	2012	2013	2014
Ramadan begins	20 Jul	9 Jul	29 Jun
Eid al-Fitr (end of Ramadan)	19 Aug	8 Aug	28 Jul
Tabaski	26 Oct	15 Oct	4 Oct
Maulid (Prophet Mohammed's birthday)	4 Feb	24 Jan	13 Jan
New Year begins	29 Nov (1433)	18 Nov (1434)	7 Nov (1435)
Eid al-Adha (Feast of Sacrifice)	28 Oct	17 Oct	6 Oct

Islamic Holidays

Islamic festivals and holidays are particularly significant on the coast. Many eateries there close until after sundown during the Muslim fasting month of Ramadan. Islamic holidays vary in date according to the lunar calendar.

School Holidays

Kenyan schools run on a three-term system much like the British education establishments on which they were originally modelled, although summer vacations tend to be shorter. Holidays usually fall in April (one month), August (one month) and December (five weeks). As few Kenyan families can afford to stay in tourist hotels, these holidays mostly have little impact on visitors, but more people will travel during these periods and popular public areas like the coastal beaches will be that bit more crowded.

Safe Travel

While Kenya is a comparatively safe African destination, there are still plenty of pitfalls for the unwary or inexperienced traveller, from everyday irritations to more serious threats. A little street sense goes a long way here, and getting the latest local information is essential wherever you intend to travel.

Banditry

The ongoing conflict in Somalia has had an effect on the stability and safety of northern and northeastern Kenya. AK-47s have been flowing into the country for many years, and the newspapers are filled with stories of hold-ups, shoot-outs, cattle rustling and general lawlessness. Bandits and poachers infiltrating from Somalia have made the northeast of the country particularly dangerous. In 2011, tourists and aid workers were kidnapped close to the Somali border, prompting Kenya to briefly invade their neighbour.

In the northwest, the main problem is armed tribal wars and cattle rustling across the Sudanese border. There are Kenyan *shiftas* (bandits) too, of course, but cross-border problems seem to account for most of the trouble in the north of the country.

Despite all the headlines, tourists are rarely targeted, as much of the violence and robberies take place far from the main tourist routes. Security has also improved considerably in previously high-risk areas such as the Isiolo–Marsabit, Marsabit–Moyale and Malindi–Lamu routes. However, you should check the situation locally before taking these roads, or travelling between Garsen and Garissa or Thika.

The areas along the Sudanese and Ethiopian borders are risky, so please enquire about the latest security situations if you're heading overland.

GOVERNMENT TRAVEL ADVICE

The following government websites offer travel advisories and information for travellers:

» **Australian Department of Foreign Affairs & Trade** (www.smartraveller.gov.au)

» **Canadian Department of Foreign Affairs & International Trade** (www.voyage.gc.ca)

» **French Ministere des Affaires Etrangeres Europeennes** (www.diplomatie.gouv.fr/fr/conseils-aux-voyageurs_909/index.html)

» **Italian Ministero degli Affari Esteri** (www.viaggiaresicuri.mae.aci.it in Italian)

» **New Zealand Ministry of Foreign Affairs & Trade** (www.mft.govt.nz/travel)

» **UK Foreign & Commonwealth Office** (www.fco.gov.uk)

» **US Department of State** (www.travel.state.gov)

Crime

Even the staunchest Kenyan patriot will readily admit that the country's biggest problem is crime. It ranges from petty snatch theft and mugging to violent armed robbery, carjacking and, of course, white-collar crime and corruption. As a visitor you needn't feel paranoid, but you should always keep your wits about you, particularly at night.

Perhaps the best advice for when you're walking around cities and towns is not to carry anything valuable with you – that includes jewellery, watches, cameras, bumbags, daypacks and money. Most hotels provide a safe or secure place for valuables, although you should also be cautious of the security at some budget places.

While pickpocketing and bag-snatching are the most common crimes, armed muggings do occur in Nairobi and on the coast. Always take taxis after dark. Conversely, snatch-and-run crimes happen more in crowds. If you suddenly feel there are too many people around you, or think you are being followed, dive straight into a shop and ask for help.

Luggage is an obvious signal to criminals that you've just arrived. When arriving anywhere by bus, it's sensible to take a 'ship-to-shore' approach, getting a taxi directly from the bus station to your hotel. You'll have plenty of time to explore once you've safely stowed your belongings. Also, don't read this guidebook or look at maps on the street – it attracts unwanted attention.

In the event of a crime, you should report it to the police, but this can be a real procedure. You'll need to get a police report if you intend to make an insurance claim. In the event of a snatch theft, think twice before yelling 'Thief!' It's not unknown for people to administer summary justice on the spot, often with fatal results for the criminal.

Although crime is a fact of life in Kenya, it needn't spoil your trip. Above all, don't make the mistake of distrusting every Kenyan just because of a few bad apples – the honest souls you meet will far outnumber any crooks who cross your path.

Money

With street crime a way of life in Nairobi, you should be doubly careful with your money. The safest policy is to leave all your valuables in the hotel safe and just carry enough cash for that day. If you do need to carry larger sums around, a money belt worn under your clothes is the safest option to guard against snatch thefts. However, be aware that muggers will usually be expecting this.

More ingenious tricks include tucking money into a length of elasticised bandage on your arm or leg, or creating a hidden pocket inside your trousers. If you don't actually need your credit card, travellers cheques or cash with you, they'll almost always be safer locked away in your hotel safe. Don't overlook the obvious

HOTEL SECURITY

Although hotels give you room keys, it is recommended that you carry a padlock for your backpack or suitcase as an extra deterrent. Furthermore, don't invite trouble by leaving valuables, cash or important documents lying around your room or in an unlocked bag. Up-market hotels will have safes where you can keep your money and passport, so it's advised that you take advantage of them. It's usually best not to carry any valuables on the street, but in times when your budget accommodation is a bit rough around the edges, you may want to consider hiding your valuables on your person and carrying them at all times. Of course, use discretion, as muggings do happen in large towns and cities. Sadly, theft is perhaps the number-one complaint of travellers in Kenya, so it can't hurt to take a few extra precautions.

and leave money lying around your hotel room in plain view. However well you get on with the staff, there will be some unlikely to resist a free month's wages if they've got a family to feed.

Scams

At some point in Kenya you'll almost certainly come across people who play on the emotions and gullibility of foreigners. Nairobi is a particular hot spot, with 'friendly' approaches a daily, if not hourly, occurrence (see p81 for examples of favourite tricks). People with tales about being refugees or having sick relatives can sound very convincing, but they all end up asking for cash. It's OK to talk to these people if they're not actively hassling you, but you should ignore any requests for money.

Be sceptical of strangers who claim to recognise you in the street, especially if they're vague about exactly where they know you from – it's unlikely that any ordinary person is going to be *this* excited by seeing you twice. Anyone who makes a big show of inviting you into the hospitality of their home also probably has ulterior motives. The usual trick is to bestow some kind of gift upon the delighted traveller, who is then emotionally blackmailed into reciprocating.

Tourists with cars also face potential rip-offs. Don't trust people who gesticulate wildly to indicate that your front wheels are wobbling; if you stop, you'll probably be relieved of your valuables. Another trick is to splash oil on your wheels, then tell you the wheel bearings, differential or something else has failed, and direct you to a nearby garage where their friends will 'fix' the problem – for a substantial fee, of course.

Terrorism

Kenya has twice been subject to major terrorist attacks: in August 1998 the US embassy in Nairobi was bombed, and in November 2002 the Paradise Hotel, north of Mombasa, was car-bombed at the same time as a rocket attack on an Israeli jet. And a handful of kidnappings launched from across the border in Somali in 2011 prompted the Kenyan military to invade their neighbour, resulting in some minor terrorist scares in Nairobi in late 2011 and warnings about possible terrorist acts from militant Somali groups in 2012. While these events caused a brief panic in the tourist industry, it now seems they were isolated incidents and that Western travellers to Kenya can expect to have a trouble-free time in the country. Visitors to the predominantly Muslim coast region should be aware that anti-American sentiment can run high here, but actual violence against foreigners is highly unlikely.

STREET KIDS

Nairobi in particular has huge problems with street children, many of whom are AIDS orphans, who trail foreigners around asking for food or change. It's up to you whether you give, but if you do the word will go around and you won't get a moment's peace. It's also debatable how much your donations will help as the older boys operate like a minimafia, extorting money from the younger kids. If you want to help out, money might be better donated to a charity, such as the **Consortium for Street Children** (www.streetchildren.org.uk), which works to improve conditions for these children.

Telephone

International call rates from Kenya are relatively expensive, though you can save serious cash by using VOIP programs like Skype. Operator-assisted calls are charged at the standard peak rate, but are subject to a three-minute minimum. You can always dial direct using a phonecard. All public phones should be able to receive incoming calls (the number is usually scrawled in the booth somewhere). If you're calling internationally using a local SIM card, rates are likely to be cheaper (as little as KSh3 per minute) than from fixed-line phones.

Calls made through a hotel operator from your room will cost an extra 25% to 50%, so check before making a call.

Reverse-charge (collect) calls are possible, but only to countries that have set up free direct-dial numbers allowing you to reach the international operator in the country you are calling. Currently these countries include the **UK** (☎0800-220441), the **USA** (☎0800-111, 0800-1112), **Canada** (☎0800-220114, 0800-220115), **New Zealand** (☎0800-220641) and **Switzerland** (☎0800-220411).

Mobile Phones

More than two-thirds of all calls in Kenya are now made on mobile phones, and coverage is good in all but the furthest rural areas. Kenya uses the GSM 900 system, which is compatible with Europe and Australia but not with the North American GSM 1900 system. If you have a GSM phone, check with your service provider about using it in Kenya, and beware of high roaming charges. Remember that you will generally be charged for receiving calls abroad as well as for making them.

Alternatively, if your phone isn't locked into a network, you can pick up a prepaid starter pack from one of the Kenyan mobile-phone companies: **Safaricom** (www.safaricom.co.ke) or **Airtel** (www.africa.airtel.com/kenya/). A SIM card costs about KSh100, and you can then buy top-up scratchcards from shops and booths across the country. International calls can cost as little as KSh3 per minute.

You can easily buy a handset anywhere in Kenya, generally unlocked and with SIM card. Prices start at around KSh2500 for a very basic model.

Phone Codes

Kenya's regions have area codes which must be dialled, followed by the local number. These area codes are listed throughout this book under the name of each town or region.

The international dialling code for Kenya is ☎254.

Phonecards

With Telkom Kenya phonecards, any phone can be used for prepaid calls – you just have to dial the **access number** (☎0844) and enter in the number and passcode on the card. There are booths selling the cards all over the country. Cards come in denominations of KSh200, KSh500, KSh1000 and KSh2000, and call charges are slightly more expensive than for standard lines.

Time

Time zone Kenya is two hours ahead of Greenwich Mean Time (GMT) all year round.

Daylight saving No.

UK and Ireland Three hours behind Kenya (two hours from end of March to end of October).

USA Kenyan time is USA Eastern Time plus eight hours (seven hours from end of March to early November) and USA Pacific Time plus 11 hours (10 hours from end of March to early November).

Western Europe Two hours behind Kenya (one hour from end of March to end of October).

Australia During the Australian winter, subtract eight hours from Australian Eastern Standard Time; during the Australian summer, subtract nine hours

SWAHILI TIME

It's news to most travellers that there is such a thing as 'Swahili time'. It's not just the fact that everyone along the coast seems to have time in bucketloads. Swahili time is six hours out of kilter with the rest of the world. Noon and midnight are six o'clock *(saa sita)* Swahili time, and 7am and 7pm are one o'clock *(saa moja)*. Just add or subtract six hours from whatever time you are told; Swahili doesn't distinguish between am and pm. You don't come across this often unless you speak Swahili, but you still need to be prepared for it.

Toilets

These vary from pits (quite literally) to full-flush, luxury conveniences that can spring up in the most unlikely places. Nearly all hotels sport flushable sit-down toilets, but seats in cheaper places may be a rare commodity – either they're a prized souvenir for trophy hunters or there's a vast stockpile of lost lids somewhere... Public toilets in towns are almost equally rare, but there are a few slightly less-than-emetic pay conveniences in Nairobi if you've only got a penny to spend.

In the more up-market bush camps you'll be confronted with a long drop covered with some sort of seating arrangement. Things are less pleasant when camping in the wildlife parks. Squatting on crumbling concrete is common. When trekking it's good practice to take soiled toilet paper out of the park with you (consider carrying sealable bags for this purpose).

Tourist Information

Local Tourist Offices

Considering the extent to which the country relies on tourism, it's incredible to think that, at the time of writing, there was still no tourist office in Nairobi. There are a handful of information offices elsewhere in the country, ranging from helpful private concerns to underfunded government offices; most can at least provide basic maps of the town and brochures on local businesses and attractions.

Diani Beach i-point (Map p242; ☎040-3202234; Barclays Centre)

Lamu (Map p274; ☎042-633449; off Kenyatta Rd)

Malindi (Map p266; ☎042-20689; Malindi Centre, Lamu Rd)

Mombasa & Coast Tourist Office (Map p228; ☎041-225428; Moi Ave)

Tourist Offices Abroad

The **Ministry of Tourism** (www.tourism.go.ke) maintains a number of overseas offices, including in the UK, USA, Canada and Italy. Most only provide information by telephone, post or email. Visit the ministry website; click on 'Contact Us' for contact details around the world.

Travellers with Disabilities

Travelling in Kenya is not easy for physically disabled people, but it's not impossible. Very few tourist companies and facilities are geared up for travellers with disabilities, and those that are tend to be restricted to the expensive hotels and lodges. However, Kenyans are generally very accommodating and willing to offer whatever assistance they can. Visually- or hearing-impaired travellers, though, will find it very hard to get by without an able-bodied companion.

In Nairobi, only the ex-London taxi cabs are spacious enough to accommodate a wheelchair, but many safari companies are accustomed to taking disabled people out on safari.

Kenyan Services

The travel agency **Travel Scene Services** (☎020-2431699; www.travelsceneafrica.com) has lots of experience with disabled travellers.

Many of the top-end beach resorts on the coast have facilities for the disabled, whether it's a few token ramps or fully equipped rooms with handrails and bath tubs.

Out on safari, other places may have varying degrees of disabled access, but in Amboseli National Park, Ol Tukai Lodge (p94) has two disabled-friendly cottages, while in Lake Nakuru National Park, Lake Nakuru Lodge (p122) has a handful of accessible rooms.

Useful Resources

For further information about disabled travel contact the following:

Access-Able Travel Source (☎303-2322979; www.access-able.com) Has lists of tour operators offering tours for travellers with disabilities.

Association for the Physically Disabled of Kenya (APDK; Map p60; ☎020-2324372; www.apdk.org; APDK House, Lagos Rd, Nairobi) Kenyan group that may be able to help disabled visitors.

Royal Association for Disability & Rehabilitation (RADAR; ☎UK 020-7250 3222; www.radar.org.uk) Publishes a useful guide called *Holidays & Travel Abroad: A Guide for Disabled People;* the latest version came out in March 2012.

Society for Accessible Travel and Hospitality (☎212-447 7284; www.sath.org; USA) The website has a section called 'African Safaris' (type 'Kenya' into the search box).

Tourism for All (☎0303-303 0146; www.tourismforall.org.uk) Advice for disabled and less-mobile senior travellers.

Visas

Tourist visas can be obtained on arrival in Kenya at Nairobi's Jomo Kenyatta international airport, and the country's land borders with Uganda and Tanzania. This applies to Europeans, Australians, New Zealanders, Americans and Canadians, although citizens from a few smaller Commonwealth countries are exempt. Visas cost US$50/€40/UK£30 and are valid for three months from the date of entry. Tourist visas can be extended for a further three-month period.

It's also possible to get visas from Kenyan diplomatic missions overseas, but you should apply well in advance, especially if you're doing it by mail. Visas are usually valid for entry within three months *of the date of issue*. Applications for Kenyan visas are simple and straightforward in Tanzania and Uganda, and payment is accepted in local currency.

Under the East African partnership system, visiting Tanzania or Uganda and returning to Kenya does not invalidate a single-entry Kenyan visa, so there's no need to get a multiple-entry visa unless you plan to go further afield. Always check the latest entry requirements with embassies before travel.

It's always best to smarten up a bit if you're arriving by air; requests for evidence of 'sufficient funds' are usually linked to snap judgments about your appearance. If it's fairly obvious that you aren't intending to stay and work, you'll generally be given the benefit of the doubt.

Visa Extensions

Visas can be renewed at immigration offices during normal office hours, and extensions are usually issued on a same-day basis. Staff at the immigration offices are generally friendly and helpful, but the process takes a while. You'll need two passport photos for a three-month extension, and prices tend to vary widely depending on the office and the whims of the immigration officials. You also need to fill out a form registering as an alien if you're going to be staying more than 90 days. Immigration offices are only open Monday to Friday; note that the smaller offices may sometimes refer travellers back to Nairobi or Mombasa for visa extensions.

Local immigration offices include the following:

Kisumu (Map p138; Nyanza Bldg, cnr Jomo Kenyatta Hwy & Wuor Otiende Rd)

Lamu (Map p274; ☎042-633032; off Kenyatta Rd) Travellers are sometimes referred to Mombasa.

Malindi (Map p266; ☎042-20149; Mama Ngina Rd)

Mombasa (Map p226; ☎041-311745; Uhuru ni Kari Bldg, Mama Ngina Dr)

Nairobi (Map p60; ☎020-222022; Nyayo House, cnr Kenyatta Ave & Uhuru Hwy; ⏰8.30am-12.30pm & 2-3.30pm Mon-Fri)

PUPIL'S PASS

If you're enrolled in a language course that extends beyond the period of your three-month visa, you are usually entitled to a visa extension. The fee for a Pupil's Pass varies. A charge will be levied by your school for sorting out the paperwork, so expect to pay a minimum of KSh3500 for a one-year pass. A deposit of KSh5000 or a letter of guarantee by an approved body registered in Kenya (your language school) is usually required, along with two photographs and a copy of your passport.

Visas for Onward Travel

Since Nairobi is a common gateway city to East Africa and the city centre is easy to get around, many travellers spend some time here picking up visas for other countries that they intend to visit. But be warned: the Ethiopian embassy was not issuing tourist visas at the time of writing, putting a major dent in the overland travel plans of many. Call ahead to see if the situation has changed.

Most embassies will want you to pay visa fees in US dollars, and most open for visa applications from 9am to noon, with visa pick-ups around 3pm or 4pm. Again, contact the embassy in question (see p362 for contact details) to check the times as these change regularly in Nairobi.

Volunteering

There are quite a large number of volunteers in Kenya, which is certainly a cause for celebration as 'voluntourism' is a great way to reduce the ecological footprint of your trip. It's also an amazing forum for self-exploration, especially if you touch a few lives and make friends along the way.

Keep in mind that there is no such thing as a perfect volunteer placement. Generally speaking, you'll get as much out of a program as you're willing to put into it; the vast majority of volunteers in Kenya walk away all the better for the experience.

Kenyan Organisations

Action for Children in Conflict (AfCiC; ☎0724509138, www.actionchildren.org, kenyadirector@actionforchildren.org; 2nd fl, Imara Plaza) A small, highly effective NGO working with Thika's children in poverty. AfCiC recruits skilled volunteers via its website for long-term placements but it also welcomes visitors for the day (KSh1500 to KSh2000) by prior arrangement.

Arabuko Sokoke Schools & Ecotourism Scheme (ASSETS; boxed text, p260) Programs (including Mida Ecocamp) near the Arabuko Sokoke Forest and Mida Creek.

A Rocha (p260), Operates the Mwamba Field Study Centre at Watamu Beach.

Kenya Youth Voluntary Development Projects (Map p56; ☎020-2726011; www.kvcdp.org; Nairobi International Youth Hostel, Ralph Bunche Rd, Nairobi) Excellent local organisation that runs a variety of three- to four-week projects, including road building, health education and clinic construction.

Taita Discovery Centre The purpose-built Kasigau Conservation Trustlands is a conservation research centre covering 680 sq km of the Taita and Rukinga ranches near Tsavo West National Park, forming a vital migration corridor for elephants and other animals between Tsavo and Mt Kilimanjaro. Courses on a huge range of conservation topics are run here, along with hands-on projects in conservation and the local community. It can be contacted through **Origin Safaris** (www.originsafaris.info).

Volunteer Kenya (Inter-Community Development Involvement; www.volunteerkenya.org) Offers a number of longer community projects focusing on health issues such as AIDS awareness, agriculture and conservation in Western Kenya.

Watamu Turtle Watch (p260) Helps protect the marine turtles that come to Watamu to lay eggs on the beach.

International Organisations

Coordinating Committee for International Voluntary Service (http://ccivs.org)

Earthwatch (www.earthwatch.org)

Frontier Conservation Expeditions (www.frontier.ac.uk)

Idealist.org (www.idealist.org)

International Volunteer Programs Association (www.volunteerinternational.org)

Peace Corps (www.peacecorps.gov)

Voluntary Service Overseas (VSO; www.vso.org.uk)

Working Abroad (www.workingabroad.com)

Worldwide Experience (www.worldwideexperience.com)

Worldwide Volunteering (www.wwv.org.uk)

Women Travellers

Within Kenyan society, women are poorly represented in positions of power. However, in their day-to-day lives, Kenyans are generally respectful towards women, although solo women in bars will attract a lot of interest

VISAS FOR NEIGHBOURING COUNTRIES

COUNTRY	VISA AVAILABLE?	VISA FEE (US$)	PASSPORT PHOTOS	HOW LONG TO ISSUE?	ADDITIONAL NOTES
Ethiopia	No	-	-	-	-
Somalia	No	-	-	-	-
South Sudan	Yes (3-month, single entry)	100	2	48 hours	Collect form 8.30am-10pm; must have letter of invitation; must pay visa fee at bank
Tanzania	Yes (3-month, single entry)	50 (US nationals US$100)	1	same day	-
Uganda	Yes (3-month, single entry)	50	1	same day	-

from would-be suitors. Most are just having a go and will give up if you tell them you aren't interested.

In most areas of Kenya, and certainly on safari, women are unlikely to experience any difficulties. The only place you are likely to have problems is at the beach resorts on the coast, where women may be approached by male prostitutes as well as local aspiring Romeos. It's always best to cover your legs and shoulders when away from the beach so as not to offend local sensibilities.

With the upsurge in crime in Nairobi and along the coast, women should avoid walking around at night. The ugly fact is that while men are likely just to be robbed without violence, rape is a real risk for women. Lone night walks along the beach or through quiet city streets are a recipe for disaster, and criminals usually work in gangs, so take a taxi, even if you're in a group.

Regrettably, black women in the company of white men are often assumed to be prostitutes, and can face all kinds of discrimination from hotels and security guards as well as approaches from Kenyan hustlers offering to help rip off the white 'customer'. Again, the worst of this can be avoided by taking taxis between hotels and restaurants etc.

Work

It's difficult, although by no means impossible, for foreigners to find jobs in Kenya. The most likely areas in which employment might be found are in the safari business, teaching, advertising and journalism. Except for teaching, it's unlikely you'll see jobs advertised, and the only way you'll find out about them is to spend a lot of time with resident expats. As in most countries, the rule is that if a local can be found to do the job, there's no need to hire a foreigner.

The most fruitful area in which to look for work, assuming that you have the relevant skills, is the 'disaster industry'. Nairobi is awash with UN and other aid agencies servicing the famines in Somalia and southern Sudan and the refugee camps along the Kenyan border with those countries. Keep in mind that the work is tough and often dangerous, and pay is usually very low.

Work permits and resident visas are not easy to arrange. A prospective employer may be able to sort the necessary paperwork for you, but otherwise you'll find yourself spending a lot of time and money at the **immigration office** (Map p60; ☎020-222022; Nyayo House, cnr Kenyatta Ave & Uhuru Hwy, Nairobi) in Nairobi.

Transport

GETTING THERE & AWAY

Nairobi is a major African hub with numerous African and international airlines connecting Kenya to the world. By African standards, flights between Kenya and the rest of Africa or further afield are common and relatively cheap, and flying is by far the most convenient way to get to Kenya.

Kenya is also a popular and relatively easy waystation for those travelling overland between southern Africa and Egypt. Finding your way here can be tricky – with several war zones in the vicinity – and such journeys should only be considered after serious planning and preparation. But they're certainly possible, and it's rarely Kenya that causes problems.

Flights, tours and rail tickets can be booked online at www.lonelyplanet.com/travel_services.

Entering the Country

Entering Kenya is generally pleasingly straightforward, particularly at the international airports, which are no different from most Western terminals. Single-entry visas are typically available on arrival for most nationalities (passport photos are not required) at Mombasa and Nairobi airports and Kenya's land borders with Uganda and Tanzania. With that said, you should contact your nearest Kenyan diplomatic office to get the most up-to-date information. For visa-requirements information current at the time of going to print, see p370.

Dressing nicely will almost always smooth your way into the country with immigration officials.

Passport

There are no restrictions on which nationalities can enter Kenya, but you will need a valid passport, and usually one with a validity of more than six months.

Air

Airports

Kenya has three international airports; check out the website www.kenyaairports.co.ke for further information:

Jomo Kenyatta International Airport (NBO; ☎020-6611000) Most international flights to and from Nairobi arrive at this airport, 15km southeast of the city. There are two international terminals and a smaller domestic terminal; you can walk easily between the terminals.

Moi International Airport (MBA; ☎041-3433211) In Mombasa, 9km west of the centre, and Kenya's second-busiest international airport. Apart from flights to Zanzibar, this is mainly used by charter airlines and domestic flights.

Wilson Airport (WIL; ☎020-3603260) Located 6km south of Nairobi's city centre on Langata Rd; some flights between Nairobi and Kilimanjaro International Airport or Mwanza in Tanzania, as well as some domestic flights.

Airlines

The following airlines fly to/from Kenya. Kenya Airways is the main national carrier, and has a generally good safety record, with just one fatal incident since 1977.

African Express Airways (www.africanexpress.co.ke)

Air India (www.airindia.com)

Air Madagascar (www.airmadagascar.mg)

Air Malawi (www.airmalawi.com)

Air Mauritius (www.airmauritius.com)

Airkenya (www.airkenya.com)

British Airways (www.britishairways.com)

Daallo Airlines (www.daallo.com)

Egypt Air (www.egyptair.com.eg)

Emirates (www.emirates.com)

Ethiopian Airlines (www.ethiopianairlines.com)

Fly 540 (www.fly540.com)

Gulf Air (www.gulfairco.com)

Jetlink Express (www.jetlink.co.ke)

Kenya Airways (www.kenya-airways.com)

CLIMATE CHANGE & TRAVEL

Every form of transport that relies on carbon-based fuel generates CO_2, the main cause of human-induced climate change. Modern travel is dependent on aeroplanes, which might use less fuel per kilometre per person than most cars but travel much greater distances. The altitude at which aircraft emit gases (including CO_2) and particles also contributes to their climate change impact. Many websites offer 'carbon calculators' that allow people to estimate the carbon emissions generated by their journey and, for those who wish to do so, to offset the impact of the greenhouse gases emitted with contributions to portfolios of climate-friendly initiatives throughout the world. Lonely Planet offsets the carbon footprint of all staff and author travel.

KLM (www.klm.com)
Monarch (www.monarch.co.uk)
Precision Air (www.precisionairtz.com)
Qatar Airways (www.qatarairways.com)
Rwandair (www.rwandair.com)
Safarilink (www.flysafarilink.com)
SN Brussels Airlines (www.brusselsairlines.com)
South African Airways (www.flysaa.com)
Swiss International Airlines (www.swiss.com)
Thomson Airways (https://flights.thomson.co.uk)
Virgin Atlantic Airways (www.virgin-atlantic.com)

Tickets

It's important to note that flight availability and prices are highly seasonal. Conveniently for Europeans, the cheapest fares usually coincide with the European summer holidays, from June to September.

It's also worth checking out cheap charter flights to Mombasa from Europe, although these will probably be part of a package deal to a hotel resort on the coast. Prices are often absurdly cheap and there's no obligation to stay at the resort you're booked into.

If you enter Nairobi with no onward or return ticket you may incur the wrath of immigration, and be forced to buy one on the spot – an uncommon but expensive exercise.

Land

Ethiopia

With ongoing problems in Sudan and Somalia, Ethiopia offers the only viable overland route into Kenya from the north. The security situation around the main entry point at Moyale is changeable – the border is usually open, but security problems often force its closure. Cattle- and goat-rustling are rife, triggering frequent cross-border tribal wars, so check the security situation carefully before attempting this crossing.

If you're heading in the other direction, remember that Ethiopian visas were not being issued in Nairobi at the time of research.

PUBLIC TRANSPORT

There were no cross-border bus services at the time of writing. If you don't have your own transport from Moyale, lifts can be arranged with the trucks from the border to Isiolo for around KSh1500 (or KSh1000 to Marsabit).

From immigration on the Ethiopian side of town it's a 2km walk to the Ethiopian and Kenyan customs posts. A yellow-fever vaccination is required to cross either border at Moyale. Unless you fancy being vaccinated at the border, get your jabs in advance and keep the certificate with your passport. A cholera vaccination may also be required.

CAR & MOTORCYCLE

Those coming to Kenya with their own vehicle could also enter at Fort Banya, on the northeastern tip of Lake Turkana, but it's a risky route with few fuel stops. There's no border post; you must already possess a Kenyan visa and get it stamped on arrival in Nairobi. Immigration are quite used to this, but not having an Ethiopian exit stamp can be a problem if you want to re-enter Ethiopia.

Somalia

There's no way you can pass overland between Kenya and war-ravaged Somalia at present, as the Kenyan government has closed the border to try and stop the flow of poachers, bandits and weapons into Kenya. Kidnappings, armed conflict and banditry are rife in the area close to the border.

Sudan

With South Sudan being granted independence, the border may reopen, but at the time of writing it was only possible to travel between the two countries either by air or via Metema on the Ethiopian border.

Tanzania

The main land borders between Kenya and Tanzania are at Namanga, Taveta, Isebania and Lunga Lunga, and can be reached by public transport. There is also a crossing from the Serengeti to the Masai Mara, which can only be undertaken with your own vehicle, and one at Loitokitok, which is closed to tourists, although you may be able to temporarily cross on a tour. Train services between the two countries have been suspended.

Although all of the routes may be done in stages using a combination of buses and local matatus, there are six main routes to/from Tanzania:

- Mombasa–Tanga/Dar es Salaam
- Mombasa–Arusha/Moshi
- Nairobi–Arusha/Moshi
- Nairobi–Dar es Salaam
- Serengeti–Masai Mara
- Nairobi–Mwanza

BUS

Following are the main bus companies serving Tanzania:

Akamba (☎0722203753; www.akambabus.com)

Easy Coach (☎020-3210711)

Riverside Shuttle (☎020-3229618; www.riverside-shuttle.com)

Simba Coaches (Abdel Nasser Rd, Mombasa)

CAR & MOTORCYCLE

All of the bus routes mentioned here are easily accomplished in your own vehicle. Theoretically it's also possible to cross between Serengeti National Park and Masai Mara National Reserve with your own vehicle, but you'll need all the appropriate vehicle documentation (including insurance and entry permit).

Uganda

The main border post for overland travellers is Malaba, with Busia an alternative if you're travelling via Kisumu. For more details on crossing the frontier, see the boxed text, p161.

BUS

Numerous bus companies run between Nairobi and Kampala. From Nairobi – and at the top end of the market – **Easy Coach** (Map p60; ☎2210711; Haile Selassie Ave) and **Akamba** (☎0722203753; www.akambabus.com) have buses at least once daily, ranging from ordinary buses at around KSh1200 to full-blown 'luxury' services with drinks and movies, hovering around the KSh2400 mark. All buses take about 10 to 12 hours and prices include a meal at the halfway point.

Various other companies have cheaper, basic services, which depart from the Accra Rd area in Nairobi.

If you want to do the journey in stages, Akamba has morning and evening buses from Nairobi to Malaba and a daily direct bus from there to Kampala. There are also regular matatus to Malaba from Cross Rd.

The Ugandan and Kenyan border posts at Malaba are about 1km apart, so you can walk or take a *boda-boda* (bicycle taxi). Once you get across the border, there are frequent matatus until the late afternoon to Kampala, Jinja and Tororo.

Buses and matatus also run from Nairobi or Kisumu to Busia, from where there are regular connections to Kampala and Jinja.

Sea & Lake

At the time of writing there were no ferries operating on Lake Victoria, although there's been talk for years of services restarting.

There's always talk of a cross-lake ferry service between Kenya, Tanzania and Uganda and one company – **Earthwise Ferries** (www.earthwiseventures.com) – even has a website. If they actually end up with a boat, they could link Kisumu with Mwanza (Tanzania) and Kampala (Uganda)

Tanzania

It's theoretically possible to travel by dhow between Mombasa and the Tanzanian islands of Pemba and Zanzibar, but first of all you'll have to find a captain who's making the journey and then you'll have to bargain hard to pay a reasonable amount for the trip. Perhaps the best place to ask about sailings is at Shimoni (p248). There's a tiny immigration post here, but there's no guarantee they'll stamp your passport so you might have to go back to Mombasa for an exit stamp.

MAJOR BUS ROUTES

FROM	TO	PRICE (US$)	DURATION (HRS)	COMPANY
Mombasa	Tanga	9	4	Simba Coaches
Mombasa	Dar es Salaam	12-16	5-8	Simba Coaches
Nairobi	Moshi	35-40	7½	Riverside Shuttle Akamba
Nairobi	Arusha	25-30	5½	Riverside Shuttle Akamba
Nairobi	Dar es Salaam	34	16-18	Akamba
Nairobi	Mwanza	21	13½	Akamba

Dhows do sail between small Kenyan and Tanzanian ports along Lake Victoria, but many are involved in smuggling (fruit mostly) and are best avoided.

Tours

Most people come to Kenya on safari – see p28 for everything you need to know – but it's also possible to reach Kenya as part of an overland truck tour originating in Europe or other parts of Africa; many also start in Nairobi bound for other places in Africa. Most companies are based in the UK or South Africa.

Acacia Expeditions (www.acacia-africa.com)

Africa Travel Co (www.africatravelco.com)

Dragoman (www.dragoman.co.uk)

Guerba Expeditions (www.guerba.co.uk)

Keystone Journeys (www.keystonejourneys.com)

Kumuka (www.kumuka.co.uk)

Oasis Overland (www.oasisoverland.com)

GETTING AROUND

Getting around Kenya is relatively easy, whether you criss-cross the country by highway bus or hire car, or cruise the clear skies and placid seas by light aircraft or dhow.

Most of Kenya's towns and cities are accessible by local bus, though it's usually necessary to arrange private transport to reach national parks and lodges. If you're a seasoned or aspiring road warrior, hiring a sturdy vehicle can also open up relatively inaccessible corners of the country.

Air

Airlines in Kenya

Including the national carrier, Kenya Airways, five main domestic operators of varying sizes run scheduled flights within Kenya. Destinations served are predominantly around the coast and the popular national parks, where the highest density of tourist activity takes place.

With all these airlines, be sure to book well in advance (this is essential during the tourist high season). You should also remember to reconfirm your return flights 72 hours before departure, especially those that connect with an international flight. Otherwise, you may find that your seat has been reallocated.

The following airlines fly domestically, mostly from Nairobi:

Airkenya (☎020-3916000; www.airkenya.com) Amboseli, Diani, Lamu, Masai Mara, Malindi, Meru, Mombasa, Nanyuki and Samburu.

Fly 540 (www.fly540.com) Eldoret, Kisumu, Kitale, Lamu, Lodwar, Malindi, Masai Mara and Mombasa.

Jetlink Express (☎020-3827531; www.jetlink.co.ke) Mombasa, Kisumu and Eldoret.

Kenya Airways (☎020-6422560; www.kenya-airways.com) Kisumu, Malindi and Mombasa.

Mombasa Air Safari (☎0734400400; www.mombasaairsafari.com) Amboseli, Diani Beach, Lamu, Malindi, Masai Mara, Meru, Mombasa, Samburu and Tsavo West.

Safarilink (☎020-6000777; www.flysafarilink.com) Amboseli, Diani Beach, Kiwayu, Lamu, Lewa Downs, Masai Mara, Naivasha, Nanyuki, Samburu, Shaba and Tsavo West.

CHARTER AIRLINES

Chartering a small plane saves you time and is the only realistic way to get to some parts of Kenya. However, it's an expensive affair, and may only be worth considering if you can get a group together.

There are dozens of charter companies operating out of Nairobi's Wilson Airport. These include the following:

Blue Bird Aviation (☎020-6002338; www.bluebirdaviation.com)

Z-Boskovic Air Charters (☎020-6006364; www.boskovicaircharters.com)

Bicycle

Loads of Kenyans get around by bicycle, and while it can be tough for those who are not used to the roads or climate, plenty of hardy visiting cyclists do tour the country every year. But whatever you do, if you intend to cycle here, do as the locals do and get off the road whenever you hear a car coming. And no matter how experienced you are, it would be tantamount to suicide to attempt the road from Nairobi to Mombasa, or from Nairobi to Nakuru, on a bicycle.

Cycling is easier in rural areas, and you'll usually receive a warm welcome in any villages you pass through. Many local people operate *boda-bodas*, so repair shops are quite common along the roadside. Be wary of cycling on dirt roads as punctures from thorn trees are a major problem.

The hills of Kenya are not particularly steep but can be long and hard. You can expect to cover around 80km per day in the hills of the western highlands, somewhat more where the country is flatter. Hell's Gate National Park, near Naivasha, is particularly popular for mountain-biking.

It's possible to hire road and mountain bikes in an increasing number of places, usually for KSh500 to KSh700 per day. Few places require a deposit, unless their machines are particularly new or sophisticated.

Boat

There has been speculation for years that ferry transport will start again on Lake Victoria, but for the foreseeable future the only regular services operating are motorised canoes to Mfangano Island from Mbita Point, near Homa Bay. An occasional ferry service also runs between Kisumu and Homa Bay.

Dhow

Sailing on a traditional Swahili dhow along the East African coast is one of Kenya's most memorable experiences. And, unlike on Lake Victoria, a good number of traditional routes are very much still in use. Dhows are commonly used to get around the islands in the Lamu archipelago (p272) and the mangrove islands south of Mombasa (see Funzi Island, p248). For more dhow destinations, see p19.

For the most part, these trips operate more like dhow safaris than public transport. Although some trips are luxurious, the trips out of Lamu are more basic. When night comes you simply bed down wherever there is space. Seafood is freshly caught and cooked onboard on charcoal burners, or else barbecued on the beach on surrounding islands.

Most of the smaller boats rely on the wind to get around, so it's quite common to end up becalmed until the wind picks up again. The more commercial boats, however, have been fitted with outboard motors so that progress can be made even when there's no wind. Larger dhows are all motorised and some of them don't even have sails.

Bus

Kenya has an extensive network of long- and short-haul bus routes, with particularly good coverage of the areas around Nairobi, the coast and the western regions. Services thin out the further away from the capital you get, particularly in the north, and there are still plenty of places where you'll be reliant on matatus.

Buses are operated by a variety of private and state-owned companies that offer varying levels of comfort, convenience and roadworthiness. They're considerably cheaper than taking the train or flying, and as a rule services are frequent, fast and often quite comfortable.

In general, if you travel during daylight hours, buses are a fairly safe way to get around. You'll certainly be safer in a bus than in a matatu. The best coaches are saved for long-haul and international routes and offer DVD movies, drinks, toilets and reclining airline-style seats. On shorter local routes, however, you may find yourself on something resembling a battered school bus.

Whatever kind of conveyance you find yourself in, don't sit at the back (you'll be thrown around like a rag doll on Kenyan roads), or right at the front (you'll be the first to die in a head-on collision, plus you'll be able to see the oncoming traffic, which is usually a terrifying experience).

There are a few security considerations to think about when taking a bus in Kenya. Some routes, most notably the roads from Malindi to Lamu and Isiolo to Marsabit, have been prone to attacks by *shiftas* (bandits) in the past; check things out locally before you travel. Another possible risk is drugged food and drink: it is best to politely refuse any offers of drinks or snacks from strangers.

The following are the main bus companies operating in Kenya; all have offices in Nairobi and/or Mombasa.

Akamba (☎0722203753; www.akambabus.com) Rift Valley, Western Kenya, Mombasa and Namanga.

Busways (☎020-2227650) Western Kenya and the coast.

Coastline Safaris (☎020-217592) Western and Southern Kenya, Mombasa.

Easy Coach (☎020-3210711) Rift Valley and Western Kenya.

Eldoret Express (☎020-6766886) Western Kenya and Rift Valley.

Kenya Bus Services (KBS; 020-2341250) Rift Valley, Western Kenya and Mombasa.

Mombasa Metropolitan Bus Services (☎041-2496008) Coast.

Costs

Kenyan buses are pretty economical, with fares starting at around KSh100 for an hour-long journey between nearby towns. At the other end of the scale, you'll seldom pay more than KSh600 for a standard journey, but so-called 'executive' services on the overnight Nairobi–Mombasa route can command prices of up to KSh1800.

Reservations

Most bus companies have offices or ticket agents at important stops along their routes, where you can book a seat. For short trips between towns reservations aren't generally necessary, but for popular longer routes, particularly the Nairobi–Kisumu, Nairobi–Mombasa and Mombasa–Lamu routes, buying your ticket at least a day in advance is highly recommended.

Car & Motorcycle

Many travellers bring their own vehicles into Kenya as part of overland trips and, expense notwithstanding, it's a great way to see the country at your own pace. Otherwise, there are numerous car-hire companies that can rent you anything from a small hatchback to a 4WD, although hire

ROAD DISTANCES (KM)

	Busia	Embu	Isiolo	Kakamega	Kericho	Kisumu	Kitale	Lodwar	Malindi	Meru	Mombasa	Nairobi	Nakuru	Namanga	Nanyuki	Nyeri
Embu	610															
Isiolo	569	184														
Kakamega	95	525	481													
Kericho	218	395	351	130												
Kisumu	138	475	431	50	80											
Kitale	154	511	467	109	230	158										
Lodwar	440	691	735	395	522	443	285									
Malindi	1087	657	877	999	869	949	985	1141								
Meru	565	154	56	477	347	427	463	729	864							
Mombasa	969	618	759	881	751	831	867	1120	118	746						
Nairobi	482	131	272	394	264	368	380	599	605	259	521					
Nakuru	325	288	244	237	107	211	223	442	762	240	644	157				
Namanga	661	314	524	596	469	548	563	779	430	468	409	180	337			
Nanyuki	487	131	84	399	269	349	385	651	795	78	677	190	175	380		
Nyeri	508	88	140	420	290	370	406	601	752	136	634	150	151	330	58	
Voi	811	460	601	723	593	673	709	960	281	588	160	329	486	249	519	476

rates are some of the highest in the world.

Automobile Associations

A useful organisation is the **Automobile Association of Kenya** (Map p77; ☎020-4449676; www.aakenya.co.ke; Sarit Centre, Westlands).

Bribes

Although things have improved markedly in recent years, police will still stop you and will most likely ask you for a small 'donation'. To prevent being taken advantage of, always ask for an official receipt – this goes a long way in stopping corruption. Also, always ask for their police number and check it against their ID card as there are plenty of con artists running about. If you're ever asked to go to court, always say yes as you just might call their bluff and save yourself a bit of cash.

Bringing Your Own Vehicle

Drivers of cars and riders of motorbikes will need the vehicle's registration papers, liability insurance and driving licence; although not necessary, an international driving permit is also a good idea. You may also need a *Carnet de passage en douane*, which is effectively a passport for the vehicle and acts as a temporary waiver of import duty. The *carnet* may also need to specify any expensive spare parts that you're planning to carry with you, such as a gearbox. This is necessary when travelling in many countries in Africa, and is designed to prevent car-import rackets. Contact your local automobile association for details about all documentation.

If you're planning to ship your vehicle to Kenya, be aware that port charges in the country are very high. For example, a Land Rover shipped from the Middle East to Mombasa is likely to cost more than US$1000 just to get off the ship and out of the port – this is almost as much as the cost of the shipping itself! Putting a vehicle onto a ship in the Mombasa port can cost another US$750 on top of this. There are numerous shipping agents in Nairobi and Mombasa willing to arrange everything for you, but check all the costs in advance.

Driving Licence

An international driving licence is not necessary in Kenya, but can be useful. If you have a British photo card licence, be sure to bring the counterfoil, as the date you passed your driving test (something car-hire companies may want to know) isn't printed on the card itself.

Fuel & Spare Parts

Fuel prices are on the rise the world over, and Kenya is no exception. Rates are generally lower outside the capital, but can creep up to frighteningly high prices in remote areas, where petrol stations are scarce and you may end up buying dodgy supplies out of barrels from roadside vendors. Petrol, spare parts and repair shops are readily available at all border towns, though if you're coming from Ethiopia you should plan your supplies carefully, as stops are few and far between on the rough northern roads.

Even if it's an older model, local spare-parts suppliers in Kenya are very unlikely to have every little part you might need so carry as many such parts as you can. Belt breakages are probably the most common disaster you can expect, so bring several spares. Also note that you can be fined by the police for not having a fire triangle and an extinguisher.

Car Hire

Hiring a vehicle to tour Kenya (or at least the national parks) is an expensive way of seeing the country, but it does give you freedom of movement and is sometimes the only way of getting to more remote parts of the country. However, unless you're sharing with a sufficient number of people, it's likely to cost more than you'd pay for an organised camping safari with all meals.

Unless you're just planning on travelling on the main routes between towns, you'll need a 4WD vehicle. Few of the car-hire companies will let you drive 2WD vehicles on dirt roads, including those in the national parks, and if you ignore this proscription and have an accident you'll be personally liable for any damage to the vehicle.

A minimum age of between 23 and 25 years usually applies for hirers. Some require you to have been driving for at least two years. You will also need acceptable ID such as a passport.

It's generally true to say that the more you pay for a vehicle, the better condition it will be in. The larger companies are usually in a better financial position to keep their fleet in good order. Whomever you hire from, be sure to check the brakes, the tyres (including the spare), the windscreen wipers and the lights before you set off.

The other factor to consider is what the company will do for you (if anything) if you have a serious breakdown. The major hire companies *may* deliver a replacement vehicle and make arrangements for recovery of the other vehicle at their expense, but with most companies you'll have to get the vehicle fixed and back on the road yourself, and then try to claim a refund.

And if you plan to take the car across international borders, check whether the company allows this – many don't, and those that do charge for the privilege.

COSTS

Starting rates for hire almost always sound very reasonable, but once you factor in mileage and the various types of insurance, you'll be lucky to pay less than KSh7500 per day for a saloon car, or KSh10,000 per day for a small 4WD.

Hiring a vehicle with unlimited kilometres is the best way to go. Rates are usually quoted without insurance, with the option of paying around KSh1000 to KSh2500 per day for insurance against collision damage and theft. It would be financial suicide to hire a car in Kenya without both kinds of insurance. Otherwise you'll be responsible for the full value of the vehicle if it's damaged or stolen.

Even if you have collision and theft insurance, you'll still be liable for an excess of KSh2500 to KSh150,000 (depending on the company) if something happens to the vehicle; always check this before signing. You can usually reduce the excess to zero by paying another KSh1000 to KSh2000 per day for an excess loss waiver. Note that tyres, damaged windscreens and loss of the tool kit are always the hirer's responsibility.

As a final sting in the tail, you'll be charged 16% value added tax (VAT) on top of the total cost of hiring the vehicle. And a final warning: always return the vehicle with a full tank of petrol; if you don't, the company will charge you twice the going rate to fill up.

Driver Rates

While hiring a 'chauffeur' may sound like a luxury, it can actually be a very good idea in Kenya for both financial and safety reasons. Most companies will provide a driver for a few thousand shillings per day – the big advantage of this is that the car is covered by the company's insurance, so you don't have to pay any of the various waivers and won't be liable for any excess in the case of an accident (though tyres, windows etc remain your responsibility).

In addition, having someone in the car who speaks Swahili, knows the roads and is used to Kenyan driving conditions can be absolutely priceless, especially in remote areas. Most drivers will also look after the car at night so you don't have to worry about it, and they'll often go massively out of their way to help you fulfil your travel plans. On the other hand, it will leave one less seat free in the car, reducing the number of people you can have sharing the cost in the first place.

HIRE AGENCIES

We recommend the following local and international hire companies:

Adventure Upgrade Safaris (Map p60; ☎0722529228; www.adventureupgradesafaris.co.ke) An excellent local company.

Avis (Map p60; ☎020-2533610; www.avis.co.ke)

Budget (Map p60; ☎020-2223581; www.budget.co.ke)

Central Rent-a-Car (Map p60; ☎020-2222888; www.carhirekenya.com) Another highly recommended local company.

Uniglobe Let's Go Travel (Map p64; ☎020-4447151; www.uniglobeletsgotravel.com)

Insurance

Driving in Kenya without insurance would be an idiotic thing to do. If coming in your own vehicle, it's best to arrange cover before you leave. Liability insurance is not always available in advance for Kenya; you may be required to purchase some at certain borders if you enter overland, otherwise you will effectively be travelling uninsured.

Most car-hire agencies in Kenya offer some kind of insurance.

Parking

In small towns and villages parking is usually free, but there's a pay-parking system in Nairobi, Mombasa, Nakuru and other main towns. Attendants issue one-day parking permits for around KSh100, valid anywhere in town. If you don't get a permit you're liable to be wheel-clamped, and getting your vehicle back will cost you a few thousand shillings. With that said, it's always worth staying in a hotel with secure parking if possible.

Road Conditions

Road conditions vary widely in Kenya, from flat smooth highways to dirt tracks and steep rocky pathways. Many roads are severely eroded at the edges, reducing the carriageway to a single lane, which is usually occupied by whichever vehicle is bigger in any given situation. The roads in the north and east of the country are particularly poor. The main Mombasa–Nairobi–Malaba road (A104) is badly worn due to the constant flow of traffic, but has improved in recent years. The never-ending stream of trucks along this main route through the country will slow travel times considerably.

Roads in national parks are all made of *murram* (dirt) and many have eroded into bone-shaking corrugations through overuse by safari vehicles. Keep your speed down, slowly increasing until you find a suitable speed (when the rattling stops), and be careful when driving after rain. Although some dirt roads can be negotiated in a 2WD vehicle, you're much safer in a 4WD.

Road Hazards

The biggest hazard on Kenyan roads is simply the other vehicles on them, and driving defensively is essential. Ironically, the most dangerous roads in Kenya are probably the well-maintained ones, which allow drivers to go fast enough to do really serious damage in a crash. On the worse roads, potholes are a dual problem: driving into them can damage your vehicle or cause you to lose control, and sudden avoidance manoeuvres from other vehicles are a constant threat.

On all roads, be very careful of pedestrians and cyclists – you don't want to contribute any more to the death toll on Kenya's roads. Animals are another major hazard in rural areas, be it monkeys, herds of goats and cattle or lone chickens with a death wish.

Acacia thorns are a common problem if you're driving in remote areas, as they'll pierce even the toughest tyres. The slightest breakdown can leave you stranded for hours in the bush, so always carry drinking water, emergency food and, if possible, spare fuel.

Certain routes have a reputation for banditry, particularly the Garsen–Garissa–Thika road, which is still essentially off limits to travellers. The roads from Isiolo to Marsabit and Moyale and from Malindi to Lamu have improved considerably security-wise in the last few years, but you're still advised to seek local advice before using any of these routes.

Road Rules

You'll need your wits about you if you're going to tackle driving in Kenya. Driving practices here are some of the worst in the world and all are carried out at breakneck speed. Indicators, lights, horns and hand signals can mean anything from 'I'm about to overtake' to 'Hello *mzungu* (white person)!' or 'Let's play chicken with that elephant', and should never be taken at face value.

Kenyans habitually drive on the wrong side of the road whenever they see a pothole, an animal or simply a break in the traffic – flashing your lights at the vehicle hurtling towards you should be enough to persuade the driver to get back into their own lane. Never drive at night unless you absolutely have to, as few cars have adequate headlights and the roads are full of pedestrians and cyclists. Drunk driving is also very common.

Note that foreign-registered vehicles with a seating capacity of more than six people are not allowed into Kenyan national parks and reserves; Jeeps should be fine, but VW Kombis and other campervans may have problems.

Hitching

Hitchhiking is never entirely safe in any country, and we don't recommend it. Travellers who hitch should understand they are taking a small but potentially serious risk; it's safer to travel in pairs and let someone know where you are planning to go. Also beware of drunken drivers.

Although it's risky, many locals have no choice but to hitch, so people will know what you're doing if you try to flag down cars. The traditional thumb signal will probably be understood, but locals use a palm-downwards wave to get cars to stop. Many Kenyan drivers expect a contribution towards petrol or some kind of gift from foreign passengers, so make it clear from the outset if you are expecting a free ride.

If you're hoping to hitch into the national parks, dream on! Your chances of coming across tourists with a spare seat who don't mind taking a freeloading stranger along on their expensive safari are slimmer than a starving stick insect, and frankly it seems pretty rude to ask. You'll get further asking around for travel companions in Nairobi or any of the gateway towns.

On the other side of the wheel, foreign drivers will be approached regularly by Kenyan hitchers demanding free rides, and giving a lift to a carload of Maasai is certainly a memorable cultural experience.

Local Transport

Boat

The only local boat service in regular use is the Likoni ferry between the mainland and Mombasa island, which runs throughout the day and night and is free for foot passengers (vehicles pay a small toll).

Boda-Boda

Boda-bodas (bicycle or motorcycle taxis) are common in areas where standard taxis are harder to find, and also operate in smaller towns and cities such as Nakuru or Kisumu. There's a particular proliferation on the coast, where the bicycle boys also double as touts, guides and drug dealers in tourist areas. A short ride should cost around KSh50 or so.

Bus

Nairobi is the only city with an effective municipal bus service, run by KBS. Routes cover the suburbs and outlying areas during daylight hours and generally cost no more than KSh50. Metro Shuttle and private City Hopper services also run to areas such as Kenyatta Airport and Karen. Due to traffic density, safety is rarely a serious concern.

Matatu

Local matatus are the main means of getting around for local people, and any reasonably sized city or town will have plenty of services covering every major road and suburb. Fares start at around KSh20 and may reach KSh100 for longer routes in Nairobi. As with buses, roads are usually busy enough for a slight shunt to be the most likely accident, though of course congestion never stops drivers jockeying for position like it's the Kenya Derby.

The vehicles themselves can be anything from dilapidated Peugeot 504 pick-ups with a cab on the back to big 20-seater minibuses. The most common are white Nissan minibuses (many local people prefer the name 'Nissans' to matatus).

Despite a briefly successful government drive to regulate the matatu industry, matatus are once again notorious for dangerous driving, overcrowding and general shady business. A passenger backlash has seen a small but growing trend in more responsible matatu companies offering less crowding, safer driving and generally better security. Mololine Prestige Shuttle is one of these plying the route from Nairobi to Kisumu.

Apart from in the remote northern areas, where you'll rely on occasional buses or paid lifts on trucks, you can almost always find a matatu going to the next town or further afield, so long as it's not too late in the day. Simply ask around among the drivers at the local matatu stand or 'stage'. Matatus leave when full and the fares are fixed. It's unlikely you will be charged more than other passengers.

Wherever you go, remember that most matatu crashes are head-on collisions – under no circumstances should you sit in the 'death seat' next to the matatu driver. Play it safe and sit in the middle seats away from the window.

Shared Taxi (Peugeot)

Shared Peugeot taxis are a good alternative to matatus. The vehicles are usually Peugeot 505 station wagons that take seven to nine passengers and leave when full.

Peugeots take less time to reach their destinations than matatus as they fill quicker and go from point to point without stopping, and so are slightly more expensive. Many companies have offices around the Accra, Cross and River Rds area in Nairobi, and serve destinations mostly in the north and west of the country.

Taxi

Even the smallest Kenyan towns generally have at least one banged-up old taxi for easy access to outlying areas or even more remote villages, and you'll find cabs on virtually every corner in the larger cities, especially in Nairobi and Mombasa, where taking a taxi at night is virtually mandatory. Fares are invariably negotiable and start around KSh250 to KSh400 for short journeys. Most people pick up cabs from taxi ranks on the street, but some companies will take phone bookings and most hotels can order you a ride. Since few taxis in Kenya actually have functioning meters (or drivers who adhere to them), it's advisable that you agree on the fare prior to setting out. This will inevitably save you the time and trouble of arguing with your cabbie over the fare.

Tuk-Tuk

They're an incongruous sight outside southeast Asia, but several Kenyan towns and cities have these distinctive motorised minitaxis. The highest concentration is in Malindi, but they're also in Nairobi, Mombasa, Nakuru, Machakos and Diani Beach; Watamu has a handful of less sophisticated motorised rickshaws. Fares are negotiable, but should be at least KSh100 less than the equivalent taxi rate for a short journey (and you wouldn't want to take them on a long one!).

Train

The Uganda Railway was once the main trade artery in East Africa, but these days the network has dwindled to two main routes: Nairobi–Kisumu (via Nakuru and Naivasha) and Nairobi–Mombasa. And it's worth remembering that train travel is more something to be experienced than a fast and efficient means of getting around the country: with a night service of around 15 hours, the Nairobi–Mombasa train is much slower than going by air or road.

For a list of destinations, fares and journey times, turn to p85. And for more on the unforgettable journey between Nairobi and Mombasa, see the boxed text, p238.

Classes

There are three classes on Kenyan trains, but only 1st and 2nd class can be recommended.

» First class consists of two-berth compartments with a washbasin, wardrobe, drinking water and a drinks service.

» Second class consists of plainer, four-berth compartments with a washbasin and drinking water.

» Third class is seats only.

No compartment can be locked from the outside, so remember not to leave any valuables lying around if you leave it for any reason. You might want to padlock your rucksack to something during dinner and breakfast. Always lock your compartment from the inside before you go to sleep. In 3rd class security can be a real problem. Note that passengers are divided up by gender.

Passengers in 1st class on the Mombasa line are treated to a meal typically consisting of stews, curries or roast chicken served with rice and vegetables. Tea and coffee is included; sodas (soft drinks), bottled water and alcoholic drinks are not. Cold beer is available at all times in the dining car and can be delivered to your compartment.

Reservations

There are booking offices at the train stations in Nairobi and Mombasa, and it's recommended that you show up in person rather than trying to call. You must book in advance for 1st and 2nd class, otherwise there'll probably be no berths available. Two to three days is usually sufficient, but remember that these services run just three times weekly in either direction. Note that compartment and berth numbers are posted up about 30 minutes prior to departure.

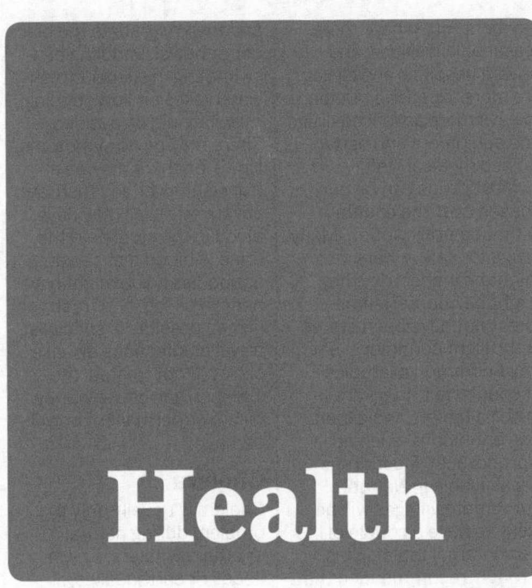

Health

If you stay up-to-date with your vaccinations and take some basic preventive mea-sures, you'd be pretty unlucky to succumb to most of the health hazards covered in this chapter. Africa certainly has an impressive selection of tropical and other diseases, but you're much more likely to get a bout of diarrhoea (in fact, you should bank on it), a cold or an infected mosquito bite than an exotic disease. When it comes to injuries (as opposed to illness), the most likely reason for needing medical help in Kenya is as a result of road accidents.

BEFORE YOU GO

It's tempting to leave all the preparations to the last minute – don't! Many vaccines don't take effect until two weeks after you've been immunised, so visit a doctor four to eight weeks before departure. Ask your doctor for an International Certificate of Vaccination (known in some countries as the yellow booklet), which will list all the vaccinations you've received. This is mandatory for the African countries that require proof of yellow fever vaccination upon entry, which includes Kenya and its neighbours, but it's a good idea to carry it anyway wherever you travel.

Insurance

Find out in advance whether your insurance plan will make payments directly to providers or will reimburse you later for overseas health expenditures (many doctors expect payment in cash). It's vital to ensure that your travel insurance will cover the emergency transport required to get you to a hospital in a major city, to better medical facilities elsewhere in Africa, or all the way home, by air and with a medical attendant if necessary. Not all insurance covers this, so check the contract carefully. If you need medical help, your insurance company might be able to help locate the nearest hospital or clinic, or you can ask at your hotel. In an emergency, contact your embassy or consulate.

Membership of the **African Medical & Research Foundation** (AMREF; www.amref.org) provides an air evacuation service in medical emergencies in Kenya, as well as air ambulance transfers between medical facilities. Money paid by members for this service goes into providing grassroots medical assistance for local people.

Recommended Vaccinations

The **World Health Organization** (www.who.int/en/) recommends that all travellers be covered for diphtheria, tetanus, measles, mumps, rubella and polio, as well as for hepatitis B, regardless of their destination.

According to the **Centers for Disease Control & Prevention** (www.cdc.gov), the following vaccinations are recommended for Kenya: hepatitis A, hepatitis B, meningococcal meningitis, rabies and typhoid, and boosters for tetanus, diphtheria, polio and measles. It is also advisable to be vaccinated against yellow fever (see p387).

Medical Checklist

It's a very good idea to carry a medical and first-aid kit with you, to help yourself in the case of minor illness or injury. Following is a list of items you should consider bringing:

- Acetaminophen (paracetamol) or aspirin
- Acetazolamide (Diamox) for altitude sickness (prescription only)
- Adhesive or paper tape
- Antibacterial ointment (eg Bactroban) for cuts and abrasions (prescription only)
- Antibiotics (prescription only), eg ciprofloxacin (Ciproxin) or norfloxacin (Utinor)
- Antidiarrhoeal drugs (eg loperamide)
- Antihistamines (for hay fever and allergic reactions)
- Anti-inflammatory drugs (eg ibuprofen)

- » Antimalaria pills
- » Bandages, gauze, gauze rolls
- » Insect repellent containing DEET, for the skin
- » Iodine tablets (for water purification)
- » Oral rehydration salts
- » Permethrin-containing insect spray for clothing, tents and bed nets
- » Pocket knife
- » Scissors, safety pins, tweezers
- » Steroid cream or hydrocortisone cream (for allergic rashes)
- » Sunscreen
- » Syringes, sterile needles and fluids if travelling to remote areas
- » Thermometer

If you're travelling through an area where malaria is a problem, particularly an area where falciparum malaria predominates, consider taking a self-diagnostic kit that can identify malaria in the blood from a finger prick.

IN KENYA

Availability & Cost of Health Care

Health care in Kenya is varied: it can be excellent in Nairobi, which generally has well-trained doctors and nurses, but is often patchy off the beaten track, even in Mombasa. Medicine and even sterile dressings and intravenous fluids might need to be purchased from a local pharmacy. The standard of dental care is equally variable, and there is an increased risk of hepatitis B and HIV transmission from poorly sterilised equipment.

By and large, public hospitals in Kenya offer the cheapest service, but will have the least up-to-date equipment and medications; mission hospitals (where donations are the usual form of payment) often have more reasonable facilities; and private hospitals and clinics are more expensive but tend to have more advanced drugs and equipment and better-trained medical staff.

Most drugs can be purchased over the counter without a prescription. Many drugs for sale in Kenya might be ineffective; they might be counterfeit or might not have been stored in the right conditions. The most common examples of counterfeit drugs are malaria tablets and expensive antibiotics, such as ciprofloxacin. Most drugs are available in Nairobi, but remote villages will be lucky to have a couple of paracetamol tablets. It is strongly recommended that you bring all medication from home.

Also, the availability and efficacy of condoms cannot be relied upon – bring all the contraception you'll need. Condoms bought in Kenya might not be of the same quality as in Europe, North America or Australia, and they might have been incorrectly stored.

There is a high risk of contracting HIV from infected blood if you receive a blood transfusion in Kenya. The **Blood Care Foundation** (www.bloodcare.org.uk) is a useful source of safe, screened blood, which can be transported to any part of the world within 24 hours.

Infectious Diseases

It's a formidable list but, as we say, a few precautions go a long way...

Bilharzia (Schistosomiasis)

This disease is spread by flukes (minute worms) that are carried by a species of freshwater snail. The parasites penetrate human skin as people paddle or swim and then migrate to the bladder or bowel. Paddling or swimming in suspect freshwater lakes or slow-running rivers should be avoided. There may be no symptoms. However, there may be a transient fever and rash, and advanced cases may have blood in the stool or in the urine. A blood test can detect antibodies if you might have been exposed, and treatment is then possible in specialist travel or infectious disease clinics. If not treated, the infection can cause kidney failure or permanent bowel damage.

Cholera

Cholera is usually only a problem during natural or other disasters, eg war, floods or earthquakes, although small outbreaks can also occur at other times. Travellers are rarely affected. The disease is caused by a bacteria and spread via contaminated drinking water. The main symptom is profuse watery diarrhoea, which causes debilitation if fluids are not replaced quickly. Most cases of cholera can be avoided by drinking only clean water and by avoiding potentially contaminated food. Treatment is by fluid replacement (orally or via a drip), but sometimes antibiotics are needed. Self-treatment is not advised.

Diphtheria

Found in all of Africa, diphtheria is spread through close respiratory contact. It usually causes a high temperature and a severe sore throat. A membrane can form across the throat, requiring a tracheotomy to prevent suffocation. Vaccination is recommended for those likely to be in close contact with the locals in infected areas. This is more important for long stays than for short-term trips. The vaccine is given as an injection alone or with tetanus, and lasts 10 years.

Hepatitis A

Hepatitis A is spread through contaminated food (particularly shellfish) and water. It causes jaundice and, although it is rarely fatal, it can cause prolonged lethargy. If you're recovering from hepatitis A, you shouldn't drink alcohol for up to six months afterwards, but once you've recovered, there won't be any long-term problems. The first symptoms include dark urine and a yellow colour to the whites of the eyes. Sometimes a fever and abdominal pain might be present. Hepatitis A vaccine (Avaxim, Vaqta, Havrix) is given as an injection: a single dose will give protection for up to a year, and a booster after a year gives 10-year protection. Hepatitis A and typhoid vaccines can also be given as a single-dose vaccine, with hepatyrix or viatim.

Hepatitis B

Hepatitis B is spread through infected blood, contaminated needles and sexual intercourse. It can also be spread from an infected mother to the baby during childbirth. Hepatitis B affects the liver, which causes jaundice and occasionally liver failure. Most people recover completely, but some people might be chronic carriers of the virus, which could lead eventually to cirrhosis or liver cancer. Those visiting high-risk areas for long periods or those with increased social or occupational risk should be immunised. Many countries now give hepatitis B as part of routine childhood vaccinations. It is given singly or can be given at the same time as hepatitis A (hepatyrix).

A course will give protection for at least five years. It can be given over four weeks or six months.

HIV

Human immunodeficiency virus (HIV), the virus that causes acquired immune deficiency syndrome (AIDS), is an enormous problem in Kenya, where the infection rate is around 6.3% of the adult population. The virus is spread through infected blood and blood products, by sexual intercourse with an infected partner, and from an infected mother to her baby during childbirth or breastfeeding. It can be spread through 'blood to blood' contacts, such as with contaminated instruments during medical, dental, acupuncture and other body-piercing procedures, and through sharing intravenous needles. If you think you might have been exposed to HIV, a blood test is necessary; a three-month gap after exposure and before testing is required to allow antibodies to appear in the blood.

Malaria

Malaria is a major health scourge in Kenya. Infection rates vary with the season (higher in the rainy season) and climate, so check out the situation before departure. The incidence of malarial transmission at altitudes higher than 2000m is rare.

Malaria is caused by a parasite in the bloodstream spread via the bite of the female anopheles mosquito. There are several types, falciparum malaria being the most dangerous and the predominant form in Kenya. Unlike most other diseases regularly encountered by travellers, there is no vaccination against malaria (yet). However, several different drugs are used to prevent malaria and new ones are in the pipeline. Up-to-date advice from a travel-health clinic is essential, as some medication is more suitable for some travellers than others. The pattern of drug-resistant malaria is changing rapidly, so what was advised several years ago might no longer be the case.

SYMPTOMS

Malaria can affect people in several ways. The early stages include headaches, fevers, generalised aches

THE ANTIMALARIAL A TO D

» A – Awareness of the risk. No medication is totally effective, but protection of up to 95% is achievable with most drugs, as long as other measures have been taken.

» B – Bites: avoid at all costs. Sleep in a screened room, use a mosquito spray or coils; sleep under a permethrin-impregnated net at night. Cover up at night with long trousers and long sleeves, preferably with permethrin-treated clothing. Apply appropriate repellent to all areas of exposed skin in the evenings.

» C – Chemical prevention (ie antimalarial drugs) is usually needed in malaria-infected areas. Expert advice is needed as the resistance patterns of the parasite can change, and new drugs are in development. Not all antimalarial drugs are suitable for everyone. Most antimalarial drugs need to be started at least a week in advance and continued for four weeks after the last possible exposure to malaria.

» D – Diagnosis. If you have a fever or flu-like illness within a year of travel to a malaria-infected area, malaria is a possibility, and immediate medical attention is necessary.

and pains, and malaise, often mistaken for flu. Other symptoms can include abdominal pain, diarrhoea and a cough. Anyone who develops a fever while in a malarial area should assume malarial infection until a blood test proves negative, even if you've been taking antimalarial medication. If not treated, the next stage can develop within 24 hours, particularly if falciparum malaria is the parasite: jaundice, reduced consciousness and coma (known as cerebral malaria), followed by death. Treatment in hospital is essential, and if patients enter this late stage of the disease the death rate may still be as high as 10%, even in the best intensive-care facilities.

SIDE EFFECTS & RISKS

Many travellers are under the impression that malaria is a mild illness, that treatment is always easy and successful, and that taking antimalarial drugs causes more illness through side effects than actually getting malaria. Unfortunately this is not true. Side effects of the medication depend on the drug being taken. Doxycycline can cause heartburn and indigestion; mefloquine (Larium) can cause anxiety attacks, insomnia and nightmares, and (rarely) severe psychiatric disorders; chloroquine can cause nausea and hair loss; and proguanil can cause mouth ulcers. These side effects are not universal, and can be minimised by taking medication correctly, such as with food.

If you decide that you really do not wish to take antimalarial drugs, you must understand the risks, and be obsessive about avoiding mosquito bites. Use nets and insect repellent, and report any fever or flu-like symptoms to a doctor as soon as possible. Some people advocate homeopathic preparations against malaria, such as Demal200, but as yet there is no conclusive evidence that this is effective, and many homeopaths do not recommend their use. Some people should not take a particular antimalarial drug, eg people with epilepsy should avoid mefloquine, and doxycycline should not be taken by pregnant women or children younger than 12. Malaria in pregnancy frequently results in miscarriage or premature labour and the risks to both mother and foetus during pregnancy are considerable. Travel in Kenya when pregnant should be carefully considered.

STAND-BY TREATMENT

If you're going to be in remote areas or far from major towns, consider taking a stand-by treatment. Emergency stand-by treatments should be seen as emergency treatment aimed at saving the patient's life and not as a routine way of self-medicating. It should be used only if you will be far from medical facilities and have been advised about the symptoms of malaria and how to use the medication. Medical advice should be sought as soon as possible to confirm whether the treatment has been successful. The type of stand-by treatment used will depend on local conditions, such as drug resistance, and on what antimalarial drugs were being used before stand-by treatment. This is worthwhile because you want to avoid contracting a particularly serious form such as cerebral malaria, which can be fatal within 24 hours. Self-diagnostic kits, which can identify malaria in the blood from a finger prick, are also available in the West.

Dengue Fever (Break-Bone Fever)

Dengue fever, spread through the bite of mosquitoes, causes a feverish illness with headache and muscle pains similar to those experienced with a bad, prolonged attack of influenza. There might be a rash. Mosquito bites should be avoided whenever possible. This disease is present in Kenya. Self-treatment consists of paracetamol and rest.

Meningococcal Meningitis

Meningococcal infection is spread through close respiratory contact and is more likely to be contracted in crowded situations, such as dormitories, buses and clubs. Infection is uncommon in travellers. Vaccination is recommended for long stays and is especially important towards the end of the dry season. Symptoms include a fever, severe headache, neck stiffness and a red rash. Immediate medical treatment is necessary.

The ACWY vaccine is recommended for all travellers in sub-Saharan Africa. This vaccine is different from the meningococcal meningitis C vaccine given to children and adolescents in some countries; it is safe to be given both types of vaccine.

Rabies

Rabies is spread by the bites or licks of an infected animal on broken skin. It is always fatal once the clinical symptoms start (which might be up to several months after an infected bite), so postbite vaccination should be taken as soon as possible. Postbite vaccination (whether or not you've been vaccinated before the bite) prevents the virus from spreading to the central nervous system.

Animal handlers should be vaccinated, as should those travelling to remote areas where a reliable source of postbite vaccine is not available within 24 hours. To prevent the disease, three injections are needed over a month. If you have not been vaccinated and receive a bite, you will need a course of five injections starting 24 hours or as soon as possible after the injury. If you have been vaccinated, you will need fewer postbite injections, and have more time to seek medical help.

Rift Valley Fever

This fever is spread occasionally via mosquito bites and is rarely fatal. The symptoms are a fever and flu-like illness.

Typhoid

This illness is spread through handling food or drinking water that has been contaminated by infected human faeces. The first symptom of infection is usually a fever or a pink rash on the abdomen. Sometimes septicaemia (blood poisoning) can also occur. A typhoid vaccine (typhim Vi, typherix) will give protection for three years. In some countries, the oral vaccine Vivotif is also available. Antibiotics are usually given as treatment, and death is rare unless septicaemia occurs.

Yellow Fever

You should carry a certificate as evidence of vaccination against yellow fever if you've recently been in an infected country, to avoid immigration problems. For a full list of countries where yellow fever exists visit the website of the **World Health Organization** (www.who.int/wer/) or the **Centers for Disease Control & Prevention** (www.cdc.gov/travel/blusheet.htm). A traveller without a legally required up-to-date certificate could possibly be vaccinated and detained in isolation at the port of arrival for up to 10 days, or even repatriated.

Yellow fever is spread by infected mosquitoes. Symptoms range from a flu-like illness to severe hepatitis (liver inflammation), jaundice and death. Vaccination must be given at a designated clinic and is valid for 10 years. It's a live vaccine and must not be given to immuno-compromised people or pregnant women. For visitors to Kenya, vaccination is not mandatory but is recommended.

Traveller's Diarrhoea

Although it's not inevitable that you will get diarrhoea while travelling in Kenya, it's certainly likely. Diarrhoea is the most common travel-related illness, and sometimes simply dietary changes, such as increased spices or oils, are the cause. To help prevent diarrhoea, avoid tap water (see p388). You should also only eat fresh fruits or vegetables if cooked or peeled, and be wary of dairy products that might contain unpasteurised milk. Although freshly cooked food can often be safe, plates or serving utensils might be dirty, so be highly selective when eating food from street vendors (ensure that cooked food is piping hot right through).

If you develop diarrhoea, drink plenty of fluids, preferably an oral rehydration solution containing water (lots), and some salt and sugar. A few loose stools don't require treatment but if you start having more than four or five stools a day, you should start taking an antibiotic (usually a quinoline drug, such as ciprofloxacin or norfloxacin) and an anti-diarrhoeal agent (eg loperamide) if you are not within easy reach of a toilet. If diarrhoea is bloody, persists for more than 72 hours or is accompanied by fever, shaking chills or abdominal pain, seek medical attention.

Amoebic Dysentery

Contracted by eating contaminated food and water, amoebic dysentery causes blood and mucus in the faeces. It can be relatively mild and tends to come on gradually, but seek medical advice if you think you have the illness as it won't clear up without treatment (which is with specific antibiotics).

Giardiasis

This, like amoebic dysentery, is caused by contaminated food or water. The illness usually appears a week or more after exposure to the parasite. Giardiasis might cause only a short-lived bout of typical traveller's diarrhoea, but may cause persistent diarrhoea. Ideally, seek medical advice if you suspect you have giardiasis, but if you are in a remote area you could start a course of antibiotics.

Environmental Hazards

Heat Exhaustion

This condition occurs following heavy sweating and excessive fluid loss with inadequate replacement of fluids and salt, and is particularly common in hot climates when taking unaccustomed exercise before full acclimatisation.

Symptoms include headache, dizziness and tiredness. Dehydration is already happening by the time you feel thirsty – aim to drink sufficient water to produce pale, diluted urine. Self-treatment: fluid replacement with water and/or fruit juice, and cooling by cold water and fans. The treatment of the salt-loss component consists of consuming salty fluids such as soup, and adding a little more salt to foods than usual.

Heatstroke

Heat exhaustion is a precursor to the much more serious condition of heatstroke. In this case there is damage to the sweating mechanism, with an excessive rise in body temperature; irrational and hyperactive behaviour; and eventually loss of consciousness and death. Rapid cooling by spraying the body with water and fanning is ideal. Emergency fluid and electrolyte replacement is usually also required by intravenous drip.

Insect Bites & Stings

Mosquitoes might not always carry malaria or dengue fever, but they (and other insects) can cause irritation and infected bites. Use DEET-based insect repellents, which are also effective against sand flies.

Scorpions are frequently found in arid or dry climates. They can cause a painful bite that is sometimes life-threatening. If you are bitten by a scorpion, seek immediate medical assistance.

Snake Bites

Basically, avoid getting bitten! Don't walk barefoot, and don't stick your hand into holes or cracks. However, 50% of those bitten by venomous snakes are not actually injected with poison (envenomed). If bitten, do not panic. Immobilise the bitten limb with a splint (such as a stick) and apply a bandage over the site, with firm pressure – similar to bandaging a sprain. Do not apply a tourniquet, or cut or suck the bite. Get medical help as soon as possible so antivenene can be given if needed.

Water

Never drink tap water unless it has been boiled, filtered or chemically disinfected (such as with iodine tablets). Never drink from streams, rivers and lakes. It's also best to avoid drinking from pumps and wells – some do bring pure water to the surface, but the presence of animals can still contaminate supplies.

WANT MORE?

For in-depth language information and handy phrases, check out Lonely Planet's *Swahili Phrasebook*. You'll find it at **shop.lonelyplanet.com**, or you can buy Lonely Planet's iPhone phrasebooks at the Apple App Store.

Swahili is the national language of Kenya (as well as Tanzania). It's also the key language of communication in the wider East African region. This makes it one of the most widely spoken African languages. Although the number of speakers of Swahili throughout East Africa is estimated to be well over 50 million, it's the mother tongue of only about 5 million people, and is predominantly used as a second language or a lingua franca by speakers of other African languages. Swahili belongs to the Bantu group of languages from the Niger-Congo family and can be traced back to the first millenium AD. It's hardly surprising that in an area as vast as East Africa many different dialects of Swahili can be found, but you shouldn't have problems being understood in Kenya (or in the wider region) if you stick to the standard coastal form, as used in this book.

Most sounds in Swahili have equivalents in English. In our coloured pronunciation guides, ay should be read as in 'say', oh as the 'o' in 'role', dh as the 'th' in 'this' and th as in 'thing'. Note also that the sound ng can be found at the start of words in Swahili, and that Swahili speakers make only a slight distinction between r and l – instead of the hard 'r', try pronouncing a light 'd'. In Swahili, words are almost always stressed on the second-last syllable. In our pronunciation guides, the stressed syllables are in italics.

BASICS

Jambo is a pidgin Swahili word, used to greet tourists who are presumed not to understand the language. If people assume you can speak a little Swahili, they might use the following greetings:

Hello. (general)	*Habari?*	ha·*ba*·ree
Hello. (respectful)	*Shikamoo.*	shee·ka·*moh*
Goodbye.	*Tutaonana.*	too·ta·oh·*na*·na

Good ...	*Habari za ...?*	ha·*ba*·ree za ...
morning	*asubuhi*	a·soo·*boo*·hee
afternoon	*mchana*	m·*cha*·na
evening	*jioni*	jee·*oh*·nee

Yes.	*Ndiyo.*	n·*dee*·yoh
No.	*Hapana.*	ha·*pa*·na
Please.	*Tafadhali.*	ta·fa·*dha*·lee
Thank you (very much).	*Asante (sana).*	a·*san*·tay (*sa*·na)
You're welcome.	*Karibu.*	ka·*ree*·boo
Excuse me.	*Samahani.*	sa·ma·*ha*·nee
Sorry.	*Pole.*	*poh*·lay

How are you?
Habari? ha·*ba*·ree

I'm fine.
Nzuri./Salama./Safi. n·*zoo*·ree/sa·*la*·ma/*sa*·fee

If things are just OK, add *tu* too (only) after any of the above replies. If things are really good, add *sana* *sa*·na (very) or *kabisa* ka·*bee*·sa (totally) instead of *tu*.

What's your name?
Jina lako nani? jee·na *la*·koh *na*·nee

My name is ...
Jina langu ni ... jee·na *lan*·goo nee ...

KEY PATTERNS

To get by in Swahili, mix and match these simple patterns with words of your choice:

When's (the next bus)?
(Basi ijayo) itaondoka lini? — (ba·see ee·ja·yoh) ee·ta·ohn·doh·ka lee·nee

Where's (the station)?
(Stesheni) iko wapi? — (stay·shay·nee) ee·koh wa·pee

How much is (a room)?
(Chumba) ni bei gani? — (choom·ba) nee bay ga·nee

I'm looking for (a hotel).
Natafuta (hoteli). — na·ta·foo·ta (hoh·tay·lee)

Do you have (a map)?
Una (ramani)? — oo·na (ra·ma·nee)

Please bring (the bill).
Lete (bili). — lay·tay (bee·lee)

I'd like (the menu).
Nataka (menyu). — na·ta·ka (may·nyoo)

I have (a reservation).
Nina (buking). — nee·na (boo·keeng)

Do you speak English?
Unasema Kiingereza? — oo·na·say·ma kee·een·gay·ray·za

I don't understand.
Sielewi. — see·ay·lay·wee

ACCOMMODATION

Where's a ...?	*... iko wapi?*	... ee·koh wa·pee
campsite	*Uwanja wa kambi*	oo·wan·ja wa kam·bee
guesthouse	*Gesti*	gay·stee
hotel	*Hoteli*	hoh·tay·lee
youth hostel	*Hosteli ya vijana*	hoh·stay·lee ya vee·ja·na

Do you have a ... room?	*Kuna chumba kwa ...?*	koo·na choom·ba kwa ...
double (one bed)	*watu wawili, kitanda kimoja*	wa·too wa·wee·lee kee·tan·da kee·moh·ja
single	*mtu mmoja*	m·too m·moh·ja
twin (two beds)	*watu wawili, vitanda viwili*	wa·too wa·wee·lee vee·tan·da vee·wee·lee

How much is it per ...?	*Ni bei gani kwa ...?*	nee bay ga·ne kwa ...
day	*siku*	see·koo
person	*mtu*	m·too

air-con	*a/c*	ay·see
bathroom	*bafuni*	ba·foo·nee
key	*ufunguo*	oo·foon·goo·oh
toilet	*choo*	choh
window	*dirisha*	dee·ree·sha

DIRECTIONS

Where's the ...?
... iko wapi? — ... ee·koh wa·pee

What's the address?
Anwani ni nini? — an·wa·nee nee nee·nee

How do I get there?
Nifikaje? — nee·fee·ka·jay

How far is it?
Ni umbali gani? — nee oom·ba·lee ga·nee

Can you show me (on the map)?
Unaweza kunionyesha (katika ramani)? — oo·na·way·za koo·nee·oh·nyay·sha (ka·tee·ka ra·ma·nee)

It's ...	*Iko ...*	ee·koh ...
behind ...	*nyuma ya ...*	nyoo·ma ya ...
in front of ...	*mbele ya ...*	m·bay·lay ya ...
near ...	*karibu na ...*	ka·ree·boo na ...
next to ...	*jirani ya ...*	jee·ra·nee ya ...
on the corner	*pembeni*	paym·bay·nee
opposite ...	*ng'ambo ya ...*	ng·am·boh ya ...
straight ahead	*moja kwa moja*	moh·ja kwa moh·ja

Turn ...	*Geuza ...*	gay·oo·za ...
at the corner	*kwenye kona*	kway·nyay koh·na
at the traffic lights	*kwenye taa za barabarani*	kway·nyay ta za ba·ra·ba·ra·nee
left	*kushoto*	koo·shoh·toh
right	*kulia*	koo·lee·a

EATING & DRINKING

I'd like to reserve a table for ...	*Nataka kuhifadhi meza kwa ...*	na·ta·ka koo·hee·fa·dhee may·za kwa ...
(two) people	*watu (wawili)*	wa·too (wa·wee·lee)
(eight) o'clock	*saa (mbili)*	sa (m·bee·lee)

I'd like the menu.
Naomba menyu. — na·ohm·ba may·nyoo

What would you recommend?
Chakula gani ni kizuri? — cha·koo·la ga·nee nee kee·zoo·ree

Do you have vegetarian food?
Mna chakula bila nyama? m·na cha·*koo*·la bee·la *nya*·ma

I'll have that.
Nataka hicho. na·*ta*·ka *hee*·choh

Cheers!
Heri! hay·ree

That was delicious!
Chakula kitamu sana! cha·*koo*·la kee·*ta*·moo *sa*·na

Please bring the bill.
Lete bili. lay·tay bee·lee

I don't eat ...	*Sili ...*	*see*·lee ...
butter	*siagi*	see·*a*·gee
eggs	*mayai*	ma·*ya*·ee
red meat	*nyama*	*nya*·ma

Key Words

bottle	*chupa*	*choo*·pa
bowl	*bakuli*	ba·*koo*·lee
breakfast	*chai ya asubuhi*	*cha*·ee ya a·soo·*boo*·hee
cold	*baridi*	ba·*ree*·dee
dinner	*chakula cha jioni*	cha·*koo*·la cha jee·*oh*·nee
dish	*chakula*	cha·*koo*·la
fork	*uma*	oo·ma
glass	*glesi*	*glay*·see
halal	*halali*	ha·*la*·lee
hot	*joto*	*joh*·toh
knife	*kisu*	*kee*·soo
kosher	*halali*	ha·*la*·lee
lunch	*chakula cha mchana*	cha·*koo*·la cha m·*cha*·na
market	*soko*	*soh*·koh
plate	*sahani*	sa·*ha*·nee
restaurant	*mgahawa*	m·ga·*ha*·wa
snack	*kumbwe*	*koom*·bway
spicy	*chenye viungo*	*chay*·nyay vee·*oon*·goh
spoon	*kijiko*	kee·*jee*·koh
with	*na*	na
without	*bila*	*bee*·la

Meat & Fish

beef	*nyama ng'ombe*	*nya*·ma ng·*ohm*·bay
chicken	*kuku*	*koo*·koo
crab	*kaa*	ka
fish	*samaki*	sa·*ma*·kee
hering	*heringi*	hay·*reen*·gee
lamb	*mwanakondoo*	mwa·na·kohn·*doh*
meat	*nyama*	*nya*·ma
mutton	*nyama mbuzi*	*nya*·ma m·*boo*·zee
oyster	*chaza*	*cha*·za
pork	*nyama nguruwe*	*nya*·ma n·goo·*roo*·way
seafood	*chakula kutoka bahari*	cha·*koo*·la koo·*toh*·ka ba·*ha*·ree
squid	*ngisi*	n·*gee*·see
tuna	*jodari*	joh·*da*·ree
veal	*nyama ya ndama*	*nya*·ma ya n·*da*·ma

Fruit & Vegetables

apple	*tofaa*	toh·*fa*
banana	*ndizi*	n·*dee*·zee
cabbage	*kabichi*	ka·*bee*·chee
carrot	*karoti*	ka·*roh*·tee
eggplant	*biringani*	bee·reen·*ga*·nee
fruit	*tunda*	*toon*·da
grapefruit	*balungi*	ba·*loon*·gee
grapes	*zabibu*	za·*bee*·boo
guava	*pera*	*pay*·ra
lemon	*limau*	lee·*ma*·oo
lentils	*dengu*	*dayn*·goo
mango	*embe*	*aym*·bay
onion	*kitunguu*	kee·toon·*goo*
orange	*chungwa*	*choon*·gwa
peanut	*karanga*	ka·*ran*·ga
pineapple	*nanasi*	na·*na*·see
potato	*kiazi*	kee·*a*·zee
spinach	*mchicha*	m·*chee*·cha
tomato	*nyanya*	*nya*·nya
vegetable	*mboga*	m·*boh*·ga

Signs

Mahali Pa Kuingia	Entrance
Mahali Pa Kutoka	Exit
Imefunguliwa	Open
Imefungwa	Closed
Maelezo	Information
Ni Marufuku	Prohibited
Choo/Msalani	Toilets
Wanaume	Men
Wanawake	Women

Other

bread	*mkate*	m·*ka*·tay
butter	*siagi*	see·*a*·gee
cheese	*jibini*	jee·*bee*·nee
egg	*yai*	*ya*·ee
honey	*asali*	a·*sa*·lee
jam	*jamu*	*ja*·moo
pasta	*tambi*	*tam*·bee
pepper	*pilipili*	pee·lee·*pee*·lee
rice (cooked)	*wali*	*wa*·lee
salt	*chumvi*	*choom*·vee
sugar	*sukari*	soo·*ka*·ree

Drinks

beer	*bia*	*bee*·a
coffee	*kahawa*	ka·*ha*·wa
juice	*jusi*	*joo*·see
milk	*maziwa*	ma·*zee*·wa
mineral water	*maji ya madini*	*ma*·jee ya ma·*dee*·nee
orange juice	*maji ya machungwa*	*ma*·jee ya ma·*choon*·gwa
red wine	*mvinyo mwekundu*	m·*vee*·nyoh mway·*koon*·doo
soft drink	*soda*	*soh*·da
sparkling wine	*mvinyo yenye mapovu*	m·*vee*·nyoh *yay*·nyay ma·*poh*·voo
tea	*chai*	*cha*·ee
water	*maji*	*ma*·jee
white wine	*mvinyo mweupe*	m·*vee*·nyoh mway·*oo*·pay

EMERGENCIES

Help!	*Saidia!*	sa·ee·*dee*·a
Go away!	*Toka!*	*toh*·ka

I'm lost.
Nimejipotea. — nee·may·jee·poh·*tay*·a

Question Words

How?	*Namna?*	*nam*·na
What?	*Nini?*	*nee*·nee
When?	*Wakati?*	wa·*ka*·tee
Where?	*Wapi?*	*wa*·pee
Which?	*Gani?*	*ga*·nee
Who?	*Nani?*	*na*·nee
Why?	*Kwa nini?*	kwa *nee*·nee

Call the police.
Waite polisi. — wa·ee·tay poh·*lee*·see

Call a doctor.
Mwite daktari. — m·*wee*·tay dak·*ta*·ree

I'm sick.
Mimi ni mgonjwa. — *mee*·mee nee m·*gohn*·jwa

It hurts here.
Inauma hapa. — ee·na·*oo*·ma *ha*·pa

I'm allergic to (antibiotics).
Nina mzio wa (viuavijasumu). — *nee*·na m·*zee*·oh wa (vee·oo·a·vee·ja·*soo*·moo)

Where's the toilet?
Choo kiko wapi? — choh *kee*·koh *wa*·pee

SHOPPING & SERVICES

I'd like to buy ...
Nataka kununua ... — na·*ta*·ka koo·noo·*noo*·a ...

I'm just looking.
Naangalia tu. — na·an·ga·*lee*·a too

Can I look at it?
Naomba nione. — na·*ohm*·ba nee·*oh*·nay

I don't like it.
Sipendi. — see·*payn*·dee

How much is it?
Ni bei gani? — ni bay *ga*·nee

That's too expensive.
Ni ghali mno. — nee *ga*·lee *m*·noh

Please lower the price.
Punguza bei. — poon·*goo*·za bay

There's a mistake in the bill.
Kuna kosa kwenye bili. — koo·na koh·sa kwayn·yay bee·lee

ATM	*mashine ya kutolea pesa*	ma·*shee*·nay ya koo·toh·*lay*·a *pay*·sa
post office	*posta*	*poh*·sta
public phone	*simu ya mtaani*	*see*·moo ya m·*ta*·nee
tourist office	*ofisi ya watalii*	o·*fee*·see ya wa·ta·*lee*

TIME & DATES

Keep in mind that the Swahili time system starts six hours later than the international one – it begins at sunrise which occurs at about 6am year-round. Therefore, *saa mbili* sa m·*bee*·lee (lit: clocks two) means '2 o'clock Swahili time' and '8 o'clock international time'.

What time is it?
Ni saa ngapi? — nee sa n·*ga*·pee

It's (10) o'clock.
Ni saa (nne). — nee sa (*n*·nay)

Half past (10).
Ni saa (nne) na nusu. — nee sa (*n*·nay) na *noo*·soo

morning	*asubuhi*	a·soo·*boo*·hee
afternoon	*mchana*	m·*cha*·na
evening	*jioni*	jee·*oh*·nee
yesterday	*jana*	*ja*·na
today	*leo*	*lay*·oh
tomorrow	*kesho*	*kay*·shoh

Monday	*Jumatatu*	joo·ma·*ta*·too
Tuesday	*Jumanne*	joo·ma·*n*·nay
Wednesday	*Jumatano*	joo·ma·*ta*·noh
Thursday	*Alhamisi*	al·ha·*mee*·see
Friday	*Ijumaa*	ee·joo·*ma*
Saturday	*Jumamosi*	joo·ma·*moh*·see
Sunday	*Jumapili*	joo·ma·*pee*·lee

TRANSPORT

Public Transport

Which ... goes to (Mbeya)?	*... ipi huenda (Mbeya)?*	... *ee*·pee hoo·*ayn*·da (m·*bay*·a)
bus	*Basi*	*ba*·see
ferry	*Kivuko*	kee·*voo*·koh
minibus	*Matatu*	ma·*ta*·too
train	*Treni*	*tray*·nee

When's the ... bus?	*Basi ... itaondoka lini?*	*ba*·see ... ee·ta·ohn·*doh*·ka *lee*·nee
first	*ya kwanza*	ya *kwan*·za
last	*ya mwisho*	ya *mwee*·shoh
next	*ijayo*	ee·*ja*·yoh

A ... ticket to (Iringa).	*Tiketi moja ya ... kwenda (Iringa).*	tee·*kay*·tee *moh*·ja ya ... *kwayn*·da (ee·*reen*·ga)
1st-class	*daraja la kwanza*	da·*ra*·ja la *kwan*·za
2nd-class	*daraja la pili*	da·*ra*·ja la *pee*·lee
one-way	*kwenda tu*	*kwayn*·da too
return	*kwenda na kurudi*	*kwayn*·da na koo·*roo*·dee

What time does it get to (Kisuma)?
Itafika (Kisumu) saa ngapi? — ee·ta·*fee*·ka (kee·*soo*·moo) sa n·*ga*·pee

Does it stop at (Tanga)?
Linasimama (Tanga)? — lee·na·see·*ma*·ma (*tan*·ga)

I'd like to get off at (Bagamoyo).
Nataka kushusha (Bagamoyo). — na·*ta*·ka koo·*shoo*·sha (ba·ga·*moh*·yoh)

Numbers

1	*moja*	*moh*·ja
2	*mbili*	m·*bee*·lee
3	*tatu*	*ta*·too
4	*nne*	*n*·nay
5	*tano*	*ta*·noh
6	*sita*	*see*·ta
7	*saba*	*sa*·ba
8	*nane*	*na*·nay
9	*tisa*	*tee*·sa
10	*kumi*	*koo*·mee
20	*ishirini*	ee·shee·*ree*·nee
30	*thelathini*	thay·la·*thee*·nee
40	*arobaini*	a·roh·ba·*ee*·nee
50	*hamsini*	ham·*see*·nee
60	*sitini*	see·*tee*·nee
70	*sabini*	sa·*bee*·nee
80	*themanini*	thay·ma·*nee*·nee
90	*tisini*	tee·*see*·nee
100	*mia moja*	*mee*·a *moh*·ja
1000	*elfu*	*ayl*·foo

Driving & Cycling

I'd like to hire a ...	*Nataka kukodi ...*	na·*ta*·ka koo·*koh*·dee ...
4WD	*forbaifor*	*fohr*·ba·ee·fohr
bicycle	*baisikeli*	ba·ee·see·*kay*·lee
car	*gari*	*ga*·ree
motorbike	*pikipiki*	pee·kee·*pee*·kee

diesel	*dizeli*	dee·*zay*·lee
regular	*kawaida*	ka·wa·*ee*·da
unleaded	*isiyo na risasi*	ee·see·yoh na ree·*sa*·see

Is this the road to (Embu)?
Hii ni barabara kwenda (Embu)? — hee nee ba·ra·*ba*·ra *kwayn*·da (*aym*·boo)

Where's a petrol station?
Kituo cha mafuta kiko wapi? — kee·*too*·oh cha ma·*foo*·ta *kee*·ko *wa*·pee

(How long) Can I park here?
Naweza kuegesha hapa (kwa muda gani)? — na·*way*·za koo·ay·*gay*·sha *ha*·pa (kwa *moo*·da *ga*·ni)

I need a mechanic.
Nahitaji fundi. — na·hee·*ta*·jee *foon*·dee

I have a flat tyre.
Nina pancha. — *nee*·na *pan*·cha

I've run out of petrol.
Mafuta yamekwisha. — ma·*foo*·ta ya·may·*kwee*·sha

GLOSSARY

The following are some common words you are likely to come across when in Kenya.

abanyamorigo – medicine man

askari – security guard, watchman

banda – thatched-roof hut with wooden or earthen walls or simple wood-and-stone accommodation

bao – traditional African board game

beach boys – self-appointed guides, touts, hustlers and dealers on the coast

bhang – marijuana

boda-boda – bicycle-taxi

boma – village

bui-bui – black cover-all garment worn by Islamic women outside the home

cardphone – phone that takes a phonecard

chai – tea, but also a bribe

chang'a – dangerous homemade alcoholic brew containing methyl alcohol

choo – toilet; pronounced *cho*

dhow – traditional Arab sailing vessel

duka – small shop or kiosk selling household basics

fundi – repair man or woman who fixes clothing or cars, or is in the building trades; also an expert

gof – volcanic crater

hakuna matata – no problem; watch out – this often means there is a problem!

harambee – the concept of community self-help; voluntary fundraising; a cornerstone of Kenyatta's ideology

hatari – danger

hoteli – basic local eatery; sometimes also called simply 'hotel'

ito – wooden 'eyes' painted on a dhow to allow it to see obstacles in the water

jinga! – crazy!; also used as an adjective

jua kali – literally 'fierce sun'; usually an outdoor vehicle-repair shop or market

kali – fierce or ferocious; eg *hatari mbwa kali* – 'danger fierce dog'

kanga – printed cotton wraparound incorporating a Swahili proverb; worn by many women both inside and outside the home

KANU – Kenya African National Union

kikoi – striped cotton sarong traditionally worn by men

kiondo – woven basket

kitu kidogo – 'a little something'; a bribe

kofia – cap worn by Muslim men

KWS – Kenya Wildlife Service

lugga – dry river bed, mainly in northern Kenya

makonde – woodcarving style, originally from southern Tanzania

makuti – thatch made with palm leaves used for roofing buildings, mainly on the coast

malaya – prostitute

mandazi – semisweet, flat doughnut

manyatta – Maasai or Samburu livestock camp often surrounded by a circle of thorn bushes

mataha – mashed beans, potatoes, maize and green vegetables

matatu – public minibuses used throughout the country

matoke – mashed plantains (green bananas)

mboga – vegetables

miraa – bundles of leafy shoots that are chewed as a stimulant and appetite suppressant

mkate mayai – fried, wheat pancake filled with mincemeat and raw egg; literally 'bread eggs'

moran – Maasai or Samburu warrior (plural *morani*)

murram – dirt or part-gravel road

mursik – milk drink fermented with cow's urine and ashes

mwizi – a thief

mzee – an old man or respected elder

mzungu – white person (plural *wazungu*)

NARC – National Alliance Rainbow Coalition

Ng'oroko – Turkana bandits

Nissan – see *matatu*

nyama choma – barbecued meat, often goat

Nyayo – a cornerstone of Moi's political ideology, meaning 'footsteps'; to follow in the footsteps of Jomo Kenyatta

panga – machete, carried by most people in the countryside and often by thieves in the cities

parking boys – unemployed youths or young men who will assist in parking a vehicle and guard it while the owner is absent

pesa – money

Peugeot – shared taxi

pombe – Kenyan beer, usually made with millet and sugar

rafiki – friend; as in 'my friend, you want safari?'

rondavel – circular hut, usually a thatched building with a conical roof

safari – 'journey' in Kiswahili

sambusa – deep-fried pastry triangles stuffed with spiced mincemeat; similar to Indian samosa

shamba – small farm or plot of land

shifta – bandit

shilingi – money

shuka – Maasai blanket

sigana – traditional African performance form

containing narration, song, music, dance, chant, ritual, mask, movement, banter and poetry

sis – white Kenyan slang for 'yuck'

siwa – ornately carved ivory wind instrument, unique to the coastal region and often used for fanfare at weddings

Tusker – Kenyan beer

ugali – staple made from maize or cassava flour, or both

uhuru – freedom or independence

wa benzi – someone driving a Mercedes-Benz car bought with, it's implied, the proceeds of corruption

wananchi – workers or 'the people' (singular *mwananchi*)

wazungu – white people (singular *mzungu*)

behind the scenes

SEND US YOUR FEEDBACK

We love to hear from travellers – your comments keep us on our toes and help make our books better. Our well-travelled team reads every word on what you loved or loathed about this book. Although we cannot reply individually to postal submissions, we always guarantee that your feedback goes straight to the appropriate authors, in time for the next edition. Each person who sends us information is thanked in the next edition – the most useful submissions are rewarded with a selection of digital PDF chapters.

Visit **lonelyplanet.com/contact** to submit your updates and suggestions or to ask for help. Our award-winning website also features inspirational travel stories, news and discussions.

Note: We may edit, reproduce and incorporate your comments in Lonely Planet products such as guidebooks, websites and digital products, so let us know if you don't want your comments reproduced or your name acknowledged. For a copy of our privacy policy visit lonelyplanet.com/privacy.

OUR READERS

Many thanks to the travellers who used the last edition and wrote to us with helpful hints, useful advice and interesting anecdotes:

Carmen, Cavillot, Tineke, Vimal Abraham, Jakub Alchimowicz, Jeffrey and Lindsay Wicharuk, France Barral, Fabio Bergamin, Vanessa Blommaert, Gretchen Boisseau, Lyn Brayshaw, Chris Burkhart, Elizabeth Caiger, Lois Cameron, Marco Coduti, Gary Cymbaluk, Christian Daul, Marjolijn De Keijzer, Remco Dijkstra, Avital Dobo, Stacey Falls, Nadine Flores Martin, Renee Ford, Minna Friborg Hansen, Jochen Fuchs, Jean Gallagher, Bianca Gideback, Gisela Glietenberg, George Gordon, Stephanie Green, Jessica Greenhalgh, Allan H. Adams, Dorothea Hampel, Alexandra Hannah, Sarah Harrison, Karni Hazan, Deniz Hircin-Kistner, David Hirst, Chris Howles, Sakshi Kapahi, Sarah Katz, Ronan Kelly, Erin Kline, Lynda Kuhn, Ben Leed, Benoit Leleux, Martijn Leusink, Sam Lovell, Jacqueline Lycklama à Nijeholt, Miguel Manzano, Dr. Marc-David Munk, Tony Maslin, Angel McClarey, Alan McCullough, Nancy McLennan, Hazel Meares, Anze Mihelic, Daffney Obare, Jane Orr, Shari Ostrow Scher, Owen Ozier, Simone Pilgram, Stig Poulsen, Michael Provenza, John Quinterno, Rosanne Roobeek, Mikkel Ryhl Faber, Rik Schuiling, Carl Slaughter, Douglas Snadden, Graham Stone, Jonathan Stonehouse, John Stonestreet, Charlotte Street, Theo Ten Velde, Markus Ulrik Bank Lentz, Jim Van Den Hoorn, Nathalie Verstraeten, Frank Willberg, Bec Willner, Tim Woods

AUTHOR THANKS

Anthony Ham

Special thanks to Peter Drango, who began as my driver and guide and quickly became a friend; he taught me so much about Kenya. Thanks also to George Muriuki (Nairobi), Dea and Lisa Shupbach (Lake Naivasha), Manja Seifert (Tsavo West) and many others. Back at home, I am in awe of my three wonderful girls – Marina, Carlota and Valentina – who endure my absences with good grace and who welcome me home with unbridled joy. One day, I will take you here.

Stuart Butler

Thank you to George Muriuki as well as the ever-patient Peter Kiega for his driving up north. Massive thanks to Charlotte and Esther as well as Patrick and Meriem Simkin, Issy and Murray and Riccardo Orizio for a great time. In Lewa thanks to William T Kipsoi for superb guiding. Thanks to Jeannette Goddar for seeing what I couldn't. On the coast cheers to Ramtu, Hassan and Abdulah for driving skills.

In Malindi a huge thanks to Mick, Tony, Ken Haji, David and Georgina for sharing waves, as well as Aidan Hartley. On Manda thanks to Rachael. Cheers once again to Toby Adamson for being a fellow magician and great travel partner. Last, but not least, huge thanks and hugs to Heather and Jake for everything.

Dean Starnes

It would be wrong not to acknowledge the legacy of work from previous editions and help and assistance from authors extraordinaire Anthony Ham and Stuart Butler. Gentlemen, it was a blast.

Big ups to the team at Lonely Planet for all their help with my pesky queries, particularly Sam Trafford, David Carroll and Brigitte Ellemor.

My life was made easier by the sage advice given to me by Elanor Harrison, Toby Jones, Eugene Nijssen, John Wambua and Ibrahim O Nandi.

ACKNOWLEDGMENTS

Climate map data adapted from Peel MC, Finlayson BL & McMahon TA (2007) 'Updated World Map of the Köppen-Geiger Climate Classification', *Hydrology and Earth System Sciences*, 11, 163344.

Cover photograph: Maasai tribe, Kenya, Tom Brakefield/Photolibrary. Many of the images in this guide are available for licensing from Lonely Planet Images: www.lonelyplanetimages.com.

This Book

This 8th edition of Lonely Planet's *Kenya* guidebook was written and researched by Anthony Ham (coordinating author), Stuart Butler and Dean Starnes. The Wildlife & Habitat chapter was written by David Lukas, and the Health chapter was updated by Anthony Ham. The previous edition was written by Matthew Firestone, Stuart Butler, Paula Hardy and Adam Karlin, with contributing author David Lukas (Wildlife & Habitat).

This guidebook was commissioned in Lonely Planet's Melbourne office and produced by the following:

Commissioning Editors David Carroll, Will Gourlay, Sam Trafford

Coordinating Editor Sonya Mithen

Coordinating Cartographer Valentina Kremenchutskaya

Coordinating Layout Designer Lauren Egan

Managing Editor Brigitte Ellemor

Managing Cartographers Adrian Persoglia, Amanda Sierp

Managing Layout Designer Chris Girdler

Assisting Editors Kim Hutchins, Helen Koehne, Dianne Schallmeiner, Kate Whitfield

Assisting Cartographers Hunor Csutoros, Mark Milinkovic, Diana Von Holdt

Assisting Layout Designer Kerrianne Southway

Cover Research Naomi Parker

Internal Image Research Liz Abbott, Rebecca Skinner

Language Content Annelies Mertens, Branislava Vladisavljevic

Thanks to Lucy Birchley, Yvonne Bischofberger, Ryan Evans, Jane Hart, Yvonne Kirk, Trent Paton, Gerard Walker

index

000 Map pages
000 Photo pages

000 Map pages
000 Photo pages

N

000 Map pages
000 Photo pages

S

T

000 Map pages
000 Photo pages

how to use this book

These symbols will help you find the listings you want:

- Sights
- Beaches
- Activities
- Courses
- Tours
- Festivals & Events
- Sleeping
- Eating
- Drinking
- Entertainment
- Shopping
- Information/ Transport

These symbols give you the vital information for each listing:

- Telephone Numbers
- Opening Hours
- Parking
- Nonsmoking
- Air-Conditioning
- Internet Access
- Wi-Fi Access
- Swimming Pool
- Vegetarian Selection
- English-Language Menu
- Family-Friendly
- Pet-Friendly
- Bus
- Ferry
- Metro
- Subway
- London Tube
- Tram
- Train

Reviews are organised by author preference.

Look out for these icons:

- TOP CHOICE Our author's recommendation
- FREE No payment required
-  A green or sustainable option

Our authors have nominated these places as demonstrating a strong commitment to sustainability – for example by supporting local communities and producers, operating in an environmentally friendly way, or supporting conservation projects.

Map Legend

Sights

- Beach
- Buddhist
- Castle
- Christian
- Hindu
- Islamic
- Jewish
- Monument
- Museum/Gallery
- Ruin
- Winery/Vineyard
- Zoo
- Other Sight

Activities, Courses & Tours

- Diving/Snorkelling
- Canoeing/Kayaking
- Skiing
- Surfing
- Swimming/Pool
- Walking
- Windsurfing
- Other Activity/ Course/Tour

Sleeping

- Sleeping
- Camping

Eating

- Eating

Drinking

- Drinking
- Cafe

Entertainment

- Entertainment

Shopping

- Shopping

Information

- Bank
- Embassy/ Consulate
- Hospital/Medical
- Internet
- Police
- Post Office
- Telephone
- Toilet
- Tourist Information
- Other Information

Transport

- Airport
- Border Crossing
- Bus
- Cable Car/ Funicular
- Cycling
- Ferry
- Metro
- Monorail
- Parking
- Petrol Station
- Taxi
- Train/Railway
- Tram
- Other Transport

Routes

- Tollway
- Freeway
- Primary
- Secondary
- Tertiary
- Lane
- Unsealed Road
- Plaza/Mall
- Steps
- Tunnel
- Pedestrian Overpass
- Walking Tour
- Walking Tour Detour
- Path

Geographic

- Hut/Shelter
- Lighthouse
- Lookout
- Mountain/Volcano
- Oasis
- Park
- Pass
- Picnic Area
- Waterfall

Population

- Capital (National)
- Capital (State/Province)
- City/Large Town
- Town/Village

Boundaries

- International
- State/Province
- Disputed
- Regional/Suburb
- Marine Park
- Cliff
- Wall

Hydrography

- River, Creek
- Intermittent River
- Swamp/Mangrove
- Reef
- Canal
- Water
- Dry/Salt/ Intermittent Lake
- Glacier

Areas

- Beach/Desert
- Cemetery (Christian)
- Cemetery (Other)
- Park/Forest
- Sportsground
- Sight (Building)
- Top Sight (Building)

OUR STORY

A beat-up old car, a few dollars in the pocket and a sense of adventure. In 1972 that's all Tony and Maureen Wheeler needed for the trip of a lifetime – across Europe and Asia overland to Australia. It took several months, and at the end – broke but inspired – they sat at their kitchen table writing and stapling together their first travel guide, *Across Asia on the Cheap*. Within a week they'd sold 1500 copies. Lonely Planet was born.

Today, Lonely Planet has offices in Melbourne, London and Oakland, with more than 600 staff and writers. We share Tony's belief that 'a great guidebook should do three things: inform, educate and amuse'.

OUR WRITERS

Anthony Ham

Coordinating Author, Nairobi, Southern Kenya, Rift Valley Anthony brings to *Kenya* more than a decade's experience in Africa. His love affair with the continent began in North and West Africa, where he has spent the last decade exploring the Sahara with Tuareg nomads and tracking down endangered elephant herds from the Malian Sahel to remote corners of southern Chad. In addition to coordinating Lonely Planet's *West Africa*, *Africa* and *Libya* guides, Anthony writes and photographs for numerous newspapers and magazines around the world, primarily covering conservation issues, nomadic and indigenous peoples and countries in conflict. When he's not in Africa, Anthony lives in Madrid with his wife, Marina, and their two daughters, Carlota and Valentina.

Read more about Anthony at:
lonelyplanet.com/members/anthonyham

Stuart Butler

Northern Kenya, Mombasa & the South Coast, The North Coast Stuart Butler grew up listening to stories of his father's childhood in Kenya and his grandparents' tales of working on the earliest English-language editions of the *Daily Nation* newspaper. When Stuart finally stepped foot in Africa, it was Kenya he chose. It didn't disappoint. Stuart now calls the south of France home. His travels, for both Lonely Planet and various surfing magazines, have taken him beyond Africa from the coastal deserts of Pakistan to the jungles of Colombia.

Read more about Stuart at:
lonelyplanet.com/members/stuartbutler

Dean Starnes

Western Kenya, Central Highlands Dean first backpacked through Kenya in 2004 as part of a greater East African adventure. After racing camels in Maralal (despite a backwards facing start, he came a respectable 14th) and dhows near Lamu, he fell in love with the diversity, culture and humour of the Kenyan people and vowed to return. Since then he has worked on Lonely Planet's *Ethiopia* (4th edition) and *East Africa* (9th edition). Dean lives in New Zealand with his wife and his wife's cat. When he's not writing for Lonely Planet, he works as a freelance graphic designer and plots new ways to shirk his responsibilities.

Contributing Author

David Lukas wrote the Wildife & Habitat chapter. David is a freelance naturalist who lives next to Yosemite National Park in California. He writes extensively about the world's wildlife, and has contributed wildlife chapters to eight Africa Lonely Planet guides ranging from *Ethiopia* to *South Africa*. He also wrote *A Year of Watching Wildlife*, which covers the top places in the world to view wildlife.

Published by Lonely Planet Publications Pty Ltd
ABN 36 005 607 983
8th edition – June 2012
ISBN 978 1 74179 673 5

10 9 8 7 6 5 4 3 2 1
Printed in China